Delphi™ 4 Bible

Delphi™ 4 Bible

Tom Swan

IDG BOOKS WORLDWIDE

IDG Books Worldwide, Inc.
An International Data Group Company

Foster City, CA ✦ Chicago, IL ✦ Indianapolis, IN ✦ New York, NY

Delphi 4™ Bible

Published by
IDG Books Worldwide, Inc.
An International Data Group Company
919 E. Hillsdale Blvd., Suite 400
Foster City, CA 94404
www.idgbooks.com (IDG Books Worldwide Web site)

Library of Congress Catalog Card No.: 98-071855

ISBN: 0-7645-3237-5

Printed in the United States of America

10 9 8 7 6 5 4 3 2 1

1B/SS/QX/ZY/FC

Distributed in the United States by IDG Books Worldwide, Inc.

Distributed by Macmillan Canada for Canada; by Transworld Publishers Limited in the United Kingdom; by IDG Norge Books for Norway; by IDG Sweden Books for Sweden; by Woodslane Pty. Ltd. for Australia; by Woodslane (NZ) Ltd. for New Zealand; by Addison Wesley Longman Singapore Pte Ltd. for Singapore, Malaysia, Thailand, Indonesia, and Korea; by Norma Comunicaciones S.A. for Colombia; by Intersoft for South Africa; by International Thomson Publishing for Germany, Austria, and Switzerland; by Toppan Company Ltd. for Japan; by Distribuidora Cuspide for Argentina; by Livraria Cultura for Brazil; by Ediciencia S.A. for Ecuador; by Ediciones ZETA S.C.R. Ltda. for Peru; by WS Computer Publishing Corporation, Inc., for the Philippines; by Unalis Corporation for Taiwan; by Contemporanea de Ediciones for Venezuela; by Computer Book & Magazine Store for Puerto Rico; by Express Computer Distributors for the Caribbean and West Indies. Authorized Sales Agent: Anthony Rudkin Associates for the Middle East and North Africa.

For general information on IDG Books Worldwide's books in the U.S., please call our Consumer Customer Service department at 800-762-2974. For reseller information, including discounts and premium sales, please call our Reseller Customer Service department at 800-434-3422.

For information on where to purchase IDG Books Worldwide's books outside the U.S., please contact our International Sales department at 650-655-3200 or fax 650-655-3297.

For information on foreign language translations, please contact our Foreign & Subsidiary Rights department at 650-655-3021 or fax 650-655-3281.

For sales inquiries and special prices for bulk quantities, please contact our Sales department at 650-655-3200 or write to the address above.

For information on using IDG Books Worldwide's books in the classroom or for ordering examination copies, please contact our Educational Sales department at 800-434-2086 or fax 317-596-5499.

For press review copies, author interviews, or other publicity information, please contact our Public Relations department at 650-655-3000 or fax 650-655-3299.

For authorization to photocopy items for corporate, personal, or educational use, please contact Copyright Clearance Center, 222 Rosewood Drive, Danvers, MA 01923, or fax 978-750-4470.

IDG BOOKS WORLDWIDE is a trademark under exclusive license to IDG Books Worldwide, Inc., from International Data Group, Inc.

ABOUT IDG BOOKS WORLDWIDE

Welcome to the world of IDG Books Worldwide.

IDG Books Worldwide, Inc., is a subsidiary of International Data Group, the world's largest publisher of computer-related information and the leading global provider of information services on information technology. IDG was founded more than 25 years ago and now employs more than 8,500 people worldwide. IDG publishes more than 275 computer publications in over 75 countries (see listing below). More than 90 million people read one or more IDG publications each month.

Launched in 1990, IDG Books Worldwide is today the #1 publisher of best-selling computer books in the United States. We are proud to have received eight awards from the Computer Press Association in recognition of editorial excellence and three from *Computer Currents'* First Annual Readers' Choice Awards. Our best-selling ...*For Dummies*® series has more than 50 million copies in print with translations in 38 languages. IDG Books Worldwide, through a joint venture with IDG's Hi-Tech Beijing, became the first U.S. publisher to publish a computer book in the People's Republic of China. In record time, IDG Books Worldwide has become the first choice for millions of readers around the world who want to learn how to better manage their businesses.

Our mission is simple: Every one of our books is designed to bring extra value and skill-building instructions to the reader. Our books are written by experts who understand and care about our readers. The knowledge base of our editorial staff comes from years of experience in publishing, education, and journalism — experience we use to produce books for the '90s. In short, we care about books, so we attract the best people. We devote special attention to details such as audience, interior design, use of icons, and illustrations. And because we use an efficient process of authoring, editing, and desktop publishing our books electronically, we can spend more time ensuring superior content and spend less time on the technicalities of making books.

You can count on our commitment to deliver high-quality books at competitive prices on topics you want to read about. At IDG Books Worldwide, we continue in the IDG tradition of delivering quality for more than 25 years. You'll find no better book on a subject than one from IDG Books Worldwide.

John Kilcullen
CEO
IDG Books Worldwide, Inc.

Steven Berkowitz
President and Publisher
IDG Books Worldwide, Inc.

*Eighth Annual
Computer Press
Awards ≥1992*

*Ninth Annual
Computer Press
Awards ≥1993*

*Tenth Annual
Computer Press
Awards ≥1994*

*Eleventh Annual
Computer Press
Awards ≥1995*

IDG Books Worldwide, Inc., is a subsidiary of International Data Group, the world's largest publisher of computer-related information and the leading global provider of information services on information technology. International Data Group publishes over 275 computer publications in over 75 countries. More than 90 million people read one or more International Data Group publications each month. International Data Group's publications include: **ARGENTINA:** Buyer's Guide, Computerworld Argentina, PC World Argentina; **AUSTRALIA:** Australian Macworld, Australian PC World, Australian Reseller News, Computerworld, IT Casebook, Network World, Publish, Webmaster; **AUSTRIA:** Computerwelt Österreich, Networks Austria, PC Tip Austria; **BANGLADESH:** PC World Bangladesh; **BELARUS:** PC World Belarus; **BELGIUM:** Data News; **BRAZIL:** Annuário de Informática, Computerworld, Connections, Macworld, PC Player, PC World, Publish, Reseller News, Supergamepower; **BULGARIA:** Computerworld Bulgaria, Network World Bulgaria, PC & MacWorld Bulgaria; **CANADA:** CIO Canada, Client/Server World, ComputerWorld Canada, InfoWorld Canada, NetworkWorld Canada, WebWorld; **CHILE:** Computerworld Chile, PC World Chile; **COLOMBIA:** Computerworld Colombia, PC World Colombia; **COSTA RICA:** PC World Centro America; **THE CZECH AND SLOVAK REPUBLICS:** Computerworld Czechoslovakia, Macworld Czech Republic, PC World Czechoslovakia; **DENMARK:** Communications World Danmark, Computerworld Danmark, Macworld Danmark, PC World Danmark, Techworld Denmark; **DOMINICAN REPUBLIC:** PC World Republica Dominicana; **ECUADOR:** PC World Ecuador; **EGYPT:** Computerworld Middle East, PC World Middle East; **EL SALVADOR:** PC World Centro America; **FINLAND:** MikroPC, Tietoverkko, Tietoviikko; **FRANCE:** Distributique, Hebdo, Info PC, Le Monde Informatique, Macworld, Reseaux & Telecoms, WebMaster France; **GERMANY:** Computer Partner, Computerwoche, Computerwoche Extra, Computerwoche FOCUS, Global Online, Macwelt, PC Welt; **GREECE:** Amiga Computing, GamePro Greece, Multimedia World; **GUATEMALA:** PC World Centro America; **HONDURAS:** PC World Centro America; **HONG KONG:** Computerworld Hong Kong, PC World Hong Kong, Publish in Asia; **HUNGARY:** ABCD CD-ROM, Computerworld Szamitastechnika, Internetto online Magazine, PC World Hungary, PC-X Magazin Hungary; **ICELAND:** Tolvuheimur PC World Island; **INDIA:** Information Communications World, Information Systems Computerworld, PC World India, Publish in Asia; **INDONESIA:** InfoKomputer PC World, Komputek Computerworld, Publish in Asia; **IRELAND:** ComputerScope, PC Live!; **ISRAEL:** Macworld Israel, People & Computers/Computerworld; **ITALY:** Computerworld Italia, Macworld Italia, Networking Italia, PC World Italia; **JAPAN:** DTP World, Macworld Japan, Nikkei Personal Computing, OS/2 World Japan, SunWorld Japan, Windows NT World, Windows World Japan; **KENYA:** PC World East African; **KOREA:** Hi-Tech Information, Macworld Korea, PC World Korea; **MACEDONIA:** PC World Macedonia; **MALAYSIA:** Computerworld Malaysia, PC World Malaysia, Publish in Asia; **MALTA:** PC World Malta; **MEXICO:** Computerworld Mexico, PC World Mexico; **MYANMAR:** PC World Myanmar; **NETHERLANDS:** Computer! Totaal, LAN Internetworking Magazine, LAN World Buyers Guide, Macworld Netherlands, Net, WebWereld; **NEW ZEALAND:** Absolute Beginners Guide and Plain & Simple Series, Computer Buyer, Computer Industry Directory, Computerworld New Zealand, MTB, Network World, PC World New Zealand; **NICARAGUA:** PC World Centro America; **NORWAY:** Computerworld Norge, CW Rapport, Datamagasinet, Financial Rapport, Kursguide Norge, Macworld Norge, Multimediaworld Norge, PC World Ekspress Norge, PC World Nettverk, PC World Norge, PC World ProduktGuide Norge; **PAKISTAN:** Computerworld Pakistan; **PANAMA:** PC World Panama; **PEOPLE'S REPUBLIC OF CHINA:** China Computer Users, China Computerworld, China InfoWorld, China Telecom World Weekly, Computer & Communication, Electronic Design China, Electronics Today, Electronics Weekly, Game Software, PC World China, Popular Computer Week, Software Weekly, Software World, Telecom World; **PERU:** Computerworld Peru, PC World Profesional Peru, PC World SoHo Peru; **PHILIPPINES:** Click!, Computerworld Philippines, PC World Philippines, Publish in Asia; **POLAND:** Computerworld Poland, Computerworld Special Report Poland, Cyber, Macworld Poland, Networld Poland, PC World Komputer; **PORTUGAL:** Cerebro/PC World, Computerworld/Correio Informático, Dealer World Portugal, Mac*In/PC*In Portugal, Multimedia World; **PUERTO RICO:** PC World Puerto Rico; **ROMANIA:** Computerworld Romania, PC World Romania, Telecom Romania; **RUSSIA:** Computerworld Russia, Mir PK, Publish, Seti; **SINGAPORE:** Computerworld Singapore, PC World Singapore, Publish in Asia; **SLOVENIA:** Monitor; **SOUTH AFRICA:** Computing SA, Network World SA, Software World SA; **SPAIN:** Communicaciones World España, Computerworld España, Dealer World España, Macworld España, PC World España; **SRI LANKA:** Infolink PC World; **SWEDEN:** CAP&Design, Computer Sweden, Corporate Computing Sweden, Internetworld Sweden, it.branschen, Macworld Sweden, MaxiData Sweden, MikroDatorn, Nätverk & Kommunikation, PC World Sweden, PCaktiv, Windows World Sweden; **SWITZERLAND:** Computerworld Schweiz, Macworld Schweiz, PCtip; **TAIWAN:** Computerworld Taiwan, Macworld Taiwan, NEW ViSiON/Publish, PC World Taiwan, Windows World Taiwan; **THAILAND:** Publish in Asia, Thai Computerworld; **TURKEY:** Computerworld Turkiye, Macworld Turkiye, Network World Turkiye, PC World Turkiye; **UKRAINE:** Computerworld Kiev, Multimedia World Ukraine, PC World Ukraine; **UNITED KINGDOM:** Acorn User UK, Amiga Action UK, Amiga Computing UK, Apple Talk UK, Computing, Macworld, Parents and Computers UK, PC Advisor, PC Home, PSX Pro, The WEB; **UNITED STATES:** Cable in the Classroom, CIO Magazine, Computerworld, DOS World, Federal Computer Week, GamePro Magazine, InfoWorld, I-Way, Macworld, Network World, PC Games, PC World, Publish, Video Event, THE WEB Magazine, and WebMaster; online webzines: JavaWorld, NetscapeWorld, and SunWorld Online; **URUGUAY:** InfoWorld Uruguay; **VENEZUELA:** Computerworld Venezuela, PC World Venezuela; and **VIETNAM:** PC World Vietnam. 5/7/98

Credits

Acquisitions Editor
Greg Croy

Development Editor
Denise Santoro

Technical Editor
Danny Thorpe

Copy Editors
Pamela Clark
Marcia Baker

Project Coordinator
Tom Debolski

Cover Design
Murder By Design

**Graphics and
Production Specialists**
Mario Amador
Stephanie Hollier
Jude Levinson
Liz Pauw

Graphics Technicians
Linda Marousek
Hector Mendoza

Quality Control Specialists
Mick Arellano
Mark Schumann

Proofreader
Mary C. Barnack

Indexer
Liz Cunningham

About the Author

Tom Swan has written over 30 books on computer programming and is a former contributing editor and columnist for *PC World, Dr. Dobb's Journal, PC Techniques* (now named *Visual Developer*), and other publications. In his personal life, Swan is an avid sailor. He recently completed a single-handed voyage under sail between Key West and Cuba, and he regularly sails the Gulf of Mexico and Caribbean waters.

In memory of Steve Glick, sailor and friend.

Preface

Delphi 4 Bible provides a complete guide and reference to programming with Delphi. You need no prior programming experience to use this book, but if you know a little Pascal, C, C++, or Visual Basic, you'll be way ahead of the pack. This book's step-by-step instructions introduce Delphi techniques from beginner to more advanced levels. Delphi's Object Pascal language and Visual Component Library are documented, and you learn how to create practical, yet snazzy, user interfaces for a variety of applications. Numerous sample applications—all provided with full source code—light the way.

About This Book

Delphi 4 Bible covers Delphi's commands, features, and techniques in four parts:

✦ **Part I: Introduction**—Chapters in this part introduce Delphi's programming environment and explain many of its commands and features. You learn how to use visual components, forms, properties, and events to create practical 32-bit applications for Windows 95, 98, and NT.

✦ **Part II: The User Interface**—Chapters in this part explain how to create user interfaces with Delphi's Visual Component Library. You learn how to program the keyboard and mouse, and build user interfaces with objects such as menus, buttons, toolbars, Coolbars, status panels, scroll bars, dialog boxes, page controls, and dockable windows. You also learn how to work with single-line strings and multiple-line text, navigate directories and files, and communicate with dialog boxes.

✦ **Part III: The Application**—Chapters in this part cover application development topics and explain how to use Delphi's advanced visual components. You learn how to program applications for graphics, multimedia animations, printer output, multiple-document interface, object-linking and embedding, and database development. You also learn how to create reports and graphical charts using Delphi's QuickReport and TeeChart component libraries.

✦ **Part IV: Advanced Techniques**—Chapters in this part present topics of interest to advanced Delphi developers. You learn how to use exceptions for error handling, use and create packages, and construct custom components and convert them to ActiveX controls. The final chapter in this part (and in the book) presents advanced programming techniques for Object Pascal. You learn about new object-oriented features such as dynamic arrays, method overloading, default parameters, file streams, multithreaded applications, and other assorted odds and ends.

Parts II and III cover most Delphi visual components. To find references to specific components, look them up in the subject index at the back of the book.

Requirements

In addition to this book, you need a copy of Delphi's Desktop, Professional, or Client/Server editions installed on your PC or network. You also need to install Windows 95, Windows 98, or Windows NT. All applications and step-by-step tutorials in this book make full use of Delphi's visual environment running in Windows. Although much information in the book applies to all versions of Delphi, you should use Version 3 or 4 for best results.

Be sure to install Delphi's source code files (usually in Delphi's Source installation directory). Many questions are easily answered by browsing a component's Pascal source code. I occasionally suggest reading a source code file for more information about a component or topic.

Any PC with an 80386, 80486, or Pentium processor, at least 32MB memory, a graphics display, and a hard disk makes an excellent Delphi development system. To develop the code for this book and to write the text, I used a stock 300MHz Pentium II computer with 128MB RAM and a 9GB hard drive. You need a printer for Chapter 14. Munchies and your favorite beverage are optional, but highly recommended.

Early Delphi releases ran on PCs with 80286 or 80386 processors using Windows 3.1. Delphi 4 requires an 80386 processor or later model, and a 32-bit operating system such as Windows 95 or Windows NT. Also on the subject of CPUs, Delphi can automatically generate corrected code for Pentium processors with the infamous floating-point-division bug, although this is less of a problem today than in years past. To enable this feature, select the Project⇨Options command, click the Compiler page tab, and switch on the Pentium-safe FDIV check box.

Version Differences

In Delphi 4, you open Project Options by selecting View⏐Project Manager... and then right-clicking the project entry (Project1, for example). This displays a pop-up menu from which you can select the Options... command to open the Project Options dialog. Use this method if you are using Delphi 4 when this book instructs you to select Project⏐Options.... Project Options is also still available on the Project Menu.

I assume in this book that you know how to use Windows and you have a mouse or similar device such as a track ball. I won't waste your time or mine explaining topics such as how to select menu commands, click buttons, and switch among windows. If you need help using Windows, consult one of the many excellent tutorials on the market or refer to the references and guides that come with the Windows operating system. I include numerous tips for effectively using Delphi's integrated development environment, but this is primarily a programming book. Most of its content focuses on how to write applications using Delphi and the Object Pascal programming language.

If you are truly getting started, install Windows first and then install Delphi, following the instructions provided with each product. If you can successfully install and run Delphi, you are ready to begin. See Appendix A for instructions about installing this book's CD-ROM files onto your hard drive.

Conventions Used in This Book

Each chapter is small enough to read in a single session. If you finish one or two chapters a day, you should be able to master Delphi 4 in about two weeks. Stay with it for another week or so and you'll be a certified guru.

I recognize, however, enough hours don't exist in a day for everyone to read every word in a large book such as this. To help you find what you need quickly — and especially so you don't waste time studying what you already know — most chapters end with three sections:

✦ **Projects** — To test your comprehension of the chapter's contents, try your hand at the suggested projects at the end of each chapter. The book's CD-ROM contains any files mentioned in this section.

✦ **Expert-User Tips** — Browse these additional tips to enhance your understanding of the chapter's topic and to pick up useful programming lore, tricks, tidbits, and techniques.

✦ **Summary** — Read this point-by-point summary to refresh your memory of the chapter's contents. You might also scan the summaries to find chapters that cover specific topics.

If you already know Pascal or if you are familiar with Delphi, first skim a chapter's Projects, Expert-User Tips, and Summary to help you decide whether you should read the chapter. Throughout the text, you find additional Notes, Tips, and Cautions that explain dozens of Delphi techniques. These sections — marked by icons in the left border of the page — can also help you find specific topics when browsing. Also notice code that uses everyday words is in italics.

Near the end of each chapter are summaries of the topics covered in the chapter. At the end of each chapter, you also find suggested projects to try and several expert-user tips. For the complete story on a specific component, look it up in the Contents and the Index. Also consult the online visual component reference on the CD-ROM. And remember: all component classes are derived from other classes, so to understand all the properties and methods available to a component, you might have to read up on several classes.

Which Delphi Versions Can You Use?

To prepare the sample applications and most of the screen illustrations in this book, I used Delphi Version 3 and an advance copy of Delphi Version 4, running under Windows 95. Some information in this book applies to all Delphi versions but, for best results, you should run Delphi Version 3 or 4. New items or items that work differently in Version 4 are noted in the text. If you are using Delphi Versions 1 or 2, you probably will have trouble running many of the sample applications; you might use an early version to get started. I don't recommend using Delphi 1 with this book except, perhaps, to get started. You may use Delphi 2 with much of this book, but I recommend you upgrade as soon as possible to Version 3 or 4 (most information and sample applications in this book works with Delphi 3). Features unique to Delphi 4 are clearly marked or noted in the text.

How to Reach Me

Of course, I never make a mistake (you believe that, right?), but if you discover an error in this book, drop me a note in care of the publisher or send an e-mail to TomSwan@compuserve.com. I spend half my time as a refugee from computer technology, so if you don't receive a quick reply, try again later. Please keep your message short and do not send large attachments electronically. For a reply via U.S. mail, please include a self-addressed, stamped envelope.

Acknowledgments

For their hard work on this book, special thanks are due, at IDG Books Worldwide, Greg Croy, Steve Sayre, and Denise Santoro; and at Inprise Corporation, Nan Borreson and Danny Thorpe. Thank you all.

Contents at a Glance

Contents

• •

Part III: The Application   489

Chapter 13: Developing Graphics Applications 491

Introduction

As you will learn in this book, with Delphi's help, you can develop complex applications in short order, regardless of your programming experience.

If you're just getting started in Windows software development, you've come to the right place to begin. If you already know your way around Delphi or you're an experienced programmer, you can read the chapters in Part I quickly—but do read them. They introduce the book's format and contain information you need to know before you can tackle more advanced topics.

If you are using Delphi Versions 1, 2, or 3—and especially if you are considering upgrading to Delphi 4—see "Migration Paths" in Chapter 1 for a comparison of Delphi programming features and a list of new items in Delphi 4.

Introducing Delphi 4

Getting started is always the hardest part of learning to use a new software development tool. (For me, just getting up in the morning is difficult enough.) With Delphi, however, you create your first application in just minutes. In this chapter, I introduce the book's layout, and I highlight key features of Delphi's visual programming environment.

Migration Paths

Delphi has now gone through four generations and each new release has increased this development product's sophistication. Because of the extensive changes that have been made to Delphi, some older applications and components might require revision before you can compile and use them in Delphi 4. However, in most cases, these changes are minor. In fact, I was able to compile this book's many projects using Delphi 4 with no modifications even though I originally wrote them using Delphi's first release. Admittedly, the book's sample applications are relatively simple, but they do cover most Delphi programming features. Only the database and OLE examples needed rewriting.

One reason for an easy upgrade path for Delphi applications is that object class interfaces have been enhanced, but not changed significantly. Object implementations have been revised, in many cases drastically, but because their class interfaces are unaltered, programs that use them need only to be recompiled to convert them for further development using newer Delphi versions. This is, after all, one of the advantages that object-oriented programming promises. It's gratifying to find one example where a promised computer technology has actually been delivered.

Key features in Delphi 1

Delphi Version 1, released about the same time as Windows 95, provided the first visual programming environment that compiles to true, native code. Although Visual Basic (VB) had been around for a while, it produces code that runs under the control of an interpreter. Delphi compiles source code text directly to native code instructions.

Note   Delphi 1 creates 16-bit native-code applications for running under Windows 3.1, Windows 95, and Windows NT. Support for 32-bit programming did not arrive until Version 2.

The key features of Delphi 1 still exist largely unmodified, though greatly enhanced, today. These features are:

✦ **A component palette of visual components that can be inserted into forms**— Each component is an object that is described programmatically as an Object Pascal class.

✦ **A property editor**—the Object Inspector window—used for assigning component property values such as captions, sizes, and colors.

✦ **An event editor**—also selected via the Object Inspector window—inserts event handlers for objects such as a procedure that is called when the program's user clicks a button.

✦ **Automatic code generation**—Delphi generates class and variables declarations, and also empty event-handler procedures. To create a new application, you drop objects into forms, select object properties, and create event handlers, which you fill in with your application's code. Automatic code generation is one of Delphi's slickest features.

✦ **Native .exe code files**—Compiled applications contain the full visual component library, making them somewhat wasteful of disk space, but very fast, and typically smaller than similar applications built with C++ class libraries, which can produce truly huge executables. (Delphi's smart linker, and trim programming language, naturally lead to a trim code file.) Most important, unlike VB, no run-time interpreter is needed to use Delphi applications.

✦ **The death of the pointer**—Pointers haven't actually passed away, they are still used and fully supported in Object Pascal. But it is no longer necessary to use pointers explicitly in most cases. The primary reason for this is that with a fully visual programming environment, memory management becomes the responsibility of the underlying component library rather than the programmer. Thus, it is rarely necessary to allocate memory to objects and to use pointers to address them. Objects are created as needed automatically and they are referenced through their visual representations. This puts pointers very much in the background, although they are still there if you need them.

✦ **Support for Visual Basic (VBX) controls**— You can't create VBX controls with Delphi 1, but you can use VBX controls by wrapping them in Delphi components.

✦ **Database programming using visual components and the Borland Database Engine**— The capability to write fully functional database applications is probably the key ingredient in Delphi's tremendous success.

Two editions of Delphi 1 are available—desktop and client-server. The desktop edition was for standalone Windows application development. The client-server edition offered additional database and networking capabilities for accessing mainframe database servers from Delphi applications. Delphi now comes in desktop, professional, and client-server flavors.

Upgrading Turbo Pascal and Borland Pascal applications to Delphi 1 requires extensive redevelopment. In fact, most applications have to be rewritten from scratch, perhaps using only snatches of the original code. In addition to its brand-new visual environment, Delphi 1's Visual Component Library (VCL) class library is largely incompatible with the earlier Borland Pascal ObjectWindows and TurboVision libraries. For this reason, porting existing code into Delphi 1 is extremely difficult for most applications.

OWL's Connection with Delphi

Technically, Delphi 1.0 was 100 percent compatible with OWL and Turbo Pascal for Windows (TPW). In fact, OWL shipped with Delphi 1.0 so that developers could recompile their programs with no modifications. However, to convert OWL applications into Delphi programs that used the new VCL components meant rewriting most applications from scratch, which many developers proceeded to do.

There were two major reasons Borland broke from the OWL model. For one, it wasn't well-suited to visual component programming because it lacked support for properties and methods—essential ingredients in the component model. OWL also needed major surgery to make the transition to 32 bits, so Borland made the logical, if painful, choice of killing the OWL and introducing visual components along with Object Pascal features to support them. (For old time's sake, in some of this book's chapters and on the CD-ROM, you'll find my original OWL icon who's been with me since TPW 1.0.)

On a final note, DOS applications written with Turbo Pascal are easily upgraded to Win32 console applications using Delphi 4.

If you are using Delphi 1, you'll find some information in this book useful. However, you may have to make changes to many sample programs and, of course, features in later releases are unavailable to you. I recommend not using Delphi 1 with this book except, perhaps, to get started.

Key features in Delphi 2

The main new feature in Delphi Version 2 is support for 32-bit programming. Other new features in Delphi 2 include:

✦ **Long and short strings** — finally doing away with the albatross of Borland Pascal — the 255-character "length-byte" string. This original string type still exists, but long strings finally freed programmers from going through an encyclopedia of contortions to store lengthy text objects in memory.

✦ **A 32-bit integer** — which broke lots of code that relied on the Integer type's former 16-bit length. Programmers discovered the validity of warnings about relying on data type byte sizes to remain unchanged.

✦ **All code and data references are now *far*** (32 bits) — which doesn't affect application programming except in cases where low-level assembly language is critical to the program.

✦ **Memory allocations limited only by the amount of available memory that can be multiple megabytes in size.**

✦ **Huge arrays that are indexed by 32-bit index values.**

✦ **Multithreaded code.**

✦ **Full support for 32-bit Windows controls such as TreeView outlines.**

✦ **Removal of support for 16-bit VBX controls** — addition of support for 32-bit OCX controls.

✦ **Improved support for Object Linking and Embedding (OLE).**

✦ **Improved Borland Database Engine and SQL links.**

✦ **Distribution in desktop, developer, and client-server editions.**

✦ **Requirement for Windows 95 or NT.** It no longer runs under Windows 3.1.

The upgrade path from Delphi 1 to Delphi 2 is fairly straightforward because existing class interfaces are largely unchanged. The key to upgrading an application is to think in 32 bits and to ferret out any code that relies on 16-bit integers and pointers. Any procedures and functions that rely on 16-bit calls must also be upgraded to 32 bits. However, these new features are pretty much automatic for most programmers who use Delphi's visual environment to construct applications.

In most cases, simply recompiling code — and also components — is all that's needed to upgrade from Delphi 1 to 2.

The same is not true of Delphi 1 applications that use 16-bit VBX controls, which Borland provided as samples that are not available in Version 2. This includes programs using the TBiSwitch, TBiGauge, TBiPict, and TChart components.

Caution

The experience with 16-bit VBX controls suggests that it is not a wise idea to use Delphi Sample components in application development. I refer *only* to those components on the Samples VCL palette; all others, and all sample code included with Delphi, are intended for use in final code.

If your application uses any 16-bit resources, you'll need to recompile them in order for Delphi's 32-bit linker to build the finished .exe code file. For example, if you import cursor bitmaps, use Image Editor to create a new 32-bit resource file in order to link the cursor images with your application.

You may use Delphi 2 with much of this book, but I recommend that you upgrade as soon as possible to Version 3 or 4.

Key features in Delphi 3

You might call this version the one that solidified Delphi's position as a top Windows development system. New features introduced in Delphi 3 include:

✦ **Support for code packages** — which enables multiple applications to share code. As a key benefit, it is no longer necessary for each compiled application to contain the entire compiled VCL, as it was for the past two versions. Code packages, however, mean that component developers must revise their products and provide compile- and run-time packages to end users. All Delphi components are now provided in package form.

✦ **Numerous enhancements to the VCL** — including new Win32 components. Sophisticated third-party report and charting components are also provided. These are fully supported components (actually, they are entire component libraries) — they are not samples.

✦ **Full support for ActiveX controls, including their creation** — Delphi 3 adds native language support for interfaces, which simplifies the use and creation of COM objects in Delphi code.

✦ **Capability to compile units to object code (.obj) files** — a long-requested change that goes back to Turbo Pascal days. This permits compiled Delphi modules to be imported into other development systems such as C++.

✦ **Enhanced client-server components and multitiered database support with the new TClientDataset and TRemoteServer components.** These components are available only in the client-server edition of Delphi 3.

✦ **Internet and intranet components with the professional and client-server editions.** These components communicate with a Web server and simplify Web application development by relieving programmers of the need to manage HTML communication protocols.

✦ **Improved integrated development environment (IDE) and code insights —** adding features that in the past were available only in third-party programming editors. The look and feel of Delphi, however, is largely unchanged.

✦ **Support for the WideString character-string type.**

✦ **Newly revised Borland Database Engine and SQL links for improved database development.**

✦ **Standard, professional, and client-server editions.** Most components and database development tools are provided in all editions. However, the client-server edition provides tools for building multitiered (that is, multiple computer) database applications using remote SQL servers and local networks. The professional edition provides capabilities for building client applications on local networks and also supports ODBC-compliant databases by way of third-party drivers.

Note   Actually, the Delphi 3 universe has a fourth dimension. If you have really deep pockets, you can acquire Delphi Enterprise edition, which includes yet more tools to connect Delphi 3 applications to data sources throughout the corporate enterprise using Borland's Entera technology. Price? Well, if you have to ask. . . .

To upgrade a Delphi 2 application to Version 3, you can usually just recompile without making any changes. However, you will probably want to take advantage of new features such as Internet support and, perhaps, ActiveX controls.

Some components in Delphi 3 are located in different categories on the VCL palette. Some other components are replaced with similar, though not identical, models. For example, the Header component is no longer available in the Additional palette; its Win32 replacement, HeaderControl, is similar but lacks some of the other component's properties and methods.

You may use Delphi 3 with most information and sample applications in this book. Features unique to Delphi 4 are clearly marked or noted in the text.

Key features in Delphi 4

Users of any previous Delphi version should be able to jump right in and get comfortable with Delphi 4. New features in Delphi 4 include the following items, most of which are covered in detail throughout the book:

✦ **A new, but still familiar, look** — Delphi's speedbar and VCL palette, which were formerly placed side by side, now rest on top of each other. This became necessary because the number of components and categories greatly exceeded the original palette's size. With Delphi 4, it is no longer necessary to scroll the palette left and right to find the components you need. (This might still be necessary on low resolution displays, however.)

✦ **Object Pascal Language Extensions** — These make several changes to Object Pascal, but all changes are advanced in nature and are unlikely to break existing code. Some changes make Object Pascal more closely resemble C++ and are particularly valuable to component developers who want to offer Delphi and C++ Builder versions of their products. New language features include dynamic arrays, method overloading, default parameters, a new 64-bit Integer data type, changes to Pascal's Real data type, and minor changes to Windows API function calls and parameters. See Chapter 21, Honing Your Delphi Skills, for information on new Object Pascal features.

✦ **Project Manager** — The old project manager has been completely revamped into a new, tree-outline model, that makes keeping track of a project's forms and files much easier. It is also now possible to create project groups, which can automate compilation of multiple projects. A project group is stored as a text Make file. This file can be used to compile projects from the DOS command line with the supplied Make utility. See "Project Manager" in this chapter for more information.

✦ **Module Explorer** — Delphi's smart code editor doubles in IQ with this new release. The Module Explorer, which normally shows to the left of the code editor window but can be undocked to a separate window, simplifies browsing in a Pascal source code unit file. The Module Explorer shows all declarations in the unit, which you can use to locate various pieces of programming in the text. For example, the Module Explorer gives you a simple way to jump from a method declaration to that method's implementation. See "Module Explorer" in this chapter for more information.

✦ **Dockable Tool Windows** — Delphi's tool windows are dockable. For example, you can undock a toolbar or other window, such as the Module Explorer, and redisplay it as a standalone window. You can also dock windows to create multipaged tool windows. For example, rather than display the Breakpoints and Watches windows separately, you can dock them into a single window and then select the individual tools by clicking page tabs. Simply click and drag the window you want to dock or undock. Hint: To dock a window, click and drag it to the edge of another, such as the code editor. Keep dragging until the window outline changes size, at which point you can release the mouse to complete the docking maneuver.

✦ **Improved Debugging** — Three new elements add improved debugging services. A CPU window shows the low-level state of an application, including CPU register values and flags. You also can view and debug your applications on the assembly language level. A Modules window now shows an application's modules, a list of source files that were compiled to build the module, and a list of global symbols and entry points. The third new window provides an Event log window that shows process control messages, breakpoint messages, Output-Debug-Strings messages, and window messages. Delphi 4 also contains advanced debugging features such as remote debugging, multiprocess debugging, cross-language debugging, and debugging of CORBA objects.

✦ **VCL Enhancements** — Several VCL enhancements and new components are available in Delphi 4. These include command lists for linking together responses to functionally similar objects such as menus and buttons, service application support for Windows NT, dockable TControl and TWinControl components for creating dockable windows and toolbars, window resize constraints, and other changes. The client-server edition includes a new TQueryClientDataSet and other components.

✦ **Multitiered Database Programming** — New components enhance client-server database programming. Connections are improved with the mconnect unit and the socket server now supports callbacks. The socket server application can also run as a Windows NT service. Other advanced database features include support for Oracle8 Abstract Data Types (ADTs) as table fields.

✦ **Support for the Microsoft Transaction Server (MTS) component model** — Delphi 4 database classes, COM classes, and even Delphi's integrated development environment now support the creation, installation, and debugging of COM objects managed by MTS. Support is also included for creating, debugging, and deploying CORBA objects.

✦ **Database Programming Enhancements** — You can browse databases and modify tables more easily by using the dataset TTable component's pop-up commands. Right-click a TTable object to gain access to the field editor and to delete, rename, and update table structures. You can also run the Database Explorer from this pop-up menu. If the table is connected to a data source, this displays the table and its information in the Explorer.

✦ **ActiveX Enhancements** — Delphi's support for ActiveX controls is enhanced to include Visual Basic data interfaces and also support for creating nonvisual ActiveX controls.

If you have Delphi 4, you can use all information and run all sample applications in this book. You may use either the desktop or professional models; you do not need the client-server edition, although I mention some of its capabilities. (It is rumored that Inprise may change the types of editions offered with Delphi 4, but this will have little effect on your use of the information in this book.)

Note

This book's information on new features in Delphi 4 can help you decide whether to upgrade from an earlier version, if you have not already done so or you are unsure about taking the plunge. If you do not yet have Delphi 4, you can use Delphi 3 with most of this book's sample code and applications.

Delphi Application Development

As with most software, the best way to learn your way around Delphi is by using it. In this section, you'll try out Delphi's visual environment. Start or switch to Delphi now. Figure 1-1 shows Delphi running in Windows 95. If your screen does not resemble the figure, select the File | New Application command.

Some buttons and windows may differ depending on your software version, operating system, and installation options. Depending on your Windows version and configuration, many title bars, borders, buttons, and other objects may differ from those shown here. These differences are largely cosmetic and, except where I indicated otherwise, they do not affect the information in this book.

Delphi's integrated development environment (IDE) has several main elements. These elements (in the order referenced in Figure 1-1) are:

✦ **Speed buttons** — These are point-and-click buttons for selected menu commands. You can learn what a button does by positioning the mouse cursor over it (don't click) and waiting a moment to see a hint box with the button's name. Get used to using Delphi's speed buttons, which in the long run will save you hours of development time, especially if you are handy with a mouse. For example, although you can run programs in other ways, the fastest method is probably to click the Run speed button (the right-pointing triangle). Some icons have been changed in Delphi 4 to better conform with Microsoft recommendations. For example, the Save project button (the second from the left) now looks like a set of disks.

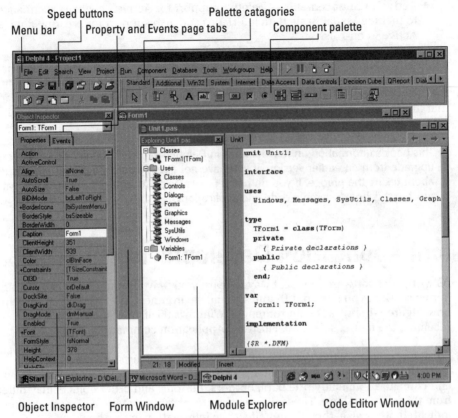

Figure 1-1: Delphi 4 running in Windows 95

✦ **Menu bar** — This is a standard Windows-style menu. Scan through Delphi's menus now to become familiar with them. Delphi 4 adds icons to many commands. These are the same icons displayed as speed buttons in the toolbar.

✦ **Component palette** — This palette contains icons that represent components in the VCL. Click a palette button to select a visual component and then click the mouse inside the form window to insert a component object. For information about a specific component, position the mouse cursor over any component button but don't click the mouse. After a moment, Delphi displays a hint box with the component's name. Move the mouse to view other component hint boxes. Use this method to locate specific components mentioned in this book.

✦ **Palette categories** — To view other component categories, click one of the page tabs shown above the VCL palette. For example, click the Dialogs page tab to display Delphi's dialog-box components.

✦ **Properties and Events page tabs** — Click one of these two page tabs at the top of the Object Inspector window to switch between a component or form's properties and events. A property represents a component's attribute, such as a button's size or a text label's font. An event represents an action, such as a mouse click or a keypress.

✦ **Object Inspector** — This window shows all of the properties and events for one or more selected components or forms. In time, you and this window will become fond friends; despite its apparent simplicity, the Object Inspector window is one of Delphi's most important programming tools. (Tip: Press F11 to bring up the Object Inspector window if it is hidden by another window, or if it was accidentally closed.)

✦ **Form window** — In most applications, a form is a visual representation of the program's main window. However, a form can represent other windows — for example, a dialog box or a child window in Multiple Document Interface (MDI) software. Simple programs may have just one form; complex applications can have dozens. The dotted grid helps you align components inserted into the form window. This grid does not appear in the final application. (Tip: Press F12 one or more times to locate this window if it is hidden by another.)

✦ **Module Explorer** — New to Delphi 4, this window shows the current module's classes, a list of other units used by this one, variables, objects, methods, and other information. To jump to a declaration or method in the code editor window, simply click any one of the entries in the Module Explorer.

✦ **Code editor window** — This window shows the Pascal source code associated with each form in the application. I'll call this the *code editor* or just the *editor window* from now on. Delphi automatically inserts most declarations and event handlers into this window, to which you can add Pascal statements that perform actions for events such as menu commands and button clicks. You can also use this window to edit other Pascal modules and text files. Select among opened files by clicking the page tabs along the top of the editor window.

✦ **Windows 95 task bar** — The Windows 95 task bar displays the Start button and icons for currently loaded applications. To activate a loaded program, just click its button in the task bar.

Tip

Press F12 to toggle between the code editor and form windows, which normally hide behind each other.

You learn more about each of Delphi's windows, commands, and other capabilities as you try out this book's sample applications. You also meet many other windows, such as the Project Manager, the Object Browser, the Integrated Debugger, the Code Editor, Code Insights, the Image Editor, Package Editor, Menu Designer, and other tools. Until you become familiar with Delphi, however, you should arrange your display so it resembles Figure 1-1.

Tip   Before continuing, select Tools|Environment Options and choose the Preferences page tab. Enable the check box, Show component captions. This makes learning about components easier, although experienced programmers may want to disable this option. Delphi does not show captions for all components; only for those that don't have a distinctive visual appearance. For example, with this option selected, a DataSource component (used in database programming) is labeled DataSource1 or another name if you changed it. Without component captions, nonvisual components are shown simply as icons, which can make it difficult to distinguish among them.

Preparing a new application

The first step after beginning a new application is to give it a name. I like to do this immediately after selecting File|New Application. Naming a new project as soon as possible prevents Delphi from saving the project in its own directories under default filenames, which wastes disk space and can cause trouble because of the way Delphi uses a module's program name to create statements and declarations.

A typical Delphi project consists of several types of files. Some files contain text, others contain binary values, bitmaps, and code. Because each application consists of many files, it's a good idea to create a separate directory on your hard disk for each new project. That way, you can easily copy an application's files to a floppy disk or a network drive for safekeeping, and you can delete old applications simply by removing their directories.

Tip   Saving projects in separate directories helps keep the application's modules well organized. Never store multiple projects in the same directory — the resulting collection of files will be more difficult to pick apart than thorns in a rose bush.

To follow along and create your first Delphi application, perform these steps now:

1. Use the Windows Explorer to create a new directory (you might call it a folder) such as C:\Projects for storing your Delphi projects. You may use a drive letter other than C: and a different name if you prefer. Inside your new directory, create a subdirectory named Hello. The finished path, C:\Projects\Hello, is now ready for holding the project's files.

2. Switch back to Delphi and select File|New Application. Alternatively, you can select File|New..., click the Page tab, and choose the Application icon — but this is the long way to the same end. If another project has already been loaded and modified, Delphi gives you a chance to save the project or discard it.

3. Before inserting components or making any other changes to the new project, select File|Save All (press Alt+FV), or click the Save All speed button. You now see two dialogs, one after the other. The first, labeled Save Unit1 As, requests a filename for the unit's main source code file. I like to name this file Main, which indicates that it contains the source for the application's main visual form. To do this, open the directory you created in Step 1, and type **Main** into the Save dialog's File name input box. Press Enter or click Save to create the file Main.pas in the open directory. Delphi automatically appends the .pas filename extension if you don't supply one. Don't change this or any other extension indiscriminately. Delphi recognizes the types of files from their extensions, and if you change them, Delphi might not be capable of creating the finished application.

4. Delphi next displays a second dialog, labeled Save Project1 As. I like to name my projects the same as their directories. For example, in this case, enter Hello for the project filename, and then press Enter or click Save. This creates the main project file, Hello.dpr, in the open directory. Delphi automatically supplies the .dpr filename extension, which stands for Delphi Project.

If Delphi does not request a project name in Step 4, you may have mistakenly selected one of two other File|Save commands, which might not save the entire project. If this happens, simply repeat Steps 3 and 4. In Step 3, you can choose File|Save Project As... (Alt+FE), but I find it easier to save my projects and any related files by selecting File|Save All (Alt+FV).

To develop more of your first Delphi application, continue with the instructions in the next section.

To ensure all project files are saved, select Tools|Environment Options, choose the Preferences page tab, and turn on the two Autosave options: Editor files and Desktop. This way, any changes to a project's files are saved automatically every time just before you run them. Don't select these options, however, if you like to make temporary changes and run them to test theories and ideas.

Setting the window caption

By default, Delphi sets the sample Hello project's form-window caption to Form1. The caption appears in the title bar under the window's top border. Follow these steps to change the caption to the program's title:

1. The Object Inspector window should display Form1: TForm1 at the top—if not, click inside the Form1 form window (the one with the dotted grid). Press F11 and F12 as needed to bring the necessary windows into view. At the top of the Object Inspector window (refer back to Figure 1-1), click the Properties page tab to display properties for the program's form. This also selects the Object Inspector window so you can make changes to object properties and events.

2. Select the Caption property. (It may already be selected by default.)

3. To modify a property, simply type or select a new value in the column to the right of the property's name. For example, change the Caption's value from Form1 to Hello Delphi Programmer! Just start typing—you don't have to highlight the text beforehand. You also don't have to press Enter after typing. If you do press Enter, however, the field is simply highlighted again. Notice the form-window caption changes as you type.

4. Save the project by selecting File | Save All. Because you have already supplied filenames, Delphi executes the command immediately—that is, it does not display the file-save dialogs that you saw when you first created the project. However, every time you add a new form to a project, you'll see one or more of these dialogs again when you save the project.

Tip

When the project is completely saved, the Save All speed button is dimmed. This is a quick way to check visually whether changes to a project's modules are safely stored on disk.

To finish your first application, continue with the instructions in the next section.

Running the application

Believe it or not, you have just finished programming your first Delphi application! To complete the development process and run the program, follow these steps:

1. Press F9, or select the Run command from the Run menu. Or, even faster, click the Run speed button (the right-facing triangle). Use one of these methods to run your application frequently during development, and to test new programming. You do not have to finish a project before running it.

2. Your computer's gears whirl, the disk turns, smoke pours out of the disk drive bays (well, I thought I saw a puff), and after a few seconds, your first application's window appears on screen. Figure 1-2 shows Hello's display in Windows 95. The program's appearance may differ depending on your operating system and desktop configuration.

3. To quit the application, double-click the system-menu button in the window's upper-left corner, or single-click the button and select Close from the system menu. If you prefer to use the keyboard, press Alt+F4 to close the application and return to Delphi. Or, you can click the window-close button in the upper-right corner.

Figure 1-2: The Hello application's display

Although the Hello application doesn't do very much, it demonstrates an important aspect of Delphi programming. Projects start out as finished applications. Contrast this to a nonvisual development system, such as a conventional C++ installation that might require you to write dozens, or more, lines of code before you can begin to test your program. Delphi programs are ready to run at most stages in their development.

Caution

After running applications from inside Delphi, always close them to return to programming mode. If you accidentally leave an application open, you will be unable to select many of Delphi's commands. if Delphi becomes recalcitrant — and especially if you cannot view the Object Inspector window by pressing F11 — the cause is probably a running application you forgot to close.

Try another quick experiment: press F9 to rerun Hello. Notice that this time, the application window appears more quickly than when you first ran the program. Delphi recognizes that you made no changes to the project, so it simply reloads the application's code file. Close the Hello program window now.

You can also use Windows Explorer to run a Delphi application. For example, open the Explorer, and browse to the C:\Projects\Hello directory. Double-click Hello.exe, or highlight that filename and press Enter. Your program's users run finished Delphi applications the same as they do other Windows programs. Remember to close the program before continuing.

It's possible to use Windows Explorer to run multiple instances of an application. For example, you can run two or more copies of Hello. You can, however, run only one program instance from inside Delphi. To run multiple instances, you must use the Explorer or the Windows Start button Run command. Close all instances of Hello before continuing.

A Delphi application is a full-fledged Windows program — you run it the same way you run other applications. You can click and drag an application's filename to your desktop, or create a shortcut to the file (click and drag using the right mouse button), and then double-click the resulting icon. Masochists who like to do things the hard way can type the program's full path name **C:\Projects\Hello\Hello.exe** using the Start button's Run command. You can also open a DOS window, change to the project directory, and enter Hello to run the program. The point is, Delphi-created applications are true compiled native-code programs. You run them just as you do other Windows software.

Compiling and linking the code

When you run an application by pressing F9, Delphi compiles and links the program to create an executable code file. Two key actions occur. First, the Delphi compiler translates the program's text into binary code. Then, the linker combines that code with other modules required for various startup chores and other tasks. The result of compiling and linking a Delphi project is a complete, executable code file that has the same name as the project, but a filename ending with the extension .exe.

To compile and link an application, but not run it, press Ctrl+F9 or select the Project|Syntax Check command. You might use these methods to verify that the program is free of errors such as minor typing mistakes.

Tip

Use Tools|Environment Options and switch on the Show compiler progress check box. This displays a dialog that shows various details of compiling and linking, and is especially useful for pinpointing errors in large applications.

Unlike other visual programming systems, Delphi generates true native code, which means that finished programs do not require a run-time interpreter. In past versions of Delphi, the resulting .exe code file was 100 percent complete, and was the only file required by your program's users. This is still true of Delphi 4. However, starting with Delphi Version 3, much of Delphi's Visual Component Library (VCL) is organized into a *package* that two or more applications can share. Depending on the types of applications you create, you might need to provide design-time or run-time packages (or both) to your end users. You definitely need to do this, for example, if you develop custom components for other Delphi programmers.

Another reason for distributing packages is to minimize the amount of duplicated code in compiled .exe files. In Delphi Versions 1 and 2, all necessary code, including code for the entire VCL, was linked into every .exe code file. If you had six different Delphi applications, their .exe code files stored six separate copies of the same VCL components. Obviously, this waste of space is undesirable, even though the resulting files are simple and fast running. Today, you may choose to distribute common code using packages that all host applications share. There aren't any speed penalties for using packages (as there are with run-time interpreters such as used by Visual Basic and Java). Chapter 20, Constructing Custom Components, explains how to create your own packages.

Note Packages are optional at the run-time application level. If you prefer to link in all code used by your application, select Project|Options..., click the Packages page tab, and disable the check box, Build with runtime packages. Custom components, however, as well as those supplied with Delphi, must be organized into packages.

Programming with Components

Before continuing with this chapter, let's pause for a quick review. You now know three essential Delphi techniques:

✦ How to create and save a new project

✦ How to modify a property such as a Caption in a Delphi form

✦ How to compile, link, and run an application by pressing F9, or by clicking the Run speed button (right-pointing triangle)

You will probably use these techniques in every application you write. Of course, programs that do nothing but display a title aren't going to burn up the best-seller charts. To give the Hello application something to do, you can insert a visual component in the program's window, and debug the code, as the following sections explain.

Tip The Open-file speed button opens individual files. To load a complete Delphi application, always click the Open-project speed button, or select File|Open... to open a project file ending with the extension .dpr. You can also select the File|Open Project... command, which has made a surprise reappearance in Delphi 4 after disappearing in Version 3.

Inserting visual components

Follow these steps to insert a visual component object into the Hello program's window:

1. Close the running Hello program if necessary to return to Delphi. Select File|Open... or click the Open-project speed button. (Do this for experience even if Hello is already open.) When the Open Project dialog appears, change directories if necessary and select Hello.dpr. Press Enter or click OK to open the project. Use this same method to open other projects mentioned in this book.

Tip If you need to pause for a breather midway through a chapter, save the project and then reload it when you are ready to continue.

2. Click the Standard page tab of the component palette and then select the Button component labeled Ok.

3. Move the mouse cursor into the form and click once to insert a Button object in the window. The location doesn't matter.

4. Make sure the Button object is selected — you should see square handles around it. If the object is not selected, click it once now. By default, Delphi names the object Button1. For a more meaningful name, select the Name property in the Object Inspector, and type **CloseButton**. That's one word, not two — don't type any spaces in it. Press Enter.

5. Notice that the Caption property and the button's text also change to CloseButton. This is normal, but you will often want a component object's Name and Caption properties to differ. In this case, for example, select the Caption property, and type **Close**. Your form window should resemble Figure 1-3.

Figure 1-3: Hello's form window in Delphi

6. Single-click the CloseButton object if necessary to select it. At the top of the Object Inspector window, select the Events page tab, which lists the actions that the button can perform. Double-click the blank space to the right of the OnClick event. Main.pas appears in the code editor, and Delphi positions the flashing cursor between the keywords begin and end. Type the following statement:

```
Close;
```

7. You have just programmed a procedure called an *event handler* for the button's OnClick event. Be sure to end the statement with a semicolon. Compare the text in your window with that in Listing 1-1.

Listing 1-1: **The CloseButton object's OnClick event handler**

```
procedure TForm1.CloseButtonClick(Sender: TObject);
begin
  Close;
end;
```

8. Save the project and then run it by pressing F9. You can now click the OK button to close the window. Because this is the program's main window, closing it also ends the application.

The preceding steps demonstrate three important aspects of programming with Delphi:

✦ You inserted a Button component object into a form window.

✦ You modified the object's *properties* to change its Name and Caption values.

✦ You programmed one of the object's *events* to perform a run-time action in response to the button's selection.

Most of your programming experience with Delphi involves using component objects, properties, and events. To create applications, you insert component objects into forms, and you program their properties and event handlers. It's that simple! And, by the way, Delphi's interface and all components were written using Delphi — powerful proof of what you can accomplish with this remarkable development system.

Debugging program statements

Programmers hate debugging as much as gardeners hate weeding. Who wouldn't rather design new code than waste time squashing bugs? Delphi can't prevent bugs, of course, but it can help you avoid many common errors by giving you a smart visual environment that automatically creates much of your application. Unfortunately, there's still plenty of room for error, and I would be fibbing if I promised that programming with Delphi is always pest free.

When the critters start chewing up your code, use Delphi's debugging commands to run your applications one step at a time and view the values of objects and variables. By slowing a program's usual breakneck speed, the cause of a problem often becomes obvious. Get used to Delphi's debugging commands now so you know how to use them when you need them — trust me, you need them!

Delphi's debugging commands are also useful for investigating how a program works. Use them frequently to examine the sample programs in this book as well as those in Delphi's Demos directory. Follow these steps to learn how to use some of Delphi's debugging features:

1. Open the Hello project if necessary.

2. If you did not insert a Close button into the form, do so now by following the instructions in the preceding section.

3. Locate the TForm1.CloseButtonClick procedure in the Main.pas editor window. Insert the following statement above Close to display a message. The two lines between begin and end should now look like this:

```
ShowMessage('Ready to close application');
Close;
```

4. Normally, you press F9 to compile, link, and run a program. This time, however, press F8 to select Delphi's Step Over command from the Run menu. This begins the program, and pauses at the first statement. (Actually, depending on your Delphi version, it may pause at the unit's initialization code, indicated by the keyword end. Press F8 a second time if this happens.) You should see the program's window. When it appears, click the Close button. Instead of ending the program, Delphi pauses it inside the CloseButtonClick procedure. This is an example of *single-stepping,* one of the most important debugging tools used during a program's development.

5. Press F8 two more times to step to the ShowMessage statement and execute it. A box with an OK button appears on screen. Click this button. Again, because you pressed F8, Delphi pauses the program at the next statement to execute, Close.

6. Press F9 to execute the Close statement and run the program to completion. After pressing F8 to single-step one or more statements, you will usually continue to run a program this way by pressing F9. The program ends, and Delphi returns from debugging back to development mode.

Another way to step through a program is by setting a *breakpoint.* When the program reaches the marked statement, Delphi halts the application before that statement executes. Follow these steps to set a breakpoint and step through the program:

1. Move the flashing cursor to the ShowMessage statement in Main.pas, and select Run⏐Add Breakpoint. Click the New button in the resulting dialog, or just press Enter. The marked statement is now highlighted in red (dark gray on monochrome monitors). Or, you can point the mouse cursor to the left of a statement and click the mouse button to set the breakpoint. Use this method to quickly toggle breakpoints on and off. You may set more than one breakpoint at different places in the program, but for this experiment, we'll set only one.

2. Press F9 to run the program. When you click the Close button, Delphi halts the code at the marked statement. Press F8 to single-step that statement and display a message. Close the message dialog by clicking its OK button, and press F9 to run the program to completion.

3. Try Step 2 again, but this time, press Alt+F4 to end the program. Because this does not execute the CloseButtonClick procedure, the program ends without stopping at the breakpoint. (Hint: Early versions of Delphi displayed a stop-sign icon when you move the cursor over a paused program's window. Newer versions no longer do this.)

4. Always try to run a program to completion. If you can't do that, select Run|Program Reset (Ctrl+F2) and start over. This may skip termination routines that delete various resources from memory, causing a gradual loss of available memory that eventually requires you to exit and restart Windows. Such is the software developer's life, but fortunately, this problem is rare.

5. To toggle a breakpoint on or off, move the mouse cursor to the extreme left of a marked statement and click the left button once. This is the easiest way to set and remove a breakpoint. You can also use the View|Breakpoints command to add, delete, disable, and perform other operations on breakpoints. Select this command now and click the right mouse button in the Breakpoint list window for a list of available commands. Remove the breakpoint from the ShowMessage statement now by selecting the pop-up menu's Delete command.

I suggest other Delphi debugging commands at the appropriate times throughout the rest of this book. However, don't wait for me to suggest single-stepping a program's statements by pressing F8 and by setting breakpoints. Use Delphi's debugging features often to investigate this book's sample applications. You'll be amazed at what you can learn just by slowing down the code and examining the program's state at strategic locations.

Code Insight

Newly introduced in Delphi 3, *code insights* automatically complete code while you type, and they also provide information about Delphi's procedure, function, and component libraries. Using code insights, you can create shells for common programming elements such as procedures and loops. You can then fill in the shells to save typing time. You can also have Delphi's code editor display parameter types for common procedures and functions, and also show properties and methods for component objects. Having this pop-up information available in the code editor helps you spend less time sorting through Delphi's online help and printed documentation—if, that is, you learn how to use code insights properly. This section will help.

Sometimes, I find code insights are more trouble than they are worth — especially on slower computers that pause too long to display context-sensitive help windows. On the other hand, I find code insights invaluable the more I use them. For instance, to create a new procedure, I simply type the word **procedure** and press Ctrl+J, the code template hot key. This creates an entire procedure shell that I can then fill in. Using other types of code insights — code completion and code parameters — I can automatically list method names and parameter argument types. In the following sections, I show examples of all of these techniques.

You probably want to customize code insights depending on your programming style, but before spending too much time doing that, it's probably best to get used to the default settings. The four basic code insight features are:

✦ Code Templates

✦ Code Completion

✦ Code Parameters

✦ Tool-tip Expression Evaluation

The following sections give tips for using code insights as well as suggestions for customizing these valuable programming tools.

Code templates

Press Ctrl+J at any time while using the code editor to display a list of code templates. Select the template you want, and Delphi automatically inserts the template into the source code at the current cursor position. Because there are numerous templates, you can save time by typing the first portion of the template you want before pressing Ctrl+J. For example, to insert an if statement into your code, type the word **if** and press Ctrl+J. Delphi lists the following four possible statement templates:

```
if statement                                 ifb
if then (no begin/end) else (no begin/end)   ife
if then else                                 ifeb
if (no begin/end)                            ifs
```

The first column describes the type of statement template. The last column gives the template's shortcut name, which you can use to edit the template if necessary. If you don't need to edit the templates, you can ignore their shortcut names.

You learn more about code templates by using them than by reading about them here, so I won't attempt to document the many available types. Spend a few minutes selecting various templates for the statements you tend to use the most. I find some templates more useful than others. For example, it takes me more time to move the cursor around in a simple if-then-else shell than it does for me to type the keywords directly—but, then, I'm a fast typist. I find other templates more useful, especially because I also use C++ and other programming languages. For instance, code templates remind me that Object Pascal exceptions use the *try* and *except* keywords, where other languages might use *try* and *catch*. Code insights help me remember the correct Object Pascal syntax, and reduce compilation errors.

Tip   Do not type a space after the first portion of the code template. Type only the first word of the statement—for example, *if, for,* or *while*—and then press Ctrl+J. Delphi adds spaces according to the template's design.

After you get used to using code templates, you might want to edit the stock set. You might also want to create your own templates. For demonstration purposes, we'll create a new commented procedure template that inserts a shell for a new procedure preceded by a comment that you can fill in to describe the code's purpose. Follow these steps:

In Delphi 7 : Tools | Editor Options | Source Options → Edit Code Templates

1. Select Tools|Environment Options.... and click the Code Insight page tab. Click the Add... button, and enter **procedureC** for the template's shortcut name, and "**procedure (commented)**" for its description.

2. Click inside the editor window next to the label, Code:. Enter the following lines or use your own design (the vertical bar indicates where you want Delphi to place the text cursor after inserting the template into a program's source code):

```
{ Purpose: |
  Date   : 00/00/00
  Author : Tom Duck
}
procedure ();
begin

end;
```

You can now add another template or you can edit existing ones. Click OK to save your changes. To use the template, type **P** and press Ctrl+J. This lists all template names that begin with *P*. Choose the new template named procedureC to insert the template into the code editor.

Note   If there is only one template when you press Ctrl+J, Delphi immediately inserts that template into the code editor. By following the preceding steps, you now have to select among two templates for the procedure keyword. To return to the default setting, open the Code Insight dialog, select the new template (procedureC), and click the Delete button. You can now type **P** followed by Ctrl+J to insert a procedure template directly into your code. Similarly, you can type **F** followed by Ctrl+J to insert a function template.

Code completion

Delphi's code completion tool also inserts text automatically into the code editor, but it differs from code templates by suggesting appropriate methods, properties, events, and arguments. This feature saves time mostly by helping prevent compiler errors rather than saving typing time. For example, you can list all possible methods for any VCL class object. By selecting from this list, you are less likely to make a syntax error, to assign an illegal value, or to attempt to call a method that doesn't exist.

I find code completion especially useful when programming with objects in source code. Rather than look up method and property names in Delphi's online help, I type a bit of code and wait a moment for the code completion insight to kick in. I then select the method or other item I want and continue typing. Remember, this doesn't save typing time so much as research time (at least that's true for me).

Follow the next steps to experiment with code completion and to see how it differs from code templates:

1. Start a new application by selecting File | New Application. You can name and save the application if you want, or just use the default names.

2. Insert a Button component from the Standard component palette into the application's form window. Double-click the button object to create a default event handler for it.

> **Tip**
>
> This is often the fastest way to create a default event handler for an object, although you can also use the Object Inspector window as described for the Hello application in this chapter.

3. The cursor should be positioned between begin and end keywords in a Button1Click procedure. Now use code completion to change the button's label when clicked. First, type the following:

```
Button1.
```

Then, wait a moment. Do not type a space after the period. You soon see the code completion suggestions for this type of object. (If the suggestions disappear, delete and retype the period to again engage code completion.) Delphi lists all the properties, constructors, procedures, and functions for this type of object. In this case, we want to assign a new string to the object's Caption property. Find the word Caption in the list, and double-click it to insert Caption into the source code. Complete the assignment by typing a new string to assign to the button's Caption property. For example, edit the source code line to read as follows:

```
Button1.Caption := 'Ouch!';
```

4. You can now run the program and click the button, which changes its text to "Ouch!"

Tip

To alter the amount of time you have to wait for the code completion insight window to pop up, use Tools|Environment Options..., select the Code Insight page tab, and drag the Delay slider to set the value you want. On my main desktop system, I use the fastest setting—one half-second. On my slower laptop, I *increase* this value so the pop-up window appears only if I intentionally wait a second or longer. This way, I can continue typing if I prefer not to see the window, which can take a moment to form. Try different settings to see what timing works best on your system.

A second way to use code completion is to press Ctrl+spacebar. This forces open the code completion window, which lists items available for this location in the source code. Contrary to other documentation you might read, this feature does not list legal values for assignment statements—it lists *all* objects that are in scope and, thus, can potentially be assigned or used in some way at this place in the program. That might be useful in assignment statements, but it is also useful in other ways, such as finding the name of a global declaration.

For example, I find this second type of code completion most useful in selecting among a program's numerous local and global variables. To begin an assignment statement, I press Ctrl+spacebar and then select a variable's name from the resulting pop-up list. This enables me to use long and descriptive variable names such as CountOfAliveObjects, and select them from a pop-up list, rather than typing such names repeatedly.

Note

Remember you can use code completion two ways. One, type an object name and a period, and then wait a moment to list object properties and methods. Two, press Ctrl+spacebar at any time to list objects that are available at this place in the source code.

Code completion requires the source code to be syntactically valid at least up to the place of insertion. If you receive the error message, "Unable to invoke Code Completion due to errors in source code," check that you haven't left out a keyword or other essential element. To see this error, move the cursor past the end of a unit's source code (after the end with a period) and press Ctrl+spacebar. Actually, there might not be any errors in this case—the space beyond the end of a unit is outside of the code's scope, which is why you receive this error message.

You have two ways to customize code completion. You can alter the time it takes for the completion window to pop up, or you can disable code completion entirely. Use Tools|Environment Options... and select Code Insight to make either modification. You might want to disable code completion on very slow computers, which might take too long to bring the completion window into view. In this case, you are probably best advised to use online help or printed documentation to look up properties, methods, and objects.

Code parameters

The third type of code insight makes it practically impossible to pass the wrong types of data to methods — one of the most common programming errors you can make. (Believe me, I know.) With this feature, a pop-up window lists all required parameters in the methods your code calls. You simply consult this information as you supply argument values for procedure and function parameters.

An experiment can show how valuable code parameters are. I also use code completion to demonstrate how to use these two types of code insights together, which you will often do. Follow these steps:

1. Start a new application and insert a Button object into the form window. Double-click the button to create a default event handler for the object.

2. In between the begin and end keywords, type **Button1.** (don't forget the period) and wait a moment. Type **sc** (case doesn't matter) to show the ScaleBy method in the code completion window, and press Enter to insert that method into the source code. (Remember this technique — when the code completion window appears, type the first few letters of the method or property you want, and then press Enter to insert it into the program.)

3. Add an open parenthesis to the partially formed Button1.ScaleBy statement and then wait a moment. You should see the following list of parameter types for the arguments you can pass to the ScaleBy method:

```
M: Integer; D: Integer
```

This text appears in a box just below the text cursor. Notice the first parameter is in bold — this indicates the parameter you are expected to type next. Enter **4** and a comma and, again, wait a moment. Now, the *D* parameter is in bold, indicating an argument value for this parameter is expected. Type **3**, a close parenthesis, and a semicolon to end the statement. When you type the parenthesis, the code parameter pop-up window disappears, indicating you have supplied all required arguments. Tip: Remember to type a comma, not a semicolon, between actual argument values — a fact that expert Pascal programmers probably know, but beginners might miss. The finished statement should look like this:

```
Button1.ScaleBy(4, 3);
```

4. You can now press F9 to compile and run the program. Like something out of *Alice in Wonderland*, the button grows larger each time you click it. It does this because the ScaleBy method scales a visual component object by *M* divided by *D*, in this case $4/3$, or about 1.33 times.

Tip The code parameter pop-up window might take a moment or two to appear, especially for procedures that take numerous arguments. As with code completion, you can alter the delay time for this option or you can disable it with the Tools|Environment Options... command.

Tool-tip expression evaluation

This code insight sounds more exotic than it actually is, but that's not to say it lacks usefulness. In fact, this feature might be the one you use most often in testing your code. To use tool-tip expression evaluation, you must run your program in debug mode. You can do this in several ways, but the two most common are to set a breakpoint or to run code in single-step mode by pressing F8.

When you do this and pause the program at some place during its execution, move the cursor over any variable to see a pop-up window of its value. This is immensely useful when investigating variables during debugging. The variable has to be in scope at that point in the program's execution — variables declared local to methods outside of the one where the program stops are not available for inspection (in fact, those variables don't exist in memory). For an example of how this feature works, follow these steps:

1. Create a new application, insert a Button object, double-click it, and insert the following statement in the Button1Click method:

```
Button1.Caption := 'Ouch!';
```

2. This is the same statement you typed for the code completion example in this section. Before running the application, insert a breakpoint on the preceding statement. Do this by clicking to the left of the line, or by using the Run|Add Breakpoint... command.

3. Press F9 to run the application and then click the button. This pauses the program at the statement for which you set the breakpoint. Because the program is paused in debug mode, you can now use tool-tip expression evaluation to examine variables. Move the cursor over the word Caption. Wait a moment, and Delphi displays the value currently assigned to this property. In a small box, you see:

```
Button1.Caption = 'Button1';
```

4. The Caption is set to this string because the program hasn't yet executed the statement at the breakpoint. Do this by pressing F9 to continue running the program and then click the button a second time. When the program again halts at the breakpoint, move the cursor over Caption, which now shows the new value assigned the last time this statement was executed.

As with code completion and code parameters, you can alter the delay time for tool-tip expression evaluation, or disable this feature by using the Tools|Environment Options… command. However, I can't think of any reason you'd want to disable this useful feature.

Tip   Tool-tip evaluation works best if compiler optimizations are turned off, because when optimizations are enabled, the compiler might rearrange code in such a way that locating variables in memory is difficult or impossible for the debugger. To disable optimizations, select Project|Options… and choose the Compiler page tab. Under Code generation, clear the Optimization check box. To make this the default setting, enable the Default check box at the bottom of the dialog window before you click OK. Be sure to enable optimization before compiling your finished program.

Module Explorer

The Module Explorer, new to Delphi 4, greatly simplifies finding your way around an application's source code files. The Module Explorer provides an outline of your program's symbols. This outline serves to document the source and also to help you find specific declarations. Figure 1-4 shows the Module Explorer from Figure 1-1.

Module Explorer

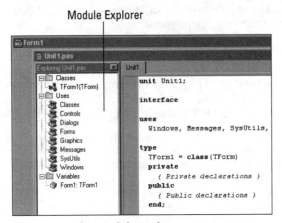

Figure 1-4: The Module Explorer

The Module Explorer is shown at the left of the code editor. It displays a tree-outline of the current unit's types, classes, properties, methods, global variables, and global routines. The Module Explorer also lists the names of units used by the current module.

To toggle between the Module Explorer and the code editor windows, press Ctrl+Shift+E. Highlight any entry in the tree-outline, and the text cursor hops to that symbol's declaration in the code editor. I find this especially helpful to locate the implementation of a method that is declared in the unit's interface section—a method declaration inside a class for example.

The Module Explorer supports incremental searching. Type the first letters of the symbol you want to find. If that symbol is a program declaration, this positions the cursor in the code editor.

Docking and undocking

You can dock and undock the Module Explorer window. To undock it, click and drag the window's top border. You'll see a thick outline, which you can drag to any location. Release the mouse button to display the Module Explorer in a separate window. You might do this, for example, on a low-resolution display. In that case, the standard Module Explorer might make the code editor too small. On my 1024×768 display, I prefer to leave the Module Explorer docked in its original location.

After undocking, you can bring up the Module Explorer window by selecting View|Module Explorer. Pressing Ctrl+Shift+E while the code editor is active also brings the Module Explorer to the front of other windows.

To dock the Module Explorer back to its original position, click and drag the window border to the left of the code editor. Continue dragging until the thick outline changes to thin (it will also be skinnier). Release the mouse button to complete docking.

You can also dock the Module Explorer to the right of the code editor window. Grab its top border with the mouse and drag the Module Explorer window to the other side of the editor. Keep dragging until the outline changes from thick to thin and then release the mouse button.

Tip   When the code editor is maximized, the thick docking window outline might disappear. You can release the mouse button at this time to complete docking.

Class completion

If you've programmed with Delphi, you probably have made plenty of mistakes typing class method declarations and their implementations in the correct formats. When I do this, I invariably forget to supply the class name and a period in the implementation; or, I accidentally copy this text to the declaration. Both mistakes lead to frustrating compilation error messages.

Using the Module Explorer's class completion feature — which you might consider as a kind of new code insight tool — the code editor can create a method shell for any declaration. To try this out, start a new application, and then follow these steps:

1. Insert a Button object into the program's main form.

2. Double-click Button1 to create a method for the object's OnClick event.

3. Click TForm1 in the Module Explorer. This moves the text cursor to the TForm1 class declaration. Locate the private keyword and just below it, type the following procedure declaration, which declares Subroutine as a member of the TForm1 class:

```
procedure Subroutine;
```

4. To complete the code, you must supply an implementation of the actual method. This is where class completion comes in handy. Position the cursor anywhere in the TForm1 class declaration, and then press Ctrl+Shift+C. Delphi generates shells for all declared methods that do not have implementations.

5. With only one unimplemented method, the cursor is positioned between Subroutine's begin and end keywords. Enter two statements to complete the method as follows:

```
procedure TForm1.Subroutine;
begin
  ShowMessage('Ready to exit');
  Close;
end;
```

6. Locate the OnClick event handler from Step 2. To do this quickly using Module Explorer, click Button1Click under TForm1's methods.

7. Type the following single statement between the begin and end keywords. The completed method should look like this:

```
procedure TForm1.Button1Click(Sender: TObject);
begin
  Subroutine;
end;
```

8. Press F9 to compile and run the program. When you click the button, the OnClick event handler calls Subroutine, which displays a message and ends the program.

Class completion also works in reverse. Enter any procedure or function in a unit's implementation section. Move the cursor to anywhere inside the procedure or function, and then press Ctrl+Shift+C to create a declaration for that method in the indicated class. To try this, delete the class declaration from TForm1's private section. Use Module Explorer to jump to Subroutine's implementation and press Crtl+Shift+C. If no prototype declaration exists for the method, Delphi adds one in the proper format to the class's private section. (You can move this declaration to a protected or public section if necessary.)

Module navigation

The Module Explorer provides another way to toggle the code editor between a method's declaration in its class and its implementation. With the cursor positioned on any method declaration, press Crtl+Shift+Down arrow or Crtl+Shift+Up arrow to jump to that method's implementation. (It doesn't seem to matter which arrow key you press because the feature is a toggle, and the direction is unimportant.)

A note in Delphi's help file indicates you can use these keys to toggle between the interface and implementation sections of a unit, but this doesn't seem to work for me. Perhaps it will be fixed in your copy of Delphi.

Files and Filename Extensions

The following sections describe the contents of many types of files that Delphi creates for an application. I'll also explain which files you may safely delete from a project directory to save room on disk.

Source code files

When you insert components into a form, and when you modify form and component properties and events, Delphi writes the text of your program in Object Pascal. This text is called the program's *source code.* At any time while developing an application, you can view the program's source code files, and you can print them for paper backups.

Experienced Pascal programmers may be tempted to modify their applications' source code. Regardless of your experience, however, you should enter new programming with extreme care. Delphi's code generator is smart, but it can't understand every change you make. For best results, follow this book's suggestions for creating applications. In time, the rules for what you can and cannot change become obvious.

Follow these steps to examine the source code for the sample Hello application and to become more familiar with the programming and files that Delphi generates:

1. If the Hello project is not open, select File | Open... to open the Hello.dpr project file.

2. Select View | Units (Ctrl+F12) or click the Select-unit-from-list speed button, and choose Main from the resulting dialog's list of modules. This displays the unit's source code in Delphi's editor window. Press Enter or click OK to close the unit dialog. Listing 1-2 shows the text you see on screen. This same text is stored on the CD-ROM as Main.pas in the Source\Hello directory.

3. Select View | Units again but this time choose the Hello module. The editor window now shows two files — select between them by clicking a page tab at the top of the window. Listing 1-3 shows the project file's text, which is stored on the CD-ROM as Hello.dpr in the Source/Hello directory.

Listing 1-2: **Hello\Main.pas**

```
unit Main;

interface

uses
  Windows, Messages, SysUtils, Classes, Graphics, Controls,
Forms, Dialogs,
  StdCtrls;

type
  TForm1 = class(TForm)
    CloseButton: TButton;
    procedure CloseButtonClick(Sender: TObject);
  private
    { Private declarations }
  public
    { Public declarations }
  end;

var
  Form1: TForm1;

implementation

{$R *.DFM}
```

```
procedure TForm1.CloseButtonClick(Sender: TObject);
begin
  Close;
end;

end.
```

Listing 1-3: **Hello\Hello.dpr**

```
program Hello;

uses
  Forms,
  Main in 'Main.pas' {Form1};

{$R *.RES}

begin
  Application.Initialize;
  Application.CreateForm(TForm1, Form1);
  Application.Run;
end.
```

Tip

To close individual files in the editor window, make that page current and press Ctrl+F4, or click the right mouse button and choose Close Page. This merely closes the page in the editor window—it does not delete the file from disk. To reopen a unit's source code file, select its name using the View|Units command.

A Delphi project's source code is stored in at least two text files — in this case, Main.pas and Hello.dpr. The Main.pas file in Listing 1-2 is an example of a unit, which contains programming for the Hello program's main-window form. All applications in this book have at least one unit, but complex projects may have many units, each stored in a separate .pas file.

The second source code file in a typical Delphi application contains the entire project's source code. For example, Hello.dpr in Listing 1-3 shows the source code for the Hello project. Every application has one and only one project file.

To print the currently selected file in the editor window, select File | Print…. You can choose from a variety of options in the resulting Print Selection dialog. For example, enable Line numbers to number each programming line, or enable the Header/page number option for a finished appearance. Enable the Syntax print option to print keywords in bold and to use italics and underlining for other program elements. Disable Syntax print for faster printing on slow, dot-matrix printers or if you prefer a relatively plain appearance in listings.

Note   Newer versions of Delphi include an option to print in color. The resulting listing shows keywords and other program elements using syntax highlighting, similar to what you see in Delphi's editor window. Of course, you need a color printer to use this feature. You also want to use Tools|Environment Options… to select the default color scheme — other settings such as Classic, for example, look better on screen than they do on paper. Experiment with short test files until you get the look you want. Unfortunately, you have to actually print a page to change printing options — changing them and canceling printing reverts to your old settings.

Unit files

Now, let's take a closer look at the source code that Delphi generates for a project, beginning with the main form's unit, Main.pas (Listing 1-2). The first line in this file states the unit's name — in this case, Main. Delphi gives the unit the same name that you specify when saving the project's unit file.

Next comes an interface directive, which makes the items that follow available to other units that use this one. The interface contains the unit's public declarations. Items not in the interface are hidden from other units.

Units may — and usually do — use other units. For example, Main uses many different units, all of which are listed in the module's uses directive. Units such as Windows, Messages, SysUtils, and others provide data and code for the Windows API, or application programming interface, and for Delphi's components. You can also create your own units and use them. For example, you might create a unit with data and code to be shared among a program's different parts.

Next in Main.pas comes a *type declaration* section, identified by the keyword type. A type — more fully called a *data type* — describes the nature of an item that can be created in memory. For example, an Integer is a data type that represents whole numbers. To use Integers, you must create one or more variables of that type that can store specific values such as 123. Other Pascal data types include characters, strings, records, and floating-point values. I'll explain more about these and other types as you meet examples of them in this book's sample applications.

A data type can also be a class, an object-oriented structure used extensively in Delphi applications. A class describes the features of an object that can be created in memory. A class encapsulates related code and data, which are collectively known as class members. Classes can inherit the members of other classes. For example, the TForm1 class in Main.pas inherits TForm's members, a class that Delphi provides for creating forms. Because of its inheritance, the TForm1 class is called a *descendant* of TForm.

The TForm1 class in Main.pas declares two additional members to those it inherits. The first member is a TButton object, named CloseButton. The second member of TForm1 is a procedure, a subroutine that performs an action. In this case, the CloseButtonClick procedure ends the program when you click the program's Close button. These are the component and event hander that you created by following the steps in this chapter—Delphi writes the code in response to your properties and events for the component objects you insert into forms.

Classes may have additional declarations, some of which might be private (for use only in the class's unit) or public (available also to statements in other units). This case has no private and public declarations. Two comments surrounded by curly braces indicate where these types of declarations can go:

```
private
  { Private declarations }
public
  { Public declarations }
```

Comments have no run-time effects. They are merely notes that describe an aspect of the program. A comment might explain a tricky statement, or it can identify the program's author, revision number, and other sundry facts. You may type anything you want between the braces except another closing brace. Comments can also extend over more than one line. Here's an example of a multiline comment:

```
{ This multiline comment occupies three lines. It
begins with an opening brace on the first line,
and ends with a closing brace. }
```

Instead of curly braces, you may use the double-character symbols (* and *)— leftovers from the early days of Pascal when many keyboards and terminals lacked curly brace characters. For example, this is a perfectly acceptable comment:

```
(* Program author: Your name goes here *)
```

You may mix different comment styles in the same program, but if you begin a comment with an opening brace, you must end it with a closing brace. Likewise, if you begin a comment with (*, you must end it with *).

A third type of comment — unique to Object Pascal, and borrowed from C++ — begins with a double slash and extends to the end of the current line. This type of comment can be only one line long. For example, you might use this type of comment to add an explanatory note to a declaration:

```
var
   Counter: Integer;  // Temporary loop counter
```

Finally, in the unit's interface section are one or more variables preceded by the keyword *var*. Units may have zero, one, or more variables. This example has only one variable:

```
var
   Form1: TForm1;
```

The declaration creates a variable named Form1 of the TForm1 class. In other words, Form1 is an object of a class that occupies space in memory. The object in this example represents the Hello program's main window, which contains a button and an event handler that performs the button's action. Again, Delphi writes this declaration when you create the form. You never have to do this manually.

A class object is similar to a variable of a data type such as an Integer. You may create one or more actual objects of any class, just as you can create multiple Integer variables.

Following its interface section is the unit's implementation, where Delphi creates statements to perform run-time actions, and where you can insert your own declarations and other programming. You can also type statements into a unit's implementation. For example, locate the procedure in which you typed the Close; statement. Here it is again for reference:

```
procedure TForm1.CloseButtonClick(Sender: TObject);
begin
   Close;
end;
```

Just before to that procedure, you find this strange-looking directive:

```
{$R *.DFM}
```

Although it looks like a comment, the dollar sign immediately following the opening brace tells Delphi that this line is a special directive that opens and reads a file ending with the filename extension .dfm (short for Delphi Form). The asterisk tells Delphi to look for a file named the same as the project, but ending with the filename extension .dfm. This file contains the form's properties entered with the Object Inspector.

On the last line of Main.pas is the keyword end followed by a period. Technically, the end keyword designates the end of the unit module, and the period signifies the end of the file. However, this is a relatively unimportant distinction. Just remember that only the final end in a unit ends with a period.

Project files

Pascal experts in the audience will recognize Hello.dpr as a Pascal program (refer to Listing 1-3). As with the Main unit, Delphi creates this text automatically. A Delphi project is actually a Pascal program. A project has two main purposes — to declare the application's unit modules and to run the program.

The first line in Hello.dpr specifies the project name in a program declaration — in this case, Hello. In the next line, a uses declaration specifies other units that the program uses.

This case has two such units. First is a standard unit, Forms, that provides the programming necessary for creating Delphi forms at run time. Second is the Main unit in the file Main.pas. The second line of the uses declaration indicates that unit Main is located in file Main.pas, and that Form1 is the name of the form object in that unit. Delphi writes all of this code automatically.

The command {$R *.RES}, which comes next, binds a binary resource file into the compiled .exe code file. Typically, resource files contain only the program's system icon, but they can have other types of resources. However, you won't use resource files as extensively in Delphi as you might with other development systems, such as C and C++.

Finally in the project are three statements between *begin* and *end* keywords, followed by a period that marks the end of the file. The first statement initializes the Application object, which provides data and code that apply to the entire application. The second statement creates the application's form object, Form1, in memory. The third and final statement runs the application. (This code differs in newer Delphi versions — if you are using an older release of Delphi, you might see only two statements, but they essentially perform the same actions described here.)

Note   Delphi automatically creates and maintains the source code for the Hello.dpr project file. You rarely, if ever, need to modify this file's statements, and for that reason, chapters in this book do not list most application project files. In most cases, you insert programming only into unit modules that correspond to your application's forms, and you insert that programming only in the unit's implementation, not its interface, section.

Filename extensions

A typical Delphi application consists of many different types of files. Each filename ends with an extension that identifies the file's contents. The following list describes the files and their filename extensions that Delphi creates for this chapter's Hello project, plus a few more. I've also indicated which files you may safely delete, in case you are short on disk space or — like me — you frequently clean house by getting rid of deadwood files.

Here are the files that Delphi creates for the Hello project, along with some others you may run into from time to time:

✦ **.~* files** — Files with names ending in .~* (for example, Main.~dp) are backup copies of modified and saved files. You may safely delete these files at any time, although you might want to keep them for recovering lost or damaged programming, or to return to a previous revision.

✦ **.bpg files** — Borland Project Group files, which can store groups of projects, are actually command-line Make text files in disguise. A Make file lists module dependencies and provides the necessary commands and information to compile and link a multimodule application. To use a Make file, you simply feed it to the Make utility, which is supplied with Delphi 4. Only experienced programmers using command-line compilation tools use this method.

✦ **.dcr files** — Delphi Component Resource files contain a component's icon as it appears on the VCL palette. You use .dcr files only when constructing custom components. You should not delete these files. If you do, Delphi substitutes a stock icon for the component when you install it into the palette.

✦ **.dcu files** — These files contain compiled code and data for a program's units. For example, Main.dcu contains the code and data declared in the Main.pas source file. You may safely delete a project's .dcu files because Delphi recreates them when you compile the application.

✦ **.dfm files** — These files contain binary values representing form properties as well as the properties of any components inserted into the form. Relationships between events and event handlers are also stored in .dfm files. Delphi copies this information into the finished .exe code file. Never delete .dfm files. Treat them with the same care as you do source code files.

✦ **.dll files** — These files contain code for dynamic link libraries. Although you may safely delete .dll files for which you have the source code, some third-party DLLs are provided only in binary form. Don't delete a .dll file unless you wrote it or you are sure of its origin.

✦ **.dof files** — These files store project options. The extension stands for Delphi Options File. If you use the Project | Options command to alter various options for this project, Delphi saves your settings in the project's .dof file. The only reason to delete these files is to revert to standard options for a project. This type of file replaces the .opt file in earlier Delphi releases.

✦ **.dpk files**—These types of files contain packages, which are most often collections of multiple units. For example, the entire VCL is provided in packages. Never delete these files. A package is actually a Pascal source code file—it encapsulates code in compiled unit (.dcu) files, but does not contain any code itself.

✦ **.dpr files**—Short for Delphi Project, .dpr files are actually Pascal source code files in disguise. In most cases, you should not modify .dpr files, although experienced Pascal programmers may do so with extreme care. Delphi creates a .dpr file when you first save a new application project. Never delete .dpr files.

✦ **.dsk files**—These files store the application's desktop configuration, but only if you selected Autosave options with the Tools | Environment Options... command. You may delete .dsk files if you don't want to preserve the arrangement of Delphi's windows, or if you want to return to a default layout. However, desktop files also store project pathnames, so if you move your projects to other locations, or if you store project modules in multiple directories, you should not delete .dsk files.

✦ **.exe files**—As you probably know, files ending in .exe are executable code files. As I mentioned, Delphi can create a complete .exe code file, which is the only one you must distribute to your application's users. You may safely delete a project's .exe file because Delphi recreates it when you compile the application.

✦ **.opt files**—See .dof files, which replace .opt files in newer versions of Delphi. The .opt file is now obsolete. If you find one—for example, when upgrading an older application—you may safely delete it after opening and saving the project using a newer version of Delphi.

✦ **.pas files**—These files contain Pascal source code. A typical Delphi application has one .pas file for each form's associated unit, although experienced Pascal developers may store other programming in .pas files. You may edit .pas files using Delphi's code editor, or with any ASCII text editor. Never delete .pas files.

✦ **.res files**—Files with names ending in .res contain binary resources such as the program's system icon and other bitmaps. Resource files figure more prominently in nonvisual Windows programming with Borland Pascal, C, or C++ than they do with Delphi. In Delphi, use the Image Editor in the Tools menu to create and modify .res files. Never make changes to the project's resource file, which is named the same as the project but ending with the filename extension .res. If you do this, when Delphi regenerates this file, any resources you added are permanently lost.

Caution   Never delete files with names ending in .dfm, .dpr, or .pas, unless of course, you want to throw away a project. These files contain the application's properties and source code. When backing up an application under development, these are the critical files to save.

Project Manager

The Project Manager in Delphi 4 is a completely new tool that replaces the old manager, which has undergone little change since Version 1. The new Project Manager greatly simplifies keeping track of a complex application's parts and pieces. You can also use the Project Manager to create Make files for compiling from a command line with the supplied Make utility. The new Project Manager is capable of grouping two or more related projects, which can then be compiled with a single command.

Figure 1-5 shows the new Project Manager window. The figure shows three of the projects on this book's CD-ROM which I combined into a single project group.

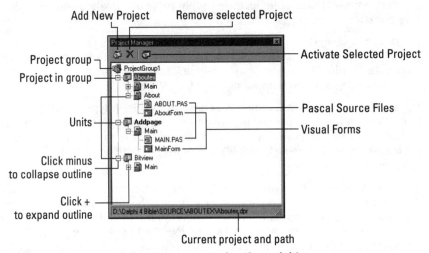

Figure 1-5: The new Project Manager window for Delphi 4

Using the Project Manager

Most of the Project Manager's commands are intuitive. Select a project to activate, and click the Activate Selected Project speed button. You can add a brand-new, and empty, project by clicking the Add New Project speed button. Or, you can delete a project with the Delete Project button. You can also add and delete individual files to one or another project.

The Project Manager's pop-up menu commands change depending on what type of item is highlighted. For example, highlight a project name and click the right mouse button for a list of commands that you can apply to the project. Highlight a filename and click the right mouse button for a list of commands that apply to individual files.

Many Project Manager commands are also available in the Project menu. These commands change to reflect the currently selected project, which is displayed in bold. You can open and close any files in any project displayed in the Project Manager window. The files do not have to be related. For example, using the information in the next section on creating project groups, you can open the source files for units in two separate, unrelated projects. This is handy for working on multiple projects which, in the past, you had to open and close individually (or load into multiple copies of Delphi).

Tip   You can dock the Project Manager window to make it easier to find. Click and drag the window's border to the left or right of the code editor, and release the mouse button when the window outline becomes skinny and thin. Undock the window by clicking and dragging its top border until the outline becomes fat, and then release the mouse button.

Creating project groups

The new Project Manager can group multiple projects, which may be useful for compiling several related projects all at once. Follow these steps to create a sample project group, which I used to prepare the image in Figure 1-5:

1. Select File|New... and choose the New page tab. Double-click the Project Group icon to create a new project group file and open the Project Manager window.

2. To give the project group a different name (ProjectGroup1 by default), save the project in any directory. If you are combining existing projects into a group, you might want to create a separate directory for the project file, but this is up to you. You can store the group anywhere you like. To save a project group, select it in the Project Manager window, and click the right mouse button in the window. Select Save Project Group... and supply a filename.

3. Open the pop-up menu again (be sure the ProjectGroup1 item is selected), and choose the Add Existing Project... command. Browse to any Delphi application directory, and open a .dpr project file to add it to the group. You can also use the Add New Project... command to create a new project for the group.

4. Save the modified group. To view the source code for the project group, again open the pop-up menu and select View Project Group Source. Listing 1-4 shows the project group source code for the projects shown in Figure 1-5. (This listing is not on the CD-ROM — it serves no practical purpose and is shown here only for demonstration.) As you can see, a project group file is actually a text Make file, which can be used with the supplied Make utility to compile multiple projects using the Delphi command-line compiler.

Listing 1-4: A project group file is actually a command-line Make file in disguise.

```
#-----------------------------------------------------------
VERSION = BWS.01
#-----------------------------------------------------------
!ifndef ROOT
ROOT = $(MAKEDIR)\..
!endif
#-----------------------------------------------------------
MAKE = $(ROOT)\bin\make.exe -$(MAKEFLAGS) -f$**
DCC = $(ROOT)\bin\dcc32.exe $**
BRCC = $(ROOT)\bin\brcc32.exe $**
#-----------------------------------------------------------
PROJECTS = Aboutex Addpage Bitview
#-----------------------------------------------------------
default: $(PROJECTS)
#-----------------------------------------------------------

Aboutex: ..\Delphi 4 Bible\SOURCE\ABOUTEX\Aboutex.dpr
  $(DCC)

Addpage: ..\Delphi 4 Bible\SOURCE\ADDPAGE\Addpage.dpr
  $(DCC)

Bitview: ..\Delphi 4 Bible\SOURCE\BITVIEW\Bitview.dpr
  $(DCC)
```

I won't go into the commands in the project group file — only experienced developers need to understand them. The importance of the group, however, is that it can simplify browsing and compiling multiple projects. This feature of the new Project Manager makes it especially appealing to programming teams who maintain multiple applications. A single group can provide access to all application source files from inside a single Delphi session.

Expert-User Tips

✦ For older Delphi versions, and especially if you are still running Windows 3.1, if you receive an "out of resources" error during installation of Delphi, the likely cause is an out-of-date or nonstandard video driver. Use the Windows Setup utility to change the driver to Standard VGA. This should enable you to install Delphi. Contact your VGA vendor for an updated driver. This should never happen with newer Delphi versions.

✦ You frequently toggle back and forth between form and editor windows, but they often hide each other and may be difficult to find. For easier switching, press F12 and F11. Try this now to see what these keys do.

✦ Delphi's hint boxes, displayed when you rest the cursor on a component icon or speed button, appear only if one of Delphi's windows is active. Hint boxes do not appear if another application or icon is active — a fact that is not always obvious due to Delphi's unconfined window arrangement. For example, if you open and click the Windows 95 Start menu bar, Delphi's hints are disabled. If you don't see a hint box after a sufficient wait, click the mouse cursor on Delphi's title bar or on another window such as the Object Inspector, and then try again.

✦ For a progress report while compiling and linking, choose the Tools | Environment Options... command, select the Preferences page tab, and enable Show compiler progress. When you next compile and link a program, Delphi displays a status report dialog that shows the file and the number of lines compiled or linked. This information isn't particularly valuable to most developers, but it verifies that something is happening during compilation. Beware: Displaying the dialog steals time from the compiler, and if you write a lot of small applications, it might take longer to display the dialog than to compile your programs.

✦ Double-click form or editor windows to expand them to full screen. If this hides Delphi's menus and buttons, press Alt to make Delphi's component palette and toolbars reappear. You can also do this by pressing Alt plus a menu hotkey — Alt+F, for instance — to open the File menu. Press Alt, if necessary, to return to the expanded window. Normally, Delphi displays an expanded editor window below the VCL palette. To expand the window to cover the entire screen, select Tools | Environment Options..., choose the Display (formerly the Editor) display page tab, and switch on Zoom to full screen.

✦ You may use the editor window to edit any Pascal source code file (usually ending with the filename extension .pas) or a text file (usually ending with .txt). Choose the File | Open... command or click the Open-file speed button. To take advantage of Delphi's syntax highlighting, the file must end with one of the filename extensions entered into the Tools | Environment Options... Editor Syntax-extensions text box. Each extension is separated with a semicolon.

✦ By convention, statements between the begin and end keywords — technically called a *block* — are indented by two spaces (refer to Listings 1-1 and 1-2). Indentation is not required, but it helps keep programs understandable by showing which statements go together. By convention, statements indented to the same level are in some way associated.

✦ On a 640×480 display, choose Tools | Environment | Options... and select the Display (formerly Editor) page tab. Set the text font to Courier New (the default) and specify a size of 9 points. This setting, which is useful on laptops, displays most of a program's source code in the default-sized editor window without requiring horizontal scrolling. If your eyes are better than mine, try a size of 8 points to see even more text. You may also want to experiment with this dialog's Keystroke mappings option, which configures the editor's keyboard commands. Select Default if you are an expert Windows user, Classic if you are familiar with Borland Pascal or C++ environments, or Brief or Epsilon if you know these editors.

✦ To test multiple running applications, start the first instance in Delphi and use the Windows Explorer to start the second. Or, to test the second or subsequent instances, start the first ones with the Explorer and then run the final instance from Delphi. Use the Run menu's debugging commands to step through the programming statements for the instance you started with Delphi.

✦ Properties and event relationships are stored in .dfm files. These are not text files — they are binary data files — and you should never use a text editor to modify them. However, if you open a .dfm file using File|Open..., Delphi displays it as text. (Try this now by opening the Hello project's Hello.dfm file.) Pascal programmers will recognize this text as object-type declarations that specify component properties and event relationships — it's not really Pascal, but a close cousin that is unique to Object Pascal. To save a printable copy of this information, choose File|Save As.... and rename the file with a .txt filename extension. You can also do the reverse — open the text file, modify it, and save it with a .dfm filename extension to convert the text back to binary. Experienced programmers might do this, for example, to modify the project's properties, although it is probably easier in most cases to use the Object Inspector window for this purpose.

 ## Projects to Try

1-1: Open the Hello project and select the form window's Close button. Change that button's Default property to True. Press F9 to compile, link, and run the modified program. To end the program, you can now press Enter, which selects the default control in a window. Back in Delphi, set the Close button's Cancel property to True. Now when you run the program, you can also press Esc to end. Usually, however, only one component in a form should have its Default or Cancel property set to True.

1-2: Try adding other components to Hello or create a new test application. A few minutes spent playing around can help you become more comfortable with Delphi's layout. View the properties and events for various components. Click and drag components in the form window, and run your applications — it doesn't matter whether you provide any events or new properties. A Delphi application is always ready to run, regardless of its current state of completion.

1-3: Select the Tools|Environment Options... command to customize Delphi's environment. Use the Editor and Colors page tabs to modify text editor features, and to select syntax-highlighting colors. Delphi can display keywords and other elements in source code files in bold, different colors, italic text, and so on. Syntax highlighting is not just for show—a good selection of colors and text features can help make programs clearer by highlighting statements, keywords, comments, and other elements.

1-4: For added safety, select the Tools|Environment Options... command, click the Preferences tab, and enable the two Autosave options. The first option, Editor files, automatically saves all files in a project when you compile and run it, or when you exit Delphi. The second option, Desktop, preserves the arrangements of Delphi's windows. With this option, when you restart Delphi, you can pick up where you left off during the previous session.

Tip

If you run a lot of short, trial programs to test Delphi features, you may want to disable the Autosave Editor files option to reduce disk activity. When developing a major application with many different files, however, this option may prevent the accidental loss of a critical file.

Summary

✦ Delphi is a rapid application development system, suitable for creating Windows prototypes and finished applications that rival or exceed the speed and efficiency of programs written in C, C++, Borland Pascal 7.0, and Visual Basic, as well as programs created by any other means.

✦ New features in Delphi 4 include Object Pascal language extensions, a new Project Manager, and Module Explorer for navigating unit source code files. Also new to Delphi are improved debugging features, VCL enhancements, and database and client-server components.

✦ A Delphi application consists of one or more form windows into which you place visual components. You can modify component and form properties, such as their Names and Captions, and you can create Pascal procedures to perform actions for events such as mouse clicks.

✦ Code insights provide templates, code completion, and parameter lists that can help you save typing time as well as time spent wading through online help screens and printed documentation. In addition to these useful editing features, tool-tip expression evaluation shows the values of variables when a program is paused in debug mode.

✦ When you run an application, Delphi compiles and links source code and other modules to create a finished .exe code file. This is typically the only file you need to distribute to your program's users.

✦ Delphi's new Project Manager can create project groups for multiple projects. This simplifies browsing among multiple project files, and also creates a Make file for compiling multiple projects with Delphi's command-line compiler. The new Module Explorer feature also makes browsing your code's parts and pieces easier than in past versions.

In the next chapter, Introducing Visual Components, you learn more about how to insert components into an application's forms. The chapter introduces Delphi's component categories with sample applications that demonstrate many properties and events found in visual components.

✦   ✦   ✦

Introducing Visual Components

Programming with visual components is easier than shooting fish in a barrel. You can make a big splash with very little effort, and best of all; you don't even have to get wet.

A visual component is an object such as a button or a text memo that you insert into a form window. Actually, a form is also a component—one that can hold other component objects. As you develop Delphi applications, you will spend most of your time inserting and modifying visual component objects, so it's important to understand them thoroughly. Visual components are literally the building blocks on which your code's foundation rests.

The Visual Component Library

With Delphi's Visual Component Library (VCL), you can create useful applications with only a dash of programming. But don't take my word for it; try the sample applications in this chapter for hands-on demonstrations of rapid application development with Delphi.

After mastering the basics of visual components in this chapter, you can find more information on specific components in the chapters of Parts II and III.

Visual component categories

To choose a component category, click a page tab such as Dialogs above Delphi's component palette (see Figure 2-1). What follows is a list of Delphi visual component categories in their onscreen order. The order and number of categories on your screen may differ depending on your version and edition of Delphi, installation options, and additional components that you may have installed. The order may also be different if you have used Tools|Environment Options... to arrange palette icons.

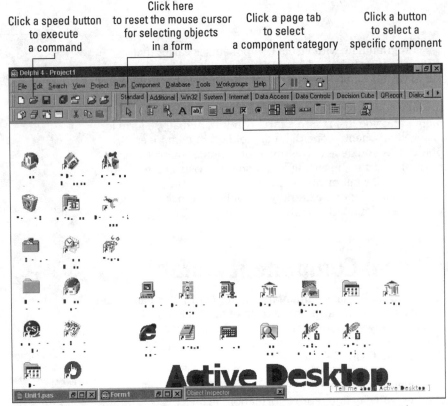

Figure 2-1: Delphi's visual component palette provides page tabs that organize components into categories.

✦ **Standard** — Standard Windows controls, such as buttons, labels, input boxes, lists, check boxes, and scroll bars.

✦ **Additional** — Custom controls, such as bit buttons with graphic images (called glyphs), toolbar speed buttons, string and graphical grids, bitmap images, graphics shapes, scroll boxes, check box lists, window splitters, static text and a simple chart tool.

✦ **Win32** — Standard 32-bit Windows 95 and NT controls including tab and page controls, image lists, rich-text editors, track and progress bars, animation windows, a date-and-time picker, tree and list view objects, status bars, and toolbars.

✦ **System** — System service components including timers, paint boxes, multimedia player controls, OLE, and Dynamic Data Exchange (DDE) objects.

✦ **Internet** — Internet and World Wide Web components and Internet/Intranet protocol tools for HTTP, HTML, FTP, and connection objects such as TCP and UDP.

✦ **Data Access** — Components for accessing databases through tables and SQL queries, and for creating reports with QReport components.

✦ **Data Controls** — Data-aware components for working with database information using controls such as navigators, edit boxes, memos, pictures, check boxes, and lists.

✦ **Decision Cube** — Components for creating decision reports such as cross tabulations with database information — client-server edition only.

✦ **QReport** — An extensive set of report objects commonly used in conjunction with data-aware controls. These components replace the ReportSmith application that was provided with early versions of Delphi. For more information on QReport components, see "Additional and Dialogs Components" in this chapter and also Chapter 17. In addition, Delphi provides a full user manual in Microsoft Word format for these extensive components. See file Qrpt2man.doc located in Delphi's Quickrpt directory.

✦ **Dialogs** — Common dialog boxes for such tasks as selecting files and directories, choosing fonts and colors, setting up print jobs, and finding or replacing data in documents.

✦ **Win3.1** — These components are provided for backward compatibility with Windows 3.1 Delphi applications. All components in this category have 32-bit replacements. Most Delphi programmers never need these components, and this category can be deleted from the component palette if you wish. To do this, use Tools | Environment Options... and click the Palette page tab.

✦ **Samples** — Sample components for which the source code programming is provided in Delphi's Source\Samples directory. These components are mostly intended as guides for creating your own components, but you may find them useful in applications. The samples have not changed much over Delphi's history, and this category can be safely deleted. Other components provide all of the capabilities demonstrated by these samples.

✦ **ActiveX** — These are third-party sample components that demonstrate how to use and program ActiveX controls using Delphi. For more information on ActiveX controls, see this book's Chapter 20, Constructing Custom Components.

✦ **MIDAS** — Components such as Provider, ClientDataSet, RemoteServer and others for creating single- and multitiered database applications — client-server edition only.

Sample applications in this chapter

Three sample applications in this chapter perform useful jobs while demonstrating techniques you typically need in Delphi programming. The MemoPad application demonstrates menu and file handling. The BitView application demonstrates how to use graphics and dialog boxes. The DClock application demonstrates how to use a Timer component to create background processes.

I urge you to create these applications on your own by following the hints and suggestions in this chapter — it's a great way to learn Delphi's techniques. Don't merely run the sample programs — you won't learn anything that way. Of course, this book's CD-ROM provides all applications and their source code files. Copy selected project directories from the CD-ROM to your hard drive (see Appendix A, How to Use the CD-ROM), and then use File | Open... to load the project's .dpr file. Press F9 to compile and run the application. You can also use the supplied files as guides if you get stuck while creating your own programs. Also see this chapter's sections "Win32 Components" and "Additional and Dialogs Components" for introductions to some of Delphi's more sophisticated components.

Table 2-1 lists this chapter's sample applications, which are stored on this book's accompanying CD-ROM in directories that match the application names. For example, you'll find the MemoPad application's files in the Memopad directory. The table also shows the component categories that each application uses.

Standard Components

With Standard components, you can create Windows control objects and common interface elements such as buttons, check boxes, and menus. Because Standard components are relatively simple to use, they also make a good introduction to visual component programming.

Table 2-1
Visual Component Sample Applications

Application	Category	Description
MemoPad	Standard	Memo pad text file editor. Demonstrates how to program main- and pop-upmenu commands, and how to read and write text files.
BitView	Standard, Additional, Dialogs	Bitmap file viewer. Opens and displays any Windows bitmap, icon, metafile, or other graphic file. Demonstrates graphical and dialog component programming.
Dclock	Standard, System	Digital clock. Shows how to program a timer component that runs concurrently with other tasks.

Designing applications with component objects

If Delphi is not running, start it now. If an application is already loaded, use File | New Application to prepare fresh form and code editor windows. Click the Standard page tab under the component palette to display component icons in this category (refer back to Figure 2-1).

Select a component icon. For example, click the button labeled with a capital *A*, which represents the Label component. Move the cursor into the form window and click the left mouse button to insert a Label component object into the form. The exact location doesn't matter. Don't drag the component into the form; instead, click the component icon, move the mouse pointer into the form, and click again to insert the object.

You can also double-click the mouse pointer on any component to insert it into the current form. After this, click and drag the component to move it. To insert several copies of the same type of component, insert one into the form and, leaving it selected, press Ctrl+C followed by Ctrl+V for each new copy.

To delete a component, select it and press Delete. Be extra cautious about doing this — you can undo only the most recent component object deletion. If you delete two component objects, only the second is recoverable. To undelete an object, select Edit | Undelete (or press Ctrl+Z).

Note

To avoid potential ambiguities in this book, the term *component* refers to an icon in the VCL palette; a *component object* (or just *object*) is an instance of a component inserted into a form. If an instruction in this book tells you to click an object or a component object, select it in the form window. A *component class* contains a component's programming. Class names begin with a *T* (for *type*); thus the Label component's programming is found in the TLabel class. Objects are typically named using their component names. Label1, Label2, and FileLabel are examples of good names because they remind you these are objects of the Label component.

Add a few other component objects to the form by selecting them from the Standard palette and clicking the mouse in the form window. After you insert several objects (the exact number and types don't matter), try the following experiments to become familiar with component arrangement commands:

✦ To move and resize a component, first select it with the mouse. (Delphi automatically selects newly inserted components.) This surrounds the component with small boxes called handles. To alter the selected component's size, click and drag a handle. To move the object on the form, click inside the component and drag the mouse.

✦ If a component is selected (it has visible handles) but you can't manipulate it — for example, pressing Delete doesn't work — click inside the form window to make it active, then try again. I like to use the F12 key to activate the form window.

✦ Click and drag the mouse in the form background to surround multiple component objects with a rubber band outline. Release the mouse to select the outlined objects. You can then click and drag inside the selected objects to move them en masse. Delphi displays dim handles around all selected component objects. You can't use these handles to size multiple objects — you can size only individual component objects, one at a time.

✦ Here's another way to select multiple objects. Click the first one to select it, and hold down the Shift key while clicking the mouse pointer on others. Choose Edit ǀ Select All if you want to select all component objects in a form.

✦ With several objects selected, shift-click any one to deselect it. In some cases, to select a large set of objects, it's easier to select them all and then deselect the ones you don't want.

✦ To deselect objects, click the mouse on the form's background. Or, with the form window active, press Esc (this is a good method to use when one or more component objects completely fill a form, making it difficult or impossible to click the window's background). You know all component objects are deselected when no handles are visible. It's important to recognize this state because you can modify a form's properties and events only when no component objects are selected.

✦ To align multiple component objects, select them and choose the Edit | Align command, which displays a dialog box. Use the buttons in this dialog to align edges, to space controls equally within their conglomerate space, and to perform other rearrangements. Try several of the dialog's options to become familiar with alignment commands.

✦ When one component object covers another, use Edit | Bring to Front and Edit | Send to Back to change the objects' relative display order. To try out these commands, insert a few CheckBox objects into a form, and then insert a GroupBox, an example of a container component. If you move the GroupBox over the buttons, it covers them. To make the buttons reappear, select the GroupBox and choose Edit | Send to Back to shove it behind the buttons. (If nothing seems to happen, the reason might be that you selected the buttons and the GroupBox. To select only the GroupBox, first deselect all objects, and then click the GroupBox.)

✦ At run time, users can press the Tab key to shift the input focus from one control to another. (The input focus refers to the current control that receives any keyboard activity.) To set the tab order, select some or all component objects and choose the Edit | Tab Order command. This brings up a dialog box that you can use to specify the order in which each control becomes active in response to Tab key presses. The dialog's commands are intuitive — simply click and drag component object names to rearrange them or select a name and click the dialog's up and down buttons.

When you select two or more component objects, the Object Inspector window shows their shared properties and events. Any changes to those values affect all selected objects. For example, to change the text style for a set of check boxes, first select them all and then enter your settings into the shared Font property.

Tip You know you are viewing shared properties and events when the Object Inspector's drop-down list is blank.

Sample application: MemoPad

This section's sample application, MemoPad, shows how to use standard Label and Memo components. The program also demonstrates how to create a simple menu bar of commands. Figure 2-2 shows MemoPad's display.

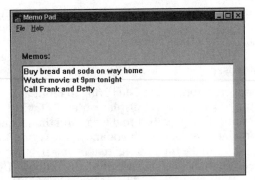

Figure 2-2: MemoPad demonstrates Label and Memo components.

Running MemoPad

To run the MemoPad application now, use File❘Open... or click the Open-project speed button to open Memopad.dpr. Press F9 to compile, link, and run the program. Type a few notes, then quit MemoPad and return to Delphi so you can inspect the application's form and components.

Choose MemoPad's File❘Save command to save your memos in a text file named Memos.txt in the current directory. MemoPad always uses this filename. Choose File❘Exit to end MemoPad, which also saves your memos automatically. (You can also use any other method to quit the program.) Choosing Help❘About displays the message dialog box shown in Figure 2-3, which identifies the application.

Figure 2-3: MemoPad's message dialog box displays when you select the program's Help|About command.

Two of the sample program's menu commands have corresponding accelerator keys users can press to select menu commands without using the mouse. Press F2 to save your memos. Press F1 to display the message dialog box. In addition, menu commands have underlined hot keys. For example, press Alt+F *X* to select File❘Exit.

Note   Delphi somewhat incorrectly terms all keyboard aliases *shortcut keys*. Technically speaking, an *accelerator key* is a combination of one or more Ctrl, Alt, or other function keys assigned to a menu command and shown to its immediate right in the menu's pop-up window. A *shortcut key* is an underlined letter in a menu or a menu command. This isn't an important problem—just be aware that a menu command's underlined keys, such as Alt+F X, are different from accelerator keys such as F1 or Ctrl+X. Any menu command can have either or both kinds of shortcut assignments.

The MemoPad program also uses a PopupMenu component to provide yet another alternative for executing commands. Move the mouse pointer anywhere inside MemoPad's window—but not on the menu bar—and click the right mouse button. As Figure 2-4 shows, this opens a small floating pop-up menu that works like a main menu but appears at the mouse position. To close this menu window, click the right mouse button outside of the pop-up menu, or select a command (or press Esc).

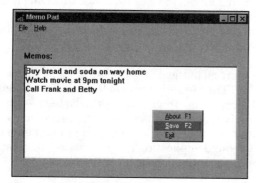

Figure 2-4: MemoPad's floating pop-up menu pops into view when you click the right mouse button.

Always give users several different methods for executing common commands. This way, beginners can select commands from the application's menus (which are relatively simple to learn how to use), but experts can memorize shortcut keys and use floating pop-up menus to execute commands quickly.

Creating MemoPad

After you become familiar with the MemoPad application, use Delphi to inspect the program's form and components. Exit MemoPad now to get back to Delphi. Select each of the program's component objects in the form window with single mouse clicks, and view their properties and events in the Object Inspector window.

Get in the habit of single-clicking component objects in form windows. For most components, if you double-click their objects, Delphi creates a blank procedure in the program's source code for the default event, usually OnClick. If this happens by accident, you can select Edit|Undo to recover or just ignore the insertion. If you accidentally create an unwanted event handler, don't worry about it—as long as you don't add any statements or comments to the procedure, Delphi removes it automatically the next time you compile the project.

Also view the statements in the Main unit (the window captioned Main.pas). If you can't find this text, bring up the code editor window with View∣Units or click the Toggle Form/Unit speed button. Or, you can press F12 one or more times until the window appears. Main.pas contains Object Pascal source code, which Delphi synchronizes with the form and its visual component objects. While developing an application, you will often switch between a form and its associated code editor window.

It's helpful to think of a form and its corresponding unit as offering different views of the same objects. The form window shows the visual appearance of a window and its controls. The editor window shows the Object Pascal commands that perform component activities such as responding to a button click or saving data in a file. Each form is typically associated with one unit (which may use other units) that may contain numerous procedures, functions, and other declarations for the form's component objects.

Don't be concerned about understanding all of the programming in MemoPad's Main.pas file, shown here in Listing 2-1. The file and others in this book are listed purely for reference. Delphi created most of the programming shown here — to program the application's tasks, I simply typed statements into the procedure declarations that Delphi inserted into the editor for the application's components. This is one of Delphi's key features for rapid application development — to create an application, you select components and then literally fill in the blanks that Delphi provides.

Listing 2-1: **Memopad\Main.pas**

```
unit Main;

interface

uses
    Windows, SysUtils, Messages, Classes, Graphics,
    Controls, Forms, Dialogs, Menus, StdCtrls;

type
    TMainForm = class(TForm)
        MainMenu1: TMainMenu;
        PopupMenu1: TPopupMenu;
        File1: TMenuItem;
        Save1: TMenuItem;
        Exit1: TMenuItem;
        Help1: TMenuItem;
        About1: TMenuItem;
        About2: TMenuItem;
        Save2: TMenuItem;
        Exit2: TMenuItem;
        MemoLabel: TLabel;
        Memo1: TMemo;
```

```
        procedure Save1Click(Sender: TObject);
        procedure Exit1Click(Sender: TObject);
        procedure About1Click(Sender: TObject);
        procedure FormActivate(Sender: TObject);
        procedure FormClose(Sender: TObject;
           var Action: TCloseAction);
     private
        { Private declarations }
     public
        { Public declarations }
     end;

var
  MainForm: TMainForm;

implementation

{$R *.DFM}

procedure TMainForm.Save1Click(Sender: TObject);
begin
  Memo1.Lines.SaveToFile('memos.txt');
end;

procedure TMainForm.Exit1Click(Sender: TObject);
begin
  Close;
end;

procedure TMainForm.About1Click(Sender: TObject);
begin
  MessageDlg(
'Memo Pad'#13#10'÷ 1995,1998 by Tom Swan'#13#10'Version 1.00',
    mtInformation, [mbOk], 0);
end;

procedure TMainForm.FormActivate(Sender: TObject);
begin
  if FileExists('memos.txt')
    then Memo1.Lines.LoadFromFile('memos.txt')
    else Memo1.Lines.SaveToFile('memos.txt');
end;

procedure TMainForm.FormClose(Sender: TObject;
  var Action: TCloseAction);
begin
  Memo1.Lines.SaveToFile('memos.txt');
end;

end.
```

Now, try to recreate the MemoPad application on your own. If you get stuck, use the files on the CD-ROM in the Source\MemoPad directory as guides, or refer to Listing 2-1. Follow these step-by-step instructions:

1. Use the Windows Explorer to create a directory such as C:\Projects\Memopad to save your application's files. If you don't want to save the application, you can store files in a directory named Temp and delete them later.

2. Start a new project. Click inside the form to select it, and change the Caption property in the Object Inspector window to Memo Pad. From now on, when I suggest changing a property, first select the component or form, and if necessary, click the Properties tab in the Object Inspector window. Then, select the property and change its value, shown to the right of the property name.

3. Change the form's Name property to MainForm. That's one word with no spaces. If you type illegal characters into a Name property, Delphi displays an error message. Names must begin with a letter or underscore, and they may contain only letters, digits, and underscores. The Name you enter corresponds to the object's programmed name. In the source code, therefore, you can refer programmatically to the form object as MainForm.

4. Choose File|Save All or click the Save All speed button to create the project's disk files. You could wait until later to save the project, but doing so now creates filenames that Delphi uses to create various elements in the program's text. I strongly urge you to save a project as soon as possible after you name its main-window form.

5. Delphi presents you with two file dialogs, one after the other. In the first dialog, titled Save Unit1 As, change to the directory from step 1, and type **Main** in the File Name box. Press Enter or click OK. In the second dialog, labeled Save Project1 As, type **MemoPad** for the filename. Press Enter or click OK. You have just created two files: Main.pas and Memopad.dpr. Delphi appends the .pas and .dpr extensions to your filenames. For quick tests and demonstrations, you can use the default names Unit1 and Project1, but in most cases, you'll want to change these to more descriptive filenames.

Tip   Unit and project filenames must be valid Pascal identifiers. Long filenames are acceptable, but they can't have any embedded spaces or other symbols such as punctuation.

6. Insert a MainMenu component into the form. Also insert a PopupMenu component. Both components are on the Standard palette. In this example, you use the default object Names, MainMenu1 and PopupMenu1, to identify the objects. Because they are relatively complex components, Delphi displays them in the form window as icons that represent their final appearances (see Figure 2-5). The icons are invisible at run time. Move both icons to the upper-

right corner of the form, or to any convenient spot that is out of the way. The exact locations don't matter. If you do not see labels for the two components as shown in the figure, select Tools | Environment Options, click the Preferences page tab, and enable the check box Show component captions in the Form designer section of the dialog window. Captions are displayed only for components such as MainMenu and PopupMenu that do not have visual appearances or labels. Buttons for example, which have their own labels and whose types are visually obvious, do not have captions.

These objects are not visible at runtime

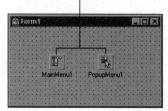

Figure 2-5: MainMenu and PopupMenu component icons show only at design time — they do not appear in the running program's window. The icon captions shown here are optional.

7. To create the menu's commands, double-click the MainMenu1 component object, which opens Delphi's Menu Designer, as shown in Figure 2-6. To create the File menu, type **&File**, and press Enter to change the Caption property for this menu object. Precede a letter with an ampersand (&) to designate the command's Alt shortcut key.

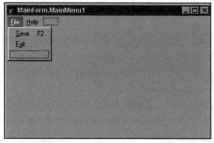

Figure 2-6: This is Delphi's Menu Designer showing the commands in MemoPad's MainMenu object.

8. The Menu Designer now highlights the next place to insert a command, in this case, below the File menu. Enter **&Save** to create the Save command. Don't press Enter (if you did, use the up-arrow key to rehighlight the command). Select the ShortCut property in the Object Inspector window, click the down arrow, and select the F2 accelerator shortcut key for this command.

Tip   It's faster just to type **F** and **2** and press Enter than it is to search for keys using this property's lengthy drop-down list.

9. Click the blank space below the Save command in the Menu Designer, and select the Caption property in the Object Inspector window. Enter **E&xit** to create the Exit key and designate the letter *X* as the command's Alt shortcut key.

Tip   When entering new menu commands, always select the Caption property before you type the command's text.

10. Using similar methods, enter the Help menu and its About command. Designate F1 as the accelerator shortcut key for the command the same way you designated F2 for Save.

11. Close the Menu Designer window to view your menu in the form window. You may inspect this menu, but for the time being, don't select a command, which creates an event handler in the unit module. (There's no harm done if you do this by accident. Just make the form window active before continuing.)

12. Double-click the PopupMenu component to reopen the Menu Designer, which this time displays a simpler style for floating pop-up menus (see Figure 2-7). Enter the About, Save, and Exit commands into this menu. Precede underlined letters with ampersands. Use each command's ShortCut property to assign accelerator shortcut keys such as F1 and F2.

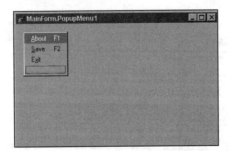

Figure 2-7: Delphi's Menu Designer showing the commands in MemoPad's PopupMenu object

13. It's not enough just to create a PopupMenu object — you must also tell the form to use it. Close the Menu Designer window, and then click inside the form's background to deselect any components. You should see MainForm: TMainForm in the Object Inspector's drop-down list. Change the form's PopupMenu property to PopupMenu1. You can type this name or select it from the property's drop-down list. This programs the form to display the PopupMenu1 object when the user clicks the right mouse button in the form window's background.

14. Press F9 to compile and run the application, which, at this stage, is unfinished. I usually do this immediately after creating a program's commands so I can test their appearance. Try out the program's menu commands (none of which work at this point), and click the right mouse button to display the floating pop-up menu, which is also inoperative. To return to Delphi, press Alt+F4, double-click the system-menu button, or click the Windows 95 close button.

You have now completed stage one of MemoPad's programming. If you want to take a breather, have lunch, or finish college, this is a good place to pause. After you are refreshed, load the MemoPad project if necessary, and follow these steps to complete the application:

1. Insert a Label component into the form window, and change its Name property to MemoLabel. Press Enter and notice that Delphi sets the object's Caption to the same text.

2. Often it is not desirable for a component object to show its internal name. To change the label's displayed text, select MemoLabel and change its Caption property to Memos:.

3. Also insert a Memo component object into the form. This time, you may leave the object's Name property set to the default, Memo1. However, delete all characters from the Lines property so the input area is blank. To do that, select Memo1's Lines property, and click the ellipsis button at right. This opens Delphi's String list editor, which you can use to delete the line Memo1 (press backspace repeatedly or highlight that text and press Del). Press Enter or select the editor's OK button to make the change stick.

4. Resize Memo1 and arrange all components to make your display match Figure 2-8. At this point, you might want to save the project and compile and run it to view the application's final appearance.

Tip

Don't wait for me to suggest trying out your applications. You can press F9 to compile and run a program at nearly any stage in its development.

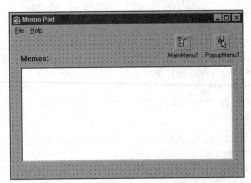

Figure 2-8: Use this image of the MemoPad
form window in Delphi as a guide when you
create the application.

5. To program MemoPad's commands, select the program's File⏐Save command
in the form window. (Do not select the command in the running application—
select it in Delphi's form window.) When you do this, Delphi inserts a
procedure, called an event handler, into the program's source code and
positions the cursor in the code editor window. There, you can type a
statement to perform the command's actions. Enter the following statement
between begin and end. The text inside the parentheses should be enclosed
with single quotation marks. Don't use double quotes. For this and other
suggested programming in this book, refer to the project's disk files or listings
(see Listing 2-1 for this example).

```
Memo1.Lines.SaveToFile('memos.txt');
```

6. In English, the statement you just entered saves Memo1's lines in a file named
Memos.txt. Lines is an object that the Memo1 component object owns—in
other words, Lines is itself an object inside the component. SaveToFile is a
method in that object that Lines can perform. The periods, called dot
notation, specify that Memo1, Lines, and SaveToFile are associated. The string
'memos.txt' represents a filename. The statement passes the string shown in
parentheses to the SaveToFile method. Notice that the statement ends with a
semicolon. Technically speaking, in Pascal, a semicolon separates one
statement from another. In this case, because there is no subsequent
statement, you can leave out the semicolon; however, it does no harm to
insert it anyway. If you place a semicolon incorrectly or if you leave a required
one out, Delphi tells you in an error message when you compile the program.

7. Complete the other MemoPad commands. Select File I Exit in the form. Enter Close; between the begin and end keywords (refer to procedure TMainForm.Exit1Click in Main.pas). As you learned in the preceding chapter, the Close procedure, just one of countless Delphi procedures you can call, closes a window. If, as in this example, that is the program's main window, Close also ends the program.

8. Return to the form window and select Help I About. Enter the following statement between begin and end. Carefully type each character exactly as shown, or if you want to cheat, copy and paste the statement from the Main.pas file. (I always advocate cheating to meet deadlines, so please don't hesitate to copy sample programming from these pages or from the accompanying CD-ROM. You do not need special permission to use this book's source code in your own work.) Type the following all on one line — it's broken into two lines here due to space limitations:

```
MessageDlg('Memo Pad'#13#10'@cw 1995,1998 by Tom
Swan'#13#10'Version 1.00', mtInformation, [mbOk], 0);
```

9. The statement creates a message dialog that displays MemoPad's copyright notice and version number. To the MessageDlg procedure, the program passes four arguments in parentheses, separated by commas. The first argument is a string, delimited with quotation marks. In this string, the notation #13#10 inserts carriage return and line feed ASCII control codes that start subsequent text on new lines. To enter the copyright symbol, use the Windows Character Map utility, or cut and paste the character from the sample files on the CD-ROM. (Or, just type **C**.) The mtInformation argument selects from several dialog styles. The [mbOk] argument is a set, which in this example has only one member, mbOk, that specifies a dialog box style with an OK button. The 0 argument is a placeholder for the dialog's help context, which MemoPad doesn't use. Once again, a semicolon ends the statement. (For more information on MessageDlg argument values, look up the procedure in Delphi's online help.)

10. To program the pop-up menu's commands, double-click the PopupMenu1 object (the one with the arrow) that you inserted into the form. This reopens the Menu Designer window. Click the Events page tab in the Object Inspector window. Select the About command in the Menu Designer, and set the OnClick event to About1Click. You can enter this event handler's name, or select it from the OnClick's drop-down menu. Set the Save command's OnClick event to Save1Click. Set the Exit command's OnClick event to Exit1Click. These are the same event handlers that you programmed for the main menu — a demonstration of how two or more events can share the same code.

11. Close the Menu Designer window. Click inside the form's background, and if necessary, select the Events page tab in the Object Inspector window. Double-click the blank space to the right of the OnActivate event, and enter the following if-then-else statement between begin and end. The statement reads the designated file's text into the component's Lines object:

```
if FileExists('memos.txt')
  then Memo1.Lines.LoadFromFile('memos.txt')
  else Memo1.Lines.SaveToFile('memos.txt');
```

The preceding statement calls a function FileExists, which returns True if the stated file is on disk, or False if not. If the file exists, the statement reads the file into Memo1's Lines. If the file does not exist, the statement saves Lines to a new file. Because the object's Lines property is empty at this point, calling its SaveToFile method creates a blank, new file. Although it may appear that many operations are taking place, the entire if-then-else construction is actually a single statement, and therefore only one semicolon is needed to separate this statement from another. If you type a semicolon at the end of the second line, Delphi displays an error message when you compile the program.

12. Select the form (it is probably already selected), and double-click the space to the right of the event OnClose. Delphi inserts a procedure for this event, which occurs when you close the program's window. Enter the following statement between begin and end to save the component's Lines in a stated file:

```
Memo1.Lines.SaveToFile('memos.txt');
```

13. Press F9 to compile, link, and run the completed program. Try out the commands and return to Delphi. Compare your program's Main.pas file with the sample file of that name on the book's CD-ROM. Some of the procedures may be in a different order depending on the order in which you inserted components into the form and the order in which you programmed the event handlers, but the statements and general layout should be the same.

Additional and Dialogs Components

In this section, you develop a bitmap viewer application that uses visual components from two other Delphi categories, Additional and Dialogs. Select those page tabs and use Delphi's hint boxes to locate the components mentioned here. (Reminder: Point the mouse cursor at a component icon and wait for the hint box to appear.)

Among other items, the Additional category provides graphics components that you can use to create bitmap images and Graphics Device Interface (GDI) shapes such as rectangles, circles, and lines. The Windows GDI provides a device-independent method for drawing and printing graphics. You access the GDI by inserting component objects into a form window.

The Dialogs category provides components that interface with common Windows dialog boxes. Although these are all Delphi components, Windows provides the actual appearance and code for the resulting dialog boxes. Using common dialog boxes gives users familiar ways to navigate disk directories, choose filenames, select fonts and colors, and search or replace values in documents.

Using the Image component

To create a bitmap in a form, insert an Image component object from the Additional category. Try it now. First choose File | New Application to clear Delphi's workspaces, and then insert an Image object into a blank form. Because the Image component doesn't have a run-time shape — because a bitmap's content defines its appearance — Delphi displays the Image object transparently as a dashed outline, which does not appear in the finished program.

With the Image object outline selected, highlight the Picture property in the Object Inspector window, and click the ellipsis button to open Delphi's Picture Editor. Or, you can simply double-click the component object. Use the Picture Editor to import any bitmap image into the application. First click the Load button and then choose a file that ends with the extension .bmp (bitmap), .ico (icon), .wmf (Windows metafile), or .emf (enhanced metafile). You can then click Save to copy the file to another disk file, Clear to erase a previously loaded image, Cancel to perform no operation, or OK to load the image into the Image component object.

If you are following along, use the Picture Editor's Load button to switch to the Data directory, on the CD-ROM. Open the Sample.ico icon file, and click OK. The file's icon appears in the form's Image component, and the Picture property changes to TIcon. Or, to insert a bitmap, select the Sample.bmp file. You can also load other images if you have some bitmaps stored on disk. You might have to resize the Image object to see the bitmap. To do this automatically, set the Image AutoSize property to True. You can resize a bitmap's image loaded into an Image component object, but an icon's image always remains a fixed size.

Tip

After loading a bitmap into an Image object, to reduce or expand the object to fit the bitmap exactly, set AutoSize to True, double-click the Image object, and click OK in the Image Editor.

Sample application: BitView

The application described in this section combines Standard, Additional, and Dialogs components to create a bitmap file viewer.

Running BitView

To try the application, open the Bitview.dpr project file in the Bitview subdirectory, and press F9. Select any .bmp bitmap file. There's a sample file if you need it in the Data directory on the CD-ROM. Figure 2-9 shows BitView in operation.

Figure 2-9: The BitView application can display any bitmap file.

You will now create your own BitView application. If you ran BitView, exit the program now before continuing.

Creating BitView

Listing 2-2 shows the BitView application's Main.pas source code. Use this file as a guide when you create the application by following the step-by-step instructions after the listing.

Listing 2-2: **Bitview\Main.pas**

```
unit Main;

interface

uses
   Windows, SysUtils, Messages, Classes, Graphics, Controls,
   Forms, Dialogs, Menus, ExtCtrls;
```

```
type
  TMainForm = class(TForm)
    BitImage: TImage;
    MainMenu1: TMainMenu;
    File1: TMenuItem;
    Open1: TMenuItem;
    Exit1: TMenuItem;
    OpenDialog1: TOpenDialog;
    procedure Open1Click(Sender: TObject);
    procedure Exit1Click(Sender: TObject);
  private
    { Private declarations }
  public
    { Public declarations }
  end;

var
  MainForm: TMainForm;

implementation

{$R *.DFM}

procedure TMainForm.Open1Click(Sender: TObject);
begin
  if OpenDialog1.Execute then
  begin
    BitImage.Picture.LoadFromFile(OpenDialog1.Filename);
    Caption := OpenDialog1.Filename;
  end;
end;

procedure TMainForm.Exit1Click(Sender: TObject);
begin
  Close;
end;

end.
```

To create your own BitView application, first choose File|New Project to clear any currently loaded project. You should be getting used to these start-up steps by now, so I won't repeat them in future hands-on tutorials. I also abbreviate some of the following steps, such as how to save a project. If you completed the previous application successfully, you should have no trouble with this one:

1. Change the form's Caption property to Bitmap Viewer. Change its Name property to MainForm.

2. Change the form's WindowState property from wsNormal to wsMaximized by selecting that value from the property's drop-down list. This displays BitView's window in full-screen mode. The other values select different window states — wsMinimized displays a window as an icon; wsNormal displays the window in its designed size at a position that Windows determines.

3. Select the Additional component category, and insert an Image component into the form. Change the object's Name property to BitImage. The object's exact location and size are unimportant.

4. With the BitImage object still selected, change its Align property to alClient. This automatically resizes the component object to the same size as the form's client area, which is the space inside the window's borders.

5. To make the bitmap inside the component object also fit within the client area requires one more change. Highlight the BitImage component's Stretch property, and double-click the property value to toggle it from False to True. (You can also type or select True or False from the property's drop-down list, but double-clicking a True/False property is the easiest way to toggle its value.) With Stretch set to True, the program displays the bitmap within the component's space. Because the component object is automatically sized to the window, so is the bitmap image. This also demonstrates how a component object and its data, though related, can sometimes require separate programming.

6. Insert a Standard MainMenu component into the form. The default Name, MainMenu1, is descriptive enough, and you don't have to change it. Double-click the menu object's icon, and create a menu named File with two commands, Open and Exit. Remember to type an ampersand ahead of an underlined shortcut key — &File, for example. If you have trouble creating the program's menu, review the steps for MemoPad. You don't have to assign accelerator-shortcut keys, but you may do so if you want. Close the Menu Designer window when you are done.

7. From the Dialogs component palette, insert an OpenDialog component into the form. As it does for menus, Delphi represents dialogs as icons that are invisible when the program runs. You can position the MainMenu1 and OpenDialog1 objects anywhere you like. Your display should resemble Figure 2-10, which shows BitView's form window under development in Delphi.

8. Select the OpenDialog1 component object, and click the ellipsis button next to the Filter property's value. This opens Delphi's Filter Editor, which you can use to specify filename filters. For example, you can specify the filter *.bmp to show only bitmap files. Enter two filters, one for .bmp files and one for All files, using Figure 2-11 as a guide. Click the dialog's OK button to save your filters. (After these numbered steps, I describe another way to form this string.)

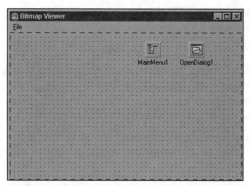

Figure 2-10: Use this image of BitView's form window in Delphi as a guide when you create the application.

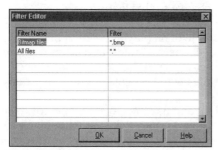

Figure 2-11: Delphi's filename Filter Editor simplifies entering filename filters.

9. All components are now in place, and you might want to save, compile, link, and run the application. Quit the program to return to Delphi. (Menu commands are still unfinished, and you can't use File|Exit to quit, so click the program's close button instead.)

10. In the form window — not in the running program — select File|Open to create a procedure for this command. In between the procedure's begin and end keywords, insert the following programming (refer to Bitview\Main.pas as a guide, or open that file and copy its statements):

```
if OpenDialog1.Execute then
begin
  BitImage.Picture.LoadFromFile(OpenDialog1.Filename);
  Caption := OpenDialog1.Filename;
end;
```

11. The preceding if statement activates OpenDialog1 by calling the object's Execute function. If that function returns True, the user closed the dialog by selecting its OK button. In that case, the program executes the two statements inside begin and end keywords. The first statement calls the LoadFromFile method for the Picture object to load the file named by the dialog's Filename property. The second statement assigns this same filename to the form's caption, thus changing the window title to the bitmap's path. The := symbol is Pascal's assignment operator, which copies the value at right to the object at left.

12. Return to the form window, select File|Exit, and insert the statement Close; between begin and end in the event-handler procedure that Delphi creates for the command.

13. Save the completed project, and press F9 to compile, link, and run. Load any bitmap file. Click the middle size button on BitView's upper-right border to shrink the window to its normal size. Resize the window with your mouse, and notice that the bitmap shrinks or expands to fit inside the window. This can make some images look weird, but at least they fit. See Project 2-4 at the end of this chapter for a suggested change to this feature.

Because the Image component is capable of displaying many types of graphics files, it's easy to upgrade BitView to display icons, metafiles, and other types of images. You can also assign a standard file filter string to the Open dialog object so it displays .bmp, .wmf, .emf, and other files with recognized graphics extensions.

To make this change, go back to Delphi and use the Object Inspector to select MainForm. Click the Events page tab, and double-click inside the blank space to the right of the OnActivate event. This creates a blank procedure for the event, which occurs when the form is activated (at the start of the program, for example). Make your procedure look like this:

```
procedure TMainForm.FormActivate(Sender: TObject);
begin
  OpenDialog1.Filter := GraphicFilter(TGraphic);
end;
```

The statement assigns the Graphics unit's GraphicFilter function to the OpenDialog1 Filter property. Rather than use the filter editor as described before, this provides all recognized graphics filename extensions for the TGraphic class.

Another cool change you can make is to add JPEG images to the standards. To do this, locate the *uses* declaration at the beginning of the program's source code, and add the JPEG unit to the others listed. The finished *uses* declaration should look like this (change in bold):

```
uses
   Windows, SysUtils, Messages, Classes, Graphics, Controls,
   Forms, Dialogs, Menus, ExtCtrls, Jpeg;
```

Now, when you run the program (press F9) the Open dialog lists .jpg and .Jpeg files along with other recognized graphics file types.

System Components

System components provide an assortment of objects for accessing system hardware and software. Components in this category include a Timer for background processing, a PaintBox for general purpose graphics, and the multimedia MediaPlayer component. Others include OLE and DDE components for data sharing.

Eventually, you meet examples of all these components in this book. In this section, you use a Timer to create a digital 24-hour clock, which also demonstrates how to perform background processes.

Using the Timer component

The Timer component is one of Delphi's simplest. It has only a few properties and a single event. You can program one or more timers to perform jobs that run concurrently with other applications, or that run in the background.

To create a Timer component, select it from the component palette's System category. Insert the component object into a blank form, change its Name property if you wish, and set the Interval to the desired event frequency in milliseconds from 1 to 65535. A value of 1000 creates a one-second timer; a value of 100 creates a $1/10$-second timer. (Delphi permits you to set a timer's interval to zero, but there's no good reason to do so.)

The Timer component offers only one event, OnTimer. Double-click the event value or you can double-click the Timer object, which does the same thing, and insert statements between begin and end to perform at the Timer's frequency.

Sample application: DClock

To demonstrate how to create a Timer event handler, this section presents a sample application, DClock. In addition to showing how to use the Timer component, the following hands-on tutorial also demonstrates how to create a fixed-sized window, which is often useful when there are no benefits in permitting users to adjust the window size.

Running DClock

Figure 2-12 shows DClock's display. Unlike in MemoPad, the clock window does not have minimize and maximize buttons, and it has no menu or commands.

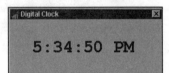

Figure 2-12: DClock's display demonstrates background processing using a Timer object.

Creating DClock

Open the DClock.dpr file now and inspect the form's component objects. Scan the program's Main.pas source code in Listing 2-3. When you are done looking around, close the application and try to create your own digital clock by following the instructions after the listing.

Listing 2-3: **Dclock\Main.pas**

```
unit Main;

interface

uses
  Windows, SysUtils, Messages, Classes, Graphics, Controls,
  Forms, Dialogs, ExtCtrls, StdCtrls;

type
  TMainForm = class(TForm)
    TimeLabel: TLabel;
    Timer1: TTimer;
    procedure Timer1Timer(Sender: TObject);
  private
    { Private declarations }
  public
    { Public declarations }
  end;

var
  MainForm: TMainForm;

implementation

{$R *.DFM}
```

```
procedure TMainForm.Timer1Timer(Sender: TObject);
begin
  TimeLabel.Caption := TimeToStr(Time);
end;

end.
```

1. Start a new project. Change the form's Caption property to Digital Clock and set its Name to MainForm. Create a directory such as C:\Projects\Dclock to store the application files, and save the project. Name the unit file Main and the project file Dclock.

2. To eliminate the window's minimize and maximize buttons, select the form (click inside its window) and double-click the BorderIcons property. (Position the mouse over the property name at left, not on its value at right.) Notice the small plus sign to the left of the property name, which changes to a minus after double-clicking. The plus sign tells you this property has one or more hidden subvalues. A minus sign indicates that the subvalues are displayed. In this case, there are three such values. Set biSystemMenu to True (its default value), and the remaining subvalues to False. Despite this change, the form in Delphi still shows minimize and maximize buttons. This is normal because it must be possible to change the window size when designing the application — you must run the program to view the window's actual appearance, which in this case, is fixed to its designed size.

3. That characteristic requires another change — removing the size buttons from the window isn't enough to prevent users from resizing the window frame. To fix the window size, select the form's BorderStyle property, and select bsSingle from the drop-down list. For the same reason mentioned in Step 2, you see the effect of this change only when you run the program.

4. Insert a Standard Label component into the form. Change the object's Name property to TimeLabel, and change its Caption to 00:00:00 AM. This ensures that the label is the proper size for the time digits inserted at run time.

5. Select TimeLabel's Font property. Click the ellipsis button to open a font-selection dialog. Choose a font, a size, and a style for your clock. I specified Bold Courier New with a size of 24 points.

6. Add a System Timer component to the form window. Because this is the program's only Timer object, the default Name, Timer1, is adequate. Set the Timer object's Interval property to 1000, for an update frequency of one second. This is the default value.

7. Select the Timer1 object, and click the Object Inspector's Events page tab. You should see only one event, OnTimer. Double-click the value to the right of the event to create a procedure in the program's source code. Or, you can more simply double-click the Timer object, which creates a handler for the default event — the only one in this component. Enter the following line between the begin and end keywords:

```
TimeLabel.Caption := TimeToStr(Time);
```

8. The preceding line converts the current time to a string and assigns the result to the label's Caption. This updates the time on screen once per second — the frequency that the OnTimer event is programmed to be called.

9. Resize the form window for a comfortable fit. (Use View | Form or press F12 to find the window if it is hidden.) Your window should resemble Figure 2-13, which shows DClock's form in Delphi. The Timer1 object's icon is not visible at run time, and you can move it to any convenient location.

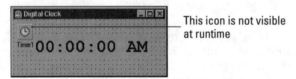

This icon is not visible
at runtime

Figure 2-13: Use this image of DClock's form window in Delphi as a guide when you create the application.

10. Press F9 to compile, link, and run the application. In a few seconds, you should see a digital clock ticking the time away. Press Alt+F4 or use the System menu's Close command (or click the Windows 95 close button) to quit and return to Delphi.

Win32 Components

You will probably use one or more Win32 components in just about every application you write. These components provide wrappers for 32-bit Windows native controls for creating multipage windows and dialogs, animations, status bars, toolbars, and Coolbars. This section introduces one Win32 component, TDateTimePicker, which you can add to any application that needs a way for users to choose a date and time. You meet most of the other Win32 components throughout this book.

For now, though, we focus on TDateTimePicker. I don't know how much time I've wasted writing code to prompt users for the date and time, but with Delphi's TDateTimePicker component, I don't need to waste any more. This component allows users to enter and select dates and times, but it goes beyond a simple prompter — it's actually a full-blown calendar system in component form.

TDateTimePicker could hardly be simpler to use. Drop one of these components into a form, and set its Kind property to dtkDate for a calendar control or to dtkTime for a time-of-day control. To learn more about this component, follow these steps:

1. Start a new application.

2. Click the Win32 page tab in Delphi's component palette.

3. Select the DateTimePicker component, and click inside the form window to insert an object of this class. Set this object's Kind property to dtkTime.

4. Repeat step 3 to insert a second DateTimePicker object into the form. Set this object's Kind property to dtkDate (the default).

You can run the application at this point by pressing F9. Figure 2-14 shows the program's display with the date component open (click the drop-down arrow to select a date by clicking it in a small calendar window).

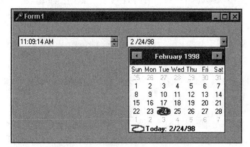

Figure 2-14: The TDateTimePicker component simplifies selecting time and date values.

After you try out the components, exit the test program and return to Delphi. Try out combinations of the following property settings:

✦ **Checked** — Toggles a check box to the left of the control's edit window. When checked, the control is active; when unchecked, the control is disabled and users cannot enter or select dates and times. This property does nothing unless ShowCheckbox is True.

✦ **Date** — The currently selected date (today is the default) as a TDate object. Use this property to obtain a date selected by the user.

✦ **DateFormat** — Select between dfShort (2/24/98) and dfLong (Tuesday, February 24, 1998) formats to display in the control's edit window. This setting affects only components with Kind set to dtkDate.

✦ **DateMode** — Choose between two modes for date controls (Kind equals dtkDate). Use dmComboBox (the default) for a drop-down calendar from which users can choose a date by pointing and clicking. Use dmUpDown to display up and down arrows that, when clicked, advance or retard the selected portion of a date. Frankly, I find this second option too difficult to use, and besides, the drop-down calendar adds a neat bit of flash to the interface, so that's the option I always use.

✦ **Kind** — As mentioned, set this to dtkDate for a date control or to dtkTime for time entry. Properties such as DateFormat with the word Date in their names are meaningful only for date controls. However, even for a time control, the Date field still returns a valid date (today unless you change it under program control).

✦ **MaxDate, MinDate** — Enter the maximum and minimum dates you want users to be able to enter in a date control (Kind equals dtkDate).

✦ **ShowCheckbox** — Set this property to True to display a check box to the left of a date or time control. When enabled (see the Checked property), the control is active and can be changed. When disabled (Checked is False), the control is dimmed and users cannot change its value. Tip: Use the Enabled property to enable and disable a TDateTimePicker object under program control. Use the ShowCheckbox and Checked properties if you want users to have the ability to enable and disable the control.

✦ **Time** — The currently selected time (now is the default) as a TTime object. Use this property to obtain a time selected by the user.

Tip

Highlight and delete the default entry in a time control's Time property. This causes the control to display 12:00:00 A.M. Deleting the Date property sets it to 12/30/89. That's Saturday, December 30, 1989!

If your program needs notification that a user has selected a new date, create an event handler to respond when the selected date changes. There are two ways to do this. Select the TDateTimePicker object in the form, and click the Events page tab on the Object Inspector. Double-click the OnChange and OnCloseUp events, and enter the following code for both procedures (or you could write a separate procedure and call it from the event handler):

```
var
  S: String;
begin
```

```
S := DateToStr(DateTimePicker1.Date);
ShowMessage('Date entered = ' + S );
end;
```

The procedure calls DateToStr (a function in the SysUtils unit) to convert the Date to a string, which is passed to ShowMessage to display the selected date in a small dialog box window. It is apparently necessary to program both OnChange and OnCloseUp events so that manual changes to date values as well as dates picked from the drop-down calendar are noted.

Expert-User Tips

✦ In most cases, after inserting a component into a form, you should give the object a Name that reflects its purpose. The usual exception to this rule is when you insert only one type of component object. For example, if your program has only one main menu, the default name — MainMenu1 — is probably adequate.

✦ Use descriptive Names such as CloseButton, AgeLabel, and NameEdit. Some programmers like to use short names — for example, B1, B2, and B3 for buttons — but if you do that, you may not recognize your objects next year or next month — or, if your memory is no better than mine, by noon tomorrow.

✦ As a rule of thumb, your programs are easier to understand and maintain if you append component names to the end of Name property values. For example, NoteMemo is probably a better name for a Memo object than NoteArea. The former name reminds you of the object's component type; the latter hides this important fact.

✦ Names must begin with a letter or underscore, and they may contain only letters, digits, and underscores. Label10 is a legal name; 10Label is not. Names may not have embedded spaces. Use capital letters to clarify long Names — for example, MainSysMenu is more readable than mainsysmenu. A Name may contain embedded underscores as in My_Main_Menu. Underscores are hard to see on screen, however, and I don't recommend using them. Names may be from 1 to 63 characters long and must adhere to Pascal identifier syntax.

✦ Unlike Names, Captions and other text-value properties may have any characters that you can type or cut and paste, in any order, including spaces and punctuation. The length of a Caption is technically limited to 255 characters, but in practice, a component object's size limits its Caption length to a much smaller value.

✦ When a form becomes full of component objects, or when one or more objects cover the window's client area, you may have trouble selecting the form. In that case, use the Object Inspector's drop-down list to select the form by name. For example, to select the main-window form in most of this book's applications, choose MainForm from the Object Inspector list. You can also use this method to select any component object inserted into a form.

✦ To align multiple components, first move one component to its proper position. Select this component first, and then select the others. The Edit | Align command aligns component objects relative to the first one you select.

✦ In the Menu Designer, press Ctrl+Ins to insert a menu command between two others. Press Ctrl+Del to delete a command. Type a single dash in a command's Caption property to insert a separator between two other commands.

✦ Select Edit | Lock Controls to enable this menu option (a check mark appears next to it). When enabled, this option prevents moving or resizing component objects, but you can still modify control properties and events. After you program a form just the way you want it, use this command to prevent accidental rearrangements of your carefully positioned objects.

✦ If you cannot move or resize selected component objects, check whether Lock Controls from the preceding tip is enabled.

✦ Newcomers to Pascal typically worry about semicolon placement, but don't be overly concerned. If you type a semicolon in the wrong place, Delphi displays an Error in statement message. In C and C++, semicolons terminate statements. In Pascal, semicolons separate statements from one another. For example, you may not insert a semicolon before an if statement's else clause because, unlike in C and C++, Pascal's if-then-else is a single statement. Refer to this book's listings for examples of correct semicolon placement. You might also spend a few moments experimenting with the code editor's code insights, which as explained in Chapter 1, insert Pascal statements in the correct syntax automatically.

✦ For a faster way to insert component objects into a form, double-click any component icon in Delphi's palette. This inserts an object of that component in the center of the current form. Use this method to insert multiple component objects — a set of check boxes, for example. Each object exactly overlays the preceding ones, and you should click and drag them to their final resting spots before doing anything else.

✦ The fastest way to insert multiple component objects of the same type is to insert one, leave it selected, and then press Ctrl+C followed by Ctrl+V for as many objects as you want. The objects are given sequentially numbered names such as Label1, Label2, and Label3.

✦ After inserting a component object into a form, double-click the object to create an event handler for its default event. This is always the first event listed in the Object Inspector window. Some components don't work this way. For example, double-clicking a MainMenu component object opens the Menu Designer window.

✦ To locate an existing event handler, double-click it in the Object Inspector window's Events page. This displays the form's unit window, and positions the cursor inside the event handler. Delphi creates a new event handler only if one does not already exist.

✦ Set a Label component object's AutoSize property to True to have the control automatically adjust its size to fit its Caption data. Set this property to False if you want the component to remain a fixed size at all times. You must use a fixed size if you set WordWrap True to display multiline labels.

✦ Editing lengthy window captions and other single-line strings can be difficult because of the Object Inspector's small size. For easier editing, enter the text anywhere in the code editor window. Highlight the text, press Ctrl+X to cut it to the Windows clipboard, switch back to the Object Inspector, highlight a text property such as Caption, and press Ctrl+V to insert your text. I like to keep numerous such strings as comments in my source code files, in between a pair of comment brackets (* and *). I can then easily edit the text and copy it (press Ctrl+C rather than Ctrl+X) to the clipboard for pasting into Caption properties. For example, insert a comment such as the following anywhere in a unit's source code:

```
(*
This is the first window caption
This is another window caption
*)
```

✦ If you want to do your own parsing of date and time entries in a TDateTimePicker control — to limit entries to specific dates, for example, only Mondays through Fridays — set the ParseInput property to True. This triggers an OnUserInput event when the user types into the control's edit window.

Projects to Try

2-1: Change various properties of MemoPad's component objects. For example, assign a different Font for the Memo1 object. Change the style of the MemoLabel component, and try out its Color property.

2-2: When you start the DClock application, it first displays 00:00:00 AM before showing the current time. To improve the display and show the time as soon as the program's window appears, create an event handler for the form's OnCreate event. Click the form background to select the form, and then choose the Events page tab in the Object Inspector. Click the down arrow to the right of the OnCreate event, and select Timer1Timer. This is the same event handler you programmed for the Timer1 component. When you run the program, it initializes TimeLabel by calling the Timer1Timer procedure, which sets the label to the current time before the window becomes visible.

2-3: Open the BitView project and select its OpenDialog1 component object. The Ctl3D property is provided for backward compatibility only, and under Windows 95 and NT, no longer has any effect. All controls in these operating systems have a 3D appearance. If you are still using an early version of Delphi and Windows 3.1, however, try changing the Ctrl3D property to False, and press F9 to compile, link, and run. When you select the program's File I Open command, you see a standard Windows dialog box, probably with a white background and a relatively plain appearance. To return to a 3D effect, change the Ctrl3D property back to True.

2-4: Open the BitView project, and select the BitImage component. Set the image's Stretch property to False, and press F9 to compile, link, and run. Open a bitmap file. It displays more quickly because adjusting image sizes takes time. Unfortunately, however, displaying full-size images may cut off areas that extend beyond the window borders. In the next chapter, you insert scroll bars into the window to solve this problem. Also refer to Chapter 10 for more information about scrolling.

Summary

✦ Visual components simplify Windows programming. To create a Delphi application, you simply insert component objects into a form, and you select and modify object properties and events.

✦ Choose among Delphi's component categories by selecting one of the page tabs above the component palette. Click the icon of the component you want, move the mouse cursor into the form, and click again to insert a component object at that location.

✦ Selecting a component displays handles around it that you can use to resize the object. You can also click and drag components to position them in the form. Select a component by single-clicking it, or choose it by name from the Object Inspector's drop-down list. You can also select multiple components by clicking and dragging an outline around them.

✦ Properties are values that specify component characteristics. For example, components such as Buttons and Labels have a Font property for selecting a text font name, point size, and style.

✦ Events represent a component's run-time actions. Double-clicking an event value inserts an event-handler procedure into the program's source code. To program the event, enter one or more Pascal statements between the procedure's begin and end keywords, which were automatically inserted by Delphi.

✦ When you select two or more components, the Object Inspector window displays their shared properties and events. Any changes you make to these values affect all selected components.

✦ Delphi maintains a visual representation of your application in the form window, and an Object Pascal source code representation in a unit window. The two representations are synchronized so that changes in one window are reflected in the other.

✦ A small plus sign to the left of a property indicates that the property has subvalues. Double-click the property value field to list and unlist these values.

✦ An ellipsis button to the right of a property's value indicates that double-clicking the value, or single-clicking the button, opens a dialog box for changing this property's setting. Some properties have both subvalues and dialog boxes.

✦ Use the TDateTimePicker component from the Win32 palette to create a control in which users can enter or select dates and times.

In the next chapter, you investigate more about forms, properties, and events. You also learn how to respond to mouse actions, how to add scroll bars to a form window, how to make a window stay on top, and how to create an opening splash screen.

✦   ✦   ✦

Introducing Forms

The word *form* can mean many things. On a construction site, a *form* is a box that shapes wet cement. We say healthy individuals are in good form. You can form a corporation and you can march the troops into formation, but nobody loves a tax form.

In Delphi, every project has at least one form object that represents the program's main window. Projects can also have multiple forms for child windows, dialog boxes, and data-entry screens. Although a form's main purpose is to hold other components such as buttons and check boxes, a form can also perform actions in response to events such as key presses and mouse clicks.

Forms are among Delphi's most versatile objects and you use them extensively to develop applications. In this chapter, you learn key features of forms and their properties and events.

Forms as Components

A form represents a window's visual appearance, but a form is not just another pretty window. A *form* is actually a Delphi component with its own set of properties and events. Unlike other components, however, a form doesn't appear on the component palette.

You normally create a form object in one of two ways: by starting a new application or by selecting the File|New Form command. Use the first method to create your application's main window form. Use the second method for additional forms — to create an About dialog, for example, or to display a startup splash screen. (More on these subjects later.)

Forms and units

When you create a new form, Delphi adds two windows to the programming environment. The form window shows the form's visual representation as it appears in the finished application. The code editor window lists the form's Object Pascal programming. The text in this window is a called a *unit*. Figure 3-1 shows the form and code editor windows for the DClock application from Chapter 2. Internally, the form is an object in the unit, which is also sometimes called a *module*.

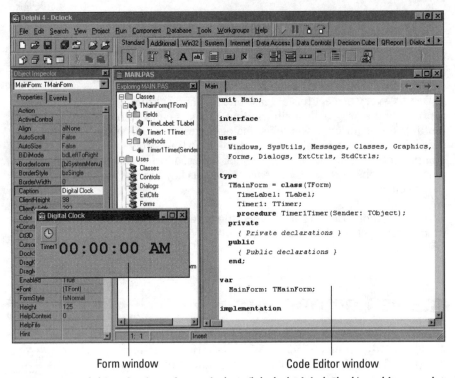

Form window   Code Editor window

Figure 3-1: Delphi maintains a form window (labeled Digital Clock) and its associated programming in the code editor window (the one labeled Main.pas).

Delphi automatically creates an Object Pascal unit for each new form you insert into an application. It is neither possible nor desirable to insert multiple form objects into one unit. Every form must have a corresponding unit. However, all units do not have forms. Some units merely provide data and code for other modules to use.

Caution

Expert Pascal programmers beware! Attempting to insert multiple forms into a unit may cause Delphi to lose its marbles. Inserting multiple form objects into a unit can disrupt Delphi's visual programming and automatic code generation capabilities. For best results, adhere to the one-form-one-unit rule. Delphi never inserts multiple forms into a unit, so the only way you experience this error is by writing units from scratch or by attempting to combine two form units into one. Don't do that.

Saving forms in projects

When saving a new project, never set a form's Name property and unit filename the same. For example, if you set a form's Name property to MainForm, do not save the form unit as Mainform.pas (I suggest using Main.pas instead). Because the unit's internal name equals its filename minus the .pas extension, using the same name for the form and the unit results in a name conflict.

To experience this error so you can avoid it in the future, follow these steps:

1. Start a new application and change the form's Name property to Main.

2. Save the project, and enter Main for the unit filename. Delphi automatically adds the .pas extension to create the actual filename, Main.pas.

3. Click the file-save dialog's OK button or press Enter. Because of the naming conflict, instead of saving the file, Delphi displays the error message, "The project already contains a form or module named Main." Click OK to close the error message window.

4. Fix the problem by changing the form's Name property to something different from its filename — for example, MainForm. You can now repeat Step 2 and save the unit as Main.pas.

To prevent this type of name conflict, which may be frequent until you become familiar with Delphi's naming rules, follow these tips for choosing Name properties and unit filenames:

✦ Append the word Form to every form's Name property. Examples of good form Names are MainForm for the program's main window, AboutForm for an About dialog, and EntryForm for a data-entry screen.

✦ Save the unit modules using their Name properties minus Form. For example, when you save the project, specify the filenames Main for the MainForm module, About for AboutForm, and Entry for EntryForm. This creates the three files Main.pas, About.pas, and Entry.pas.

Selected form properties

Specific examples throughout this book demonstrate many properties of form objects. Many properties have obvious purposes, and I won't explain them further here. (It doesn't take a genius to understand the purpose of a form's Height and Width properties.) Also, you have already met many form properties such as Caption, Name, and BorderStyle. The following describes less obvious form-object properties that you can view and edit in the Object Inspector window.

> **Note**   Be aware that some properties are inherited by the TForm class from other classes such as TComponent. In general, the same is true of most component classes — if you look up a class in your printed documentation, you need to inspect the class's ancestral hierarchy to find all properties and methods for the class.

✦ **ActiveControl** — Set this to any component object such as a Button or CheckBox to give that object the input focus when the form window first becomes visible. The input focus is not permanent; users can still press Tab to move the focus to other components.

✦ **AutoScroll** — Set to True to have scroll bars automatically appear and disappear in a window depending on whether more information extends beyond the window borders. This is the default value, which also affects form scaling. If AutoScroll is False, both the form's client area and the window rectangle are scaled; if True, only the form client area is scaled. Usually, with scaled forms, you should set AutoScroll to False. For more information about using scroll bars, see "Form Frameworks" in this chapter.

✦ **Cursor** — Specifies a cursor shape to display when the mouse cursor moves into the window's client area. Select one of the values from this property's drop-down list.

✦ **Enabled** — Normally set to True to have the form respond to mouse, timer, or keyboard events. Set to False to disable event handling. Don't do this for main-window forms. Set this property to False only for forms that the program manages. (The splash-screen method explained in this chapter uses this feature.)

✦ **HorzScrollBar** — Sets a horizontal scroll bar's values. The scroll bar appears only if the subvalue Visible is True and if Range is greater than ClientWidth. Double-click the property name (not its value) to open these subvalues.

✦ **Icon** — Selects an associated icon to represent the form window. If the form is the program's main window, the Icon property specifies the system icon that Windows displays when you minimize the window.

✦ **KeyPreview** — Set to True if you want the form to receive most keyboard events before they go to the focused control. If False, all keyboard events go to the selected control. Regardless of KeyPreview's setting, the form never receives navigation key events such as generated by pressing the Tab, BackTab, and cursor arrow keys, unless the current control (an input box, for example) processes those keys.

✦ **Menu** — Specifies which MainMenu component to use for the form's menu bar. Delphi normally sets this property to the form's first MainMenu object, but you can change it to another menu. See Chapter 5 for more information.

✦ **ObjectMenuItem** — Used with OLE applications. See Chapter 16 for more information.

✦ **PixelsPerInch** — Designates how the application creates a form window scaled to pixels per inch. Use with Scaled to create forms that appear similar in size in different screen resolutions. If Scaled is False, PixelsPerInch has no effect. This property's name is somewhat misleading because its value does not equal the number of pixels in one inch. Instead, Delphi determines PixelsPerInch based on the system font size, and then uses this value to scale the form window.

✦ **Position** — Determines the method for calculating a form's size and position. The default setting, poDefault, displays the window in its designed size and position; poDefaultPosOnly positions the window as designed, but calculates its size at run time; (Windows determines the initial size of the run-time form); poDefaultSizeOnly sizes the window as designed, but positions it at run time (Windows determines where the window appears); and poScreenCenter centers the window in the display.

✦ **Scaled** — Set to True to use the PixelsPerInch property and create a form that is automatically scaled relative to the font size. This helps you create applications that look good regardless of display resolution. Set to False to not scale a form. Scaling is especially important to ensure that text is displayed correctly in the form's controls on systems that use large fonts. This is even more critical in Windows 98 and NT 5.0, in which users can select arbitrary font scales.

✦ **Tag** — No preset meaning. Use Tag to store any integer (whole number) value you wish — for example, a version number, or a code or count that the program inspects at run time.

✦ **VertScrollBar** — Same as HorzScrollBar, but configures the form's vertical scroll bar subproperties.

✦ **Visible** — Set to True to make a component visible; False to hide it until the program calls the component object's Show method. A form's Visible property is normally False because applications automatically make their forms visible at the proper times. For a form used as a child window or dialog box, however, you might set Visible to False to hide the window until needed.

✦ **WindowMenu** — In Multiple Document Interface (MDI) applications, designates the menu to display titles of opened windows. Set this property to any menu item (usually the one labeled "Window") in the form's MainMenu object.

Note   See Chapter 15, Developing MDI Applications, for more information about MDI applications and using forms to create child windows.

Selected form events

As with form properties, examples throughout this book demonstrate many form events; others — for example, such as OnClick and OnDblClick — are self-evident. Following are less obvious events displayed in a selected form's Object Inspector window:

✦ **OnActivate** — Called when the program activates the form — that is, when it first receives the input focus as for example, when you switch back to the program from another application. See also OnDeactivate.

✦ **OnClose** — Called when the form closes. See also OnDestroy.

✦ **OnCloseQuery** — Called just before the form closes, usually when the application calls the Close procedure. You can use this event to prevent data loss by prompting users to save changed files before the application ends, or to prevent a form from closing. See "Closing a Window" in this chapter for more information.

✦ **OnCreate** — Called once when the program creates a form object in memory. Use this event to perform one-time initializations.

✦ **OnDeactivate** — Called when the user switches away from the application. See also OnActivate.

✦ **OnDestroy** — Called just before a form object's destruction. Use this event to release any system-held resources or to perform critical cleanup chores. If the form is the program's main window, OnDestroy is your last, best opportunity to perform actions before the program terminates.

✦ **OnDonner, OnBlitzen** — Called in response to jingling bells heard on the rooftop. (Just checking whether you're still paying attention.)

✦ **OnDockDrop, OnDockOver** — These two events are called in response to window docking maneuvers. Other related events are OnEndDock, OnStartDock, and OnUndock. See "Creating Docking Controls" in Chapter 12 for more information.

✦ **OnDragDrop, OnDragOver** — Part of Delphi's drag-and-drop services. See Chapter 16, Developing with the Clipboard, DDE, and OLE, for more information on data transfers, DDE, and OLE.

✦ **OnHide** — Used to perform actions when a form is hidden. For example, an OnHide event handler could release memory or other resources when a form is not visible.

✦ **OnKeyDown** — Called when the user presses any key, including function and special keys. Use this event to interpret multikey activity, such as pressing the Alt and Shift keys, perhaps in combination with a function key. It is possible for a program to receive multiple OnKeyDown events without receiving intervening OnKeyUp events. Usually set KeyPreview to True when using this event.

✦ **OnKeyPress** — Called when the user presses a single ASCII or control key, but not a function or other special key. Use this event to detect character keypresses. This event occurs after OnKeyDown but before OnKeyUp. Usually set KeyPreview to True when using this event.

✦ **OnKeyUp** — Called when the user releases any key, including function and special keys. One OnKeyUp event matchs every OnKeyDown event. Use this event along with OnKeyDown to fine-tune keyboard activity — for example, in a game that performs actions (perhaps via a Timer component) while the user holds down a certain key combination. An OnKeyUp event occurs for every OnKeyDown event, but not necessarily in strict down-up-down-up consecutive order (Windows always sends key down and key up messages in order, but the message pairs might not be consecutive — down 1, down 2, up 1, up 2 is possible). Usually set KeyPreview to True when using this event.

✦ **OnMouseDown** — Called when the user clicks any mouse button and the mouse cursor is positioned over the form's client area. Delphi calls the Windows API GetCapture for an OnMouseDown event to ensure that the object receives subsequent OnMouseMove and OnMouseUp events. This feature is controlled by the csCaptureMouse flag in the TControl class's ControlState property.

✦ **OnMouseMove** — Called when the user moves the mouse cursor within the form's client area. You can also determine whether the user has pressed the Shift, Alt, or Ctrl keys while moving the mouse.

✦ **OnMouseUp** — Called when the user releases a mouse button that previously generated an OnMouseDown event, regardless of the mouse cursor's position.

✦ **OnPaint** — Called when the form's contents require updating — for example, after the user moves another window aside. For more information on graphics programming, see Chapter 13, Developing Graphics Applications.

✦ **OnResize** — Called after the window changes size. This can be in response to dragging the window's size button, and minimizing or maximizing the window. Note that the window has already been resized when your application receives this event.

✦ **OnShow** — Called just before a window becomes visible. Use this event to perform initializations before the window appears.

When processing Tab keystrokes in OnKeyDown events, always check the Shift flags. If the user presses Alt+Tab to switch away from the application, the OnKeyDown event receives that key combination. If you do not check for the Alt key in the Shift flags, your program might interfere with the operation of Windows.

Form Templates

You can construct your own forms from scratch, or you can select from one of several preprogrammed form templates supplied with Delphi. The templates are easy to use and modify, and they are especially valuable for quickly getting prototypes up and running.

As demonstrated in the following sections, you can also create your own form templates to provide a common base for new programs, standard data-entry screens, custom dialog boxes, and many other applications.

Using form templates

Try the following steps to create an About dialog using a preprogrammed form template that displays a copyright notice and other information about your application.

Note

Early versions of Delphi required selecting Options|Environment and enabling the Gallery option. Use on New Form, to bring up a dialog window of available form templates. Newer releases of Delphi automatically display a similar, though more extensive, dialog when you select the New… command.

1. Begin a new project, and create a directory such as C:\Projects\Aboutex for its files. Change the form's Name to MainForm and its Caption to About Box Example. Save the project in the directory you created. Name the unit Main and the project Aboutex.

2. To add a second form to the project, select File|New…. As shown in Figure 3-2, this brings up the New Items (formerly titled Browse Gallery) dialog which lists form and other templates. Table 3-1 describes selected templates in the New Items dialog—you'll meet some of the others throughout this book.

3. Click the Forms page tab in the New Items dialog window. Choose the About Box template with the mouse or by pressing Tab or arrow keys. Press Enter or click OK to insert this form into the application and close the New Items dialog.

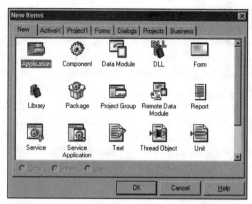

Figure 3-2: Delphi's New Items dialog form and other templates

4. You should see the blank About dialog window illustrated in Figure 3-3. By default, the form's Name property is set to AboutBox. Change this Name to AboutForm. Also change AboutForm's Caption to About This Program, or to any other text.

Figure 3-3: The unmodified AboutBox form-template window

Note

I strongly suggest including the component name, such as Form, in its Name property.

5. Save the project, and when Delphi presents the file-save dialog, enter About for the AboutForm unit filename. This creates a new Object Pascal module, About.pas, in the current directory. The project now has two forms — one for the program's main window (MainForm) and one for an About dialog (AboutForm). Each form has an associated Object Pascal module: Main.pas for MainForm and About.pas for AboutForm. In addition, the file Main.dfm stores MainForm's properties; About.dfm stores AboutForm's properties. You might want to view the project's filenames with the Windows Explorer at this stage.

6. Modify AboutForm's Label component objects as you wish. Insert your program's name, a copyright notice, and any other text you want. You can also insert additional Label and other components into AboutForm's window. Any changes you make affect only this application—the form template remains unblemished for future uses. Figure 3-4 shows a sample finished AboutForm dialog.

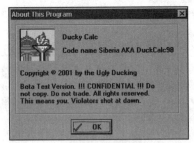

Figure 3-4: The finished AboutForm from the AboutEx application

7. If you compile and run the program at this stage, it displays only a blank window. Although MainForm automatically becomes visible, the AboutForm dialog hides until needed. To display the dialog, first add a Button component to MainForm. Keep the default Name, Button1, and change the Caption to "Click Me!," or to any other text. Size the button and MainForm window as you wish. Double-click the Button1 object in the form to create an OnClick event handler, and enter this statement between begin and end:

```
AboutForm.ShowModal;
```

8. The preceding statement calls AboutForm's ShowModal function. This displays a modal dialog, which you must close before continuing to use the application. A modeless dialog permits menus and other commands to operate normally while the dialog remains open. Chapter 12 explains more about modal and modeless dialogs.

9. If you try to compile the application at this point, you receive an error message because the Main unit module doesn't yet recognize the AboutForm object in the About module. Try this — newer versions of Delphi can add the necessary programming to *use* the AboutForm unit. Answer Yes when

prompted. Or, to insert the programming manually, click the error window's Cancel button and bring up Main unit in the code editor (you can press Ctrl+F12 and select Main from the View Unit dialog). Locate the uses directive at the top of Main, which lists other modules used by this one. Between the last module name and semicolon, type a comma and the word About. Make sure the directive still ends with a semicolon. For example, your uses directive might look like the following, but the exact order and number of modules may differ depending on the changes you made to the AboutForm window. The new entry is shown here in bold:

```
uses
    Windows, Messages, SysUtils, Classes, Graphics,
    Controls, Forms, Dialogs, StdCtrls, About;
```

10. Now that Main imports, or uses, the About unit module, the preceding statement that calls ShowModal compiles. Press F9 to compile, link, and run the application. When its main window appears, click the button to display the AboutForm dialog. Close the dialog and the program to return to Delphi.

You can use similar steps to program a menu command that displays AboutForm. Instead of a Button, insert a MainMenu component into MainForm, and double-click the object to create the menu's commands. Select a command such as Help|About in the form window to create an event handler, and enter the same statement you typed for Button1's OnClick event.

Another, and sometimes better way to import a unit into another is to add a fresh *uses* directive in the host unit's implementation section. This is what Delphi does automatically if you answer Yes to the error dialog in Step 9. To do this manually, delete the About unit name and the preceding comma from the Main unit's uses directive you modified in Step 9. Locate the word *implementation* in this same unit, and just below that line, add a uses directive to import the About module. The two lines should now look like these:

```
implementation
uses About;
```

The main difference between this method and adding About to the Main module's uses directive at the top of that unit is that items in a unit's implementation are private to that module. Using units in a module's implementation also helps prevent circular reference errors, which are caused by two units using one another. This is allowed, but requires the units to have uses directives in their implementation sections. Circular unit references in uses directives in the units' interface sections is never allowed. And, by the way, no matter how many units use another unit, only one copy of each unit is loaded into memory. The uses directives merely make a unit's declarations available so that the program can refer to variables and call methods and use other imported items.

Table 3-1
Selected New Item Templates

Template	Category	Description
Application	New	Begins a new application; same as selecting the File|New Application command.
Component	New	Prompts you for information about a new component you want to create. Until you learn more about Delphi programming, you probably won't use this template.
Form	New	General-purpose blank form; same as selecting the File|New Form command. Use this template to create a program's main window, child windows, and custom dialog boxes.
Unit	New	Begins a new unit that does not have an associated form. Use this template to create units with declarations, procedures, and functions that you want other units to share.
About box	Forms	Displays a copyright notice, version number, and other program information. Usually displayed in response to a Help|About... command.
Dual list box	Forms	Two interactive lists, with buttons for transferring selected items from one list to the other. Useful for selecting among options, files, and other information sets.
Tabbed pages	Forms	Standard dialog box with OK, Cancel, and Help buttons, a GroupBox area that can hold other components, and a set of page tabs displayed at top. Useful for complex dialogs that have too many controls to fit on one screen, such as an Options dialog. Users can select page tabs to view other parts of the dialog.
Standard Dialog	Dialogs	Similar to a blank form, but with OK and Cancel buttons. This category has a few similar templates that add Help buttons and place all buttons at the bottom or right side of the window.
Password Dialog	Dialogs	Small dialog with an input box, OK, and Cancel buttons. Use it to request a password from users. The password is not visible while typing.

Tip Think of a unit's interface section (at top) as a public area that makes items visible to other units. Think of the implementation section (at bottom) as a private area where the business programming of the unit takes place. Units can use only items – types, variables, methods, and other declarations – that appear in an imported unit's interface. Only the unit itself can use the items declared in its implementation. As a general rule, except for modifying a unit's uses directive, you should type new programming only into a form unit's implementation. Delphi automatically programs the interface section of a form unit, and any changes you make to this section might conflict with Delphi's code generation capabilities.

Tip When you first save a project with multiple forms, Delphi presents a gaggle of file-save-as dialogs, one for each unnamed module. At best, this can be confusing. At worst, it can cause even skilled programmers to run screaming for the nearest watering hole. To guard against accidentally misnaming module files in applications with numerous forms, create each new form individually. Enter its Name and Caption, and then select File|Save All to name and save the new module. It takes a little more time to save each new form as you create it, but this method is potentially less disorienting than saving multiple forms all at once.

Creating Object Repository templates

Creating your own form and application templates is a great way to share programming or to develop software shells. For example, if your program's users require several data-entry screens that differ in minor ways, you can save time by creating templates for commonly shared elements. Programming teams can also save time and effort by developing templates for new projects, demos, and prototypes.

You can save any form, or even an entire application, as a template. You do this by inserting your form or application into Delphi's *Object Repository*. This is simple and easy to do, and it's a great way to customize Delphi with your own template designs. Follow these steps to add any form or application to the Object Repository:

Note The book's CD-ROM does not include files for the following tutorial. Use these steps to convert your own forms and applications into templates.

1. Develop and save your application, or open any existing project. Bring up your target form's window (press Shift+F12, if necessary, or choose the View|Form command). You must be viewing the form window, not the code editor, to add a form to the Object Repository.

2. Press Alt+F10 or single-click the right mouse button with the mouse cursor inside the target form's window. This displays a floating pop-up menu. Choose the command Add To Repository.

3. You are prompted for a Title, a Description, a Page (select one from the drop-down list, or enter a new page name), and optional Author information. Click the Browse button to select an icon to display for your template, either one from Delphi's Images\Icons directory, or one of your own design. When you are satisfied with your entries, click OK. Your template is now in the Object Repository, and appears in the New Items dialog when you select Delphi's File I New... command.

If you want to create a template for an entire application — a nifty way to provide application shells as starting places for new programs — open the application project file and select the Project I Add To Repository command. Enter information and select an icon as in Step 3. You can then select this template using File I New... to begin a new application using the template as a shell.

Note

The Object Repository stores information about your templates. The actual data and source code files are the originals. Adding a form or application to the Object Repository does *not* copy source code and forms into Delphi, it merely creates an entry that refers to the original files. As a result, after adding a form or application to the Object Repository, any changes you make to the original files affect the template for all future uses via File|New.... One advantage of this is that you can modify, debug, and upgrade your templates without having to remove and reload them into the Object Repository.

The source files for Delphi's default templates are in the Objrepos directory in your Delphi installation. You can edit these files to modify the default templates, but you might want to save copies of the originals. You can further edit the template entries in the New Items dialog by using the Tools I Repository... command. Use the resulting dialog to display objects in each of the New Items pages, to delete templates (the original source files are unaltered), and to rename page tabs.

In a shared environment, such as a network with many programmers needing access to form and application templates, you need to set up a path called the "Shared Repository Directory." This path is stored in the Windows registry. To change it, use the Tools I Environment Options... command and select the Preferences page tab. Enter a shared pathname where Delphi looks for the Object Repository file, DELPHI32.dro. This path is *not* the same as the one mentioned in the preceding paragraph. The default path is Delphi's \bin installation directory. Copy the original DELPHI32.dro file to your shared directory if you change its path name.

Note

Delphi controls access to a shared Object Repository file by using a lock file named DELPHI32.drl. This is done to prevent two or more programmers writing to the Object Repository simultaneously. However, if Delphi exits abnormally while the Object Repository is being modified, the file lock might not be removed. To recover full access to the repository, simply delete DELPHI32.drl.

Deleting Object Repository templates

Follow these steps to delete a form or application template from the Object Repository:

1. Select Tools I Repository... to bring up the Object Repository editor window.

2. Select the page name where the template is stored — this is the same name as the page tab displayed by the File I New... command. The templates for this page are displayed in the Objects window.

3. Select the template you want to discard and click the Delete Object button. Answer Yes when prompted to finish the deletion.

4. You can also delete an entire page of templates with the Delete Page button.

Deleting a template does not erase its files. They remain in their original directories. To restore a deleted template, simply add it back to the Object Repository. You may delete Delphi's standard form templates, but these are highly useful objects and you should not remove them without good reason. Some of the sample applications and step-by-step tutorials in this book assume that one or more standard templates are available. If you can't find a mentioned template, it's possible that some nasty creature modified your Object Repository, and you either have to recreate it or reinstall Delphi.

Using a Dialog for a Main Window Form

In some cases, you might want to change the main window to a different form. For example, it's often useful to use a dialog or other form template as an application window. The resulting interface is simple and clean, and it doesn't require a menu bar. Users run the program by clicking buttons and selecting other controls in the window.

Follow these steps to change an application's main window to another form or template:

1. Start a new application.

2. Select File I New... and choose a form template from the New Items dialog window, also known as the Object Repository. For this demonstration, click the Dialogs page tab and choose the Dialog with Help form template.

3. Choose View I Project Manager (see Figure 3-5). Highlight the Project1 entry, and right-click the mouse to bring up a pop-up menu. Select the Options command, and in the resulting Project Options dialog, click the Forms page tab, and change the entry in the "Main form" edit box to OKHelpRightDlg (you

can most easily do this by selecting the object's name from the drop-down list). Click OK. You have now specified that OKHelpRightDlg is to be used as the application's main form.

Figure 3-5: Delphi's Project Manager window

4. You should again be viewing the Project Manager window. Use this window to delete the application's old main form, which is no longer needed. To do that, highlight Unit1 in the Project Manager window, click the right mouse button for a pop-up menu, and select Remove from project command. Answer No if Delphi prompts you to save Unit1.pas. This discards the project's default form and its source code unit file. The old form also disappears from the display, leaving only the OKHelpRightDlg window and its source code file.

5. Close the Project Manager window or shove it aside. Save the project using File | Save All... and, as usual, name the unit Main and the project Test (the exact names are unimportant).

6. Compile, link, and run the application by pressing F9. Figure 3-6 shows the program's main window — a stylish dialog box with OK, Cancel, and Help buttons. Because you didn't supply any event handlers for the dialog's buttons, the buttons don't do anything.

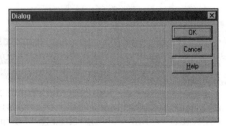

Figure 3-6: A dialog template used as a main window

Closing a Window

Why is it we close things up but shut them down? I don't know, but whichever way you like to travel, closing a window correctly is as important as getting one up and running.

As you have learned, in the program's source code, you can close any Delphi form object by calling its Close procedure. If the window is the application's main one, this also ends the program. To try this, start a new application and insert a Button object into the main form. Create an event handler by double-clicking the Button, and call Close like so:

```
begin
  Close;    { <-- insert this statement here }
end;
```

Although this appears simple enough, calling Close sets several behind-the-scenes actions into motion. You don't have to program these activities — they are automatic, but it's important to understand the process. Internally, Close calls another function, CloseQuery, which returns True if it is okay for the window to close. If CloseQuery returns False, the call to Close is canceled and the window does not close. If CloseQuery returns True, the program activates the OnClose event handler (if there is one) for this form.

Delphi's closure sequence provides several good opportunities to perform actions when forms close. Internally, CloseQuery activates the OnCloseQuery event handler, which you can use to determine whether it is safe to close the form window. For example, your OnCloseQuery event handler might check whether the user saved critical data. If not, the program can display a warning, or it can cancel the request to close the window. Figure 3-7 illustrates the actions that occur when you call Close.

A simple example demonstrates how to use OnCloseQuery to confirm a user's intention to end a program by closing its main window. Start a new application, and then follow these steps:

1. Insert a Button component into the form. Double-click the Button and enter Close; between the resulting event handler's begin and end keywords.

2. Press F9 to compile, link, and run the program. Click the Button object to exit and return to Delphi. This demonstrates normal form closure. By tapping into this process, you can add a confirmation box that permits users to change their minds about ending the program.

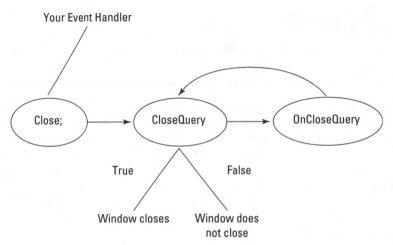

Figure 3-7: Delphi performs these actions when a program calls a window's Close event.

3. Back in Delphi, select the form by clicking in its background. Be sure the Button1 object is not selected. Go to the Events page in the Object Inspector window, and double-click the mouse cursor in the value field to the right of the OnCloseQuery event. Enter the programming in Listing 3-1. For reference, the listing shows the entire event handler — enter only the statements between the begin and end keywords. On disk, you find this listing in the OnClose directory. The programming displays a message dialog with Yes and No buttons. If the user chooses Yes, MessageDlg returns the value mrYes, and the if statement sets CanClose to True. If the user chooses No, the program sets CanClose to False.

4. Press F9 to run the program. This time, when you click the window's button, the message dialog requests confirmation as shown in Figure 3-8. Choose Yes to end. Choose No to cancel the close request.

Note

Carefully enter the programming in Listing 3-1 exactly as shown, or copy it from the CloseQuery.pas file on the CD-ROM in the Source\Misc directory. If you enter this, notice the mix of square brackets and parentheses in this code, which may look similar on the printed page.

Figure 3-8: Confirmation message dialog

Listing 3-1: **An OnCloseQuery event handler**

```
procedure TForm1.FormCloseQuery(Sender: TObject;
  var CanClose: Boolean);
begin
  if MessageDlg('End the program?',
    mtConfirmation, [mbYes, mbNo], 0) = mrYes
    then CanClose := True
    else CanClose := False;
end;
```

Form Frameworks

The following sections describe some other neat things you can do with forms, such as attaching scroll bars, making a window stay on top of other windows, and creating a startup splash screen.

Quick-and-dirty scroll bars

A *scroll* is one of the most ancient known devices for viewing information in a relatively small space. Today, scrolling has become one of modern computing's most accepted display tricks for viewing large documents on small screens. Besides being a useful interface tool, a scroll bar is literally a link to the past.

As you probably know, a *scroll bar* is a Windows control you click, drag, and poke to scroll information in a window. Click a scroll bar's buttons to browse at slow speed (a line at a time, for example), or click inside the shaded bar to page through data more quickly. The scroll bar's thumb box indicates the relative position of the window's view. Drag the thumb box for another view. For example, to move to the document's midpoint, drag the thumb box to the center of the bar.

In Windows 95, scroll bar thumb boxes grow to indicate how much information is not displayed in a window — a large thumb box indicates that very little information is out of view, while a small thumb box indicates there's a lot of off-screen information. You don't have to perform any special programming to take advantage of this feature.

Adding scroll bars to a form

Adding scroll bars to a form is easy, but you can make several refinements for smoother scrolling. Follow these steps to add scroll bars to the BitView application from Chapter 2.

1. Copy the BitView sample application from Chapter 2 to a new directory named Mybits (or another name). Copy only the Bitview.dpr, Main.dfm, and Main.pas files. Do not copy any other files, especially those such as desktop files ending in .dsk which may contain pathnames to the original Bitview directory. For reference, this tutorial's finished files are in the Bitview2 directory on the CD-ROM.

2. Open the BitView project (be sure to change to the directory you created from Step 1). Single-click inside the outlined BitImage component object, which fills the form's client area. (Or, select BitImage from the Object Inspector's drop-down list.) In the Object Inspector's Properties page, double-click the bitmap's Stretch property to change True to False. With Stretch disabled, the program no longer adjusts bitmaps to fit BitImage's size, and therefore, you need to add scroll bars to view pictures larger the window.

3. Set MainForm's WindowState property to wsNormal so the window displays in its designed size rather than full screen. (Select MainForm from the Object Inspector's drop-down list.) Also, change MainForm's Caption to Bitmap Viewer With Scroll Bars.

4. To add a horizontal scroll bar to the form, double-click the form's HorzScrollBar property to open its five subvalues. Click the property name, not its value. Set Range to 1000 and make sure that Visible is True (the default value). When you press Enter or move to another Property, a horizontal scroll bar appears in the form window. If not, specify a larger range.

5. To add a vertical scroll bar to the form, repeat the preceding step for MainForm's VertScrollBar property. The final form window now shows horizontal and vertical scroll bars.

6. Press F9 to run the modified application. Open any bitmap file such as Sample.bmp in the Data directory. Resize the window, and use its scroll bars to move the image up, down, left, and right.

In general, you can use similar steps to add scroll bars to any informational component aligned to the window's client area. For each scroll bar property, make sure:

✦ The subvalue Visible is True.

✦ The subvalue Range is greater than the form's ClientWidth property. A value from 1000 to 2000 is usually adequate.

Quick-and-dirty scroll bars are useful for prototypes and for testing scrolling operations; however, for smoother scrolling, you will want to make several refinements to finished applications as described next.

Fine-tuning scroll bars

Experienced Windows users expect scroll bars to perform as though choreographed in a ballet. Following are some of the dance steps that if not followed exactly, will bring jeers from your program's users:

✦ Scroll bars should not appear until the user opens a document in the window.

✦ The appearance of a scroll bar should indicate that more information is available by scrolling. For example, in a text window, a vertical scroll bar indicates the document contains more lines than the window can show.

✦ Resizing the window, or loading another document, should display or remove scroll bars as necessary. For example, if maximizing a window causes the entire document to come into view, scroll bars should disappear. If you load a large document, scroll bars should come back into view if necessary.

✦ The scroll bar's thumb position should indicate the relative viewing location in the document — or, to state that in technical terms, scroll bar ranges should mirror the document's size.

In the following tutorial, you make all of the preceding improvements to the BitView application. Listing 3-2 shows the final Main.Pas form unit file from the Source\Bitview2 directory on the CD-ROM.

Open the modified BitView project file from the preceding section, or start with fresh copies of the project's .dpr, .dfm, and .pas files. Then, follow these steps:

1. Double-click MainForm's HorzScrollBar and VertScrollBar properties, and set the Range subvalues for each property back to 0. This removes the scroll bars from the form and ensures that they do not appear until the user opens a bitmap file.

2. Click MainForm's Events page tab in the Object Inspector. Double-click the value field next to the OnResize event to create an event-handler procedure named FormResize. The program calls this procedure whenever the window size changes, regardless of how that action occurs. Enter the following two statements between begin and end (also refer to Listing 3-2 at this section's end if you need more help):

```
HorzScrollBar.Range := BitImage.Picture.Width;
VertScrollBar.Range := BitImage.Picture.Height;
```

3. The preceding statements set the Range properties in the form's horizontal and vertical scroll bar objects equal to the width and height of the BitImage object's Picture. With these changes, scroll bars automatically mirror the image size. As you will discover, however, these changes alone are not enough to ensure smooth scrolling.

4. Press F9 to compile, link, and run the application. Open a bitmap file. At this stage, no scroll bars appear until after you resize the window. To display scroll bars upon opening a new file requires modifying the File | Open event handler. Quit the program now to return to Delphi.

5. To locate the correct event handler, select File | Open from the form window. Because a procedure already exists for this command, Delphi positions the cursor at the first statement in the event handler. Insert the following line after the statement that assigns a filename to the form's Caption property. This is inside the innermost begin and end keywords. (Refer to Listing 3-2 at the end of this section if you need help positioning the statement.)

```
FormResize(Sender);
```

6. Press F9 to compile, link, and run the application. Open a bitmap file. Scroll bars automatically appear if the image doesn't fit inside the program's window. Change the window's size if necessary, and try out the scroll bar operations.

The statement you added in Step 5 calls an existing event handler from inside another procedure. In earlier examples, you learned how to set two or more events to the same handler, thus sharing existing code among multiple processes. Here, you are using another code-sharing technique, but in this case, you called an event-handler procedure from inside another one that performs additional actions — in this case, loading a bitmap file from disk.

As a result of the new statement, when you load a bitmap document the program automatically adjusts scroll bar ranges, which causes the scroll bars to appear or disappear as necessary.

Tip

When calculating an image's size, be sure to use the correct Height and Width properties. For example, the expression BitImage.Picture.Height obtains the height of the bitmap loaded into the BitImage component. The expression BitImage.Height refers to the component object's height, not to the height of the data in that object, which is the value you probably want.

Listing 3-2: Bitview2\Main.pas

```
unit Main;

interface
```

```
uses
  Windows, SysUtils, Messages, Classes, Graphics, Controls,
  Forms, Dialogs, Menus, ExtCtrls;

type
  TMainForm = class(TForm)
    BitImage: TImage;
    MainMenu1: TMainMenu;
    File1: TMenuItem;
    Open1: TMenuItem;
    Exit1: TMenuItem;
    OpenDialog1: TOpenDialog;
    procedure Open1Click(Sender: TObject);
    procedure Exit1Click(Sender: TObject);
    procedure FormResize(Sender: TObject);
  private
    { Private declarations }
  public
    { Public declarations }
  end;

var
  MainForm: TMainForm;

implementation

{$R *.DFM}

procedure TMainForm.Open1Click(Sender: TObject);
begin
  if OpenDialog1.Execute then
  begin
    BitImage.Picture.LoadFromFile(OpenDialog1.Filename);
    Caption := OpenDialog1.Filename;
    FormResize(Sender);
  end;
end;

procedure TMainForm.Exit1Click(Sender: TObject);
begin
  Close;
end;

procedure TMainForm.FormResize(Sender: TObject);
begin
  HorzScrollBar.Range := BitImage.Picture.Width;
  VertScrollBar.Range := BitImage.Picture.Height;
end;

end.
```

Quick-and-dirty ListBox scroll bars

Here's an even simpler way to add scroll bars to a window. The technique is especially useful for displaying lengthy lists. Try these steps:

1. Start a new project and insert a ListBox component object from the Standard palette into the form.

2. Select the ListBox object's Items property value, and click the ellipsis button to open Delphi's string editor. Enter 20 or so lines of text (or copy some lines from a text file). Close the editor. If you wish, use the Font property to choose a font size and style for the ListBox text.

3. Set the ListBox's Align property to alClient. This expands the ListBox object to fill the form window, which you might also want to resize at this time.

4. Press F9 to compile, link, and run. A vertical scroll bar automatically appears when the window is too short to display all lines of text in the ListBox control. (You have also just created a handy text viewer.)

The preceding steps add only vertical scroll bars to ListBox component objects. To create a horizontal scroll bar, insert the following statement in an event handler — a form's OnActivate event, for example:

```
ListBox1.Perform(LB_SETHORIZONTALEXTENT, 1000, 0);
```

The statement calls the VCL-internal Perform procedure, inherited by components such as ListBox from the TControl class. Perform sends a Windows message, in this case LB_SETHORIZONTALEXTENT, to the control for which the component serves as an interface. The value 1000 is the width of the data in the list box in pixels — an approximation in this case. The zero is a meaningless placeholder.

Keeping your form window on top

Some programs — for example, clocks, system resource utilities, and toolbars — are easier to use if they remain on top of other windows. Here's how to make a form window always stay on top of things. Now, if I could just figure out how to make my pen do that on my actual desktop, I'd be thrilled.

 The following tutorial's files are stored in the Source\Ontop directory in this book's accompanying CD-ROM.

1. Start a new application. Name the form MainForm and set its Caption to On Top Demo. Save the project in a directory such as C:\Projects\Ontop. Name MainForm's unit Main and the project file Ontop.

2. Insert a MainMenu object into MainForm. Double-click the object icon and create a menu named Demo with two commands: Stay on top and Exit. Close the Menu Designer.

3. Back in the form window, select the Exit command and enter **Close;** between the begin and end keywords. Select the Stay on top command and enter the programming shown in Listing 3-3. After the last step of this tutorial, I explain how this programming works. The source code text is located on disk in the Main.pas file in the OnTop directory.

4. Press F9 to run the completed program. Select the Stay on top command to cause the window to stay on top of other application windows. Notice that selecting the command adds a check mark to it. Select the command again to delete the check mark.

Listing 3-3: **Stay on top demonstration**

```
procedure TMainForm.Stayontop1Click(Sender: TObject);
begin
  with Sender as TMenuItem do
  begin
    Checked := not Checked;
    if Checked
      then FormStyle := fsStayOnTop
      else FormStyle := fsNormal;
  end;
end;
```

The procedure in Listing 3-3 demonstrates two key Delphi programming techniques. The Sender parameter to this procedure represents the command object that the user selected. However, the parameter's type is TObject, on which all Delphi objects are based. Thus, any object descendent of TObject can be passed to the procedure. To use that object requires telling Delphi what it actually is.

That's done here in a with statement, which tells Delphi to treat Sender as a TMenuItem object. This gives the program access to the menu command's properties, one of which is Checked. Setting this parameter to its opposite value with the expression not Checked inserts and removes a check mark from the menu.

The second technique that Listing 3-3 demonstrates is in the if statement that sets the form's FormStyle to one of two values — fsStayOnTop or fsNormal. The same FormStyle property is available in the Object Inspector window, but to have a window stay on top in response to a user command, as shown here, the program itself must assign the property value at run time.

This brings up an important point. In addition to setting property values using the Object Inspector window at design time, you can also assign most object property values at run time. For example, create a procedure for an event handler, or insert a Button object and double-click it. Insert an assignment such as the following between begin and end:

```
Caption := 'A New Window Title!';
```

When you run the program, click the button to change the form's title. Notice that the statement can also be written

```
MainForm.Caption := 'A New Window Title!';
```

Although that works, it refers directly to the MainForm object, making the resulting code less generally useful. On the other hand, it is more explicitly clear. The former statement could change the caption of any window; the latter can change only MainForm's caption. To change the text of the Button object, use a statement such as:

```
Button1.Caption := 'Click Me Again!';
```

Creating a startup splash screen

Well-written Windows programs display a startup notice, sometimes called a *splash screen*. With a little splishin' and splashin', you can add a significant flash factor to your program's display.

Because the project itself creates the program's main window, and because the splash screen must appear before that happens, the project file has to create its own splash. This means you must modify the source code to the project file, which is usually not necessary in Delphi programming.

The following tutorial's files are in the Splashin subdirectory. Figure 3-9 shows the program's splash screen, which appears as a borderless, fixed-size window with no title bar, system menu, or buttons.

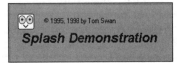

Figure 3-9: A startup splash screen

1. Start a new project. Name the form MainForm and set its Caption to Splashin Demo. Save the project in a directory such as C:\Projects\Splashin. Name MainForm's unit Main and the project file Splashin.

2. Insert a Button component into MainForm. Change the Button's Name property to ExitButton and its Caption to Exit. (Hint: Type **E&xit** in the Caption to designate the letter *x* as a shortcut key. Users can then press Alt+X to select the button.) Just for fun, enlarge the button and resize the form window as shown in Figure 3-10. Create a handler for ExitButton's OnClick event (you can simply double-click the Button object), and insert the statement Close; between the procedure's begin and end keywords.

Figure 3-10: Splashin's MainForm window in Delphi

3. Select the File I New Form command or click the New Form speed button. This brings up the Browse Gallery dialog, which presents several preprogrammed forms. (If you don't see the dialog, use Options I Environment to enable the Use on New Form check box under the Gallery label.) Choose the Blank form template and press Enter or click OK to close the Browse Gallery dialog.

4. You have just added a second form to the application. Change this form's Name property to SplashForm. Delete its Caption. Also, change its BorderStyle property to bsNone and set the three subvalues under BorderIcons to False. Some of these values are optional, and you might want to experiment with different window styles after you finish the tutorial. Figure 3-11 shows the sample SplashForm window in Delphi that you create in the next several steps (the exact contents of the window, however, are up to you).

5. Save the project. When Delphi prompts you for a unit filename, be sure the correct directory is current (C:\Projects\Splashin if you are following along). Enter **Splash** for SplashForm's unit filename.

6. Set SplashForm's Enabled property to False. This is one of the rare times when you don't want users to be able to give keyboard and mouse commands to a window. In this case, we want the program to have total control over SplashForm's display.

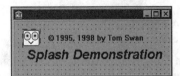

Figure 3-11: SplashIn's SplashForm
window in Delphi

7. Resize the SplashForm window. Because the window has no outline, insert a
   Bevel component object from the Additional category. This helps define the
   window's edges. Set Bevel1's Align property to alClient. Also, change the
   object's Shape to bsFrame and its Style to bsRaised. These values are up to
   you — try different settings after you finish the tutorial.

8. Insert Image and Label component objects into SplashForm. You can insert
   any graphical items you want to display during the program's startup.
   However, don't insert any buttons or other interactive controls. The
   application itself displays and removes the splash dialog.

9. This is an optional step. Set the SplashForm's FormStyle property to
   fsStayOnTop, and change Position to poScreenCenter. Here again, the settings
   depend on your preferences, but it's probably a good idea to center a splash
   screen and to have its window always stay on top of others.

10. Select View|Project Manager. Highlight the Splashin project, and click the
    right mouse button for a pop-up menu. Select the Options command. In the
    resulting Project Options dialog, select the Forms page tab. Notice that
    MainForm and SplashForm are in the Auto-create forms list. Highlight each
    form and click the right-arrow button to move it to Available forms. All Delphi
    forms are automatically created in memory at run time, which consumes
    memory and system resources. In cases such as this one, where the program
    creates a form at run time, you should remove that form from the Auto-create
    list. Close the Project Manager window.

11. Next, modify the project's source code to display the splash dialog before the
    main window becomes visible. This is one of the rare cases in which you need
    to insert statements into the project file. To do that, select the View|Project
    Source command. Modify the statements between begin and end to match the
    Splash.dpr project file in Listing 3-4. I explain more about this programming
    after these steps.

12. If you compile and run the program at this stage, it displays and removes the
    startup splash dialog so quickly you might not have the chance to see it. To
    force the dialog to remain visible for a few seconds, select the program's
    MainForm (the one with the big button). Create a handler for the form's
    OnCreate command. Preceding the begin keyword, add a longInt variable
    named currentTime. Between begin and end, insert two statements: a call to

the Windows GetTickCount function to set currentTime to the number of seconds that Windows has been running and a while statement that delays for an additional four seconds. (GetTickCount returns the number of milliseconds that Windows has been running. Dividing this value by 1000 converts it to seconds.) Refer to Listing 3-5, Main.pas, for these statements.

13. Press F9 to compile, link, and run. The program displays the startup splash dialog, waits a few seconds, removes the dialog, and displays the main window.

Listing 3-4: **Splashin\Splashin.dpr**

```
program Splashin;

uses
  Forms,
  Main in 'MAIN.PAS' {MainForm},
  Splash in 'SPLASH.PAS' {SplashForm};

{$R *.RES}

begin
  SplashForm := TSplashForm.Create(Application);
  SplashForm.Show;
  SplashForm.Update;
  Application.CreateForm(TMainForm, MainForm);
  SplashForm.Close;
Application.Run;
end.
```

Listing 3-4, Splashin.dpr, demonstrates how a program can create a form object at run time. To do that, call the Create method in the object's class, as this statement demonstrates:

```
SplashForm := TSplashForm.Create(Application);
```

That statement creates the object, and assigns it to SplashForm, which is defined in the Splash.pas module. The object now exists in memory, but it is not yet visible. To make it appear and to update its contents, call the object's Show and Update methods:

```
SplashForm.Show;
SplashForm.Update;
```

Listing 3-5: **Splashin\Main.pas**

```pascal
unit Main;

interface

uses
  Windows, SysUtils, Messages, Classes, Graphics, Controls,
  Forms, Dialogs, StdCtrls;

type
  TMainForm = class(TForm)
    ExitButton: TButton;
    procedure ExitButtonClick(Sender: TObject);
    procedure FormCreate(Sender: TObject);
  private
    { Private declarations }
  public
    { Public declarations }
  end;

var
  MainForm: TMainForm;

implementation

{$R *.DFM}

procedure TMainForm.ExitButtonClick(Sender: TObject);
begin
  Close;
end;

{ The following procedure pauses for a few seconds so
  the Splash dialog remains visible for a predetermined
  length of time. }

procedure TMainForm.FormCreate(Sender: TObject);
var
  CurrentTime: LongInt;
begin
  CurrentTime := GetTickCount div 1000;
  while ( (GetTickCount div 1000) < (CurrentTime + 4) ) do
    Sleep(1);
end;

end.
```

You can use similar steps to create and display any form at run time. Be sure, however, that the form is not auto-created (use the Project Manager's Options command to check).

Note

Calling Update after Show is necessary here only because the programming exists outside the application's main message loop, which processes Windows messages. No paint messages are therefore processed and, thus, calling Update is necessary. Usually, you only have to call Show to display a window.

After you are done using a form object, hide it from display and then delete the memory it occupies. The freed memory is then available for other objects. For example, after creating the main window (which in this case pauses for several seconds so you can see the splash window), the demonstration program uses this statement to get rid of the splashy dialog:

```
SplashForm.Close;
```

Listing 3-5 also demonstrates some useful techniques for MainForm's OnCreate event. First, the procedure calls GetTickTime, a Windows function that returns the number of milliseconds that have passed since Windows was started. This value divided by 1000 equals the number of elapsed seconds.

To pause for a few seconds, the program assigns the divided value to CurrentTime, a variable of the LongInt type. A while loop then uses a complex-looking expression to test whether GetTickTime (again divided by 1000) is less than the previously saved time plus four. The *while* loop calls the Windows Sleep function (the 1 argument specifies the number of milliseconds to sleep). This ensures that other processes are given a chance to run while our CPU-intensive loop steals the show. After four seconds, the while loop's expression is no longer true, and the procedure ends. This proves that time indeed passes despite our best efforts to slow it down — if this trick fails, the universe is okay, but your computer's clock is probably busted.

The demonstration program pauses only because it has nothing else to do. If your program's OnCreate event performs many initializations, you may not need to insert an artificial pause. However, computers are becoming faster every day, and instructions that take four seconds today might zip by in the future. For safety, call GetTickCount to test whether at least a certain amount of time has passed before ending your splash form's OnCreate event handler.

Introducing Data Modules

A data module is a separate form that can contain nonvisual component objects. Data modules are never visible in the finished application — they provide a kind of storehouse for components that you might want to share among an application's other forms and units. A data module is also a handy place to keep nonvisual objects such as MainMenu and Timer components. You can use a data module to move the object icons out of other forms, where they simply clutter the display.

Note   Data modules are particularly valuable in database programming as explained in Chapter 17, Developing Database Applications. However, you may use data modules in any application.

On the CD-ROM   Follow the next steps to learn how to create and use a data module. Figure 3-12 shows the sample program's design-time display in Delphi. The finished files are on the CD-ROM in the DMTest directory.

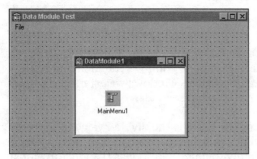

Figure 3-12: Use a data module to move nonvisual component icons such as MainMenu out of visible forms and reduce clutter.

1. Start a new application. Name the main form MainForm, and set its Caption to Data Module Test. Save all files, naming MainForm's unit Main.pas and the project DMTest.dpr.

2. Select File | New Data Module. A form window with a white background appears. You may insert only nonvisual component objects into this window. If you attempt to insert a visual object such as a Button, you receive an error message.

3. Select File | Save All a second time. When prompted for a name for Unit2, enter Module1 and click OK. This names the data module's source file Module1.pas, and also displays that label in the code editor window. The application now has two forms.

4. Insert a MainMenu object from the Standard palette into the data module window, which is named DataModule1. You can change this name in your own applications, but for this demonstration, we use the default name.

5. Double-click the MainMenu object, and create a File menu with an Exit command. Double-click the Exit command to insert an event handler for it into the data module's source code. Enter the following statement between begin and end:

```
MainForm.Close;
```

6. Compile by pressing F9. You receive an error message because DataModule1 refers to MainForm, which is in another unit. To make that reference, the data module must *use* MainForm's unit. Either insert the text uses Main; in the data module's implementation section, or answer Yes if Delphi prompts you to make this change automatically. (If Delphi can determine which units are missing from a uses directive, it can enter their names automatically, but it will not do so without your permission.)

7. You can now compile and run the application, but it does not display the MainMenu object in the program's window. To do that, the Main module must also use the data module. Another uses directive does the trick. Make sure the Main module is displayed in the code editor, select File|Use Unit..., and choose Module1 from the list (there's only one entry). Click OK to add uses Module1; to the Main module's implementation. You can type this statement manually if you prefer.

8. Finally, press F12 to bring up the main form window, and click inside it to display its property values in the Object Inspector window. Set the Menu property to DataModule1.MainMenu1 by selecting that name from the drop-down list. This tells the main form to use the nonvisual object, MainMenu1, stored in the DataModule1 object. Press F9 to compile and run the finished application.

Carefully review the preceding steps and examine the program's source code files in Listing 3-6 and Listing 3-7. Pay particular attention to the uses directives in each listing. This is an example of a circular unit reference, which as I mentioned, is permitted only with uses directives in unit implementation sections. Notice that each unit refers to the other. Technically speaking, using a data module requires only the host unit (MainForm in this case) to use the data module's unit. However, for that module's MainMenu object to close the MainForm, it too must use Main's unit. This is typical, and data modules are often used circularly this way.

Tip   You may insert a data module into the Object Repository, just as you do any other form. Be sure, however, to give the module a unique name (don't use its default name DataModule1 for example). This avoids name conflicts among multiple modules and forms in the Object Repository.

Listing 3-6: **DMTest\Main.pas**

```pascal
unit Main;

interface

uses
  Windows, Messages, SysUtils, Classes, Graphics, Controls,
  Forms, Dialogs;

type
  TMainForm = class(TForm)
  private
    { Private declarations }
  public
    { Public declarations }
  end;

var
  MainForm: TMainForm;

implementation

uses Module1;

{$R *.DFM}

end.
```

Listing 3-7: **DMTest\Module1.pas**

```pascal
unit Module1;

interface

uses
  Windows, Messages, SysUtils, Classes, Graphics, Controls,
Forms, Dialogs,
  Menus;

type
  TDataModule1 = class(TDataModule)
    MainMenu1: TMainMenu;
    procedure DataModuleFormExit1Click(Sender: TObject);
  private
```

```
   { Private declarations }
public
   { Public declarations }
end;

var
  DataModule1: TDataModule1;

implementation

uses Main;

{$R *.DFM}

procedure TDataModule1.DataModuleFormExit1Click(
  Sender: TObject);
begin
  MainForm.Close;
end;

end.
```

The Splitter Component

The Additional palette contains numerous components that are unique to Delphi. These are custom controls that either enhance standard controls, or that provide services you will probably need but will not find among Windows' native control designs. For example, the BitBtn component, which you have seen in action and will see used again throughout this book, enhances a Windows button control with graphics for a more interesting, and more informative, appearance.

One of the components on this palette that I find most useful is Splitter (class name TSplitter). Use it to create a multipanel window that users can adjust by clicking and dragging. Lots of Windows applications have similar split windows, and this control is one of the most generally useful. It is also easy to use. Try these steps:

1. Start a new application.

2. Drop a Memo component from the Standard palette onto the form. Set this object's Align property to alLeft. This aligns Memo1 against the window's left edge.

3. Click the Additional page tab and drop a Splitter component onto the form to the right of Memo1. The control jumps to the right edge of Memo1 like a magnet to iron. Notice that Splitter1's Align property is alLeft, the same as the setting of the object to its immediate left.

4. Go back to the Standard palette and drop a second Memo component onto the form to the right of Memo1 and Splitter1. Set Memo2's align property to alClient. In most all cases, you should set the final panel of a split window to align to the window's client area so that this object fills the remaining space left over by resizing other objects.

Run the application by pressing F9. Click and drag the Splitter bar between the two Memo components to resize them.

Try a few options with the Splitter component. Select Splitter1 from the test application, and try out these property settings:

✦ **Beveled** — Set this to True or False for a small adjustment to the splitter bar's appearance. Personally, I like the default setting of True.

✦ **Cursor** — This should usually be left to its default setting, crHSplit. There isn't much reason to change the cursor appearance, but you can use a different one if you want.

✦ **MinSize** — Assign the minimum size to limit split panel widths or heights. Although this value is set to 30 by default, that is a meaningless value and should normally be changed under program control — in a form's OnCreate event handler, for example. A good formula is to assign a value equal to a fraction of the window's width — $1/4$ of the client area width, for instance. Be sure to update MinSize in the Form's OnResize event, so that if the user resizes the entire window, the minimum pane size is adjusted accordingly.

✦ **ResizeStyle** — Use one of three possible settings: rsLine to display a straight line while clicking and dragging that shows where the window split will be when the user releases the mouse; rsNone to display no line; or rsUpdate to resize the split objects continuously while clicking and dragging. Typically, you use rsLine when splitting objects such as bitmaps that take time to redraw. Use rsUpdate for Memo and other objects that can be redrawn quickly. I never use rsNone because this gives little indication except for the cursor shape that a resize operation is in effect.

✦ **Width** — I prefer the minimum value of 1 here, although 3 is the default. With a width of 1 and Beveled set to True, the splitter looks like the edge of a Memo or other object rather than a separate control. Users who have trouble using a mouse might find it hard to grab hold of the splitter bar, in which case you should use a larger setting or make it optional and assign the Width property at run time with a statement such as:

```
procedure TForm1.Edit1Exit(Sender: TObject);
begin
  Splitter1.Width := StrToInt(Edit1.Text);
end;
```

You can split windows vertically as well as horizontally—it's all a matter of how you set the object Align properties. To try this, follow the preceding steps, but change the Align properties of the Memo1 and Splitter1 objects to alTop. The Align property of Memo2 should be alClient. Run the application and click and drag the Splitter bar to resize the Memo objects' widths.

Tip A horizontal Splitter component's Height property controls its thickness. The Width property controls a vertial Splitter's thickness.

Expert-User Tips

✦ At times, Delphi may report that an event handler is referenced but not available, and request permission to delete the event. Usually, when this happens, you should answer Yes, especially if the event is one that you have been trying to kill. But if the event is one that you think should not be deleted, you may have accidentally erased an event handler's assignment. Answer No in that case, and double-click the event (or select a handler from the drop-down list) to recover the procedure.

✦ Use File I Open... to open a form's .pas unit file to inspect its programming. However, this does not add the form to the current project. To do that, select File I Add to project. The form does not appear automatically. To make it visible, choose View I Forms... or use the Project Manager, also accessed through the View menu. To bring up the form's unit, choose View I Units....

✦ If you are familiar with other text editors that display files in separate windows, you may be tempted to close Delphi's editor window before editing another module. Resist this temptation. Delphi uses a single editor window for all unit modules in a project, and closing this window closes all opened modules. However, this does not delete the files—it merely closes them in the editor window. To switch to another module, use View I Units... or select the module from the editor window's page tabs. Because of Delphi's single-window text editor, you can open all of a project's units without cluttering the display with dozens of windows, so you may as well leave them all open.

✦ If you prefer to have multiple edit windows, select View I New Edit Window.

✦ Scroll bar properties have additional subvalues that you might use in special circumstances. To view these values, double-click a form's HorzScrollBar or VertScrollBar property. The Increment value determines how many units the thumb box moves when you click a scroll bar's arrow buttons. The Margin determines how far the scroll bar sits from the form's edge. The Position represents the current location of the thumb box.

✦ If two or more windows are set to stay on top, they revert to normal overlapping windows. There's nothing you can do about this. Everybody — that is, every window — can't be on top all the time.

✦ You can import a template from the Object Repository in three ways: Copy, Inherit, or Use. These options are displayed as radio buttons when you select File I New... to open the New Items dialog, which lists the Object Repository's contents. All three options are not available for all types of templates.

- The Copy option copies the template into your application. Saving those copies then creates a separate copy of the items, and future changes to the template's original files are *not* reflected in your application.

- The Inherit option creates a new, derived class for use in your application and to which you may add new programming. Any changes to the original template files are automatically incorporated in your application when you recompile. This makes the Inherit option the most generally useful and flexible way to use templates — for example, to upgrade an application, you simply modify the original template files, compile them, and then compile all applications that use those templates. You do not have to reimport the templates.

- The third and final option, Use, uses the original template files directly. For example, the source code for a form is opened directly in the code editor window. Any changes you make to the form in your application are saved in the template's original files. Don't use this option if you want to preserve a template's original design. Use it only when you want to share templates directly among multiple applications. This is the least flexible option, but is useful for templates such as data modules.

Projects to Try

3-1: Design and add a system icon to the sample BitView application. Use the Windows Paintbrush or Delphi's Image Editor to create an icon file with the filename extension .ico. Or, copy an existing icon file from a network, shareware, or public domain disk. Select MainForm, and double-click its Icon property. Use the resulting dialog to open your icon file. Delphi copies the icon image into the finished .exe code file — you do not have to distribute the .ico file to your program's users.

3-2: Customize Delphi's AboutBox form template. Insert your copyright, company name, and other common information. You might also want to customize the AboutBox template to display a company logo (use an Image component).

3-3: Create a form template for obtaining Yes and No answers to various prompts. For example, the dialog might display a question and have Yes and No buttons. If you get stuck, refer to the YesNo project on the book's CD-ROM. Open the project and follow this chapter's instructions to insert the YesNoDlg form into the Object Repository. Name the form unit Yesno.pas.

3-4: Advanced. Write your own text-file lister using BitView2 as a guide. In place of the Image component, use Memo. You do not have to add scroll bars to the form window, although you may do so if you wish. However, it's easier to select the form's Memo component and set its ScrollBar property to ssBoth. If you get stuck, refer to the ListText project on this book's CD-ROM.

3-5: Use a Splitter component to create two views of your file lister program from project 3-4.

Summary

✦ Every project has at least one form object that represents the program's main window. However, projects may have multiple forms.

✦ A form is a component, but it doesn't appear on the component palette. Create a form by starting a new project or by selecting File I New Form.

✦ Every form has a corresponding unit module that lists the form's programming. The form's Name property and its unit filename must differ. (Tip: To keep your form names and files straight, use a Name such as EntryForm and save its source code unit in a file named Entry.pas.)

✦ A form is more than a representation of the program's window. Forms also have properties and events that you can program to select window characteristics and to perform actions.

✦ Form and application templates are useful for creating common screens, prototypes, and demos. Use the File I New... command to select from several supplied templates, or you can create your own and add them to Delphi's Object Repository.

✦ You may designate any form as an application's main window. For example, you can use a dialog box for a simple and clean application interface that doesn't require a menu bar.

✦ The OnCloseQuery event confirms or cancels a window's closure. Use this event to help prevent data loss.

✦ Scroll bars enable windows to display more information than fits in the window's borders. It's easy to add quick-and-dirty scroll bars to windows, but in finished applications, you should make several refinements to your windows' scroll bars as explained in this chapter.

✦ Assign a form's FormStyle property to fsStayOnTop to have that window stay on top of other application windows. You may assign this value in the Object Inspector, or at run time.

✦ A project may have multiple forms as the Splashin program demonstrates. Delphi normally creates form objects at run time, a fact that may have consequences on memory and other resources in large applications. To create a form object under program control, use the Project Manager to highlight the project, click the right mouse button, and select the Options command. In the Forms page, remove the form from the Auto-create forms list. The form object is no longer created automatically.

✦ A data module can hold nonvisual objects such as MainMenu components. This moves the components out of the way and helps better organize the program. To use a data module, insert its unit name in a uses directive in a form unit's implementation section. Data modules can be stored in the Object Repository.

✦ Use the Splitter component to create multipane windows that users can resize at run time by clicking and dragging the Splitter bar.

In the next chapter, you begin learning how to use Delphi components and forms to design attractive user interfaces. You also learn how to program two of the computer's most important input devices: the keyboard and the mouse.

✦   ✦   ✦

The User Interface

Creating an efficient user interface isn't easy. Of course, most people with a suitable laboratory can sew together check boxes, buttons, input fields, and menus to conceive a monster that looks like a Windows application. But it takes hard work and careful planning to build handsome interfaces that attract users rather than scare the wits out of them.

The chapters in this part cover Delphi components and techniques for assembling practical and friendly application interfaces. You learn the gory details about creating graphical user interfaces and using component objects such as menus, buttons, toolbars, status panels, lists, scrollbars, dialog boxes, plus other application body parts.

Programming the Keyboard and Mouse

Some day—let's hope soon—talking to a computer will seem as natural as gossiping with the neighbors. But until voice-recognition hardware and software undergo major improvements, the keyboard and the mouse are likely to remain the primary input tools for conversing with software applications. Computers can talk fairly well, but they just don't know how to listen.

As experienced developers know, an application's input capabilities literally define its ease of use. Even one needless keystroke or mouse command is enough to aggravate expert users who don't want to type and click more than absolutely necessary. Because ease of input is crucial to a program's success, the subjects of keyboard and mouse handling are appropriate places to begin the investigations of Part II into the development of application user interfaces with Delphi's Visual Component Library.

About Parts II and III

Part II of this book covers user-interface design techniques using Delphi components such as menus, buttons, and other interface-related objects. Part III explains application-specific topics such as graphics and data sharing, and covers advanced objects in the Visual Component Library. To make the most of this information, you should know how to perform the following tasks:

✦ Start a new Delphi application

✦ Assign Name and Caption properties to a form

✦ Save the project and assign filenames

✦ Insert component objects into a form

✦ Insert a new form into an application

✦ Modify form and component object properties

✦ Create procedures for form and component events

If you are unfamiliar with any of the preceding items, all of which were introduced in Part I, read the preceding three chapters and complete one or more of the step-by-step tutorials. If you are pressed for time, you don't have to memorize every word. Just be sure you understand how to do the preceding tasks before continuing.

Components covered

The chapters in Parts II and III begin with a list and brief descriptions of covered components and related classes. Most chapters also refer to other components in hands-on tutorials and sample applications. Where applicable, the component's palette category is listed. This chapter uses several components, but it focuses on the TForm class, described next:

✦ Form — Application windows are objects of the Form component, which is programmed in the TForm class. A Form object typically contains other components such as buttons, edit boxes, and other items that create the application's user interface. Palette: none.

Note

Delphi prefaces a component's Pascal class name with the letter *T*, meaning data type. For example, *TButton* is the class name for the Button component. In this book, I use class names only when necessary — for example, in a variable declaration that requires a component's class name.

Tutorials and property tables

To shorten step-by-step instructions and to avoid restating the obvious (such as how to save unit and project files), the upcoming hands-on tutorials are more abbreviated than in Part I. In addition, some tutorials list property values in tables. Table 4-1 demonstrates the property-table format used throughout the rest of this book.

Table 4-1
Sample Property-Table Format

Component	Name	Property	Value
Form	MainForm	Caption	Window Demo
Label	XCoordLabel	Caption	X Coordinate
		Alignment	taRightJustify
		Font.Name	Arial
		Font.Size	24
Edit	Edit1	Text	

The first line of a property table lists the form that holds subsequent component objects. For example, Table 4-1 indicates that you should change the Name property of the program's default form to MainForm, and set its Caption to Window Demo. You should then insert the other listed objects into MainForm's window.

Except where noted otherwise, all sample main-window forms in this book are named MainForm. On the CD-ROM, MainForm's unit module, Main.pas, is stored in a subdirectory that matches the project name such as BitView and OnTop. Other form modules are similarly named. For example, NextForm's unit module would be named Next.pas.

The second line of Table 4-1 indicates you should insert a Label component object into MainForm and change its Name to XCoordLabel. Set this object's Caption to X Coordinate, and change its Alignment and Font properties to the indicated values. For object placement and size, refer to figures in the book, and to the supplied files.

A period separates a property and its subvalue. For example, the Property column of Table 4-1 indicates that you should set the Font property's Name subvalue to Arial and its Size subvalue to 24 points.

The final line of Table 4-1 tells you to insert an Edit component object into MainForm, but to leave the object's Name set to the default value, Edit1. The blank last column indicates that you should clear the object's Text property by highlighting and deleting this value.

Property tables do not include noncritical or obvious settings such as window width and height values. The tables also do not list window dressing such as the Bevels used in the KeyInfo project to organize the window's display. (Peek ahead to Figure 4-1.) I explain many of these extra goodies throughout this book, but I don't want to waste space documenting obvious matters at the expense of more important information.

By convention, in this book most component Name properties end with the component's identifier. For example, you know that XCoordLabel in Table 4-1 is a Label component object. The usual exception to this rule is a default name such as Edit1, which Delphi assigns.

On the Keyboard

Delphi applications can use two fundamental methods for receiving keyboard input. The first and easiest, is to use a component object, such as Edit, that automatically responds to keypresses. For more general-purpose keyboard handling, however, you can create procedures in a form that handle any combination of three events (they are listed for a form object in the Object Inspector window):

✦ **OnKeyDown** — Called when you press any key, including function keys and special keys such as Shift, Alt, and Ctrl

✦ **OnKeyPress** — Called when you press an ASCII character-generating key, including control keys

✦ **OnKeyUp** — Called when you release any key

Each of these events receives at least one parameter, named Key, which represents a pressed key. In the OnKeyDown and OnKeyUp events, Key is an unsigned (that is, positive only) Word value that represents a Windows virtual key code. In the OnKeyPress event, Key is a Char value that represents an ASCII character. Even though both variables are named Key, they represent different keyboard information. All ASCII characters have corresponding virtual key codes, but the reverse is not true — there are many virtual keys with no ASCII counterparts.

Windows represents keystrokes with virtual key code symbols prefaced with vk_. For example, vk_alt is the virtual key code for the Alt key. For more information about virtual key codes, search for functions VkKeyScan and VkKeyScanEx in the Microsoft Win32.hlp file supplied with Delphi. If you don't have this file or can't locate the definitions (they seem to be missing in some editions), search for Vk in Windows.pas, located in Delphi's Source\Win directory.

Responding to keyboard events

A sample application, KeyInfo, demonstrates how to program a form's three keyboard events. Figure 4-1 shows KeyInfo's display. Locate and run this program by loading its project file from the Keyinfo directory and pressing F9. Press various keys — including function, Ctrl, Shift, and Alt — and observe the values displayed to the right of the window's labels:

✦ **Keypress character** — This label shows ASCII characters. For keys with no visible symbol, an empty box is displayed.

✦ **Key down value** — This label shows the key's numeric value. When you press a multiple key combination such as Shift+Alt+A, this box shows the value of the last key pressed (*A* in this example).

✦ **Key down shift** — This label shows the current shift state. For example, when you press the Alt and Ctrl keys together, the program displays Alt+Ctrl, and the Key down value shows the numeric value of the key last pressed (Ctrl in this case).

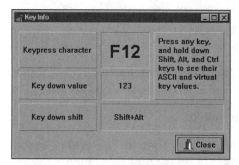

Figure 4-1: KeyInfo displays keyboard events.

Even though KeyInfo shows information for most keypresses, the program continues to respond to standard keyboard commands. For example, pressing Enter selects the Close button and ends the program. Pressing F10 selects the system menu icon, after which you can press the spacebar or Enter to open the menu, or press Esc to return to normal operation.

Creating KeyInfo

Follow the numbered steps in this section to recreate the KeyInfo sample application. Table 4-2 shows significant component and form property values.

Table 4-2
KeyInfo's Properties

Component	Name	Property	Value
Form	MainForm	Caption	Key Info
Label	CharLabel	Caption	
		Alignment	taCenter
		AutoSize	False
		Font:Name	Arial
		Font:Size	24
		Font:Style	[fsBold]
Label	ValueLabel	Alignment	taCenter
		AutoSize	False
Label	ShiftLabel	Alignment	taLeftJustify
		AutoSize	False

The following instructions assume that you have created a new project, changed its main-window form Name to MainForm, and saved the unit module as Main and the project as Keyinfo.

To create the KeyInfo sample application:

1. Insert Bevels and Labels into a form to organize the window as shown in Figure 4-1. The exact placement of these items is unimportant. Use Delphi's default property Names for all of them.

2. Insert a BitBtn component from the Additional category. Change its Kind to bkClose and its Name to CloseBitBtn.

3. Insert three Label components into the center indented Bevels shown in Figure 4-1. Name them CharLabel, ValueLabel, and ShiftLabel respectively, and delete their Captions. Refer to Table 4-2 for other property values. Adjust the Font properties for a pleasing display — for example, you might want to make the CharLabel Font large and bold.

4. Select MainForm, and create event handlers for OnKeyDown, OnKeyPress, and OnKeyUp. Insert the programming shown in Listing 4-1 for these three procedures. I explain how the statements work after the listing.

5. Press F9 to compile, link, and run.

You can find KeyInfo's complete source code on the book's accompanying CD-ROM in the KeyInfo directory; Listing 4-1 lists its Main.pas file.

Listing 4-1: Keyinfo\Main.pasunit Main;

```
interface

uses
  Windows, SysUtils, Messages, Classes, Graphics, Controls,
  Forms, Dialogs, Buttons, StdCtrls, ExtCtrls;

type
  TMainForm = class(TForm)
    Label2: TLabel;
    CharLabel: TLabel;
    Label3: TLabel;
    Label4: TLabel;
    ValueLabel: TLabel;
    ShiftLabel: TLabel;
    Bevel1: TBevel;
    Bevel2: TBevel;
    Bevel3: TBevel;
    Label1: TLabel;
    Bevel4: TBevel;
    Bevel5: TBevel;
    Bevel6: TBevel;
    Bevel7: TBevel;
    CloseButton: TBitBtn;
    procedure FormKeyDown(Sender: TObject; var Key: Word;
      Shift: TShiftState);
    procedure FormKeyPress(Sender: TObject; var Key: Char);
    procedure FormKeyUp(Sender: TObject; var Key: Word;
      Shift: TShiftState);
  private
    { Private declarations }
  public
    { Public declarations }
  end;

var
  MainForm: TMainForm;

implementation
```

(continued)

Listing 4-1 *(continued)*

```
{$R *.DFM}

const
  ctrl_A = 1;      { ASCII value for Ctrl+A }
  ctrl_Z = 26;     { ASCII value for Ctrl+Z }

  FunctionKeys: array [vk_f1 .. vk_f12] of string[3] =
    ('F1', 'F2', 'F3', 'F4', 'F5', 'F6', 'F7', 'F8',
     'F9', 'F10', 'F11', 'F12');

procedure TMainForm.FormKeyDown(Sender: TObject; var Key: Word;
  Shift: TShiftState);
var
  s: string;
begin
{- Show integer Key value }
  ValueLabel.Caption := IntToStr(Key);
{- Show Key shift state }
  s := '';
  if ssShift  in Shift then s := s + 'Shift+';
  if ssAlt    in Shift then s := s + 'Alt+';
  if ssCtrl   in Shift then s := s + 'Ctrl+';
  if Length(s) > 0 then
    Delete(s, Length(s), 1); { Delete final '+' }
  ShiftLabel.Caption := s;
{- Do function key labels }
  if Key in [vk_f1 .. vk_f12] then
    CharLabel.Caption := FunctionKeys[Key]
  else
    CharLabel.Caption := '';  { Erase old character label }
{- Disable Spacebar to prevent selecting Close button }
  if Key = vk_space then
    Key := 0;
end;

procedure TMainForm.FormKeyPress(Sender: TObject; var Key:
Char);
begin
  if Ord(Key) in [ctrl_A .. ctrl_Z] then
    CharLabel.Caption := Chr(Ord(Key) + Ord('A') - 1)
  else
    CharLabel.Caption := Key;
  ValueLabel.Caption := IntToStr(Ord(Key));
end;

procedure TMainForm.FormKeyUp(Sender: TObject; var Key: Word;
  Shift: TShiftState);
```

```
begin
{- Erase the three labels when user releases key(s) }
  CharLabel.Caption := '';
  ValueLabel.Caption := '';
  ShiftLabel.Caption := '';
end;

end.
```

Inside KeyInfo

Two constants, ctrl_A and ctrl_Z in the Main unit's implementation section, declare the ASCII values for Ctrl+A and Ctrl+Z keys. The program uses these values to define a range of control keys so that, when you press Ctrl+Q, for example, the Keypress character label shows that value.

A third constant defines function key strings such as F1 and F2, also for display in the Keypress character label. This typed constant array is automatically initialized to the values shown in parentheses, and in this case, is indexed with the virtual key codes vk_f1 through vk_f12. Given a string variable named FunctionS, the following statement sets the string equal to F3:

```
FunctionS := FunctionKeys[vk_f3]; {Assign F3 key to FunctionS}
```

The keyboard event handler, FormKeyDown, receives a Key value equal to the virtual key code for a pressed key. First, the procedure assigns the Key value to the ValueLabel object's Caption property in order to display that value under the Key down value label in the window. Because a Captain is a string, however, you cannot assign Key directly to it. This would not work:

```
ValueLabel.Caption := Key;  { ??? }
```

Note

Throughout this book, I use three question marks in comment braces, { ??? }, to indicate a questionable practice or a faulty statement you should avoid using in your own programs.

Instead, you have to convert Key to a string value. In this case, you can do that by passing Key to Delphi's IntToStr function, which accepts a Word argument and returns a string:

```
ValueLabel.Caption := IntToStr(Key);
```

The next statement in FormKeyDown assigns the null string to *s*. This initializes the string for the upcoming *if* statements:

```
s := '';
```

Tip To convert a string to an integer value, use the StrToInt function.

To create a null string, type two single quotation marks (apostrophes) with no space between them. Assigning a null string to a string variable with the := operator erases the string's characters.

Three *if* statements build the string *s* to show combination key values such as Shift+Ctrl. The statements use the Shift parameter, of type TShiftState, passed to the procedure. Delphi declares the TShiftState data type as:

```
TShiftState =
  set of (ssShift, ssAlt, ssCtrl, ssRight, ssLeft,
  ssMiddle, ssDouble);
```

A variable such as Shift — a set of TShiftState values — can hold zero, one, or more values. For example, you could assign this set to Shift to represent the Shift and Ctrl keys:

```
Shift := [ssShift, ssCtrl];
```

Pascal represents the set using single bits, so this is an efficient method for storing multiple items in a very small space.

A series of *if* statements determines which of the possible values (if any) are in the Shift set. Examine the first of these statements:

```
if ssShift in Shift then s := s + 'Shift+';
```

In English, this states if the value ssShift is in the Shift set, the program appends the string Shift+ to the end of the string variable *s*. Similar statements check for other set values, and append additional strings onto *s*.

After forming the string, the variable *s* is either empty or it lists the names of various special keys, separated with plus signs. If the string is not empty, it ends with an extra plus sign, which this statement deletes:

```
if Length(s) > 0 then
  Delete(s, Length(s), 1);
```

Pascal's Length procedure returns the length in characters of any string. If that length is greater than zero, the *if* statement here calls Delete to erase the final character. To Delete, you pass the string, the position at which the deletion is to begin, and the number of characters to delete from that location. Because the first character in a string is in position 1 — in other words, at the string index 1 — passing the string's length to Delete's second parameter deletes the last character in the string.

To display the completed string, the program assigns it to the ShiftLabel component's Caption property:

```
ShiftLabel.Caption := s;
```

To handle function keys, another *if* statement tests whether Key is in the set of virtual key codes vk_f1 through vk_f12. If so, the program assigns one of the unit's constant strings from the FunctionKeys array to CharLabel's Caption. Otherwise, the program sets this field to the null string, erasing any text shown in this area.

The FormKeyDown procedure also assigns a null string to CharLabel.Caption to erase any character displayed in that field:

```
CharLabel.Caption := '';
```

Finally, in FormKeyDown, an *if* statement tests whether Key equals vk_space. I added this statement because pressing the spacebar selects the current control object — in this case, CloseButton. Notice the Key variable in FormKeyDown's header (its first line) is preceded by var. This means the parameter is variable and assigning a value to it passes that value back to FormKeyDown's caller. Thus, setting Key equal to zero disables this key (because zero represents no particular key):

```
if Key = vk_space then
   Key := 0;  { Disable SpaceBar }
```

The other two procedures are relatively easy to understand. FormKeyUp assigns null strings to the Caption properties in CharLabel, ValueLabel, and ShiftLabel; this erases these labels when you release a key.

FormKeyPress receives a Key value equal to an ASCII character. If the ordinal value of Key is in the set of values defined by the range of control-code constants, ctrl_A through ctrl_Z, then the program sets CharLabel's Caption to ^A', ^B', and so on. (The caret is often used as a symbol for a control key.) This is necessary because a control code has no associated visible symbol.

The *else* clause handles noncontrol characters, merely assigning Key directly to CharLabel's Caption. Note that you can assign a Char variable such as Key to a string such as Caption — one of the few areas in which Pascal bends its usual strong type-checking rules.

Finally, the program sets ValueLabel's Caption field to the string equivalent of Key's ordinal value. When you press *Q,* for example, this statement assigns the string 81 to Caption.

Previewing keypresses

The KeyInfo application uses event handlers in a form to respond to keypresses. Many components also respond to keyboard activity, and it's often necessary to decide whether a component or the form should be first to receive a specific keyboard event.

Windows uses the input focus to determine where to send keyboard events. For example, the currently selected component in a form has the input focus and, therefore, it receives all keyboard events. If the component doesn't handle the event, for example, because it is not programmed to use a certain key such as Esc or Ctrl, that event is passed to the component's owner, which is usually the form. Figure 4-2 shows this relationship between a component, a form, and the input focus.

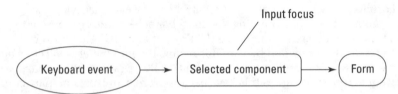

Figure 4-2: Keyboard events normally go to the selected component and then to the form.

To send keyboard events to the form before the selected component receives those events, set the form's KeyPreview property to True. For example, you might do this to modify certain keys or to prevent users from typing unwanted characters such as digits or punctuation symbols. Figure 4-3 illustrates the relationship between a component, the form, and the input focus when KeyPreview is True.

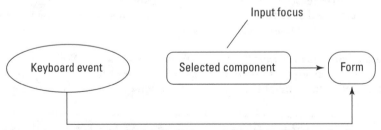

Figure 4-3: Set KeyPreview to True to receive keyboard events in the form before the selected component receives those events.

A simple experiment demonstrates the value of the KeyPreview property, which you can use to restrict input in text-editing components. Start a new project, and follow these steps:

1. Insert an Edit component into the form. You needn't change its Name or other properties.

2. Change the form's KeyPreview property from False to True by double-clicking its value.

3. Change to the Events page in the Object Inspector, and double-click the form's OnKeypress event to create a handler. Be sure to do this for the Form1 object, not for Edit1. Type the following statement between begin and end to convert lowercase characters to uppercase:

```
Key := Upcase(Key);
```

4. Press F9 to compile and run the program. If Delphi displays file-save dialogs, save the unit and the project under the default names in a temporary directory.

5. Type some text into Edit1. The program automatically converts lowercase letters to uppercase whether or not you press Caps Lock or Shift.

6. Exit the program, set KeyPreview to False, and then press F9 to compile and run. The program no longer converts characters to uppercase. This happens because the Edit1 control now has the input focus — rather than the form — and, therefore, the control receives keyboard events first.

KeyPreview is also useful for limiting the kinds of characters that users can enter. For example, to prevent users from typing digit keys into an Edit component, add this statement to the form's OnKeypress event handler and set KeyPreview to True:

```
if Key in ['0' .. '9'] then
  Key := Chr(0);
```

This *if* statement checks whether the Key parameter passed to the event handler is in the set of characters from '0' to '9'. If so, the second line of the statement assigns the character value of zero to Key. Because a zero ASCII character value has no meaning, this prevents any input into the Edit component when it receives the modified Key.

The preceding *if* statement uses some valuable Pascal techniques that may be new to you. The expression '0' .. '9' is called a range. It is composed of two values separated by a two-dot ellipsis. Pascal interprets this expression as equivalent to the series of characters:

```
'0', '1', '2', '3', '4', '5', '6', '7', '8', '9'
```

You may also compose ranges of integer values. For example, the range 5 .. 8 is equivalent to the series of values 5, 6, 7, 8. Be sure to understand, however, that ASCII characters and integer values are not equivalent. The range '0' .. '9' equals the series of ASCII digit characters. The range 0 .. 9 (without quotation marks) equals the series of integer values from zero to nine. You can only stuff ordinal values (those represented by integer values) into a set. You cannot, for example, create a set of strings, because Pascal can't represent string values with single bits. An array is the appropriate data type for collections of complex values such as strings, records, and class objects.

The preceding *if* statement also shows how to assign a specific ASCII value to a variable of the type Char. Because it is impossible to type a character with the ASCII value 0, another method is needed to assign this value to Key. Because the Key parameter is a Char variable, you can assign any character to it with a statement such as:

```
Key := 'Q';
```

However, you cannot assign an ASCII value directly to a Char variable. This does not work:

```
Key := 81;   { ??? }
```

The value 81 is not a character, even though it happens to be the ASCII value for *Q*. You can't assign zero directly to Key:

```
Key := 0;   { ??? }
```

Pascal is finicky about such assignments because the assigned value must match the variable's type. The solution is to convert the value to the proper data type, which you can do here by using the Chr function. The following statements show three logically equivalent methods for assigning the *Q* character to Key:

```
Key := Chr(81);  { Calls Pascal Chr to convert 81 to a Char }
Key := Char(81); { "Casts" the value 81 to the type Char }
Key := 'Q';      { Directly assigns the character Q to Key }
```

Creating a while-key event

Some programs need to perform actions while users hold down a key. For example, a graphics design system could use the technique to adjust a color shade from light to dark while you hold down an arrow key. A game might shoot a weapon while you hold down the spacebar. The technique's possibilities are endless, and as the following hands-on tutorial demonstrates, the programming isn't difficult.

One of this book's sample programs, KeyCount, illustrates how to create while-key events. This program is created in Listing 4-2, and can also be found on the book's accompanying CD-ROM in the KeyCount directory. Although KeyCount has no practical value, it increments and decrements an integer value while you press and hold the up- or down-arrow keys—thus demonstrating the necessary basics for creating while-key events.

Compile and run KeyCount. Press and hold the up- or down-arrow keys to increment or decrement the integer value in the center of the program's window. Press Alt+F4 to end. Figure 4-4 shows the program's display. Listing 4-2 lists the program's Main.Pas unit.

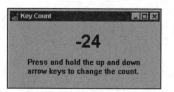

Figure 4-4: KeyCount's display after pressing the down-arrow key for a while

Listing 4-2: **Keycount\Main.pas**

```
unit Main;

interface

uses
  SysUtils, WinTypes, WinProcs, Messages, Classes, Graphics,
Controls,
  Forms, Dialogs, ExtCtrls, StdCtrls;

type
  TMainForm = class(TForm)
    Label1: TLabel;
    Label2: TLabel;
    Timer1: TTimer;
    procedure FormCreate(Sender: TObject);
    procedure FormKeyDown(Sender: TObject; var Key: Word;
      Shift: TShiftState);
    procedure FormKeyUp(Sender: TObject; var Key: Word;
      Shift: TShiftState);
    procedure Timer1Timer(Sender: TObject);
  private
    { Private declarations }
```

(continued)

Listing 4-2 *(continued)*

```
    Count: Integer;
    KeyPressed: Word;
  public
    { Public declarations }
  end;

var
  MainForm: TMainForm;

implementation

{$R *.DFM}

procedure TMainForm.FormCreate(Sender: TObject);
begin
  Count := 0;
end;

procedure TMainForm.FormKeyDown(Sender: TObject; var Key: Word;
  Shift: TShiftState);
begin
  if ((Key = vk_up) or (Key = vk_down)) then
  begin
    KeyPressed := Key;
    Timer1.Enabled := True;
  end;
end;

procedure TMainForm.FormKeyUp(Sender: TObject; var Key: Word;
  Shift: TShiftState);
begin
  Timer1.Enabled := False;
end;

procedure TMainForm.Timer1Timer(Sender: TObject);
begin
  if KeyPressed = vk_up then
    Inc(Count)
  else if KeyPressed = vk_down then
    Dec(Count);
  Label1.Caption := IntToStr(Count);
end;

end.
```

The following step-by-step tutorial shows you how to create the KeyCount application and how to program a while-key event. Table 4-3 shows the program's significant property values.

Table 4-3 **KeyCount Properties**			
Component	*Name*	*Property*	*Value*
Form	MainForm	Caption	KeyCount
Label	Label1	Caption	0
		Font:Name	Arial
		Font:Size	24
		Font:Style	[fsBold]
Label	Label2	Caption	(enter text from Figure 4-4)
		WordWrap	True
		AutoSize	False
Timer	Timer1	Interval	100

To create the KeyCount sample application:

1. To create the text at the bottom of the program's window, insert a Label component (Label2 in Table 4-3), and change its WordWrap property to True and its AutoSize property to False. Adjust the object's size, and then select the Caption property. Don't press Enter as you type. Instead, allow the lines to wrap around automatically within the component and window boundaries.

2. Create two global variables, so named because they are available globally to all parts of a unit module. The first variable, named Count, of type Integer, holds the current counter value, displayed at the center of the window. The second variable, named KeyPressed, of type Word, holds a virtual key value. Declare these variables by switching to the program's Main.pas unit window, and enter these lines after the var keyword (use Listing 4-2 as a placement guide):

```
Count: Integer;
KeyPressed: Word;
```

3. To initialize Count to zero when the program runs, double-click the form's OnActivate event value and enter this assignment between begin and end:

```
Count := 0;
```

4. The program needs two other event handlers — one for a keypress and another for the key's release. Double-click the form's OnKeyDown event and enter the programming from Listing 4-2 between begin and end. Study this programming carefully. If the Key value is vk_up or vk_down (representing the up- and down-arrow keys) then the program saves the Key value in the global KeyPressed variable. The program also engages the Timer1 component with the following statement. After this statement, the timer begins calling its OnTimer event handler:

```
Timer1.Enabled := True;
```

5. Create another handler for the form's OnKeyUp event. This event disables the timer by setting its Enabled property to False. After this statement, the timer no longer calls its OnTimer handler:

```
Timer1.Enabled := False;
```

6. Finally, select the Timer1 object and create a handler for its OnTimer event (the only one that Timers have). The programming for this event increments or decrements Count depending on whether KeyPressed equals vk_up or vk_down. The timer event displays the current count by converting Count to a string with the standard IntToStr procedure and assigning the result to Label1's Caption.

Integer variables can store negative and positive values from –32,768 to 32,767. Word variables can store only positive values from 0 to 65,535. Variables of either data type can represent only whole numbers, not fractions.

When you need to add or subtract 1 from an ordinal value, use Pascal's Inc and Dec functions as the Timer1Timer procedure demonstrates. For example, if Count is an Integer variable, instead of statements such as these:

```
Count := Count + 1;  { ??? }
Count := Count - 1;  { ??? }
```

you can write

```
Inc(Count);
Dec(Count);
```

You can't use Inc and Dec on properties, however, and the procedures have little, if any, positive effect on run-time performance. These are not procedure calls, even though that's what they look like. They are actually reduced to CPU instructions that increment or decrement a value stored in a memory location. Delphi's smart optimizer replaces expressions such as $x := x + 1$ and $y := y - 1$ with the equivalent Inc() and Dec() instructions.

WinTypes, WinProcs, changing Enter to Tab

Although Windows expects users to press the Tab key to move from one input field to another, many computer users naturally press Enter for this purpose. Unfortunately, pressing Enter usually selects an OK button, which closes the window or saves current entries before you have the chance to complete them all. This can be highly frustrating.

For a simple solution to this problem, follow these steps to reprogram the keyboard so pressing Enter works similarly to pressing Tab:

1. Insert three or more Edit components into a form. The default Names are adequate, but you can change them if you wish.

2. Insert a BitBtn object and change its Kind to bkClose.

3. Set the form's KeyPreview property to True.

4. Change the form's ActiveControl to Edit1 (or to the Name of any Edit component object).

5. Create a handler for the form's OnKeyPress event. Enter the programming shown in Listing 4-3. Press F9 to compile and run, and then try pressing Tab and Enter. The window closes on pressing Enter only when the Close button is selected. This text is on the CD-ROM in the KeyMouse directory, in file Enter2Tab.pas.

Listing 4-3: **Making Enter behave like Tab**

```
procedure TForm1.FormKeyPress(Sender: TObject; var Key: Char);
begin
  if Key = #13 then
  begin
    Key := #0;
    SelectNext(ActiveControl, True, True);
  end;
end;
```

The *if* statement in Listing 4-3 checks whether Key represents the Enter key, which has the ASCII value 13 in decimal. The expression #13 is another way to represent an ASCII character value in Pascal. If Key equals Enter, an assignment statement sets Key to null. This effectively disables Enter.

SelectNext is a method of the TWinControl class, a base class for all visible controls that can receive the input focus. Call SelectNext to advance or retard the focus to the next control. The method is defined as:

```
procedure SelectNext(CurControl: TWinControl;
  GoForward, CheckTabStop: Boolean);
```

✦ **CurControl** — Usually, this should equal the form's ActiveControl. However, you may specify a different control object to move the focus starting from a control other than the current one — for example, to select the first edit field in a data-entry form.

✦ **GoForward** — Set this parameter True to move the focus to the next control. Set it False to move the focus to the previous control.

✦ **CheckTabStop** — Set this parameter True to move the focus to the next or previous control in tab order. Set it False to move the focus to the next or previous control regardless of whether the control's TabStop property is True.

Posting messages

Instead of calling SelectNext, you may also post a Windows message to change the focus to another control. For example, in Listing 4-3, you may replace the call to SelectNext with the following statement, which demonstrates how to post a message:

```
PostMessage(Handle, WM_NEXTDLGCTL, 0, 0);
```

The statement posts the Windows message WM_NEXTDLGCTL, which changes the focus to the next control in the tab-order lineup. The Handle argument represents the form's window — a value that various Windows procedures need in order to know which window should receive a certain message. The two zero arguments are unused.

Although this technique works, posting messages this way risks making your code nonportable and is less object-oriented than calling the SelectNext class method. There's nothing technically wrong with posting Windows messages to controls and other windows, but when a method exists to perform an operation, it is always preferable to call the method.

Mouse Traps

Some users motor a computer mouse like a Porsche racing down a mountain switch-back. Others delicately pedal a mouse as though it needed training wheels. But whether you love 'em or hate 'em, computer mice are here to stay, and the success of your software may depend on how well you program your application's mouse events, as I explain next.

Single- and double-clicking

You have already used mouse-click events to perform various actions. For example, to take an action if the user clicks the right mouse button, you can simply program an OnClick event handler for any form or most components. To respond to a double-click, use the OnDblClick event. You can program either or both events for the same form or component. The events occur for the default mouse button, usually the left one. Remember, however, that users can change the default button with the Windows Control Panel.

The OnClick and OnDblClick events are adequate for many, if not most, mouse chores. But for finer control over mousing around, you can create handlers for these three events, which are available to forms and most components:

✦ **OnMouseDown** — Called when the user presses any mouse button

✦ **OnMouseMove** — Called when the user moves the mouse cursor

✦ **OnMouseUp** — Called when the user releases a mouse button

Procedures for these events receive additional information about mouse activity — for example, which button the user pressed, and the mouse cursor's location. To inspect some of this information, start a new project and create empty event handlers for each of the three events. Examine the procedure declarations. For example, here's the declaration for the OnMouseDown event:

```
procedure TForm1.FormMouseDown(
    Sender: TObject;
    Button: TMouseButton;
    Shift: TShiftState;
    X, Y: Integer);
```

✦ **Sender** — Represents the object that received this event. If two or more components share the same event handler, you can use Sender to determine which object was clicked. (More on this later.)

✦ **Button** — One of three values: mbRight, mbLeft, or mbMiddle. Use this parameter to determine which mouse button the user pressed.

✦ **Shift** — A set of zero or more values: ssShift, ssAlt, ssCtrl, ssRight, ssLeft, ssMiddle, and ssDouble. Use this parameter to determine whether the user was pressing the Shift, Alt, or Ctrl keys (or a combination of those keys) while clicking the mouse. You can also use this parameter to determine which mouse button the user clicked.

✦ ***x, y*** — The form or component pixel location of the mouse cursor's hot spot. Use these values to select objects in windows, to draw graphics, and to begin a click-and-drag operation. (Some copies of Delphi's documentation incorrectly state these values are relative to the screen. They are actually relative to the window's client area, with the coordinate 0,0 at the upper-left corner.)

It's best not to require the use of a middle mouse button, except in special circumstances when you can be certain that a third mouse button is available. Most PCs have a two-button mouse.

The OnMouseUp event handler declares the same parameters as OnMouseDown, but is called when the user releases the mouse button. The OnMouseMove event handler also receives the same parameters except for Button.

To distinguish between the left and right mouse buttons, you should normally use the Button parameter. For example, to sound a beep when the user presses the right or middle mouse buttons — which you might do to indicate that the program does not recognize them — insert an event handler for a form's OnMouseDown event and insert the following statement:

```
if (Button = mbRight) or (Button = mbMiddle)
  then MessageBeep(0);
```

Note   The terms *right* and *left* are relative to the user's system mouse preferences settings. Remember, mbLeft actually refers to the primary mouse button, while mbRight refers to the alternate button. The terms *left* and *right* are holdovers from earlier days of Windows when it wasn't possible to switch them.

Use the Shift parameter to determine whether the user also pressed a key while clicking the mouse. For example, to beep the speaker if the user clicks the left mouse button while also pressing the Ctrl key, you can use this statement:

```
if (Button = mbLeft) and (ssCtrl in Shift)
  then MessageBeep(0);
```

The first part of the expression is true if Button equals mbLeft, indicating a left button click. The second part tests whether ssCtrl or another possible value is in the set of Shift values passed to the procedure.

You can also use the Shift parameter to determine which button the user clicked. For example, the following statement produces the identical result as the preceding one, but checks whether ssLeft is in the Shift set of values:

```
if (ssLeft in Shift) and (ssCtrl in Shift)
  then MessageBeep(0);
```

You can extend this method to test for other keys such as Alt:

```
if (ssLeft in Shift) and
   (ssCtrl in Shift) and
   (ssAlt  in Shift)
  then MessageBeep(0);
```

In such cases, it is often easier to define the possible key values as a literal set in brackets, and compare it to Shift:

```
if [ssLeft, ssCtrl, ssAlt] = Shift
  then MessageBeep(0);
```

The two techniques are not exactly equivalent, however. The former method beeps the speaker if ssLeft, ssCtrl, and ssAlt are in Shift regardless of whether other values are also in the set. The latter method beeps the speaker if only the three stated values are in Shift. For example, the first technique would enable users to also hold down a Shift key; the second method would not. As this indicates, sets are handy, but you must think carefully about what you are trying to achieve.

Don't mistake the Shift parameter for the Shift key. To determine whether a Shift key was held down during a mouse event, use a statement such as:

```
if (ssShift in Shift) then
...
```

Use the *x* and *y* parameters to determine the location of the mouse cursor's hot spot during a mouse up, down, or move event. For example, to display mouse coordinates when the user clicks the mouse button, insert two Label components into a form and create a handler for the form's OnMouseDown event. (Be sure to select the form event.) Insert these statements between begin and end:

```
Label1.Caption := IntToStr(X);
Label2.Caption := IntToStr(Y);
```

Run the program and click the mouse inside the window. The two labels show the mouse cursor position relative to the window's client area.

Return to sender

I promised earlier in this chapter to explain how to use the Sender parameter passed to many event handlers, such as OnMouseDown. When several objects share an event handler, you can use Sender to determine which object received the event.

For an example of this useful technique, follow these steps:

1. In a form window, insert three buttons named by default Button1, Button2, and Button3. (Tip: Insert one button, press Ctrl+C to copy it to the clipboard, and then press Ctrl+V twice to paste two more objects. This is faster than inserting multiple objects one by one, but you must also modify the button Captions or they will all be labeled Button1.)

2. Click and drag a rubber band outline to select the three buttons. You should see dim handles around them. The Object Inspector window now shows the buttons' shared properties and events.

3. Select the Object Inspector's Events page, and double-click the OnMouseDown event value. This creates an event handler that the three buttons share. In other words, clicking any one button at run time calls this same procedure.

4. Obviously, the shared procedure needs a method to determine which button you clicked, and this is where Sender comes in. In the OnMouseDown procedure, enter the variable declaration and statements in Listing 4-4. On the CD-ROM, this text is in the KeyMouse directory in file WhichButton.pas.

5. Press F9 to run the program. When you click a button, a message confirms which button object you selected.

Listing 4-4: **Sender example**

```
procedure TForm1.Button1MouseDown(Sender: TObject; Button:
TMouseButton;
  Shift: TShiftState; X, Y: Integer);
var
  s : string;
begin
  if Sender = Button1 then
    s := 'Button1'
  else if Sender = Button2 then
    s := 'Button2'
  else if Sender = Button3 then
```

```
      s := 'Button3'
   else s := 'Unknown Object';
   ShowMessage('You clicked ' + s);
end;
```

In Listing 4-4, a nested if-then-else statement compares Sender to Button1, Button2, and Button3. Depending on Sender's value, the program sets a string variable to the appropriate button name. A final *else* clause sets the variable to Unknown Object just in case Sender doesn't match one of our three buttons.

The final statement in Listing 4-4 calls ShowMessage to display a note about the button you selected. You can pass any string to ShowMessage. Notice how a plus sign adds the string assigned by the preceding if-then-else statement to the literal string "You clicked".

The nested if-then-else statement in Listing 4-4 is one statement, not several. It is therefore separated from the next statement by one semicolon.

When using Sender, you often need to tell Delphi what type of object the parameter represents. You can then assign values to the Sender's properties. For example, to change each button's Caption after it is selected, the following does not work:

```
   Sender.Caption := 'Clicked';  // ???
```

You cannot do this because Sender is of type TObject, from which all Delphi components descend. In other words, all components are TObjects just as oaks, spruces, and maples in a forest are all trees. To access the button Caption properties, use a with-do statement to tell Delphi that Sender is actually a TButton object — like a particular kind of tree. Insert this statement into the procedure in Listing 4-4:

```
   with Sender as TButton do
      Caption := 'Clicked';
```

The with-do expression tells Delphi to treat Sender as a TButton object, which has a Caption property. When you run the modified program, each button's label now changes to Clicked after you select it. Using *as* does not convert Sender to a TButton component — it merely views Sender as the specified type of object. It is your responsibility to ensure that Sender really is the type of object you specify. You can't use the keyword *as* to change an object into another of a different type.

Mouse cursors

You can specify one of several stock cursor shapes for any form or component. For example, start a new application and change the form's Cursor property from crDefault to crCross. Press F9 to compile and run, and move the mouse cursor over and away from the program's window. The cursor automatically changes to a cross, then back to an arrow when you move it away from the window's client area.

Components may also have associated cursor shapes that indicate the types of operations users can select or perform. For example, add a GroupBox component to the form and set its Cursor property to crHSplit. Press F9 to compile and run. When you move the mouse pointer into the GroupBox, the cross hair changes to a split-cursor shape, which typically indicates that clicking and dragging the mouse changes the relative sizes of a split window.

Custom mouse cursors

You can also create your own cursor shapes for any form or component. This is not difficult to do, but requires some extra work and a little programming.

1. Run Delphi's Image Editor from the Tools menu to create or modify a cursor image, usually a 2-color, 32×32 pixel bitmap.

2. Save your image in a file with the extension .cur. You can also find numerous cursor files on bulletin boards or public domain and shareware disks. Also check out the files in Images\Cursors in Delphi's directory.

If you didn't install Delphi's cursor files and you don't have time to create one, use the Sample.cur file in the Data subdirectory on this book's CD-ROM.

3. You next have to import the cursor as a resource into a Delphi application. Resources are stored inside the program's compiled .exe code file, but during development, it's more convenient to store them separately in .res files. Compiling and linking the program binds the .res file data into the finished code file — you don't have to distribute .res files to end users.

4. Use Delphi's Image Editor to create a resource file, perhaps named Cursor.res. Use File|New to create a new resource file, and then right-click inside the resource window to create bitmap, cursor, and icon resource objects. These objects are given default names such as CURSOR_1. You may change this name if you want.

   Save the resource file, and copy it to a temporary directory. On the CD-ROM, you may use the sample Cursor.res file in the Data directory.

5. You can use the Image Editor to create a cursor image file, as well as other types of images such as bitmaps. As a resource, however, a cursor has a

resource name to which a program can refer — plain cursor images are unnamed. The cursor resource is also bound directly into the program's compiled .exe code file.

To use the cursor resource, the program must carry out three steps:

- Combine the resource into the program's compiled code file
- Load the resource into memory at run time
- Save a handle to the resource for use in the program

Delphi takes care of the first step when you compile and link the program. You perform the other two steps by adding instructions and statements to the program.

6. Start a new application, and in the Pascal unit source code file, insert this command after the keyword *implementation*, following the similar-looking existing command that reads the program's .dfm form file. The two lines should look like these:

```
{$R *.DFM}
{$R Cursor.res}
```

7. Change the filename, Cursor.res, if necessary. (You could also enter Cursor without a filename extension.) The command tells the linker to read the resource file, which may contain multiple resources, and insert the resources into the finished .exe code file. You can import any resource from a .res file using this same type of command, and you may insert as many such commands as needed into a Pascal unit file. In Delphi programming, however, you probably do this only for bitmaps, cursors, and icons as described here. Other Delphi tools such as the Menu editor make using resources unnecessary.

Note The {$R filename} command executes during compilation and linking, not at run time. You do not have to supply the .res file with the finished application.

8. Next, insert program code to load the cursor image from the .exe file into memory at run time. For example, to load and enable the cursor before the form window becomes visible, create a handler for the form's OnCreate event. Declare an integer constant to identify the cursor. For example, insert these lines before the begin keyword:

```
const
  newCursorID = 2;
```

You may use any positive integer value not already used for another cursor. If you have multiple cursors (or other resources), declare integer constants for each.

9. Finish the OnCreate event handler by adding programming to load the cursor resource into memory. Listing 4-5 shows the final procedure.

Listing 4-5: **Loading a cursor resource**

```
procedure TForm1.FormCreate(Sender: TObject);
const
  newCursorID = 2;
begin
  Screen.Cursors[newCursorID] :=
    LoadCursor(HInstance, 'Cursor1');
  Cursor := newCursorID;
end;
```

The two statements in Listing 4-5 demonstrate the proper way to load a cursor resource and use it in a form or other component. The Screen variable, of type TScreen, represents various display aspects, and serves as a kind of parent to the application. (Look up the TScreen in Delphi's online help for more information about this extensive data type.) Screen.Cursors provides a list of cursor images, and is technically called an array property. To assign a value to Cursors, use the Windows LoadCursor function as shown here to load the cursor resource into memory, named here 'Cursor1'. (This string is not case sensitive — you can enter resource names in uppercase or lowercase.) The HInstance argument refers to the current task, or instance, of the program. Windows uses HInstance to find the proper .exe code file that contains the specified cursor resource.

Assign the result of LoadCursor to the Cursors array property, and specify the constant identifier in brackets. To enable the cursor for the form, assign the constant identifier also to the Cursor member of the form or other component.

Note The singular Cursor specifies the currently assigned cursor; the plural Cursors refers to the array property that lists all available cursors. When you compile and run the program, move the mouse cursor into the window to see the new cursor shape.

You may question the validity of the assignment to Cursors in Listing 4-5. Despite appearances, Cursors is not a Pascal array. It is an array property. As such, references to Cursors actually call read and write procedures that return and insert cursor resources. A reference to Cursors[X] initiates a search for a cursor identified as *X*. An assignment to Cursors[X] deletes any cursor identified as *X* before inserting a new cursor into the property. Behind the scenes, Cursors is implemented as a linked list and is technically a sparse associated array, but this is a fact TScreen conveniently hides.

Tip

Delphi cannot load 16-bit .res files—those, for example, from a Windows 3.1 application. To update them to 32-bit, create new resource files using Image Editor.

Sketching with the mouse

On the
CD-ROM

Using the mouse techniques you have learned in this chapter, you can program click-and-drag operations for a variety of purposes. The next sample application, Sketch, demonstrates the necessary basics for clicking and dragging. Locate this project in the Sketch directory. (A similar program is in Delphi's directories—use the one supplied with this book's CD-ROM.) Run Sketch and click and drag the mouse inside the application's window to draw simple shapes. Double-click the mouse cursor in the window to erase the display. Listing 4-6 shows the program's source code.

Listing 4-6: **Sketch\Main.pas**

```
unit Main;

interface

uses
  SysUtils, WinTypes, WinProcs, Messages, Classes, Graphics,
Controls, Forms, Dialogs, Menus;

type
  TMainForm = class(TForm)
    MainMenu1: TMainMenu;
    Demo1: TMenuItem;
    Erase1: TMenuItem;
    Exit1: TMenuItem;
    N1: TMenuItem;
    procedure FormMouseDown(Sender: TObject; Button:
    TMouseButton; Shift: TShiftState; X, Y: Integer);
    procedure FormMouseMove(Sender: TObject; Shift:
    TShiftState; X, Y: Integer);
    procedure FormMouseUp(Sender: TObject; Button:
    TMouseButton;
    Shift: TShiftState; X, Y: Integer);
    procedure FormDblClick(Sender: TObject);
    procedure Erase1Click(Sender: TObject);
    procedure Exit1Click(Sender: TObject);
    procedure FormCreate(Sender: TObject);
```

(continued)

Listing 4-6 *(continued)*

```
private
  { Private declarations }
public
  { Public declarations }
  Dragging: Boolean;
end;

var
  MainForm: TMainForm;

implementation

{$R *.DFM}

procedure TMainForm.FormCreate(Sender: TObject);
begin
  Dragging := False;
end;

procedure TMainForm.FormMouseDown(Sender: TObject; Button:
  TMouseButton; Shift: TShiftState; X, Y: Integer);
begin
  Dragging := True;
  Canvas.MoveTo(X, Y);
end;

procedure TMainForm.FormMouseMove(Sender: TObject; Shift:
  TShiftState; X, Y: Integer);
begin
  if Dragging then
    Canvas.LineTo(X, Y);
end;

procedure TMainForm.FormMouseUp(Sender: TObject; Button:
  TMouseButton; Shift: TShiftState; X, Y: Integer);
begin
  Dragging := False;
end;

procedure TMainForm.FormDblClick(Sender: TObject);
begin
  Erase1Click(Sender);
end;

procedure TMainForm.Erase1Click(Sender: TObject);
begin
  Canvas.Brush := Brush; { Assign form's brush to Canvas }
```

```
    Canvas.FillRect(MainForm.ClientRect);  { Repaint form
background }
    end;

procedure TMainForm.Exit1Click(Sender: TObject);
begin
  Close;
end;

end.
```

Follow these steps to recreate the Sketch application and to learn how to implement click-and-drag mouse operations:

1. Go to the unit window, and in the TMainForm class's public section, declare a variable Dragging, of type Boolean. (See Listing 4-6.) The program sets this variable to True to indicate that a click-and-drag operation is in effect. When False, Dragging indicates normal mouse operation.

2. Initialize the Dragging variable to False by inserting a procedure for the form's OnCreate event. Insert this statement into the procedure:

```
Dragging := False;
```

3. To implement the click-and-drag operation, insert procedures for each of the three form events, OnMouseDown, OnMouseMove, and OnMouseUp. Insert the programming from Listing 4-6 into the event handlers. I explain this programming after the last step in this tutorial.

4. Add a menu component and insert commands for erasing the display and exiting the application. The erase command can use statements such as the following to fill the window's client area with the current background color. First, assign the form's Brush property to the drawing Canvas's Brush, and then call FillRect to fill the Canvas with that color (Chapter 13 explains more about Canvases and graphics):

```
Canvas.Brush := Brush;
Canvas.FillRect(MainForm.ClientRect);
```

5. Specify your Erase procedure for the form's OnDblClick event. You can now select the menu command or double-click the mouse to erase the window's contents.

6. Compile, link, and run the application by pressing F9.

When you click the mouse, OnMouseDown sets the Dragging flag True, and calls the MoveTo procedure in the form's Canvas to set the current graphics position to the mouse coordinates. Any visible drawing takes place at this location. When you release the mouse, OnMouseUp sets Dragging False, canceling the click-and-drag operation.

When you move the mouse, OnMouseMove checks whether Dragging is True — if so, it calls the Canvas's LineTo procedure to draw a visible line from the most recent current graphics position to the new mouse position, which becomes the graphics position for the next drawing operation. If Dragging is False, OnMouseMove performs no actions.

The Sketch application merely demonstrates clicking and dragging — it doesn't preserve your drawings. Also, covering Sketch's display with another window erases any drawing. Chapter 13 explains methods for creating more practical graphics applications.

Expert-User Tips

- ✦ KeyCount's FormKeyDown procedure assigns the current key value to KeyPressed before enabling the timer. Reversing the order of these two statements would be an error because timers begin ticking as soon as you set their Enabled property to True. Never do that until after preparing any and all conditions required by a Timer component's OnTimer event.

- ✦ You may use a third-party resource editor such as Borland's Resource Workshop or C++ Builder, to create .res files for use in Delphi applications. Combine the resource file into the finished code file by inserting the directive {$R filename.res} following a unit's implementation keyword.

- ✦ Experienced programmers use uppercase and lowercase to help distinguish among a program's identifiers. By convention, constant identifiers such as newCursorId begin with lowercase letters; variables such as Count begin with uppercase letters. Procedures such as LoadCursor also begin with uppercase letters. These are not rigid rules, and you can adopt another convention if you want. Just be sure to follow some convention to keep your code as understandable as possible.

- ✦ Programming the Tab key is often difficult because of the way Windows uses this key to shift the focus from one control to another. To recognize Tab-key events in Delphi applications, insert programming into an OnKeyUp event. (The OnKeyDown and OnKeyPress events do not receive Tab keypresses.) For example, insert the programming from Listing 4-7 into a form's OnKeyUp event handler to display a message when you press Tab or Shift+Tab. This text is on the CD-ROM in the KeyMouse directory in file Tab.pas.

Listing 4-7: **Receiving Tab and Shift-Tab keypresses in a form's OnKeyUp event handler**

```
procedure TForm1.FormKeyUp(Sender: TObject; var Key: Word;
  Shift: TShiftState);
var
  S: string;
begin
  if Key = vk_Tab then
  begin
    S := 'Tab Key Pressed';
    if ssShift in Shift then
      S := 'Shift-' + S;
    ShowMessage(S);
  end;
end;
```

 Projects to Try

4-1: Create a keyboard version of the Sketch program. You need a few Integer variables to represent the current drawing position. Program event handlers for incrementing and decrementing the current position when the user presses the keyboard's arrow keys, and call the form Canvas MoveTo and LineTo methods to draw lines.

4-2: Write a test program that displays a message or beeps the speaker (the exact response doesn't matter) when both mouse keys are clicked. You need a Boolean flag that, when True, indicates the first mouse button was clicked but not released. The event handler for the second button can check whether the flag is True, and in that way, program the two buttons to work similarly to Ctrl and Alt keys.

4-3: Add a custom pen-shaped cursor to the sample Sketch application.

4-4: Advanced. Add menu commands to select among different cursors for the Sketch application. Hint: Load each cursor resource, identified by a unique constant, and in the menu command procedures, assign the selected constant to the form's Cursor property.

Summary

✦ Add keyboard handling to applications in two ways: use Edit or other input-aware components, or insert procedures for a form's OnKeyDown, OnKeyPress, or OnKeyUp events.

✦ OnKeyDown and OnKeyUp events represent keys using virtual key codes such as vk_up and vk_shift. OnKeyPress events represent keys as ASCII characters.

✦ Windows uses the input focus to determine where to send keyboard events. Normally, keyboard input goes first to the currently selected component. Set a form's KeyPreview property to True to redirect any keyboard activity destined for the current component object first to the form's keyboard events.

✦ Use a Timer component to create a while-key event, which is useful for performing actions repeatedly while the user holds down a specified key.

✦ Use the OnKeyPress event to modify key values. For example, use the technique in this chapter to change Tab keys to Enter so that users can press Enter to move the input focus from one input control to another.

✦ The OnClick and OnDblClick mouse events are adequate for most mouse-handling chores. For finer control over mouse activity, insert procedures for the OnMouseDown, OnMouseMove, and OnMouseUp events. These events receive additional information such as whether a key is pressed and the mouse cursor location.

✦ Use the Sender parameter, which is passed to most event handlers, to determine which object received an event. This method is most useful when multiple objects share the same event handler.

✦ Change a form or component's Cursor property to display a different cursor shape when the mouse moves over the form or component. You can select from a number of supplied cursors.

✦ You can also design and load a custom cursor as a resource in a .res file. Use an {$R filename} directive to combine the resource file data into the compiled .exe code file. For an event such as OnCreate, call the Windows LoadCursor function and assign the result to the form or component's Cursors (plural) array using an integer constant index. Assign the index to the Cursor property (singular) to enable the custom cursor image.

In the next chapter, we discuss one of the most recognizable user-interface features in most Windows applications: the menu bar. Programming menu bars is easy with Delphi's Menu Designer and you can use a number of options in your program's menus, such as check marks, icons, and dynamic menus.

✦   ✦   ✦

Constructing Menus

The word *menu* comes from the Latin for *minute,* meaning very small or detailed. As every Windows user knows, a pop-up menu is a detailed list of commands, such as Open and Exit. In most applications, a menu bar lists the names of one or more pop-up menus. You can also create floating pop-up menus that appear when you click the right mouse button.

Browsing a cleverly designed menu is like slipping on a favorite sweater, and you can't spend too much effort making your application's menus comfortable to use. As this chapter explains, Delphi provides three menu components and a number of related techniques for constructing easy-to-use menus with sophisticated features that users will appreciate.

Components

Delphi's three menu components are:

+ **MainMenu** — Use this component to create a window's menu bar, which is always displayed below the top border and caption. To create dynamic menus — those that change at run time according to various program operations, such as opening a new form window — you can insert multiple MainMenu objects into forms and follow instructions in this chapter to merge the menus' commands. Palette: Standard.

+ **PopupMenu** — Use this component to create floating pop-up menus, which appear when the user clicks the right mouse button with the mouse cursor over the window's client area. You can also define other ways to display a floating pop-up menu at any screen location. Palette: Standard.

✦ **MenuItem** — Each item in a pop-up or a floating pop-up menu is an object of the TMenuItem class. The MenuItem component, however, does not appear on the VCL palette. Although it's usually easiest to create these objects with Delphi's Menu Designer, as this chapter explains, you can also use program statements or resource scripts to create menu items. (Although TMenuItem is the class name, I refer to this component as MenuItem from now on to be consistent with other component names.) Palette: None.

Pop-Up Menus

Technically speaking, a pop-up menu is the window you see when you open an item on a window's menu bar. A floating pop-up menu can appear anywhere on screen. The two types of menus are otherwise the same. This section explains programming techniques that apply to both types of pop-up menus. Use the MainMenu component to create pop-up menus on a window's menu bar. Use the PopupMenu component to create floating pop-up menus.

Main menus

Most Windows programs have a main menu, which you can create using a MainMenu component. As you have learned from other examples in this book, you create a main menu by inserting a MainMenu object into the program's main-window form. Double-click the object to open Delphi's Menu Designer, and enter your program's commands.

Create a program's main menu by following three main steps:

1. Use Project | Options to select the Forms page tab and set Main form to the program's main-window form. This is the default setting for single-window applications.

2. Insert a MainMenu object into the main-window form.

3. Set the form's Menu property to the MainMenu object's name.

Although only one main menu can be in an application, except for two restrictions, any form, even a dialog box, can have a menu bar. Simply insert a MainMenu object into the form. The restrictions are: The form's BorderStyle property may not equal bsDialog, and its FormStyle may not equal fsMDIChild. (MDI child windows may own MainMenu objects, but as Chapter 15, Developing MDI Applications, explains, these menus are merged into the main window's menu bar.)

Floating pop-up menus

To create a floating pop-up menu that appears when users click the right mouse button, follow these steps (also see the section, "Floating Pop-up Menus," later in this chapter):

1. Insert a PopupMenu object into a form. Delphi names the object PopupMenu1 by default.

2. Double-click the PopupMenu1 object and use the Menu Designer to enter the menu's commands.

3. Assign PopupMenu1 to the form's PopupMenu property.

Menu items

Every item in a menu is an object of the TMenuItem class. Delphi automatically creates these objects when you design your menus with the Menu Designer. You may, however, create MenuItem objects with program statements, and you often refer to these objects in statements. For example, to add a check mark to a menu command, assign True to a MenuItem object's Checked property. You can also perform operations on all MenuItems contained in a MainMenu or PopupMenu object by referring to the Items array in that object.

As with all objects, adopting a good naming convention is the key to creating maintainable menus. Delphi automatically chooses MenuItem names such as File1, Open1, and Save2, which are adequate only for quick tests and demos. I change these names using the following guidelines:

✦ For menu-bar labels, I append the word Menu to MenuItem object names — for example, FileMenu for the File menu object, and EditMenu for the Edit menu.

✦ For commands in pop-up menus, I preface the command with the menu-bar label. For example, MenuItem command objects in the File menu are named FileOpen, FileSave, and FileSaveAs. Objects in the Edit menu have names such as EditCut, EditCopy, and EditPaste. Some Delphi application wizards append *Item* to these names such as FileOpenItem, and EditCutItem. You might want to do the same, especially if you plan on using wizards to create new application shells.

Objects such as FileMenu (representing the File menu) and OpenFile (representing the Open command in the File menu) are objects of the same TMenuItem class, as are all menu items — even separator bars that divide commands into categories.

Set the MenuItem's Caption property to the text you want to display in the menu bar or a command. When designing a new menu, I find it easiest to type in all my menu Captions, and then change the default MenuItem object Names, but you can enter these values in any order.

You can also assign values to MenuItem objects at run time to create dynamic menus that insert and delete commands according to the program's needs. For example, try these steps:

1. Insert a MainMenu object into a form and double-click it to open the Menu Designer.

2. Create a File menu with an Exit command (type **&File** and **E&xit** to underline the *F* and *x* shortcut keys).

3. Select each menu item either in the Menu Designer or in the form. Change the property name File1 to FileMenu. Change Exit1 to FileExit.

You now have a MainMenu object that owns two MenuItem objects, FileMenu and FileExit. You can enter statements to program these menu items for a variety of purposes. For example, add a button to the form and double-click it to create an event handler. Then, insert this statement between begin and end:

```
with FileExit do
  Visible := not Visible;
```

Also, insert a Close; statement for the File|Exit command's procedure. Run the program and click the button to toggle the Exit command on and off. Using the Visible property is an effective way to create dynamic menus with commands that appear and disappear according to various program conditions.

Or, you can disable a menu item by setting its Enabled property to True or False. For example, change the preceding code to:

```
with FileExit do
  Enabled := not Enabled;
```

Command simulations

To simulate selecting a command, call any MenuItem's Click method. This can be useful, for example, when you want an event handler to perform the same task as a pop-up menu command. If that command object is OptionsProject, you can execute the command's event handler with the following statement:

```
OptionsProject.Click;  { Simulate selecting Options|Project }
```

Click has no effect on a MenuItem object that labels a menu in a window's menu bar. However, the MenuItem still receives the OnClick event for any user activity such as clicking the mouse on the menu item's name. You could use this event to perform actions such as changing the names of commands in a menu, or inserting check marks.

The Items property

You can also get to MenuItem objects by using the Items property, which is an element of MainMenu, PopupMenu, and MenuItem components. Items is a TMenuItem object, which you can use to call methods such as Items.Insert, or as an array in expressions such as MyMenu.Items[N]. In a MainMenu object, the Items property contains the menu bar's pop-up menu items. For example, in a program with three pop-up menus — File, Edit, and Help — the following statements change the first menu's name to Presto-Chango, disable the Edit menu, and make the Help menu invisible:

```
with MainMenu1 do
begin
  Items[0].Caption := 'Presto-Chango';
  Items[1].Enabled := False;
  Items[2].Visible := False;
end;
```

Each MenuItem object also has an Items property, which you can use to access menu commands. For example, to disable the File|Exit command, assuming this is the only command in the menu, you can use this statement

```
FileMenu.Items[0].Enabled := False;
```

This has the same effect as the following statement, which is probably simpler in most cases:

```
FileExit.Enabled := False;
```

As a general rule, to perform tasks for individual MenuItem objects, it's easiest to refer to their object names, as in the preceding example. To set multiple properties, however, it may be more convenient to use the Items property. Either technique accesses the same MenuItem objects, so use whichever makes sense. For example, the following statement uses an Integer variable in a *for* loop to disable all commands in the FileMenu:

```
for I := 0 to FileMenu.Count - 1 do
  FileMenu.Items[I].Enabled := False;
```

By the way, because the preceding statement refers to FileMenu twice, you can simplify the code by using a *with* statement. Even though the result has one more line, it is logically more efficient:

```
with FileMenu do
  for I := 0 to Count - 1 do
    Items[I].Enabled := False;
```

The *with* statement tells Delphi to use FileMenu's Count and Items, eliminating the need to preface those names with FileMenu and a period. This saves typing, and can help the compiler produce more efficient code. Try to use *with* as often as you can.

FileMenu's Count property equals the number of MenuItem objects in the Items array. Because the first array index is 0, the last object index equals Count - 1. Always consider this when writing loops to process the Items property as an array.

Multiway menus

Any item in a pop-up menu can have an attached submenu. As Figure 5-1 shows, you can carry this idea to extremes, but it's best not to go too far overboard. Although multiway menus are useful for organizing complex command structures, they can be difficult to use.

Note   Windows 95 simplifies menu selection by not requiring users to click the mouse button multiple times. This makes multiway menus easier to use than in past Windows versions. Limiting the amount of nesting to two levels is still wise, though. Three levels is almost always too many.

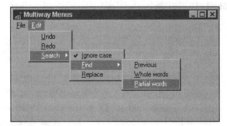

Figure 5-1: Multiway menus nest complex command structures. This display is from the MultiMen program on the book's CD-ROM.

To create submenus in the Menu Designer, follow these steps:

1. Create a menu command such as Search (see Figure 5-1).

2. Highlight the command and press Ctrl+right arrow. This creates a submenu you can edit as you do other pop-up menu windows.

3. Repeat these steps to create additional nesting levels.

Multiway menus require no special programming. You create event handlers for their commands the same as you do for single-level pop-up menus. In other words, menu nesting is purely visual. Therefore, regardless of nesting level, all MenuItem objects in a MainMenu or PopupMenu object must have unique Name properties.

Menu item shortcut keys

You can make two types of shortcut key assignments for menu commands. You can preface a letter with & to designate an Alt key. For example, if you set a MenuItem's Caption to &Configure, users can press Alt+C to open the Configure menu.

A second type of shortcut key is called an *accelerator*. Usually, accelerator keys are combinations of alphanumeric, Ctrl, Shift, arrow, and function keys. They are called *accelerators* because users can press them to select commands without having to open a menu window.

Do not enter shortcut key labels in MenuItem Captions. Delphi automatically appends the key names. For example, enter E&xit for the FileExit object's Caption, and set that object's shortcut key to Alt+X. Delphi automatically displays the command as Exit Alt+X in the pop-up menu.

You can select shortcut keys from that property's drop-down list. However, because this list has so many entries, I find it easier to enter the key label as text. For example, instead of pressing Alt+X, I type the five characters **A L T** + **X** into the ShortCut property and press Enter. You must do this to assign keys such as Enter which are not in the drop-down list — type **E N T E R,** for example. You can also create character shortcuts by entering **A, B, C, 1, 9** or any other key you can type.

Table 5-1 lists some standard accelerator shortcut key assignments for common menu items. Windows 95 applications more closely follow these standards than in past Windows versions, and it's a good idea to use them in your applications. These aren't strictly rigid rules, and key usage depends on the application — for example, you might use the Ins key to insert a field rather than toggle an editor's insert/overtype switch. (I disagree with Alt+F4 as the official standard File|Exit key. Everybody and their aunts and uncles know that Alt+X is the standard program-exit accelerator.)

Table 5-1
Standard Accelerator Shortcut Keys

Command	Menu	Shortcut
Cascade	Window	Shift+F5
Collapse all	Tree	Ctrl+* (keypad)
Collapse item	Tree	- (keypad minus)
Copy	Edit	Ctrl+C
Cut	Edit	Ctrl+X
Delete	Edit	Del
Exit	File	Alt+X (officially Alt+F4)
Expand all	Tree	* (keypad star)
Expand item	Tree	+ (keypad plus)
Expand/Collapse	Tree	Enter
Find	Edit	Ctrl+F
Find next	Edit	F3
Insert/Overtype	Edit	Ins
New	File	Ctrl+N
Open	File	Ctrl+O
Paste	Edit	Ctrl+V
Print	File	Ctrl+P
Replace	Edit	Ctrl+H
Save	File	Ctrl+S
Search	Help	F1
Select all	Edit	Ctrl+A
Tile	Window	Shift+F4
Undo	Edit	Ctrl+Z

Check marks

Adding and removing check marks from menu commands couldn't be easier. Simply set any MenuItem's Checked property to True to display a check mark, or to False to erase one. You can do this at design time or at run time using a statement such as:

```
EditInsert.Checked := True;
```

In designing your program's user interface, think carefully whether to make a checkmarked command operate as a toggle or as a selection from a group of related commands. For example, a game's Level menu might list difficulty levels, only one of which can be selected at a time. An Insert command in an Edit menu should probably be an on/off toggle, though.

Create a toggle by using Pascal's *not* operator as in this statement, which you might enter into the MenuItem's OnClick event handler:

```
with EditInsert do
  Checked := not Checked;
```

Elsewhere in the program, use Checked in an *if* statement to select an action:

```
if EditInsert.Checked then
  ... { do something if menu item is checked }
```

Run the Checks application and try the Level menu. The program uses check marks in two ways: to select among nine levels, and to toggle an Insert command on and off. Click the window's button to display the current level settings. Figure 5-2 shows the program's window.

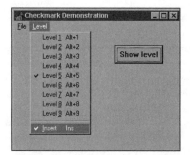

Figure 5-2: The Checks application demonstrates how to use check marks as toggles and to select one of a set of commands, such as the nine levels shown here.

Listing 5-1 shows the form's source code, which demonstrates how a series of menu commands can share the same event handler. To create the LevelClick procedure, declare it as shown in the TMainForm class, and enter the procedure's statements in the unit's implementation section. The procedure turns off check marks for commands Level1 through Level9, and then sets the Sender's Checked property to True. The expression TMenuItem(Sender) casts Sender as a TMenuItem object. To use the LevelClick procedure, assign it to the OnClick event for each MenuItem, Level1 through Level9.

Listing 5-1: **Checks\Main.pas**

```
unit Main;

interface

uses
   Windows, SysUtils, Messages, Classes, Graphics, Controls,
   Forms, Dialogs, Menus, StdCtrls;

type
  TMainForm = class(TForm)
    MainMenu1: TMainMenu;
    FileMenu: TMenuItem;
    FileExit: TMenuItem;
    LevelMenu: TMenuItem;
    Level1: TMenuItem;
    Level2: TMenuItem;
    Level3: TMenuItem;
    Level4: TMenuItem;
    Level5: TMenuItem;
    Level6: TMenuItem;
    Level7: TMenuItem;
    Level8: TMenuItem;
    Level9: TMenuItem;
    ShowButton: TButton;
    N1: TMenuItem;
    LevelInsert: TMenuItem;
    procedure FileExitClick(Sender: TObject);
    procedure LevelClick(Sender: TObject);
    procedure ShowButtonClick(Sender: TObject);
    procedure LevelInsertClick(Sender: TObject);
  private
    { Private declarations }
    function GetLevel: Integer;
  public
    { Public declarations }
  end;

var
  MainForm: TMainForm;

implementation

{$R *.DFM}

const
```

```
    highLevel = 9;    { Highest level command }

procedure TMainForm.FileExitClick(Sender: TObject);
begin
  Close;
end;

procedure TMainForm.LevelClick(Sender: TObject);
var
  I: Integer;
begin
  with LevelMenu do
    for I := 0 to highLevel - 1 do
      Items[I].Checked := False;
  TMenuItem(Sender).Checked := True;
end;

function TMainForm.GetLevel: Integer;
var
  I: Integer;
begin
  GetLevel := -1;
  with LevelMenu do
    for I := 0 to highLevel - 1 do
      if Items[I].Checked then
        GetLevel := I + 1;
end;

procedure TMainForm.ShowButtonClick(Sender: TObject);
var
  S: string;
begin
  S := 'Level = ' + IntToStr(GetLevel) + ' — Insert:';
  if LevelInsert.Checked
    then S := S + 'ON'
    else S := S + 'OFF';
  ShowMessage(S);
end;

procedure TMainForm.LevelInsertClick(Sender: TObject);
begin
  with Sender as TMenuItem do
    Checked := not Checked;
end;

end.
```

Function GetLevel shows how to interrogate MenuItem objects through the Items array to determine which command has a check mark. The function returns -1 if no command is checked, or it returns the level, 1 through 9.

When you click the button, ShowButtonClick creates a string that shows the current level (by calling the GetLevel function) and the current setting of the Insert toggle. Delphi's handy ShowMessage procedure displays the final result.

Floating Pop-up Menus

Borrowing a phrase from the real estate business, floating and nonfloating pop-up menus have only three important differences: location, location, location. You program PopupMenu objects the same as MainMenu objects, but instead of appearing in a menu bar, a floating pop-up menu can appear at any screen location. The MemoPad application from Chapter 2 demonstrates how to create and use floating pop-up menus.

To create a floating pop-up menu, simply insert a PopupMenu component into a form, double-click the object, and enter its commands using the Menu Designer the same way you do for MainMenu components. Assign the PopupMenu object to the form's PopupMenu property, and you're done.

Most often, floating pop-up menu commands share the same event handlers as a window's main menu, but this isn't a rule. You can program separate event handlers for floating pop-up menus if you want.

The right mouse button

To program right-mouse-button clicks to display a floating pop-up menu, assign the PopupMenu object's name to a form's PopupMenu property. The menu appears when users click the right mouse button in the form window.

You can also assign PopupMenu objects at run time, which you might do to change between two or more floating pop-up menus depending on various program conditions. In a button's event handler, or in a procedure for a menu command, use a statement such as this to assign a PopupMenu object to a form's PopupMenu property:

```
PopupMenu := PopupMenu2;  { Assign PopupMenu2 to PopupMenu }
```

Other ways to float

Call the PopupMenu component's *Popup* method to display a floating pop-up menu in response to events other than a right-mouse-button click. Pass screen *x* and *y* coordinates to *Popup* as in this statement:

```
PopupMenu1.Popup(100, 100);
```

Popup's *x* and *y* coordinates are relative to the Windows screen, with (0,0) at the upper-left corner.

When passing mouse-click coordinates to *Popup*, because those values are relative to the active window, call the ClientToScreen function to convert to screen-relative coordinates. First declare a variable of type TPoint:

```
var
   Pt: TPoint;
```

Then, in a form's MouseDown event handler, enter these statements:

```
Pt.X := X;
Pt.Y := Y;
Pt := ClientToScreen(Pt);
PopupMenu1.Popup(Pt.X, Pt.Y);
```

The first two lines assign the mouse coordinates *x* and *y* passed to the event handler to the TPoint variable. The third line calls ClientToScreen in the TControl class, which is one of TForm's distant ancestors. This converts Pt from window-client-relative coordinates to screen-relative values. The last line passes the converted *x* and *y* values to PopupMenu's *Popup* method.

Dynamic Menus

Delphi provides several techniques for creating menus that change dynamically at run time. You can:

✦ Change a window's entire menu bar

✦ Insert and delete pop-up menus

✦ Add and remove commands

✦ Merge menu objects

The following sections explain these techniques and more.

Changing menus

The easiest way to change a window's menu is to assign a different MainMenu object to a form's Menu property. First, insert two or more MainMenu objects into the form and use the Menu Designer to enter their commands. Then, perhaps in a command or a button event handler, enter a statement such as:

```
Menu := MainMenu2;
```

When you run the program, the menu bar changes from its design-time assignment to MainMenu2. The menu bar automatically changes its visual appearance when the program executes the preceding assignment statement.

Inserting and deleting menus

You can merge menu objects (see "Merging MainMenu objects," later in this chapter) but there's a much simpler method you can use to insert and delete entire pop-up menus in a window's menu bar. To try this technique, insert a single MainMenu object into a form, double-click the object, and use the Menu Designer to enter menus and commands.

Next, create a handler for the form's OnCreate event. Insert statements like the following to make selected pop-up menus invisible:

```
OptionMenu.Visible := False;
WindowMenu.Visible := False;
```

Finally, in response to a button click or a menu command (or any other event), set a menu item's Visible property to True. The menu automatically appears. This is a good method for programming a quick-and-dirty Advanced Menus command that expands menus to their full regalia. Invisible menu items remain active, however, and still receive OnClick events. If those menu items have associated shortcut keys, users can still select them even if the commands are not visible.

Changing menu items

To change a command's text, simply assign a new Caption to any MenuItem object. For example, you might program an Undo command to inform users what can be undone:

```
EditUndo.Caption := '&Undo deletion';
```

Adding, inserting, and deleting menu items

You can add, insert, and delete commands from any pop-up menu object of the TMenuItem class. For example, you can append filenames to the end of a File menu's FileMenu object. Or, you can use the technique to modify a pop-up menu's commands at run time.

The first step in adding or inserting a menu item is to create a TMenuItem object. First, declare a variable like this in an event handler:

```
var
  MI: TMenuItem;
begin
  ...
end;
```

In the procedure body, create a new TMenuItem object by calling the Create method, and pass the parent object, which is usually the parent menu for the new command item:

```
MI := TMenuItem.Create(FileMenu);
```

You now have a new menu object referenced as MI. Assign the object's caption and other properties using statements such as the following:

```
MI.Caption := '&New command';
MI.Visible := True;
MI.ShortCut := ShortCut(vk_F1);
```

When you are done configuring the new menu item, add it to the bottom of a pop-up menu by calling *Add*:

```
FileMenu.Add(MI);  { Add menu item to bottom of File menu }
```

At this point, the FileMenu object assumes ownership of MI, and deletes that object at the proper time. You do not have to delete the memory allocated to MI by Create.

You may use MI again to create another menu item, but for each one, you must call the Create method as shown here. For example, you cannot simply assign a different caption to MI and add it to the menu. For experienced Pascal programmers: MI is actually a pointer to a dynamically allocated object. In programs, you do not have to dereference this pointer — simply use it as you would a variable of the addressed type.

Or, you can insert a menu item between others. Suppose you have a separator line object named FileSep. To insert MI above that line, first locate the separator's index and assign it to an Integer variable:

```
Index := FileMenu.IndexOf(FileSep);
```

Then, instead of calling *Add,* insert MI by calling the Insert method and passing it the Index value and the new menu object:

```
FileMenu.Insert(Index, MI);  { Insert menu item at Index }
```

You can also delete menu items by index value. Call TMenuItem's Delete method:

```
FileMenu.Delete(Index);
```

Or, you can delete a menu item object by calling Remove. For example, this deletes the Exit command from the File menu:

```
FileMenu.Remove(FileExit);
```

You can modify the contents of a pop-up or main menu through the Items property. Use Items as an array of TMenuItem objects. For example, MyMenu.Items[I] refers to the TMenuItem object at index I in MyMenu.

Assigning code to menu items

When you create a new menu item, you should also assign it an event handler to perform an action when users select the command. This takes three steps:

1. Declare the event handler procedure in the form's class.

2. Implement the procedure in the unit's implementation section.

3. Assign the procedure to the menu item's OnClick event.

For example, add the following declaration to the TForm1 class (usually add this and other declarations in the class's private or public sections; in this case, put it in the private part):

```
procedure NewCommandClick(Sender: TObject);
```

Next, implement the procedure anywhere in the unit's implementation section:

```
procedure TForm1.NewCommandClick(Sender: TObject);
begin
  ShowMessage('New command executed!');
end;
```

Notice the method's implementation identifies the procedure using the class name, a dot, and the procedure name. In this way, the method is owned by the form object created using the TForm1 class. Finally, declare a TMenuItem variable such as MI, create the object, assign the properties you want, and assign the event handler to the OnClick event:

```
MI := TMenuItem.Create(FileMenu);
MI.Caption := '&New command';
MI.OnClick := NewCommandClick;
```

Insert or add the new object into a menu. When users select it, the program calls NewCommandClick.

Of course, you can assign an existing menu-command event handler to a new menu item's OnClick event. Just use the final line from the preceding example, and change NewCommandClick to the existing procedure's name.

Adding filenames to a file menu

MenuItem objects do not have to be commands. They can also be informational — for example, the names of recently opened files. You can use Add, Insert, and Delete to manage this list — just create TMenuItem objects and assign filenames to the Caption properties. However, I find it's easier to insert dummy commands into the File menu and to assign filenames to them as users open new files.

The FileMenu sample application on the book's CD-ROM in the Source\FileMenu directory shows the necessary code. Figure 5-3 shows the program's File menu with four recently opened files. You can select these names like any other command, and each has an Alt+N key, where *N* is the underlined number. The code to manage the filename list is a bit tricky, as Listing 5-2 shows.

Figure 5-3: A common interface technique lists recently opened files in the File menu. The programming can be tricky, as the FileMenu application demonstrates.

Listing 5-2: Filemenu\Main.pas

```pascal
unit Main;

interface

uses
  Windows, SysUtils, Messages, Classes, Graphics, Controls,
  Forms, Dialogs, StdCtrls, Menus, Buttons;

type
  TMainForm = class(TForm)
    MainMenu1: TMainMenu;
    FileMenu: TMenuItem;
    FileExit: TMenuItem;
    OpenButton: TButton;
    OpenDialog: TOpenDialog;
    FileOpen: TMenuItem;
    FileSep1: TMenuItem;
    FileSep2: TMenuItem;
    FileName1: TMenuItem;
    FileName2: TMenuItem;
    FileName3: TMenuItem;
    FileName4: TMenuItem;
    BitBtn1: TBitBtn;
    procedure FileExitClick(Sender: TObject);
    procedure OpenButtonClick(Sender: TObject);
    procedure FileName1Click(Sender: TObject);
  private
    { Private declarations }
  public
    { Public declarations }
  end;

var
  MainForm: TMainForm;

implementation

{$R *.DFM}

procedure TMainForm.FileExitClick(Sender: TObject);
begin
  Close;
end;

{- Prompt for filename and add name to File menu }
procedure TMainForm.OpenButtonClick(Sender: TObject);
var
```

```
    S: string;
    I, K: Integer;
begin
  if OpenDialog.Execute then with FileMenu do
  begin
    if not FileSep2.Visible then
      FileSep2.Visible := True;   { Make separator visible }
    K := IndexOf(FileName1);
    for I := Count - 1 downto K + 1 do
    begin   { Move current filenames down one position }
      S := Items[I - 1].Caption;
      S[2] := Chr(Ord('0') + (I - K + 1));   { Alt-Shortcut }
      Items[I].Caption := S;
      Items[I].Visible := Items[I - 1].Visible;
    end;
    FileName1.Caption := '&1 ' + OpenDialog.Filename;
    FileName1.Visible := True;
    ShowMessage('Adding: ' + OpenDialog.Filename);
  end;
end;

{- Get filename selected from File menu }
procedure TMainForm.FileName1Click(Sender: TObject);
var
  Filename: string;
begin
  with Sender as TMenuItem do
  begin
    Filename := Caption;
    System.Delete(Filename, 1, 2);
  end;
  ShowMessage('Selected: ' + Filename);
end;

end.
```

Tip

Procedure FileName1Click in Listing 5-2 shows how to resolve a common conflict that may give you trouble from time to time. The procedure calls the Pascal Delete procedure to remove the underlined Alt key labels added to each filename. However, the preceding *with* statement tells Delphi to use TMenuItem members, one of which is also named Delete. I resolved this name conflict by prefacing Delete with System and a period, which tells the compiler to use the Delete string procedure found in the System unit, not the TMenuItem method of the same name. Other commonly used generic names you may need to qualify include Insert, Text, Assign, and Close.

Follow these steps to create a File menu and add recently opened filenames to the bottom of the menu window:

1. Insert a MainMenu component into a form and use the Menu Designer to create a File menu with a separator (enter a hyphen in the Caption property) and four dummy filename menu items. See Figure 5-4 for an example. Name the menu FileMenu, and the dummies FileName1, FileName2, FileName3, and FileName4. Name the separators FileSep1 and FileSep2. Table 5-2 lists significant component names and properties.

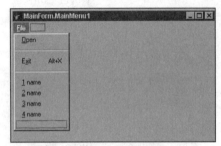

Figure 5-4: The FileMenu application's menu opened in Delphi's Menu Designer, with four dummy filename items.

2. Set Visible to False for the separator and all dummy menu items. The program makes them visible as users open new files.

3. Create an event handler for the first dummy entry by selecting it in the Menu Designer. See FileName1Click in the sample listing, which simply displays the selected filename. Assign this same event handler to the other dummy items.

4. Insert an OpenDialog object into the form.

5. Create an event handler for an Open command or button, and insert the programming from the demonstration's OpenButtonClick procedure.

Using shortcut keys

Delphi's Menus unit, added to any program with a MainMenu or PopupMenu object, provides four subroutines that are useful for assigning and using accelerator shortcut keys. To follow along, insert a MainMenu object into a form, and use the Menu Designer to create a menu with at least one item named Demo. I use the default Name Demo1 here.

Table 5-2
FileMenu Application Component Properties

Component	Name	Property	Value
Form	MainForm	Caption	Dynamic File Menu
Button	OpenButton	Caption	Open file
BitBtn	BitBtn1	Kind	bkClose
OpenDialog	OpenDialog	Filter	All files (*.*)|*.*
MainMenu	MainMenu1		
MenuItem	FileOpen	Caption	&Open
MenuItem	FileExit	Caption	E&xit
MenuItem	FileSep1	Caption	-
Component	Name	Property	Value
MenuItem	FileSep2	Caption	-
		Visible	False
MenuItem	FileName1	Caption	&1 name
		Visible	False
MenuItem	FileName2	Caption	&2 name
		Visible	False
MenuItem	FileName3	Caption	&3 name
		Visible	False
MenuItem	FileName4	Caption	&4 name
		Visible	False

Use the ShortCut function to assign an accelerator key to a menu item. Delphi defines the function as follows:

```
function ShortCut(Key: Word; Shift: TShiftState): TShortCut;
```

Using ShortCut, you can assign F9 to Demo1's ShortCut key property (to follow along, add this statement to a button's event handler):

```
Demo1.ShortCut := ShortCut(vk_F9, []);
```

Delphi automatically displays shortcut keys in the pop-up menu to the right of the Demo command. You don't have to modify the menu item's caption.

The empty brackets specify a null set of shift keys. To assign Alt+F9, specify a TShiftState value in brackets:

```
Demo1.ShortCut := ShortCut(vk_F9, [ssAlt]);
```

Because the shift state is a Pascal set, you can specify multiple values separated by commas. For example, this statement assigns Ctrl+Shift+A as the shortcut (the order of values in the set doesn't matter):

```
Demo1.ShortCut := ShortCut(Ord('A'), [ssCtrl, ssShift]);
```

You cannot specify the *A* key using the virtual key code vk_A, even though this and other alphanumeric codes are listed in Delphi's online help and also the source code file Windows.pas in Delphi's Source\RTL directory. Use Pascal's Ord function and a literal character in single quotation marks to specify ASCII character keys.

To break apart a shortcut key into its separate values, call ShortCutToKey, which is defined as follows:

```
procedure ShortCutToKey(ShortCut: TShortCut;
  var Key: Word; var Shift: TShiftState);
```

Pass a menu item's ShortCut property to the first parameter. The procedure assigns the ShortCut's virtual key code to Key and its set of shift-state values to Shift.

Another function, TextToShortCut, interprets a string value as a shortcut key assignment. For example, specify Alt+X as a string with this statement:

```
Demo1.ShortCut := TextToShortCut('Alt+X');
```

You can use this method to prompt users to enter a shortcut key value, perhaps in a configuration utility that lets users program their own menu commands:

```
var
  S: string;
begin
  S := InputBox('Input Dialog', 'Enter shortcut key', '');
  if Length(S) > 0 then
    Demo1.ShortCut := TextToShortCut(S);
end;
```

The InputBox function is especially handy for prompting users for string values. The first string is the dialog's caption, the second is a prompt displayed in the dialog window, and the third (null here) is the default string value returned if the user does not enter a string value.

Perform the reverse operation with ShortCutToText, which is defined as follows:

```
function ShortCutToText(ShortCut: TShortCut): string;
```

For example, you can display a menu item's shortcut key as a string in a dialog box:

```
ShowMessage('Demo1 shortcut = ' +
  ShortCutToText(Demo1.ShortCut));
```

Enabling and disabling commands

I already explained in this chapter how to enable and disable menu items by setting the Enabled property to True or False. When Enabled is False, the menu item's caption is dimmed in the pop-up menu window, and users cannot select it.

In practice, it takes careful planning to dim the proper commands at the correct times. The easiest approach is to write a procedure that configures an entire menu according to global flags and other values. For example, define a Boolean FileIsOpen variable, and write a procedure to enable or disable a File menu's Open, Save, and other commands according to the variable's value.

The ToDo application on this book's CD-ROM in the Source\ToDo directory shows how to do this for a common File menu. The program's form class, TMainForm, declares a procedure named EnableMenu:

```
procedure EnableMenu;
```

The program implements the procedure as shown in Listing 5-3. The statements enable and disable the commands in the program's File menu according to the program's file-open and file-saved states. The text of this listing is located in the ToDo project's Main.pas file on the CD-ROM.

> ### Listing 5-3: **Procedure EnableMenu from the ToDo sample**

```
applicationprocedure TMainForm.EnableMenu;
var
  I: Integer;
begin
  with FileMenu do
  begin
    for I := 0 to Count - 1 do          { Enable File commands }
      Items[I].Enabled := True;
    if not FileDirty then
    begin  { No edits }
```

```
        FileSave.Enabled := False;       { Must use Save as }
        if Length(Filename) = 0 then      { i.e. file not named }
        begin { No edits; no name }
          FileSaveAs.Enabled := False;    { Nothing to save }
          FilePrint.Enabled := False;     { Nothing to print }
        end;
      end;
    end;
  end;
```

The ToDo program uses a flag, FileDirty, to indicate whether changes have been made to an opened file. Procedure EnableMenu uses this flag to enable the menu's Save command, which remains dim (and therefore unselectable) if the file data is unchanged. The procedure also enables and disables other commands such as Save As and Print.

To use EnableMenu, create a handler for FileMenu's OnClick event, and call the procedure. As a result, the menu's commands are configured before the pop-up menu window becomes visible. For example, here's the OnClick event handler from ToDo:

```
procedure TMainForm.FileMenuClick(Sender: TObject);
begin
  EnableMenu;  { Enable/disable commands before menu opens }
end;
```

In a more complex application, it might be best to write a menu-enabling procedure for each of the program's menus, File, Edit, Window, and so forth. Call the procedures from OnClick event handlers for each MainMenu item. However, this does not prevent users from selecting commands by pressing shortcut keys. The safest course is for each command to perform its own validation. For example, a File|Save command could simply exit without taking any action if no file is open, and therefore, nothing needs to be saved.

Merging and unmerging MainMenu objects

Any form can have multiple MainMenu objects that you can merge into one another to create dynamic menus. This technique is especially useful in programs with two or more forms. When the program displays a secondary form, its MainMenu commands automatically merge with the program's main window. For example, a configuration dialog could use this technique to merge a new set of commands into the menu bar. When the user closes the dialog, the merged commands automatically disappear.

Merging MainMenu objects

The key element in merging menus is the GroupIndex byte value in the TMenuItem class. This value, which may range from 0 to 255, determines the effect of the merge. Use equal GroupIndex values to replace one menu with another. Use lesser values to insert menus to the left. Use higher values to insert menus to the right.

Assign GroupIndex values in multiples of 10 to make it easier to insert new menus between existing ones. However, in OLE applications (see Chapter 16), Windows requires you to use specific GroupIndex values to enable menu merging for in-place editing.

Follow these steps to merge two MainMenu objects in the same form and experiment with the technique:

1. Insert two MainMenu objects into a form window. I use the default object names MainMenu1 and MainMenu2, but you could change these names if you want.

2. Double-click MainMenu1 and use the Menu Designer to create a Demo menu with a command Advanced. Delphi names the menu item Demo1 by default. Select Demo1 in the Object Inspector window, and set Demo1's GroupIndex value to 0 (the default value).

3. Double-click MainMenu2, and create an Extra menu with a command Exit. Delphi names the menu item Extra1 by default. Select Extra1 in the Object Inspector window, and set Extra1's GroupIndex value to 1.

4. Create an event handler for the Advanced command by selecting it in the form or in the Menu Designer, and insert the following statement between begin and end:

```
MainMenu1.Merge(MainMenu2);
```

5. Create an event handler for the Exit command. (Because MainMenu2 is not shown in the form, you must use the Menu Designer to select the command.) Insert a Close statement for this command's procedure.

6. Press F9 to run the program. Select the Demo⎮Advanced command to merge the secondary menu, and make the Exit command available.

Try other GroupIndex values. For example, set GroupIndex to 1 for both Demo1 and Exit1. Selecting the Advanced command then causes the Extra menu to replace Demo. Or, set the GroupIndex to a higher value in Demo1 than in Exit1. The Advanced command now inserts the Extra menu to the left of Demo.

Unmerging MainMenu objects

Undo the effect of a menu merge by calling the UnMerge method for any MainMenu object. For example, insert a button into the form window and use the following statement in the button's OnClick event handler. Clicking the button removes MainMenu2 from MainMenu1:

```
MainMenu1.UnMerge(MainMenu2);
```

Merging MainMenu objects in multiple forms

When merging MainMenu objects in two or more forms, use the AutoMerge property to determine whether merging is automatic or occurs under program control. Try these steps to experiment with multiple-form menu merging:

1. Insert a MainMenu object into a form, double-click it, and use the Menu Designer to create a Demo menu with a single command, Show form. Still in Menu Designer, single-click the Demo menu, and then use the Object Inspector to set GroupIndex to 0 (the default value). Notice the Menu object is named Demo1 and is an object of the TMenuItem class. Be sure to select the menu objects using the Menu Designer, not the form in which the menu appears.

2. Add a second blank form to the project using the File|New Form command. Resize this form window, which is named Form2, and move it aside.

3. Into Form2, insert a separate MainMenu object, and set its AutoMerge property to True. Notice the object is named MainMenu1, the same as the other MainMenu object. Because the objects are in separate forms, there is no name conflict. Double-click Form2's MainMenu1 object and use the Menu Designer to create an Advanced menu with a Close command. Select this command and insert a Close; statement in the event handler.

4. While still in Form2 and using the Menu Designer, single-click the Advanced menu item and set its GroupIndex property to 1. (If necessary, double-click Form2's MainMenu1 object to get back to Menu Designer.) Switch to Form1, select the Demo|Show form command, and enter this statement in the resulting event handler:

```
Form2.Show;
```

5. Add the following uses declaration just below Unit1's implementation keyword:

```
uses Unit2;
```

6. Do the same for Unit2, but refer to Unit1 as follows (each unit now uses the other):

```
uses Unit1;
```

7. Finally, create an event handler for Form2's OnClose event. Insert this statement into the procedure:

```
Form1.MainMenu1.UnMerge(MainMenu1);
```

8. Press F9 to run the program. Select the Demo|Show form command, and notice the main window now has an Advanced menu item. Select this menu's Close command to close the secondary window and restore the merged menu to its original format.

The preceding steps may seem a bit complex the first time you do them. The technique is useful, however, when the appearance of a sublevel window dictates a change to the program's set of menus — for example, when programming a Find dialog window. When merging MainMenu objects in multiple forms, remember these tips:

✦ Insert one MainMenu object into each form. Set AutoMerge to False for the main window's object. Set AutoMerge to True for all other MainMenu objects. If you don't want automatic merging, set AutoMerge to False for all menus, and call Merge to perform menu merges as you did for single-form merging.

✦ Add the secondary unit module names (Unit2, Unit3, and so on) to a uses declaration in Unit1. This tells the main module to use the secondary ones.

✦ Add the main module unit name (for example, Unit1) to a new uses declaration in each secondary module.

✦ Call UnMerge for the main form's MainMenu object to remove a menu automatically when the secondary form closes. See Step 7 in the preceding tutorial for sample code. Despite the AutoMerge setting, unmerging is never automatic when a form closes (though perhaps it should be).

✦ Call Show to display a secondary form window as a child or modeless dialog of the main window parent.

✦ Delphi names each MainMenu object MainMenu1 in each form. For a clearer program, select better names for these objects such as MainFormMainMenu and FindFormMainMenu.

MDI and OLE applications require different menu merging techniques. See Chapters 15 and 16 for more information on MDI and OLE programming.

Modifying the system menu

The system menu appears when you click the program icon in a window's upper-left corner. Most applications shouldn't need to add commands to this menu — also, Delphi automatically handles the menu's standard commands. However, if you need to modify the system menu for a special application, here's how.

The system menu is owned by Windows, not the application. Therefore, you cannot use a MainMenu object to access the system menu. To add a command, call the Windows AppendMenu function. To respond to the command's selection, add a message-handler procedure to the form's class. Follow these steps to try out the technique and add an About... command to the system menu:

1. Create a handler for the main-window form's OnCreate event. Insert the programming for procedure FormCreate from Listing 5-4 (this text is on the CD-ROM in the SysMenu project's Main.pas file).

2. Declare a constant to represent the new command. Use any small value such as hexadecimal $00A0 (100 decimal). Windows uses the low four bits of this value for command flags, which should be zero. The easiest way to satisfy this requirement is to assign values in hexadecimal with the last digit equal to 0. For example, add this declaration to the unit's implementation:

```
const
  cm_About = $00A0;
```

3. In the form's class (TForm1 by default), insert the following message-handler declaration in the class's private section. The first line declares the procedure, which must have the single TWMSysCommand variable parameter as shown. The second line tells Delphi to call this procedure when the form receives a wm_Syscommand message from Windows. This message indicates that the user has selected a system-menu command:

```
procedure WMSysCommand(var Message: TWMSysCommand);
  message wm_SysCommand;
```

4. Implement the WMSysCommand procedure as shown in Listing 5-4. Run the program and select the system menu's About... command to display a message dialog.

In Listing 5-4, the WMSysCommand procedure demonstrates how to handle a message in a form class. The procedure receives a TWMSysCommand variable that describes a message's contents. In this variable, field CmdType represents the value of a selected command. If that value equals our cm_About constant, a case statement calls ShowMessage to display a dialog box. To perform default processing for other system menu commands, the procedure calls inherited for unhandled CmdType values.

The form's OnCreate event handler demonstrates how to get the window handle for a system menu. The procedure stores this handle in a variable, MenuH, of type HMenu (handle to a menu). First, GetSystemMenu returns the menu handle for the form window—the Handle argument in this statement belongs to the form. The Windows AppendMenu function adds the About... command to this menu.

Listing 5-4: **Adding commands to an application's system menu**

```
procedure TForm1.WMSysCommand(var Message: TWMSysCommand);
begin
  case Message.CmdType of
    cm_About: ShowMessage('About command selected!');
  else
    inherited;  { Default processing }
  end;
end;

procedure TForm1.FormCreate(Sender: TObject);
var
  MenuH: HMenu;
begin
  MenuH := GetSystemMenu(Handle, False);
  AppendMenu(MenuH, mf_String, cm_About, 'About...');
end;
```

Next, the OnCreate event handler repeats the preceding two steps but, this time, the program passes the Handle from the Application object to GetSystemMenu. This is necessary to modify the system menu for a minimized application, for which the form window is hidden from view.

Portable Menus

Many application menus have similar commands, and you can save time by developing portable menus for sharing among multiple programs. Two basic tools are used to create portable menus: templates and resources.

Menu templates

Delphi has several built-in menu templates you can import into MainMenu and PopupMenu objects. To import a template:

1. Insert one of those two objects into a form.

2. Double-click it to open the Menu Designer.

3. Click the right mouse button or press Alt+F10 to open a floating pop-up menu.

4. Select Insert From Template.

5. Choose your menu poison (a stock File menu, for example).

After inserting a menu template, a good idea is to rename all the menu item objects according to the guidelines I mentioned. This takes only a few moments, but greatly contributes to readable code. Always do this before writing statements that refer to objects by name. Menu Designer's default names, such as Edit1 and Save1, are not very descriptive. These would be better named FileEdit and FileSave to indicate to which menu they belong. FileEditItem and FileSaveItem are even better names because they remind you they are objects of the TMenuItem class.

Tip

If you import a menu template into a PopupMenu object, Delphi creates a nested menu as though the floating pop-up menu were a menu bar turned on its side. Try this! This is a good interface technique not often used.

You can also save any menu as a template. Use the Menu Designer's Save as Template command to store your favorite menus with stock templates. Delphi stores menu templates in the Delphi32.dmt file, located in Delphi's \bin directory.

Name properties and event handlers are not stored with menu templates because these will likely be different in each application. Menu templates are strictly MenuItem objects. They don't contain any code. If you need to save code with your menu templates, create a test program for each menu, and then after importing the template into a new application, copy and paste statements from the test module.

Menu resource scripts

Another way to create portable menus is to design them the "old-fashioned way," using resource script commands. You can also use this technique to import menus from other applications — those developed in C or C++, for example.

On the
CD-ROM

Listing 5-5 and Listing 5-6 show a sample menu script. Multimen.inc is an include file that defines constants to represent menu items. Multimen.mnu is a resource script that declares the menu's text and layout. You can find both files in the Multimenu subdirectory on this book's CD-ROM.

Listing 5-5: **Multimen.inc**

```
const
  id_Menu      = 100;
  cm_FileMenu  = 101;
  cm_FileExit  = 102;
```

Listing 5-6: **Multimen.mnu**

```
#include multimen.inc

id_Menu MENU
BEGIN
  POPUP "&File"
  BEGIN
    MENUITEM "E&xit", cm_FileExit
  END
  POPUP "&Edit"
  BEGIN
    MENUITEM "&Undo", 201
    MENUITEM "&Redo", 202
    POPUP "&Search"
    BEGIN
      MENUITEM "&Ignore case", 301, CHECKED
      POPUP "&Find"
      BEGIN
        MENUITEM "&Previous", 401
        MENUITEM "&Whole words", 402
        MENUITEM "&Partial words", 403
      END
      MENUITEM "&Replace", 303
    END
  END
END
```

To use the Multimen.mnu script, insert a MainMenu or PopupMenu object into a form. Double-click the object to open the Menu Designer, and select the Insert From Resource command. Open the .mnu script file. (By the way, this is how I created the nested menu for the MultiMen application in this chapter.)

Caution

After importing a menu script into a Delphi application, you can use the Menu Designer to modify your menu's commands. However, you cannot easily modify the original script and merge it back into the application.

Delphi's menu script loader is nonstandard in one way. All menu items on a menu bar must have at least one command item. Windows and Delphi applications, however, permit a menu item with no commands on a menu bar. Selecting the command-less item does not open a menu window but immediately executes the item as a command.

Menu Designer does not permit command-less menu resources, and therefore, a resource script cannot have two POPUP commands in succession, as in this example:

```
POPUP "&Demo"
POPUP "&Help"
```

Menus with no commands are unusual, therefore this problem is a minor one. However, Borland Pascal 7.0 and most C and C++ development systems support command-less menus, and you may find an occasional resource script that Delphi cannot read. You can fix the problem by adding BEGIN and END keywords to the POPUP menus. Use code such as:

```
POPUP "&Demo"
BEGIN
END
POPUP "&Help"
BEGIN
END
```

Menu Designer Tips

Delphi's Menu Designer has an intuitive interface that's easy to master. However, the following are a few tips that may be less than obvious:

✦ Press Ins to insert a blank menu item ahead of the currently highlighted one. Highlight a menu bar item and press Ins to insert a new pop-up menu in the menu bar.

✦ Press Del to delete a menu item. Be careful when pressing Del — you cannot undo a menu deletion.

✦ Enter a single hyphen into a menu item's Caption to display a separator line. This line appears in the correct size in the form and in the run-time window, but in the Menu Designer, the separator is as tall as a normal menu command so you can select and edit it as any other menu item.

✦ To create a nested menu, highlight any menu item and press Ctrl+right arrow. Press Esc to return to a previous level, or use the mouse and the arrow keys to navigate through the menu.

✦ Drag-and-drop menu items to rearrange them. Try this with a sample menu; it's the easiest way to perform major surgery on a menu's layout.

ActionLists

A well-constructed user interface provides numerous ways to accomplish the same tasks. This accommodates users of different skill levels, and can reduce the agony of learning how to use a new application. For example, rather than use only menu commands to drive a program, a better interface might provide buttons and toolbars to execute the same commands.

For programmers, however, the more paths to interface-nirvana, the more work it takes to create reliable code. In a program with only a few dozen commands, adding buttons and toolbars that share the same code greatly complicates the interactions between those commands and the program's state. Just to name one example, it is frequently difficult to disable inappropriate commands correctly at the correct times. It also takes diligence to reduce duplications in the source code — for instance, writing the same operation for two different command objects two different ways, which might lead to future bugs.

Delphi 4 introduces the concept of an *action list* to help with these problems. The ActionLIst component located on the Standard palette can store one or more Action objects. Each Action object is a kind of anchor to which other objects can attach. To provide common properties and events for two or more other objects such as menu items and buttons, you simply program the Action to do what you want and attach it to the other objects. Each of those objects take on the characteristics of the Action component as though you had programmed each individually.

> **Note** The ActionList component is programmed in the TActionList class. An Action component is of the TAction class. Only ActionList appears on the palette — Command objects are created by the action list editor, which this section explains how to use. This arrangement is similar to the way a MainMenu component object stores individual MenuItems.

The Actions project in Listing 5-7 demonstrates how to program a CommandList component. Figure 5-5 shows the program's design-time appearance inside Delphi. This program demonstrates how an ActionList object stores an Action object that provides common attributes and programming for two or more other objects. To run the program, follow these steps:

1. Open the Actions project using Delphi (you must have Version 4 for this demonstration).

2. Run the program by pressing F9.

3. Enter Quit into the edit box to enable the Exit button and command of that same name.

4. You can then select either the menu item or click the button to end the program and return to Delphi.

Figure 5-5: Enter Quit into the edit box to enable the program's Exit menu command and button. This demonstrates how to use the ActionList component.

Listing 5-7: **Actions\Main.pas**

```pascal
unit Main;

interface

uses
  Windows, Messages, SysUtils, Classes, Graphics, Controls,
  Forms, Dialogs, Menus, ActnList, StdCtrls;

type
  TForm1 = class(TForm)
    MainMenu1: TMainMenu;
    Edit1: TEdit;
    Button1: TButton;
    Label1: TLabel;
    ActionList1: TActionList;
    Demo1: TMenuItem;
    Exit1: TMenuItem;
    ExitAction: TAction;
    procedure ExitActionExecute(Sender: TObject);
    procedure ExitActionUpdate(Sender: TObject);
  private
    { Private declarations }
  public
    { Public declarations }
  end;

var
  Form1: TForm1;
```

```
implementation

{$R *.DFM}

procedure TForm1.ExitActionExecute(Sender: TObject);
begin
  Close;  // Exit program
end;

procedure TForm1.ExitActionUpdate(Sender: TObject);
var
  Flag: Boolean;
begin
// Set Flag True if user types Quit into Edit1
  if Lowercase(Edit1.Text) = 'quit'
    then Flag := True
    else Flag := False;
  Button1.Enabled := Flag;  // Enable or disable Button1
  Exit1.Enabled := Flag;    // Enable or disable Menu item
end;
```

On the CD-ROM

To learn how to use the ActionList component, follow these steps to recreate the Actions application on the CD-ROM in the Source\Actions directory:

1. Start a new application. Insert MainMenu, Edit, Button, Label, and ActionList objects (one each).

2. Double-click MainMenu1 and create a Demo menu with an Exit command. This creates the Exit1 object, which does not appear in the form.

3. Set the Enabled properties to False for the Button1 and Exit1 objects (select the Exit1 object using the Object Inspector drop-down list). This sets the initial properties for the two command objects that, when enabled via their shared ActionList, exit the program.

4. Double-click the ActionList object. Like MainMenu and other nonvisual components, an ActionList object shows up as an icon on the form, but is not visible at run time. You are now viewing the action list editor in which you can create shared Action objects (see Figure 5-6).

Figure 5-6: To open Delphi 4's action list editor shown here, double-click an ActionList object.

5. Click the New Action speed button (it's the first on the left) to create an Action object. This is named Action1 by default. In this demonstration, we use only one Action object, but you can add as many Actions as you need to a single ActionList component.

6. Using the Object Inspector's drop-down list, select the Action1 object created in the preceding step. (This is probably already selected.)You will normally want to change this object's name to reflect its purpose. In this case, change the Name property to ExitAction. Set the Caption property to E&xit.

7. Click the ExitAction object's Events tab in the Object Inspector. Double-click each of the two events, OnExecute and OnUpdate, to create event handlers. Fill in these procedures using the listing as a guide — I explain the programming after these steps.

8. The final step in the process of creating an ActionList is to link controls that are to share Action object properties and events. To do this, select the Exit1 object using the Object Inspector drop-down list, and set its Action property to ExitAction. Similarly, select the Button1 object and set its Action property also to ExitAction. The events and properties of ExitAction are now shared by the menu item and button. Notice that the shared object Captions change to the ExitAction's Caption property.

9. Run the program by pressing F9. Enter Quit into the edit box to enable the command objects, which when selected, execute the shared ExitAction OnExecute event, and end the program.

Note   The Action property, of the TAction class, is new to Delphi 4, and is declared as a private member in various other classes such as MenuItem, Button, BitBtn, SpeedButton, and other components.

Each Action object such as ExitAction in the demonstration program has two events, OnExecute and OnUpdate. The OnExecute event handler provides programming that executes when any other object such as a Button or MenuItem is selected. Those other objects set their Action property to ExitAction to link to the shared code, which, in this case, simply ends the program by calling Close.

Similarly, an Action's OnUpdate event provides the opportunity to alter multiple shared objects. In the demonstration program, I programmed the ExitActions's OnUpdate event to set the Button1 and Exit1 Enabled properties to True or False, depending on whether the Edit1 Text property equals "quit" (case doesn't matter). The OnUpdate event is called repeatedly while the application is idle, so don't add lengthy programming here. Setting Enable properties to True or False as done in the demonstration is a typical good use for an Action object's OnUpdate event.

Tip

Insert an ActionList object into a data module (see Chapter 3, Introducing Forms). This reduces clutter in your visible forms, and also provides easy access to the ActionList and its Action objects for other modules. Simply "use" the data module in any form.

Expert-User Tips

✦ Although MenuItems are components, you cannot select them all in the form window to program shared properties and events. To create a shared event for multiple MenuItem objects, write one procedure for the first or any other item, and assign it to the other objects one by one in the Object Inspector window. There doesn't seem to be any easier way to do this. Alternatively, you can assign procedures to the objects' OnClick event at run time — perhaps in the form's OnCreate handler.

✦ Increment MenuItem Tag fields in the object's OnClick event handlers. Print these values before the program terminates for a report on menu command usage. Use this data to better organize menu items — putting more frequently used commands on top, for example.

✦ Insert a copy of a selected menu command into the top of a menu. As users select commands, they tend to appear nearer the top of the menu window. You might use this technique to make frequently selected commands more readily accessible — font names, for example.

✦ In the Menu Designer, set a MenuItem object's Break property to mbBarBreak (vertical separator) or to mbBreak (no separator) to create horizontally segmented pop-up menus. View the resulting menu in the form — you see no visible change in the Menu Designer. These features are rarely used in Windows software, but are handy for building some types of complex menus, especially those with numerous commands that cause the menu window to extend far beyond the window's bottom border.

✦ Use the Alignment property in PopupMenu objects to alter the location of the menu window relative to the mouse cursor. For example, set Alignment to paCenter to center the top of the window at the mouse cursor. Alignment works only with floating pop-up menus assigned to a form's PopupMenu property.

✦ The ActionList component provides the Images property which you can use to store bitmap images to be displayed by other visual objects such as MenuItems and BitBtns. Add your Images to the ActionList. To associate each image with individual Action components, use the Action object's ImageIndex property. These properties make it easier to associate common bitmaps with multiple components.

 Projects to Try

5-1: Write a program for a standard File menu template. Add code from this chapter to implement Open, Save, Save As, and other commands. Also add code from the FileMenu sample application to append filenames to the bottom of the menu. Save the result as a shell for beginning new file-related projects (very useful for prototypes).

5-2: Modify the FileMenu sample application to permit users to specify the number of displayed names in the File menu.

5-3: Advanced: Write a program that lets users build a new menu at run time. Include commands for entering accelerator shortcut keys.

5-4: Advanced: Using your code from project 5-3, write menus in resource script form for importing into Delphi applications.

5-5: Reprogram Menu Designer's templates to use more descriptive TMenuItem object names. To do this, insert a MainMenu object into a form, double-click it, and load each template into Menu Designer. Modify the object names by selecting them in Menu Designer and changing their Name properties in Object Inspector. For example, you might change the File|Save command's object Save1 to FileSaveItem. Finally, using Menu Designer, save the template under the same or a different name.

5-6: Reprogram the Actions project. Transfer the ActionList objects to a data module (see Chapter 3). Modify the MenuItem and Button objects to access the list's ExitAction, for example, as DataModule1.ExitAction.

Summary

✦ Use the MainMenu object to create main-window menu bars.

✦ Use the PopupMenu object to create floating pop-up menus that appear when users click the right mouse button. You can also call the Popup method to display floating pop-up menus at any screen location.

✦ All items in MainMenu and PopupMenu objects are objects of the TMenuItem class. Assign values to CheckMark, Visible, and Enable properties (and others) in TMenuItem objects to create dynamic menus.

✦ Use the Items property in MainMenu, PopupMenu, and MenuItem objects to access any MenuItem objects that the three types of menu objects contain. Limit array index values to the range 0 to Count - 1. Items is a TMenuItem, which has an array property; thus, you may call methods such as Insert for Items, or you can use it as an array.

✦ Use standard accelerator shortcut keys when possible. You may assign nearly any key combination as an accelerator shortcut. For fine-tuning shortcut key assignments at run time, use the ShortCut, ShortCutToKey, TextToShortCut, and ShortCutToText functions described in this chapter.

✦ The easiest way to create dynamic menus is to insert multiple MainMenu objects in a form and assign them at run time to the Menu property. You can also assign PopupMenu objects to a form's PopupMenu property.

✦ Another easy method for creating dynamic menus is to set the Visible property in MenuItem objects to True and False. This makes menu items — or even entire menus on the menu bar — appear and disappear under program control.

✦ Use the Add, Delete, Insert, and Remove methods to modify menu items at run time. For example, you can use these procedures to insert filenames at the bottom of a File menu. I find it easier to create dummy menu items for this purpose and set their Visible properties to True as users open new files.

✦ You may create new TMenuItem objects at run time. Call the Create method to create each object, and use Add or Insert to inject the item into a menu. Assign an event handler procedure to the item's OnClick event.

✦ Merge multiple MainMenu objects by setting MenuItem GroupIndex values and AutoMerge properties as described in this chapter. You may merge MainMenu objects in the same form, or in different forms. MDI and OLE applications use different menu merging techniques.

✦ It's tricky to do, but you can add commands to an application's system menu. The steps in this chapter show how to do this, and also demonstrate how to create event handlers for Windows messages.

✦ Use menu templates and resource scripts to create portable menus for sharing among multiple applications. You can also create your own menu templates.

✦ Delphi 4 adds the ActionList component to the Standard palette. Use ActionList to create Action objects with properties and events that other components such as MenuItem and Button objects can share.

Delphi makes a science out of the lowly Windows button control, as you discover in the next chapter. Of course, you can create standard-issue buttons, check boxes, and radio buttons, but you can spruce up your application's user interface in a hurry by using Delphi's graphical BitBtn and other component objects. We also look at static text and up-down controls.

✦   ✦   ✦

Attaching Buttons and Check Boxes

◆ ◆ ◆ ◆

CHAPTER 6

In This Chapter

Components

Basic buttons

Colorful buttons

Button groups

Spin buttons

Static text

Up-down button controls

◆ ◆ ◆ ◆

Buttons and check boxes are the nuts and bolts of a graphical user interface, and Delphi provides a virtual tool chest of push buttons, radio buttons, check boxes, speed buttons, and bitmap buttons. You can assemble groups of button objects, and you can use organizational components such as bevels and panels to arrange a busy window full of buttons and other controls.

In this chapter, I explain how to use Delphi's button objects and related components such as GroupBox, RadioGroup, SpinEdit, and SpinButton. I also explain how to create and use colorful bitmap images, called glyphs, that appear on BitBtn and SpeedButton components. You can also display glyphs in SpinButton controls. Finally, I discuss static text controls (which add features such as borders to standard label text), and also Win32 up-down buttons, which resemble SpinButtons but are native to 32-bit Windows.

Note This chapter introduces the SpeedButton and Panel components. See the next chapter for more information on using these components to construct toolbars and status panels.

Components

Delphi's button-related components are:

> ◆ **Bevel** — This purely visual component looks like a rectangular indentation in a window. A Bevel can also display horizontal and vertical lines, affectionately known to interface designers as speed bumps and dips, that are useful for dividing a window into sections. Palette: Additional.

✦ **BitBtn** — You might call this component "a push button with flair." A BitBtn works like a Button component, but can display a colorful icon, called a glyph, that visually represents the button's action. Palette: Additional.

✦ **Button** — This is a standard Windows button control encapsulated in a Delphi component. I explain about Buttons in this chapter, but you probably want to use BitBtns instead. Palette: Standard.

✦ **CheckBox** — This also is a standard Windows control, composed of a label with a box that users can toggle on and off. It's highly useful for designing dialog boxes with sets of program options. Palette: Standard.

✦ **GroupBox** — Another standard Windows control, this component logically groups multiple RadioButtons and other objects. Users can press Tab to move among multiple GroupBoxes, and then press the arrow keys to select from the grouped controls. Also see the RadioGroup component, which simplifies grouping RadioButton objects. Palette: Standard.

✦ **Panel** — This component provides a platform for segmenting a busy window and for creating toolbars and status panels (discussed in the next chapter). A Panel object can appear as a raised surface, or it can look indented and have a variety of beveled borders. Panels never receive the input focus. They are purely visual, and serve as containers for other controls. Palette: Standard.

✦ **RadioButton** — You can insert multiple RadioButton objects into a GroupBox or Panel component, but in most cases, the RadioGroup object is easier to use for creating RadioButton sets. You can also insert sets of RadioButtons directly into forms. Palette: Standard.

✦ **RadioGroup** — This component is similar to a GroupBox, but is easier to use for grouping multiple RadioButton objects. Simply enter strings into a RadioGroup's Items property to create your buttons. Palette: Standard.

✦ **SpeedButton** — Usually, you use SpeedButtons to create toolbars, as the next chapter explains. However, you can insert individual SpeedButtons in forms. This chapter's Calc32 application — a 32-bit programmer's calculator provided on the book's CD-ROM — uses SpeedButtons this way. Palette: Additional.

✦ **SpinEdit** — Located on the Samples VCL palette, this component demonstrates custom component design, but it is also useful in its own right. I also explain in this chapter how to use the related SpinButton component. Palette: Samples.

✦ **StaticText** — Use this relatively new component to create static text labels with visual features such as a sunken border. For creating sectional windows, this is easier than combining multiple Panel and Label components. Palette: Additional.

✦ **UpDown** — This component accesses the 32-bit Windows up-down control, which is similar to the sample SpinButton control, also discussed in this chapter. Palette: Win32.

Basic Buttons

Windows offers three standard types of buttons, which Delphi encapsulates in components. The three buttons and their corresponding components are:

✦ **Push buttons**—Button component

✦ **Check boxes**—CheckBox component

✦ **Radio buttons**—RadioButton component

The three types of components recognize similar events. For example, you can insert statements into an OnClick event handler to perform actions when users select a button, a check box, or a radio button. For finer control over button selection, use the OnMouseDown or OnKeyDown events. You can also program actions for a button's release by creating a procedure for an OnMouseUp event.

Preface any character in a button Caption property with an ampersand to designate an Alt-shortcut accelerator key. For example, users can press Alt+C to select a button with the Caption &Close. As in menu items, the accelerator key can be any letter in the Caption property. For example, the Caption E&xit designates Alt+X as the button's shortcut key.

Push buttons

Push buttons are easy to use. Just insert a Button object into a form, and assign a string to the Caption property for the button's label. As you have seen in several other examples, to perform actions when users click a button, create an event handler for the button's OnClick event, and insert statements between begin and end.

For a default button, change the Default property to True. Only one button in a form (usually labeled OK) should be the default, which users can select by pressing Enter. To associate a button (usually labeled Cancel) with the Esc key, set the button's Cancel property to True. Regardless of the Cancel and Default settings, however, you still have to create event handlers for the buttons.

Buttons and other controls assume the form's Font. For a pleasing display, change the form's Font to a TrueType font such as Arial. However, when doing this, be sure to choose a font that is available on all Windows installations. The typical fonts available on a Windows 95 installation are listed here. You can also select different fonts for individual buttons and other controls.

Note

TrueType fonts are scalable in size; bitmap fonts are also scalable, but look best in their listed point sizes.

✦ **True Type Fonts** — Arial; Arial Bold; Arial Bold Italic; Arial Italic; Courier New; Courier New Bold; Courier New Bold Italic; Courier New Italic; Symbol; Times New Roman; Times New Roman Bold; Times New Roman Bold Italic; WingDings

✦ **Bitmap Fonts** — Courier 10,12,15; Modern; MS Sans Serif 8,10,12,14,18,24; Roman; Script; Small Fonts; Symbol 8,10,12,14,18,24

On rare occasions, you might want to force users to select a particular push button, an OK button, for example. You can't do this by setting the button's Default property to True because users can still press Tab to shift the focus to another button such as Cancel. This can be confusing, especially to novice computer users who, until they gain experience, may fail to notice the faint outline around the focused control.

One solution to this problem is to disable all buttons and other objects on a form by setting their Enabled properties to False. To do that, declare an Integer variable I, and use code such as the following:

```
for I := 0 to ComponentCount - 1 do
  if Components[I] is TWinControl then
    TWinControl(Components[I]).Enabled := False;
```

The preceding code accesses the Components array in a form to set the Enabled properties of all control objects to False. An *if* statement tests whether the object is a TWinControl (the grandparent class from which control objects such as buttons are derived). If so, the program sets the control's Enabled property False by casting Components[I] to a TWinControl object. The cast is necessary because the Components array's contents are of the general type, TComponent, which doesn't have an Enabled property.

After executing the preceding code, all controls on the form are disabled and displayed in a dim style. To finish the programming, enable one button and change the focus to that button. This is the only button that users can select:

```
OKButton.Enabled := True;    { Enable button and set the focus }
OKButton.SetFocus;           { so pressing Enter selects it. }
```

Check boxes

CheckBox components are among Windows' simplest, but most useful, interface-design tools. Insert a CheckBox object into a form, and set its Checked property True to display a check mark in the box, or False for no check mark. At run time, you can detect whether a CheckBox is on or off using code such as this:

```
if MyCheckBox.Checked
  then {do something};
```

A CheckBox is usually an on-and-off toggle, but it can also be a three-way switch that is either on, disabled, or off. A disabled CheckBox has a grayed check mark in its box. To create a three-way CheckBox, set its AllowGrayed property True, and then set State to one of three initial values: cbChecked, cbGrayed, or chUnchecked (the default). Users can now select the CheckBox to turn it on or off, or to disable it.

If AllowGrayed is False and State is cbGrayed, a disabled check mark appears in the CheckBox control. Users can select the control to switch it on and off, but they cannot return the check box to its disabled state.

You may color a CheckBox's background by selecting a value for the Color property. For example, set Color to clBtnShadow to color a CheckBox control the same as the system setting for button shadows. Or, select a fixed color such as clOlive from the Color property's drop-down list.

You cannot color a Button object as you can a CheckBox. This is a Windows limitation. For more colorful buttons, use BitBtn instead of Button components.

In many cases, you create multiple check boxes. I find it's easiest to do this by first inserting one CheckBox object, pressing Ctrl+C to copy it to the clipboard, and then pressing Ctrl+V repeatedly to paste new objects into the form window. (These keys may differ depending on your Environment Options — open the Edit menu to check.) I then select each object, change its Name and Caption properties, and move each object to its final position.

Radio buttons

The third and final standard Windows control is a radio button, which Delphi encapsulates in the RadioButton component. Radio buttons are like potato chips — one is never enough. You always use at least two RadioButton objects. (A CheckBox is more appropriate than a RadioButton for an individual on/off control.) You can color RadioButton objects as you can CheckBoxes.

When a form contains multiple RadioButton objects, users can toggle only one button at a time on/off. But when you insert multiple sets of radio buttons, they function as a single set, which is probably not what you want. The solution is to group each set of controls so that users may select one button from each set, and press Tab to shift the focus from one set to another (and to other controls). I explain more about grouping control objects in the section "Button Groups," later in this chapter. Also, see "Using Radio Groups" for an alternate radio button grouping technique.

RadioButton objects provide a double-click event that is not available for push buttons and check boxes. Double-click the OnDblClick event value in the Object Inspector to create the event handler. Users can then single-click the radio button control or they can double-click the object to perform a different action.

Colorful Buttons

For a more eye-catching display, use a BitBtn object instead of a standard Windows Button. The BitBtn component works like a push button, but it can display a colorful bitmap, called a *glyph,* that reminds users what the button does. Looks may be deceiving, but a little makeup goes a long way, and glyphs can help dress up an otherwise drab window. You can select glyphs from a library of stock images or you can create your own. You can also choose from several predefined BitBtn objects with default glyphs that represent standard operations such as Yes, No, Close, Help, Ignore, and Retry.

Delphi also provides the SpeedButton component, which is similar to a BitBtn with a glyph bitmap and, usually, no Caption. As the next chapter explains, you can use SpeedButtons and Panels to create toolbars, but you also can insert independent SpeedButtons into a form window. This chapter's Calc32 application—a 32-bit programmer's integer calculator—demonstrates how to use SpeedButtons as individual controls.

Bitmap buttons

The BitBtn component is the first one on the Additional VCL palette. The easiest way to use this component is to insert it into a form, and then set its Kind property to one of the values shown in Figure 6-1—for example, bkHelp. Set Kind to bkCustom to display your own glyph image or none. If you don't display a glyph on a BitBtn, however, you may as well use a Button component.

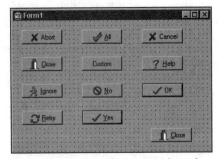

Figure 6-1: A sample form with each type of BitBtn object. Labels show the values inserted into the objects' Kind properties.

Tip If you set a BitBtn's Kind property to bkClose, users can select the button to close its form window. The button does this by internally setting ModalResult to a value such as mrOk. You do not have to write your own code to do this. However, if you do not want a Close BitBtn to close the window, first set Kind to bkClose and then change it to bkCustom. The button label and glyph stay the same, but you can now assign your own event handler to the object's OnClick event.

You may assign an image to a BitBtn object. Double-click the object's Glyph property value to open the Picture Editor. Select Load and specify a bitmap file. You can find a bunch of sample files in Delphi's Images\Buttons directory. After loading a bitmap, select Save to copy the image to a new file. Select OK to copy the bitmap image to the BitBtn object. These steps also work for SpeedButtons.

You do not have to supply the bitmap file with your application's code file. However, you may want to copy Delphi's bitmap and other files to your development directories in order to build a complete set of source files for your application.

To adjust the location of a BitBtn's glyph relative to its caption, set the Layout property to blGlyphBottom, blGlyphLeft, blGlyphRight, or blGlyphTop. Try these on sample BitBtn objects to see their effects. For a standard appearance, use the default value blGlyphLeft, which places the glyph to the left of the button caption. Also adjust the Margin property to separate images from button borders—0 for no separation, 1 for a single-pixel space, 2 for two pixels, and so on. To center a glyph, set Margin to -1.

For more information on glyph bitmaps, see "More About Glyphs," after the next section on SpeedButtons.

Modifying the Display Style of BitBtn Objects Using the Style Property

Early versions of Delphi allowed modifying the display style of BitBtn objects using the Style property. For reference, I list the descriptions of this property's settings, but they are now obsolete, although they might have a visual effect under Win32s and Windows 3.1 (bsAutoDetect is the default value for BitBtn objects):

✦ **bsAutoDetect**—Automatically uses the bsNew style for Windows 95 and the bsWin31 style for Windows 3.1.

✦ **bsNew**—Always uses the new Windows 95 button style, with thinner shadow effects on the bottom and right edges.

✦ **bsWin31**—Always uses the Windows 3.1 button style, with denser shadows on the bottom and right edges.

Speed buttons

SpeedButton objects usually appear on toolbars, but you can also create individual SpeedButtons as I explain here. SpeedButtons can also display colorful icons called *glyphs*. See the next chapter for more information on using SpeedButtons and Panels to create toolbars.

In general, you program SpeedButton events as you do push buttons, but SpeedButtons recognize only five events. Use OnClick and OnDblClick to perform actions for mouse clicks and double-clicks. Use OnMouseDown, OnMouseMove, and OnMouseUp for finer control over button selection—for example, inspecting the OnMouseDown Shift parameter to determine whether a key was pressed. (See Chapter 4 for information on this parameter's TShiftState data type.)

A SpeedButton's primary advantage over other button types is its capability to function in two manners: as an on/off toggle or as a "sticky" button that stays down when you push it. These characteristics made SpeedButtons the ideal choice for my 32-bit programmer's calculator, which you can find on this book's CD-ROM in the Calc32 directory. Figure 6-2 shows Calc32's display. It has SpeedButton objects that can function as on/off toggles (such as the digit entry keys) and "sticky" buttons that stay down when you click them (such as the Memory, Decimal, Hexadecimal, and Binary buttons under the Calc menu item).

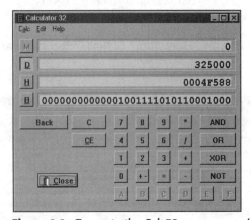

Figure 6-2: To create the Calc32 programmer's calculator, I used SpeedButton objects that function as on/off toggles and "sticky" buttons that stay down when you click them.

Another reason to use SpeedButtons concerns resources. SpeedButtons do not have window handles and associated structures internal to Windows, so a form with a dozen SpeedButtons uses less memory than a dozen standard buttons. SpeedButton objects also display more quickly than standard controls.

Calc32 is a 32-bit integer calculator, suitable for programming tasks such as figuring out bit patterns and converting between hexadecimal, binary, and decimal. Calc32 is intuitively simple to use. Click the *D*, *H*, or *B* buttons to select decimal, hexadecimal, or binary input. Enter values using the keyboard or by clicking buttons. The display fields near the top of the window always show values in three radices regardless of input mode. Values stored in the memory field (M) are always decimal. Calc32 does not support floating-point values.

Calc32's source code is too long to list here; of course, all source files are on the CD-ROM. I refer to sections of the code from time to time. To examine the application, open the Calc32.dpr project file in the Calc32 directory.

Calc32 demonstrates that SpeedButtons do not have to display glyph images to be useful. To create the program's buttons, I entered Caption properties such as 1, 2, 3, C, and CE, and I set Glyph to None (the default value).

I chose SpeedButtons for Calc32 rather than standard Button components because two or more SpeedButtons can operate like a group of RadioButtons. To do this, assign GroupIndex values to define SpeedButton groups. If GroupIndex equals 0 (the default value), a SpeedButton works like a spring-loaded on/off switch. Other positive GroupIndex values create groups of SpeedButton objects. For example, set a series of SpeedButton GroupIndexes to 3. Users may then select only one SpeedButton in that group, and selecting one button automatically toggles off the currently selected control.

In Calc32, the memory (*M*), decimal (*D*), hexadecimal (*H*), and binary (*B*) SpeedButtons all have GroupIndex values equal to 1. Selecting one of these buttons pops up one of the others. The selected button stays down until you select another in the group.

One of the problems I had writing Calc32 was assigning event handlers for groups of SpeedButton objects. I wanted to use my own procedure names rather than the ones that Delphi assigns by default. To do that, I performed the following steps:

1. First, I chose one object of the group — for example, the hexadecimal *A* button.

2. I double-clicked the object to create an event handler named by default, ButtonAClick.

3. Next, I used Delphi's Search|Replace command to rename every occurrence of ButtonAClick to DigitButtonClick, which more accurately describes what the procedure does.

4. Finally, I selected all of the buttons in the group, including the original button from Step 1. Using the Object Inspector's Events page tab, I set the shared OnClick event to DigitButtonClick.

Glyphs

A *glyph* is a Windows bitmap displayed on a BitBtn or SpeedButton object. Although there's no restriction on glyph size, the standard image is 16-by-16 pixels, in 16 living colors. In a component, a Glyph property is an object of the TBitmap type.

As shown in Figure 6-3, glyphs may contain from one to four separate images, stored side by side in the bitmap file, each of which must be equal in width and height (usually 16-by-16 pixels). Delphi displays each image to represent a different button state:

1. Up (normal display)

2. Disabled (dimmed; Enabled = False)

3. Down (shifted and possibly dimmed)

4. Stay down (SpeedButtons only)

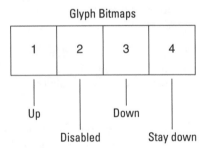

Figure 6-3: Glyph bitmaps may have from one to four side-by-side images, each of which has a different purpose. For example, Delphi uses the second image to display a disabled button.

To display a button in its normal state, Delphi uses the first image. To display a button in its pushed state, Delphi displays the glyph's third image. If the glyph doesn't have a third image, Delphi instead shifts the bitmap down and to the right. Figure 6-4 shows expanded and normal views of the Alarmrng.bmp file supplied with Delphi. Because the bitmap lacks third and fourth images, Delphi shifts the glyph's bits down and to the right to represent pushed button states. You can supply images 3 and 4 to animate a BitBtn or SpeedButton when it's selected.

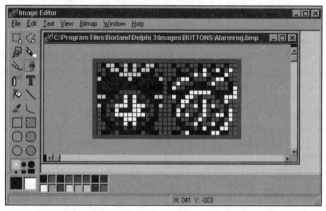

Figure 6-4: The Alarmrng.bmp file contains a two-part glyph. Delphi uses the first image for normal, unpushed buttons, and the second image for disabled buttons.

Loading and assigning glyph bitmaps

When loading a glyph bitmap, set the NumGlyphs property to the number of images it contains. This must be a value from 1 to 4. Normally, Delphi figures out the correct value from the bitmap's size. For example, Delphi assumes that a 32-bit-wide × 16-bit-tall bitmap contains two 16 × 16 glyphs.

You can assign glyph images when you design a form, or you can load bitmap files at run time, perhaps to animate a BitBtn or SpeedButton object, or simply to change its appearance based on an external condition. To load a glyph at run time, insert a BitBtn object into a form, double-click it, and insert these statements into the OnClick event handler (modify the pathname according to where you installed Delphi):

```
BitBtn1.Glyph.LoadFromFile(
  'c:\delphi\images\buttons\alarm.bmp'); { Or another file }
BitBtn1.NumGlyphs := 2;                  { Important step! }
```

The first statement calls the LoadFromFile procedure for the Glyph object to load the Alarm.bmp file supplied with Delphi. The second statement sets the number of glyphs to 2.

Note Always set NumGlyphs to the proper value when loading glyph bitmaps at run time. Delphi automatically calculates the number of glyphs in a bitmap file only at design time.

You can also assign any TBitMap object to a BitBtn's or SpeedButton's Glyph property. However, it's important to understand that Delphi makes a copy of the bitmap to insert into the button object. It is your responsibility to delete from memory any original TBitMap objects that you create. When loading bitmaps from disk files and assigning the resulting bitmap directly to a Glyph property, you do not have to delete anything because the image is copied directly into the object. However, suppose you define a separate TBitMap object, perhaps because you want to use it for more than one purpose. First, declare the TBitMap object, referenced here as MyImage:

```
var
  MyImage: TBitMap;
```

Create the bitmap object in memory by calling the TBitMap class's Create method:

```
MyImage := TBitMap.Create;  { Create MyImage object }
```

You now have an object in memory, referenced by MyImage, into which you can load a bitmap file. You can then assign the object to a BitBtn or a SpeedButton's Glyph property. You can also use MyImage for other purposes. Here's the rest of the code:

```
MyImage.LoadFromFile('c:\delphi\images\buttons\alarm.bmp');
BitBtn1.Glyph := MyImage;
{ ... insert other uses for MyImage here }
MyImage.Free;
```

The first statement calls LoadFromFile for MyImage. The second statement copies the object to a BitBtn's Glyph property. Insert other uses for MyImage where the comment indicates. When you are done using the TBitmap object, free its memory by calling Free. This last step is essential; if you forget to free a TBitmap that you create, portions of it remain in memory even after the program terminates. Delphi applications automatically free any objects owned by another parent object; however, the program must free any other structures such as bitmap pixels associated with an object. If the program doesn't free such structures, the only way to recover the lost memory is to exit the application. This is so because 32-bit Windows allocates resources on a per-process basis. When the process ends (for example, the user exits an application), any orphaned resources are automatically recovered. In 16-bit Windows, however, the only way to recover lost resources is to exit and restart Windows.

A glyph's background color equals the color of the single pixel in the lower-left corner. All other pixels in the glyph of that same color are considered to be transparent—in other words, whatever the user selects as the background color for buttons replaces the glyph's designated background pixels. If users color their buttons fire-engine red, your glyph backgrounds will be equally red-faced, but at least they'll still appear to float on the button surface. Unfortunately, however, any fixed red pixels will blend in with the button's red color, effectively disappearing. The most effective way to guard against this problem is by using as many different colors as possible in your glyph images. That way, your glyphs still look right even to users who actually like Windows' "Hotdog Stand" desktop color scheme.

Note

Normally, the glyph's transparent (background) color defaults to the first pixel in the bitmap data at the bottom-left corner. You can use the TBitmap TransparentColor and the TransparentMode properties to override this default characteristic, however. For example, assign a TColor value such as clAqua to TransparentColor. This automatically changed TransparentMode to tmFixed. To return to using the bottom-left pixel as the transparent color value, set TransparentMode back to its default value, tmAuto.

How to animate a glyph

You can animate glyph bitmaps to display different images when, for example, users click a BitBtn object. Follow these steps to try out the technique:

1. Insert a BitBtn object into a form. I use the default name BitBtn1 here.

2. Select BitBtn1's Glyph property, click the ellipsis button, and load the bitmap file Dooropen.bmp from Delphi's Images\Buttons directory.

3. Insert the following declarations into the TForm1 class's public section (they could also go in the private section):

```
DoorShutBmp: TBitmap;
DoorOpenBmp: TBitmap;
```

4. Initialize the bitmap objects and load images into them by inserting these statements into the form's OnCreate event (copy the two bitmap files to the current directory from Delphi's Images\Buttons directory):

```
DoorShutBmp := TBitmap.Create;
DoorOpenBmp := TBitmap.Create;
DoorShutBmp.LoadFromFile('doorshut.bmp');
DoorOpenBmp.LoadFromFile('dooropen.bmp');
```

5. Free the images by inserting these statements into the form's OnDestroy event handler:

```
DoorShutBmp.Free;
DoorOpenBmp.Free;
```

6. Create a handler for BitBtn1's OnMouseDown event (be sure to select the button object, not the form). Insert this statement into the procedure:

```
BitBtn1.Glyph := DoorShutBmp;
```

7. Create another handler for BitBtn1's OnMouseUp event, and insert this statement into the procedure:

```
BitBtn1.Glyph := DoorOpenBmp;
```

8. Press F9 to run the program. When you click the BitBtn1 object, the door shuts. When you release the mouse, the door opens.

Another way to animate a glyph is by creating one bitmap containing separate images for the button's up and down states. For example, you could combine the Dooropen.bmp and Doorshut.bmp bitmap files, and assign the resulting four-part glyph to a BitBtn object. This way, you eliminate the need to load and free individual bitmap objects at run time.

Button Groups

In busy windows — configuration dialogs, for example — it's a good idea to categorize multiple buttons into groups. Organize button object groups in three general ways:

✦ Use Bevel and Panel objects to create sections in a form that appear indented or raised. Insert buttons into these objects.

✦ Insert buttons into a GroupBox component.

✦ Create a RadioGroup object, which can automatically generate multiple RadioButtons. Simply enter button labels into the RadioGroup's Items array (more on this later).

Using Bevels and Panels

Bevels and *Panels* are visual aids that can help you produce an attractive display. The Bevel component is on the Additional VCL palette; the Panel component is on the Standard palette. Drop these objects onto a form to experiment with the components.

Panel objects can respond to events such as OnClick and OnMouseDown. Panels are akin to simple buttons that don't appear pushed when you click them. The Bevel component looks like a Panel, but is purely visual and recognizes no events. Panels are also useful for creating toolbars and status panels, as the next chapter explains. Panels have window handles, and therefore, they use more system resources than Bevels. However, Panels can contain other controls such as Buttons; Bevels are purely visual, and because they lack window handles, Bevels cannot contain Buttons or other controls.

Figure 6-5 shows a default form with a Panel object and a Bevel object. The Panel has a default caption (Panel1 in the figure), but you can delete the Caption property value to display a blank surface.

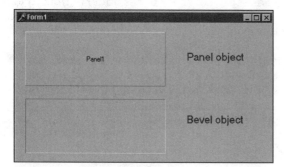

Figure 6-5: A default form with Panel and Bevel objects, which are useful for organizing a busy display into visual sections.

Adjust the BevelOuter, BevelWidth, BorderStyle, and BorderWidth properties for different Panel appearances. Adjust the Shape property to alter Bevel object appearances. (It may seem confusing that Panels use Bevel*xxx* properties to set their appearances, but this is just a naming oddity of no significance. Panels and Bevels are separate types of components.)

Bevels don't have to be boxy. You can also use them to create dividing lines, which some programmers imaginatively call speed bumps and speed dips because they resemble the traffic control barriers in a supermarket parking lot. For example, set a Bevel object's Shape property to bsBottomLine to display a horizontal speed dip, which is useful for carving a window into top and bottom sections. Use bsLeftLine or bsRightLine to create vertical barriers. Change Style to bsRaised to create speed bumps. Figure 6-6 shows examples of a speed bump and speed dip. To make these more visible here, I set the two Bevels' Shape properties to bsBox; however, you normally set them to bsBottomLine, bsFrame, bsLeftLine, bsRightLine, or bsTopLine to create single-line speed bumps and dips.

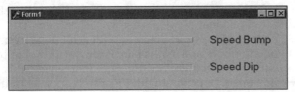

Figure 6-6: A default form with speed bump and speed dip.

Using GroupBoxes

A GroupBox is a standard Windows control that Delphi encapsulates in a component. Use GroupBoxes to create sets of check boxes, radio buttons, and other controls. Users can press Tab to move from one GroupBox to another, and they can press arrow keys and the spacebar to select among grouped controls.

GroupBoxes are mostly useful for organizing radio buttons into logical sets. For example, you can insert several radio buttons into each of two GroupBox objects. Users can then select one button from either set. If you don't insert radio buttons into GroupBoxes, users can only select one of the buttons in the window.

Figure 6-7 shows a default form with two GroupBox objects, each with three radio buttons. To create this window:

1. Insert the two GroupBox components first.

2. Insert RadioButtons into the GroupBox objects.

3. Clicking the mouse pointer inside the GroupBox to insert a RadioButton (or other control) tells Delphi to associate the inserted object with the GroupBox.

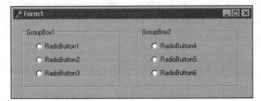

Figure 6-7: GroupBoxes are used to organize radio buttons into logical sets.

For tabbing to work correctly, at least one RadioButton of each group must be selected. Set the Checked property to True for one RadioButton object in each GroupBox. This is a Windows restriction on grouped radio button controls.

If you insert RadioButtons before you create their GroupBoxes, the buttons will not operate as distinct groups. Dragging the RadioButtons into a GroupBox is no help — the objects remain associated with the component in which they were initially dropped (the form or another container control). If you experience this problem, select the RadioButtons, cut them to the clipboard, select the intended GroupBox, and paste the RadioButtons from the clipboard into the selected container. You can also delete the buttons and reinsert them from the VCL palette directly into a GroupBox object, but then you lose whatever property changes you've made to the controls.

To group radio buttons or other control objects at run time, set the button object's Parent property to a target GroupBox. (You can do this only at run time because the Parent property is not available in the Object Inspector window.) For example, to associate three RadioButton objects with GroupBox1, use statements such as these, perhaps in a form's OnCreate event handler:

```
RadioButton1.Parent := GroupBox1;
RadioButton2.Parent := GroupBox1;
RadioButton3.Parent := GroupBox1;
RadioButton1.Checked := True;  { Select one grouped button }
```

A good way to tell if RadioButtons are properly grouped is to drag the GroupBox object. If the RadioButtons follow along like ducks behind their mother, they are associated with that group. If not, the buttons are probably associated with the form. Cut and paste the buttons to fix the problem.

You can also group CheckBox objects, but because these controls operate individually, there's usually no good reason to group them. In most cases, it's probably just as well to use Panel or Bevel objects to visually organize sets of CheckBox objects.

To get radio button groups working as you want when users press the Tab key, you'll probably have to fuss with your form's tabbing order. After creating the GroupBox objects and inserting RadioButton controls, select the form and choose Edit I Tab Order to set the order in which users can press Tab to move among the groups. Next, select each GroupBox object, and again use Edit I Tab Order, but this time, to affect the tab order of the grouped RadioButton objects.

Using RadioGroups

Most developers soon realize that GroupBoxes and RadioButtons are as ornery as bulls in a ring. For a less painful way to create radio button groups, insert a RadioGroup component into a form. Do not insert RadioButton objects into the RadioGroup. Instead, select the RadioGroup's Items property, and double-click its value or click the ellipsis button to open Delphi's String list editor. Enter labels for each radio button in the order you want them to appear. That's all you have to do to create sets of RadioButton controls in a RadioGroup object.

Optionally set the RadioGroup's Columns property to the number of columns for displaying RadioButtons. Figure 6-8 shows four radio buttons in a RadioGroup with Columns equal to 1. Figure 6-9 shows the same RadioGroup object with Columns set to 2.

Figure 6-8: Four radio buttons in a RadioGroup with Columns equal to 1

Figure 6-9: The same buttons from Figure 6-8 but with Columns equal to 2

Use the ItemIndex property to detect the currently selected button. Set ItemIndex to -1 (the default value) to deselect all buttons in the group. Set it to 0 to select the first button, 1 to select the second button, and so on.

You can also create radio buttons in RadioGroup objects at run time. For example, use this variable and procedure to let users enter new radio buttons into a group:

```
var
  S: String;
begin
  if InputQuery('Input', 'Enter Radio Button', S) then
    RadioGroup1.Items.Add(S);
end;
```

The Items array is a string list of type TStrings. Call the list's Add method to insert a new string, which also causes the RadioGroup to create a new RadioButton object using the string as a label. The Items Count property equals the number of strings in the Strings property, and therefore, also equals the number of RadioButtons owned by the RadioGroup. ItemIndex equals the currently selected button's index.

Use these values to iterate through button labels, as in the following sample statement, which calls AnyProcedure (not shown):

```
for I := 0 to RadioGroup1.Items.Count _ 1 do
  AnyProcedure(RadioGroup1.Items.Strings[I]);
```

Or, use a *with* statement to make the preceding code more understandable, and to reduce the two references to RadioGroup1 to one reference:

```
with RadioGroup1, Items do
  for I := 0 to Count - 1 do
    AnyProcedure(Strings[I]);
```

Notice the special syntax for *with*, using commas to separate multiple identifiers. The first line in the preceding example is equivalent to:

```
with RadioGroup1 do with Items do
```

Use ItemIndex to determine the selected button. For example, an *if* statement can take an action for a particular button identified by its label:

```
with RadioGroup1, Items do
  if Strings[ItemIndex] = 'Button2' then...
```

Always set one button to its on state for each RadioGroup object; otherwise, users cannot press Tab to shift the focus to the group (a Windows oddity). Either set ItemIndex to 0 when you design the RadioGroup object, or insert the following code into the form's OnCreate event handler:

```
with RadioGroup1, Items do
if Count > 0 then
  ItemIndex := 0
else
  ItemIndex := -1;
```

You can also use this code in another event handler for RadioGroups that the program builds at run time; in which case you must allow for the possibility that the group has no buttons. In that case, you should set ItemIndex to -1 as demonstrated here.

The TRadioGroup class descends from TCustomGroupBox, which is the immediate ancestor of TGroupBox. GroupBox rules and regulations therefore apply equally to RadioGroup objects. For example, to enable tabbing between groups, preselect one button in each group by setting ItemIndex to a value from 0 to Items.Count - 1.

RadioGroup objects contain two lists that represent the grouped RadioButtons. The Items array contains a string list of button labels, and is available at design time and at run time. The Components array, which is available only at run time, contains references to the actual RadioGroup objects.

To investigate the Components array and related items, insert a RadioGroup object into a form, and enter several button labels into the Item's string list. Insert a Button object and create an OnClick event handler with these statements:

```
with RadioGroup1 do
 if ItemIndex >= 0 then
   ShowMessage('You selected ' + Items.Strings[ItemIndex]);
```

Run the program and click the button to display the currently selected radio button's label. Quit and return to Delphi, and then set a debugger breakpoint on the *with* statement. To do that, single-click the mouse cursor at the extreme left of the line, or move the flashing keyboard cursor to the line and select Run | Add Breakpoint. Either way, Delphi colors the statement stop-sign red, which indicates that the program will halt just before this statement executes.

Run the program again, and click the button. The program halts at the breakpoint. Move the flashing cursor to anywhere in the RadioButton1 identifier, and press Ctrl+F7 to open the debugger's Evaluate/Modify dialog. You should see RadioGroup1 in the Expression field and a list of property values in the Result box. If not, enter RadioGroup1 in the Expression field and click Evaluate. This is a useful technique listing members of objects that are not publicly available through the Object Inspector window.

Lengthy lists of values in objects and records are difficult to decipher in the Evaluate/Modify dialog. To display each property by name along with its value, enter ",R" (don't type the quotes, but don't neglect the comma ahead of R) after the identifier in the Expression field. For example, if you are following along, type the expression **RadioGroup1,R** and press Enter.

 Tip   Enable tool-tip expression evaluation using Tools|Environment Options and clicking the Code Insights page tab. You can then move the cursor to an object name such as RadioGroup1, pause a moment, and see that object's value displayed in a small pop-up window.

You should now see the following values, plus lots of others, in the Evaluate/Modify dialog. Click Evaluate if not. The property name is followed by its associated class method. For example, here are the first two lines from the Result field:

```
Components:<GetComponent>;
ComponentCount:<GetComponentCount>;
```

The Components array contains the RadioButton objects that belong to the RadioGroup. ComponentCount equals the number of those objects. Use these two values to access individual RadioButtons in the RadioGroup object. For example, to set the Checked property to False for all RadioButtons in a group, you can use a *for* loop such as this:

```
with RadioGroup1 do
for I := 0 to ComponentCount - 1 do
  TRadioButton(Components[I]).Checked := False;
```

Or, to switch on a particular button, use this statement:

```
with RadioGroup1 do
   TRadioButton(Components[2]).Checked := True;
```

When referring to the Components array, you must tell the compiler what type of objects the array contains. Do that by using the class name (TRadioButton here) as though it were a function that returns an object of the specified type. Pass the indexed Components reference to this type cast construction. You can then access object properties such as Checked.

If you are following along, get back to Delphi, and press F9 to continue running the program, which is paused at the breakpoint. Quit the program to return to Delphi's design mode. You can then remove the breakpoint or start a new project.

RadioGroups are also useful for designing opinion-survey, option, and multiple-choice forms. Create several RadioGroup objects, and enter blank spaces, punctuation marks, digits or any other characters into the Items array. In this case, you probably don't want full labels — you just want to display the RadioButton control's circles. Set the Columns property equal to the number of buttons, and shrink the RadioGroup object as small as possible. Figure 6-10 shows a hypothetical example that uses RadioGroups for a pychological profile inspired by a psychologist friend who hands out similar tests at parties.

Some versions of Delphi's documentation state that you can put other types of controls (other than radio buttons) into a TRadioGroup object. This is incorrect. You can insert only radio buttons into a RadioGroup object.

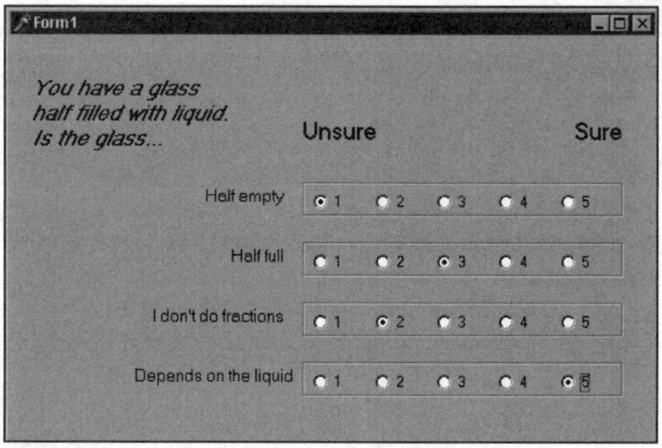

Figure 6-10: RadioGroups are useful for creating multiple-choice quizzes and opinion surveys as in this hypothetical profile.

Other kinds of RadioGroups

As you may know, you can insert RadioButton objects directly into form windows. If you need only one set of radio buttons, you don't have to insert them into a GroupBox and you don't need to use a RadioGroup object. Just insert as many radio buttons as you need into any form.

Although it's not widely known (but not exactly a big secret), you can also group multiple RadioButton objects in Panel components. Try this:

1. Insert two Panels into a form, and then insert several RadioButtons into each panel.

2. Set the Checked property of one RadioButton in each group to True.

3. Run the program.

As this experiment shows, there's no operational difference between a GroupBox and a Panel — at least in terms of their capability for grouping together multiple radio buttons. A GroupBox caption, however, appears on its top border — a Panel displays its caption inside, and you may need to erase it to make room for radio buttons and other controls.

One advantage in using Panels as group boxes is the Panel component's 3D graphics capability, which the GroupBox lacks. As Figure 6-11 illustrates, you can use Panels to create fancy RadioButton sets. The text below each set of RadioButtons shows the property values that produce the illustrated 3D effects. The Fancy application, which has no significant code, is in the Source\Fancy directory in this book's accompanying CD-ROM.

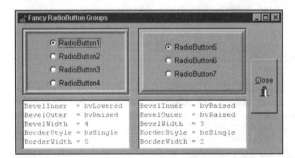

Figure 6-11: The Fancy sample application demonstrates how to use Panel objects to create 3D RadioButton groups.

It's also possible to insert objects of different types into GroupBox and Panel components. For example, a Panel might contain three RadioButtons and two CheckBoxes. Users can press Tab to move among the groups, and the end result might be useful in programs that are largely keyboard driven. Because users select CheckBoxes individually, however, inserting them into GroupBox and Panel components isn't usually advantageous.

Spin Buttons

The Samples page tab on the VCL palette provides two additional button controls, SpinButton and SpinEdit. Assign your own glyphs to these objects' DownGlyph and UpGlyph properties to display custom up and down arrows or other shapes. The two components are:

- ✦ **SpinButton**—A double component with up and down buttons. Clicking one of the buttons calls the OnDownClick or OnUpClick event handler.
- ✦ **SpinEdit**—A SpinButton attached to an edit field. Clicking the button's up or down arrows increases or decreases an integer value in the edit field. Users can also enter values into this field, which also recognizes cut, copy, and paste commands.

Using SpinButton components

To use SpinButton's components, follow these steps:

1. Insert a SpinButton component into a form and insert code into its OnDownClick and OnUpClick event handlers. To follow along, also insert a Label object into the form, and declare the following variable in the TForm1 class's private section:

```
private
  Count: Integer;
```

2. Create a handler for the form's OnCreate event and initialize Count to zero:

```
Count := 0;
```

3. Create event handlers for the SpinButton's OnDownClick and OnUpClick events. Use the programming in Listing 6-1 to increment and decrement Count, and to display Count's value in the label.

Listing 6-1: **Use a SpinButton component and this programming in the OnDownClick and OnUpClick events to increment and decrement a Count variable and display it in a Label object.**

```
procedure TForm1.SpinButton1DownClick(Sender: TObject);
begin
  Dec(Count);
  Label1.Caption := IntToStr(Count);
end;

procedure TForm1.SpinButton1UpClick(Sender: TObject);
begin
  Inc(Count);
  Label1.Caption := IntToStr(Count);
end;
```

Use the UpGlyph and DownGlyph properties in the SpinButton component to display glyphs for the object's up and down buttons. Either select from Delphi's stock arrow bitmaps, or create your own glyphs.

SpinButton glyphs may not contain multiple images, and therefore, to use Delphi's supplied bitmaps (which all contain double images) you must convert them to single-image glyphs. Do that by copying the files you want to another directory — the Arrow1d.bmp and Arrow1u.bmp files, for example, from Delphi's Images\Buttons directory. Open these files in the Image Editor from the Tools menu. For each file, select Image|Attributes, change Width from 32 to 16 (or make it equal to Height), and deselect Scale image to fit. You can then save the converted image. This is the easiest way I've found to chop down a multi-image glyph to a single-image bitmap.

Of course, you can also create your own glyphs using any bitmap editor. Either way, you can now insert your glyphs into a SpinButton object. For example, try these steps:

1. Insert a SpinButton object from the Samples page tab on the VCL palette. Be sure to select the SpinButton component, not SpinEdit.

2. Click the DownGlyph property's ellipsis to open the Image Editor. Load a modified down-arrow image file such as Arrow1d.bmp.

3. Repeat Step 2 for the UpGlyph property to load the modified Arrow1u.Bmp.

4. Depending on the glyph bitmap sizes, you may have to adjust the SpinButton object's dimensions to show the glyphs in full.

Using SpinEdit components

The SpinEdit component combines a SpinButton with an Edit input field to create a spin button with full editing capabilities, including cut, copy, and paste commands. Figure 6-12 shows sample SpinEdit and SpinButton objects from the SpinButt application on the CD-ROM in the Source\SpinButt directory. Listing 6-2 shows the application's source code.

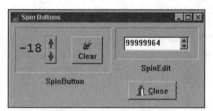

Figure 6-12: The SpinButt sample application shows SpinEdit and SpinButton objects.

SpinButton and SpinEdit controls are superceded by the relatively new UpDown component. Unless you are using an earlier version of Delphi, or if you need to provide backwards compatibility, you might want to use UpDown objects instead of SpinButtons and SpinEdits. However, there's nothing wrong with these components, and you should not hesitate using them if they provide the features you need. After the next section, I explain how to use the new UpDown component.

Listing 6-2: **Spinbutt\Main.pas**

```
unit Main;

interface

uses
   SysUtils, Windows, Messages, Classes, Graphics, Controls,
   Forms, Dialogs, Spin, StdCtrls, ExtCtrls, Buttons;

type
   TMainForm = class(TForm)
     SpinButton1: TSpinButton;
     Label1: TLabel;
     SpinEdit1: TSpinEdit;
```

(continued)

Listing 6-2 *(continued)*

```
    SpinEdit: TLabel;
    SpinLabel: TLabel;
    BitBtn1: TBitBtn;
    Bevel1: TBevel;
    Bevel2: TBevel;
    BitBtn2: TBitBtn;
    procedure FormCreate(Sender: TObject);
    procedure SpinButton1DownClick(Sender: TObject);
    procedure SpinButton1UpClick(Sender: TObject);
    procedure BitBtn1Click(Sender: TObject);
    procedure SetSpinButtonCaption;
  private
    { Private declarations }
    Count: Integer;
  public
    { Public declarations }
  end;

var
  MainForm: TMainForm;

implementation

{$R *.DFM}

const
  minCount = -99;
  maxCount = 99;

procedure TMainForm.SetSpinButtonCaption;
begin
  SpinLabel.Caption := IntToStr(Count);
end;

procedure TMainForm.FormCreate(Sender: TObject);
begin
  Count := 0;
end;

procedure TMainForm.SpinButton1DownClick(Sender: TObject);
begin
  if Count > minCount then Dec(Count);
  SetSpinButtonCaption;
end;
```

```
procedure TMainForm.SpinButton1UpClick(Sender: TObject);
begin
  if Count < maxCount then Inc(Count);
  SetSpinButtonCaption;
end;

procedure TMainForm.BitBtn1Click(Sender: TObject);
begin
  Count := 0;
  SetSpinButtonCaption;
end;

end.
```

The SpinEdit component has an internal Button object of the SpinButton type. (The name Button is an unfortunate choice—it is not a Button component, but rather a SpinButton object named Button.) Use a SpinEdit's Button as you do a stand-alone SpinButton. For example, to assign up and down glyph images of type TBitmap, you can insert statements such as these:

```
SpinEdit1.Button.UpGlyph := NewUpGlyph;
SpinEdit2.Button.DownGlyph := NewDownGlyph;
```

Static Text (TStaticText)

Delphi offers a relatively new component for displaying labels, StaticText, on the Additional palette. Similar to the Standard Label component, the StaticText component is useful for creating interactive labels that users can click with the mouse.

Note

Technically speaking, the TStaticText class is similar to TLabel, except that TStaticText is derived from TWinControl. Label objects, in other words, don't have window handles; StaticText objects do. In cases where an accelerator key must belong to a control with a window handle, use StaticText instead of Label.

The StaticText component has three properties not found in the Label component. The new properties are:

✦ **BorderStyle**—Set this to sbsNone (no border), sbsSingle (single black line border), or sbsSunken (three-dimensional appearance). Except for sbsNone, you might want to set AutoSize to False; otherwise, the control size is set automatically depending on how much Caption text it displays.

✦ **TabOrder**—Set this to the tab order of the StaticText item. Because this component has a window handle, it may receive the input focus (although users can't type into it).

✦ **TabStop**—Set this True to add the StaticText object to the list of others that receive the input focus when the user presses Tab.

Two Label component styles are not found in StaticText. These are:

✦ **Transparent**—When this property is True, the background of a Label object does not obscure any other control or the window. In conjunction with the Color property, you can set Transparent to False to explicitly color the background (which also displays the text faster than when Transparent is True). StaticText objects are never Transparent, and therefore, they lack this property. However, to create a StaticText control that *looks* transparent, simply set its Color property the same as whatever object is beneath the text.

✦ **WordWrap**—With Label objects, you can optionally set this property True to automatically break long lines of text between words. StaticText objects always wrap lengthy text within their defined size. Set AutoSize False when displaying lengthy text in a StaticText component; otherwise, the control does not wrap its text but instead displays one line, no matter how long.

Note   The Label and StaticText components respond to the same set of events. However, as explained next, providing visual feedback that a Label has been clicked is more difficult, and usually requires graphics programming, than it is for a StaticText object.

On the CD-ROM   The StaticText component is useful for creating text objects that users can select by clicking with the mouse. The StaticDemo application in Listing 6-3 demonstrates how to do this, and also illustrates the three different styles of StaticText objects. The program is on the CD-ROM in the Source\StaticDemo directory. Figure 6-13 shows the program's display.

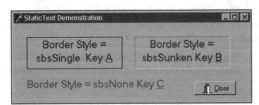

Figure 6-13: The StaticDemo application demonstrates StaticText sytles, and also shows how to create text items that users can click with the mouse.

Listing 6-3: **StaticDemo\Main.pas**

```pascal
unit Main;

interface

uses
  Windows, Messages, SysUtils, Classes, Graphics, Controls,
  Forms, Dialogs,  StdCtrls, Buttons;

type
  TMainForm = class(TForm)
    StaticText2: TStaticText;
    StaticText1: TStaticText;
    StaticText3: TStaticText;
    BitBtn1: TBitBtn;
    procedure StaticText1MouseDown(Sender: TObject;
      Button: TMouseButton; Shift: TShiftState; X, Y: Integer);
    procedure StaticText1MouseUp(Sender: TObject;
      Button: TMouseButton; Shift: TShiftState; X, Y: Integer);
    procedure StaticText1Click(Sender: TObject);
  private
    { Private declarations }
  public
    { Public declarations }
  end;

var
  MainForm: TMainForm;

implementation

{$R *.DFM}
var
  SavedStyle: TStaticBorderStyle;

{ Change static text border style to indicate its selection }
procedure TMainForm.StaticText1MouseDown(Sender: TObject;
  Button: TMouseButton; Shift: TShiftState; X, Y: Integer);
begin
  with Sender as TStaticText do
  begin
    SavedStyle := BorderStyle;
    if BorderStyle = sbsSunken
      then BorderStyle := sbsSingle
      else BorderStyle := sbsSunken;
  end;
end;
```

(continued)

Listing 6-3 *(continued)*

```
{ Reset static text border style when mouse button released }
procedure TMainForm.StaticText1MouseUp(Sender: TObject;
  Button: TMouseButton; Shift: TShiftState; X, Y: Integer);
begin
  with Sender as TStaticText do
    BorderStyle := SavedStyle;
end;

{ Make a sound when text object is clicked }
procedure TMainForm.StaticText1Click(Sender: TObject);
var
  S: String;
begin
  MessageBeep(0);
  S := TStaticText(Sender).Name;
  ShowMessage('You selected ' + S);
end;

end.
```

The demonstration program shows one way to give visual feedback when users click a StaticText object. The MouseDown and MouseUp event handlers are assigned to all three of the StaticText objects in the program's form, each of which has a different BorderStyle property value.

When the user clicks the mouse on one of the StaticText objects, the MouseDown event handler saves the current BorderStyle in a global variable and then changes the style to something else. So the user receives a visual confirmation that the control recognizes the mouse click. When the user releases the mouse, the MouseUp event handler resets the BorderStyle property to its saved value, which restores the control's original appearance.

In both of these cases, it is necessary to use a statement like this:

```
with Sender as TStaticText do
  BorderStyle := SavedStyle;
```

The Sender parameter passed to the event handlers equals the object that the user clicked. Because the form also has a BorderStyle property, which is of a different type, it is necessary to use a *with* statement or other indicator to tell the compiler which BorderStyle property to use. Another way to do that is to use a statement such as:

```
StaticText1.BorderStyle := sbsSunken;
```

Without the object name and a period, BorderStyle is ambiguous. When using the BorderStyle property in a program statement, if you receive the error message "Incompatible types: 'TFormBorderStyle' and 'TStaticBorderStyle'," use one of the preceding two techniques to resolve the conflict.

The third and final event handler in the sample application sounds a tone to indicate the StaticText object was selected, and also displays a message containing the object's name. This demonstrates how you can use the Sender property to determine which StaticText item the user selected. Or, you could program separate OnClick event handlers for each StaticText component.

Up-Down Button Controls

Another relatively new component makes it easy to create up and down buttons, which are typically used to select values or scroll through a set of items in an edit window or label. The only way to do this in early versions of Delphi was to use the Sample SpinButton component, demonstrated earlier in this chapter. However, because this is only a Sample component, and not one of Delphi's official standards, programmers are reluctant to use it for fear that Borland might not support SpinButton objects in the future.

For my money, the UpDown component on the Win32 palette is superior to SpinButton, and I recommend using UpDown objects from now on. They are simple to associate with other controls such as StaticText and Edit objects, and as native Windows controls, they ensure a consistent appearance with other software interfaces.

To compare UpDown and SpinButton components, I wrote the sample UpDown Demo application on the CD-ROM. Figure 6-14 shows the application's display. Listing 6-4 shows the program's source code. Open the UpDownDemo.dpr project file and press F9 to compile and run the program in Delphi. Click the buttons to the left of the StaticText items. The UpDown object is automatically associated with its text object; the SpinButton object requires programming to do the same.

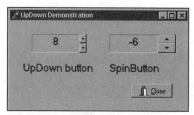

Figure 6-14: The UpDownDemo application compares a native Win32 UpDown component with Delphi's SpinButton on the Samples palette.

Listing 6-4: **UpDownDemo\Main.pas**

```pascal
unit Main;

interface

uses
  Windows, Messages, SysUtils, Classes, Graphics, Controls,
  Forms, Dialogs, StdCtrls, Spin, ComCtrls, Buttons;

type
  TMainForm = class(TForm)
    UpDown1: TUpDown;
    SpinButton1: TSpinButton;
    Label1: TLabel;
    Label2: TLabel;
    BitBtn1: TBitBtn;
    StaticText1: TStaticText;
    StaticText2: TStaticText;
    procedure SpinButton1UpClick(Sender: TObject);
    procedure SpinButton1DownClick(Sender: TObject);
  private
    { Private declarations }
  public
    { Public declarations }
  end;

var
  MainForm: TMainForm;

implementation

{$R *.DFM}

{ These constants and the two event handlers are needed
  by SpinButton components to associate them with another
  control, a StaticText object in this demonstration. The
  new UpDown component needs none of this programming because
  it can be automatically associated with another control. }
const
  Min = -10;
  Max = +10;

{ Respond to user clicking the SpinButton's Up button }
procedure TMainForm.SpinButton1UpClick(Sender: TObject);
var
  V: Integer;
begin
  V := StrToInt(StaticText2.Caption);
  if V = Max
    then V := Min
```

```
      else inc(V);
  StaticText2.Caption := IntToStr(V);
end;

{ Respond to user clicking the SpinButton's Down button }
procedure TMainForm.SpinButton1DownClick(Sender: TObject);
var
  V: Integer;
begin
  V := StrToInt(StaticText2.Caption);
  if V = Min
    then V := Max
    else dec(V);
  StaticText2.Caption := IntToStr(V);
end;

end.
```

None of the programming in the sample listing is needed with UpDown controls —
they are easy to associate with text labels and edit fields. For example, in this
case, to associate the UpDown control with its text item at left, I simply set the
UpDown1 object's Associate property to StaticText1. The control takes care of all
the display details of converting numeric values to strings and displaying them in
the text window. These steps are done manually for the SpinButton control as
shown in the listing.

UpDown component properties

The UpDown component offers a number of interesting properties you can try.
Some of the more useful properties are:

 ✦ **AlignButton** — Set this property to udLeft or udRight to glue the buttons to
   one side or the other of an associated control. This property has no effect
   unless Associate is set to the name of another control. When this property is
   used, attempts to manually change the position of the UpDown buttons
   relative to the associated control will not work.

 ✦ **ArrowKeys** — When True, this property enables keyboard up- and down-arrow
   keys to "click" the control's buttons. The UpDown object must have the input
   focus (set TabStop to True).

 ✦ **Associate** — Set this property to the name of another object, which will most
   likely be a Label, StaticText, or Edit component. Use AlignButton to place the
   UpDown control to one side or the other of its associated control. Associating
   a control with an UpDown object is all you need to do to provide automatic
   sequencing of values in the control.

✦ **Cursor** — Select a cursor shape if you want it to change when users point the mouse to the UpDown buttons.

✦ **Increment** — Each time the user clicks a button the value of the UpDown control varies by the value set in Increment.

✦ **Max, Min** — Limit the control's range by setting these two values. Normally, Min should be less than Max; however, if Min is greater than Max, the UpDown control appears to work backwards (clicking the up button, for instance, reduces the control's value). Unless you really want to confuse your program's users, be sure that Min is less than Max.

✦ **Orientation** — Although named UpDown, the component can display its buttons horizontally (udHorizontal) or vertically (udVertical). Use whichever setting you want.

✦ **Position** — The Position property equals the current value of the UpDown control. (So, why didn't they name it Value?) Read this property at run time to determine the currently selected value.

✦ **Thousands** — Set to True if you want punctuation between sets of three digits in controls with Position values of four or more digits.

✦ **Wrap** — When this property is False, increments and decrements halt when the control reaches its maximum or minimum value. When this property is True, values wrap around. For example, if Max equals 100, attempting to increment the control to 101 causes it to wrap around to the value of Min.

Responding to events

UpDown buttons can respond to a few events, but only two are probably needed: OnChanging and OnClick. Delphi calls the OnChanging event handler when the Position value of the UpDown component is about to change. The event handler procedure is declared something like this:

```
procedure TMainForm.UpDown1Changing(Sender: TObject;
  var AllowChange: Boolean);
```

As usual, Sender indicates the component that triggered the event. Inside the event handler, set AllowChange to True to enable the UpDown control to alter the value of Position. Set AllowChange to False to cancel the control's operation, and not change Position's value. Usually, you use this event handler to provide explicit limits on the value of Position, and also when an UpDown object is not associated with another control. For example, rather than disable an UpDown object, you might use the value of a check box to determine whether to allow users to click the control. The programming for the OnChanging event handler might be written like this:

```
begin
  if CheckBox1.Checked
    then AllowChange := True
    else AllowChange := False;
end;
```

The second UpDown component event you are likely to use is OnClick. This event fires before OnChanging. Use OnClick to respond to the user's selection of the control's arrow buttons. The OnClick event handler procedure is declared as:

```
procedure TMainForm.UpDown1Click(Sender: TObject;
    Button: TUDBtnType);
```

Sender indicates which UpDown button was selected in the case where multiple controls share the same event handler. The Button parameter indicates which of the two arrow buttons the user clicked. When Button equals btNext, the user clicked the up or right arrow; when Button equals btPrev, the user clicked the down or left arrow.

You might use an OnClick event handler to perform some operation before the value of the UpDown control changes. Remember that OnClick fires before OnChanging, and that only when OnChanging returns AllowChange equal to True does the value of Position change up or down by the amount set in Increment.

Expert-User Tips

✦ A GroupBox can have a PopupMenu separate from a form's PopupMenu. Assign any PopupMenu object to a GroupBox's PopupMenu property, similar to the way you designate a form's PopupMenu. Using multiple GroupBox objects in a form is a good way to design multiple floating pop-up menus that depend on where users click the right mouse button.

✦ To create buttons that appear and disappear in response to commands or various program conditions, set a button's Visible property to True or False. You may do this for any of the components described in this chapter, as well as most other Delphi components.

✦ Double-click any value in a Color property (click the value at right; not the name) to open the Color Editor window. Select any color, or use the Define Custom Colors button to open another part of the editor that allows programming custom colors using red, green, and blue values, or alternatively, hue, saturation, and luminance values.

✦ Enter text into a SpeedButton's Hint property, and set ShowHint to True. Users then see a small hint box when they rest the mouse cursor on the button.

✦ Use a BitBtn's Spacing property to adjust the amount of space between a glyph image and the button's caption. The default value is 4. Use -1 to center the text between the image and the button edge. Set Spacing to 0 if you want no extra pixels between the image and the text. The SpeedButton component, which has no Caption, also has a Spacing property that you can use to adjust glyph placement.

✦ Although Panels are most useful as purely visual objects, you may create event handlers for them. For example, create an OnClick handler to perform an action when users click a Panel object. Another highly useful event is OnResize, typically used for Panels aligned to a window's client area. When users resize the window, the Panel's OnResize event handler can adjust the positions of controls inside its window.

✦ The SpinButton component described in this chapter uses an object of the undocumented TTimerSpeedButton class. Based on TSpeedButton, a TTimerSpeedButton creates a Timer object that repeatedly simulates a button click while you hold down the mouse. The component does this by calling its own Click method, which simulates an OnClick event. See the Spin.pas file in Delphi's Source\Samples directory for the source code to the TTimerSpeedButton class.

✦ Any container control can group radio buttons, check boxes, and other component objects. For example, if you want two radio button groups without borders, use TPanels as the containers and turn off their borders.

✦ Use the OnClick and OnChanging events with an UpDown component when it is not associated with another control. Normally, when associated with an edit or text control, UpDown events are not needed.

Projects to Try

6-1: Write a program that displays Bevel and Panel objects in many possible configurations. You'll find this useful as a guide to creating new Bevels and Panels in applications. Your program should allow users to input object properties and instantly see their effects.

6-2: Modify Calc32 to use double-precision 64-bit integer values. Hint: Use the Int64 data type.

6-3: Create glyphs for Calc32's SpeedButtons and generally spruce up the calculator's user interface.

6-4: Try the animation technique suggested in this chapter. First, combine the Doorshut.bmp and Dooropen.bmp files using Delphi's Image Editor. The resulting file should contain four separate glyph images, each of the size 16-by-16 pixels. Assign the modified glyph to a BitBtn object and run the program —the door shuts when you click the button. You might want to start a library of animated glyph images.

6-5: Write a glyph catalog program (Glyphlst) that displays all the glyph patterns in Delphi's Images\Buttons directory.

6-6: Write a program that displays four SpeedButton objects showing the four possible states of its glyph bitmap (use the AllowAllUp, Down, and Enabled properties). To the SpeedButtons, assign a glyph bitmap at run time, perhaps selected from a file directory.

6-7: Advanced. Write a floating-point calculator, using Calc32 as a guide. Use the Double (8-byte) or Extended (10-byte) data types to store values internally.

Summary

✦ Windows provides three types of standard buttons — push buttons, check boxes, and radio buttons. Delphi encapsulates these standard controls into Button, CheckBox and RadioButton components.

✦ Use the form's Components array to access all objects — for example, to disable all but one button control in a window.

✦ CheckBoxes normally operate as on/off toggles, but they can also be three-way switches by setting AllowGrayed True. Users can then check the box to enable, disable, and gray its check mark.

✦ You may color CheckBox and RadioButton controls, but due to a limitation in Windows, you may not color Button objects. For a more colorful button, use the BitBtn component.

✦ BitBtn and SpeedButton components can display bitmap glyphs that represent a control's purpose. A glyph is a Windows bitmap represented as a TBitmap object, and is usually 16-by-16-pixels in 16 colors. However, there are no restrictions on a glyph's size. A glyph may have from one to four separate images that represent a button's various states.

✦ SpeedButton objects normally appear in toolbars (see the next chapter), but as this chapter's Calc32 application demonstrates, you also can use SpeedButtons as stand-alone objects.

✦ Use the GroupBox component to logically group multiple controls. GroupBoxes usually contain RadioButton objects, but they may contain other controls. Users can press Tab to move the focus from one GroupBox to another.

✦ Use the RadioGroup component for a simpler method of creating sets of RadioButtons. Enter button labels into the RadioGroup's Items property.

✦ Panel and Bevel objects are purely visual components, but they are useful for organizing a busy display full of buttons and other controls.

✦ The Samples page tab on the VCL palette provides two additional button controls, SpinButton and SpinEdit. Assign your own glyphs to these objects' DownGlyph and UpGlyph properties to display custom up and down arrows or other shapes.

✦ Use the StaticText component to create labels that have window handles. The StaticText component is useful also for creating text areas that users can click like buttons.

✦ Use the UpDown component instead of SpinButtons and SpinEdits to associate up and down arrows with labels, static text, and edit objects.

The next chapter explains how to use SpeedButton and Panel components to create toolbars and status panels — two interface elements that practically every Windows application should have. We also take a look at a relatively new invention: Coolbars.

✦   ✦   ✦

Creating Toolbars, Coolbars, and Status Panels

One of the hallmarks of a well-written Windows program is a toolbar of speed buttons for quickly selecting commands with a mouse. Toolbar buttons are to the mouse what hot keys are to the keyboard — shortcuts for power users who don't want to waste time opening menus to select commands. This chapter explains how to create toolbars in Delphi applications.

This chapter also explains how to create Coolbars, which can contain one or more *bands* that can hold any windowed control. For example, a Coolbar can display a set of buttons, a drop-down list, check boxes, Internet hot-link buttons, and other controls. (If you have Microsoft's Internet Explorer, you are familiar with Coolbars — there's one at the top of the Explorer window that displays browser buttons and the URL address selector.) Users can click and drag the mouse to reorganize Coolbar panels.

A related interface element is a status panel, which usually appears at the bottom of a window, and is often divided into multiple sections. For example, a text editor's status panel might display the line and column numbers for the current cursor position. Or, a panel can display the date and time to remind clock watchers how late they are on their deadlines. This chapter shows different ways to create status panels using Delphi components, and also with Win32 StatusBar objects.

Note Because Delphi has different ways to create toolbars and status panels (but only one way to create a Coolbar), this chapter uses the generic terms *toolbar, Coolbar,* and *status panel* for these interface elements. The capitalized words ToolBar, Coolbar, and StatusBar refer to Delphi's Win32 components.

Components

Following are some Delphi components for creating toolbars, Coolbars, and status panels:

✦ **Animate** — Coolbars often contain an Animate object to provide some animated graphics for an otherwise boringly static display. This chapter's Coolbar demonstration shows how to create an attractive animated icon, which has the practical purpose of letting users know that the program is actively running. Palette: Win32.

✦ **CoolBand** — Objects of this component type, which is not on the VCL palette, are stored in and managed by a Coolbar object. Each CoolBand may hold another windowed control such as a ToolBar or ComboBox. Palette: None.

✦ **Coolbar** — Similar to a toolbar in style, but much more sophisticated in operation, a Coolbar is a multisectional object that is divided into areas called bands (see the CoolBand component). Delphi's Coolbar component provides a wrapper for a Windows Coolbar control, which can display and manage any number of windowed controls (specifically, those components that are descended from TWinControl). Users can configure Coolbars at run time by clicking and dragging with the mouse. Palette: Win32.

✦ **Panel** — Use this component to create a platform for building toolbars and status panels. You can alter the platform's 3D appearance to make it look like an indented crater or a raised plateau. When used as a toolbar, a Panel object holds SpeedButtons, but a Panel may also serve as a general-purpose container that can hold other panels and text for building sectional display areas. Palette: Standard.

✦ **SpeedButton** — This chapter explains how to use SpeedButtons to build toolbars using Panel objects. Also review the preceding chapter for more information on the SpeedButton component's properties and events. Palette: Additional.

✦ **StatusBar** — One way to create a status panel is to use a StatusBar component, which is a wrapper for a native 32-bit Windows control. StatusBars, which typically appear at the bottom of a window, contain one or more StatusPanel components to segment their displays. Palette: Win32.

✦ **StatusPanel** — This component forms a section, called a panel, of a StatusBar, and is displayed and maintained by the StatusBar component. (Don't confuse this component with the more general-purpose Panel.) Palette: None.

✦ **ToolBar** — This component provides an alternate way to create toolbars in an application window. The ToolBar component is a wrapper for a native 32-bit Windows control that can display ToolButton objects in a variety of styles. Use a ToolBar to give your applications a Web-browser-like appearance and to meet Windows 98 interface guidelines. Palette: Win32.

✦ **ToolButton** — A ToolBar can display and maintain one or more ToolButton objects, which are similar to SpeedButtons. Like SpeedButtons, ToolButtons can display icons, but they can also display text labels. Also, ToolButtons can have several associated images that change their appearance when the user points to or clicks a button. Palette: None.

Toolbars

The Tabs application in this chapter demonstrates toolbar and status panel techniques. Figure 7-1 shows a sample toolbar for Tabs. Although the program's source code is too lengthy to list entirely here, all source files are on the CD-ROM in the Source\Tabs directory. Open the Tabs.dpr project file to inspect the application files. This is an example of a program that uses multiple units, all but one of which are associated with visual forms. For example, the Inidata unit in the Source\Inidata directory provides initialization file services for the Tabs application.

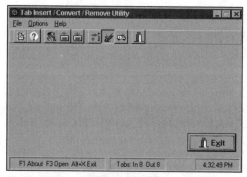

Figure 7-1: The Tabs application removes and inserts tab control codes in text files, and can also convert tab interval settings.

The Tabs application is more than a demonstration program—it's a useful utility that you might want to keep on your disk long after you're done with this book. Use Tabs to insert and remove tab control codes from text files, and also to convert files with different tab settings. For example, Tabs can convert a file that uses four-space tabs to one that uses standard eight-space tabs. The program can also convert tabs to spaces, or replace spaces with tabs (which is also a file compression technique, though not often thought of as such). To use the program, select the Convert, Remove, or Insert SpeedButtons, then click the Open button to open a file. Answer Yes to process the file. Use the Options commands and buttons to configure the program.

Be sure to back up all files *before* processing with Tabs! Some combinations of tab options can produce unwanted effects, and you might need to try different settings to get the results you want. After processing a file, it might not be possible to recover that file's original text formatting, so backups are essential. I designed the program to save original files renamed with the extension .bak, but I strongly suggest that you keep separate backup copies of your original files *in addition* to those that Tabs creates.

By the way, I originally wrote Tabs in Turbo Vision for DOS using Turbo Pascal. It took only a few hours work to convert the program for Delphi, and about ten minutes to convert it to Delphi 3 and 4 (only a few changes to the Inidata unit were needed, plus minor display adjustments). All the user-interface programming is new, but the tab-processing procedures and functions are largely unchanged from the original code.

Creating a toolbar

A toolbar consists of a Panel object and one or more SpeedButtons. To create a toolbar, follow these steps:

1. Insert a Panel component into a form. The default Panel Height value is 41. I prefer 25, but you can use any value you want.

2. Assign an appropriate Name to the Panel such as ToolbarPanel. This is the name that Tabs uses.

Although Delphi provides the Win32 ToolBar components for creating toolbars, this section shows how to create toolbars using other types of objects. Because ToolBars are typically inserted into a Coolbar, I discuss the ToolBar component along with this chapter's Coolbar information.

3. Set the ToolbarPanel's Align property to alBottom or alTop, depending on whether you want the toolbar to appear at the top or bottom of the window. You can also design toolbars to appear at the left (alLeft) or right (alRight) borders, although the standard location is at the top of the window's client area, just below the window's menu bar.

4. For a toolbar with two or more rows of SpeedButtons, insert multiple panels into a form and set their Align properties to alTop. This stacks the panels like appliances bolted under a countertop. You can then insert SpeedButtons into the Panel objects.

5. After creating the Panel, delete its Caption and insert as many SpeedButton objects as you need. Always create the Panel first, and then drop SpeedButtons onto it — this lets Delphi know that the Panel is to own the SpeedButtons. I name my SpeedButtons OpenSB and ConfigSB, which reminds me of the object component types. You probably want to create OnClick event handlers for all buttons, or you can share handlers with menu commands and buttons.

That's all you need to do to create a toolbar of SpeedButtons. Simple, no?

However, there's more to toolbar management than meets the eye. For instance, you probably want to add Hint text to each button. To do that, type a brief description in a SpeedButton's Hint property, and set ShowHint to True. A small information box then pops into view when the mouse cursor rests on the button for about a second. There's little reason not to add hints to your toolbar buttons — they go a long way toward making programs easy to use.

Panels can also respond to events. For example, you can create an OnClick event handler for a Panel object to perform an action when the user clicks, not on a button, but inside the Panel itself. Later in this chapter, I explain how to use this feature to create a floating toolbar that users can click and drag around the window. In general, however, it's probably best not to handle events for Panels — users intuitively know that they can click buttons in toolbars, but providing a clickable toolbar might be more confusing than helpful. (A Coolbar is probably a better choice if you want to provide this level of interaction in your user interface. See Coolbars in this chapter for more information on creating run-time configurable toolbars.)

SpeedButtons

When designing a toolbar, consider whether you need spring-loaded buttons that pop back up as soon as you release the mouse button, or a set of objects that operate like radio buttons. For example, you can create a "sticky" SpeedButton that stays down when pushed; and you can also create SpeedButton sets in which clicking one button deselects another.

A spring-loaded SpeedButton is the easiest to create. Just insert a SpeedButton object into a toolbar Panel, and create a handler for its OnClick event. (See the preceding chapter for more information on programming SpeedButtons, assigning them glyph bitmaps, and animating button images.) Spring-loaded buttons are useful for operations such as opening a file, printing, and other tasks that commence immediately. Alternatively, you can create an on/off SpeedButton that stays down when you click it, and then pops up when you click it again.

On/off (sticky) SpeedButtons

This type of sticky toolbar button is useful for options that select program features. In a word processor, for example, a sticky SpeedButton might choose text styles such as bold face, italics, and underlining. Users might click a button once to convert selected text to bold; and then click the button again to return text to normal.

Follow these steps to create a sticky on/off SpeedButton:

1. Set the SpeedButton's GroupIndex to any nonzero value that no other control in the toolbar uses.

2. Set the SpeedButton's AllowAllUp property to True.

3. Optionally set the SpeedButton's Down property to True to display the button initially in its pressed state.

A sample application, Toolbar1, demonstrates spring-loaded and sticky SpeedButtons. The program's files are on the CD-ROM in the Source\Toolbar1 directory. Figure 7-2 shows the program's display. The left SpeedButton is sticky; it stays down when you click it. Do that now and select Close, which prompts you for confirmation before ending the program, as shown in Figure 7-3. Release the left SpeedButton to exit normally without displaying a message dialog. Listing 7-1 shows the program's source code.

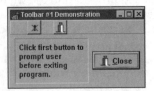

Figure 7-2: The Toolbar1 demonstration uses two SpeedButtons in a simple toolbar. The left button is a sticky SpeedButton that stays down when you click it.

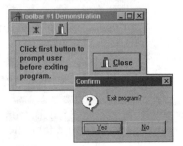

Figure 7-3: When the toolbar's leftmost SpeedButton is down, Toolbar1 requests confirmation before ending.

Listing 7-1: **Toolbar1\Main.pas**

```pascal
unit Main;

interface

uses
  SysUtils, Windows, Messages, Classes, Graphics,
  Controls, Forms, Dialogs, StdCtrls, Buttons, ExtCtrls;

type
  TMainForm = class(TForm)
    Panel1: TPanel;
    PromptSB: TSpeedButton;
    ExitSB: TSpeedButton;
    CloseBitBtn: TBitBtn;
    Label1: TLabel;
    Bevel1: TBevel;
    procedure ExitSBClick(Sender: TObject);
    procedure FormActivate(Sender: TObject);
  private
    { Private declarations }
  public
    { Public declarations }
  end;

var
  MainForm: TMainForm;

implementation

{$R *.DFM}

procedure TMainForm.ExitSBClick(Sender: TObject);
begin
  if not PromptSB.Down then
    Close
  else if MessageDlg('Exit program?',mtConfirmation,
    [mbYes, mbNo], 0) = mrYes then
    Close;
end;

procedure TMainForm.FormActivate(Sender: TObject);
begin
  ExitSB.Glyph := CloseBitBtn.Glyph;
end;

end.
```

Toolbar1's Main.pas file demonstrates two interesting techniques for working with SpeedButtons. For a sticky button, you can use an *if* statement to detect whether the button is down. For example, see the first line in procedure ExitSBClick, which executes a statement if the PromptSB button is not down:

```
if not promptSB.Down then ...
```

Secondly, the module shows how to steal a glyph from another object for displaying on a SpeedButton's face. Notice in Figure 7-2 that the SpeedButton on the right and the Close push button have the same glyph. The SpeedButton steals this image at run time by executing the following statement in the form's OnActivate or OnCreate event handler:

```
ExitSB.Glyph := CloseBitBtn.Glyph;
```

SpeedButton groups

Creating a set of sticky SpeedButtons that operate like radio buttons is a fairly basic procedure. Just select all buttons in the group and set their GroupIndex properties to any nonzero value that is not used by any other toolbar control. With this setup, clicking an unselected button causes the currently selected button to pop back up.

Initially, all buttons may be in the up state. Once users click a button, however, at least one button is always down. If you want users to be able to deselect all buttons in a group, set the AllowAllUp property to True for each button which can return to an up state.

At design time, you may set a SpeedButton's Down property to True to initially display it in a down state. For this to work, however, you must set the button's GroupIndex to a nonzero value. Use a unique value among all buttons unless you intend to group them as you would a set of radio buttons.

Tip   If a SpeedButton's Down property refuses to change to True, set the button's GroupIndex property to any unused nonzero value. If the SpeedButton gets stuck in the down position — that is, if Down refuses to change back to False — set AllowAllUp to True. You can then reset Down to pop up the button.

The Tabs program (refer back to Figure 7-1) demonstrates how to program a group of toolbar SpeedButtons to operate like radio buttons. Run Tabs and select the Insert, Remove, and Convert buttons to select the operation you want to perform on a text file. One of these three buttons is always in the down state. The other toolbar buttons in Tabs operate as spring-loaded push buttons.

Dynamic toolbars

By using a combination of MouseDown, MouseUp, and OnClick events, you can create dynamic toolbars that users can configure at run time. The sample application Toolbar2, shown in Figure 7-4, demonstrates these techniques and also shows some ways to manipulate component objects and event handlers using program statements. The program's files are on the CD-ROM in the Source\Toolbar2 directory.

Figure 7-4: Click the SpeedButtons in Toolbar2's form to move them into the toolbar. You can then click the buttons to perform their actions.

Run the program and click the SpeedButton objects in the form to move them into the toolbar. After moving a button into the toolbar, click the button to perform an action such as displaying a calendar (See Figure 7-5). Click the Calendar button again to remove the calendar. You must move the Exit SpeedButton into the toolbar before you can click it to end the program. Listing 7-2 shows the program's source code.

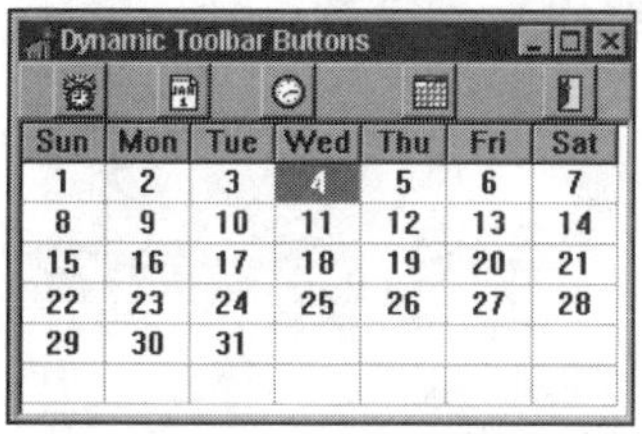

Figure 7-5: After moving Toolbar2's SpeedButtons into the toolbar, click the Calendar button to display a monthly calendar.

Listing 7-2: **Toolbar2\Main.pas**

```
unit Main;

interface

uses
  SysUtils, Windows, Messages, Classes, Graphics,
  Controls, Forms, Dialogs, ExtCtrls, StdCtrls, Buttons, Grids,
  Calendar;
```

(continued)

Listing 7-2 *(continued)*

```pascal
type
  TMainForm = class(TForm)
    ToolbarPanel: TPanel;
    RingSB: TSpeedButton;
    DateSB: TSpeedButton;
    TimeSB: TSpeedButton;
    CalendarSB: TSpeedButton;
    ExitSB: TSpeedButton;
    Label1: TLabel;
    Label2: TLabel;
    Label3: TLabel;
    Label4: TLabel;
    Label5: TLabel;
    Label6: TLabel;
    Bevel1: TBevel;
    Calendar1: TCalendar;
    procedure SBMouseDown(Sender: TObject;
      Button: TMouseButton; Shift: TShiftState; X, Y: Integer);
    procedure SBMouseUp(Sender: TObject; Button: TMouseButton;
      Shift: TShiftState; X, Y: Integer);
    procedure RingSBClick(Sender: TObject);
    procedure DateSBClick(Sender: TObject);
    procedure TimeSBClick(Sender: TObject);
    procedure CalendarSBClick(Sender: TObject);
    procedure ExitSBClick(Sender: TObject);
  private
    { Private declarations }
    function InToolbar(Sender: TObject): Boolean;
  public
    { Public declarations }
  end;

var
  MainForm: TMainForm;

implementation

{$R *.DFM}

const
  isNotInToolbar = 0;     { SpeedButton Tag flag }
  isInToolbar    = 1;     { SpeedButton Tag flag }

{- Returns True if Sender is in the toolbar }
function TMainForm.InToolbar(Sender: TObject): Boolean;
begin
  with Sender as TSpeedButton do
```

```
    if Tag = isNotInToolbar then
    begin
      Tag := isInToolbar;    { Set Tag flag }
      Result := False;       { Return function result = False }
    end else
      Result := True;        { Return function result = True }
end;

{- Assign OnClick event handlers for buttons not in toolbar }
procedure TMainForm.SBMouseDown(Sender: TObject;
  Button: TMouseButton; Shift: TShiftState; X, Y: Integer);
begin
  with Sender as TSpeedButton do
  if Tag = isNotInToolbar then
  begin { Assign OnClick event handler to a button }
    if Sender = RingSB then
      RingSB.OnClick := RingSBClick
    else if Sender = DateSB then
      DateSB.OnClick := DateSBClick
    else if Sender = TimeSB then
      TimeSB.OnClick := TimeSBClick
    else if Sender = CalendarSB then
      CalendarSB.OnClick := CalendarSBClick
    else if Sender = ExitSB then
      ExitSB.OnClick := ExitSBClick;
  end;
end;

{- Move buttons into the toolbar }
procedure TMainForm.SBMouseUp(Sender: TObject;
  Button: TMouseButton; Shift: TShiftState; X, Y: Integer);
begin
  with Sender as TSpeedButton do
  if Tag = isNotInToolbar then
  begin   { Move button into the toolbar }
    Parent := ToolbarPanel;  { ToolBar now owns the button }
    Top := 0;                { Reposition button }
  end;
end;

{- Respond to Ring button click }
procedure TMainForm.RingSBClick(Sender: TObject);
begin
  if InToolbar(Sender) then
    MessageBeep(0);
end;
```

(continued)

Listing 7-2 *(continued)*

```
{- Respond to Date button click }
procedure TMainForm.DateSBClick(Sender: TObject);
begin
  if InToolbar(Sender) then
    ShowMessage('The date is ' + DateToStr(Date));
end;

{- Respond to Time button click }
procedure TMainForm.TimeSBClick(Sender: TObject);
begin
  if InToolbar(Sender) then
    ShowMessage('The time is ' + TimeToStr(Time));
end;

{- Respond to Calendar button click }
procedure TMainForm.CalendarSBClick(Sender: TObject);
begin
  if InToolbar(Sender) then
  with Calendar1 do
  begin
    Align := alClient;
    Visible := not Visible;
  end;
end;

{- Respond to Exit button click }
procedure TMainForm.ExitSBClick(Sender: TObject);
begin
  if InToolbar(Sender) then
    Close;
end;

end.
```

To create Toolbar2, perform the following steps:

1. Insert a Panel and several SpeedButton objects into the form.

2. Create OnClick event handlers such as RingSBClick and DateSBClick for each button.

3. Then, in the Object Inspector, highlight each OnClick event handler and press Del to delete it. This leaves the procedure in the source module, but decouples it from the button object — this is necessary because the first time that users click the button the program moves it into the toolbar rather than performing an action.

To indicate whether a button is in the toolbar, the program inspects the button's Tag field, which can equal one of the two constants, isNotInToolbar or isInToolbar. The program defines these constants just after the implementation keyword in the unit module. Function InToolbar returns True or False depending on Tag's value and changes that value to isInToolbar.

Tip

> You can use an object's Tag field for any integer value. As demonstrated here, a typical use is a flag that indicates some fact about the object's state.

Each of the SpeedButtons share the same MouseDown and MouseUp event handlers. In procedure SBMouseDown, an *if* statement checks whether Tag equals isNotInToolbar, in which case we can assume the user has clicked a button to move it into the toolbar. To ensure that the next use of that button executes an action, SBMouseDown reattaches the button's OnClick event handler, which was decoupled earlier.

On releasing the mouse, procedure SBMouseUp again checks whether Tag equals isNotInToolbar. If so, the procedure moves the button into the toolbar by setting the SpeedButton object's Parent property to the toolbar Panel, and setting the button's Top property to 0, which repositions the button relative to the Panel's border. These two statements perform the necessary actions:

```
Parent := ToolbarPanel;
Top := 0;
```

Each OnClick event calls the InToolbar function to detect whether the button has been moved to the toolbar. If InToolbar returns True, the event handler performs the button's action. By the way, take a look at how the CalendarSBClick procedure switches the calendar object on and off simply by toggling its Visible property with the statement:

```
Visible := not Visible;
```

Floating toolbars

Toolbar panels do not have to be cemented in place. You can also create toolbars that users can click and drag to any location inside a form window. The Toolbar3 sample application, shown in Figure 7-6, explores this useful technique, which is especially valuable in programs with busy displays, or those that show large graphics images. The program's files are on the CD-ROM in the Source\Toolbar3 directory. Users can simply drag a floating toolbar out of the way rather than having to scroll the window. To try this program, click and drag the toolbar's top border. Select any button, which simply confirms your choice. Turn off the check box to fix the toolbar in place. Click Reset to return the toolbar to its startup location. The program's source code in Listing 7-3 explains the details of creating a draggable Panel object. After the listing, I explain how the program works.

Note Delphi 4 now provides dockable windows, which greatly simplify the techniques in this section. You might still use these methods if you are using an earlier version of Delphi, but see "Creating Docking Controls" in Chapter 12 for another way to create dockable windows that can be used as floating toolbars.

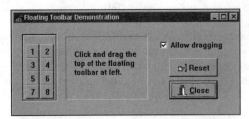

Figure 7-6: Toolbar3 demonstrates how to create a floating toolbar of SpeedButtons.

Listing 7-3: **Toolbar3\Main.pas**

```
unit Main;

interface

uses
   SysUtils, WinTypes, WinProcs, Messages, Classes, Graphics,
   Controls, Forms, Dialogs, Buttons, ExtCtrls, StdCtrls;

type
   TMainForm = class(TForm)
     FloatingToolbar: TPanel;
     SpeedButton1: TSpeedButton;
     SpeedButton2: TSpeedButton;
     SpeedButton3: TSpeedButton;
     SpeedButton4: TSpeedButton;
     SpeedButton5: TSpeedButton;
     SpeedButton6: TSpeedButton;
     SpeedButton7: TSpeedButton;
     SpeedButton8: TSpeedButton;
     BitBtn1: TBitBtn;
     Label1: TLabel;
     Bevel1: TBevel;
     AllowDraggingCB: TCheckBox;
     ResetBitBtn: TBitBtn;
     procedure FormCreate(Sender: TObject);
     procedure SpeedButton1Click(Sender: TObject);
```

```
    procedure FloatingToolbarMouseDown(Sender: TObject;
      Button: TMouseButton; Shift: TShiftState; X, Y: Integer);
    procedure FormMouseUp(Sender: TObject;
      Button: TMouseButton; Shift: TShiftState; X, Y: Integer);
    procedure FormMouseMove(Sender: TObject;
      Shift: TShiftState; X, Y: Integer);
    procedure ResetBitBtnClick(Sender: TObject);
    procedure AllowDraggingCBClick(Sender: TObject);
  private
    { Private declarations }
    Dragging: Boolean;
    XOffset, YOffset: Integer;
    procedure MoveToolbar(X, Y: Integer);
  public
    { Public declarations }
  end;

var
  MainForm: TMainForm;

implementation

{$R *.DFM}

{- Initialize }
procedure TMainForm.FormCreate(Sender: TObject);
begin
  Dragging := False;
end;

{- Display number of selected SpeedButton in toolbar }
procedure TMainForm.SpeedButton1Click(Sender: TObject);
begin
  ShowMessage('You selected button number ' +
    IntToStr(TSpeedButton(Sender).Tag));
end;

{- Start dragging operation on clicking in toolbar }
procedure TMainForm.FloatingToolbarMouseDown(Sender: TObject;
  Button: TMouseButton; Shift: TShiftState; X, Y: Integer);
begin
  if AllowDraggingCB.Checked then
  begin
    Dragging := True;       { Dragging opertion in effect }
    SetCapture(Handle);     { Send all mouse messages to form }
    XOffset := X;           { Save mouse coordinates to compute }
    YOffset := Y;           { offset from top-left corner }
  end;
```

(continued)

Listing 7-3 *(continued)*

```
end;

{- End dragging operation on releasing mouse button }
procedure TMainForm.FormMouseUp(Sender: TObject;
  Button: TMouseButton; Shift: TShiftState; X, Y: Integer);
begin
  if Dragging then        { Ignore if not dragging }
  begin
    MoveToolbar(X, Y);    { Move toolbar to final location }
    Dragging := False;    { End dragging operation }
    ReleaseCapture;       { Return message handling to normal }
  end;
end;

{- Move toolbar if dragging operation in progress }
procedure TMainForm.FormMouseMove(Sender: TObject; Shift:
  TShiftState; X, Y: Integer);
begin
  if Dragging then        { Ignore if not dragging }
    MoveToolbar(X, Y);    { Move toolbar to mouse location }
end;

{- Move the toolbar to mouse location X and Y }
procedure TMainForm.MoveToolbar(X, Y: Integer);
begin
  FloatingToolbar.Left := X - XOffset; // Adjust location of
  FloatingToolbar.Top := Y - YOffset;  // panel top-left corner
end;

{- Reset toolbar to startup location }
procedure TMainForm.ResetBitBtnClick(Sender: TObject);
begin
  with FloatingToolbar do
  begin
    Left := 24;
    Top := 24;
  end;
  AllowDraggingCB.Checked := True;
end;

procedure TMainForm.AllowDraggingCBClick(Sender: TObject);
begin
  with Label1 do
    Enabled := not Enabled;
end;

end.
```

To create a floating toolbar, insert a Panel object into a form window and assign it an appropriate Name property. In Toolbar3, I used the name FloatingToolbar, and I changed the object's width to 50 — exactly twice the width of a SpeedButton. The toolbar's Height is less critical. Make it tall enough to hold your buttons plus a little at the top for a border. Users can click and drag in this area to move the toolbar to another location.

The sample toolbar's BevelInner and BevelOuter properties are both set to bvRaised, but you may want to experiment with other Panel styles and settings. The SpeedButtons in the Panel are standard issue. Simply insert as many buttons as you need.

To manage dragging you need three variables, declared in TMainForm's private section. These variables are:

✦ **Dragging** — A Boolean variable that, when True, indicates that a dragging operation is in progress.

✦ **Xoffset** — The number of pixels between the left edge of the toolbar Panel and the mouse's X-coordinate. This makes dragging more realistic by allowing users to click the mouse anywhere in the Panel's visible surface.

✦ **Yoffset** — The number of pixels between the top of the toolbar Panel and the mouse's Y-coordinate.

In addition to these variables, the class declares one private procedure, MoveToolbar. Pass the X- and Y-coordinates of the mouse location (from a MouseMove event, for example) to move the toolbar to this location.

Write an OnCreate event handler for the form and set the Dragging variable to False. This is the only required initialization.

Next, create an OnMouseDown event for the FloatingToolbar object. Be sure to do this for the Panel object, not for the form. Toolbar3 checks whether the Allow dragging check box is on — if not, the procedure ends, which effectively prevents the toolbar from moving.

Four statements begin a dragging operation (refer to the MouseDown event handler in the listing):

```
if AllowDraggingCB.Checked then
  begin
    Dragging := True;
    SetCapture(Handle);
    XOffset := X;
    YOffset := Y;
  end;
```

First, the program sets Dragging to True so other procedures can detect a dragging operation is in progress. SetCapture, a Windows API function, sends all mouse messages to the active window — thus, while dragging, users cannot use the mouse to shift to other tasks. Finally, two assignments initialize XOffset and YOffset to the mouse coordinates, which are relative to the Panel object for which the MouseDown event occurred.

When you release the mouse button, the form's MouseUp event takes over. Do not create this event for the Panel — you must create the MouseUp event for the *form,* even though the dragging operation began for the Panel. In fact, when creating any kind of draggable object, the MouseUp event must be for the form, despite the fact that the MouseDown event is for the object. The reason for this is because SetCapture, called in the MouseDown event handler, causes all mouse messages to be sent to the active window. This window is the form — not its child Panel — and therefore, during a SetCapture, the Panel never receives MouseMove and MouseUp events.

The MouseUp event first checks whether Dragging is True. If so, MoveToolbar shifts the toolbar to its final position at the mouse coordinates x and y adjusted for the panel's offset. The procedure sets Dragging to False, canceling the dragging operation, and calls ReleaseCapture to return mouse messages to their normal traffic patterns.

Tip   Always pair a call to SetCapture with ReleaseCapture or your program's customers will lose mouse control. If this happens, you might lose your customers.

The final wrinkle in creating a floating toolbar is the form's MouseMove event. Again, because of the call to SetCapture, you must create this handler for the form's event, not the toolbar's. The procedure checks whether Dragging is True, indicating that a click-and-drag operation is underway, and if so, calls MoveToolbar to move the toolbar Panel to the mouse location. Because the toolbar owns its SpeedButton objects, those objects follow along automatically — you don't have to reposition them; you have to move only the Panel object.

The other procedures in Toolbar3 have obvious purposes. MoveToolbar relocates the FloatingToolbar object by assigning new values to its Left and Top properties. Subtracting the mouse offset values from X and Y allows users to click the mouse anywhere in the Panel's visible surface. (Try assigning X and Y without subtracting the offsets to see why this step is necessary.)

Procedure ResetBitBtnClick, called when you click the Reset button, returns the floating toolbar to its start-up location. It is always a good idea to include this capability in case users lose track of the toolbar, which can easily happen when resizing the program's window.

Status Panels

A status panel resembles a toolbar, but usually displays text rather than SpeedButton objects. Status panels typically appear at the bottom of a window, and may have subsections that make them easier to read. For example, Microsoft Word, which I used to write this book, displays the current page number, line and column values, and keyboard indicators in subdivided status panels. Fortunately, it no longer displays the time, which only reminds me how late I usually am finishing these books! Figure 7-7 shows the status panel from the Tabs program. The panel shows function and Alt keys, the current input and output tab-width settings, and the current time. Each subsection in the panel is itself a separate Panel object.

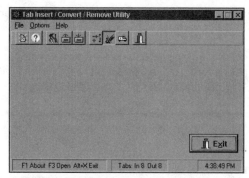

Figure 7-7: The Tabs program displays a sectional status panel at the bottom of the window's border.

You might also display online help or error messages in a status panel. Delphi makes it easy to create sectional status panels, but learn about a few gotchas, so they don't getcha.

Note   Although Delphi provides the Win32 StatusBar component for creating status panels, this section shows how to create status panels using other types of objects. The last section of this chapter explains how to use the StatusBar component.

Creating a status panel

To create a status panel, follow these steps:

1. Insert a Panel object into a form window to serve as the base for each panel subsection.

2. Give this main Panel a Name such as StatusPanel, and change its Height property to 25. You can use a smaller value, but remember, not all computer users are 18 years old with 20–20 vision, so don't make your panels too small.

3. For a nice 3D effect, set the Panel's BevelInner property to bvLowered, and set BevelOuter to bvRaised (the default value).

4. Set BorderWidth to 0 (the default value).

5. Delete the Caption.

6. To affix the Panel to the window's bottom border, change Align to alBottom.

Of course, you are free to use other styles and to position the Panel wherever you want.

Tip

Many successful Windows programs use 8-point MS Sans Serif font for a status panel's text. With this font, you can pack nearly 100 characters into a maximized window's status panel on a standard 640×480 display. This font also tends to look good with higher resolutions.

Sectioning a status panel

To divide a status panel into sections, insert additional Panel objects into StatusPanel (the main Panel object). Choose easy-to-remember names for each subpanel. For example, Tabs names its subpanels KeyPanel, TabPanel, and TimePanel. Use the same 3D settings as for the main Panel, but set BevelOuter to None. To automatically align subpanels, change their Align properties to alLeft or alRight.

When you set Align to alLeft or alRight, each subpanel automatically joins any other panels in the main status bar. After initially setting Align, reset this property to alNone. You can then click and drag the subpanel to another location — to increase the amount of space between sections, for example. This is how I created the raised spaces between the subpanels in the Tabs application (see Figure 7-7).

Table 7-1 lists significant properties for the StatusPanel and subpanel objects in the Tabs application. You might find this information useful in constructing your own subdivided status panels.

Updating a status panel

To change the text in a status panel, simply assign strings to Caption properties. For example, to display the time, Tabs executes this statement in a Timer object's OnTimer event handler:

```
TimePanel.Caption := TimeToStr(Time);
```

Table 7-1
Tabs Status Panel Object Properties

Component	Name	Property	Value
Panel	StatusPanel	Align	alBottom
		BevelInner	bvLowered
		BevelOuter	bvRaised
		Height	25
Panel	KeyPanel	Align	alLeft
		BevelInner	bvLowered
		BevelOuter	bvNone
		Font:Name	MS Sans Serif
		Font:Size	8
Panel	TabPanel	Align	alNone
Panel	TimePanel	Align	alRight

This causes the time to advance automatically. The Timer's Interval is set to 1000 milliseconds (one second). You might also assign literal Caption strings to display static text items at run time, or you can simply type strings into Caption properties using the Object Inspector.

However, avoid the urge to poke individual characters into subpanel Captions. For example, it is a futile exercise to enter individual hour, minute, and second digits into the TimePanel Caption — an approach that many Delphi programmer's have needlessly wasted hours programming. It's a whole lot easier, and probably more efficient, to reassign the entire Caption string every second, even though this may seem wasteful.

You might find it necessary, on occasion, to display text on top of a status panel's subdivisions. For example, you could display an online hint or an error message. Temporarily, you want to overwrite the subpanels to display the message, and then, when the user presses a key or uses the mouse, you can restore the status panel to normal.

This technique is easy to implement. Set the main panel's Alignment to taLeftJustify, and hide the subpanels when you want to display the message. Assign a string to the main panel's Caption property. Finally, reverse these steps to restore the status panel to normal. For example, the Tabs program displays an error message using code similar to the following. First, the program hides the two subpanels that display function key labels and the tab-width settings (the time subpanel at the extreme right isn't in the way, and it can remain visible):

```
KeyPanel.Visible := False;
TabPanel.Visible := False;
```

Next, a *with* statement sets the main StatusPanel's Alignment, and assigns text to the Caption property:

```
with StatusPanel do
begin
  Alignment := taLeftJustify;
  Caption := 'Error #45: Now look what you''ve done!';
end;
```

Note

Type two single quote marks to enter a quote mark character into a string. See the preceding Caption assignment statement for an example.

You can also set the Alignment property at design time with the Object Inspector, in which case you can simply assign a string to Caption. To restore the status panel to normal — after a Timer expires, for example, or on receipt of keyboard or mouse events — assign a null string to the main panel, and set the subpanel Visible properties to True. For example, execute this code:

```
StatusPanel.Caption := '';
KeyPanel.Visible := True;
TabPanel.Visible := True;
```

Using the Format function

Delphi's Format function is especially helpful for preparing strings to display in status panels, but you can use this utility function for other string-formatting purposes. You might want to look up Format in Delphi's online help before reading the following notes and suggestions. If you know C or C++, you recognize Format as Pascal's equivalent to the sprintf() function.

Pass two or more arguments to Format and assign the function result to a string variable, or pass it directly to a non-varstring parameter in a procedure or function. Delphi defines Format and its parameters as follows:

```
function Format(const Format: string;
  const Args: array of const): string;
```

✦ **Format** — a literal or variable string that contains format specifiers that the Format function uses to create the output string.

✦ **Args** — an open array of one or more arguments — such as integers, floating-point variables, characters, and strings — to be inserted into the output string. There must be one argument for each format specifier in the Format string. (Technically speaking, you can have more arguments than format specifiers, but you receive a run-time error if you declare too few.) Enclose arguments in brackets and separate multiple arguments with commas.

Note

Pascal permits a procedure or function name to be the same as a parameter, thus the Format function's first parameter is named Format. In a function, however, assigning a value to the function name is ambiguous if a parameter uses that same name. In that case, you can assign the function result to the reserved Result keyword.

Format is useful for inserting one string into another. For example, declare a string variable such as the following (if you want to follow along, insert a Button and a Label component into a form and enter the following code in the Button's Onclick event handler, before the begin keyword):

```
var
   Proc: string;
```

Assign a string to Proc and then use Format to insert that string into another (insert this code between begin and end):

```
Proc := 'Pentium II';
Label1.Caption := Format('I wish my PC had a %s CPU', [Proc]);
```

The first line assigns a literal string to Proc. The second line uses Format to insert Proc into a literal string, replacing the format specifier %s with Proc's value. Notice that Proc is encased in brackets because the second argument passed to Format is an open array, which resembles a Pascal set in usage, but is actually a variable list of parameters that can be of any types. The final result is the label:

```
I wish my PC had a Pentium II CPU
```

You can also use Format to insert numeric values into strings. For example, declare a floating-point, double-precision variable:

```
var
   Balance: double;
```

Assign a value to Balance, and insert it into a string using the Format specifier %8.2f, which converts the value to a string in eight columns and two decimal places:

```
Balance := 159.72;
Label2.Caption := Format('Your balance is $%8.2f', [Balance]);
```

Executing those two statements sets Label2's Caption to the following string (notice that the eight columns include the decimal point):

```
Your balance is $  159.72
```

Format specifiers begin with a percent sign followed by a letter, called the type, that represents the type of information to insert into the string and also how that information is to be displayed. For example, %d indicates a decimal value, %x indicates a hexadecimal value, %s is a Pascal or null-terminated string, and %f or %g indicate floating-point values. It is your responsibility to supply a value in Args for each format specifier. It is also your responsibility to supply values of the indicated types.

Between the % sign and type letter (*d, x, s,* and others) may be several other kinds of information, such as a left-justification indicator (-), a column-width value, and a precision (preceded by a decimal point). For example, the specifier %6.3f formats a floating-point value in six columns and three decimal places. The specifier %-8x left-justifies an integer value in hexadecimal within eight columns.

Tip

Argument index overrides in brackets simplify repeating values. For example, this statement

```
Format ('%s %d %0:s %d', ['test',10])
```

produces the string *test 10 test 10*. If you have a few values that need to be placed in several spots in your string, you can make the format specifiers hop around between arguments. This saves memory that is otherwise wasted on redundant arguments. Be sure to count carefully that enough arguments exist for each repeating override.

A few more examples can help you to use and understand Format. First, define some typed constants (which are similar to variables, but have declared data types and default values):

```
const
   XInt: Integer = 123;
   XLongInt: Longint = 12345678;
   XChar: Char = '@';
   XString: string = 'My dog has knees';
   XSingle: Single = 3.14159;
```

```
XDouble: Double =  9.8695877281;
XExtended: Extended = 9.51413;
```

Insert Label objects into a form to display each of these values. In a Button or other event handler, insert the following statements (your Label object Names may differ from mine):

```
Label3.Caption  := Format('XInt (dec) = %d', [XInt]);
Label4.Caption  := Format('XInt (hex) = %x', [XInt]);
Label5.Caption  := Format('XLongInt   = %d', [XLongInt]);
Label6.Caption  := Format('XChar      = %s', [XChar]);
Label7.Caption  := Format('XString    = %s', [XString]);
Label8.Caption  := Format('XSingle    = %f', [XSingle]);
Label9.Caption  := Format('XDouble    = %G', [XDouble]);
Label10.Caption := Format('XExtended  = %G', [XExtended]);
```

Running the program and clicking the button displays the following lines:

```
XInt (dec) = 123
XInt (hex) = 7B
XLongInt   = 12345678
XChar      = @
XString    = My dog has knees
XSingle    = 3.14
XDouble    = 9.8695877281
XExtended  = 9.51413
```

Also insert a Label object to display the formatted string result:

```
Pi=3.141593, Frac=0.141593, Int=3
```

Format can also insert multiple values into strings. Enter as many format specifiers as you need, of any types, and supply, in brackets, that many arguments separated by commas. For example, Listing 7-4 contains sample code that you can insert into a Button's OnClick event handler. The text is on the CD-ROM in the Source\Format directory in file Format.pas.

Finding components

Use the FindComponent function to search a form or other object's Components array by name. This array refers to all of another object's components, and it offers a handy way to perform multiple operations on those objects — resizing all of a form's buttons, for example, on a toolbar or status panel. First, define a variable of the general component type TComponent:

```
var
  C: TComponent;
```

Listing 7-4: **Setting a Label object's caption to a formatted string with multiple arguments**

```
procedure TForm1.Button1Click(Sender: TObject);
var
  R1, R2: Double;
  S: string;
begin
  R1 := Frac(Pi);
  R2 := Int(Pi);
  S := Format('Pi= %8.7G,  Frac=%8.6F,  Int=%G',
    [Pi, R1, R2]);
  Label1.Caption := S;
end;
```

Then, to find a component by name, use a statement such as this:

```
C := FindComponent('MyComponent');
```

After that statement, if C is not nil, it refers to the component named MyComponent. If C is nil, no object of the requested name exists. You usually follow calls to FindComponent with an *if* statement such as this:

```
if C <> nil then
  { ... perform action on C here }
```

Even better, use the Pascal *is* operator to confirm that C really is the type of object you think it should be:

```
if C is TListBox then
  { ... perform action on ListBox object C here }
```

Notice the statement uses the component's class name, which begins with *T*. The *if* statement compares the type of object *C* with the component's class name. You can use similar programming whenever you need to determine the type of a component object.

Tip

When using *is* to test whether an object returned by FindComponent is a particular type, you do not also have to test whether the function result is nil. For example, if the expression "C is TListBox" is true, then *C* cannot be nil.

Look at a finished procedure that calls FindComponent. To use the code, insert several CheckBox components into a form, plus a Button. Double-click the Button object and use the following procedure as its OnClick event handler (this text is on the CD-ROM in the Source\FindComp directory in file Findcomp.pas). Run the program and click some of the CheckBox objects. Click the Button to toggle all CheckBoxes on and off.

```
procedure TForm1.Button1Click(Sender: TObject);
var
  C: TComponent;
  I, J, K: Integer;
begin
  K := 0;
  for I := 0 to Form1.ComponentCount - 1 do
  begin
    C := FindComponent('CheckBox' + IntToStr(I + 1));
    if C is TCheckBox then
      with C as TCheckBox do
        Checked := not Checked;
  end;
end;
```

FindComponent returns a TComponent object, and you also usually have to use some additional programming to inform the compiler what type of component C really is. You can do this several ways. You can use a *type-cast expression* of the component type with C in parentheses. For example, this sets a CheckBox True:

```
TCheckBoxBox(C).Checked := True;
```

Or, you can use a *with* statement to tell Delphi to treat C as a particular type of component:

```
with C as TCheckBox do
begin
  Checked := False;
  ...
end;
```

This is generally preferred over type casting, and is safer. Delphi blindly accepts the type-cast expression, even if object C is not of an appropriate type. Using the *as* keyword, if in this example C is not an object of the TCheckBox class, Delphi generates an Invalid Type Cast exception error.

Be careful when using FindComponent along with Pascal's *with* statement. Although you will usually want to search a form's Component array, other objects also have this array, and inside a *with* statement, you might end up searching another component list. To resolve this kind of problem, either don't call FindComponent inside a *with* statement, or use an expression such as MainForm.FindComponent to refer to the object with the Components array that you want to search.

Keyboard status panels

One of the classic elements of a well-groomed status panel is a set of keyboard toggle indicators. These typically show the settings of the Caps Lock, Num Lock, Scroll Lock, and Ins keys. The CapsLock application, which is shown in Figure 7-8, demonstrates the technique. The program's files are on the CD-ROM in the Source\CapsLock directory. Listing 7-5 shows the program's Main.pas source code. There are several possible approaches for creating keyboard toggle indicators, but the one that I think looks the best shows dimmed text for keys in the off state and dark (normal) text for keys in the on state. However, accomplishing this with TPanel objects is not exactly straightforward, as I explain after the listing.

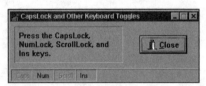

Figure 7-8: The CapsLock application displays the on/off states of the Caps Lock, Num Lock, Scroll Lock, and Ins keys.

Listing 7-5: **Capslock\Main.pas**

```
unit Main;

interface

uses
  SysUtils, Windows, Messages, Classes, Graphics,
  Controls, Forms, Dialogs, ExtCtrls, StdCtrls, Buttons;

type
  TMainForm = class(TForm)
    StatusPanel: TPanel;
    CapsLockPanel: TPanel;
    NumLockPanel: TPanel;
    ScrollLockPanel: TPanel;
    InsPanel: TPanel;
    BitBtn1: TBitBtn;
    Label1: TLabel;
    Bevel1: TBevel;
    CapsLockLabel: TLabel;
```

```
      NumLockLabel: TLabel;
      ScrollLockLabel: TLabel;
      InsLabel: TLabel;
      procedure FormKeyDown(Sender: TObject; var Key: Word;
        Shift: TShiftState);
      procedure FormActivate(Sender: TObject);
    private
      { Private declarations }
    public
      { Public declarations }
      procedure UpdateKeyPanel;
    end;

var
  MainForm: TMainForm;

implementation

{$R *.DFM}

procedure TMainForm.UpdateKeyPanel;
begin
  CapsLockLabel.Enabled :=
    GetKeyState(VK_CAPITAL) and 1 = 1;
  NumLockLabel.Enabled :=
    GetKeyState(VK_NUMLOCK) and 1 = 1;
  ScrollLockLabel.Enabled :=
    GetKeyState(VK_SCROLL)  and 1 = 1;
  InsLabel.Enabled :=
    GetKeyState(VK_INSERT)  and 1 = 1;
end;

procedure TMainForm.FormKeyDown(Sender: TObject; var Key: Word;
  Shift: TShiftState);
begin
  UpdateKeyPanel;
end;

procedure TMainForm.FormActivate(Sender: TObject);
begin
  UpdateKeyPanel;
end;

end.
```

To create a keyboard toggle status panel, follow these steps:

1. Insert a TPanel object into a form and modify it as explained in this chapter. For example, set Height to 25 and select a 3D style.

2. Align the panel with the window bottom.

3. Insert subpanels into the main TPanel, and name these CapsLockPanel, NumLockPanel, and so on.

4. Delete all panel Captions.

Displaying dim text in TPanel objects (see Figure 7-8) is less than straightforward because this component does not dim its Caption text when TPanel's Enabled property is False. Because of this limitation, the CapsLock application inserts four Label objects into each subpanel. To display a dim label for a key that is off, the program sets the Label's Enabled property to False; to display a normal label for a key that is on, the program sets Enabled to True. The program does not assign text to the subpanel Captions.

Procedure UpdateKeyPanel shows how to obtain the current settings of the Caps Lock, Num Lock, Scroll Lock, and Ins keys. The procedure calls the Windows API function GetKeyState, to which you can pass any virtual key code. GetKeyState returns an integer value. If that value's least significant bit equals 1, the key is toggled on; otherwise, the key is off. A logical AND expression examines this bit, resulting in a Boolean True or False value. Assigning that value to the Label object's Enabled property displays it in dim or normal style.

To show key values properly when the program starts and when the user presses one of the labeled keys, CapsLock creates two event handlers for the form — OnActivate and OnKeyDown. Each of these event handlers calls the UpdateKeyPanel procedure to update the status panel.

Tip
To detect changes to Caps Lock, Num Lock, Scroll Lock, and Ins keys in a form's OnKeyDown event handler, set the form's KeyPreview property to True.

Coolbars

A *Coolbar,* also known less colorfully as a *rebar,* is a multisectional container object that can hold other windowed controls. Those controls, which can be any objects of classes derived from TWinControl, reside on one or more bands that divide the Coolbar into sections. Each band is itself an object of the TCoolBand class. At run time, users can click and drag bands to shuffle and combine them to customize the Coolbar's display. While designing the program, you can do the same to arrange Coolbar bands however you wish.

Figure 7-9 shows a sample Coolbar from this section's demonstration program, CoolDemo, located in the Source\Cooldemo directory on the CD-ROM. The sample Coolbar has two bands, one on top of the other. The topmost band holds four buttons, which in the demonstration don't perform any real actions — they are just for show. The second band holds a DateTimePicker object, and also displays the label "Date selector."

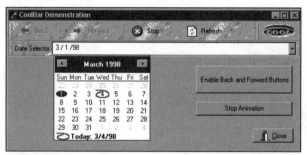

Figure 7-9: The CoolDemo application demonstrates how to create and use a Coolbar, which in this case, holds four buttons and a DateTimePicker object.

Coolbars will become more commonplace as Windows 98 gains acceptance. If you are revising an existing Delphi application, you might want to consider replacing your toolbars with Coolbars. This gives your programs a consistent look with other Windows software. This section explains how to create a Coolbar, how to section it into bands, and how to add various types of components to those bands.

For another example of a Coolbar, see the Delphi demonstration Web browser program in Delphi's Demo\Coolstuff directory.

Creating Coolbars

Creating a Coolbar is as easy as pie — just insert a Coolbar component from the Win32 VCL palette into a form. By default, the Coolbar glues itself to the top of the window. You can change this arrangement by selecting a different value for the Coolbar's Align property, but in most cases, the top of the window, just under a menu bar if there is one, is where Coolbars should be displayed, as seen in Figure 7-9.

Listing 7-6 shows CoolDemo's source code in file Main.pas, located in the Source\CoolDemo directory on the CD-ROM. I explain the programming in this listing at the appropriate places in this and the next sections.

Listing 7-6: **CoolDemo\Main.pas**

```
unit Main;

interface

uses
  Windows, Messages, SysUtils, Classes, Graphics, Controls,
  Forms, Dialogs, ComCtrls, ToolWin, Images, StdCtrls, Buttons;

type
  .TMainForm = class(TForm)
    Coolbar1: TCoolbar;
    ToolBar1: TToolBar;
    NavigatorImages: TImageList;
    NavigatorHotImages: TImageList;
    DateTimePicker1: TDateTimePicker;
    ToolButton1: TToolButton;
    ToolButton2: TToolButton;
    ToolButton3: TToolButton;
    ToolButton4: TToolButton;
    ToolButton5: TToolButton;
    BitBtn1: TBitBtn;
    BitBtn2: TBitBtn;
    Animate1: TAnimate;
    Button1: TButton;
    procedure BitBtn1Click(Sender: TObject);
    procedure Button1Click(Sender: TObject);
  private
    { Private declarations }
  public
    { Public declarations }
  end;

var
  MainForm: TMainForm;

implementation

{$R *.DFM}

procedure TMainForm.BitBtn1Click(Sender: TObject);
var
  TF: Boolean;   // True or False flag
  S: String;
begin
  TF := ToolButton1.Enabled;
  ToolButton1.Enabled := not TF;
  ToolButton2.Enabled := not TF;
```

```
  if TF
    then S := 'Enable'
    else S := 'Disable';
  BitBtn1.Caption := S + ' Back and Forward Buttons';
end;

procedure TMainForm.Button1Click(Sender: TObject);
begin
  Animate1.Active := not Animate1.Active;
  if Animate1.Active
    then Button1.Caption := 'Stop Animation'
    else Button1.Caption := 'Begin Animation';
end;

end.
```

To become familiar with Coolbars, run CoolDemo now by loading the Cooldemo.dpr project file into Delphi from the Source\Cooldemo directory, and pressing F9. Click the large button to enable and disable the first two buttons in the Coolbar's topmost band. Notice that when you move the mouse pointer over a button, it appears to grow out from the screen and its icon changes from black and white to a colored image. You provide these images using one or more ImageList objects, as I explain later in this section.

To reconfigure the Coolbar's organization, click and drag one of the two vertical bars (they look like round pegs to me) at far left in a Coolbar band. For example, pick up the lower band and move it toward the top — this combines the bands to sit side-by-side as shown in Figure 7-10. (You might have to try several times to get the effect you want.)

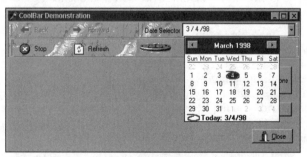

Figure 7-10: Click and drag a Coolbar band's vertical bar to rearrange the Coolbar's organization as shown here using the CoolDemo application.

Each band in a Coolbar may have a text label. To create a label, click the ellipsis next to a Coolbar object's Bands property. This opens the Coolbar Bands Editor. Select any band (or add one if necessary by clicking the Add New button), and then enter your label into the Text property using Delphi's Object Inspector.

Note The only way to access individual band objects is through the Coolbar Bands Editor. Although each band is an object of the TCoolBand class, the objects are not individually declared in the form class and, therefore, are not listed in the Object Inspector drop-down list.

Coolbar properties

Following are a few notes about selected Coolbar properties. You might need to read this and the next few sections before you understand the purpose of some properties.

✦ **Align** — Normally, Coolbars sit at the top of a window, but you can set Align to alBottom, alRight, or alLeft to alter the default setting of alTop. Custom applications might set this property to alNone for a fixed-size Coolbar, or to alClient to fill the window with the Coolbar background. When Align is alTop or alBottom, Vertical is set to False. When Align is alLeft or alRight, Vertical is set to True. Be aware of this interaction between the two fields.

✦ **AutoSize** — You almost always set this property to True, its default value, so the Coolbar automatically adjusts its size to fit within the window's boundaries. However, you may set this property to False if you want to position a Coolbar manually.

✦ **Bands** — Double-click this value, or click the ellipsis button to the right, to open the Coolbar Bands Editor. Use the Editor to add, delete, and rearrange a Coolbar's bands, each of which is an object of the TCoolBand class. The Bands Editor is the only way you can access individual bands at design time. Select a band using the Editor and then enter property values in the Object Inspector window as you do for other components.

✦ **Bitmap** — Assign any bitmap file to this property to color the Coolbar's background. Ideally, the bitmap should be symmetrical, so that when replicated over the Coolbar image, the final visual effect is seamless. It's best to use light colored or light gray images — dark ones make it difficult to see text and buttons on Coolbar bands. If you don't want to use a bitmap image for a Coolbar's background, you might set the Color property to customize your display. If you don't assign a Bitmap or Color value, the Coolbar is colored the same as a common button face (Color = clBtnFace).

✦ **EdgeBorders** — This property has four subvalues that you can set by double-clicking the small plus sign to the left of EdgeBorders in the Object Inspector window. Each subvalue is a True or False setting — try various combinations to see their effects. The four subvalues are: ebLeft, ebTop, ebRight, and ebBottom. To create a Coolbar with no visible boundaries, set all four subvalues to False, clear the Bitmap property, and set Color to clBtnFace. The resulting Coolbar is invisible at run time, but functions just as well as one with visible boundaries.

✦ **ShowText** — To display labels in a Coolbar's bands, select the bands using the Bands Editor, and enter your labels into the Text property using the Object Inspector. Set the Coolbar's ShowText property to True to display band labels. These are also displayed in the Bands Editor.

✦ **Vertical** — This property affects how bands are displayed in a Coolbar. Set Vertical to False to display bands horizontally, one on top of the other (the default). Set Vertical to True to display bands vertically, side-by-side. Set the Align property for the Coolbar, which affects its position in the window, *before* altering Vertical. This is necessary because assigning Align property values might change the value of Vertical (see Align).

Because a Coolbar usually holds bands of numerous other controls, it is often difficult to select the Coolbar object using the mouse in Delphi. If this happens, use the Object Inspector drop-down list to select the object — for example, open the CoolDemo application and select Coolbar1 to inspect the demonstration Coolbar's property values.

CoolBand properties

Following are notes about CoolBand properties. Remember, the only way to access individual band objects is to click the ellipsis next to the Coolbar's Bands property, and open the Bands Editor. You can then highlight an individual band and use the Object Inspector to set its properties. Because the Coolbar owns the CoolBand objects, they do not show up in the Object Inspector's drop-down list of components.

✦ **Bitmap** — Each band may have its own bitmap image to display in its background. If you assign a bitmap file to this property, it overrides any Bitmap value assigned to the Coolbar. Rather than use a Bitmap, you can also change the Color property of an individual band.

✦ **Break** — Set this property to True to position the band on a new line at the left side of the Coolbar. When Break is False, the band is displayed next to any previous band and does not begin on a new line.

✦ **Control** — Each band may hold one windowed control. Usually, this property is set automatically to the component that you drop onto a Coolbar, but you may set Control to any object of a class derived at some place in its hierarchy from TWinControl.

✦ **FixedBackground** — Normally, set this property to True so that the Coolbar's bitmap is displayed continuously behind all bands. When FixedBackground is False, the Coolbar bitmap is displayed separately for each band. Depending on the type of bitmap image you are using, this might be useful. However, for a seamless appearance, FixedBackground should be True. See also the ParentBitmap property.

✦ **FixedSize** — When this property is True, users cannot resize the band. Normally, this property is False (the default).

✦ **HorizontalOnly** — In cases where a specific band must be shown only horizontally — a ToolBar, for example — set this property to True. If the parent Coolbar's Vertical property is also True, the band will be invisible. You might use this property to hide selected bands when all bands are arranged vertically, but it's hard to imagine a practical use for this obscure setting. For most applications, use the default value of False.

✦ **ImageIndex** — A band may display an icon image by setting this property to the image's index value in its ImageList object. That object must be assigned to the Coolbar's Images property.

✦ **ParentBitmap** — When this property is True, the band shows the same bitmap image assigned to the Coolbar (the band's parent). Assigning an image to the band's Bitmap property automatically sets ParentBitmap to False.

Adding ToolBars to Coolbars

After dropping a Coolbar component onto a form, you'll want to section it into bands. You can do this in two ways:

✦ Click the ellipsis next to the Coolbar's Bands property in the Object Inspector window. This opens the Coolbar Bands Editor (see Figure 7-11), which you can use to add, delete, and reorder bands.

✦ Drop a windowed control such as a ComboBox, ToolBar, or as in the demonstration program, a DateTimePicker into the Coolbar. This automatically creates a new band to hold the windowed control.

Most Coolbars display one or more buttons to create a toolbar. To do that, first drop a Coolbar onto the form, and then drop a ToolBar object (also found on the Win32 palette) onto the Coolbar. Click the ToolBar using the right mouse button, and select the New Button command to create toolbar buttons. Each button is an object of the TToolButton class (this is not on the VCL palette — you must use the New Button command to create these types of buttons).

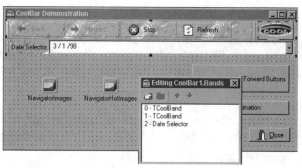

Figure 7-11: Use the Coolbar Bands Editor to create, delete, and rearrange bands in a Coolbar object.

Tip

For a classic toolbar look, follow these tips: Set the ToolBar object's AutoSize property to True, and set each ToolButton object's AutoSize property to False. Set the ToolBar's Flat property to True. To modify button sizes, select the ToolBar and assign values to the ButtonHeight and ButtonWidth properties. All buttons in a ToolBar must be of the same size, which is determined by the ToolBar, not by the individual buttons as with most other Delphi components.

Coolbars look more stylish with a background such as the stone-like image in CoolDemo (refer back to Figure 7-9). This looks best with a ToolBar that has its Flat property set to True, which causes the background to shine through the ToolBar buttons. To create the visual effect in CoolDemo, I assigned the Coolbar's Bitmap property to the image on the CD-ROM in Source\Data\Background.bmp image. You can use any bitmap for a Coolbar Bitmap, but the sample is specially designed to be replicated for a seamless background of any size.

The first time you add buttons to a ToolBar, they are bare. "Images and HotImages" in this chapter explains how to add icon graphics to ToolBar buttons. To display a text label — which you can do with or without also displaying icons — select each ToolButton object, and enter your label into the Caption property using the Object Inspector. To make the captions visible, select the ToolBar object, and set the ShowCaptions property to True.

Note

You can insert a ToolBar object directly into a form — the ToolBar doesn't have to reside in a Coolbar band. The programming techniques are the same for stand-alone ToolBar objects as described here for the CoolDemo application.

Toolbar properties

Following are notes about selected Toolbar properties. Remember, even though this section discusses ToolBars in conjunction with Coolbars, you can insert stand-alone Toolbar objects into a form. They don't have to live inside Coolbars.

✦ **Align**—Most Toolbars are best displayed at the top of a window, but you can change this property to align the bar to the window's bottom (alBottom), left (alLeft), or right (alRight) edge. For a floating or fixed-size toolbar, set Align to alNone. Set it to alClient to fill the window's client area—a useful technique for interfaces that are populated solely by a group of buttons, like a touch-screen order-entry system for instance.

✦ **AutoSize**—When this property is True, the Toolbar automatically adjusts its size to accommodate its buttons with no wasted space. You probably want to change this value to True (it's False by default) in most applications.

✦ **ButtonHeight, ButtonWidth**—Assign values to these two properties before creating ToolBar buttons. All buttons in a ToolBar are the same size. The values are expressed in pixels.

✦ **DisabledImages**—Assign an ImageList object to this property, and assign ImageIndex values for each of a ToolBar's buttons. Disabled buttons display the icons from this ImageList object. If you don't assign an ImageList object to this property, disabled button icons are automatically dimmed using the bitmaps from the Images property (if assigned).

✦ **Flat**—For a classic Web-browser-like appearance, and especially when inserting a ToolBar into a Coolbar, you want to set this property to True. Also assign a Bitmap to the Coolbar, and set the ToolBar's Transparent property True. The ToolBar then takes on the appearance of its parent Coolbar, as do the ToolBar's buttons.

✦ **HotImages**—Assign an ImageList object to this property, and assign ImageIndex values for each of a ToolBar's buttons. These icons are displayed when the user moves the mouse cursor over the buttons. Typically, the icons are the same as in the Images property, but are colored differently. This causes the buttons to appear to light up when the mouse cursor points to them. The hot images are not used for disabled buttons (those with Enabled properties equal to False).

✦ **Images**—Assign an ImageList object to this property, and assign ImageIndex values for each of a ToolBar's buttons. These icons are displayed on the buttons unless the they are disabled or the user points to a button using the mouse (see the DisabledImages and HotImages properties).

✦ **Indent**—Increase this value to display extra space at the left edge of the ToolBar before the first button object.

✦ **ShowCaptions**—Set this value to True to show the Caption properties of the buttons in a ToolBar object.

✦ **Transparent**—Set this property to True to show the parent object's bitmap or color as the ToolBar's background. When inserting a ToolBar into a Coolbar, you probably set this and the Flat property to True for a classic look.

✦ **Wrappable** — When True, the ToolBar buttons wrap around onto new rows if they do not all fit within the ToolBar's boundaries. The individual button objects must have their Wrap properties also set to True for this effect to work properly.

ToolButton properties

Following are notes about selected ToolButton properties. To add a button to a ToolBar, click the right mouse button and select the New Button command from the pop-up menu. To select an individual button object, click its image in the ToolBar, or you can select the ToolButton by name in the Object Inspector window.

✦ **AllowAllUp** — Set this to True to permit all buttons of a group to be deselected. When False, one button of the group must be selected (and should initially be chosen by setting its Down property True). This property has no effect unless the button's Style is set to tbsCheck, and its Grouped property is True.

✦ **AutoSize** — When this property is True, the button automatically adjusts its size to fit in the ToolBar. For most applications, however, you can leave this value set to False and set the ToolBar's AutoSize property True. These settings together probably give you the control you want over button sizes.

✦ **Caption** — Assign a short label to this property, and set the ToolBar's ShowCaptions field True, to display captions in buttons.

✦ **Command** — Assign a command from a CommandList object to share that command's event handler with the button. This is the handler that is executed when the user clicks the button. Or, you may assign an event handler to a ToolButton's OnClick event (just as you do for common Button objects). Using a CommandList, however, simplifies the chore of sharing commands among multiple objects — a pop-up menu, main menu, and ToolBar button, for example. See the Commands demonstration program on the book's accompanying CD-ROM in the Source\Commands directory, and also the discussion of the CommandList component in Chapter 5.

✦ **Down** — This property is True if the button is in its down (depressed) state. When grouping multiple buttons that have Styles set to tbsCheck and AllowAllUp properties set to True, at least one button in the group should have its Down property initialized to True. You can do this using the Object Inspector, or by assigning True to the button's Down property with a program statement. A good place to do this is in the form's OnCreate event handler.

✦ **Enabled** — Set to True to display the button in its normal appearance, and also to enable OnClick events for it. Set to False to display the button using its disabled icon if one is assigned. (See the ToolBar DisabledImages and Images properties.)

✦ **Grouped** — Assign True to this property to create groups of buttons that operate interactively with one another. The buttons must also have Styles set to tbsCheck. Set AllowAllUp to True if all buttons are permitted to be deselected; otherwise, at least one button of the group must be selected at all times (that is, its Down property must be True).

✦ **ImageIndex** — This value indicates which icon to display from the ImageList object assigned to the ToolBar's Images property (and also its DisabledImages and HotImages properties, if these are used). The first image index is always zero, the next is 1, the next 2, and so on. Set this property to –1 if you don't want to display an icon image on a button.

✦ **Indeterminate** — When this property is True, the button is displayed using a grayed-out color, but if Enabled is also True, the button can still be selected. The purpose of this field is to provide a visual clue to users that a button may be selected, but that it might be inappropriate to do so given the program's current state — switching to another process, for example, during a lengthy sort or print job. You can also inspect this field in the button's OnClick event handler, and if the property is True, display a confirmation message or warning that the user has selected a potentially inappropriate command.

✦ **Style** — Use this property to select among different types of buttons. A plain button Style equals tbsButton, the default. Set all grouped buttons' Styles to tbsChecked — this doesn't display a check mark, but creates a sticky button that stays down when clicked until clicked again. You can also use this style to create stand-alone option buttons — they don't have to be grouped. (Also see the following tip.)

✦ **Wrap** — Set to True to enable this button to wrap around onto a new row if it doesn't fit in the ToolBar's boundaries. The ToolBar's Wrappable property must also be set to True for this effect to work properly.

Tip   To create a visual separator between other buttons, set Style to tbsDivider or tbsSeparator (they are the same). This type of button is purely for display and cannot be clicked. To display a down arrow at right inside the button, set Style to tbsDropDown. This does not create a pop-up menu for the button — to do this, insert a PopupMenu object from the Standard palette into the form, double-click the object to create the pop-up menu's commands, and assign the PopupMenu object to the button's DropDownMenu property. Clicking this type of button at run time opens the menu from which users can select commands.

Images and HotImages

Buttons in a Coolbar's ToolBar should normally display icon graphics that indicate what the buttons do. This requires using another component from the Win32 palette: ImageList. Insert one or more objects of this type into a form, and then use the objects to manage one or more icon images for display on ToolBar buttons. (You can use ImageList objects for other purposes as well when you need a storage vessel to hold icons.)

Figure 7-12 shows two ImageList objects in the CoolDemo form window inside Delphi. The ImageList objects — named NavigatorImages and NavigatorHotImages — show up at design time as icons, but are invisible when the program runs. To make the icons more visible here, I set the form's background to white; on your display the background is colored normally depending on your Windows display settings. To add, delete, and rearrange ImageList icons, double-click an ImageList object. This opens the ImageList editor window illustrated in Figure 7-13.

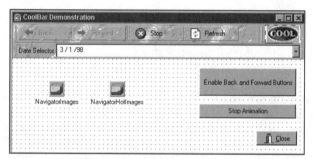

Figure 7-12: The CoolDemo application's design-time form, showing two ImageList objects as icons that are invisible when the program runs.

Index integer values

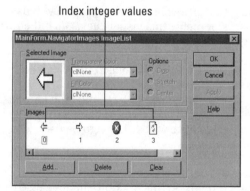

Figure 7-13: Open the ImageList editor window by double-clicking an ImageList component object.

Use the Add button in the ImageList editor to open any icon or other bitmap file, and insert the image into the list. To change the order of listed images, click and drag them to the positions you want. Select any image and click Delete to delete it from the list. Click the Clear button to erase all images.

Note The ImageList editor can adjust the Transparent and Fill colors of a bitmap image, and can also crop, stretch, or center an image. Click the appropriate buttons in the editor to perform these actions. Because icons are fixed in size and color, these options are disabled for icons.

Refer to Figure 7-13. Notice each icon is assigned an index integer value, starting with zero for the first image. You use these index values to assign specific images to ToolBar buttons. Two important steps make this work:

1. Select the ToolBar and assign an ImageList object to the Images property. This links the ToolBar to a set of images — the button icons in this example.

2. Select each individual button in the ToolBar, and assign to the button's ImageIndex property the index value of the image you want.

Those are the minimum steps required to display icon images on ToolBar buttons. However, you might want to take advantage of two other ways to show icon images. You might do this to provide different images when buttons are disabled, and when the user moves the mouse cursor over a button. Using different images (or the same images colored differently) for these actions gives the interface a tremendous boost in the visual feedback department.

CoolDemo uses one of those methods to color buttons when the mouse cursor points to them. To see the effect, run the program again and move the mouse over the four sample buttons. (Click the large plain button to enable the first two ToolBar buttons.) As you can see, each button seems to light up when you pass the mouse cursor over its image. Most users perceive this visual cue as an indicator that the button is "ready" for clicking.

To create that effect in CoolDemo, I created another ImageList object named NavigatorHotImages (actually this is the same object as found in the Delphi demonstration Web browser program). This ImageList object holds the identical icons as the other list, but the images are brightly colored. Assigning the ImageList object to the ToolBar's HotImages property causes these icons to be used when the mouse cursor moves over a button at run time.

The third way to use ImageList objects in ToolBars is to assign yet a third set of icons to the DisabledImages property. I did not do this in CoolDemo because the default disable icons — taken from the ImageList assigned to the Images property and automatically dimmed — are usually adequate. However, you can assign DisabledImages if you want to use specific images for buttons that have their Enabled properties set to False. You could animate an icon — to close a door, for example, or show another sort of image — when a button is disabled.

Tip

To use the icons shown in this chapter's CoolDemo application, simply copy (select and press Ctrl+C) the NavigatorImages and NavigatorHotImages objects one at a time into your application form window (press Ctrl+V).

Coolbar animations

A cool thing to do with a Coolbar is to add an animated icon, which indicates that the program is running, and also adds some flashy graphics to the display. The CoolDemo application displays a spinning "Cool" disk, which I borrowed from Delphi's Web browser demonstration program. The animation is a standard audiovisual interface file (.avi), stored in the Source\Data\Cool.avi file (and also provided with Delphi in the Demo\CoolStuff directory).

It's easy to add an animation to a Coolbar. Simply drop an Animate component object from the Win32 palette onto a Coolbar. Make sure you drop the Animate object onto the Coolbar, not the ToolBar. This makes it easier to position the Animate component where you want it. (A ToolBar may hold an Animate object, however.)

Dropping an Animate component onto a Coolbar creates a new band for the animation. You probably want to move this band to a new location — for example, CoolDemo displays its animated icon to the right of its ToolBar. To move the animation band:

1. Select the Animate object and set its AutoSize property to False.

2. Then, still inside Delphi, drag the band's vertical bar to the far left and drop the band to the right of the ToolBar, or to wherever else you want it. This may take a few tries until you achieve the effect you want — best to save the project before beginning to configure the Coolbar bands.

3. Assign the name of the .avi file to the Animate object's FileName property.

4. Set the Active property True to begin the animation, which automatically repeats.

To start and stop an animation at run time, assign True or False to the Active property. CoolDemo does this in a Button's OnClick event handler using the statements:

```
Animate1.Active := not Animate1.Active;
if Animate1.Active
  then Button1.Caption := 'Stop Animation'
  else Button1.Caption := 'Begin Animation';
```

This code sets Active to its opposite True or False state, and then changes the button caption accordingly.

Note   Windows limits the size of an AVI image that the Animate control can display, and therefore, these same restrictions apply to the Delphi Animate component which accesses the Windows control. For example, the image display size must be less than 64K and the file cannot be compressed. Other limitations may also apply depending on the configuration and total length of the AVI file. Don't be too surprised, therefore, if your Animate control is unable to play every AVI file you find.

Other Coolbar controls

As I mentioned, you can add any windowed control to a Coolbar band. The only rule is that the component must be of a class that is derived from TWinControl at some place in the class's hierarchy. For example, you can add a ComboBox component to a Coolbar because the TComboBox class is derived from TCustomComboBox, which is in turn derived from TWinControl. However, you can't add a TShape object to a Coolbar because the TShape class is not derived from TWinControl.

Note   It is technically possible to drop a nonwindowed control object onto a Coolbar, but this does not create a new band for the control. For best results, limit the controls that you add to Coolbars to components of classes derived from TWinControl.

To demonstrate how a Coolbar can hold any windowed control, I dropped a DateTimePicker object from the Win32 palette onto CoolDemo's Coolbar object. Refer back to Figure 7-9, or run the CoolDemo program, to view this control. Because the DateTimePicker object resides on a Coolbar band, users can resize and move the control to another location by clicking and dragging the band's vertical bar at far left.

To display the label "Date selector" to the left of the TDateTimePicker object, I opened the Bands Editor (by clicking the ellipsis next to the Coolbar's Bands property), and selected the band that holds the TDateTimePicker. I next entered the label into the band object's Text property. Unlike many other components with labels, you must use the Text property—TCoolBand objects do not have a Caption field.

Note   To display labels in Coolbar bands, the Coolbar object's ShowText property must be set to True.

StatusBars

As explained earlier in this chapter, one way to create a status panel is to insert a Panel object into a form. This technique gives you a wide variety of display options, but there's a simpler way to achieve good-looking status panels by using the StatusBar component from the Win32 palette. In most cases, this component is all you need to create status bars in your application windows.

To avoid confusion, I call the interface element a *statusbar* when it uses the StatusBar component; and a *status panel* when it uses the Delphi Panel component.

Creating a StatusBar

Statusbars normally sit at the bottom of the window, and they provide various bits of information about the program's state. Each statusbar may be divided into panels (not to be confused with the Panel component), each of which can display text or graphics. In most cases, you should display information in statusbars that users need to find at a glance such as line and column numbers, cursor positions, file sizes, keyboard reminders, and error messages. You can also optionally add a window gripper to the bottom-right corner of a statusbar—this makes resizing a thin-bordered window easier.

Figure 7-14 shows a sample statusbar from the Status project, located on the book's accompanying CD-ROM in the Source\Status directory. To run the program, and view its source code, complete the following steps:

1. Open the Status.dpr project file and press F9.

2. Move the mouse cursor inside the window to update the X and Y coordinate values displayed in the statusbar's first two panels.

3. Click the Force Exception button to display an error message in the middle panel.

4. Grab the resize gripper with the mouse and drag to resize the window—notice that the statusbar automatically resizes, but only the message panel changes length.

Many of these features are enacted under program control, which as I explain following the program listing, demonstrates several common techniques in statusbar programming.

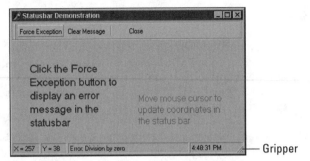

Figure 7-14: A statusbar is divided into panels, each of which can display text or graphics. Notice the window resize gripper at the statusbar's lower-right corner.

To create a statusbar, drop a StatusBar component from the Win32 palette onto a form. Normally, the object jumps to the bottom of the window, where most statusbars are displayed. However, as with other components, you can alter the Align property to place the statusbar on any window edge (alLeft, alRight, alTop, or alBottom) , or to fill the window's client area (alClient).

Each StatusBar object may have one or more panels, each of which is an object of the TStatusPanel class. To create a panel, follow these steps:

1. Select the StatusBar object in the form's window.

2. Click the ellipsis next to the Panels property. This opens the Status Panels Editor (see Figure 7-15).

3. Click the Add New icon to add a new panel.

4. Click Delete Selected to delete the highlighted panel.

Use the up-and-down arrow buttons to move a selected panel up or down in the list.

This editor is the only way to access individual panel objects at design time. Using the editor, highlight the panel you want to modify, and then use the Object Inspector to enter property values.

StatusBar properties

The StatusBar object has several properties that you can use to configure the entire statusbar. Remember that each panel in a statusbar is accessible only through the Status Panels Editor, which opens when you click the ellipsis next to the StatusBar's Panels property. Selected StatusBar properties include the following:

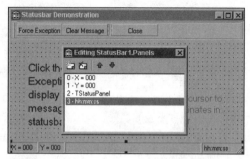

Figure 7-15: Use the Status Panels Editor to create, delete, and arrange a StatusBar object's panels.

✦ **Canvas** — Use this object to paint text and graphics in a StatusBar panel. You don't have to do this for text-only panels. You use this field only with owner-draw panels, which I discuss in detail near the end of this chapter (see Owner draw StatusBar panels).

✦ **Panels** — This property is an array of TStatusPanel objects, each of which defines the appearance and content of an individual StatusBar panel. At design time, click the ellipsis next to this property to open the Status Panels Editor. At run time, you can access the individual StatusPanel objects using this array — for example, to change a panel's text.

✦ **SimplePanel** — If you need only a single-panel statusbar, set this property True and ignore the Panels array. Use the next field, SimpleText, to display a message in this simple statusbar. You can also use this field to temporarily convert a multipanel statusbar to a simple one — to display a lengthy message, for example. Just set SimplePanel to True in a program statement, and assign text to SimpleText. To return the statusbar to its multipanel appearance, set SimplePanel to False.

✦ **SimpleText** — Assign any string to display in a statusbar that has its SimplePanel field set to True. To display text in a multipanel statusbar, use the Panels array.

✦ **SizeGrip** — Set this property to True to display an optional window resize gripper at the statusbar's lower-right corner. This makes it easier for users to resize windows by clicking and dragging with the mouse.

StatusPanel properties

Each panel in a StatusBar is an object of the TStatusPanel class. Although this is a component, it does not show up in the VCL palette. The only way to create and modify TStatusPanel objects is by using the Status Panels Editor (click the ellipsis button next to the StatusBar object's Panels property). Use the editor to add, delete, and rearrange panels. Select individual panels and then use the Object Inspector to modify the following properties:

✦ **Alignment** — This property affects how text is displayed in the panel. Set to taLeftJustify (the default) to display text flush against the left boundary; use taRightJustify to display text against the right boundary; or use taCenter to center text inside the panel's width.

✦ **Bevel** — Panels have three display options. Use pbLowered (the default) for a sunken 3D effect, pbRaised for a raised panel, or pbNone for a flat appearance.

✦ **Style** — Normally set to psText so that Windows automatically updates the text content inside the panel. If you set this to psOwnerDraw, you are responsible for displaying the panel's content in a StatusBar OnDrawPanel event handler, using the StatusBar's Canvas property. A bit later in this chapter, I explain how to use the style and event to display graphics in StatusBar panels (see "Owner-draw StatusBar panels").

✦ **Text** — Assign the text string to display in the panel. The text is aligned according to the Alignment property, and is automatically displayed if Style is set to psText. You may use this property to store the panel's text if Style is set to psOwnerDraw, but in that case you are responsible for displaying the text in the panel.

✦ **Width** — This is the panel's width in pixels. Although the StatusBar automatically resizes when the window size changes, you might want to control the widths of individual panels. For example, run the Status sample application and resize the window — notice that only the large middle panel changes length; the others stay the same size. This requires some programming, as I explain following the program's listing next.

The Status sample application

The Status application, located in the Source\Status directory on the book's accompanying CD-ROM, demonstrates several key elements of StatusBar programming. Listing 7-7 shows the Status program's source code. Refer back to Figure 7-14 for an illustration of the program's display.

Listing 7-7: **Status\Main.pas**

```
unit Main;

interface
```

```
uses
  Windows, Messages, SysUtils, Classes, Graphics, Controls,
  Forms, Dialogs, ComCtrls, StdCtrls, Buttons, ExtCtrls,
  ToolWin;

type
  TMainForm = class(TForm)
    Label1: TLabel;
    StatusBar1: TStatusBar;
    Timer1: TTimer;
    Coolbar1: TCoolbar;
    ToolBar1: TToolBar;
    ToolButton1: TToolButton;
    ToolButton2: TToolButton;
    ToolButton3: TToolButton;
    ToolButton4: TToolButton;
    Label2: TLabel;
    procedure FormMouseMove(Sender: TObject;
      Shift: TShiftState; X, Y: Integer);
    procedure FormResize(Sender: TObject);
    procedure Timer1Timer(Sender: TObject);
    procedure ToolButton1Click(Sender: TObject);
    procedure ToolButton2Click(Sender: TObject);
    procedure ToolButton4Click(Sender: TObject);
    procedure Label1MouseMove(Sender: TObject;
      Shift: TShiftState; X, Y: Integer);
  private
    { Private declarations }
  public
    { Public declarations }
  end;

var
  MainForm: TMainForm;

implementation

{$R *.DFM}

{ Rather than use literal index values, this section defines
  descriptive contants for the statusbar's four panels }
const
  XPanelIndex       = 0;
  YPanelIndex       = 1;
  MessagePanelIndex = 2;
  TimePanelIndex    = 3;

{ Update X and Y coordinate values in the statusbar }
```

(continued)

Listing 7-7 *(continued)*

```
procedure TMainForm.FormMouseMove(Sender: TObject;
  Shift: TShiftState; X, Y: Integer);
begin
  StatusBar1.Panels[XPanelIndex].Text := 'X = ' + IntToStr(X);
  StatusBar1.Panels[YPanelIndex].Text := 'Y = ' + IntToStr(Y);
end;

{ Calculate width of middle panel so the others stay the
  same size when the window resizes. }
procedure TMainForm.FormResize(Sender: TObject);
const
  Fudge = 25;   // Allow extra space for width calculation
var
  W: Integer;   // Width of fixed-size panels
begin
  with StatusBar1 do
  begin
    W := Panels[XPanelIndex].Width +
      Panels[YPanelIndex].Width + Panels[TimePanelIndex].Width;
    Panels[MessagePanelIndex].Width := Width - (W + Fudge);
  end;
end;

{ Display the time in the rightmost statusbar panel }
procedure TMainForm.Timer1Timer(Sender: TObject);
begin
  StatusBar1.Panels[TimePanelIndex].Text := TimeToStr(Time);
end;

{ Force an exception to occur and display its message
  in a statusbar panel. The call to ShowMessage is never
  made, but is included to prevent the compiler from
  optimizing out the integer division. }
procedure TMainForm.ToolButton1Click(Sender: TObject);
var
  K, J: Integer;
begin
  K := 100; J := 0;
  try
    K := K div J;  // Force divide by zero exception
    ShowMessage(IntToStr(K) + ':' + IntToStr(J));
  except on E: Exception do
    begin
      MessageBeep(0);
```

```
      StatusBar1.Panels[MessagePanelIndex].Text :=
        'Error: ' + E.Message;
    end;
  end;
end;

{ Clear the text from middle statusbar panel }
procedure TMainForm.ToolButton2Click(Sender: TObject);
begin
  StatusBar1.Panels[MessagePanelIndex].Text := '';
end;

{ End the program }
procedure TMainForm.ToolButton4Click(Sender: TObject);
begin
  Close;
end;

{ Translate mouse coordinates when the cursor moves over
  one of the two large labels, and pass the results on
  to the MainForm's OnMouseMove event handler. }
procedure TMainForm.Label1MouseMove(Sender: TObject;
  Shift: TShiftState; X, Y: Integer);
var
  T: TLabel;  // Refers to Sender as a TLabel object
begin
  T := Sender as TLabel;  // Initialize T
  // Pass coordinates to MainForm's event handler
  MainForm.FormMouseMove(Sender, Shift, T.Left + X, T.Top + Y);
end;

end.
```

The Status program displays a four-panel statusbar at the bottom of the window. To create the panels, I opened the Status Panels Editor (by clicking the ellipsis next to the StatusBar's Panels property) and added four panel objects. I initially set the third panel's width to 250, leaving the others set to the default width, 50. I also entered text into all but the larger panel, just to show something at design time to remind me of a panel's purpose. This isn't strictly necessary, however. Figure 7-16 shows the form's design-time appearance. The Timer icon is invisible at run time — this object provides a Timer event that the program uses to update the time in the rightmost panel.

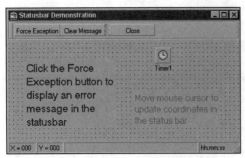

Figure 7-16: The Status program's form window at design time

For demonstration purposes, the first two panels in the sample program's StatusBar display the mouse cursor's *x* and *y* coordinates. Run the program and move the mouse cursor inside the program's window — the coordinates are shown in the StatusBar. Two procedures update this information. The first is the MainForm object's OnMouseMove event handler, which executes the statements:

```
StatusBar1.Panels[XPanelIndex].Text := 'X = ' + IntToStr(X);
StatusBar1.Panels[YPanelIndex].Text := 'Y = ' + IntToStr(Y);
```

This shows how to access individual panels in a StatusBar using the Panels array. The index values in brackets can be literal whole numbers (the first panel's index is always zero), however I defined descriptive constants such as XPanelIndex (see the *const* declarations about midway through the listing). Because you might add and subtract, or rearrange panels, while designing your program, it's a good idea to use descriptive constants rather than literal integers. If you change the StatusBar's panels, you can simply update the constant assignments accordingly.

The program's two large text objects, which tell you to click the Force Exception button and to move the mouse cursor, receive their own mouse move events. For this reason, a second procedure is necessary to update the *x* and *y* coordinate values in the StatusBar when the mouse cursor passes over the text. This is a bit tricky, and is accomplished in the Label1MouseMove procedure, which is also attached to the second label's OnMouseMove event. The label objects have their own coordinate system, with [0,0] at the upper-right corner. To display the mouse position relative to the window's client area, it is necessary to add the position of each label [Left, Top] to the coordinates received by the Labels' OnMouseMove event.

Updating the time in a StatusBar panel is simple. To do this, I inserted a Timer object into the form, and programmed its OnTimer event handler to execute the statement:

```
StatusBar1.Panels[TimePanelIndex].Text := TimeToStr(Time);
```

Again, using a constant TimePanelIndex is safer and more descriptive than a literal integer index value to access the Panels array. Simply setting the Text property of this panel is all that's needed to display the time every second, the default frequency of the Timer's event.

To simulate an error message display—one of the most typical uses for a StatusBar panel—the ToolButton1Click event handler purposely divides an integer variable by zero. This causes the except portion of the *try-except* block to beep the speaker and display the exception's Message field using the code:

```
MessageBeep(0);
  StatusBar1.Panels[MessagePanelIndex].Text :=
  'Error: ' + E.Message;
```

Once again, I used a descriptive constant to access the proper StatusBar panel in the Panels array. Setting the Text property displays the error message. To clear that message, another ToolButton event handler assigns a null string to this same property:

```
StatusBar1.Panels[MessagePanelIndex].Text := '';
```

Note When you run a program from inside Delphi, if an exception occurs, Delphi's debugger displays the current program state and might open the CPU window. If this happens, select Tools|Environment Options, click the Debugger page tab, and highlight Delphi Exceptions in the Exceptions list box. To prevent interrupting the program and to enable it to handle exceptions normally, set the Handled By button to User Program. To return to interrupting the program on receiving an exception, change this button back to Debugger.

When you resize the Status program's window, the StatusBar automatically resizes to fit along the window's bottom edge. However, this default effect isn't good enough to achieve what I wanted—to have the coordinate and time panels stay fixed in size, and to have only the larger message panel grow and shrink as needed. Accomplishing this effect took a little programming. To see this, run Status and resize the window. Examine how only the third StatusBar panel changes in length.

To provide a place for the code that controls the panel widths, Status uses an OnResize event handler for the program's form window. This event is called when the window is initially displayed, and also at any time the window size changes. To update the panel widths, the event handler executes this code:

```
with StatusBar1 do
begin
  W := Panels[XPanelIndex].Width +
    Panels[YPanelIndex].Width + Panels[TimePanelIndex].Width;
  Panels[MessagePanelIndex].Width := Width - (W + Fudge);
end;
```

Variable *W* is set to the sum of the widths of the three fixed-size panels. This value, plus a "fudge factor," is subtracted from the StatusBar's total width. The result equals the target width of the message panel, which is simply assigned to that panel's Width property. As a result of this code, resizing the window changes only the third panel's length. The coordinate and time panels remain fixed in size.

Owner-draw StatusBar panels

When you need more control over how items are displayed in a StatusBar panel, you can request notification that a panel requires updating. You might use this opportunity to draw graphics in panels, or to display text using different fonts. This is called an owner-draw StatusBar panel (or, in more general terms, an owner-draw control).

Normally, Windows takes care of displaying text in StatusBar panels. All you need to do is assign that text, for example, in an event handler. Simply assign any string to a panel object's Text property using a statement like this:

```
StatusBar1.Panels[2].Text := 'Insert mode';
```

Assigning a string to a panel's Text property immediately displays that text. If later on the panel needs updating — for instance, when the window size changes or when it is uncovered by another window — Windows automatically redisplays the StatusBar panel's text using the string saved in the Text property.

To take over this responsibility, set a panel's Style property to psOwnerDraw using the Status Panels Editor (click the ellipsis next to the StatusBar's Panels property). You can do that for selected panels, or for them all. With this style selected, whenever Windows requires the panel to display its contents, an OnDrawPanel event is triggered for the StatusBar object. Into this procedure, you can insert the programming statements you need to display items in StatusBar panels.

Note   The OnDrawPanel event is associated with the StatusBar object. Each Panel in that object must have its Style property set to psOwnerDraw for the event to be triggered for that panel.

On the CD-ROM   As an example of how to do this, the StatusOD project (that's OD for "Owner Draw"), demonstrates how to change the font styles of text items in StatusBar panels, and also how to draw an icon image inside a panel. Figure 7-17 shows the program's display. Listing 7-8 shows the program's source code. The program's files are on the book's accompanying CD-ROM in the Source\StatusOD directory. To load this program into Delphi, open the StatusOD.dpr file, and press F9 to compile and run.

Figure 7-17: Owner-draw StatusBar panels make it possible to change text fonts and display graphics as the StatusOD program demonstrates.

Listing 7-8: **StatusOD\Main.pas**

```
unit Main;

interface

uses
  Windows, Messages, SysUtils, Classes, Graphics, Controls,
  Forms, Dialogs, Images, ComCtrls;

type
  TMainForm = class(TForm)
    StatusBar1: TStatusBar;
    ImageList1: TImageList;
    procedure StatusBar1DrawPanel(StatusBar: TStatusBar;
      Panel: TStatusPanel; const Rect: TRect);
  private
    { Private declarations }
  public
    { Public declarations }
  end;

var
  MainForm: TMainForm;

implementation

{$R *.DFM}

procedure TMainForm.StatusBar1DrawPanel(StatusBar: TStatusBar;
  Panel: TStatusPanel; const Rect: TRect);
var
  SavedStyles: TFontStyles;
begin
```

(continued)

Listing 7-8 *(continued)*

```
with StatusBar, Canvas do
begin
  SavedStyles := Font.Style;  // Save current font styles
  // Set font style or draw an icon depending
  // on which Panel needs updating.
  case Panel.Index of
    0 : Font.Style := [fsBold];
    1 : Font.Style := [fsItalic];
    2 : ImageList1.Draw(Canvas,
          Rect.Left + 2, Rect.Top + 2, 0);
    3 : Font.Style := [fsBold, fsItalic];
  end;
  // Draw text in all panels except the third,
  // which displays an icon.
  if Panel.Index <> 2 then
    TextRect(Rect, Rect.Left, Rect.Top, Panel.Text);
  Font.Style := SavedStyles;  // Restore saved font styles
  end;
end;

end.
```

Procedure StatusBar1DrawPanel in the listing shows how to program owner-draw StatusBar panels. Each panel in the demonstration program has its Style property set to psOwnerDraw. This causes the StatusBar's OnDrawPanel event handler to receive notification when the panel requires redrawing. This might be when the program first starts, when the window changes size, or when another statement elsewhere in the program assigns a new string to a panel's Text property. In all cases, the OnDrawPanel event handler is called to update the panel's contents. In this example, because the StatusBar has four panels, the OnDrawPanel event is called four times: once for each panel, whenever the StatusBar requires updating.

One of the first jobs of the event handler is to determine which panel needs to be drawn. The easiest way to do this is to use the Panel parameter's Index property. This equals the index value that accesses the panel object in the StatusBar's Panels array. This relationship might be best understood programmatically—the following is a true statement:

```
StatusBar.Panels[Panel.Index] = Panel;
```

The event handler receives a StatusBar parameter that represents the object containing the panel. The Panel object is referenced by the Panel parameter. A third parameter, Rect, gives the dimensions of the panel onscreen — if the window is changing size, this record contains the new size of the panel.

To draw text in different styles, the sample program assigns sets of style constants to the StatusBar.Canvas's Font property. I'm jumping ahead a little here — the concept of a Canvas is discussed in Chapter 13, Developing Graphics Applications. Think of a Canvas as a surface on which you can paint inside a windowed control. In the case of a StatusBar, the Canvas provides the surface on which to paint or draw text inside an individual panel.

A *with* statement in the procedure simplifies some of the code. For example, to assign the fsBold font style to the Canvas's Font.Style property, the case statement executes the statement:

```
Font.Style := [fsBold];
```

Font styles are sets, and therefore, even though only one value is specified, it must be in brackets. If a *with* statement hadn't been used, this statement would be written:

```
StatusBar.Canvas.Font.Style := [fsBold];
```

Both statements are equivalent, but the *with* statement simplifies the former statement by telling Delphi to use the Font property in the StatusBar's Canvas by default. After setting a font's style, the program calls a StatusBar's Canvas method to display text using that style. This statement:

```
TextRect(Rect, Rect.Left, Rect.Top, Panel.Text);
```

draws the Panel object's Text value using the Rect passed as a parameter to the event handler. The first mention of Rect here specifies the boundaries for the output — if drawing the text exceeds the size of the panel, it is clipped to fit. The next two values specify the location of the text item's top-left corner. The final parameter is, of course, the string to draw.

Drawing graphics in a panel is just as easy. To do this in the sample program, the case statement calls the Draw method in the program's ImageList object:

```
ImageList1.Draw(Canvas,
  Rect.Left + 2, Rect.Top + 2, 0);
```

You don't have to use an ImageList object, but it is the simplest way to import graphics bitmaps, and especially so for icons. The ImageList component efficiently stores such images as a *single* bitmap in memory. Simply specify the index number of the image you want (0 in this case, passed as the last argument to Draw), and the ImageList object retrieves that much of the image. Notice how the Draw statement specifies the Canvas of the StatusBar1 object.

Expert-User Tips

✦ Assign a value to the application object's HintPause property to alter the time delay for a hint box to appear. The default value is 800 milliseconds. For example, to program a faster-appearing hint box, you can assign 250 ($^1/_4$ second) to Application.HintPause. You might do this in any event handler (use the form's OnCreate event to configure hints at startup).

✦ Hint boxes are yellow with black text, which resembles the original Post-It® Notes. To change this color, you can assign a new TColor value to the application's HintColor property. For example, to create red hints, assign clRed to Application.HintColor. (Look up the TColor data type in Delphi's online help for more information.) Keep in mind that users can change the color of hint boxes by modifying Windows system settings.

✦ When designing segmented status panels with multiple TPanel components, select a font for the main panel, and then set the ParentFont property to True for each subpanel. Each subdivision then uses the main panel's font settings. This is easier than assigning font properties for each subpanel.

✦ You can use TPanel objects as platforms for displaying text anywhere in a form window—you don't have to restrict TPanels for use as toolbars and status panels. For example, Delphi's Compiling information dialog uses TPanels to display progress information during compilation. To see this window, choose the Options⏐Environment command, select the Preferences page tab to enable Show compiler progress, and compile a sample application.

✦ Insert a Panel into a form and set its Align property to alClient. This causes the Panel to completely fill the form window. Select values for BevelInner and BevelOuter, and try various BevelWidth and BorderWidth settings (25 and 10, for example). You can achieve some interesting window interiors by using a Panel as a window's background. (If components disappear, select the Panel and choose Edit⏐Send to Back.)

✦ Rather than use a glyph bitmap, you can use the SpeedButton Font property to display symbols. Set the button's Font to a TrueType font such as WingDings. The Caption still displays ASCII text characters. This works for any text item with a Font property.

✦ When using the Format function, a common mistake is forgetting to enter arguments in brackets. Remember that Format's Args parameter is an open array — in other words, a variable-length parameter list. For example, the expression [V1,V2,V3] passes to Args the variables V1, V2, and V3.

✦ The TCoolbar and TToolBar classes are each derived from the abstract class, TToolWindow, which defines the abstract characteristics of a window with a custom client area and borders. This makes TCoolbar and TToolBar siblings (they share the same parent class). To understand more about the Coolbar and ToolBar components, you might also want to study the online and printed documentation for the TToolWindow abstract class.

✦ A Coolbar is a windowed control, and it may be inserted into another Coolbar to create a multilevel concoction. You might use this technique to create Coolbars with some bands arranged vertically and others horizontally — in fact, this is the only way to achieve that effect. However, be sure you truly need the added complexity of a multilevel Coolbar before going hog-wild with this idea.

Projects to Try

7-1: Create a toolbar that users can move to the window's top, bottom, right, or left borders. In addition to assigning a new value to the Panel's Align property, you have to adjust SpeedButton Left and Right properties to new relative positions within the toolbar Panel object boundaries.

7-2: Create a status panel that shows the date and time. (Hint: Refer to the Toolbar2 application's source code.) Test your application by running it overnight to be sure it changes the date at midnight.

7-3: Design a floating color-selection toolbar, using the Toolbar3 application as a guide.

7-4: Experiment with run-time clicking and dragging of objects such as Buttons and SpeedButtons. Use programming similar to that in Toolbar3 to respond to OnMouseDown, OnMouseMove, and OnMouseUp events.

7-5: Write a test program with a status panel that displays an error message. Use the Format function to create a string from an integer error code. Add buttons or menu commands to the program to simulate various types of errors.

7-6: Insert the date and time into a status panel.

7-7: Design a form template with the status panel from the CapsLock sample application (refer back to Figure 7-8 and Listing 7-5).

7-8: Convert the Tabs program on the CD-ROM in the Source\Tabs directory to use Win32 ToolBar and StatusBar objects.

Summary

✦ Use the Panel component to create toolbars and status panels. Typically, toolbars contain SpeedButton objects. Status panels display text.

✦ SpeedButtons can be spring-loaded (they pop back up when you release the mouse) or they can be sticky (they stay down when clicked).

✦ Group together SpeedButton objects by setting their GroupIndex properties to the same nonzero, positive integer value. The SpeedButtons then operate like a set of RadioButtons — only one button in the group may be down. Set AllowAllUp to True to permit all buttons in the group to be in the off state.

✦ Design floating toolbars by creating OnMouseDown, OnMouseMove, and OnMouseUp event handlers. Call the Windows SetCapture function to initiate a click-and-drag operation. Always pair every call to SetCapture with a call to ReleaseCapture. See Chapter 12 for information on Delphi 4's new docking window capabilities which you can also use to create floating toolbars.

✦ A status panel resembles a toolbar, but usually displays text instead of buttons. Subdivide a status panel by inserting Panel objects into a main Panel. Display text in panel subdivisions by assigning strings to the Caption property. Alternatively, insert Label objects into each subpanel and assign text to the Label Captions — you can also display dimmed text in status panels this way by setting a Label object's Enabled property to False.

✦ Use Delphi's Format function to create formatted strings. The function resembles the standard C and C++ function *sprintf()*. Format is especially useful in creating strings for display in status panels, but it is a handy function for many other purposes as well.

✦ A classic status panel displays the settings of the Caps Lock, Num Lock, Scroll Lock, and Ins keys, as this chapter's CapsLock program demonstrates. Call the Windows GetKeyState function to obtain key-toggle settings.

✦ A Coolbar component from the Win32 palette can hold bands of windowed controls such as Win32 ToolBars and drop-down lists. Users can rearrange Coolbar bands at run time.

✦ The StatusBar component from the Win32 palette provides a simple way to create a multipanel statusbar in a window.

In the next chapter, you learn how to use Delphi's list components such as ListBox and ComboBox. You also investigate list classes such as TList, TStrings, and TStringList.

✦   ✦   ✦

Making Lists

✦   ✦   ✦   ✦

In This Chapter

Components

List components

String and other lists

✦   ✦   ✦   ✦

If there's one data structure that, sooner or later, every programmer uses, it's a list. It's not too surprising then, to discover that one of the most useful Windows controls is the list box. With this control, and the related combo box, which adds a text-entry area to a list box, you can create string lists for just about any purpose. You can sort list-box data, and you can choose from several different types of list box and combo box styles — for example, to permit multiple selections, or to incrementally search a drop-down list based on partial entries.

Delphi also provides several related list-making classes, such as TList, TStrings, and TStringList. These are all useful weapons in the battle to create sophisticated user interfaces, and as you discover in this chapter, Delphi provides a rich assortment of tools for maintaining just about any imaginable type of list.

Components

The following is a list of Delphi's components for making lists:

✦ **ComboBox** — This standard Windows control combines a ListBox with an Edit object. Depending on the ComboBox object's style, users can choose from listed entries, which optionally appear in a drop-down box, or they can enter new data into the Edit control. Palette: Standard.

✦ **ListBox** — Use this general-purpose, standard Windows control to create lists of strings from which users can select entries using keyboard and mouse commands. As this chapter explains, ListBox objects provide a TStrings array named Items that provides easy access to ListBox data. Palette: Standard.

✦ **StringGrid** — Despite its name, this component is capable of storing string and bitmap (or other) data. This makes StringGrid especially useful for creating lists of named objects, as demonstrated by this chapter's GlyphLst application, which displays the filenames and bitmaps for every glyph icon image supplied with Delphi. Palette: Additional

List Components

The two standard Delphi components, ListBox and ComboBox, can probably handle the bulk of your program's list-selection requirements. As you learn in this section, Delphi enhances these standard Windows controls to provide easy access to listed data. For example, with simple statements, you can transfer ListBox and ComboBox strings to and from text files. This section's sample application — a ToDo List utility — demonstrates this technique, and also shows how to transfer strings between two ListBox objects using one of Delphi's dialog-box templates. You can find the ToDo application in the Source\ToDo directory on the CD-ROM.

ListBoxes

The ListBox component provides a number of interesting properties that enable you to select among various styles. For example, ListBox objects normally have a dark outline border, but you can set BorderStyle to bsNone for a borderless list. (By the way, this configuration looks good with a ListBox inserted into a Bevel.) Assign a value to the Columns property to display listed items in more than one column. This value is zero by default — set it to two or more to create columnar lists.

There are many different ways to insert data into a ListBox object. At design time, click the ellipsis button for the Items property to open Delphi's String list editor and enter your listed items. Or, you can copy text from another file into the editor. This method stores the listed strings in the program's .exe code file and automatically inserts the strings into the ListBox object.

To insert strings into a ListBox at run time, a program can call methods for the Items property of the TStrings class. Every ListBox object provides an Items object for easy access to listed data. For example, to prompt users for new strings and enter them into a ListBox, you can use programming such as this:

```
var
  S: String;
begin
  S := InputBox('Test Program', 'Enter a string', '');
  if Length(S) > 0 then
    ListBox1.Items.Add(S);
end;
```

Notice you call Add for the Items object that ListBox1 owns. The ListBox itself does not have an Add method — that method belongs to Items. However, you can simplify the preceding code by using a *with* statement like this:

```
with ListBox1.Items do
  Add(S);
```

The *with* statement tells Delphi to use the methods and other declarations in Items by default. To get strings out of a ListBox, use Items as an array. For example, define a string variable such as:

```
var
  S: String;
```

Next, assign any ListBox string to *S* by specifying an Item integer index with the statement, which appears to access Items as an array of Strings:

```
S := ListBox1.Items[0];
```

Appearances are deceiving in this case because Items isn't actually an array — it is a TListBox class property you use in the same way as you do Pascal arrays. To store its data, the Items property owns a Strings array used in statements that specify index values in brackets. The following statement, for example, is exactly equivalent to the preceding one:

```
S := ListBox1.Items.Strings[0];
```

Because the Strings array is the default for Items, its name needn't be specified. Doing so does no harm, however, so use whichever type of statement you prefer. Whatever method you use to index a ListBox's strings, always limit the index to the range 0 to Items.Count — 1. If you don't, Delphi raises an exception. Use a *for* loop, for example, to access all of a ListBox's strings:

```
for I := 0 to ListBox1.Items.Count - 1 do
begin
  S := ListBox1.Items[I];
  ShowMessage(S);  { Or do something else with S }
end;
```

For lengthy lists, you might want to supply data from a text file users can prepare and edit with the Windows Notepad. To load a text file's strings into a ListBox, call the LoadFromFile method for Items as in this example:

```
ListBox1.Items.LoadFromFile('C:\data\file.txt');
```

Call AddStrings to add multiple strings from one ListBox (or any other component with a TStrings property) to another. For example, this statement appends strings from ListBox2 to any strings already in ListBox1:

```
ListBox1.Items.AddStrings(ListBox2.Items);
```

To swap two listed items, call Exchange, as in this code, which swaps the first and last strings in a ListBox:

```
with ListBox1.Items do
   if Count >= 2 then Exchange(0, Count - 1);
```

Notice, here again, the range of strings is from index values 0 to Count –1. To delete a string from a ListBox, call the Delete method, which requires the item's integer index. For example, this statement deletes the fourth item from ListBox1 (the first item's index is zero, so the fourth one is identified by an index value equal to 3):

```
ListBox1.Items.Delete(3);
```

Rather than specify a literal index, or in cases where you don't know an item's index, to find that index value, call IndexOf, which returns –1 if the specified item doesn't exist:

```
Index := ListBox1.Items.IndexOf('Item to find');
if Index >= 0 then
begin
   { ... ok to use Index }
end;
```

Call the Clear method to delete all items from a list:

```
ListBox1.Items.Clear;
```

Scrolling in ListBoxes

Like a box of Cracker Jack, ListBoxes come with a free surprise — if there are more lines to display than fit within the ListBox's space, a vertical scroll bar automatically appears. When the ListBox can display all items, the vertical scroll bar automatically disappears.

Two properties affect vertical scrolling. ItemHeight indicates the height in pixels of one text line. Set IntegralHeight to True to ensure that only full text lines appear in the ListBox's borders. Set IntegralHeight False to permit partial lines at the bottom of the ListBox.

When you select a Font for a ListBox, or for a form that contains a ListBox, Delphi automatically adjusts ItemHeight to a corresponding value. To override this automatic adjustment, you must set Style to lbOwnerDrawFixed or lbOwnerDrawVariable. For more information on creating owner-draw controls, see "Using the TStrings class," later in this chapter.

ListBoxes can also display horizontal scroll bars. To enable horizontal scrolling, call the ListBox's inherited Perform method, which sends a message to the Windows ListBox control to which the ListBox component provides an object-oriented interface. The message to send in this case is LB_SETHORIZONTALEXTENT. Along with the message, pass a horizontal scrolling range in pixels, plus a third unused argument which is always zero. For example, this statement adds horizontal scroll bars to a ListBox, with a maximum scrolling range of 1000 pixels:

```
ListBox1.Perform(LB_SETHORIZONTALEXTENT, 1000, 0);
```

Instead of passing a literal range such as 1000, a better program would set the horizontal scrolling range to the width, in pixels, of the longest string. Listing 8-1 shows how to determine this value. The program calls TextWidth in the ListBox's Canvas (an object that gives you access to the Windows graphics device interface, or GDI). TextWidth returns the width, in pixels, of a string for the Canvas's current font. After the *for* loop executes, variable *K* equals the maximum string width, in pixels, which the program passes to the ListBox using the LB_SETHORIZONTALEXTENT Windows message.

On the CD-ROM

To keep horizontal scroll bar ranges in synch with a ListBox's data, perform the steps illustrated in Listing 8-1 after every addition and deletion, and after changing the ListBox's font. On the CD-ROM, this listing is in the Source\Lists directory in file Adjust.pas. Use it to adjust ListBox horizontal scroll bar ranges to the width in pixels of the longest listed string.

Listing 8-1: **Code to adjust ListBox horizontal scroll bar ranges**

```
var
  I, J, K: Integer;
begin
  with ListBox1 do
  begin
    K := 0;
    for I := 0 to Items.Count _ 1 do
    begin
      J := Canvas.TextWidth(Items[I]);
      if J > K then K := J;
    end;
    Perform(LB_SETHORIZONTALEXTENT, K, 0);
  end;
end;
```

Horizontal scroll bars are not recommended for multicolumn ListBox objects. However, you may adjust column width by sending the ListBox object a LB_SETCOLUMNWIDTH message using a statement such as this:

```
ListBox1.Perform(LB_SETCOLUMNWIDTH, 100, 0);
```

Creating a ListBox

This book's ListFont application on the CD-ROM in the Source\ListFont directory demonstrates how to insert a list of system font names into a ListBox, and then use those names to display a string in each font style. Figure 8-1 shows the program's display. Run ListFont and select any font to display the sample text in the font's default style. Click the Size button to select a new point size. Only TrueType fonts are scaleable to all sizes. Listing 8-2 shows the program's source code.

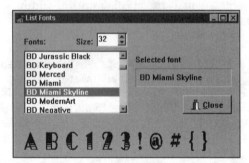

Figure 8-1: ListFont loads system font names into a ListBox object.

To insert a list of font names into a ListBox, the FontList program executes the following statement in the form's OnCreate event handler:

```
FontListBox.Items := Screen.Fonts;
```

To sort the font list alphabetically, set the ListBox's Sorted property to True.

Listing 8-2: **Listfont\Main.pas**

```
unit Main;

interface

uses
  SysUtils, Windows, Messages, Classes, Graphics,
```

```
    Controls, Forms, Dialogs, StdCtrls, Spin, Buttons, ExtCtrls;

type
  TMainForm = class(TForm)
    FontListBox: TListBox;
    Label1: TLabel;
    SampleLabel: TLabel;
    SpinEdit1: TSpinEdit;
    Label3: TLabel;
    FontNameLabel: TLabel;
    Label2: TLabel;
    Bevel1: TBevel;
    CloseBitBtn: TBitBtn;
    procedure FormCreate(Sender: TObject);
    procedure FontListBoxDblClick(Sender: TObject);
    procedure FontListBoxKeyDown(Sender: TObject;
      var Key: Word; Shift: TShiftState);
    procedure SpinEdit1Change(Sender: TObject);
    procedure CloseBitBtnClick(Sender: TObject);
  private
    { Private declarations }
  public
    { Public declarations }
  end;

var
  MainForm: TMainForm;

implementation

{$R *.DFM}

procedure TMainForm.FormCreate(Sender: TObject);
begin
  FontListBox.Items := Screen.Fonts;
end;

procedure TMainForm.FontListBoxDblClick(Sender: TObject);
begin
  with FontListBox do
  if ItemIndex >= 0 then
  begin
    SampleLabel.Font.Name := FontListBox.Items[ItemIndex];
    FontNameLabel.Caption := SampleLabel.Font.Name;
  end;
end;

procedure TMainForm.FontListBoxKeyDown(Sender: TObject;
```

(continued)

Listing 8-2 *(continued)*

```
  var Key: Word; Shift: TShiftState);
begin
  if Key in [VK_RETURN, VK_SPACE] then
    FontListBoxDblClick(Sender);
end;

procedure TMainForm.SpinEdit1Change(Sender: TObject);
begin
  SampleLabel.Font.Size := SpinEdit1.Value;
end;

procedure TMainForm.CloseBitBtnClick(Sender: TObject);
begin
  Close;
end;

end.
```

FontList uses two techniques for selecting font names from the FontListBox object. In the ListBox's OnDblClick event handler, an *if* statement first checks whether the ListBox's ItemIndex property is greater than or equal to zero. If so, the user has selected an item from the ListBox and not simply double-clicked hot air. The two subsequent statements assign the selected font's name from Items to the SampleLabel's Font.Name property. Simply assigning the Font property a new Name changes the font of the sample text displayed at the bottom of the window. Lastly, FontList assigns the font name to the Caption of another label, which displays the selected font inside an indented bevel just for looks.

In most cases, you also want users to be able to select ListBox items by pressing Enter and possibly the spacebar. The ListFont demo enables these keys in the FontListBox's OnKeyDown event handler. The procedure checks whether Key is in the set of two values VK_RETURN and VK_SPACE, and if so, calls the FontListBoxDblClick handler. This simulates a double-click event when you press Enter or the spacebar.

Using Pascal's *in* operator and a set of values is often more convenient, and possibly more efficient, than multiple logical OR expressions. For example, note the following:

```
  if (Key = VK_RETURN) or
     (Key = VK_SPACE ) or
     (Key = VK_F9    ) then {...}
```

Instead of the preceding, you can test whether Key is in the set of three values with this statement:

```
if Key in [VK_RETURN, VK_SPACE, VK_F9] then {...}
```

Selecting listed data

In some ListBoxes, you want users to be able to select only one item at a time. In others, you want to enable multiple selections. Single-item selection is easy — just use the default ListBox settings with property MultiSelect set to False. To enable multiple-item selection, set MultiSelect to True.

In addition to MultiSelect, set ExtendedSelect True or False depending on the type of multiple-item selection you want. When MultiSelect is False, ExtendedSelect has no effect (you can leave it set to its default True value). But when MultiSelect is True, ExtendedSelect configures multiple-item selection in one of two ways:

✦ **ExtendedSelect = True** — Users must press Ctrl and click the mouse to select multiple items. In addition, pressing Shift selects all items between the previously selected line and the one clicked. Pressing Ctrl+Shift and clicking does the same and retains any other individually selected items. Selecting a new item without pressing Ctrl or Shift unhighlights any previous selections, and clicking a selected item deselects it.

✦ **ExtendedSelect = False** — Users do not have to press any keys to select multiple items. Selecting a new item does not remove highlighting from previous selections.

You can assign these property values in the Object Inspector window or at run time with statements like these:

```
ListBox1.MultiSelect := True;
ListBox1.ExtendedSelect := False;
```

With MultiSelect True and ExtendedSelect False, it is your responsibility to remove highlights from selected items — when users press Esc, for example. A simple way to do this is by toggling the ExtendedSelect property on and off as Listing 8-3 demonstrates. Use this code in a ListBox's OnKeyDown event handler.

When MultiSelect is True, the SelCount property indicates the number of selected items. If there are no selected items, SelCount equals zero. With ExtendedSelect False, use this OnKeyDown event handler to unhighlight selected items in a ListBox when users press Esc.

Listing 8-3: **An OnKeyDown event handler to unhighlight selected items**

```
procedure TForm1.ListBox1KeyDown(Sender: TObject;
  var Key: Word; Shift: TShiftState);
begin
  if Key = VK_ESCAPE then
  with ListBox1 do
  begin
    ExtendedSelect := True;
    ExtendedSelect := False;
  end;
end;
```

SelCount always equals -1 if MultiSelect is False, regardless of whether an item is selected. When MultiSelect is True, ItemIndex indicates the most recently clicked item, regardless of whether that item was selected or deselected. These anomalies can trip you up. For best results, do not use SelCount with single-entry ListBoxes, and do not use ItemIndex in multiple-entry ListBoxes.

Listing 8-4 suggests one way to obtain multiple selections from a ListBox. MultiSelect must be True for this code to work properly. To try the technique, follow these steps:

1. Insert two ListBox objects into a form.

2. Enter some strings into ListBox1's Items property. Set ListBox1's MultiSelect property to True.

3. Insert a Button into the form and use the listing for the Button's OnClick event handler.

4. Run the program and click the button to transfer selected items from ListBox1 to ListBox2.

Selecting ListBox items at run time

Sometimes selecting ListBox items using program statements is useful — for example, to restore a program window to a saved state or to make preset selections from data sets. Clicking button *A* might automatically select items 3, 6, and 9; clicking button *B* would select items 2 and 7; and so forth.

Listing 8-4: **Obtaining multiples selections from a list box**

```
procedure TForm1.Button1Click(Sender: TObject);
var
  I: Integer;
begin
  ListBox2.Clear;
  for I := 0 to ListBox1.Items.Count _ 1 do
    if ListBox1.Selected[I] then
      ListBox2.Items.Add(ListBox1.Items[I]);
end;
```

To select items in a single-entry ListBox at run time, assign a value to the ItemIndex property. For example, the following statement selects the sixth item (the first item's index is zero, so the sixth item's index equals five):

```
ListBox1.ItemIndex := 5;
```

This does not work when MultiSelect is True, however. In this case, to select items at run time, assign True to entries in the Selected array. For example, the following two statements select the third and sixth items in ListBox1. Delphi automatically adjusts SelCount and ItemIndex to the proper values following each assignment:

```
ListBox1.Selected[2] := True;
ListBox1.Selected[5] := True;
```

Because the Selected array is inaccessible when MultiSelect is False, you might want to use an *if* statement such as the following to select the sixth item in ListBox1. This code works correctly for single-entry and multiple-entry ListBoxes:

```
with ListBox1 do
if MultiSelect then
  Selected[5] := True
else
  ItemIndex := 5;
```

Using ListBox data

As a practical example of using two ListBoxes and transferring data between them using Button objects, the ToDo application edits a simple list of projects to do. I used Delphi's Dual list box form template to create the program's window. I then modified the stock form for the ToDo program. Figure 8-2 shows ToDo's display. Throughout the rest of this chapter, I explain some of ToDo's source code, which is too lengthy to print in full here.

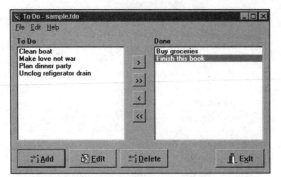

Figure 8-2: The ToDo application demonstrates how to use Delphi's Dual list box form template to transfer data between two ListBox objects.

The Dual list box form template provides most of the code needed to implement double ListBox transfers. To inspect this code, insert a new form into a project and select Dual list box from the template gallery. Open the form's unit module to see how Delphi manages the two ListBoxes.

Creating sorted ListBoxes

As mentioned, creating a sorted ListBox is easy — just set the Sorted property to True. The ListBox automatically maintains sorted order for additions and deletions. If you change an item, however, the list may become unordered because Windows performs the sorting, not the Delphi component. For example, this statement assigns the string Zebra to ListBox1's first item:

```
ListBox1.Items[0] := 'Zebra';
```

To place the Zebra at the end of the corral where it probably belongs, simply toggle the Sorted property off and then back on. These statements force the ListBox to resort its data:

```
ListBox1.Sorted := False;
ListBox1.Sorted := True;
```

ComboBoxes

ComboBoxes are great for creating selection lists with optional editing capabilities. The ComboBox component merges an input box (similar to Delphi's Edit component) with a ListBox. Users can select items from the list and they can enter new data into the edit control's window. The three basic ComboBox styles are:

✦ **Simple (Style = csSimple)** — The ListBox is always visible. Users can select an item from the list, or they can enter a new item into the edit window.

✦ **Drop-Down (Style = csDropDown)** — The ListBox drops down when users click the down-arrow button next to the edit window — they can also press Alt+Down. As with the Simple style, users can select an item from the list, or they can enter a new item into the edit control. Incremental searching is also enabled for this style — type one or more characters and press the up- or down-arrow key to select the entry that most closely matches your input.

✦ **Drop-Down-List (Style = csDropDownList)** — As with the Drop-Down style, the ListBox drops into view on clicking the down-arrow button. With this style, the edit box is "read-only," and users must select a listed entry. However, users may type the first letter of an item to select it. For example, press the *P* key repeatedly to select all entries that begin with *P*.

Note   Unlike ListBox controls, ComboBoxes cannot display horizontal scroll bars. This is a limitation in Windows.

The Combos application illustrates the three ComboBox styles. Figure 8-3 shows the program's display. Listing 8-5 shows its source file.

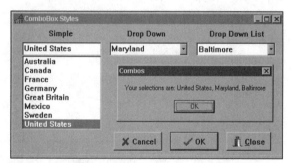

Figure 8-3: The Combos application illustrates the three ComboBox styles: Simple, Drop-Down, and Drop-Down-List.

The Combos listing shows the correct way to obtain selections from a ComboBox object. In most cases, you should do this by referring to the object's Text property, which holds the text displayed in the edit control's window. You may use ListBox methods to obtain selections, for example, by referring to the Items array:

```
if ItemIndex >= 0 then
  S1 := SimpleCB.Items[ItemIndex];  // ???
```

Listing 8-5: **Combos\Main.pas**

```pascal
unit Main;

interface

uses
  SysUtils, Windows, Messages, Classes, Graphics,
  Controls, Forms, Dialogs, StdCtrls, Buttons;

type
  TMainForm = class(TForm)
    SimpleCB: TComboBox;
    DropDownCB: TComboBox;
    DropDownListCB: TComboBox;
    Label1: TLabel;
    Label2: TLabel;
    Label3: TLabel;
    CancelBitBtn: TBitBtn;
    OKBitBtn: TBitBtn;
    CloseBitBtn: TBitBtn;
    procedure CancelBitBtnClick(Sender: TObject);
    procedure OKBitBtnClick(Sender: TObject);
    procedure CloseBitBtnClick(Sender: TObject);
  private
    { Private declarations }
  public
    { Public declarations }
  end;

var
  MainForm: TMainForm;

implementation

{$R *.DFM}

procedure TMainForm.CancelBitBtnClick(Sender: TObject);
begin
  Close;
end;

procedure TMainForm.OKBitBtnClick(Sender: TObject);
var
  S1, S2, S3: string;
begin
  S1 := SimpleCB.Text;
  S2 := DropDownCB.Text;
  S3 := DropDownListCB.Text;
```

```
    ShowMessage('Your selections are: ' +
      S1 + ', ' + S2 + ', ' + S3);
  end;

  procedure TMainForm.CloseBitBtnClick(Sender: TObject);
  begin
    OKBitBtn.Click;   { Simulate OK button click }
    Close;            { End program }
  end;

  end.
```

This technique is questionable because it does not properly pick up user entries from the Text field. For best results, get selections from the Text property unless you need to perform actions on entries in the ListBox window. For example, this statement copies the selection from the SimpleCB ComboBox to a string variable S1:

```
  S1 := SimpleCB.Text;
```

At design time, enter list items into a ComboBox's Items property. Enter or clear the Text property to change the string edit area, to which Delphi assigns the object's name by default.

ComboBoxes provide some other methods you might find useful for designing your program's interface. Use the DroppedDown property to determine whether a ComboBox is hanging down:

```
  if DropDownCB.DroppedDown then
    {... do something if ComboBox is open }
```

Assign True or False to DroppedDown to open and close the list portion of a ComboBox under program control. For example, insert a ComboBox object and a Button in a form, and use this statement in the Button's OnClick event handler to open and close the ComboBox list window:

```
  with ComboBox1 do
    DroppedDown := not DroppedDown;
```

To select all text in a ComboBox's edit area, call the SelectAll method. This highlights the edit control's text — it does not select all listed items as the method's name seems to suggest. For example, you might use this statement in an OnKeyDown event handler to highlight the edit control's text when users press a certain key:

```
  SimpleCB.SelectAll;
```

ComboBoxes are single-entry objects. Only ListBox components handle multiple selections.

Calling Clear erases all listed entries and any text in the edit window box from a ComboBox object. To delete all text from a ComboBox, use this statement:

```
ComboBox1.Clear;
```

If you want to delete only the text from the edit control, assign a null string to the ComboBox's Text property:

```
ComboBox1.Text := '';
```

You can also use the methods discussed earlier to make changes to listed items through the Items array. For example, this adds a new entry to a ComboBox's list box:

```
ComboBox1.Items.Add('Aardvark');
```

String and Other Lists

The ListBox and ComboBox objects are visual tools for creating selection lists in windows. Most programs also need internal list-making capabilities using objects not on Delphi's VCL palette. This section discusses three classes you can use for managing string and other lists in your applications. In alphabetical order, the three classes are:

✦ **TList** — A general-purpose list-making class.

✦ **TStringList** — A class that applications can use to create lists of strings and objects. TStringList allocates memory for string storage. Use this type to create stand-alone variables when you need a place to store lists of Strings.

✦ **TStrings** — An abstract class that component properties use to manage lists of strings and other objects. TStrings objects do not allocate any memory for storage. The only time you use this type of list is when referring to component object properties. You never create stand-alone variables of this type.

Note   The preceding classes aren't strictly user-interface tools, but I want to introduce them here in Part II anyway because of their key importance in Delphi application development. However, I also discuss the StringGrid component, which uses string lists and is a highly valuable tool for creating practical user interfaces.

Using the TList class

Delphi uses the TList class as the basis for creating general-purpose lists. You can also use TList as a container class for storing objects of any type in lists. In most cases, to use TList, you need to create two of your own classes—one for the object items to store in the list, and one for the list itself. For example, you might create a class in a unit module's implementation part as follows. Items in the list are objects of your class's type, which might be defined in a unit's interface like this:

```
type
  TAnyItem = class
    Data: Integer;
    constructor Create(Data1: Integer);
  end;
```

As declared here, TAnyItem is a class data type that provides an integer variable named Data. Although not of practical use, TAnyItem demonstrates the basics for creating a list of objects. In addition to its Data member, the class has a constructor named Create for initializing objects of the class. Always name the constructor Create. Implement the constructor as you would any procedure, but use the keyword constructor in place of procedure, and preface the method name with TAnyItem and a period. The following goes in the unit's implementation section:

```
constructor TAnyItem.Create(Data1: Integer);
begin
  Data := Data1;
  inherited Create;
end;
```

The constructor saves the Data1 parameter in the object's Data variable and then calls the inherited Create method in the ancestor class. Calling the inherited Create gives the ancestor class the opportunity to perform its own initializations, whatever they happen to be. (In object-oriented programming, we don't need to know all the gory details of an ancestor class's methods.) In this case, the ancestor is TObject, the granddaddy (or perhaps it's the grandmother) of all Delphi classes, even of those you create yourself.

Note Think of a class constructor as an initializer that prepares the internal elements of a new object. For each object of the class, the program must call the Create constructor to initialize the object.

You also need a class for the list. There's rarely any good reason to reinvent the wheel so, to take advantage of the methods that TList provides, derive the new class from TList. The new class inherits the properties and methods from TList. In other words, the new class is the same as Tlist, plus whatever other capabilities you decide to add. To create the derived class, use this declaration in the unit's implementation:

```
type
  TAnyList = class(TList)
    destructor Destroy; override;
  end;
```

The TAnyList class overrides the Destroy destructor in the ancestor TList class. This is necessary because TList objects normally do not destroy the objects they contain. To add this capability to the derived class, implement the destructor, also in the unit's implementation, as follows:

```
destructor TAnyList.Destroy;
var
  I: Integer;
begin
  for I := 0 to Count - 1 do
    TAnyItem(Items[I]).Free;
  inherited Destroy;
end;
```

First, a *for* loop calls Free for all TAnyItem objects on the list. The TList class maintains a Count of items. The Items property contains pointers to (addresses of) objects in the list. To call a method such as Free requires a type-cast expression as shown, which, in this example, informs the compiler that Items[I] is not just a pointer, but a TAnyItem object. Finally, the new destructor calls the inherited Destroy to give the TList class an opportunity to perform its own cleanups.

Armed with these basics, you can use TList to create lists of any kind of objects. The StrList sample program demonstrates the necessary steps. Figure 8-4 shows the program's display. Listing 8-6 gives the program's source code. Run the program, click Add, and enter a string. Repeat these steps several times to create a list of string objects in memory.

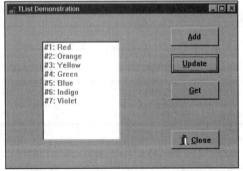

Figure 8-4: The StrList application demonstrates how to use Delphi's TList class to create lists of objects in memory.

Click Update to transfer the listed objects to the ListBox control. (You won't see your strings until after you click Update.) Click Get and enter a string to search the list. I explain more about the code after the listing.

Listing 8-6 **Strlist\Main.pas**

```
unit Main;

interface

uses
   SysUtils, Windows, Messages, Classes, Graphics,
   Controls, Forms, Dialogs, StdCtrls, Buttons;

type
   TMainForm = class(TForm)
     AddButton: TButton;
     CloseBitBtn: TBitBtn;
     GetButton: TButton;
     ListBox1: TListBox;
     UpdateButton: TButton;
     procedure FormCreate(Sender: TObject);
     procedure FormDestroy(Sender: TObject);
     procedure AddButtonClick(Sender: TObject);
     procedure UpdateButtonClick(Sender: TObject);
     procedure GetButtonClick(Sender: TObject);
   private
     { Private declarations }
   public
     { Public declarations }
   end;

var
   MainForm: TMainForm;

implementation

{$R *.DFM}

type

{- New class of items to insert in a list }
   TStrItem = class
     S: string;
     I: Integer;
     constructor Create(S1: string; I1: Integer);
```

(continued)

Listing 8-6 *(continued)*

```
    end;

{- Derived class to hold TStrItem objects }
  TStrList = class(TList)
    destructor Destroy; override;
    function FindItem(S1: string): TStrItem;
  end;

var
  StrList: TStrList;       { List of TStrItems }
  ItemCount: Integer;      { Number of items inserted }

{- Create a new instance of TStrItem }
constructor TStrItem.Create(S1: String; I1: Integer);
begin
  S := S1;                 { Save string parameter }
  I := I1;                 { Save integer parameter }
  inherited Create;        { Call inherited Create }
end;

{- Destroy instance of TStrList }
destructor TStrList.Destroy;
var
  I: Integer;
begin
  for I := 0 to Count - 1 do
    TStrItem(Items[I]).Free;  { Free all TStrItems }
  inherited Destroy;          { Call inherited destroy }
end;

{- Return object identified by S1 or nil for no match }
function TStrList.FindItem(S1: string): TStrItem;
var
  I: Integer;
  P: TStrItem;
begin
  for I := 0 to Count - 1 do
  begin
    P := TStrItem(Items[I]);  { P refers to a TStrItem object }
    if Uppercase(P.S) = Uppercase(S1) then  { Match? }
    begin               { Found match }
      Result := P;      { Return P as function result }
      Exit;             { Exit function immediately }
    end;
  end;
  Result := nil;        { No match; return nil }
end;
```

```
{- TMainForm event handlers }

procedure TMainForm.FormCreate(Sender: TObject);
begin
  StrList := TStrList.Create;  { Create new StrList object }
  ItemCount := 0;              { Initialize insertion count }
end;

procedure TMainForm.FormDestroy(Sender: TObject);
begin
  StrList.Free;  { Also destroys listed items }
end;

{- Button event handlers }

procedure TMainForm.AddButtonClick(Sender: TObject);
var
  StrItem: TStrItem;  { New item to insert }
  S: string;          { User input string }
begin
  S := '';
  if InputQuery(Caption, 'Enter item', S) then
  if Length(S) > 0 then
  begin
    Inc(ItemCount);
    StrItem := TStrItem.Create(S, ItemCount);
    StrList.Add(StrItem);
  end;
end;

procedure TMainForm.UpdateButtonClick(Sender: TObject);
var
  I: Integer;
  P: TStrItem;
begin
  ListBox1.Clear;
  with StrList do
  for I := 0 to Count - 1 do
  begin
    P := TStrItem(StrList.Items[I]);
    ListBox1.Items.Add(Format('#%d: %s', [P.I, P.S]));
  end;
end;

procedure TMainForm.GetButtonClick(Sender: TObject);
var
  S: string;
```

(continued)

Listing 8-6 *(continued)*

```
  P: TStrItem;
begin
  UpdateButton.Click;
  S := '';
  if InputQuery(Caption, 'Enter item name', S) then
  if Length(S) > 0 then
  begin
    P := StrList.FindItem(S);
    if P <> nil then
      ShowMessage(Format('%s, Number = %d', [P.S, P.I]))
    else
      ShowMessage('No such item');
  end;
end;

end.
```

StrList demonstrates how to create an associative list, which requires two classes. The first class, TStrItem, declares two data members — a string, *S*, and an integer value, *I*. The class also declares a Create constructor to initialize these variables. The second class, TStrList, which is derived from TList, declares two methods: a destructor and a function, FindItem, that searches a list for an object identified by a string argument.

To create the list object, the program defines a variable, StrList, of the TStrList class. If you prefer, these variables could also go into the form's class.

The TStrItem constructor assigns string and integer parameters to the class's *S* and *I* variables. This initializes new objects to be inserted into the list. Notice that the constructor calls the inherited Create, even though TStrItem is a new class that is not derived from any other. This step isn't strictly necessary, but you should do it anyway because, in Delphi's Pascal, all classes are derived from the Adam-and-Eve ancestor TObject.

Because new classes are automatically derived from TObject, all Delphi classes and objects are related. Among other advantages, this means you can pass an object of any class type to a TObject parameter in a procedure or function.

TObject provides a default Create constructor and a default Destroy destructor, plus message-dispatching code. By examining Delphi's run-time library source code, you can find TObject's Pascal declaration in the file System.pas, located in the Source\Rtl\Sys path. As you discover by browsing this information, TObject's methods are written using in-line Assembly language statements. This code used to be stored separately in files Clsf.asm and Clsh.asm; it is now in System.pas. (You don't need the source code to use TObject, but if you do much programming with Delphi, you can learn a lot by browsing component methods such as these.)

You needn't derive classes explicitly from TObject, although you may if you wish. For example, the following two class declarations are equivalent:

```
type
  TNewClass1 = class
    {...}
  end;
  TNewClass2 = class(TObject)
    {...}
  end;
```

The TStrList destructor, Destroy, calls Free for each TStrItem object on the list. It then calls the inherited Destroy. You might use similar code in other methods — for example, one that clears objects from the list.

Function FindItem searches the list of objects for one that matches a string parameter. A *for* loop iterates through the list using TList's Count. To simplify the code, a statement assigns each listed object to *P*:

```
P := TStrItem(Items[I]);
```

P is a variable of the list-object class, TStrItem. Despite appearances, however, *P* does not contain the data of an object instance. *P* contains a pointer reference to a TStrItem object instance. In Delphi, all class-object variables, such as *P*, are references — that is, they are pointers that refer to objects in memory. If you know other versions of Pascal, the preceding code may appear to copy an entire TStrItem object to *P*, but that's not what happens in Delphi's Object Pascal. All that's assigned is the reference address of the TStrItem object in the list's Items array. All class variables — that is, objects — are references.

Inside the *for* loop, an *if* statement compares the object's string (P.S) with the argument (S1) passed to FindItem. The statement uses Delphi's Uppercase function to compare the strings without regard for case. If the strings match, the program assigns *P* to the function's Result, and then exits the function immediately by calling Pascal's built-in Exit procedure. If there's no match, the final statement assigns nil to the function Result.

Although FindItem's declared result is TStrItem, the function actually returns a reference to a TStrItem object. This is just one additional benefit of Delphi's rule that all class-object variables are references. Consequently, Delphi permits assigning nil to FindItem's Result to indicate that it refers to no object.

StrList's OnCreate event handler for the program's form creates a new list by executing the following statement, which calls the TStrList Create method. An assignment statement constructs a TStrList object in memory, and it initializes the StrList variable to refer to that object:

```
StrList := TStrList.Create;
```

One of Delphi's cardinal rules is that you must free the objects you create. In this case, for example, the form's OnDestroy event handler frees the list object by calling the Free method, inherited from TList:

```
StrList.Free;
```

Because the TStrList destructor frees all listed objects, freeing the list properly disposes of all memory allocated to the list and to its contained objects.

To add new objects to the list, AddButton's OnClick event prompts you to enter a string. These two statements create a new TStrItem object and add it to the list by calling TList's Add method:

```
StrItem := TStrItem.Create(S, ItemCount);
StrList.Add(StrItem);
```

In the example program, when you click the Update button, its OnClick event handler transfers all listed object string and integer values to a ListBox component object. The expressions P.I and P.S refer to the data in each TStrItem object on the list. Similar expressions in GetButtonClick display object strings and integers after calling FindItem to search the list.

Creating an Array of TObject References

In complex applications, it might be convenient to create an array of TObject references to various components in a form. All classes derive from TObject, and therefore, an array of TObjects can refer to any Delphi object. For example, you can insert a set of component objects into a TObject array, and then use the array to perform operations on all objects. The ObjList application (see Listing 8-7) demonstrates the necessary techniques. The program's form window contains six CheckBox objects. Click the form's On/Off button to disable and enable the CheckBoxes. The program accomplishes this task by declaring a pointer to an array of TObjects, and then using GetMem to allocate memory for the number of CheckBoxes in the form. The form's OnCreate event handler assigns each CheckBox to the CheckBoxArray elements (remember, these are all references). The button's OnClick event handler uses a *for* loop to toggle each CheckBox object's Enabled property on and off. Finally, the form's OnDestroy event handler calls FreeMem to dispose of the allocated memory. Figure 8-5 shows the program's display.

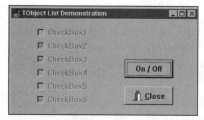

Figure 8-5: ObjList demonstrates how to create an array of TObject references for performing operations on sets of objects.

Listing 8-7: **Objlist\Main.pas**

```pascal
unit Main;

interface

uses
  SysUtils, WinTypes, WinProcs, Messages, Classes, Graphics,
  Controls, Forms, Dialogs, StdCtrls, Buttons;

type
  TMainForm = class(TForm)
    CheckBox1: TCheckBox;
    CheckBox2: TCheckBox;
    CheckBox3: TCheckBox;
    CheckBox4: TCheckBox;
    CheckBox5: TCheckBox;
    CheckBox6: TCheckBox;
    OnOffButton: TButton;
    BitBtn1: TBitBtn;
    procedure FormCreate(Sender: TObject);
    procedure FormDestroy(Sender: TObject);
    procedure OnOffButtonClick(Sender: TObject);
  private
    { Private declarations }
  public
    { Public declarations }
  end;
```

(continued)

Listing 8-7 *(continued)*

```pascal
var
  MainForm: TMainForm;

implementation

{$R *.DFM}

const
  numCheckBoxes = 6;

type
  PObjectArray = ^TObjectArray;
  TObjectArray =
    array[0..65520 div SizeOf(TObject)] of TObject;

var
  CheckBoxArray: PObjectArray; //Pointer to array of checkBoxes

procedure TMainForm.FormCreate(Sender: TObject);
begin
  GetMem(CheckBoxArray, numCheckBoxes * SizeOf(TObject));
  CheckBoxArray^[0] := CheckBox1;
  CheckBoxArray^[1] := CheckBox2;
  CheckBoxArray^[2] := CheckBox3;
  CheckBoxArray^[3] := CheckBox4;
  CheckBoxArray^[4] := CheckBox5;
  CheckBoxArray^[5] := CheckBox6;
end;

procedure TMainForm.FormDestroy(Sender: TObject);
begin
  FreeMem(CheckBoxArray, numCheckBoxes * SizeOf(TObject));
end;

procedure TMainForm.OnOffButtonClick(Sender: TObject);
var
  I: Integer;
begin
  for I := 0 to numCheckBoxes - 1 do
    with CheckBoxArray^[I] as TCheckBox do
      Enabled := not Enabled;
end;

  end.
```

Using the TStringList class

Delphi provides another class, TStringList, that uses a TList object to create string lists. TStringList is derived from TStrings, the class that components use for string-list properties. (I explain more about TStrings in the next section.) By using TStringList, you can create associative lists of strings and other objects, and you can assign those lists to a TStrings property in any Delphi component object.

One of the most common uses for TStringList objects is to read and write text files. In the distant past, because TStringList used Pascal strings, lines could be no longer than 255 characters. This restriction no longer exists now that Object Pascal Strings can be virtually any length. Listing 8-8 shows how to use TStringList to create a new text file. To try the code, create a project and insert two Button objects into the form. Also insert a Memo component. Enter the statements from Listing 8-8 into Button1's OnClick event handler.

Listing 8-8: This OnClick event handler demonstrates how to use TStringList to create a text file.

```
procedure TForm1.Button1Click(Sender: TObject);
var
  SL: TStringList;
begin
  SL := TStringList.Create;
  try
    SL.Add('This is the first line');
    SL.Add('This is the second line');
    SL.Add('This is THE END');
    SL.SaveToFile('Anyname.txt');
  finally
    SL.Free;
  end;
end;
```

The sample program first creates a TStringList object named SL. It then adds some strings to the list, and calls SaveToFile to write them to a text file named Anyname.txt. The procedure calls Free to delete the string list object from memory. Always free the objects you create. The *try-finally-end* statement block ensures that, even if any statement after *try* causes an exception, SL is freed. (See Chapter 19 for more information on exception handling.)

Listing 8-9 demonstrates how to read a text file into a TStringList object. If you are creating the project, use this code for Button2's OnClick event handler. The procedure creates a TStringList object SL, and then calls LoadFromFile to read lines from Anytext.txt into the list object. An assignment copies this data to the Memo1 object's Lines property, an object of type TStrings.

Because TStringList is derived from TStrings, you can assign any TStringList object to a component object's TStrings property. You also can assign any TStrings property to a TStringList object.

Listing 8-9: This OnClick event handler demonstrates how to use a TStringList object to read a text file.

```
procedure TForm1.Button2Click(Sender: TObject);
var
  SL: TStringList;
begin
  SL := TStringList.Create;
  try
    SL.LoadFromFile('Anyname.txt');
    Memo1.Lines := SL;
  finally
    SL.Free;
  end;
end;
```

Listing 8-9 demonstrates how to read a text file into an independent TStringList object, which you might want to do for a variety of list-handling purposes. However, you can more simply load a Memo component's Lines by calling its LoadFromFile method. This statement does all the work of Listing 8-9:

```
Memo1.Lines.LoadFromFile('Anyname.txt');
```

Use AddStrings to attach multiple string lists to a TStringList object or a TStrings property. For example, if you have three TStringLists — T1, T2, and T3 — you can insert them into a Memo object's Lines property with the following statements. The first assignment replaces Memo's text with strings from T1. The next two assignments append the other two lists:

```
with Memo1, Lines do
begin
  Lines := T1;
  AddStrings(T2);
  AddStrings(T3);
end;
```

TStringList is valuable, not only for string lists, but also for creating associations between strings and objects. The next section explains how to use this capability to display bitmaps in a ListBox control.

Using the TStrings class

TStrings is an abstract class, which means programs cannot create objects of this type. (Object-oriented gurus say that you cannot *instantiate* the class.) You may use TStrings only as a property of a component object. For example, you can store a list of strings and other objects in a ListBox's Items property, a TStrings object. To create your own list objects, use the TList and TStringList classes as described in the preceding sections.

Because TStringList is derived from TStrings, the information in this section applies to both classes. Anything you can do with a TStrings property you can do with a TStringList object.

Using the StringGrid component

A StringGrid object is an advanced list box that is capable of associating strings and other objects such as bitmaps. StringGrid can display tables of string data, each of which might be associated with another object.

The next program, GlyphLst, demonstrates how to use StringGrid to create an associative array of strings and bitmaps. The demonstration displays all of Delphi's glyph bitmaps and their filenames in an owner-draw StringGrid object. (See Chapter 6 for an introduction to glyphs.) The term *owner-draw* means the program, rather than Windows, takes over responsibility for drawing each item in a StringGrid cell. Figure 8-6 shows GlyphLst's display. The program's source code is in Listing 8-10. On the CD-ROM, you can find the program's files in the Source\GlyphLst directory. I inserted comments into the code to explain many of the statements, which use some techniques not yet introduced.

If you did not install Delphi in the default directories on drive C:, modify the path name string in constant glyphPath, located just after the unit's implementation keyword.

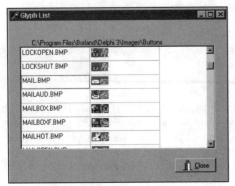

Figure 8-6: GlyphLst displays an owner-draw
ListBox of all the glyph bitmaps supplied
with Delphi.

Listing 8-10: **Glyphlst\Main.pas**

```
unit Main;

interface

uses
  Windows, Messages, SysUtils, Classes, Graphics, Controls,
  Forms, Dialogs, StdCtrls, Buttons, Grids;

type
  TMainForm = class(TForm)
    PathLabel: TLabel;
    BitBtn1: TBitBtn;
    GlyphList: TStringGrid;
    procedure FormCreate(Sender: TObject);
    procedure FormClose(Sender: TObject;
      var Action: TCloseAction);
    procedure GlyphListDrawCell(Sender: TObject;
      Col, Row: Integer; Rect: TRect; State: TGridDrawState);
  private
    { Private declarations }
  public
    { Public declarations }
  end;

var
  MainForm: TMainForm;

implementation
```

```
{$R *.DFM}

const glyphPath =
 'C:\Program Files\Borland\Delphi 4\Images\Buttons';

// Reads all glyph bitmaps and stores their filenames and
// images in the GlyphList TStringGrid object.
procedure TMainForm.FormCreate(Sender: TObject);
var
  SearchRec: TSearchRec;    { Directory scan result record }
  K: Integer;               { while-loop control variable }
  Bitmap: TBitmap;          { Holds bitmaps. Do not Free! }
  Index: Integer;           { TStringGrid cell index }
begin
  Show;   { Make form visible while loading bitmaps }
  Screen.Cursor := crHourGlass;   { Show hourglass cursor }
  Index := 0;
  try
    PathLabel.Caption := glyphPath; { Show path above ListBox }
    { Start scan }
    K := FindFirst(glyphPath + '\*.*', faAnyFile, SearchRec);
    try
      while K = 0 do   { Scan directory for file names }
      begin
        if SearchRec.Name[1] <> '.' then {No '.' or '..' paths}
        begin
          Bitmap := TBitmap.Create;   { Create bitmap object }
          try { Get bitmap and load from list }
            Bitmap.LoadFromFile(glyphPath + '\'
              + SearchRec.Name);
            if Index = GlyphList.RowCount then  // Expand list
              GlyphList.RowCount := Index + 1;
            GlyphList.Cells[0, Index] := SearchRec.Name;// Name
            GlyphList.Objects[1, Index] := Bitmap;    // Bitmap
            inc(Index);
          except
            Bitmap.Free; { Executed if ANYTHING goes wrong }
            raise;       { Pass any exceptions up call chain }
          end;
        end;
        K := FindNext(SearchRec);   { Continue directory scan }
      end;
    finally
      FindClose(SearchRec);
    end;
  finally
```

(continued)

Listing 8-10 *(continued)*

```
    Screen.Cursor := crDefault;  { Restore normal cursor }
  end;
end;

// Frees memory occupied by all glyph bitmaps. The TStringGrid
// object does NOT do this automatically.
procedure TMainForm.FormClose(Sender: TObject;
  var Action: TCloseAction);
var
  I: Integer;
begin
  for I := 0 to GlyphList.RowCount - 1 do
    TBitmap(GlyphList.Objects[0, I]).Free;
end;

// Draw each glyph bitmap. The TStringGrid object is smart
// enough to draw its filename text objects with no further
// help. This code draws only the bitmaps in the second column.
procedure TMainForm.GlyphListDrawCell(Sender: TObject;
  Col, Row: Integer; Rect: TRect; State: TGridDrawState);
var
  Bitmap: TBitmap;
begin
  if col = 1 then  // Be sure to refer to the bitmap column
  begin
    { Get bitmap object }
    Bitmap := TBitmap(GlyphList.Objects[1, Row]);
    if Bitmap <> nil then
    begin  { Draw bitmap in column cell }
      GlyphList.Canvas.BrushCopy(
        Bounds(Rect.Left + 2, Rect.Top + 2, Bitmap.Width,
          Bitmap.Height), Bitmap,
          Bounds(0, 0, Bitmap.Width, Bitmap.Height), clRed);
      { The preceding clRed argument gives the transparent
        glyph substance. Change this to any solid color, or
        change it to 0 to see why this is necessary. }
    end;
  end;
end;

end.
```

GlyphLst demonstrates some key techniques you can use in all applications with a StringGrid object. The program's main form contains only three components: Label1, BitBtn1, and GlyphList, of the TStringGrid class. (Ordinarily, I would name this object GlyphStringGrid, but I kept the name GlyphList because the original version of this program used a List object rather than the more sophisticated StringGrid component.)

I modified the GlyphList object properties to create a two-column list. The program displays glyph filenames in the first column. The second column shows the bitmaps associated with each glyph. To program the sample application's StringGrid, I changed these key properties:

✦ **ColCount = 2** — This is the number of columns, which can be changed at run time.

✦ **DefaultColWidth = 128** — Sets the width of each column. Because this is a row and column grid, each cell is the same width.

✦ **FixedCols = 0; FixedRows = 0** — These settings remove the gray row and column headers, which you see on a default StringGrid object. These values are normally set to 1 to reserve one column and one row for header information such as column labels.

You may often want to take over drawing of each cell in a StringGrid object. You do this simply by creating a handler for the StringGrid's OnDrawCell event. This creates what's known as an *owner drawn control*. For each cell in the grid, Delphi calls the event handler which paints whatever you like inside the cell boundaries. Another property, DefaultDrawing, affects how the StringGrid object and your event handler work together, as described here:

✦ **DefaultDrawing = True** — StringGrid paints the cell's background and displays any text data associated with the cell before calling the OnDrawCell event handler. After the handler returns, Delphi draws a focus rectangle around the currently selected cell.

✦ **DefaultDrawing = False** — Your OnDrawCell event handler is responsible for all background and foreground drawing in each cell.

The GlyphLst program uses the first option: DefaultDrawing = True. The StringGrid's OnDrawCell event handler fills each pair of cells with the glyph's filename and its associated bitmap. Each call to the GlyphListDrawCell procedure contains three important pieces of information passed as parameters. These are:

✦ **Col** — The cell's column number

✦ **Row** — The cell's row number

✦ **Rect** — The drawing boundaries of the cell's rectangle

The first column and row are each numbered zero. In this case, we have no header columns or rows — if you use them, however, remember that you need to draw these cells too. GlyphList doesn't use headers.

Two properties hold a StringGrid's string and associated object data for each cell. The Cells property is declared as:

```
property Cells[ACol, ARow: Integer]: string;
```

Each cell is a string object, plain and simple. The Objects property is declared similarly, but it can hold any kind of class object, as long as it is descended from TObject:

```
property Objects [ACol, ARow: Integer]: TObject;
```

Together, Cells and Objects provide access to string and other data for each cell of a StringGrid object. Displaying this data is a simple matter of accessing it through these arrays. Because text data is drawn automatically, our event handler first checks that Col equals 1. If so, then the StringGrid is requesting that the application draw graphical data. This data is stored in the grid's Objects property. Assuming that Bitmap is a temporary object of the TBitmap class, this statement:

```
Bitmap := TBitmap(GlyphList.Objects[1, Row]);
```

obtains a reference to the Bitmap object stored at column 1, and the indicated row. After obtaining this reference, the program draws it by calling the StringGrid's BrushCopy procedure for the object's Canvas. Examine this statement in the listing, and notice how the Rect parameter is used to position the image inside each grid cell. The clRed argument in this statement causes the glyph to be transparent.

Note   If you are familiar with Windows programming, Canvas is Delphi's equivalent to a *device context*. Don't be concerned if you don't know what device contexts are — you learn about them and more about Canvas in Chapter 13.

To prepare for drawing each grid, the program uses an OnCreate event handler for the main form window. Because it might take a while to load each glyph bitmap file, procedure FormCreate begins by setting the Screen cursor to crHourGlass. It then calls FindFirst to locate the first matching file. A Bitmap object is created with the statement:

```
Bitmap := TBitmap.Create;
```

That object is then used to load the bitmap image from disk using the statement:

```
Bitmap.LoadFromfile(glyphpath + '\' + SearchRec.Name;
```

The Name property in the SearchRec variable holds the results from calling FindFirst. To provide room in the grid to hold another filename and bitmap, the program executes this code:

```
if Index = GlyphList.RowCount then
   GlyphList.RowCount := Index + 1;
```

Simply expanding RowCount by one increases the amount of information the StringGrid can hold and display. Two additional statements next assign the filename and bitmap image to the grid cell:

```
GlyphList.Cells[0, Index] := SearchRec.Name;
GlyphList.Objects[1, Index] := Bitmap;
```

The Cells property holds each cell's string data, which, in this example is assigned the glyph's filename from the SearchRec record. The Objects property is optionally used to associate other data with each cell's string — in this case, the program assigns the glyph bitmap image that was just loaded from disk.

It's important to understand the assignment to Objects merely associates the bitmap with that cell in the grid. The statement does not copy the bitmap to a new location. For this reason, a new Bitmap object must be created by calling TBitmap.Create for each new object assigned to the StringGrid's Objects array.

All of this code takes place inside a *try-except* block, so if anything goes wrong — a disk error occurs, for example, or the program runs out of memory — the current Bitmap object is freed and the exception is passed to the event handler's caller. If all goes well after processing each glyph, the program calls FindNext. This is a typical way of interating through a list of files — call FindFirst to start the process and then call FindNext repeatedly until that function returns a nonzero value, indicating that the filename search is complete.

Notice the event handler uses two *finally* clauses at its end, each of which is associated with a *try* block. FindClose ends the filename search, and releases system resources held for the SearchRec object. It is a good idea to call FindClose inside a *finally* block to ensure that this procedure is called even if an exception occurs somewhere in the associated *try* block.

Less critical, but still a good idea, is to reset the screen cursor to crDefault in a *finally* clause. This ensures that the cursor returns to its normal shape even if an error occurs in the procedure.

A StringGrid object is not capable of releasing object data assigned to its Objects array. It automatically manages memory used by the Cells property, but it is your responsibility to do this for items such as bitmaps assigned to Objects. This is necessary because StringGrid doesn't know what type of data you have assigned to

Objects. Although typically used to refer to Bitmap objects, it is possible to assign any type of object to the array. This generality comes at the expense of making you responsible for freeing any memory occupied by those objects.

A good place, and usually the best, to clean up a StringGrid object is in a form's OnClose event handler. In GlyphLst, for example, the following *for* loop frees all of the Bitmap objects stored as references in the Objects array:

```
var
  I: Integer;
begin
  for I := 0 to GlyphList.RowCount - 1 do
    TBitmap(GlyphList.Objects[0, I]).Free;
end;
```

The RowCount property indicates how many items have been stored in the StringGrid. Using this value, it's a cinch to create a *for* loop that calls TBitmap.Free for each Bitmap object referenced by the Objects array.

For most information on string lists, also examine the ToDo sample application on the book's CD-ROM in the Source\Todo directory. This program demonstrates various TStrings techniques. For example, Listing 8-11 shows the procedure that ToDo uses to move a selected item from one ListBox to another. Notice the TCustomListBox parameter. This class is TListBox's immediate ancestor. You could use TListBox as the parameter type, but using TCustomListBox ensures that the procedure works for any other objects of classes derived from TCustomListBox.

Listing 8-11: ToDo uses this procedure to move selected items from one ListBox to another.

```
procedure TMainForm.MoveSelected(List: TCustomListBox;
  Items: TStrings);
var
  I: Integer;
begin
  for I := List.Items.Count _ 1 downto 0 do
    if List.Selected[I] then
    begin
      Items.AddObject(List.Items[I], List.Items.Objects[I]);
      List.Items.Delete(I);
    end;
  FileDirty := True;
end;
```

The ToDo program calls MoveSelected using a statement such as the following, which transfers selected entries from the ListBox objects SrcList to DstList:

```
MoveSelected(DstList, SrcList.Items);
```

In MoveSelected (refer to the listing), parameter List is the destination ListBox; parameter Items is the source TStrings. A *for* loop scans List from bottom to top (note the use of Pascal's downto keyword). The scan must go in this direction because any deletions at item *N* alter the indexes of items N+1....

If a listed item is selected, AddObject copies the List's string and any associated object to parameter Items, of type TStrings. The procedure then deletes the original item. Calling Delete removes the string indicated by the passed index argument (I), and also sets Objects[I] to nil. Thus, one call to Delete removes a list's string and any associated object. However, it does not dispose of that object's memory — you always must do that by calling Free.

Expert-User Tips

+ Look up more information on lb_ messages in Delphi's online Windows API help. Calling Perform to send a message — to enable horizontal scroll bars in list boxes, for example — is roughly, but not exactly, equivalent to calling the Windows SendMessage function. Perform calls the VCL WndProc (window procedure); SendMessage calls the procedure for the topmost window associated with a window handle.

+ You can also use TStringList (or a TStrings component property) to create associative lists of strings and objects. The techniques are similar to those demonstrated by the GlyphLst application, which uses a StringGrid component.

Projects to Try

8-1: Write an application that uses a ListBox component to sort a text file.

8-2: Write code that reverses the order of entries in a ListBox or ComboBox object.

8-3: Write a procedure that loads a directory's filenames into a TStringList object.

8-4: Improve the GlyphLst application by adding a File menu with commands for changing directories. Note: To prevent the program from attempting to load huge bitmaps into the ListBox, you might want to add code that rejects Bitmap objects larger than a preset size.

8-5: Advanced. Create an owner-draw ListBox that displays sample strings in the fonts' styles. (Note: Some fonts are symbolic, and you have to display the font name separately from its sample string.)

Summary

✦ Delphi's ListBox and ComboBox components are invaluable for adding selectable lists to application interfaces. You can select from a number of styles to create multiple-selection lists and to permit users to enter new data into a ComboBox's edit window.

✦ Delphi also provides the related list-making classes TList, TStrings, and TStringList. Use TList and TStringList to create independent list objects in memory. You cannot create TStrings objects — only components may use TStrings as a property's class type.

✦ All classes in Delphi are derived from TObject. This means that all class objects in Delphi applications are related.

✦ Because TStringList is derived from TStrings, anything you can do with a TStrings property (such as a ListBox's Items property) you can do with an independent TStringList object.

✦ The StringGrid component provides a general-purpose row-and-column control that can hold string, and optionally, related information for each cell in the grid. Typically, the related information is a Bitmap object, but it could be any other object of a class descended from TObject. The StringGrid properties Cells and Objects operate like two-dimensional arrays, through which the program may access a grid's contents.

✦ A TStringList object or TStrings property provides access to string data through the Items property, or through the equivalent Items.Strings array. Associated object data is available through the Objects array.

✦ It is your responsibility to free the objects you create. This is especially important when using the Objects array of a StringGrid object. The best place to free a grid's objects is usually in the form's OnClose event handler.

✦ TList, TStringList, and TStrings automatically free only string data. If you insert other objects into a list, you must free those objects by calling Free.

You can find dozens more uses for string lists in Delphi's text-based components such as Memo, Notebook, and TabbedNotebook, which you meet in the next chapter.

✦   ✦   ✦

Working with Single-Line Strings

CHAPTER

9

In This Chapter

Components

Character strings

Built-in text dialogs

Single-line text components

In the old days of computing, we programmers were lucky if our terminals had uppercase and lowercase letters plus a few standard punctuation symbols. Fortunately, we could select from a wide range of display colors — as long as it was green or orange. Today, with Windows and other graphical user interfaces, scaleable TrueType fonts and full-color monitors create limitless opportunities for interface designers, but as one consequence, programmers are faced with a completely new set of rules and regulations for working with character strings and other text objects.

This chapter examines single-line strings and text components from two points of view — internal storage and external display. The old days of text-based terminals are pretty much gone for good, and creating a successful interface for a graphical operating system now demands attention to many new string storage and display techniques.

Components

The following are Delphi's components for working with single-line strings:

✦ **Edit** — One of the simplest-looking controls in Windows, but also one of the most versatile, the Edit component can handle most single-line input tasks. The Edit object automatically supports cut, copy, and paste operations, and it comes with built-in keyboard and mouse-handling features. Palette: Standard.

✦ **Label** — You have already used the Label component in previous chapters, but Labels have other uses that may not be obvious. For example, a Label can designate a hot key for other controls that don't support keyboard selection. Palette: Standard.

✦ **MaskEdit** — You might think of this component as an Edit box with brains. Use a MaskEdit component to create validated data-entry fields — for example, a telephone number input box that requires operators to enter digits in defined positions. Palette: Additional.

Character Strings

Delphi provides a healthy assortment of string operators, functions, and procedures. Before taking a look at string and text components, you need to thoroughly understand Delphi's two string formats as well as their operators and functions. The following sections provide some background information on Delphi's String data type.

Types of strings

When Delphi 2 moved into the 32-bit operating system arena, the long-established Pascal String data type underwent a long-needed transformation. In the past, a String object was an array of up to 256 8-bit characters, with the first byte of this array assigned the string's length in characters. This so-called *length-byte* string is still available as Object Pascal's ShortString type. The only reason to use this string nowadays is for backwards compatibility.

New to Object Pascal is the AnsiString data type. With this type, strings of virtually unlimited length are possible. In most cases, the strings you create are of this type. Pascal's String data type automatically defaults to this type of string.

Note

The lowercase word string refers to any type of string data. The capitalized word String refers specifically to Object Pascal's data type.

You can change the String data type to represent either type of string using the $H compiler directive. In the default state, {$H+}, a String is the same as AnsiString. In the {$H-} state, a String reverts to the old length-byte format. It's best in most cases to use the default setting and to make use of the new AnsiString data type. Use the alternate setting only if you must compile code that expects String to be the old length-byte format.

Another type of string is the WideString, which can store characters for languages that need larger character variables. WideString objects store Unicode, 16-bit characters, which permit text in a particular language to be easily transported (and in some cases displayed unambiguously) to a variety of computer systems.

Note

32-bit OLE uses WideStrings for all string data. In terms of memory management, WideString and AnsiString objects are used similarly. Both can create string variables of virtually unlimited length.

Long and short Strings

Strings are easy to create and use. Define a String variable using a *var* declaration, either in a unit's implementation section, or in a procedure or function:

```
var
   S: String;
```

This creates an empty string object, which can hold from zero to any practical number of characters. The object is also known as a *dynamic string* because its size changes dynamically according to the length of the actual string data assigned to the object. After declaring the String variable, you can assign a literal string to *S*:

```
S := 'Click!';
```

Variable *S* can subsequently be assigned to the Caption property of a control such as a Button. This statement, for example, changes a Button object's text to the character data in the String variable:

```
Button1.Caption := S;
```

You may make similar assignments to any String property. You can also use any String object as an array of characters. The first character in the String has the index 1, so that this assignment:

```
S[2] := 'X';
```

assigns *X* to the second character of the String variable *S*. Single characters are of the data type Char, which is equivalent to AnsiChar (8-bit characters). In most programs, you can simply use String and Char variables without concern for their underlying types. However, if you must use wide characters, you should declare your string objects of the WideString type and your character variables of the WideChar type. Delphi doesn't currently support automatic switching between normal 8-bit and wide character strings.

If you prefer, you may still use Object Pascal's original length-byte string. You can create one of these creatures, now known as a ShortString, in two basic ways. Use that data type name in a declaration such as:

```
var
   SS: ShortString;
```

That creates a variable, SS, that is capable of holding up to 255 characters. Because this is usually wasteful (it's unlikely that your short strings are all of this maximum length), another and usually better way to create a short string is to specify a maximum length in brackets:

```
var
   SS: String[4];
```

Notice that you use the identifier String, not ShortString, to create a restricted-size ShortString object. As declared here, SS is five bytes in length — four bytes for its character data, and one for its length stored as the byte value at SS[0].

Note

> Short strings can impact performance negatively — another good reason not to use them. For example, all of Delphi's string-manipulation routines accept long string parameters. If you pass short strings to these routines, they are internally converted to and from long strings, wasting time and memory. For best performance, use Pascal's String data type, and use ShortStrings only when absolutely necessary.

You may compare String objects alphabetically using the usual logical operators: <, >, <=, >=, and =. For example, the following code shows how to compare two String objects alphabetically:

```
var
   S1, S2: String;
begin
   S1 := 'ABCDEFG';
   S2 := 'abcdefg';
   if (S1 > S2) then
      ShowMessage('S1 > S2')
   else
      ShowMessage('S1 <= S2');
end;
```

C and C++ programmers take note: It is also possible using Object Pascal to define a null-terminated string as an array of Char. This creates a data type that is equivalent to null-terminated strings in programming languages such as C++. For example, the following defines a 64-character string plus one byte reserved for the terminating null:

```
var
  S: array[0 .. 64] of Char;
```

Although this is allowable, it's usually best to use Pascal Strings rather than null-terminated character arrays. Delphi's String functions are highly optimized, easier to use, and generally more reliable than writing your own string manipulation functions — even if you are familiar with C and C++ null-terminated strings and string pointers. As a general rule, you need null-terminated strings only to pass arguments to Windows functions or for use with library procedures and functions that require this data type.

Note
Long strings are always null-terminated, although no string procedures or functions require this as a rule. Because they are null-terminated, long strings are type-cast compatible with PChar pointers.

Built-In Text Dialogs

Just in case you haven't discovered Delphi's string input and output dialogs, I mention them here. They are handy tools for displaying messages and prompting users for input. Try these — single-line text utilities have dozens of uses.

Displaying text messages

Delphi provides five message dialogs, one of which is almost sure to meet your needs. Figures 9-1 through 9-5 show the five dialogs in order of complexity.

✦ ShowMessage procedure displays only static messages, as shown in Figure 9-1.

Figure 9-1: ShowMessage displays a string in a dialog box with an OK button.

✦ ShowMessagePos procedure is the same as ShowMessage but with *x*- and *y*-coordinate parameters that specify the screen-relative location of the dialog box (see Figure 9-2).

Figure 9-2: ShoMessagePos dialogs contain x- and y- coordinate parameters.

✦ The MessageBox procedure encapsulates the Windows API MessageBox function. In Figure 9-3, under Windows 3.1, this function displays an old-style, non-3D dialog that's as outdated as a hand-cranked telephone. For better-looking results, use one of the following two functions instead. Under Windows 95, MessageBox produces the same visual results as MessageDlg and MessageDlgPos. (All controls in Windows 95, NT, and Windows 98 have a 3D appearance.)

Figure 9-3: The MessageBox dialog encapsulates the Windows API MessageBox function.

✦ The MessageDlg procedure provides a wide variety of options for displaying messages and prompting for answers to questions. You can select an icon to display (for example, the information balloon shown in Figure 9-4), and you can choose the types and number of buttons to offer.

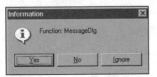

Figure 9-4: The MessageDlg dialog box enables you to elect an icon, like the information balloon shown here, for display.

✦ The MessageDlgPos procedure is the same as MessageDlg except that it also provides *x*- and *y*-coordinate parameters for positioning the dialog window anywhere on the Windows desktop, as shown in Figure 9-5.

Figure 9-5: You can position the MessageDlgPos dialog anywhere on the Windows desktop.

ShowMessage and ShowMessagePos are procedures that display messages. They are suitable only for displaying static messages. MessageBox, MessageDlg, and MessageDlgPos are functions, and they return a value that indicates which button was clicked to close the dialog window. Use one of these functions to prompt users for answers to questions or to confirm choices — for example, "Are you positively sure you want to erase your hard drive?".

The MsgDlg application on the CD-ROM in the Source\MsgDlg directory demonstrates the five types of message-display dialogs. All but one of the methods are fairly simple to use. One, MessageBox, requires using string techniques not yet introduced. I explain these following the listing. Figure 9-6 shows the program's display. Listing 9-1 lists the program's source code.

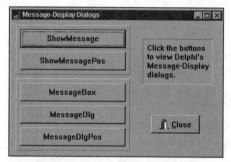

Figure 9-6: Run MsgDlg to experiment with the five types of message-display dialogs.

Listing 9-1: **Msgdlg\Main.pas**

```
unit Main;

interface

uses
  SysUtils, Windows, Messages, Classes, Graphics,
  Controls, Forms, Dialogs, StdCtrls, ExtCtrls, Buttons;

type
  TMainForm = class(TForm)
    Button1: TButton;
    Button2: TButton;
    Button3: TButton;
    Button4: TButton;
    Button5: TButton;
    BitBtn1: TBitBtn;
    Label1: TLabel;
    Panel1: TPanel;
    Bevel1: TBevel;
    Panel2: TPanel;
    procedure Button1Click(Sender: TObject);
```

(continued)

Listing 9-1 *(continued)*

```
    procedure Button2Click(Sender: TObject);
    procedure Button3Click(Sender: TObject);
    procedure Button4Click(Sender: TObject);
    procedure Button5Click(Sender: TObject);
  private
    { Private declarations }
  public
    { Public declarations }
  end;

var
  MainForm: TMainForm;

implementation

{$R *.DFM}

procedure TMainForm.Button1Click(Sender: TObject);
begin
  ShowMessage('Procedure: ShowMessage');
end;

procedure TMainForm.Button2Click(Sender: TObject);
begin
  ShowMessagePos('Procedure: ShowMessagePos', 10, 20);
end;

procedure TMainForm.Button3Click(Sender: TObject);
var
  TheText, TheCaption: String;
begin
  TheText := 'Function: MessageBox';
  TheCaption := 'MessageBox Demonstration';
  if Application.MessageBox(PChar(TheText), PChar(TheCaption),
    MB_DEFBUTTON1 + MB_ICONEXCLAMATION + MB_OKCANCEL) = IDOK
    then ShowMessage('You selected OK')
    else ShowMessage('You selected Cancel');
end;

procedure TMainForm.Button4Click(Sender: TObject);
var
  W: Word;
  S: String;
begin
  W := MessageDlg('Function: MessageDlg',
    mtInformation, [mbYes, mbNo, mbIgnore], 0);
  case W of
```

```
        mrYes:    S := 'Yes';
        mrNo:     S := 'No';
        mrIgnore: S := 'Ignore';
      end;
      ShowMessage('You selected ' + S);
    end;

    procedure TMainForm.Button5Click(Sender: TObject);
    var
      W: Word;
      S: String;
      X, Y: Integer;
    begin
      X := 50; Y := 75;
      W := MessageDlgPos('Function: MessageDlgPos',
        mtWarning, mbAbortRetryIgnore, 0, X, Y);
      case W of
        mrAbort:  S := 'Abort';
        mrRetry:  S := 'Retry';
        mrIgnore: S := 'Ignore';
      end;
      ShowMessage('You selected ' + S);
    end;

    end.
```

ShowMessage is easy to use. Just pass it any string or string variable to display a message. Remember that Delphi permits you to concatenate strings with the plus operator — a fact that makes ShowMessage handy for displaying all sorts of values as well as for debugging errant variables. For example, to display the value of an Integer Count variable, use a statement such as this:

```
ShowMessage('Count = ' + IntToStr(Count));
```

ShowMessagePos is the same as ShowMessage but adds *x*- and *y*- coordinate values, relative to the screen. To display the preceding message at the upper-left corner of the Windows desktop, use this statement:

```
ShowMessagePos('Count = ' + IntToStr(Count), 0, 0);
```

MessageDlg and MessageDlgPos return a value that indicates which button was clicked to close the dialog window. Because you determine which buttons the dialog displays, you have to check for only those buttons — you don't need to encode responses for every possible return value. A *case* statement is usually the cleanest construction. First, define a Word variable *W* and assign MessageDlg or MessageDlgPos to it with a statement such as this:

```
W := MessageDlg('Function: MessageDlg',
  mtInformation, [mbYes, mbNo, mbIgnore], 0);
```

Then, use a *case* statement to take an appropriate action based on which button the user selected:

```
case W of
  mrYes:    { action for Yes    };
  mrNo:     { action for No     };
  mrIgnore: { action for Ignore };
end;
```

MessageDlgPos is the same as MessageDlg but adds *x-* and *y-* coordinate parameters for positioning the dialog on the Windows desktop. The coordinates are relative to the screen, but you can convert them to client-relative values to display dialogs within the program's window space. This makes for a friendlier interface because users tend to look for messages in specific locations relative to the application's window.

MessageBox is more complex to use. You need to pass it null-terminated strings plus a logical grouping of constants such as MB_OKCANCEL to select various options:

```
function MessageBox(Text, Caption: PChar;
  Flags: Longint): Integer;
```

The first two parameters are of type PChar, which in Delphi represents a pointer to a character. Because long strings are null terminated, you can cast them to PChar pointers for passing to Windows functions such as these. For example, procedure Button3Click declares two string variables:

```
var
  TheText, TheCaption: String;
```

To these variables, the program assigns literal strings using two statements:

```
TheText := 'Function: MessageBox';
TheCaption := 'MessageBox Demonstration';
```

Pass the two strings, type-cast to PChar pointers, to the MessageBox function. The program does this using an *if* statement to test the function result, which indicates which button was clicked to close the dialog box window. The *if* statement shows how to type-cast strings to PChar pointers:

```
if Application.MessageBox(PChar(TheText), PChar(TheCaption),
  MB_DEFBUTTON1 + MB_ICONEXCLAMATION + MB_OKCANCEL) = IDOK
  then ShowMessage('You selected OK')
  else ShowMessage('You selected Cancel');
```

The expressions PChar(TheText) and PChar(TheCaption) pass the long string variables to the Windows function, which expects to receive null-terminated strings in these positions. The MessageBox function returns the value of the button the user clicked. If equal to IDOK, then the first message is shown using ShowMessage. If not, the user clicked Cancel, and the second message is displayed.

Function Button3Click in the sample listing shows how to use MessageBox, but I recommend that you instead use MessageDlg or MessageDlgPos, which are simpler in design and accept Pascal string arguments. Delphi defines MessageDlg and its parameters as:

```
function MessageDlg(const Msg: string; AType: TMsgDlgType;
  AButtons: TMsgDlgButtons; HelpCtx: Longint): Word;
```

✦ **Msg** — Pass a literal, variable, or constant string to display in the dialog box.

✦ **AType** — Set this parameter to a constant such as mtWarning or mtError to select an appropriate icon and dialog caption.

✦ **AButtons** — Set this parameter to the set of buttons you want to display in the dialog. Surround the set with brackets. For example, pass the expression [mbYes, mbNo, mbCancel] to display Yes, No, and Cancel buttons. Delphi automatically adds appropriate glyphs to each button (they are BitBtn component objects). Alternatively, rather than define your own button set, pass a predefined set, such as mbYesNoCancel, mbOkCancel, or myAbortRetryIgnore. These are already Pascal sets — don't surround them with brackets.

✦ **HelpCtx** — Set this parameter to zero unless you are defining a help context for the message box.

Look up MessageDlg for more information on possible values you can pass to this function and to MessageDlgPos.

Listing 9-2 demonstrates how to use screen-relative coordinates to position items in windows. Define a TPoint variable *P*, set its *X* and *Y* members to 0, and call ClientToScreen, which returns a TPoint record with those values converted to equivalent screen coordinates. You can then call MessageDlgPos as shown (or call ShowMessagePos) to position the message box at the upper-left corner or another location of the application window's client area. The listing text on the CD-ROM is in the Strings directory in file Position.pas.

Listing 9-2: Use this code to position a message dialog within the application's window.

```
var
  W: Word;     { Result of MessageDlgPos }
  P: TPoint;   { Coordinate X, Y record }
begin
  P.X := 0;   { Assign client X value }
  P.Y := 0;   { Assign client Y value }
  P := ClientToScreen(P);  { Convert P to screen coordinates }
  W := MessageDlgPos('Function: MessageDlg',
    mtInformation, [mbYes, mbNo, mbIgnore], 0,
    P.X, P.Y);  { Pass converted X, Y to function }
end;
```

If you pass *X* and *Y* equal to –1 to ShowMessagePos or MessageDlgPos, the functions display their dialog windows at default locations selected by Windows.

Prompting for text input

On the CD-ROM

Programming is often a process of give and take. The preceding message dialogs give users information. To take input from users, call the InputBox or InputQuery functions, which display the dialog shown in Figure 9-7. InputBox returns a string; InputQuery returns a Boolean True or False value, but the two functions are otherwise equivalent. Listing 9-3 demonstrates how to use InputBox and InputQuery. Copy these procedures to a program's unit as OnClick event handlers for two Button objects in a form, and run the program to experiment with the InputBox and InputQuery functions. This isn't a complete program — to use the code, insert two Button objects into a form and copy the two procedures into OnClick event handlers for each Button. The listing text on the CD-ROM is in directory Strings in file Input.pas.

Figure 9-7: Call the InputBox or InputQuery functions to prompt users for single-line text strings. Both functions display the dialog shown here.

Listing 9-3: **Using InputBox and InputQuery**

```
procedure TForm1.Button1Click(Sender: TObject);
var
  S: String;
begin
  S := InputBox('Test', 'Enter a string', '');
  if Length(S) > 0 then
    ShowMessage('You entered: ' + S);
end;

procedure TForm1.Button2Click(Sender: TObject);
var
  S: String;
begin
  S := '';
  if InputQuery('Test', 'Type QUIT to end', S) then
    if Uppercase(S) = 'QUIT' then
      Close;
end;
```

InputBox takes three string arguments: a caption, a prompt, and a default string value, which can be variable or constant. The sample listing passes a null string to InputBox for the default string, returned if users enter no changes. InputBox displays the default string highlighted in the dialog. The function also returns the default string if users click the Cancel button. If users click OK, InputBox returns the text entered in the dialog's Edit control. For example, use InputBox to prompt for a filename:

```
S := InputBox('Test', 'Enter filename', 'Readme.Txt');
ShowMessage('You entered: ' + S);
```

On the CD-ROM

InputQuery is the same as InputBox, but it returns True if users click OK, or False if users click Cancel. InputQuery deposits user input into the default string, which must be a variable. The function is ideal for prompting users to enter strings such as filenames that default to known paths. For example, insert Button and Memo objects into a form, and then use the programming in Listing 9-4 to prompt for a filename, which defaults to this book's Readme.txt file in the Source directory. The selected file's text is shown in a Memo object. The listing text on the CD-ROM is located in the Strings directory in file Query.pas.

Listing 9-4: How to prompt for a filename

```
procedure TForm1.Button1Click(Sender: TObject);
var
   Filename: String;
begin
   Filename := '\Delphi 4 Bible\Source\Readme.Txt';
   if InputQuery('Test', 'File?', Filename) then
      Memo1.Lines.LoadFromFile(Filename);
end;
```

Single-Line Text Components

Delphi offers three single-line text input and output components: Label, Edit, and MaskEdit. They are relatively simple to use, but the following sections describe some less obvious techniques that are valuable.

Labels

Labels are simply text objects you can insert into forms and other container components, such as a Panel. As you have discovered from this book's examples so far, Labels have numerous properties. You can set a Label's Font to alter its text style, you can display wrap-around text by setting WordWrap True, and you can change a Label's color with the Color property.

> **Tip**
> The Color property selects a Label's background color. Use the Font property to select a Label's foreground text color.

In most cases, Labels are noninteractive — they simply label another component, or they provide some onscreen information. One of the less obvious uses for a Label is to provide an accelerator hot key for another control that normally doesn't support keyboard selection. Follow these steps to try out this useful technique:

1. Insert three Edit objects and three Label objects into a form. Position each label to the immediate left of an Edit control.

2. Change Label1's Caption to &One. The ampersand designates a subsequent letter (*O* in this case) as the accelerator hot key.

3. Select Label1's FocusControl property, click the down arrow, and choose Edit1. When Label1 receives the input focus, it passes the focus to the indicated control.

4. Repeat Steps 2 and 3 for the other two Labels. Set Label2's Caption to &Two, and Label3's to T&hree. Assign Label2's FocusControl to Edit2, and Label3's to Edit3.

5. Run the program and press Alt+O, Alt+T, and Alt+H to shift the focus to the labeled Edit boxes.

To center a Label horizontally with an Edit or other associated control, first select the Edit control, press and hold the Shift key, and click the corresponding Label. Choose Delphi's Edit I Align... command, choose the Vertical Centers radio button, and press Enter or click OK.

Edit boxes

For general-purpose single-line input, you can't beat Delphi's Edit component. The following are some tips about selected Edit component properties:

✦ Set AutoSelect to True to highlight an Edit object's contents when the object receives the input focus.

✦ Set CharCase to ecNormal for normal entry. Set it to ecUpperCase or ecLowerCase to limit entry to uppercase or lowercase.

✦ Set HideSelection False if you want highlighted text to remain selected when users shift the focus to another control. Set HideSelection to True for normal operation — selected text is unhighlighted when the focus leaves the Edit control.

✦ Set MaxLength to the maximum number of characters you want users to enter. Although you can set this property to zero for unlimited input length, in practice, you use relatively small values. The amount of text that you can insert in an Edit box is virtually unlimited. In early versions of 16-bit Delphi, text was limited to 255 characters. This restriction is removed in 32-bit versions of Delphi; however, Windows 95 and 98 (but not NT) restrict text to a maximum of 64K.

✦ The Edit component does not have a Caption property. Use a Label, as explained in the preceding section, to give Edit objects captions and hot-key accelerators. To display an object, insert characters into the Text property, or assign a string at run time.

✦ To display text-screen DOS characters, set OEMConvert to True, and change Font to TrueType MS LineDraw. Set OEMConvert to False if you don't want ANSI characters converted (this is the normal setting for Windows). To support ASCII extended characters in DOS filenames, OEMConvert should be True.

Edit components also provide numerous events. Some of the more useful of these are:

✦ **OnChange** — Called when the control's contents change in any way. If you enable this event, be aware that it is called for each character entered into the control. To filter characters entered into an Edit control, you should instead use the OnKeyPress event.

✦ **OnClick** — Called when the user single-clicks the mouse in the Edit control. Note that this event handler is not called when the Edit control receives the focus by other means — when users press Tab, for example.

✦ **OnDblClick** — Called when the user double-clicks the mouse in the Edit control. The normal response for this event copies the Edit control's Text property to another object such as a ListBox.

✦ **OnEnter** — Called when the control receives the input focus — that is, when users select the control, tab to it, or click it with the mouse.

✦ **OnExit** — Called when the control loses the input focus — that is, when users shift the focus to another control.

✦ **OnKeyPress** — Called for every keypress. Generally, this event is the correct one to use for filtering keyboard input. For example, to prevent users from typing certain keys, if the event handler's Key parameter equals a target value, set Key to #0 to disable it.

Using OnEnter and OnExit events

The OnEnter and OnExit events are particularly useful for designing attractive interfaces. For example, you can use these events to color the focused Edit control, which can help draw the user's attention to the current field in a window with numerous input areas. First, declare a variable OldColor of type TColor in the form class's private section, something like this:

```
TForm1 = class(TForm)
  Edit1: TEdit;
private
  OldColor: TColor;
...
public
...
end;
```

Next, create an OnEnter event handler for an Edit object. Assign the object's Color to the OldColor variable, and then select the color you want for the control's background. With this code, when users shift the focus to the control, its background changes to yellow:

```
procedure TForm1.Edit1Enter(Sender: TObject);
begin
  OldColor := Edit1.Color;
  Edit1.Color := clYellow;
end;
```

Also, create a handler for the Edit object's OnExit event. Assign the OldColor value to the object's Color property. When users shift the focus away from the control, the program restores its background to the saved color:

```
procedure TForm1.Edit1Exit(Sender: TObject);
begin
  Edit1.Color := OldColor;
end;
```

On the
CD-ROM

Telephonic mnemonics

The TelName application on the CD-ROM in the Source\TelName directory demonstrates how to use Edit objects. This program uses Delphi to paint a pretty new face on some code I wrote for my Dr. Dobb's column, "Algorithm Alley," a few years back. (I am no longer writing the column.) The program solved one of my pet peeves — cutesy telephonic mnemonics in advertisements that read something like "To reach us by phone, just dial 1-800-CALL-US-NOW." It takes me forever and a day to look up the corresponding numbers on the telephone dial, so I wrote a program to convert the mnemonics to numbers. I also wrote the converse code that displays all possible permutations of any number. In my area, for example, the common exchange 293 can spell words such as AWE, AXE, and AYE, leading to some interesting mnemonics. (I have it in mind to request AWE-SOME for my next telephone number.)

To use TelName, enter a telephonic mnemonic in the Telephone name Edit control. Click the Number button to convert the name to its equivalent number. Or, enter a number in the Telephone number Edit control, and click Names to insert all possible mnemonic permutations into the window's list box. Note: On a telephone dial, digits 1 and 0 have no corresponding letters, and letters *Q* and *Z* have no corresponding digits.

Long telephone numbers in TelName produce numerous ListBox entries, which may cause Windows to run out of resources. The number of entries equals 3n where *n* is the number of digits. Four digits produce 81 entries. Six digits produce 729 entries. For best results, type a maximum of three or four digits into the Telephone number Edit control before clicking Names. For example, to see what your telephone number spells, instead of entering all digits, enter the area code, exchange, and number separately.

Note

Due to superior memory management, this is far less of a problem with Windows 95, 98, and especially NT than it was with Windows 3.1.

Figure 9-8 shows TelName's display. For best results, limit numbers to three or four digits before clicking Names. Listing 9-5 shows the program's source code. For an explanation of how the algorithm works, and on permutations in general, see my article, "Algorithm Alley: Telephonic Mnemonics," *Dr. Dobb's Journal,* June 1993.

Figure 9-8: TelName converts telephonic mnemonics to equivalent telephone numbers, and can show all possible alphabetic permutations for any number.

Listing 9-5: **TelName\Main.pas**

```pascal
unit Main;

interface

uses
  SysUtils, Windows, Messages, Classes, Graphics, Controls,
  Forms, Dialogs, StdCtrls, Buttons, Mask;

type
  TMainForm = class(TForm)
    Label1: TLabel;
    Label2: TLabel;
    ListBox1: TListBox;
    CloseBitBtn: TBitBtn;
    NamesBitBtn: TBitBtn;
    NumberBitBtn: TBitBtn;
    NameEdit: TEdit;
```

```
    NumbEdit: TEdit;
    procedure FormCreate(Sender: TObject);
    procedure NumberBitBtnClick(Sender: TObject);
    procedure NamesBitBtnClick(Sender: TObject);
    procedure NumbEditKeyPress(Sender: TObject; var Key: Char);
    procedure NameEditKeyPress(Sender: TObject; var Key: Char);
  private
    { Private declarations }
    function TelNameToNum(TelName: String): String;
    procedure ListNames(TelNum: String);
  public
    { Public declarations }
  end;

var
  MainForm: TMainForm;

implementation

{$R *.DFM}

var
{ Array of telephone dialog letters }
  TelDial: array[0 .. 9] of String;

{ Return telephone digit that corresponds to C }
function DigitToLetter(C: Char): Char;
var
  I, J: Integer;
begin
  C := Upcase(C);
  for I := 0 to 9 do
    for J := 1 to 3 do
      if (C = TelDial[I][J]) then
      begin
        Result := Chr(I + Ord('0'));
        Exit;
      end;
  Result := C;   { Default }
end;

{ Return ordinal value of digit character C }
function ValueOfChar(C: Char): Integer;
begin
  Result := Ord(C) - Ord('0');
end;
```

(continued)

Listing 9-5 *(continued)*

```
{ Return number for a telephone alphabetic name }
function TMainForm.TelNameToNum(TelName: String): String;
var
  I: Integer;
begin
  Result := '';
  for I := 1 to Length(TelName) do
    Result := Result + DigitToLetter(TelName[I]);
end;

procedure TMainForm.ListNames(TelNum: String);
var
  S: String;  { Temporary string }

  { Find N alphabetic permutations of digits in TelNum }
  procedure Permute(N: Integer);
  var
    I, Digit: Integer;
  begin
    Digit := ValueOfChar(TelNum[N]);
    for I := 1 to 3 do
    begin
      S[N] := TelDial[Digit][I];  { Insert letter }
      if (N = Length(TelNum)) then
        ListBox1.Items.Add(S)     { Add string to ListBox }
      else
        Permute(N + 1);  { Call Permute recursively }
    end;
  end; { Permute }

begin
  if Length(TelNum) > 0 then
  begin
    S := TelNum;      { Assign to temporary string }
    Permute(1);       { Start permutations }
  end;
end;

{ Initialize global variables }
procedure TMainForm.FormCreate(Sender: TObject);
begin
  TelDial[0] := '   ';  TelDial[1] := '   ';
  TelDial[2] := 'ABC';  TelDial[3] := 'DEF';
  TelDial[4] := 'GHI';  TelDial[5] := 'JKL';
  TelDial[6] := 'MNO';  TelDial[7] := 'PRS';
  TelDial[8] := 'TUV';  TelDial[9] := 'WXY';
end;
```

```
{ Do Number button click }
procedure TMainForm.NumberBitBtnClick(Sender: TObject);
begin
  NumbEdit.Text := TelNameToNum(NameEdit.Text);
  NumbEdit.SetFocus;
end;

{ Do Names button click }
procedure TMainForm.NamesBitBtnClick(Sender: TObject);
begin
  ListBox1.Clear;
  ListNames(NumbEdit.Text);
  ListBox1.SetFocus;
end;

{ Click Names button for Enter key in Number Edit object }
procedure TMainForm.NumbEditKeyPress(Sender: TObject;
  var Key: Char);
begin
  if Key = #13 then
  begin
    NamesBitBtn.Click;
    Key := #0;
  end;
end;

{ Click Number button for Enter key in Name Edit object }
procedure TMainForm.NameEditKeyPress(Sender: TObject;
  var Key: Char);
begin
  if Key = #13 then
  begin
    NumberBitBtn.Click;
    Key := #0;
  end;
end;

end.
```

TelName demonstrates some useful interface and string-handling techniques. Two labels provide accelerator hot keys for the Edit controls, using the methods discussed earlier. For example, the Telephone name label prefaces the *n* in name with an ampersand, and the Label object's FocusControl property is set to NameEdit. With these property values, pressing Alt+N selects the labeled Edit object.

The program's Number and Names buttons demonstrate how to shift the focus to another control after a button's selection. This is useful for promoting a logical progression through a group of controls. For example, when you click the Number button, the program converts a telephonic mnemonic in the Telephone name Edit box to a number. Users may want to modify that number to list other possible spellings, so the Number button's OnClick event handler shifts the focus away from itself to the NumbEdit object. The following two statements handle the Number button's selection:

```
NumbEdit.Text := TelNameToNum(NameEdit.Text);
NumbEdit.SetFocus;
```

The first statement converts the NameEdit object's text — for example, boat — to an equivalent telephone number (2628). The second statement calls NumbEdit's SetFocus method to shift the focus to the next Edit object.

Clicking the Names button performs a similar task, using these three statements in the OnClick event handler:

```
ListBox1.Clear;
ListNames(NumbEdit.Text);
ListBox1.SetFocus;
```

First, the procedure clears the ListBox's current entries. It then calls ListNames, which permutes a telephone number into all possible alphabetic mnemonics. The last statement shifts the input focus to the ListBox so users can press arrow keys to view the listed results.

Providing efficient keyboard operations for graphical software is a black art that's not often practiced well. In addition to permitting keyboard control over commands, a well-designed user interface uses methods such as SetFocus to minimize keypresses. Even though it's safe to say that most all Windows systems have a mouse input device, a finished application should be completely operable from the keyboard.

TelName takes two other measures to improve keyboard handling. When you press Enter in an Edit box, the input focus normally shifts to the next control in tab order. This offers an excellent opportunity for performing any needed processing on the Edit control's contents, thereby eliminating one button click. For example, run TelName and enter boat in the Telephone name Edit control. When you press Enter, the program shifts the focus to the Telephone number Edit area, and it converts boat to the equivalent number. Press Enter again to shift to the ListBox and insert all possible permutations of that number. When you try this, the effect seems obvious, but achieving a smooth keyboard interface often requires much thought and testing.

To reprogram the Enter key to accomplish these interactive tasks, TelName uses two OnKeyPress event handlers for the NumbEdit and NameEdit objects. In NumbEditKeyPress, for example, the program checks for a carriage return (the expression #13 represents an ASCII character with a value of 13). To process the information in the Edit window, the program simulates a button click with the statement:

```
NamesBitBtn.Click;
```

After that, the program throws out the carriage return because the button already shifts the focus to the next Edit window, and we don't want the current control to receive that character. To throw away the Enter keypress, simply set Key to ASCII null with this assignment:

```
Key := #0;
```

The procedure ListNames calls the nested Permute procedure to find all alphabetic combinations of a number passed as the TelNum parameter.

Masked Edit boxes

The *MaskEdit* component provides a formatted Edit control that restricts users to entering required symbols at defined positions. A secondary string, called the *EditMask,* defines input rules. For example, a *mask* can define a formatted telephone number that requires users to enter a seven-digit phone number. Follow these steps to experiment with MaskEdit:

1. Insert a MaskEdit object from the Additional VCL palette into a form. Also enter an Edit object and Button object.

2. The MaskEdit component provides a property, EditMask, that defines the control's input format. You can assign a mask at design time by modifying this property. To do the same at run time, double-click Button1 and enter this statement into its OnClick event handler:

```
MaskEdit1.EditMask := Edit1.Text;
MaskEdit1.SetFocus;
```

3. Run the program and enter 999\-9999;1;_ into the Edit1 object. Enter all punctuation as shown (note the final underscore). Click the button to copy that text to the MaskEdit object's EditMask property. The mask specifies a seven-digit telephone number (I explain more about the mask's format later).

4. Enter text into MaskEdit to experiment with your mask.

You can also test masks by clicking the ellipsis button for a MaskEdit object's EditMask property. This opens Delphi's Input Mask Editor dialog, which is shown in Figure 9-9. Select a sample mask, and enter test strings into the Test Input edit control. Load .dem (Delphi Edit Mask) files by clicking the Masks button. Delphi provides several sample files with telephone number, date, time, and other formatting masks in a variety of languages. Listing 9-6 shows the text from Denmark.dem, located in Delphi's Bin subdirectory.

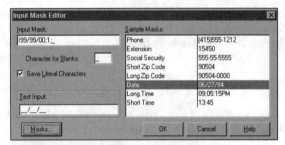

Figure 9-9: Delphi's Input Mask Editor dialog provides sample masks for a MaskEdit component's EditMask property.

Listing 9-6: **Denmark.dem illustrates the format for an edit mask text file.**

```
Phone | 48140001 | 00 09 99 99;1;_
Phone with Country | 48140001 | \+45 00 00 00 00;1;_
Social Security | 1234567890 | 000000\-0000;1;_
Zip Code | 3450 | 0000;1;_
Zip Code with Country | DK3450 | !>LL\-0000;1;_
Date | 260195 | 90\.90\.\1\900;1;_
Date (Windows) | 260195 | 90/90/00;1;_
Long Time | 210515 | !90:00:00;1;_
Short Time | 1345 | !90:00;1;_
```

For a table of script characters that you can use to construct masks, search for EditMask in Delphi's online help. An EditMask is a string of symbols that designate literal characters, input character sets, and control codes. A mask consists of three parts separated by semicolons:

✦ One or more characters that designate allowable input character sets

✦ The digit 1 to save literal characters in the input—hyphens in a telephone number, for example—or the digit 0 not to save literal characters

✦ The character to display for blanks in the MaskEdit window— this is usually an underscore or a blank

A sample telephone EditMask string illustrates how to construct each part of a complete mask. Here's the mask:

```
!\(999\)000\-0000;1;_
```

At run time, this mask causes the MaskEdit object to display the following input template:

```
(___)___-____
```

In the mask string, a leading exclamation point tells the control to discard trailing blanks from the resulting input. If you don't begin a mask with an exclamation point, trailing blanks are preserved. Type a back slash to designate a literal character—there are three in this example: the opening and closing parentheses around the number's three-digit area code, and the hyphen that separates the exchange and number. The control shows these characters in the edit window, and the text cursor automatically skips over them during typing.

A 9 in the mask indicates that users may enter a digit or nothing into this position. Use 0 to require a digit. Use capital *A* to permit alphanumeric entry; use capital *C* to require a character. See Delphi's online help for other mask symbols.

The second part of the edit mask (;1 in the preceding example) indicates whether to save literal characters in the resulting input. Enter ;0 to discard literals. With this option, the program receives a formatted telephone number such as (800)555-1212 as the string of digits 8005551212.

The third and final part of an edit mask designates the character to display for input positions in the mask template. Usually, you should specify an underscore or a blank, but you may use a different character if you wish. For example, change the preceding mask's trailing underscore to a period.

Periods and other punctuation characters in proportional fonts result in MaskEdit templates that occupy less space than the final input. For a better-looking template when using a period as the input position character, select a monospace font such as Courier New for the MaskEdit control.

You may create your own .dem files of mask templates for loading into Delphi's Input Mask Editor dialog. This is just a plain text file with the filename extension .dem. Each line in the file consists of three parts: the mask's name, a sample input, and the edit-mask string. For example, here's the Zip Code entry from Denmark.dem:

```
Zip Code | 3450 | 0000;1;_
```

Note Delphi provides several .dem files for various countries and language locales. These files contain input masks that follow local formatting customs. To find the files, look in Delphi's \bin installation directory.

Password entry

You can use an Edit or MaskEdit object to provide a password-entry box (this also applies to the database DBEdit component). Designate any character other than #0 in the PasswordChar property. For example, enter * or # in this property for a sample Edit object and run the program. Users can enter text into the control, but only the password character shows on screen.

Always give users the chance to confirm a password by typing it twice. One of the easiest methods for doing that is to insert two Edit or MaskEdit objects into a form. This form might be a dialog that a command displays, or that the program shows on startup before allowing access to information. Create a handler for the form's OnCloseQuery event. Listing 9-7 is an example of a program that compares the two Edit controls. The program allows the form to close only if the two passwords match. When using this program, use two Edit objects and this OnCloseQuery event handler to prevent a form from closing unless the two password input controls match.

Listing 9-7: Comparing two Edit controls

```
TS: The following line of code exceeds 64 characters in length.
Please break the line. Thanks. - DSprocedure
TForm1.FormCloseQuery(Sender: TObject;
  var CanClose: Boolean);
begin
  if Edit1.Text <> Edit2.Text then
  begin
    ShowMessage('Password incorrect!');
    CanClose := False;
    Edit1.SetFocus;
  end;
end;
```

Or, you can insert a Password Dialog form into an application. Follow these steps to try out this template:

1. Start a new project, and select File | New Form or click the New form speed button. Choose Password Dialog from the Browse Gallery dialog.

2. Insert a Button into the main form. Double-click the button and enter these statements into the Button object's OnClick event handler:

```
PasswordDlg.ShowModal;
ShowMessage(PasswordDlg.Password.Text);
```

3. Add Unit2 to Unit1's *uses* directive near the top of the Unit1 source code module.

4. Run the program and click the button. Enter a password in the dialog box. When you click OK, the program displays your entry in a ShowMessage dialog. Notice that the host program accesses the dialog's password text as the expression PasswordDlg.Password.Text. (Password is an Edit object that PasswordDlg owns.)

Expert-User Tips

✦ To conserve stack space, preface procedure and function string parameters with *const*. This tells Delphi that the procedure uses, but does not change, the string. Consequently, Delphi can pass the string by reference rather than copying the string's characters, which wastes stack space. (Strings are not stack allocated in the current version of Delphi, but *const* still saves possible hidden string references in *try-finally* blocks, which can create large stack frames.) For example, define a procedure like this to create a constant string parameter:

```
procedure MySubroutine(const S: String);
begin
end;
```

✦ Set Label's ShowAccelChar to False to disable the Label's capability to provide an accelerator key for other controls. You might want to do this, for example, to display ampersand characters in a Label's Caption. However, you can display an ampersand simply by typing two of them. The Label Caption &&Amp displays as &Amp.

✦ For limiting Edit control entry to uppercase or lowercase, rather than write a keyboard filter for the control's OnKeyDown event, select a value for the CharCase property. You may set CharCase to ecLowerCase, ecNormal, or ecUpperCase.

✦ Label objects do not have window handles, and therefore, they consume less memory than Edit objects. To conserve memory, always use a Label rather than an Edit object for read-only text.

✦ MessageDlg and MessageDlgPos normally display glyph bitmaps on their buttons. If you don't want glyphs on buttons, insert the following statement in the main form's OnCreate event handler:

```
MsgDlgGlyphs := False;
```

✦ Set a Label object's Transparent property to True for displaying text labels on top of graphic images such as bitmaps.

✦ A Label is a nonwindowed control, and as such, it cannot appear on top of a windowed control, such as a Button. If you cannot force a Label to appear on top of another component with the Edit | Bring to Front and Edit | Send to Back commands, you may be attempting the impossible. Try another approach to get the interface effect you want, or use the TStaticText component.

✦ The Edit component's Modified property, a Boolean True or False value, indicates whether any changes have been made to the control's contents since creating the Edit object or since setting Modified to False. After accepting input from an Edit object, set Modified to False. You can then inspect this property to determine whether the Edit object's contents have changed.

✦ You can access a MaskEdit object's text using two properties, EditText or Text. If the object's mask specifies that literal characters should be saved, EditText and Text have the identical content, and you can use either one to obtain the control's text. If the mask does not specify saving literal characters, EditText represents the text that users see in the MaskEdit window, and Text represents that same text minus its literal characters.

✦ To restrict MaskEdit entries to uppercase or lowercase, set the CharCase property to ecLowerCase or ecUpperCase. To permit uppercase and lowercase input, set CharCase to its default value, ecNormal. This may be simpler than specifying uppercase and lowercase entry using mask symbols.

✦ When concatenating strings, keep in mind that every use of the plus operator consumes memory for temporary storage. In many cases, you can use the Format function to reduce memory usage For example, to concatenate three strings A, B, and C, and assign the result to S, use a statement such as:

```
S := Format('%s%s%s', [A, B, C]);
```

This is logically equivalent to the following statement:

```
S := A + B + C;
```

 Projects to Try

9-1: Design a module that displays error messages using MessageDlg or MessageDlgPos.

9-2: Write a test program that lets users program accelerator hot keys for one or more Edit objects. You might include this code in a configuration utility or menu command.

9-3: Create MaskEdit objects for entering e-mail addresses for various services such as the Internet and CompuServe. Store your templates in a .dem text file.

9-4: Write a general-purpose password entry dialog, or improve upon Delphi's Password Dialog template. Your template should provide the means for users to confirm a password by entering it twice.

Summary

✦ Delphi's Label, Edit, and MaskEdit components can handle most of an application's single-line string requirements.

✦ Delphi supports two fundamental kinds of strings — AnsiString and ShortString. The String data type defaults to AnsiString unless using the {$H-} option, in which case Strings are ShortStrings. Pascal's 255-character length-byte strings are equivalent to ShortStrings. The String (and AnsiString) data types create virtually unlimited-length dynamic strings. Memory management is automatic when using these String types. The {$H-} option is useful only for compiling older Delphi and Pascal code.

✦ Delphi also provides a WideString type, which stores Unicode 16-bit character values. Wide strings are typically used in applications for languages such as Japanese, which cannot fully represent their characters using 8-bit bytes. They also allow the unambiguous display of text in various languages.

✦ Try to use Pascal Strings for all of your string-handling needs. Pascal string procedures and functions are highly optimized, and because String is a built-in type, you can use strings in expressions. For example, to concatenate two or more strings, simply add them together with plus operators, as in the expression S1 + S2 + S3. You can also compare Pascal strings using the <, >, <=, >=, and = <>, operators. You must call functions such as StrComp to compare null-terminated strings.

✦ To display messages, call ShowMessage or ShowMessagePos. To display messages and prompt users to click a button — for example, to request permission to delete a file — call MessageDlg or MessageDlgPos. You may also call the standard Windows MessageBox function, but this requires you to use null-terminated strings.

✦ To prompt users for single-line text entries, call InputBox or InputQuery. These functions can handle most single-line input needs, and they save you the time and effort of developing your own input dialogs with Edit components.

✦ As you probably know, you can use Label objects for labels and other static text items in forms. However, a Label object can also provide an accelerator hot key for another control such as Edit or MaskEdit that doesn't support Alt-key selection.

✦ For general-purpose single-line input needs, use the Edit object. This component has numerous properties and events that you can use to provide input areas. An Edit object is a virtual single-line text editor, and it automatically supports keyboard and mouse operations, including cut, copy, and paste.

✦ Try to make your applications operable with the keyboard and the mouse. For an example, run the TelName application, which demonstrates efficient keyboard interface techniques such as setting the focus on receiving a button click.

✦ Use a MaskEdit object to provide template-based Edit controls. Insert or select a mask for a MaskEdit object's EditMask property — for example, to require users to enter a telephone number or a date using a specific format.

✦ For password entry, assign a character to the PasswordChar property of an Edit or MaskEdit object (this also works for the database DB-Edit component). The objects display only that character for all input.

You're just beginning to scratch the surface of Delphi's text input and output capabilities. In the next chapter, you investigate components for managing multiple-line text objects.

✦   ✦   ✦

Working with Multiple-Line Text

Sooner or later, all programmers set out to write their own, personal text editors with features they've dreamed of using. Some of these ambitious souls actually manage to get a prototype up and running, but few ever finish the job. Designing even a simple text editor with minimal commands for inserting text, cutting and pasting lines, and reading and writing files is a tremendously painstaking chore. And, no, I never completed my own text editor, which remains in sorry state on a disk somewhere. I hope I never get the bright idea to finish it.

Fortunately, with Delphi's multiple-line text components, I probably never need to work on that code again. A single Memo object provides all the capabilities of the Windows Notepad editor. Just insert a Memo object into a form and wave your magic wand for an instant text editor.

In this chapter, you use the Memo and StringGrid components to build multiple-line text objects into your application's user interface. I also discuss related topics such as clipboard transfers and how to use the ScrollBar and ScrollBox components, which you almost always need when working with multiple-line text.

Components

The following are Delphi's components for working with multiple-line text:

✦ **Memo** — Practically a word processor in its own right, the Memo component adds Notepad-like capabilities to an application. This chapter's Readme text file viewer — which you can call from another application such as an installation utility — demonstrates how to use Memo objects. Palette: Standard.

✦ **ScrollBar** — This general-purpose component adds scroll bars to a form, or it can operate independently as a range-selection control. For example, in this chapter, you use a ScrollBar to create a color selection dialog. Palette: Standard.

✦ **ScrollBox** — You might call this one a container object with wheels. Use a ScrollBox to create scrollable objects, panels, text displays, options dialogs, and other complex interface elements that need scrolling capabilities. Palette: Additional.

✦ **StringGrid** — This highly capable component, which was introduced in the preceding chapter, organizes string lists into a row-and-column format accessible as a two-dimensional array. With just this component, you have most of the interface elements needed to create tables and spreadsheets. This chapter's CharGrid application, which is similar to the Windows Character Map utility, demonstrates how to use StringGrid objects to create selectable spreadsheets. Palette: Additional.

Thanks for the Memos

The Memo component encapsulates the standard Windows multiple-line Edit control. However, Memo is not just an old control in a new wrapper — it's a sophisticated multiline text editor that exemplifies the advantages of object-oriented programming. For example, the standard Windows Edit control makes managing text buffers tedious and error prone. The Memo component, which encapsulates the Edit control in a Delphi class (TMemo), bashes those barriers with intelligently designed methods for accessing multiline text in buffer or string-list formats.

Creating read-only Memos

Read-only Memo objects are useful for informational displays. For example, see the Fancy application in Chapter 6, which uses two Memo objects to display property values for various Panel 3D styles. Using a Memo object for read-only lists is a lot easier than creating multiple Labels.

To create a read-only Memo, set three properties to the values listed in Table 10-1.

Table 10-1
Read-Only Memo's Properties

Property	Setting	Description
Enabled	False	Prevents users from selecting text in the Memo window.
TabStop	False	Prevents users from tabbing to the Memo object.
ReadOnly	True	Prevents users from making any changes or entering new text into the Memo's text.

After setting these values, assign text to the Memo object's Lines property. Click the ellipsis button to open Delphi's String list editor, and type or copy and paste your text.

In 16-bit versions of Delphi, the Memo component can hold up to 32K of text. Each line in a Memo object can be no longer than 1,024 characters, provided that the line's display width is no longer than 30,000 pixels. These Windows limitations are removed in newer 32-bit versions of Delphi, and Memo objects can now potentially hold a virtually unlimited amount of text, although Windows 95 still restricts the total amount to 64K.

Text file input and output

The Memo component's Lines property is a TStrings object, and therefore, you can use the string-list techniques from Chapter 8 to read, write, and modify a Memo object's text. For example, this displays the first line in a Memo object:

```
ShowMessage(Memo1.Lines[0]);
```

Call the Lines LoadFromFile method to read a text file into a Memo object. Call SaveToFile to write a Memo object's contents to disk. With just these two procedures, you can construct your own Notepad-like editor.

On the CD-ROM

As an example of text-file handling, the Readme application displays a read-only copy of a text file in a Memo component that another program — for example, an installation utility — can call to display application notes. When designing your program's interface, you might include Readme to display application notes rather than use the tired old method of calling Notepad, which enables users to inadvertently change your program's readme file. After the Readme listing, I also explain how to run the program from inside another Delphi application — for example, you might use the technique in a program installer. Figure 10-1 shows Readme's display. Listing 10-1 shows the source code, which is located on the CD-ROM in the Source\Readme directory.

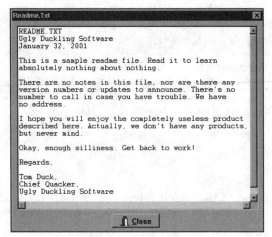

Figure 10-1: The Readme application demonstrates how to create a read-only text file viewer.

Listing 10-1: **Readme\Main.pas**

```
unit Main;

interface

uses
   Windows, SysUtils, Messages, Classes, Graphics,
   Controls, Forms, Dialogs, StdCtrls, Buttons;

type
   TMainForm = class(TForm)
      Memo1: TMemo;
      BitBtn1: TBitBtn;
      procedure FormActivate(Sender: TObject);
   private
      { Private declarations }
   public
      { Public declarations }
   end;

var
   MainForm: TMainForm;

implementation

{$R *.DFM}
```

```
procedure TMainForm.FormActivate(Sender: TObject);
var
  FileName: string;
begin
  if ParamCount >= 1
    then FileName := ParamStr(1)
    else FileName := 'Readme.Txt';
  Memo1.Lines.LoadFromFile(FileName);
  Caption := FileName;
end;

end.
```

Readme's main form OnActivate event handler shows how to obtain a parameter passed from another process to an application. (Enter test parameters with Run | Parameters.) The global variable ParamCount equals the number of parameters, each of which is available through the ParamStr function, which returns a Pascal string. Pass the parameter's index to ParamStr. The parameter indexed by 0 equals the application's path name — display it in a Button's OnClick event handler with the statement:

```
ShowMessage(ParamStr(0));   { Show application pathname }
```

In Readme, if ParamCount is greater than or equal to one, the program assigns a passed parameter to the FileName string; otherwise, it sets FileName to the default file, Readme.Txt. A single statement loads that file's text into a Memo object:

```
Memo1.Lines.LoadFromFile(FileName);
```

After that, the program sets the form's Caption to the FileName string. When using Memo objects to display text files, use a Label, Caption, or other text object to display the path name so users know which file they are viewing.

Although Readme doesn't write to disk, you can do that easily by calling the SaveToFile procedure for a Memo object's Lines property. The procedure creates a new file, or it overwrites a file if one exists by that name. To guard against accidentally overwriting an existing file, call FileExists before calling SaveToFile, as in this sample code (assume FileName is a String variable):

```
FileName := 'C:\Anyfile.Txt';
if FileExists(FileName) then
  ShowMessage('File exists')
else
  Memo1.Lines.SaveToFile(FileName);
```

To pass parameters to programs, use the Windows 95 or 98 Start button's Run command. Enter C:\Path\Readme Filename.txt to run Readme and pass it a parameter "Filename.Txt." When running programs inside Delphi, choose the Run|Parameters command, and enter one or more parameters to pass to the program the next time you compile and run it in debug mode.

Although you can run Readme as a stand-alone application, I designed it to be called from another program, such as an installation utility. To demonstrate this technique, which you can use to run any executable program—it works also for batch and DOS PIF files—examine the Runme application located on the book's CD-ROM in the Readme directory. Load the program into Delphi, and press F9 to compile and run. Select the Click Me button to run the Readme application. Figure 10-2 shows Runme's display. To run the Readme program, select the Click Me button (see Figure 10-1). Listing 10-2 lists the program's source code, which is located in the Source\Readme directory.

If Runme doesn't display the expected Readme.txt file, follow these steps. Load the Readme.dpr file into Delphi and press Ctrl+F9 to compile. Then, load Runme.dpr and press F9. Both projects are on the CD-ROM in the Source\Readme directory. You should now be able to click Click Me to run the Readme demonstration. If you experience trouble, it's probably because the program expects to find Readme.txt in the current directory, which you might have changed while using Delphi. Recompiling and running each demonstration program ensures that Readme.exe can find the Readme.txt file.

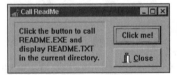

Figure 10-2: The Runme application demonstrates how an application can run another program.

Listing 10-2: **Readme\Test.pas**

```
unit Test;

interface

uses
    Windows, SysUtils, Messages, Classes, Graphics,
    Controls, Forms, Dialogs, ExtCtrls, StdCtrls, Buttons;
```

```
type
  TTestForm = class(TForm)
    ClickMeButton: TButton;
    Label1: TLabel;
    Bevel1: TBevel;
    BitBtn1: TBitBtn;
    procedure ClickMeButtonClick(Sender: TObject);
  private
    { Private declarations }
  public
    { Public declarations }
  end;

var
  TestForm: TTestForm;

implementation

uses FMXUtils;

{$R *.DFM}

(* 16-bit version; still works but WinExec is obsolete
procedure TTestForm.ClickMeButtonClick(Sender: TObject);
var
  K: Integer;  { Result of calling WinExec }
begin
  K := WinExec('Readme.Exe Readme.Txt', SW_SHOWNORMAL);
  if K < 32 then
    ShowMessage('Error running README.EXE');
end;
*)

{ 32-bit version; calls ExecuteFile in FMXUtils unit, which
  is located in Delphi's Demos\Doc\Filmanex folder }
procedure TTestForm.ClickMeButtonClick(Sender: TObject);
var
  H: THandle;
begin
  H := ExecuteFile('Readme.exe', 'Readme.txt', '.',
        SW_SHOWNORMAL);
  if Integer(H) < 32 then
    ShowMessage('Error running Readme.exe');
end;


end.
```

The Click Me button's OnClick event handler demonstrates how to run a program from within another. In earlier Delphi versions, the correct way to do this was to call the WinExec function. This still works, but is obsolete. Under 32-bit Windows 95, Windows 98, and Windows NT, it is recommended that applications call the Windows API ShellExecute function.

Doing this requires more work than you probably want. Fortunately, there's an easier solution, as shown in the listing. Delphi's Demos and Doc directories contain a separate unit, FMXUtils.pas, in the Filemanex folder. Add this unit to a project using the Project | Add to project command. In addition, add the following declaration to the form unit, just below its implementation keyword:

```
uses FMXUtils;
```

Statements can now call the unit's ExecuteFile function as shown in the sample application to run another program. You can even execute data files, which opens them inside their associated applications. For example, pass a text file to ExecuteFile to open that file using the default application for the file's type — the Windows Notepad utility, probably.

Caution   If you have trouble compiling and running the Runme application on this book's CD-ROM, the cause is probably that Delphi's FMXUtils.pas is not where the project expects to find it. Use Windows Explorer to locate this file, then use the Project|Add to project command to add the unit to Runme. Use Project|Remove from project to remove the old reference to FMXUtils.pas.

The ExecuteFile function and its parameters are declared as follows:

```
function ExecuteFile(const FileName, Params,
  DefaultDir: string; ShowCmd: Integer): THandle;
```

✦ **FileName** — Pass a string filename or a complete path name in this parameter.

✦ **Params** — Pass in this string any parameters, options, or filenames you want to pass to the code file in FileName. The demonstration passes Readme.txt in this parameter.

✦ **DefaultDir** — Set this string to the directory where ExecuteFile looks for FileName. Note that if Params is another filename, this setting does not cause the executed program to look in the specified directory.

✦ **ShowCmd** — This can be any SW_SHOW… constant such as SW_SHOWNORMAL to display an application's window in its normal start-up state, or another value such as SW_SHOWMAXIMIZED to open the window to full screen on starting the program. See the Win32.hlp file for other SW_SHOW constants you can pass to ExecuteFile.

Like WinExec, ExecuteFile (and the Windows API ShellExecute function), if successful, returns an integer value greater than or equal to 32. Any value less than 32 indicates an error. The return value is actually the instance handle of the target application, although this fact is of little practical value. The obsolete WinExec function returned this value as an integer, making it easier to use as such. The newer ExecuteFile (and ShellExecute) functions return the result value as a handle. To inspect its integer value requires using a type-cast expression such as:

```
if Integer(H) < 32 then
  ShowMessage('Error running Readme.exe');
```

Finally, try the following OnClick event handler. Add the FMXUtils.pas unit to the project, add *uses FMXUtils;* just below the implementation keyword, and then insert a Button object to a form. Program the Button's handler as follows:

```
procedure TForm1.Button1Click(Sender: TObject);
var
  H: THandle;
begin
  H := ExecuteFile('C:\Windows\Sol', '', '', SW_SHOWNORMAL);
end;
```

Unused string parameters are passed null (empty) strings. Press F9 to compile and run the program, and then click the button to execute the Windows Solitaire game.

The following is the now obsolete 16-bit code that does the same thing under Windows 3.1. This still works, but should be replaced with the newer programming in the preceding example.

```
{ This is the obsolete 16-bit method.
  Don't use this technique any longer. }
procedure TForm1.Button1Click(Sender: TObject);
var
  K: Integer;
begin
  K := WinExec('C:\Windows\Sol', SW_SHOWMAXIMIZED);
end;
```

Managing text in your Memo objects

Naturally, you want to add, delete, insert, and modify text in your Memo objects. Successfully programming these and other tasks requires a good understanding of how Memo objects provide access to their text lines. You can access a Memo object's text:

✦ As the string value of the Text property, which does not appear in the Object Inspector and is available only at run time. Use this property only when you want to manipulate a Memo object's text as one (possibly massive) object. This property value is no longer limited to 255 characters, as it was originally in Delphi Version 1.

✦ As a list of strings in the Lines property, using the methods described in Chapter 9 for TStrings and TStringList objects. This is generally the most versatile way to access a Memo object's text, and is always the best way when you need to process that text's lines individually.

To display and use a Memo object's text as a single string, use the Text property. This is inherited from TControl, but is not listed in the Object Inspector window. For example, insert Memo and Button components into a form, and use this statement in the Button's OnClick event handler to display the Memo's text:

```
ShowMessage(Memo1.Text);
```

Paste some text into the Memo1 object's window and click the button. This used to truncate Memo's contents to a maximum of 255 characters, but now that Delphi's components use the dynamic String data type, this problem no longer occurs.

For accessing individual lines in a Memo object, use the Lines property. Because this is an object of the TStrings type, you can transfer text between other objects that have TStrings properties. For example, use a statement such as this to copy a ListBox's Items to a Memo's Lines:

```
Memo1.Lines := ListBox1.Items;
```

You might use the reverse technique to enable users to enter ListBox items using Memo's text-editing features. Simply perform the assignment in the other direction, perhaps in a Button's OnClick event handler:

```
ListBox1.Items := Memo1.Lines;
```

To insert new text into a Memo object, you can assign strings to the Text property. But be careful with this method — it replaces the entire contents of the Memo, regardless of size:

```
Memo1.Text := 'I''d rather be sailing!';
```

You are not seeing double — the two single quotes create an apostrophe inside a string. Although the preceding statement works just fine, it's usually just as well (if not better) to use the Lines property. This adds a string to the Lines list:

```
Memo1.Lines.Add('Bananas are not Oranges');
```

Clear a Memo's contents by calling the Clear method like this:

```
Memo1.Lines.Clear;
```

However, because the Memo component has its own Clear method, you may call Clear without referring to Lines. This statement is equivalent to the preceding one:

```
Memo1.Clear;
```

Determine whether a Memo object is empty by inspecting the Count property of Lines:

```
if Memo1.Lines.Count = 0 then
  ShowMessage('You just clicked this button!')
else
  Memo1.Clear;
```

Accessing the Memo text buffer

As I mentioned, in most cases, you can easily access a Memo object's text through its string-list Lines object. However, if you need to perform operations directly on text buffers, you can access a Memo object's text as an array of Char bytes. This might be useful in some applications, although with Object Pascal's unlimited-length String data type, the techniques aren't as valuable as they once were. Nevertheless, this section explains the basics. Even if you don't use these methods, this section can help you to upgrade older applications that use null-terminated string buffers with Memo objects.

There are five methods for working with Memo text as arrays of Char — in other words, as null-terminated strings. The methods in the order I describe them are:

- ✦ **SetTextBuf** — Copies text into a Memo object — Equivalent to the Windows message wm_SetText

- ✦ **SetSelTextBuf** — Replaces selected text in a Memo object with new text — Equivalent to the Windows message em_ReplaceSel

- ✦ **GetTextLen** — Returns the number of characters in the Memo object's buffer — This value does not include the buffer's terminating null. Equivalent to the Windows message wm_GetTextLength

- ✦ **GetTextBuf** — Copies a Memo object's text to a program Char array or PChar-addressed buffer — Equivalent to the Windows message wm_GetText

- ✦ **GetSelTextBuf** — Copies selected text from a Memo object to a program Char array or PChar-addressed buffer — Equivalent to the Windows message em_GetSel followed by a string copy of selected text

You may use these methods with arrays of Char bytes, or with PChar pointers. You may pass an array of Char to a PChar. For example, given the following declarations, you can pass either *S* or *P* to any PChar parameter:

```
var
  S: array[0 .. 128] of Char;
  P: PChar;
```

These statements copy *S* and the string addressed by *P* to a Memo's text buffer (I assume you have initialized the strings somewhere else):

```
Memo1.SetTextBuf(S);   { Copy array S to Memo1 }
Memo1.SetTextBuf(P);   { Copy string at P to Memo1 }
```

In the following discussion, I use PChar pointers because these are more efficient, especially for large text buffers. However, the same techniques work with arrays of Char. Listing 10-3 shows how to use SetTextBuf to copy a null-terminated string to a Memo object. (In case you want to try the code, it's in the form of an OnClick event handler for a Button object.) First, StrAlloc allocates memory for a 128-character string. Then, StrCopy copies literal text to the addressed memory. The expressions #13#10 insert new-line control codes at the ends of the first three lines. SetTextBuf copies the string into the Memo1 object. After that, StrDispose deletes the allocated memory.

Listing 10-3: This OnClick event handler demonstrates how to insert text into a Memo object.

```
procedure TForm1.Button1Click(Sender: TObject);
var
  P: PChar;
begin
  P := StrAlloc(128);
  try
    StrCopy(P,
      'Red skies at night,'#13#10 +
      ' Sailor''s delight;'#13#10 +
      'Red skies at morning,'#13#10 +
      ' Sailor take warning.');
    Memo1.SetTextBuf(P);
  finally
    StrDispose(P);
  end;
end;
```

Although I want to show here how to use PChar and text buffers, it's important to understand that with Object Pascal's String data type, programming such as in Listing

10-3 is no longer necessary. The preceding procedure can be replaced with the following, which is easier to program and works perfectly well. It's also safer because there's no chance of forgetting to dispose of the text buffer created by calling StrAlloc:

```
procedure TForm1.Button1Click(Sender: TObject);
var
  S: String;
begin
  S :=
    'Red skies at night,'#13#10 +
    ' Sailor''s delight;'#13#10 +
    'Red skies at morning,'#13#10 +
    ' Sailor take warning.';
  Memo1.Text := S;
end;
```

Memo objects (as well as Edit and other text components) manage their own string-buffer memory. For example, when you call SetText, Memo copies the string data into its own memory. It is still your responsibility to delete dynamic strings that you create, even after you assign them to a Memo object.

Call SetSelTextBuf to replace selected (that is, highlighted) text in a Memo object. For example, run a test program with the event handler in the preceding listing, and then insert another Button OnClick procedure with the code from Listing 10-4 to replace selected text with new characters in a Memo by calling SetSelTextBuf. Select some or all text in the Memo object, and click the second button to replace that text with the new jingle.

Listing 10-4: OnClick event handler to replace selected text with new characters in a Memo

```
procedure TForm1.Button2Click(Sender: TObject);
var
  P: PChar;
begin
  P := StrAlloc(128);
  try
    StrCopy(P,
      'How happy is the sailor''s life,'#13#10 +
      'From coast to coast to roam;'#13#10 +
      'In every port he finds a wife,'#13#10 +
      'In every land a home.');
    Memo1.SetSelTextBuf(P);
  finally
    StrDispose(P);
  end;
end;
```

If no text is selected in the Memo object, SetSelTextBuf inserts the new text at the current cursor position. To replace all of the text completely in a Memo, call the SelectAll method before calling SetSelTextBuf.

To copy the text from a Memo object into a Char array, call GetTextBuf or GetSelTextBuf. Determine the required size of the buffer by calling GetTextLen, allocate that much memory plus one byte for a null terminator, and call GetTextBuf to copy a Memo object's text into the allocated space. Call GetSelTextBuf to copy only selected text into the buffer.

Listing 10-5 demonstrates how to use GetTextLen and GetTextBuf. The procedure first determines Memo1's buffer length. If that length is greater than zero, the code calls StrAlloc, which allocates Len+1 bytes and assigns the memory's address to *P*. GetTextBuf copies Memo1's text to the allocated memory, after which a *for* loop exclusive-ORs each character in the buffer with hexadecimal FF. This encrypts the Memo object's text, which SetTextBuf copies back into the object. Finally, StrDispose deletes the allocated memory. Try this procedure and click the button to toggle text to and from its encrypted form. The procedure copies Memo1's text to a dynamic buffer, encrypts each character with an exclusive-OR operation, and then copies the processed buffer back into the Memo object.

Listing 10-5: Use this OnClick event handler to encrypt and decode a Memo object's text.

```
procedure TForm1.Button3Click(Sender: TObject);
var
  I, Len: Integer;
  P: PChar;
begin
  Len := Memo1.GetTextLen;
  if Len = 0 then
    ShowMessage('Text buffer is empty!')
  else begin
    P := StrAlloc(Len + 1);
    try
      Memo1.GetTextBuf(P, Len);
      for I := 0 to Len do
        P[I] := Chr(Ord(P[I]) xor $ff);
      Memo1.SetTextBuf(P);
    finally
      StrDispose(P);
    end;
  end;
end;
```

The listing demonstrates an important aspect of working with PChar pointers. Although a PChar variable is a pointer to a Char byte, you can use it as though it were an array. For example, this statement assigns the letter *A* to the first character of a string buffer addressed by *P*:

```
P[0] := 'A';
```

In Listing 10-5, you can replace GetTextBuf with GetSelTextBuf to copy only selected text from a Memo object to your buffer. The two functions are otherwise the same. (If you try this, select all text each time before clicking the button, or the text is not properly decoded.)

Understanding Enter and Tab keypresses

Depending on your interface needs for a Memo object, pressing Enter and Tab can have varying effects. For example, you might want users to enter multiple lines into a Memo window—in that case, you probably want an Enter keypress to begin a new line. If you don't want Enter to act that way, you can program the key to shift the focus to another control. You also can determine whether pressing Tab inserts a tab control code into a Memo's text, or shifts to the next control in tab order.

Set the WantReturns property to True to insert new lines into a Memo's text when users press Enter. Set WantReturns to False to send Enter keypresses to the form. However, this setting requires an appropriate setting for the form's KeyPreview property. Usually, if WantReturns is True, KeyPreview should be False so the control, not the form, receives the Enter keypress. If WantReturns is False, KeyPreview should normally be True; otherwise, the form still does not receive the Enter keypress in its OnKeypress event handler.

Set WantTabs to True to insert tab control codes into a Memo's text when users press Tab. Set WantTabs to False to shift the focus to another control on receiving a Tab keypress. When WantTabs is True, a Memo object is like the Hotel California— you can check in by pressing Tab, but you can never press Tab to leave.

Pressing Ctrl+Enter always starts a new line in a Memo object, regardless of the value of WantReturns. Similarly, pressing Ctrl+Tab always inserts a tab control code regardless of the setting for WantTabs.

By sending a Memo object a Windows message, you can change the spacing of tab controls. The following code demonstrates the technique with code that you can use in a form's OnCreate event handler. The TabStops typed-constant array has only one Integer value—in this case, set to 18. Because most fonts are proportional, Windows measures tab stops in dialog box units rather than in characters, as is common with text-only displays and monospace character sets. (The default tab setting is 32 dialog units.) The sample OnCreate event handler calls the Perform method (all components have it) to send Memo an em_SetTabStops message. The one parameter specifies TabStops has only a single entry, which is repeated for all tabs. Look up the em_SetTabStops in the Win32.hlp file for more information on setting tabs in text controls.

The following code also demonstrates how to pass a variable to a message's LParam parameter by type-casting it to a Longint value. In this example, the @ sign specifies the address of the TabStops array. The full expression Longint(@TabStops) passes the array's address as a Longint, 32-bit, value:

```
procedure TForm1.FormCreate(Sender: TObject);
const
  TabStops: array[0 .. 0] of Integer = (18);
begin
  Memo1.Perform(em_SetTabStops, 1, Longint(@TabStops));
end;
```

To pass more than one tab stop, change the constant declaration in the preceding code to something like this:

```
const
  TabStops: array[0 .. 3] of Integer = (4, 8, 12, 16);
```

And also change one to four in the call to Memo1.Perform. If you are only passing a single tab stop as in the listing, you don't have to create an array. You can instead declare TabStops as an integer value (which, after all, is really the same as an "array" that has only one value).

Text and the Clipboard

Though of limited utility, the Windows clipboard is a popular way station for transmitting information to and from applications. Most Windows users quickly learn how to cut and copy text, even though they may not realize they are using the clipboard to perform these actions. Because the Edit, MaskEdit, and Memo components automatically support cut, copy, and paste, using these objects is all you need to do to provide clipboard services in your application.

Note   Database components TDBEdit, TDBMaskEdit, TDBImage, and TDBMemo also support the clipboard methods described here.

To make the clipboard easier to use, especially for beginners who haven't yet mastered the subtleties of Windows keyboard commands, call the CopyToClipboard, CutToClipboard, and PasteFromClipboard methods in the Edit, MaskEdit, and Memo components. For example, to cut selected text from a Memo object to the clipboard, use this statement, perhaps in a Button's OnClick event handler, or in the procedure for a menu's Edit | Cut command:

```
Memo1.CutToClipboard;
```

The other procedures work similarly and require no parameters. The key to success is to realize that CopyToClipboard and CutToClipboard operate only on selected text. To copy all of a Memo's text to the clipboard, precede the operation with a call to SelectAll:

```
Memo1.SelectAll;
Memo1.CopyToClipboard;
```

Scrolling Down the River

Several components provide automatic scrolling capabilities that require no programming. For example, the Memo component displays vertical and horizontal scroll bars as needed to provide access to text. Scrolling works exactly as expected —you don't need to worry about any magic settings.

For other scrolling tasks, you have two choices. You can insert a ScrollBar component into a form or you can use a ScrollBox object to provide a scrollable platform that can contain other objects. The next two sections explain how to scroll down the river with these two useful components.

Scrolling with ScrollBar

On the CD-ROM

The ScrollBar component creates a stand-alone scroll bar object that you can insert into a form or another container. Simply by writing one event handler, you can create code that responds to changes in the scroll bar's position. You can have as many ScrollBar objects as you need—they make useful interface devices for selecting values within low-to-high ranges. As an example of this concept, try the Test application in the Source\ColorDlg directory on the CD-ROM. Run the Test application in the ColorDlg directory, and click the Test button to display the color-selection dialog shown here. The dialog demonstrates how to use ScrollBar objects as value selectors—in this case, to choose red, green, and blue values for a sample color, shown in Figure 10-3 as the right box. The source code for the Test application is shown in Listing 10-6.

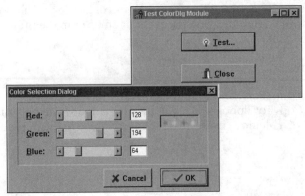

Figure 10-3: The Color Selection Dialog demonstrating how to use ScrollBar objects

Listing 10-6: \ColorDlg\ColorDlg.pas

```pascal
unit Colordlg;

interface

uses
  Windows, SysUtils, Messages, Classes, Graphics,
  Controls, Forms, Dialogs, StdCtrls, Buttons, ExtCtrls;

type
  TColorDlgForm = class(TForm)
    RedSB: TScrollBar;
    GreenSB: TScrollBar;
    BlueSB: TScrollBar;
    RedLabel: TLabel;
    GreenLabel: TLabel;
    BlueLabel: TLabel;
    RedEdit: TEdit;
    GreenEdit: TEdit;
    BlueEdit: TEdit;
    ColorEdit: TEdit;
    OkBitBtn: TBitBtn;
    CancelBitBtn: TBitBtn;
    Bevel1: TBevel;
    procedure FormCreate(Sender: TObject);
    procedure SBChange(Sender: TObject);
    procedure EditChange(Sender: TObject);
    procedure FormActivate(Sender: TObject);
    procedure OkBitBtnClick(Sender: TObject);
```

```
      procedure CancelBitBtnClick(Sender: TObject);
    private
      RedPos, GreenPos, BluePos: Integer;   { For undo }
      EditControls: array[0 .. 2] of TEdit;
      ScrollBars: array[0 .. 2] of TScrollBar;
      procedure UpdateColor;
    public
      ColorResult: TColor;   { Selected color }
    end;

var
  ColorDlgForm: TColorDlgForm;

implementation

{$R *.DFM}

{- Update ColorResult using scrollbar positions }
procedure TColorDlgForm.UpdateColor;
begin
  ColorResult := RGB(
    RedSB.Position, GreenSB.Position, BlueSB.Position);
  ColorEdit.Color := ColorResult;   { Show color }
end;

{- Initialize TObject control arrays }
procedure TColorDlgForm.FormCreate(Sender: TObject);
begin
  EditControls[0] := RedEdit;
  EditControls[1] := GreenEdit;
  EditControls[2] := BlueEdit;
  ScrollBars[0] := RedSB;
  ScrollBars[1] := GreenSB;
  ScrollBars[2] := BlueSB;
end;

{- Update values in Edit boxes for ScrollBar changes }
procedure TColorDlgForm.SBChange(Sender: TObject);
begin
  with Sender as TScrollBar do
    EditControls[Tag].Text := IntToStr(Position);
  UpdateColor;
end;

{- Update scrollbar positions for Edit box changes }
procedure TColorDlgForm.EditChange(Sender: TObject);
begin
```

(continued)

Listing 10-6 *(continued)*

```
    with Sender as TEdit do
      ScrollBars[Tag].Position := StrToInt(Text);
  end;

  {- Save scrollbar positions for possible undo }
  procedure TColorDlgForm.FormActivate(Sender: TObject);
  begin
    RedPos := RedSB.Position;
    GreenPos := GreenSB.Position;
    BluePos := BlueSB.Position;
  end;

  {- Respond to OK button. Accept changes. }
  procedure TColorDlgForm.OkBitBtnClick(Sender: TObject);
  begin
    ModalResult := mrOk; { Close Window. Color in ColorResult. }
  end;

  {- Respond to Cancel button. Undo changes. }
  procedure TColorDlgForm.CancelBitBtnClick(Sender: TObject);
  begin
    RedSB.Position := RedPos;
    GreenSB.Position := GreenPos;
    BlueSB.Position := BluePos;
    ModalResult := mrCancel;
  end;

  end.
```

Table 10-2 lists some of the significant properties for the ColorDlg form's component objects, which demonstrate a few interesting interface techniques. Three labels designate Alt accelerator shortcut keys in their Caption properties, and set their FocusControl values to the appropriate Edit box. For example, run the Test program and press Alt+G to select the GreenEdit object.

Each of the three ScrollBars in the window has a LargeChange value often. This affects the amount of scrolling when users click inside the bar — in most cases, you should set LargeChange higher than SmallChange (usually equal to one), which affects the amount of scrolling for the ScrollBar's arrow buttons. The ColorDlg ScrollBars also set their Max value to 255. Delphi's TColor data type represents colors as combinations of red, green, and blue (RGB), each in the range from 0 to 255.

Table 10-2
ColorDlg Form Component Properties

Component	Name	Property	Value
Form	ColorDlgForm	Caption	Color Selection Dialog
Label	RedLabel	Caption	&Red:
		FocusControl	RedEdit
Label	GreenLabel	Caption	&Green:
		FocusControl	GreenEdit
Label	BlueLabel	Caption	&Blue:
		FocusControl	BlueEdit
ScrollBar	RedSB	LargeChange	10
		Max	255
		Tag	0
ScrollBar	GreenSB	Tag	1
ScrollBar	BlueSB	Tag	2
Edit	RedEdit	Tag	0
Edit	GreenEdit	Tag	1
Edit	BlueEdit	Tag	2

Notice also from Table 10-2 that the ScrollBar and Edit components set their Tag values to zero, one, and two. The program uses these values to relate the components at run time. To see how this works, examine the TColorDlgForm class in Listing 10-6. The private section defines these two arrays of objects:

```
EditControls: array[0 .. 2] of TEdit;
ScrollBars: array[0 .. 2] of TScrollBar;
```

The arrays provide handy means for accessing each of the form's Edit and ScrollBar objects. Remember, TEdit and TScrollBar variables are references, so these two arrays actually contain pointers to the objects, not the objects themselves. To initialize the arrays, the form's OnCreate event handler assigns objects to array positions, equal to the Object Tag values. For example, this statement assigns the first slot in EditControls to refer to the RedEdit component object:

```
EditControls[0] := RedEdit;
```

After preparing the component reference arrays, the program can use Tag values as indexes to access individual objects. For example, examine the SBChange procedure, which handles scroll bar OnChange events. Each ScrollBar object's OnChange event is set to this same handler. In the procedure, the Sender parameter passed to the procedure is the ScrollBar object that has changed. To update the associated Edit control so its integer value matches the ScrollBar's position, the procedure uses a *with* statement to treat Sender as a TScrollBar object, and then executes this statement:

```
EditControls[Tag].Text := IntToStr(Position);
```

IntToStr converts the ScrollBar's integer Position property to a string, and assigns the result to the Edit control's Text property, using the EditControls array and the Tag index to refer to the associated Edit control.

The EditChange procedure performs a similar task. When you enter a new value into an Edit window, the resulting OnChange event calls EditChange. The procedure uses a *with* statement to treat Sender as a TEdit object, and then executes this statement:

```
ScrollBars[Tag].Position := StrToInt(Text);
```

Function StrToInt converts the Edit control's Text property to an integer value, which the statement assigns to the ScrollBar's Position. This causes the thumb box in the scroll bar to move to a position that matches the Edit control. The ScrollBar's array and the Tag property make it easy to select the ScrollBar associated with the Edit control that generated the OnChange event.

The two procedures, SBChange and EditChange, handle all OnChange events for the dialog's six ScrollBar and Edit objects. The procedures could handle practically any number of associated objects, and they demonstrate a useful technique for reducing code size. When you have numerous associated component objects in a window, consider using an array and a Tag index to refer to them in shared event handlers.

Procedure UpdateColor shows how to use ScrollBar Position values. In this case, the RGB function returns a LongInt value given three constituent bytes that represent red, green, and blue colors. The program assigns the resulting color to the ColorResult variable, declared in the TColorDlgForm class's public section.

UpdateColor also displays the current color selection using a cheap trick that is faster than the obvious graphics approach. In one version of the program, I had used a Shape component object to display the sample color, but due to the way Windows works, each color change caused Shape to erase itself to white, which might produce an annoying flash between color assignments. (Depending on your system, however, you might not see this.) To solve the problem, I used an Edit component, set Enabled and TabStop to False, and set ReadOnly to True. You can't select or enter text into the resulting Edit object. Procedure UpdateColor assigns ColorResult to the Edit object's Color property, which doesn't erase itself between updates. When you need a simple colored box, try an Edit component instead of Shape.

ColorDlg implements an *undo* feature, which all dialogs that have Cancel buttons need. In this case, the form's OnActivate event handler saves the current ScrollBar Position value in three class variables—RedPos, GreenPos, and BluePos. If the user clicks Close to end the dialog, the button's OnClick event handler assigns the saved values back to the ScrollBar Position properties.

At first glance, those assignments might not seem enough to completely undo all changes to the dialog. What's not obvious is that assigning new values to the ScrollBar generates OnChange events. Thus, the three assignments in the CancelBitBtnClick handler cause three calls to SBChange, which resets the Edit controls and updates the sample color window. Trace these events by pressing F8 and F7 to run the Test program, or set breakpoints at strategic spots, and verify the sequence that occurs when you click Cancel.

To use the color selection dialog, add ColorDlg.pas to any project and insert ColorDlg to the main form's *uses* directive. Call the ShowModal function to display the dialog window:

```
ColorDlgForm.ShowModal;
```

ShowModal returns a value that indicates which button was clicked to end the dialog. You can inspect this value and take appropriate action. For example, rather than call ShowModal as in the preceding line, use this slightly more complex code:

```
with ColorDlgForm do
if ShowModal = mrOk then
  ShowMessage(Format('Color value = $%-.6x', [ColorResult]));
```

If ShowModal returns mrOk, ShowMessage displays the ColorResult value from ColorDlgForm, using Format to insert the value in hexadecimal into the message dialog. The funny-looking text, "%-.6x", formats ColorResult as a left-justified (-) hexadecimal (x) value in six columns padded to the left with zeros (.6).

Forms and other components use the TControlScrollBar class as a property for horizontal and vertical scroll bars. This class has the same properties and methods as the TScrollBar class, which you can use as independent objects in a form.

Scrolling with ScrollBox

A *ScrollBox* is like a Panel that can scroll up, down, left, and right. The *ScrollBox component* is a container that can hold other objects such as buttons, labels, Edit input boxes, radio buttons — even other ScrollBox panels. When you're thirsty for a general-utility scrolling platform, a ScrollBox is bound to hit the spot.

Creating ScrollBox objects is easy. Just insert one into a form, and size it or set Align to alClient to have the panel completely fill the window's client area. This is a good setting for creating scrollable dialog boxes and data-entry forms with too many controls to fit comfortably in a single window. Scrolling is automatic, and scroll bars appear as needed to provide users with access to controls beyond the window's borders.

Tip   Another way to get a form to scroll is to simply set its AutoScroll property to True. ScrollBox objects are still useful in many situations, however, as this section demonstrates.

Design your ScrollBox objects in their fully open capacity. For example, you might maximize the form window, and insert all controls where you want them. After designing the window, shrink the design form back to its final size.

ScrollBoxes are also useful for scaling windows for different display resolutions. For example, you can design a full-screen entry form for 1024×768 displays that still works correctly on laptops with 640×480 resolutions. On a laptop, users have to scroll the window to reach all controls.

Controls that can receive the input focus (such as edit controls and buttons) automatically scroll into view. Try inserting a dozen Edit objects into a ScrollBox. Run the program, and press Tab. As the input focus changes, the current Edit input box automatically scrolls into view.

Sometimes, you may need to display a specific control. For example, users might select a program command or click a button. You can call the object's SetFocus method, or you can call the ScrollBox's ScrollInView procedure. For example, to ensure that Edit7 is in view, execute a statement such as this:

```
ScrollBox1.ScrollInView(Edit7);
```

Components and controls

As you become more familiar with containers such as the ScrollBox component, you discover the need to access components in various ways. Although all component objects are available by name, such as Label2 or Edit9, it's not always convenient to refer to objects individually. In a form or ScrollBox (or a Panel) with dozens of buttons, it's just plain silly, not to mention inefficient, to write code such as this:

```
Button1.Enabled := False;
Button2.Enabled := False;
...
Button38.Enabled := False;
```

Containers such as forms and ScrollBoxes provide the Components array, which you can use to access all of a parent's owned objects. ComponentCount equals the number of those components. You can use these properties to write loops such as this:

```
for I := 0 to ComponentCount - 1 do
   Components[I].Enabled := False;
```

Containers also provide similar array and count properties, Controls and ControlIndex. However, these properties provide access only to components that are also child windows. The Components and ComponentCount properties provide access to component objects. The Controls array lists the window relationships among component objects. The Components array lists the object relationships. These are not always the same. For example, a ScrollBox owns its components as child window controls. The form that owns the ScrollBox owns those same objects as components.

These concepts are not purely academic—you can use them to your advantage in writing code that affects groups of objects. To better understand the difference between the Controls and Components arrays, run the ContComp (Controls and Components) application on the CD-ROM in the Source\ContComp directory. The sample program lists components and controls in four list boxes for a ScrollBox and for the main window form. Figure 10-4 shows the program's display. Listing 10-7 gives the program's source code, which includes two procedures that you can use to investigate the control and component relationships of your application's forms. The code provides valuable insights that help you to fine-tune your program's code. I explain more about this after the listing.

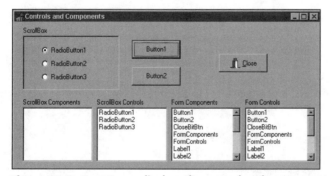

Figure 10-4: ContComp displays the control and component relationships of its own objects for a ScrollBox, which contains three RadioButton controls, and the form window.

Listing 10-7: **ContComp\Main.pas**

```pascal
unit Main;

interface

uses
  Windows, SysUtils, Messages, Classes, Graphics,
  Controls, Forms, Dialogs, StdCtrls, Buttons;

type
  TMainForm = class(TForm)
    ScrollBox1: TScrollBox;
    Label1: TLabel;
    RadioButton1: TRadioButton;
    RadioButton2: TRadioButton;
    RadioButton3: TRadioButton;
    Button1: TButton;
    Button2: TButton;
    ScrollBoxComponents: TListBox;
    ScrollBoxControls: TListBox;
    FormComponents: TListBox;
    FormControls: TListBox;
    Label2: TLabel;
    Label3: TLabel;
    Label4: TLabel;
    Label5: TLabel;
    CloseBitBtn: TBitBtn;
    procedure FormCreate(Sender: TObject);
  private
    { Private declarations }
  public
    { Public declarations }
  end;

var
  MainForm: TMainForm;

implementation

{$R *.DFM}

procedure ListControls(ListBox: TListBox;
  Control: TWinControl);
var
  I: Integer;
begin
  with Control do
  for I := 0 to ControlCount - 1 do
```

```
      ListBox.Items.Add(Controls[I].Name);
end;

procedure ListComponents(ListBox: TListBox;
  Component: TComponent);
var
  I: Integer;
begin
  with Component do
  for I := 0 to ComponentCount - 1 do
    ListBox.Items.Add(Components[I].Name);
end;

procedure TMainForm.FormCreate(Sender: TObject);
begin
  ListControls(ScrollBoxControls, ScrollBox1);
  ListComponents(ScrollBoxComponents, ScrollBox1);
  ListControls(FormControls, MainForm);
  ListComponents(FormComponents, MainForm);
end;

end.
```

To investigate control and component relationships in your own applications, copy the ListControls and ListComponents procedures into any unit module. You probably won't want to include the code in the final application, so I didn't bother making them members of a class. In any event handler (the sample program uses the form's OnCreate procedure), call the two procedures to insert owned controls and components into ListBoxes. Pass a ListBox and a component object as arguments. You may pass any TComponent-derived object to ListComponents and any TWinControl-derived object to ListControls. However, the object components must provide Controls and Components arrays.

Getting back to ScrollBoxes, as Figure 10-4 shows, ScrollBox1 does not own the three RadioButton component objects. However, the objects are child windows of the ScrollBox. From this information, you can write an efficient procedure to perform operations on all of the ScrollBox's controls. For example, try the OnClick event handler in Listing 10-8 for a third Button in the ContComp program to disable the ScrollBox's RadioButtons. The code accesses each Button through the ScrollBox's Controls.

Refer once again to Figure 10-4 (or run the ContComp program) and examine the FormComponents and FormControls lists. The form owns all of the component objects in this program, despite the fact that the three RadioButtons are inside the ScrollBox. However, a control as a child window may have only one parent; therefore, the form's Controls array does not list the RadioButtons.

Listing 10-8: An OnClick event handler to add a button

```
procedure TMainForm.Button3Click(Sender: TObject);
var
  I: Integer;
begin
  with ScrollBox1 do
  for I := 0 to ControlCount - 1 do
    Controls[I].Enabled := False;
end;
```

An object's ComponentIndex property equals that object's index in its owner's Components array. Likewise, an object's ControlIndex equals the object's index in its owner's Controls array. If *T* is a Label object owned by a form, and if *K* equals T.ComponentIndex, then TheForm.Components[K] refers to *T*. Similarly, if *T* is a control that is a child window of a form, TheForm.Controls[K] refers to *T*. If you spend some time investigating these relationships, you discover many opportunities for efficiently accessing component objects through the Controls and Components arrays.

StringGrids

We now go through an example of what has to be one of Delphi's most versatile components, the StringGrid. (The preceding chapter introduced this useful component.) Practically a full-blown spreadsheet, StringGrid organizes string and other object data into a row-and-column table layout. The CharGrid application on the CD-ROM in the Source\CharGrid directory demonstrates how to use StringGrid. As shown in Figure 10-5, the program displays a StringGrid that shows all the symbols in any Windows font. Select a font from the Font ComboBox. Double-click any character in the grid to add it to the To Copy Edit window. Or, you can also click the Select button. Click the Copy button to copy the chosen characters to the clipboard. You can then switch to another application and paste the characters into any text input field. Listing 10-9 shows CharGrid's source code.

Use CharGrid to insert hard-to-type characters such as copyright © and trademark ® symbols into Pascal strings.

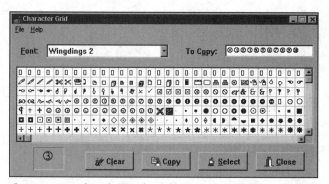

Figure 10-5: The CharGrid application demonstrates how to use Delphi's StringGrid component.

Listing 10-9: **CharGrid\Main.pas**

```
unit Main;

interface

uses
  Windows, SysUtils, Messages, Classes, Graphics, Controls,
  Forms, Dialogs, Grids, StdCtrls, Buttons, ExtCtrls, Menus,
  About;

type
  TMainForm = class(TForm)
    StringGrid1: TStringGrid;
    FontCB: TComboBox;
    FontLabel: TLabel;
    CloseBitBtn: TBitBtn;
    CopyEdit: TEdit;
    CopyLabel: TLabel;
    SelectBitBtn: TBitBtn;
    ClipBitBtn: TBitBtn;
    CharLabel: TLabel;
    Bevel1: TBevel;
    ClearBitBtn: TBitBtn;
    MainMenu1: TMainMenu;
    FileMenu: TMenuItem;
    FileExit: TMenuItem;
    HelpMenu: TMenuItem;
    HelpAbout: TMenuItem;
```

(continued)

Listing 10-9 *(continued)*

```
      procedure FormCreate(Sender: TObject);
      procedure FontCBChange(Sender: TObject);
      procedure FontCBKeyDown(Sender: TObject; var Key: Word;
        Shift: TShiftState);
      procedure StringGrid1DblClick(Sender: TObject);
      procedure StringGrid1KeyDown(Sender: TObject;
        var Key: Word; Shift: TShiftState);
      procedure StringGrid1SelectCell(Sender: TObject;
        Col, Row: Longint; var CanSelect: Boolean);
      procedure FileExitClick(Sender: TObject);
      procedure HelpAboutClick(Sender: TObject);
      procedure SelectBitBtnClick(Sender: TObject);
      procedure ClipBitBtnClick(Sender: TObject);
      procedure ClearBitBtnClick(Sender: TObject);
  private
    { Private declarations }
  public
    { Public declarations }
  end;

var
  MainForm: TMainForm;

implementation

{$R *.DFM}

{ Initialize controls }
procedure TMainForm.FormCreate(Sender: TObject);
var
  Ascii, IRow, ICol: Integer;
begin
{ Initialize FontCB ComboBox with font names }
  FontCB.Items := Screen.Fonts;
{ Show current StringGrid font in FontCB's edit box }
  FontCB.ItemIndex :=
    FontCB.Items.IndexOf(StringGrid1.Font.Name);
{ Insert characters into grid }
  Ascii := 0;
  with StringGrid1 do
  for IRow := 0 to RowCount do
    for ICol := 0 to ColCount do
    begin
      Cells[ICol, IRow] := Chr(Ascii);
      Inc(Ascii);
    end;
{ Assign sample character and font }
```

```
  with StringGrid1 do
    CharLabel.Caption := Cells[Row, Col];
    CharLabel.Font.Name := StringGrid1.Font.Name;
end;

{ Change grid, edit box, and sample to selected font }
procedure TMainForm.FontCBChange(Sender: TObject);
begin
  StringGrid1.Font.Name := FontCB.Text;
  CopyEdit.Text := '';   { Optional: Erase current entries }
  CopyEdit.Font := StringGrid1.Font;
  CharLabel.Font.Name := StringGrid1.Font.Name;
end;

{ Close FontCB drop-down list on pressing Enter or Esc }
procedure TMainForm.FontCBKeyDown(Sender: TObject;
  var Key: Word; Shift: TShiftState);
begin
  if Key in [vk_Return, vk_Escape] then
  begin
    FontCB.DroppedDown := False;
    Key := 0;
  end;
end;

{ Grid double-click event handler }
procedure TMainForm.StringGrid1DblClick(Sender: TObject);
begin
  with CopyEdit, StringGrid1 do
    Text := Text + Cells[Col, Row];
end;

{ Select character on pressing Enter or Space }
procedure TMainForm.StringGrid1KeyDown(Sender: TObject;
  var Key: Word; Shift: TShiftState);
begin
  if Key in [vk_Return, vk_Space] then
    StringGrid1DblClick(Sender);  // Same as double-click grid
end;

{ Show selected character }
procedure TMainForm.StringGrid1SelectCell(Sender: TObject; Col,
  Row: Longint; var CanSelect: Boolean);
begin
  CharLabel.Caption := StringGrid1.Cells[Col, Row];
end;

{ File|Exit menu command }
```

(continued)

Listing 10-9 *(continued)*

```
procedure TMainForm.FileExitClick(Sender: TObject);
begin
  Close;
end;

{ Help|About menu command }
procedure TMainForm.HelpAboutClick(Sender: TObject);
begin
  AboutForm.ShowModal;
end;

{ Select button click handler }
procedure TMainForm.SelectBitBtnClick(Sender: TObject);
begin
  StringGrid1DblClick(Sender);  // Same as double-clicking grid
end;

{ Copy selected characters to clipboard }
procedure TMainForm.ClipBitBtnClick(Sender: TObject);
begin
  with CopyEdit do
  begin
    if SelLength = 0 then
      SelectAll;        { Select all text if none selected }
    CopyToClipboard;   { Copy selected text to clipboard }
  end;
end;

{ Clear text in copy-to edit box }
procedure TMainForm.ClearBitBtnClick(Sender: TObject);
begin
  CopyEdit.Text := '';
end;

end.
```

The StringGrid component operates like a two-dimensional ListBox. The RowCount
property specifies the number of rows; ColCount specifies the number of columns.
On the simplest level, you can use these values to access a grid's string data
through the Cells two-dimensional array. For example, the sample form's OnCreate
event handler assigns all possible ASCII values to the program's StringGrid1 object
with these statements (Ascii, IRow, and ICol are Integer variables):

```
Ascii := 0;
with StringGrid1 do
for IRow := 0 to RowCount do
  for ICol := 0 to ColCount do
  begin
    Cells[ICol, IRow] := Chr(Ascii);
    Inc(Ascii);
  end;
```

You can also access a grid's strings through the Rows and Cols arrays, which are single-dimensional string arrays. Each element of Rows and Cols is a TStrings string-list object. To load a row's data from a disk file, for example, you can use a statement such as:

```
with StringGrid1 do
Rows[0].LoadFromFile('C:\YourFile.Txt');
```

Or, you might load multiple rows with code such as this:

```
with StringGrid1 do
for I := 0 to RowCount do
  Rows[I].LoadFromFile('C:\YourFile.Txt');
```

When making numerous additions to a StringGrid's rows and columns this way (and in general when adding strings to TStrings and TStringList objects), surround lengthy processes with BeginUpdate and EndUpdate to reduce display chatter. For example, the preceding example might be smoother when coded as follows:

```
with StringGrid1 do
for I := 0 to RowCount do
with Rows[I] do
try
  BeginUpdate;
  Rows[I].LoadFromFile('C:\YourFile.Txt');
finally
  EndUpdate;
end;
```

It's a good idea to use a *try-finally* block as shown to ensure that EndUpdate is called, even if any exceptions occur in the two statements under *try*.

Most StringGrid capabilities are the same as for TStrings, which you've already examined in depth, so I won't discuss StringGrid further here. However, the sample program demonstrates an unrelated but useful technique for ComboBox drop-down lists that you might find helpful. In the FontCB object's OnKeyDown event handler, if the passed Key parameter is vk_Return or vk_Escape, the procedure sets the ComboBox's DroppedDown property to False. It then sets Key to zero. Run the program, open the Font list, and press Enter or Esc to close the list window. This small touch helps make CharGrid's keyboard interface friendlier.

The StringGrid's OnKeyDown event handler shows how to program keys for a StringGrid object. Here, if Key equals vk_Return or vk_Space the procedure calls StringGrid1DblClick, which simulates the double-clicking of a grid cell. For this technique to work, you must install a handler for the grid's OnDblClick event.

Tip

In general, I find it easiest to program mouse events first (such as OnClick and OnDblClick), and then to add keyboard operations, I simply call the mouse handlers from OnKeyDown or OnKeyPress procedures.

Expert-User Tips

✦ The Windows API ShellExecute function returns immediately — it does not pause the current application to run another, as some programmers mistakenly assume. After application *A* calls ShellExecute to run application *B*, it is perfectly safe to close application *A* while *B* remains running. *A* and *B* are independent coprocesses — it is immaterial which one started the other.

✦ StringGrid normally fixes its first row and column in place because you most likely display headers in these cells. If you don't need headers (as in the CharGrid application), release the entire grid by setting FixedCols and FixedRows to zero.

✦ A form's OnActivate event is called when the form receives the input focus due to the user switching back to the form from another one in the same application. The OnActivate event is not equivalent to the Windows wm_Activate message.

✦ StringGrid's VisibleColCount and VisibleRowCount indicate how many nonfixed columns and rows are visible in a grid. The Row and Col variables indicate the cell that has the current input focus.

✦ To enable cell editing in StringGrid objects, set the Options.goEditing subproperty to True. If you want users to be able to press Tab to move from cell to cell, set Options.goTab to True.

✦ To enable row and column resizing by clicking and dragging the mouse, set a StringGrid's Options.goRowSizing and Options.goColSizing subproperties to True. To enable clicking and dragging rows and columns to new positions, set Options.goRowMoving and Options.goColMoving to True.

✦ When a component is created, it inserts itself into its owner's Components list. Ownership means that the child components are destroyed when their owner is destroyed. A parent determines a display context. Without a parent, a control would be invisible. All components that you create at design time are owned by a form.

Projects to Try

10-1: Use ExecuteFile in Delphi's FMXUtils unit to construct a control-panel application that displays application icons. Users should be able to click an icon to run programs. You might provide this program along with products composed of multiple utilities.

10-2: Write a replacement for the Windows Notepad that's more suitable for listing program source code. Your program should use a monospace font (or it should have a Font command to select fonts). Elsewhere in this book (for example, see Chapter 12), you learn about search-and-replace commands as well as printing, which you can add to your ultimate text editor. However, this project is still a useful exercise in using the Memo component.

10-3: Write code to copy selected text to and from multiple Memo objects.

10-4: Write a program that sorts a Memo object's strings. (Hint: You might use a ListBox, which automatically sorts data when its Sorted property is set to True, or you can write code that implements a sorting algorithm.)

10-5: Write a program that encrypts and decrypts text files. Add password protection to the program.

10-6: Add individual color samples for red, green, and blue to the ColorDlg dialog.

Summary

✦ The Memo and StringGrid components provide multiple-line text-handling objects. Memo is like having the Windows Notepad utility in a component. StringGrid is practically a full-blown spreadsheet that organizes string lists in a row-and-column format.

✦ The 16-bit version of Memo could hold only up to 32K of text. The newer 32-bit model, which uses the Object Pascal String data type, can potentially hold a virtually unlimited amount of text, but is limited by Windows to 64K.

✦ You can access Memo's text as one data object by using the Text property. For accessing Memo text as individual strings, use the Lines property. It's also possible, though no longer recommended, to access Memo data as an array of Char by calling methods such as GetTextBuf and SetTextBuf.

✦ Text components, such as Memo and Edit, provide automatic clipboard cut, copy, and paste transfers. However, you can call CopyToClipboard, CutToClipboard, and PasteFromClipboard in Edit, MaskEdit, and Memo components to perform clipboard transfers under program control.

✦ The obsolete WinExec function is still available, but no longer recommended. To run applications externally to your programs (or to open files in their default applications), use the Windows API ShellExecute function. The easiest way to do this in Delphi is to add the FMXUtils unit (located in Delphi's Demos\Doc\Filemanex directory) using the Project | Add to project command. Also add a uses *FMXUtils;* statement to the form unit's implementation. You can then call the ExecuteFile function provided in FMXUtils. ExecuteFile calls the Windows API ShellExecute function.

✦ Use a ScrollBar component as a range-selection object. Use a ScrollBox object to provide a scrollable Panel-like surface that can hold other controls.

✦ In a container object such as a form or a ScrollBox, the Components array lists all components owned by the object. The Controls array lists all components that are child windows. These arrays do not necessarily list the same components. Use the programming in this chapter's ContComp application to investigate the component and control relationships among objects. Understanding these relationships can help you to write efficient code — for example, a loop that disables all child controls in a ScrollBox without affecting other objects on the form.

✦ A StringGrid provides a row-and-column format for storing string and other object data. Use the two-dimensional Cells array to access individual cells. Use the Rows and Cols single-dimensional arrays to access a grid's data as string lists.

Dealing with disk files, filenames, directories, and related matters is a major part of most software development projects. In the next chapter, you learn about Delphi's directory navigation and related file components.

✦   ✦   ✦

Navigating Directories and Files

Effective directory and file management is essential in any file-based application. Even the simplest utility probably needs to read and write option settings in a Windows initialization (.ini) file, and programs almost always need at least one of the file-handling techniques described in this chapter.

Delphi provides four directory and file components that you can use to construct file-selection and directory-navigation dialogs. In this chapter, these components are used to build a file-selection dialog and program that can run any executable program. You also learn how to use the TIniFile object to read and write .ini files. For a practical example of .ini file handling, this chapter explains the inner workings of a moderately complex utility program, SysColor, a system-colorizer that can alter onscreen colors such as button shadows and window title bars. The program reads and writes color settings in a Windows .ini file.

Components

Following are Delphi's directory and file components:

♦ **DirectoryListBox** — Displays and permits users to change the current directory and subdirectories. In most cases, you relate a DirectoryListBox object with a FileListBox to display files as users browse a disk's directory tree. Palette: Win3.1.

✦ **DriveComboBox**—Shows and permits selecting all drives connected with the system. You normally relate a DriveComboBox with a DirectoryListBox so users can switch to another drive and browse its directories. Palette: Win3.1.

✦ **FileListBox**—Displays files in the current directory. A FileListBox object can display all files or those matching one or more wildcard filters, such as *.pas and *.txt. You normally relate a FileListBox with an Edit control to provide users with a means to enter and edit filenames. Palette: Win3.1.

✦ **FilterComboBox**—Lists wildcard filters that users can select to limit the types of files that a related FileListBox displays. Palette: Win3.1.

Note

Although the preceding components are in the Win3.1 directory, they are still valuable for creating custom file managers and other directory browsing controls. The components work perfectly well with Windows 95, 98, and NT.

Creating a Directory Dialog

Delphi's four directory and file components provide an Erector set of tools you can use to build file-selection dialogs. In this section, you meet each component, and then you use them to construct a file-selection dialog that you can put to work in your application's File I Open, File I Save, and other file-handling commands.

As you probably realize, Delphi also provides OpenDialog and SaveDialog components on the Dialogs palette (see Chapter 12). Use the following techniques when you need to customize these standard dialog boxes—for example, to add a wildcard filter editor, as one of this chapter's projects suggests.

DirectoryListBox

Figure 11-1 shows the custom dialog box you create later in this section. In the dialog, the DirectoryListBox object displays a directory tree outline. Users can double-click and use the keyboard to select directories in this window.

You can use a DirectoryListBox alone in a window, but you usually also want to display files in selected directories. To do that, assign the name of a FileListBox object to the DirectoryListBox's FileList property. This is easiest to do in the Object Inspector window, but you may make the assignment at run time with code such as the following. Insert DirectoryListBox and FileListBox objects into a form, and then insert this statement into the form's OnCreate event handler:

```
DirectoryListBox1.FileList := FileListBox1;
```

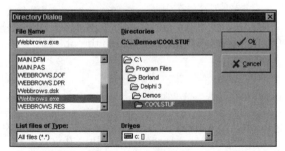

Figure 11-1: The custom dialog box in this chapter uses Delphi's four directory and file components: DirectoryListBox, DriveComboBox, FileListBox, and FilterComboBox.

Delphi shows the current directory and file lists at design time, but you must run the program to select new directories and files, and to scroll the windows.

To show the currently selected path as a string, insert a Label object into the form (usually, it should go above the DirectoryListBox). Assign the Label's name to the DirectoryListBox's DirLabel property. Or, to make the association at run time, insert this statement into the form's OnCreate event handler:

```
DirectoryListBox1.DirLabel := Label1;
```

The DirectoryListBox component assigns directory paths, including the current drive letter, to the Label's Caption. To display deeply nested paths, the component replaces the root directories with an ellipsis. This keeps the Label relatively short (about 24 characters maximum, or approximately the width of an unmodified DirectoryListBox object). For example, DirectoryListBox displays this path:

```
C:\Program Files\Borland\Delphi 4\Demos\COOLSTUFF
```

as the shortened Caption:

```
C:\...\Demos\COOLSTUFF
```

The Drive property gives the currently selected drive letter. For example, this sets a char *C* to the drive letter:

```
C := DirectoryListBox1.Drive;
```

Use the Directory property to determine the currently selected path.

To display full path names that are not shortened with an ellipsis, do not assign a Label object name to the DirLabel property. Instead, insert a Label into the form, and in the DirectoryListBox's OnChange event handler, assign the object's Directory string to the Label's Caption.

DriveComboBox

Unless you need to permit access only to a specific drive, you probably want to insert a DriveComboBox object and relate it to a DirectoryListBox. If you are following along, insert a DriveComboBox object into the form (usually, it goes below the DirectoryListBox). Assign a DirectoryListBox's name to the DriveComboBox's DirList property, or use this statement in the form's OnCreate event handler:

```
DriveComboBox1.DirList := DirectoryListBox1;
```

When users select a different drive, the DirectoryListBox automatically updates its tree. If you also associated a FileListBox with the DirectoryListBox, the file list is also updated.

The full list of available drives is available through the DriveComboBox's Items property, an object of type TStrings. You can assign this list to any other TStrings property, or to a TStringList variable. For example, to display all available drives, insert a ListBox into the form, and add this statement to the form's OnCreate event handler:

```
ListBox1.Items := DriveComboBox1.Items;
```

FileListBox

As you can probably guess, a FileListBox displays filenames in the current directory. Most often, a DirectoryListBox is associated with a FileListBox. This way, the list automatically changes when users browse through directories.

You usually also add two more components: an Edit control and a FilterComboBox. If you are following along, insert the Edit control now (the next section explains how to use FilterComboBox). Usually, the control goes above the FileListBox. Assign the Edit object's Name to the FileListBox's FileEdit property, or insert this statement into the form's OnCreate event handler:

```
FileListBox1.FileEdit := Edit1;
```

When you run the program, the Edit control initially shows the filter *.*, which selects all files. As users select filenames, the FileListBox inserts them into the Edit window. Users can also type entries and filters into the control.

To create a read-only Edit control that users cannot modify, but that still displays the current file selection, set the Edit object's ReadOnly property to True. To also prevent users from tabbing to the control and highlighting its text, set Enabled False.

Obtain the selected file in a FileListBox's FileName property. This string includes the current drive letter and path. For example, to select files by double-clicking, create a handler for the FileListBox's OnDblClick event, and insert this statement:

```
ShowMessage(FileListBox1.FileName);
```

Run the program and double-click filenames to display them in the ShowMessage window. To also select files by pressing Enter, create a handler for the FileListBox's OnKeyPress handler, and insert this code to call the double-click procedure if Key equals a carriage-return control code:

```
if Key = #13 then
  FileListBox1DblClick(Sender);
```

If you don't need the full path name in a FileListBox's FileName string, pass it to one of Delphi's File-Management functions: ExtractFileExt, ExtractFileName, and ExtractFilePath. To try these functions, insert three Labels into the form (if you are following along, Delphi names them Label2, Label3, and Label4). Assign pieces of selected file paths with this code in the FileListBox's OnDblClick event handler:

```
with FileListBox1 do
begin
  Label2.Caption := ExtractFileExt(FileName);
  Label3.Caption := ExtractFileName(FileName);
  Label4.Caption := ExtractFilePath(FileName);
end;
```

Users can select multiple files in a FileListBox if its MultiSelect property is True. With this setting, users can highlight multiple filenames by pressing the Shift and Ctrl keys while clicking the mouse pointer. If you choose this option, you need to write code and insert an OK button to provide the selection list to the application.

An Edit control associated with a FileListBox in its FileEdit property displays the most recently selected filename when MultiSelect is True. Instead of an Edit object, however, you might want to insert a ListBox into the form for displaying selected filename strings.

Listing 11-1 shows how to create a list of multiple filename selections. If you are following along, insert another ListBox into the form (Delphi names it ListBox2), and insert a BitBtn with its Kind property set to bkOk. Insert the programming in Listing 11-1 into the BitBtn's OnClick event handler.

Listing 11-1: **This OnClick event handler demonstrates how to create a list of multiple selections in a FileListBox object.**

```
procedure TForm1.BitBtn1Click(Sender: TObject);
var
  I: Integer;
begin
  ListBox2.Clear;
  if FileListBox1.SelCount > 0 then
  for I := 0 to FileListBox1.Items.Count - 1 do
    if FileListBox1.Selected[I] then
      ListBox2.Items.Add(FileListBox1.Items[I]);
end;
```

If SelCount is greater than 0, the user has selected at least one filename. The *for* loop uses the Count property in Items to determine how many total filenames the FileListBox displays. For each item *N*, if Selected[N] is True, the program adds that item to ListBox2's Items string list. Replace the ListBox in Listing 11-1 with a TStringList object if you need a list of filename selections not related to a component such as a ListBox.

You can improve the efficiency of the code in Listing 11-1 by using a *with* statement, but I prefaced properties with the object name to make it clear what the statements are doing. To make this change, replace the statements after the call to ListBox2's Clear method with the following:

```
with FileListBox1, Items do
if SelCount > 0 then
for I := 0 to Count - 1 do
  if Selected[I] then
    ListBox2.Items.Add(Items[I]);
```

FilterComboBox

Use a FilterComboBox to provide a selectable list of wildcard filters such as *.pas and *.ini. If you are following along, insert a FilterComboBox object into the form (usually, it goes under a FileListBox). To update the current file list automatically when users select a filter, assign the name of the FileListBox object to the FilterComboBox's FileList property. Or, insert this statement into the form's OnCreate event handler:

```
FilterComboBox1.FileList := FileListBox1;
```

Open Delphi's Filter editor by clicking the ellipsis next to the FilterComboBox's Filter property. Enter filters into the editor in this format:

```
All files (*.*)        | *.*
Text files (*.Txt)     | *.Txt
Pascal files (*.pas )  | *.pas
```

The strings in the left column appear in the FilterComboBox. The strings in the right column are the actual filters passed to the FileListBox. If that object has an associated Edit control, selecting a new filter also inserts it into the Edit window.

Putting the directory dialog together

If you have been following along, your form looks something like the jumbled dialog in Figure 11-2. In this section, you clean up the mess with a better-looking file-selection dialog you can use for many file- and directory-handling chores. Listing 11-2 shows DirDlg's source code (you can find it on the CD-ROM in the Source\DirEx directory). There's not a lot of code in this module — most of the dialog's operations are automatic and result from associating the file and directory objects.

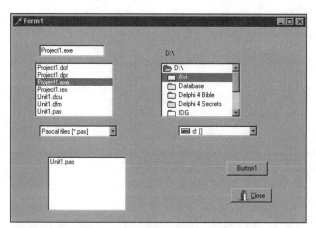

Figure 11-2: The raw (and messy) dialog box created in the preceding sections showing Delphi's file and directory components

Listing 11-2: The DirDlg module in the DirEx subdirectory

```
unit Dirdlg;

interface

uses
  SysUtils, Windows, Messages, Classes, Graphics,
  Controls, Forms, Dialogs, StdCtrls, Buttons, FileCtrl;

type
  TDirDlgForm = class(TForm)
    FileListBox: TFileListBox;
    DirectoryListBox: TDirectoryListBox;
    DriveComboBox: TDriveComboBox;
    FilterComboBox: TFilterComboBox;
    FileNameEdit: TEdit;
    FileNameLabel: TLabel;
    DirectoriesLabel: TLabel;
    DirLabel: TLabel;
    ListFilesLabel: TLabel;
    DrivesLabel: TLabel;
    OkBitBtn: TBitBtn;
    CancelBitBtn: TBitBtn;
    procedure FileListBoxDblClick(Sender: TObject);
  private
    { Private declarations }
  public
    { Public declarations }
  end;

var
  DirDlgForm: TDirDlgForm;

implementation

{$R *.DFM}

procedure TDirDlgForm.FileListBoxDblClick(Sender: TObject);
begin
  OkBitBtn.Click;
end;

procedure TDirDlgForm.DriveComboBoxChange(Sender: TObject);
begin
  DirectoryListBox.Drive := DriveComboBox.Drive;
  FileListBox.Drive := DriveComboBox.Drive;
  FileListBox.Directory := DirectoryListBox.Directory;
end;

end.
```

A test program in the DirEx directory shows how to use the DirDlg dialog. The form's ShowModal function returns the value of ModalResult, which an application can inspect to find out which button was clicked to close the dialog's window. For example, Listing 11-3, extracted from the DirEx test program, displays a selected filename in a ShowMessage dialog if ShowModal returns mrOk. To make that happen, the dialog's OK and Cancel buttons set their ModalResult properties to mrOk and mrCancel respectively. You can also assign values to ModalResult at run time with a statement such as:

```
ModalResult := mrOk;
```

Listing 11-3: **ShowModal displaying the file-selection dialog (refer to Figure 11-1)**

```
procedure TMainForm.TestBitBtnClick(Sender: TObject);
begin
  with DirDlgForm do
  if ShowModal = mrOk then
    ShowMessage('Selected file = ' + FileNameEdit.Text);
end;
```

Developing Directory-Based Utilities

As you build forms such as the file-selection dialog in the preceding section, you may want to use them in other applications. To organize your application's source code, it's usually best to create a separate directory for each program module. One or more programs can use these modules simply by adding them to the project.

As an example of this concept, and to show how to use the file-selection dialog in a practical utility, DirExec duplicates the Explorer's capability to run any executable code file. The program can also open any file in the Windows registration database. For example, DirExec opens the Notepad editor to display a text file ending in .txt.

Try creating this application yourself — it gives you some experience using Delphi's Project Manager to set up multiple module development projects. Create a directory for your program, and start a new project. View the Project Manager, and click the Add button. Change to a copy of the Source\DirEx directory from the CD-ROM, and choose the DirDlg.pas file. This adds the DirDlg module to the program's project. You must also add the module's unit name to the host program's *uses* directive. You can then add buttons or commands to the project to open the dialog for selecting file-names. Use Listing 11-4 as a guide. After the listing, I explain how the program runs applications and opens registered files. Figure 11-3 shows the program's display.

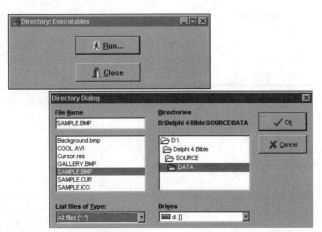

Figure 11-3: The DirExec application demonstrates how to use this chapter's file-selection dialog to run other programs and to open registered files.

Listing 11-4: **DirExec\Main.pas**

```
unit Main;

interface

uses
  SysUtils, Windows, Messages, Classes, Graphics,
  Controls, Forms, Dialogs, StdCtrls, Buttons, ShellAPI,
  DirDlg;

type
  TMainForm = class(TForm)
    RunBitBtn: TBitBtn;
    BitBtn2: TBitBtn;
    procedure RunBitBtnClick(Sender: TObject);
  private
    { Private declarations }
  public
    { Public declarations }
  end;

var
  MainForm: TMainForm;

implementation
```

```
{$R *.DFM}

function ExecuteFile(const FileName, Params, Dir: String;
  ShowCmd: Integer): THandle;
begin
  Result := ShellExecute(Application.MainForm.Handle, nil,
    PChar(FileName), PChar(Params), PChar(Dir), ShowCmd);
end;

procedure TMainForm.RunBitBtnClick(Sender: TObject);
begin
  with DirDlgForm do
  if ShowModal = mrOk then
  if ExecuteFile(FileNameEdit.Text, '',
    DirectoryListBox.Directory,SW_SHOW) <= 32 then
    MessageDlg('Unable to open file or program',
      mtError, [mbOk], 0)
  else
    Application.Minimize;
end;

end.
```

In the preceding chapter, you learned how to use the FMXUtils unit's ExecuteFile function to run other programs. (The unit is found in Delphi's Demos\Doc\Filemanex directory.) This function merely calls a Windows API function, ShellExecute, which is available without using FMXUtils. ShellExecute can also open any registered file — for example, those with names ending in .txt and .bmp.

The DirExec example (refer to Listing 11-4) includes a function, ExecuteFile, that you can cut and paste into any application. The function calls ShellExecute with five parameters:

- ✦ The current application's window handle (found in the Handle property in the Application's MainForm)

- ✦ Nil for an optional operation (specify 'Print' here to print a file rather than open it)

- ✦ Three null-terminated strings

Because ShellExecute is a Windows API function, you cannot feed it Pascal strings. The three strings represent the filename, any parameters, and the directory path.

ShellExecute returns the instance handle of the opened application. If valid, this value is greater than 32, a fact that the test program's Run button OnClick event handler uses to display an error message with MessageDlg. Notice the call to Application.Minimize near the end of the listing. This step is optional, but moves the program window out of the way of the selected application.

Drag-and-Drop Files

Any program that can display a text file should enable drag-and-drop services so users can drag filenames from the Windows File Manager and drop them into the application's Memo or other component object. Delphi doesn't provide drag-and-drop files directly, but you can add this feature with only a little extra effort.

The first step is to inform Windows that your program's window can accept drag-and-drop files. Do that in the form's OnCreate event handler by adding this statement:

```
DragAcceptFiles(Handle, True);
```

Also, insert the ShellAPI unit into the module's *uses* directive. ShellAPI declares DragAcceptFiles and its parameters as:

```
procedure DragAcceptFiles(Wnd: HWnd; Accept: Bool);
```

✦ **Wnd** — A handle to the current window, the one to which filenames can be dragged and dropped. Usually, you should pass the Handle property of the form that accepts the file drop.

✦ **Accept** — Set this parameter to True to inform Windows that this window accepts dragged and dropped filenames. Set this parameter to False to disengage dragging and dropping. Microsoft recommends doing this before the program ends — in Delphi applications, you can disable dragging and dropping in a form's OnDestroy event handler.

For any window that calls DragAcceptFiles, when you drag a filename from the Windows File Manager to that window and release the mouse button, Windows sends the window a wm_DropFiles message. Along with the message is the file's name. To receive this message, insert a message handler into a protected section of your form's class. (The declaration can go anywhere in the class, but is usually in a private or protected section.) For example, add the following lines between the private and public declarations in a form's class declaration:

```
protected
  procedure WMDropFiles(var Msg: TMessage);
    message wm_DropFiles;
```

Protected procedures are in a kind of never-never land between private and public declarations. Only class methods and methods in derived classes can access protected methods. This differs from private declarations, which are accessible only to members of the class, but not to any derived classes. Any statement can access a class's public declarations — they are like the laundry hanging between buildings. Protected items are in the hallway — you have to be in the building to get at them. Private declarations are in your own room. As long as you keep the door locked, nobody can touch them but you.

Implement the WMDropFiles method to perform an action when users drop a filename into the window. The procedure should have the general format shown in Listing 11-5. The comment indicates where you can perform an action with a dropped filename.

Listing 11-5: **Implement the WMDropFiles method with this type of code.**

```
{ Handle wm_DropFiles message }
procedure TMainForm.WMDropFiles(var Msg: TMessage);
var
  Filename: array[0 .. 256] of Char;
begin
  DragQueryFile(
    THandle(Msg.WParam),
    0,
    Filename,
    SizeOf(Filename));
  { ... Perform action with dropped filename }
  DragFinish(THandle(Msg.WParam));
end;
```

In WMDropFiles, a null-terminated string, FileName, holds the dropped filename. You can make this string longer if necessary, but 256 characters should be enough for even the most deeply nested path names. Call DragQueryFile to obtain the dropped information. ShellAPI defines this function as:

```
function DragQueryFile(Drop: THandle; FileIndex: Word;
  FileName: PChar; cb: Word): Word;
```

✦ **Drop** — A handle to an internal structure that contains information about dragged and dropped filenames. Usually, you should pass to Drop the Msg.WParam field from the wm_DropFiles message cast to a THandle object.

✦ **FileIndex** — Set this parameter to $FFFF (equal to -1 in hexadecimal) to request the number of dropped filenames. Pass a value from zero to the number of dropped filenames minus one to copy the names to the FileName parameter.

✦ **Filename** — An array of Char large enough to hold a complete path name, usually at least 256 bytes. Insert a null-terminated string into the array, or pass nil to request the number of dropped files. Pass nil also to request the size of a specific filename in bytes.

✦ **cb** — The size of the Filename buffer in bytes.

If you pass -1 to the FileIndex parameter, DragQueryFile returns the number of dropped files. Declare a Word variable to hold the function result:

```
var
  NumFiles: Word;
```

Next, call DragQueryFile to determine the number of filenames dropped into the window:

```
NumFiles := DragQueryFile(
  THandle(Msg.WParam),
  $FFFF,
  nil,
  0);
```

In many cases, you need to accept only a single filename. As a practical example, the DropFile application on the CD-ROM (in the Source\DropFile directory) demonstrates how to program a Memo object to accept drag-and-drop filenames. Run DropFile and drag any text filename from the Windows File Manager into the program's Memo window, which reads the file from disk and displays its lines. Figure 11-4 shows the program's display. Listing 11-6 shows the program's source code.

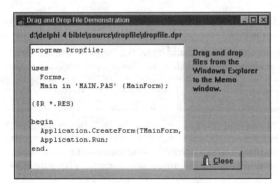

Figure 11-4: The DropFile program showing the program's DropFile.dpr project file, which I dragged to the Memo object's window from the Windows File Manager.

Listing 11-6: **DropFile\Main.pas**

```
unit Main;

interface

uses
  SysUtils, Windows, Messages, Classes, Graphics,
  Controls, Forms, Dialogs, StdCtrls, Buttons, ShellAPI;

type
  TMainForm = class(TForm)
    Memo1: TMemo;
    BitBtn1: TBitBtn;
    Label1: TLabel;
    FileNameLabel: TLabel;
    procedure FormCreate(Sender: TObject);
    procedure FormDestroy(Sender: TObject);
  private
    { Private declarations }
  protected
    procedure WMDropFiles(var Msg: TMessage);
      message wm_DropFiles;
  public
    { Public declarations }
  end;

var
  MainForm: TMainForm;

implementation

{$R *.DFM}

{ Handle wm_DropFiles message }
procedure TMainForm.WMDropFiles(var Msg: TMessage);
var
  Filename: array[0 .. 256] of Char;
begin
  DragQueryFile(
    THandle(Msg.WParam),
    0,
    Filename,
    SizeOf(Filename));
  with FileNameLabel do
  begin
```

(continued)

Listing 11-6 *(continued)*

```
Caption := LowerCase(FileName);
Memo1.Lines.LoadfromFile(Caption);
  end;
  DragFinish(THandle(Msg.WParam));
end;

{ Tell Windows this window can accept drag-and-drop files }
procedure TMainForm.FormCreate(Sender: TObject);
begin
  DragAcceptFiles(Handle, True);
end;

{ Disable drag-and-drop files (recommended) }
procedure TMainForm.FormDestroy(Sender: TObject);
begin
  DragAcceptFiles(Handle, False);
end;

end.
```

To enable drag-and-drop filenames, the DropFile form's OnCreate event handler calls DragAcceptFiles. To cancel dragging and dropping, the OnDestroy procedure calls the same function, but passes False to the second parameter.

The TMainForm class declares a WMDropFiles message handler. When Windows issues a wm_DropFiles message to the window, parameter Msg contains the passed information. The procedure's implementation uses this information in a call to DragQueryFile to obtain the dropped filename. Because this name is a null-terminated string, the program passes it to StrPas to convert the text to a Pascal string, assigned to the FileNameLabel's Caption and passed to the Memo1 object's LoadFromFile method. I added a call to LowerCase to convert the filename to lowercase, which is easier on the eyes (at least on my eyes).

One problem with the foregoing techniques is they don't work when dragging filenames onto a minimized application's icon. The reason is Delphi's main form window is not visible when the program is minimized. To implement dragging and dropping for this condition, you have to add code for the application's window handle. This is the window that shows the minimized icon — it is not the same window used by the form.

Follow these steps to add minimized-icon dragging and dropping to the DropFiles application. Add a second call to DragAcceptFiles in the form's OnCreate event handler. The statement tells Windows that the Application's window can accept drag-and-drop files:

```
DragAcceptFiles(Application.Handle, True);
```

To disable dragging and dropping for this window, add a similar statement to the form's OnDestroy event handler, but pass False to the second DragAcceptFiles parameter:

```
DragAcceptFiles(Application.Handle, False);
```

The Application object does not handle messages in the same way as a form class. The messages arrive in a raw state, just as they are passed around by Windows, and you need a special procedure to handle them. Declare the procedure as follows (its name is unimportant) in the form class's protected section. For example, add this declaration below the one for WMDropFiles:

```
procedure AppOnMsg(var Msg: TMsg; var Handled: Boolean);
```

Parameter Msg is of type TMsg, which is defined by Delphi in Windows.pas as:

```
tagMSG = packed record
hwnd: HWnd;
  message: UINT;
  wParam: WPARAM;
  lParam: LPARAM;
  time: DWORD;
  pt: TPoint;
end;
TMsg = tagMSG;
```

It is in this form that messages arrive in Application. In this case, we are interested in only one message, wm_DropFiles. In addition, we want to recognize that message only when the application is minimized. Listing 11-7 shows how to write the handler.

The AppOnMsg procedure inspects Message.Msg for a wm_DropFiles message. If the application is also minimized (IsIconic returns True), the procedure calls DragQueryFile to obtain the filename and load its text into the sample program's Memo object.

Listing 11-7: **Insert this message handler into DropFiles to enable drag-and-drop files for the application's minimized icon.**

```
procedure TMainForm.AppOnMsg(var Msg: TMsg; var Handled:
Boolean);
var
  Filename: array[0 .. 256] of Char;
begin
  with Application do
  if (Msg.Message = wm_DropFiles) and IsIconic(Handle) then
  begin
    DragQueryFile(THandle(Msg.WParam),
      0, Filename, SizeOf(Filename));
    with FileNameLabel do
    begin
      Caption := LowerCase(FileName);
      Memo1.Lines.LoadfromFile(Caption);
    end;
    DragFinish(THandle(Msg.WParam));
  end;
end;
```

There's one final step in making all of this code work properly. You have to assign the message handler (AppOnMsg in this example) to the Application's OnMessage event handler. To ensure that the program receives all intended messages, perform this step as early as possible — in the form's OnCreate event handler, for example. Create a handler for DropFile's OnCreate event, and insert this statement:

```
Application.OnMessage := AppOnMsg;
```

You can now run DropFile and minimize its window on the Windows desktop. Drag a text filename from the File Manager and drop it on the icon. When you open DropFile's window, you see the file's text in the Memo object.

Reading and Writing .ini Files

Delphi's TIniFile class simplifies the tedious chore of reading and writing Windows initialization files identified by the .ini extension. The TIniFile class is not a component, and it does not appear on Delphi's VCL palette. For this reason, you have to create and free TIniFile objects, and call their methods, completely under program control.

In most programs, you need two procedures to read and write .ini file settings. For example, you can store options and other settings, which experienced users can modify by loading the .ini file into a text editor. To create or update the file, first create a TIniFile object. Declare it like this:

```
var
   IniFile: TIniFile;
```

Then, in the procedure's body, create the IniFile object by calling TIniFile's Create method:

```
IniFile := TIniFile.Create('YourProg.ini');
```

When you are done using the IniFile object, free it with this statement:

```
IniFile.Free;
```

If you don't include drive and path name information in the filename string, the .ini file is created in the Windows directory. This is usually best, but some programmers create .ini files in the application's home directory. Wherever you locate the file, after creating the IniFile object, call its methods to read and write initialization settings. Each setting must be in a bracketed section, followed by one or more values. For example, here are the first three lines from the SysColor.ini file, created by the SysColor application described later in this section:

```
[SysColor]
Scroll Bar=12632256
Background=4210688
```

You can read .ini file settings into a TStrings or TStringList object in two ways. Define the object:

```
var
   StringList: TStringList;
```

Create the string list and call ReadSectionValues for the IniFile object to load the list with the initialization file's settings. For example, use statements such as these:

```
StringList := TStringList.Create;
IniFile.ReadSectionValues('SysColor', StringList);
```

The first statement creates the string list. The second calls ReadSectionValues, passing the section name [SysColor] without brackets as a string and the StringList object. Each item in the string list includes the item's name, an equal sign, and a value, with no spaces around the equal sign. Alternatively, to load only the item names, call ReadSection like this:

```
IniFile.ReadSection('SysColor', StringList);
```

IniFile also provides methods to read and write individual values. For example, SysColor writes a CheckBox setting with the statement:

```
IniFile.WriteBool('Options', 'Save settings',
   SaveCheckBox.Checked);
```

The first argument, 'Options', specifies the section into which the item is to go. The second argument is the name of this item, and the final argument is its value. If Checked is True, the resulting .ini file lines look like this:

```
[Options]
Save settings=1
```

To read a setting, call one of the IniFile class's Read methods. For example, SysColor loads the Save settings CheckBox value with the statement:

```
SaveCheckBox.Checked :=
   IniFile.ReadBool('Options', 'Save settings', False);
```

The other read and write methods — ReadInteger, ReadString, WriteInteger, and WriteString — work similarly, but read and write values of the indicated types.

After reading .ini file settings into a string list, youcan locate specific settings. Do that by indexing the Values array of the target string list. For example, if *T* is a TStringList object loaded by an IniFile object's ReadSectionValues method, then Values[S] equals the string value of the item identified as *S*. You can assign that value to a string:

```
S := T.Values['Button color'];
```

But, you probably want to convert it to an integer or other binary value for use in the program. Do that by calling a conversion function such as StrToImt:

```
K := StrToInt(T.Values['Button color']);
```

The SysColor Utility

A full-length program, SysColor, puts the foregoing concepts into action. The program's source code is a bit long to list completely here, so I present portions of it at a time. Explanations of each portion follow the listings. Of course, the complete source is on the CD-ROM in the Source\SysColor directory. Figure 11-5 shows the program's display. See the "How to Use Syscolor" sidebar for instructions.

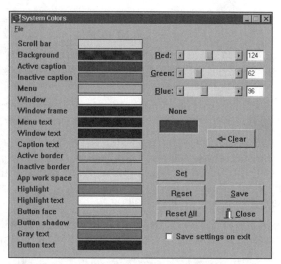

Figure 11-5: SysColor displays and enables you to select 19 Windows system colors, such as the windows background color, and active or inactive window title color.

Using the Windows Explorer, add SysColor.exe to the Taskbar's Start menu. This automatically loads your saved color settings the next time you start Windows. You can leave SysColor running or quit the application without affecting color settings.

How to Use SysColor

Now that you've studied SysColor, you're ready to use it. Notice the labeled color rectangles show current color settings. Click any color box to select it and transfer its color to the large sample box, initially labeled None. The box shows the selected color and its name. Click Clear to disassociate the sample box with any selected color (this is useful for testing color values without affecting a labeled setting).

Use the Red, Green, and Blue scroll bars to adjust color values, or you can enter integers from 0 to 255 in the three Edit controls to the right of the scroll bars. The large sample box shows the new color. If you selected a labeled color rectangle, it also shows this color as you change it.

Click the Set button to transfer the labeled colors to Windows. For example, change Active caption to fire-truck red and click Set. You see the active window caption change to a red background that can surely help wake you up in the morning.

(continued)

(continued)

Click the Reset button to return the labeled colors to their original settings when you started the program. Follow this by clicking Set if you want to restore the Windows system colors to their original values.

Click the Reset All button to reset labeled colors to their startup values as well as restore the Windows system colors. This button performs the same actions as clicking Reset followed by Set.

Click the Save button to save the current color selections in SysColor.ini, located in the Windows directory. The next time you run SysColor, it displays the saved values in the labeled color rectangles. If you don't want to use saved colors, simply delete SysColor.ini and rerun the program, which displays the current Windows color values.

Click the Close button to end the program (or you can choose the File|Exit command). If the Save settings on exit check box is enabled, the program updates SysColor.ini when you quit. Disable the check box if you don't want to automatically save your color selections.

Listing 11-8 shows SysColor's interface section. The numbered Label and Shape components display the labeled color rectangles in the window. (Chapter 13 introduces Shape and other graphics techniques.)

Listing 11-8: **SysColor\Main.pas (interface section)**

```
unit Main;

interface

uses
  SysUtils, Windows, Messages, Classes, Graphics,
  Controls, Forms, Dialogs, StdCtrls, Buttons, ExtCtrls,
  AboutDlg, IniFiles, Menus;

const
  maxColors = 19;              { Number of Windows system colors }
  redMask = $000000FF;             { Red value extraction mask }
  greenMask = $0000FF00;          { Green value extraction mask }
  blueMask = $00FF0000;            { Blue value extraction mask }
  iniFileName = 'SysColor.ini'; { In the Windows directory }

type
  TMainForm = class(TForm)
    BlueEdit: TEdit;
    BlueLabel: TLabel;
```

```
BlueSB: TScrollBar;
ClearBitBtn: TBitBtn;
CloseBitBtn: TBitBtn;
ColorEdit: TEdit;
ColorLabel: TLabel;
FileAbout: TMenuItem;
FileExit: TMenuItem;
FileMenu: TMenuItem;
GreenEdit: TEdit;
GreenLabel: TLabel;
GreenSB: TScrollBar;
Label1: TLabel;
Label2: TLabel;
Label3: TLabel;
Label4: TLabel;
Label5: TLabel;
Label6: TLabel;
Label7: TLabel;
Label8: TLabel;
Label9: TLabel;
Label10: TLabel;
Label11: TLabel;
Label12: TLabel;
Label13: TLabel;
Label14: TLabel;
Label15: TLabel;
Label16: TLabel;
Label17: TLabel;
Label18: TLabel;
Label19: TLabel;
MainMenu1: TMainMenu;
N1: TMenuItem;
RedEdit: TEdit;
RedLabel: TLabel;
RedSB: TScrollBar;
ResetAllBitBtn: TBitBtn;
ResetBitBtn: TBitBtn;
SaveBitBtn: TBitBtn;
SaveCheckBox: TCheckBox;
SetBitBtn: TBitBtn;
Shape1: TShape;
Shape2: TShape;
Shape3: TShape;
Shape4: TShape;
Shape5: TShape;
Shape6: TShape;
Shape7: TShape;
Shape8: TShape;
```

(continued)

Listing 11-8: *(continued)*

```
      Shape9: TShape;
      Shape10: TShape;
      Shape11: TShape;
      Shape12: TShape;
      Shape13: TShape;
      Shape14: TShape;
      Shape15: TShape;
      Shape16: TShape;
      Shape17: TShape;
      Shape18: TShape;
      Shape19: TShape;
      procedure ClearBitBtnClick(Sender: TObject);
      procedure EditChange(Sender: TObject);
      procedure FileAboutClick(Sender: TObject);
      procedure FileExitClick(Sender: TObject);
      procedure FormClose(Sender: TObject;
        var Action: TCloseAction);
      procedure FormCreate(Sender: TObject);
      procedure FormDestroy(Sender: TObject);
      procedure ResetAllBitBtnClick(Sender: TObject);
      procedure ResetBitBtnClick(Sender: TObject);
      procedure SaveBitBtnClick(Sender: TObject);
      procedure SaveCheckBoxClick(Sender: TObject);
      procedure SBChange(Sender: TObject);
      procedure SetBitBtnClick(Sender: TObject);
      procedure ShapeMouseDown(Sender: TObject;
        Button: TMouseButton; Shift: TShiftState; X, Y: Integer);
        private
      IniFile: TIniFile;
      IniItemList: TStringList;
      EditControls: array[0 .. 2] of TEdit;
      ScrollBars: array[0 .. 2] of TScrollBar;
      Shapes: array[0 .. maxColors - 1] of TShape;
      CurrentShape: TShape;
      procedure UpdateColor;
      procedure InitSysColorArray;
      procedure ChangeSystemColors;
      procedure SetScrollBars(C: TColor);
      procedure LoadSettings;
      procedure SaveSettings;
    public
      { Public declarations }
    end;

var
  MainForm: TMainForm;

implementation

{$R *.DFM}
```

The program defines a few constants near the top of the listing:

✦ maxColors equals the number of Windows system colors

✦ redMask, greenMask, and blueMask are 32-bit, unsigned, hexadecimal integers used to extract individual color values from TColor objects

For example, the expression C and greenMask isolates a TColor's green color value. iniFileName is the name of the program's initialization file. Because the name does not include a drive letter or any path information, its location is the Windows directory.

The TMainForm class declares numerous objects that construct the window's interface. Each Label object's number matches the corresponding Shape (for example, Label7 goes with Shape7). This relationship is not arbitrary, and as I explain in a moment, when you have a lot of related components, you can take advantage of Delphi's automatic object naming conventions to write code for related objects. Most of the other objects and event handlers are self-explanatory, so I explain only the elements I added to TMainForm's private section. Six private data members were added:

✦ **IniFile** — This object is constructed in the form's OnCreate event handler and destroyed in OnDestroy. IniFile provides access to the Syscolor.ini file for various procedures. The object opens and closes that file as needed to read and write its settings, so it's more efficient to declare the object in the form's class than it is to declare TIniFile objects in individual procedures. Also, if it were declared locally to a procedure, the .ini file would be opened and closed each time the procedure is called. Putting the variable in the form class gives the variable the same lifetime of the form object.

✦ **IniItemList** — This is a string list of identifiers for the SysColor.ini file, which stores color settings as 32-bit decimal integers. For example, the IniItemList entry for the SysColor.ini setting Background=4210688 is the string 'Background'. I find that it's helpful to keep the item labels in a separate string list, which I explain more about later in this chapter.

✦ **EditControls** — This is an easy-access array to the three Edit windows next to the scroll bars. (Chapter 10's ColorDlg application also uses this array.)

✦ **ScrollBars** — This is also an easy-access array to the three ScrollBar objects. (Chapter 10's ColorDlg application uses this array, too.)

✦ **Shapes** — This array contains references to the 19 Shape objects that display Windows system colors. Using an array simplifies the code — for example, rather than write 19 event handlers, the program can use the array to refer to color rectangle n with the expression Shapes[n]. As SysColors demonstrates, object-reference arrays can help streamline code, and you may find them valuable in many situations.

✦ **CurrentShape** — This is a reference to the currently selected color rectangle. When equal to nil, nothing is selected. Alternatively, I could have used an integer index into the Shapes array to indicate the current color, perhaps with

–1 representing no selection. However, because all Delphi objects are references (that is, they are address values), it is often best to define variables such as CurrentShape that refer to the actual target object. For example, the program can assign Shapes[n] to CurrentShape, and then use the CurrentShape reference to perform actions on the selected object.

In addition to its data members, SysColor defines six private procedures in the TMainForm class. Following are brief introductions to each procedure—complete descriptions of how they work follow their implementations:

✦ **UpdateColor**—This procedure sets the large color sample box, an Edit object named ColorEdit, to the color that the three ScrollBars represent. The procedure also sets the CurrentShape's color if one is selected. In addition, UpdateColor saves the current color in a global SysColorArray array.

✦ **InitSysColorArray**—This procedure initializes the global SysColorArray, which stores the current Windows system colors along with the currently modified color set. The array makes it easy for the program to reset colors to their start-up values. The program also uses the SysColorArray to update the SysColor.ini file.

✦ **ChangeSystemColors**—This procedure transfers to Windows the current color selections. For each color, all active applications receive a wm_SysColorChange message that indicates the application should update its windows, buttons, and other affected items. Delphi applications automatically perform these updates—you don't have to write code to support wm_SysColorChange messages.

✦ **SetScrollBars**—This procedure sets the three ScrollBars' Position properties to values that match a color passed as an argument.

✦ **LoadSettings**—This procedure reads the SysColor.ini file, if it exists.

✦ **SaveSettings**—This procedure creates or updates the SysColor.ini file's color settings.

Understanding SysColor's global declarations and initialization procedures

Listing 11-9 shows SysColor's global declarations and initialization procedures. Explanations follow the listing.

Listing 11-9: SysColor\Main.pas (globals and initializations)

```
type
{ Holds current system colors }
  SysColorRec = record
```

```
    OriginalColor: TColor;   { Color on starting program }
    CurrentColor: TColor;    { New color selected by user }
  end;

var
{ Array of SysColorRec values }
  SysColorArray: array[0 .. maxColors - 1 ] of SysColorRec;

{ Update sample colors from scrollbar positions }
procedure TMainForm.UpdateColor;
begin
{ Update color edit box (the large sample window) }
  ColorEdit.Color :=
    RGB(RedSB.Position, GreenSB.Position, BlueSB.Position);
{ Update labeled Shape color box and SysColorArray }
  if CurrentShape <> nil then with CurrentShape do
  begin
    Brush.Color := ColorEdit.Color;
    SysColorArray[Tag - 1].CurrentColor := Brush.Color;
  end;
end;

{ Load system colors into the SysColor array }
procedure TMainForm.initSysColorArray;
var
  I: Integer;
begin
  for I := 0 to maxColors - 1 do with SysColorArray[I] do
  begin
    OriginalColor := GetSysColor(I);
    CurrentColor := OriginalColor;
    Shapes[I].Brush.Color := OriginalColor;
  end;
end;

{ Change system colors to values in SysColorArray }
procedure TMainForm.ChangeSystemColors;
var
  I: Integer;
  InxArray: Array[0 .. maxColors - 1] of Integer;
  ClrArray: Array[0 .. maxColors - 1] of TColor;
begin
  for I := 0 to maxColors -1 do
  begin
    InxArray[I] := I;
    ClrArray[I] := SysColorArray[I].CurrentColor;
  end;
  SetSysColors(maxColors, InxArray[0], ClrArray[0]);
end;
```

The SysColorRec data type declares a record of two TColor values. OriginalColor is the color value obtained from Windows at startup. CurrentColor is the color value shown in a labeled color rectangle. The SysColorArray holds 19 SysColorRec records, one for each Windows system color.

Procedure UpdateColor calls the Windows RGB function to combine the three ScrollBar Position properties into a TColor-compatible LongInt 32-bit integer. Assigning this value to the ColorEdit object's Color property updates the large color sample below the scroll bars.

If the user has selected a labeled color (CurrentShape is not equal to nil), UpdateColor also assigns the new color to the CurrentShape's Brush.Color subproperty, and saves the color in the SysColorArray. Notice that the Shape's Tag equals its index in SysColorArray.

Procedure InitSysColorArray shows how to obtain the current color settings from Windows. A *for* loop calls the API GetSysColor function with an argument *I* equal to the color's index. The loop saves each color in SysColorArray, and displays it by updating the Shape's Brush.Color subproperty. This is a good example of how useful object-reference arrays such as Shapes can be.

Procedure ChangeSystemColors transfers the 19 color values to Windows by calling the API function SetSysColors. This function requires three arguments: the number of colors, an array of color-index integers, and an array of the 32-bit color values. The statement that calls SetSysColors passes the addresses of the two arrays, InxArray and ClrArray, by indexing their first elements.

Look up SetSysColors in Delphi's online API reference. The two arrays are declared as untyped *var* parameters. To give an array's address to such a parameter, pass its first element, as procedure ChangeSystemColors demonstrates.

Using SysColor's form-maintenance event handlers

Listing 11-10 shows three form-maintenance event handlers, which are responsible for initializing SysColor's objects and for performing clean-up chores when the program ends. Explanations follow the listing.

Procedure FormCreate handles the form's OnCreate event. The procedure initializes variables and calls methods to bring the display to life. The first *for* loop shows a useful technique for setting up an object-reference array. Let's look at it closely:

```
for I := 0 to maxColors -1 do
  Shapes[I] :=
    TShape(FindComponent('Shape' + IntToStr(I + 1)));
```

Listing 11-10: **SysColor\Main.pas (form-maintenance event handlers)**

```
{ Initialize TObject control arrays }
procedure TMainForm.FormCreate(Sender: TObject);
var
  I: Integer;
begin
{ Construct IniFile object instance }
  IniFile := TIniFile.Create(iniFileName);
{ Miscellaneous initializations }
  CurrentShape := nil;  { No selected labeled color shape }
{ Assign object references to easy-access arrays }
  EditControls[0] := RedEdit;
  EditControls[1] := GreenEdit;
  EditControls[2] := BlueEdit;
  ScrollBars[0] := RedSB;
  ScrollBars[1] := GreenSB;
  ScrollBars[2] := BlueSB;
{ Assign Shape color box object references to Shapes array }
  for I := 0 to maxColors -1 do
    Shapes[I] :=
      TShape(FindComponent('Shape' + IntToStr(I + 1)));
{ Create item list from Labels for Ini file read/write }
  IniItemList := TStringList.Create;
  with IniItemList do
  for I := 0 to maxColors -1 do
    Add(TLabel(FindComponent(
      'Label' + IntToStr(I + 1))).Caption);
{ Load current colors and possible Ini file settings }
  InitSysColorArray;  { Initialize SysColor array }
  LoadSettings;       { Load SysColor.ini settings if present }
end;

{ Save settings if SaveCheckBox selected }
procedure TMainForm.FormClose(Sender: TObject;
  var Action: TCloseAction);
begin
  if SaveCheckBox.Checked then
    SaveSettings;  { Save settings in SysColor.ini }
end;

{ Last chance to clean up }
procedure TMainForm.FormDestroy(Sender: TObject);
begin
  IniItemList.Free;
  IniFile.Free;
end;
```

The goal is to assign to Shapes a reference to each of the Shape objects, each representing one labeled color rectangle in the window. Function FindComponent returns a reference to the object of the name passed as a string. To refer to Shape1, Shape2, . . ., Shape19, the program uses IntToString to convert the *for* loop's control variable plus one to a string, which is attached to Shape. To complete the assignment, the program casts FindComponent's return value to a TShape object. You can find many uses for FindComponent, especially when building arrays of object references such as Shapes.

A similar *for* loop in the same procedure creates the list of identifiers for the SysColor.ini file. After creating IniItemList, a TStringList object, the loop inserts the program's Labels as the .ini file's settings. Here again, FindComponent returns the object references to Label1, Label2, . . ., Label19. The program casts the function's return value to a TLabel object and inserts into IniItemList that object's Caption field. Finally, FormCreate calls InitSysColorArray to obtain the current Windows color settings. After this, LoadSettings reads SysColor.ini, if it exists.

Procedure FormClose handles the form's OnClose event. The procedure calls SaveSettings to update or create SysColor.ini if you enabled the Save settings on exit CheckBox. Procedure FormDestroy handles the OnDestroy event. This is the last chance the program has to clean up before going to that big bit bucket in the sky. Typically, as demonstrated here, this event is a good opportunity to free memory allocated to objects. In this case, the program frees the IniItemList string list object that the form's OnCreate event handler created.

Handling events for ScrollBar, Edit, and Shape objects

Listing 11-11 shows how SysColor handles events for ScrollBar, Edit, and Shape objects. Together, these procedures select and change the window's color rectangles. Explanations follow the listing.

Listing 11-11: **SysColor\Main.pas (Scrollbar, Edit, and Shape event handlers)**

```
{ Set scrollbar positions to match color C }
procedure TMainForm.SetScrollBars(C: TColor);
begin
{ The following assignments also update Edit boxes }
  RedSB.Position   := C and redMask;
  GreenSB.Position := (C and greenMask) shr 8;
  BlueSB.Position  := (C and blueMask) shr 16;
end;

{ Update values in Edit boxes for ScrollBar changes }
```

```
procedure TMainForm.SBChange(Sender: TObject);
begin
  with Sender as TScrollBar do
    EditControls[Tag].Text := IntToStr(Position);
  UpdateColor;
end;

{ Update scrollbar positions for Edit box changes }
procedure TMainForm.EditChange(Sender: TObject);
begin
  with Sender as TEdit do
    ScrollBars[Tag].Position := StrToInt(Text);
end;

{ Select color shape on mouse down event }
procedure TMainForm.ShapeMouseDown(Sender: TObject;
  Button: TMouseButton; Shift: TShiftState; X, Y: Integer);
var
  P: TLabel;    { Pointer to matching TLabel object }
begin
  CurrentShape := TShape(Sender);   { Save clicked Shape }
  P := TLabel(FindComponent(
    'Label' + IntToStr(CurrentShape.Tag)));
  if P <> nil then
    ColorLabel.Caption := P.Caption;   { Show color name }
  SetScrollBars(CurrentShape.Brush.Color); {Synch scroll bars}
end;
```

Procedure SetScrollBars updates the three ScrollBar Position properties to match the red, green, and blue subvalues in TColor parameter *C*. Assigning values to Position moves the ScrollBar's thumb box (also called a scroll box) to a relative position within the control's range. Three logical *and* expressions use the redMask, greenMask, and blueMask constants to isolate subvalues in color *C*. The *shr* (shift right) operators move the isolated values to the least significant positions in the resulting integers, which are assigned to Position.

Chapter 10 explains how procedures SBChange and EditChange handle OnChange events for the ScrollBar and Edit objects. The objects' Tag values equal their indexed positions in the object-reference arrays EditControls and ScrollBars. With these arrays, the Scrollbar and Edit controls can share the same event handlers and cooperate, so that if you enter a value into an Edit window, the ScrollBar's thumb box follows along. Likewise, moving the thumb box updates the Edit window's value.

Procedure ShapeMouseDown handles clicking of a labeled color rectangle. Because Shape components are not selectable Windows controls, they don't have OnClick events. However, you can recognize mouse clicks for these and other nonwindow objects by creating an OnMouseDown event handler such as ShapeMouseDown.

The procedure first assigns to CurrentShape a reference to the selected Shape, passed to the procedure in parameter Sender. The program next calls FindComponent to locate Labeln, where *n* equals the Shape's Tag value. Using Tags with FindComponent this way is an efficient means for forming relationships among objects and for taking advantage of Delphi's naming conventions. Normally, you should name objects according to their purposes, but in this case, it's easier to work with the 38 Labels and Shapes using their default names, Label1, Label2, . . ., Label 19, Shape1, Shape2, . . ., Shape 19.

Creating, reading, and updating the SysColor.ini file

The final SysColor code fragment in Listing 11-12 shows how the program creates, reads, and updates the SysColor.ini file. Explanations follow the listing.

Procedure LoadSettings reads SysColor.ini, if the file exists. Studying this code line by line provides insights you can use in your own initialization-file-handling routines. For holding the file's settings, LoadSettings creates a TStringList object, IniValueList. The program then calls ReadSectionValues for the IniFile object. The 'SysColor' argument indicates the section in the .ini file to read, in this case, section [SysColor]. Each element in the resulting IniValueList object is a string in the form:

```
Identifier=Value
```

Listing 11-12: **SysColor\Main.pas (SysColor.ini file procedures)**

```
{ Load colors and options from SysColor.ini if present }
procedure TMainForm.LoadSettings;
var
  IniValueList: TStringList;
  I: Integer;
begin
  IniValueList := TStringList.Create;
  try
  { [SysColor] settings }
    IniFile.ReadSectionValues('SysColor', IniValueList);
    for I := 0 to IniValueList.Count - 1 do
    with SysColorArray[I] do
    begin
      CurrentColor := StrToInt(
        IniValueList.Values[IniItemList[I]]);
```

```
      OriginalColor := CurrentColor;
    end;
  { [Options] settings }
    SaveCheckBox.Checked :=
      IniFile.ReadBool('Options', 'Save settings', False);
  finally
    IniValueList.Free;
  end;
  ChangeSystemColors;
  InitSysColorArray;
end;

{ Create or update SysColor.ini color settings only }
procedure TMainForm.SaveSettings;
var
I: Integer;
begin
{ [SysColor] settings }
  for I := 0 to IniItemList.Count - 1 do
    IniFile.WriteString('SysColor', IniItemList[I],
      IntToStr(SysColorArray[I].CurrentColor));
end;

{ Write check box setting to SysColor.ini }
procedure TMainForm.SaveCheckBoxClick(Sender: TObject);
begin
  IniFile.WriteBool('Options', 'Save settings',
    SaveCheckBox.Checked);
end;
```

To obtain the Value portion of each setting, use the Values array in the IniValueList string-list object. LoadSettings uses this technique to assign color values to the SysColorarray. Examine this assignment carefully:

```
CurrentColor := StrToInt(
  IniValueList.Values[IniItemList[I]]);
```

The expression IniItemList[I] refers to one of the identifier labels created back in the form's OnCreate event handler (see procedure FormCreate and the statements starting from with IniItemList...). These strings represent the Identifier portion of the setting Identifier=Value. Use the Identifier string as an index in the Values array to obtain that setting's Value. This is also a string, so to assign it to CurrentColor, the program calls StrToInt.

LoadSettings uses another .ini file technique to read the Save settings on exit CheckBox. Call ReadBool for the IniFile object, passing the section header ('Options'), the setting identifier ('Save settings'), and a default value. If the setting exists, ReadBool returns it. If not, it returns the default value, assigned here to SaveCheckBox's Checked property. Call the similar ReadInteger and ReadString functions to read integer and string values.

After loading the .ini file's settings, LoadSetting frees the IniValueList object. The procedure calls ChangeSystemColors to transfer the loaded colors to Windows. The final call to InitSysColorArray reinitializes the array by obtaining those saved colors back from Windows. This ensures that the values in the array are the ones actually used — they may differ in some cases due to the way Windows selects closely matching colors depending on the display driver's capabilities.

Procedure SaveSettings is simpler than LoadSettings. A *for* loop calls the IniFile's WriteString method to write the current color settings. To WriteString, pass the .ini file's section header ('SysColor'), the Identifier portion of each setting (InitItemList[I]), and a string representing the Value portion. Here, IntToStr converts the CurrentColor value from the SysColorArray. When done writing all colors, SaveSettings frees the IniFile object.

Notice that SaveSettings does not save the SaveCheckBox's Checked property. When I tried to do exactly that in an earlier version, I realized that saving this CheckBox created a catch-22 situation. You could check the box, which saved it to the .ini file, but if you unchecked it, the file was not updated, causing the box to be set again from the old file the next time SysColor started.

The solution is to update SaveCheckBox's value every time the CheckBox changes. Procedure SaveCheckBoxClick handles this task for the control's OnClick event. The procedure calls WriteBool to save the current setting (which has already changed by the time the OnClick event handler is called). This points out a good rule of thumb in using .ini files for saving program options — you may need to update individual elements if their values affect whether the .ini file is updated.

Examining a sample SysColor.ini file

Listing 11-13 shows a sample SysColor.ini file. Refer to this listing while you investigate SysColor's.ini file-handling routines.

The rest of SysColor's listing, which you can find on the CD-ROM in the Source\SysColor directory, provides event handlers for the window's buttons and CheckBox. These handlers, which have obvious purposes, merely call other procedures in the program, so I won't list or discuss them here. I added comments to the listing, however, in case you want to investigate the program further.

Listing 11-13: **Sample SysColor.ini file**

```
[SysColor]
Scroll Bar=12632256
Background=4210688
Active caption=8755968
Inactive caption=8421440
Menu=12632256
Window=16777215
Window frame=0
Menu text=0
Window text=0
Caption text=16777215
Active border=4227072
Inactive border=8421440
App work space=12632256
Highlight=32768
Highlight text=16777215
Button face=12632256
Button shadow=8421504
Gray text=8421504
Button text=0

[Options]
Save settings=0
```

Expert-User Tips

✦ If you store .ini files in specific paths, be sure to give users the option of selecting an alternate location. In most cases, it's best to store .ini files in the Windows directory, but this is not a requirement. To store .ini files in the program's installed directory, use function ParamStr(0) to obtain the application's path.

✦ Call DiskFree to determine the amount of available disk space, which you might want to add to this chapter's file-selection dialog. Examine other file and directory functions by searching Delphi's online help for "File-management routines."

✦ Don't go hog-wild with this chapter's message-handling techniques. Before writing a message handler for an application or form, thoroughly investigate whether the capability you need already exists as an event handler.

✦ In C, a statement may assign signed values such as -1 to unsigned WORD parameters. Pascal type-checking rules do not permit this practice, but the work-around is easy. For example, to pass -1 to a Windows API function WORD parameter, use the hexadecimal equivalent constant $FFFF.

✦ Always remember to free the objects you create. When creating global dynamic objects such as TStringLists, create them in the form's OnCreate event handler. Call Free for each created object in the form's OnDestroy handler.

✦ Don't write initializations to system.ini or win.ini, which are obsolete and are largely replaced by the Windows registry.

 Projects to Try

11-1: Write a general-purpose .ini file editor.

11-2: Add a section to the SysColor.ini file that saves the program's window position. Running SysColor should move the window back to its last-known position.

11-3: Write your own wildcard filter editor, similar to Delphi's, and add it to this chapter's customizable directory dialog. Write the user's filters to an initialization (.ini) file.

11-4: Write a file utility that can change file attributes such as the Archive and ReadOnly settings. Use the FileGetAttr and FileSetAttr functions in Delphi's file-management routines (search for them online).

11-5: Advanced — This chapter introduces many of the techniques needed to create a custom file Explorer utility. There's always a good market for programs of this nature that enhance standard Windows tools. As an advanced project, consider writing your own replacement for the Windows Explorer utility. You could, for example, add a feature that keeps multiple disk drives open — something that the stock Explorer cannot do.

11-6: Advanced — SysColor updates all Windows system colors, even if the color values haven't changed. This results in lots of messages whizzing among application event buffers. Write a more efficient version that updates only the minimum number of colors when users click the Set button.

Summary

✦ Use the file and directory components described in this chapter only when you need a custom file-selection dialog. The next chapter explains how to use Delphi's OpenDialog and SaveDialog components, which are usually more than adequate for file and directory interface objects.

✦ Use the DirectoryListBox, DriveComboBox, FileListBox, and FilterComboBox components to construct custom file-selection dialogs. By associating these objects, you enable them to work together so that, for example, when users change directories in a DirectoryListBox, the associated FileListBox automatically updates its contents.

✦ Add ShellAPI to a module's *uses* directive, and call ShellExecute to run programs or load registered files. For example, you can display a text file in the Windows Notepad utility simply by opening a .txt file with ShellExecute.

✦ Delphi components do not recognize drag-and-drop filenames, but you can easily add this capability by writing a procedure that responds to the wm_DropFiles message. To enable drag-and-drop files, call DragAcceptFiles in the form's OnCreate event handler.

✦ When you minimize an application, its main form is hidden. For this reason, implementing drag-and-drop files for a program minimized as an icon requires the Application object to respond to the wm_DropFiles message. To program a response for that or for any other Windows message, assign a message handler to the Application's OnMessage property. You must perform this assignment at run time.

✦ Initialization files store options, settings, and other values. Use the TIniFile class to construct an object for which you can call methods such as ReadSectionValues, ReadBool, and WriteString to read and write .ini file settings.

✦ This chapter's SysColor utility demonstrates practical .ini file-handling methods. The program also illustrates numerous application interface techniques and Pascal programming concepts.

The next chapter covers Delphi's dialog components, and reveals tips for writing your own modal and modeless dialog windows.

✦   ✦   ✦

Communicating with Dialog Boxes

In This Chapter

Components

Dialog modes

Common dialogs

Paged dialogs

Searching with dialogs

Page controls

Constraining window size

Creating docking controls

In Windows, a *dialog box* is technically a window of a particular style that lacks minimize and maximize buttons, and usually contains check boxes, radio buttons, and other interactive controls. In Delphi, however, any form can have dialog box characteristics, and the dividing lines between an application's dialogs and its other windows blur in the light of the modern graphical user interface.

You might think of a dialog box, as I mean it here, as a program's voice and ears. It gives users a way to select options and enter input. It can post messages, ask questions, and receive responses. In this chapter, you learn about Delphi's common-dialog components, as well as the TabControl, PageControl, and TabSheet components, which make it easy to create dialogs and other windows with page-tab controls like the VCL palette page tabs in Delphi, and multipage dialog boxes. I also explain in this chapter two new programming techniques in Delphi 4 — how to create docking windows, and how to add constraints on window sizes.

For reference and completeness, this chapter also explains how to use the older Win 3.1 Notebook, TabbedNotebook, and TabSet components. New applications should use TabControl, PageControl, and TabSheet, but you need information on these older components if your application must run under Windows 3.1 or if you are upgrading older software to use the newer components.

Components

Following is a list of Delphi's common-dialog components:

✦ **ColorDialog** — This component encapsulates the Windows common color dialog. Use it for a general-purpose color-selection tool. Palette: Dialogs.

✦ **FindDialog** — This component encapsulates the Windows common find dialog. Use it to perform data searches. Palette: Dialogs.

✦ **FontDialog** — This component encapsulates the Windows font-selection dialog. Use it to permit users to choose text fonts, and to set the foreground color for displayed text. Palette: Dialogs.

✦ **Notebook** — This component provides a multipage container that you can use with a TabSet object to provide tabbed toolbars and other interactive control sets. Palette: Win3.1.

✦ **OpenDialog** — This component encapsulates the Windows common file-open dialog. Use it to select files and browse directories, typically in response to a File | Open command. Palette: Dialogs.

✦ **PageControl** — With this component, you can create page-tab windows with very little programming required. Each page in a PageControl is a separate TabSheet object. Onto these objects, you simply drop other controls such as buttons, check boxes, radio buttons — anything you like. Users can click the PageControl's page tabs to select among its pages and access the control on each page. It's a great way to pack a lot of controls into a small space — for example, in a program with extensive options. Palette: Win32.

✦ **ReplaceDialog** — This component encapsulates the Windows common replace dialog. Use it to perform search-and-replace operations. Palette: Dialogs.

✦ **SaveDialog** — This component encapsulates the Windows common file-save dialog. Use it to enter or select filenames, and to browse directories, typically in response to a File | Save as command. Palette: Dialogs.

✦ **TabbedNotebook** — This component provides a multipage panel-like object that resembles a stack of file folders with labeled tabs on the top edge. Users can select TabbedNotebook pages by clicking tab labels, which makes this component especially suitable for complex options dialogs with too many controls to fit comfortably in a single window. Palette: Win3.1.

✦ **TabControl** — Similar to a PageControl, a TabControl object creates multipaged dialogs. However, a TabControl is a single component object — its "pages" are mere illusions, which you are responsible for controlling at run time. You might use a TabControl with a set of other controls that have different contents — a series of edit fields, for example — depending on the page-tab selected. This differs from a PageControl in which each page is a separate TabSheet object that can hold its own unique set of buttons and other controls. Palette: Win32.

✦ **TabSet** — This component provides a toolbar of selectable tabs, which you can use in conjunction with other components to provide them with a page-turning capability. This chapter's TabEdit application demonstrates how to use a TabSet object to create a multipage text editor. Palette: Win3.1.

✦ **TabSheet** — A PageControl stores one or more TabSheet objects, which hold the controls that appear on each page of a multipage dialog or window. To create a TabSheet, right-click inside a PageControl object and select the New Page command from the pop-up menu. Palette: None.

Dialog Modes

Applications use dialogs in one of two ways: as modal windows that retain the input focus until closing, or as modeless windows that permit users to switch away from them. For example, an options dialog is typically a modal window that users must close before continuing to use the application. However, a search-and-replace dialog is typically modeless so that users can start a search, switch to an edit window, and then continue searching.

Modal dialogs

Call a form's ShowModal method to display a modal dialog. Users must close the dialog window before the program continues. For example, if MyDialog is a form, a menu command or button OnClick event handler might bring up the dialog window with the statement:

```
MyDialog.ShowModal;
```

Usually, the dialog's Close, Cancel, or other form-closing buttons assign a value to ModalResult, which ShowModal returns. To determine whether users clicked the dialog's OK button, use a statement such as the following to examine ShowModal's return value:

```
if MyDialog.ShowModal = mrOk then
{ ... take action if user clicked OK button }
```

In the dialog modules, assign to ModalResult the value you want ShowModal to return. Either set the button's ModalResult property to mrOk (standard Button and BitBtn components do this for you automatically), or in the form's OK button OnClick event handler, use a statement such as:

```
ModalResult := mrOk;
```

The value assigned to ModalResult must be nonzero so that ShowModal returns.

Returning Other Types of Objects from a Modal Dialog

ShowModal returns an integer value. To return other types of objects from a modal dialog, add a function to the form's class to return the data you need. For example, declare a String function in the form class's public section:

```
TYourForm = class(TForm)
...
public
  function GetStringResult: String;
end;
```

Implement the function to return the result of the dialog such as an Edit control's Text property:

```
function TYourForm.GetStringResult: String;
begin
  with Edit1 do
  if Length(Text) = 0 then
    Result := 'Default string'
  else
    Result := Text;
end;
```

Call ShowModal to display the dialog form window and then call the "get result" function immediately after:

```
if YourForm.ShowModal = mrOk then
  S := YourForm.GetStringResult;
```

Modeless dialogs

As Windows defines it, a modeless dialog is a child window that doesn't capture the input focus, and that permits users to run the application normally while the dialog box is on display. In Delphi, however, a modeless dialog is simply any form window that the program selectively makes visible. To display a form as a modeless dialog, call the Show method:

```
MyDialog.Show;
```

Calling Show sets the form's Visible property to True and calls BringToFront to display the dialog box on top of other potentially obscuring windows. To hide the dialog window, set Visible to False:

```
MyDialog.Visible := False;
```

To determine whether a modeless dialog is active, inspect its Visible property.

Common Dialogs

Four common dialog components—FontDialog, ColorDialog, OpenDialog, and SaveDialog—provide font, color, and filename selection windows. The TabEdit application on the CD-ROM demonstrates how to use these components. TabEdit's source code is too long to list in full here, so I present the listings in relatively small snippets. Of course, all of the program's source code is on the CD-ROM in the Source\TabEdit directory. Figure 12-1 shows TabEdit's display. Load TabEdit's project file into Delphi to inspect the entire program.

```
Tabbed Text Editor                         _ □ ×
File  Edit  Options  Help

unit About;

interface

uses WinTypes, WinProcs, Classes, Graphics, Forms, Control
   Buttons, ExtCtrls;

type
   TAboutForm = class(TForm)
      Panel1: TPanel;
      OKButton: TBitBtn;
      ProgramIcon: TImage;

About.pas  Main.pas  Test.txt  Test2.txt
```

Figure 12-1: TabEdit provides a multipage text editor, similar to Delphi's code editor.

Note TabEdit uses Win3.1 components to create its multiple pages, selected by clicking page tabs at the bottom of the window. Later in this chapter, I explain how to use the newer PageControl, TabSheet, and TabControl components to create multipage windows and dialogs.

Font and color dialogs

As Listing 12-1 shows, the FontDialog and ColorDialog components are effortless to use. Insert these objects into a form and call their Execute methods to display them as modal dialogs. If Execute returns True, the user clicked OK to close the dialog window, and you can copy or use the FontDialog's Font property or the ColorDialog's Color property to obtain the user's selection.

Listing 12-1: The FontDialog and ColorDialog components are easy to use.

```
procedure TMainForm.OptionsFontClick(Sender: TObject);
begin
  if FontDialog1.Execute then
    Memo1.Font := FontDialog1.Font;
end;

procedure TMainForm.OptionsBackgroundClick(Sender: TObject);
begin
  if ColorDialog1.Execute then
    Memo1.Color := ColorDialog1.Color;
end;
```

The ColorDialog component offers three options, which you can program using the Object Inspector or by assigning True or False to three properties at run time:

✦ **cdFullOpen** — When this option is False, a dialog provides a color selection grid from which users can pick colors. When cdfullOpen is True, the color dialog shows its full selection palette complete with red, green, blue, and other color-value controls. On relatively slow computers, it can take several seconds for Windows to construct the full dialog, so don't use this option if you know your application needs to run on slow systems. Users can still open the full dialog by clicking the Define custom colors button.

✦ **cdPreventFullOpen** — Set to True to prevent users from opening the full color-selection dialog (the Define custom colors button is permanently disabled). You might use this option to limit colors to a predefined set.

✦ **cdShowHelp** — Set to True to display a Help button. Set to False if your program doesn't implement online help. If your program has online help, set cdShowHelp to True and assign an appropriate value to the dialog's HelpContext property.

The FontDialog component offers many more options, some of which are obvious — fdTrueTypeOnly, for example, and fdFixedPitchOnly. Following are some tips about less obvious options:

✦ **fdAnsiOnly** — Set to True to display only fonts that implement the Windows character set. For example, when fdAnsiOnly is True, the font dialog does not list the WingDings symbol font.

✦ **fdEffects** — Set to False to disable strikeout, underline, and color options. You should always disable these features if your program doesn't use them. Unfortunately, however, it's not possible to enable and disable the three options selectively (a Windows limitation). This is an all-or-nothing option.

✦ **fdNoFaceSel** — Normally, the dialog displays the current font in the edit portion of the font-list combo box. Set fdNoFaceSel to True if you want the edit control to be blank when the dialog appears.

✦ **fdNoSimulations** — Set to True to prevent listing GDI-simulated fonts. This switch has no effect on screen fonts; only for printer device fonts.

✦ **fdNoSizeSel, fdNoStyleSel** — These switches determine whether size and style options are initially selected (highlighted). If you want users to select a new font, but you don't want to display the current font's characteristics, set these two options and fdNoFaceSel to True.

✦ **fdWysiwyg** — Set to True to list only fonts that are available to both the printer and the screen. When fdWysiwyg is False, users can select fonts that may not print as displayed. If the affected text appears only on screen and is never printed, set this option to False.

✦ **fdLimitSize** — Set to True only when also specifying MinFontSize and MaxFontSize property values to limit size choices to a specific range.

Note   FontDialog can also be used to select fonts specific to, or compatible with, a particular printer.

Open and Save dialogs

As a text editor, TabEdit is a useful program in its own right, but it also serves as a template for any file-handling program. The first step is to write two procedures — one to read a file from disk, and the other to create or write file data. I usually write these procedures separately, rather than code file input and output in menu-command event handlers. This makes the program's file procedures available to any routines that need them. Listing 12-2 shows TabEdit's LoadFile and SaveFile procedures.

LoadFile and SaveFile use Pascal exceptions to try statements that might fail. In case of errors, an *except* statement block displays a message dialog. Chapter 19 explains more about exception handling, but it's very easy to use. Just put all statements that might generate exceptions — for example, SaveToFile, in a *try* block. Insert the procedure's error response in the *except* block, and finish with an *end* keyword. The *on-do* portion of the *except* block traps specific exception objects (EReadError and EWriteError in this case). It's important to trap only the exceptions you want to handle, and to allow others to continue to Delphi's default exception handlers.

Listing 12-2: **TabEdit's file input and output procedures**

```
{ Read file from disk }
procedure TMainForm.LoadFile(const Path: String);
begin
  with Pages[TabSet1.TabIndex] do
  try
    Memo1.Lines.LoadFromFile(Path);
    Dirty := False;
    Page.Clear;
    SetFilename(Path);
  except on e: EReadError do
    MessageDlg('Error reading file', mtError, [mbOk], 0);
  end;
end;

{ Write current file to disk }
procedure TMainForm.SaveFile(Index: Integer);
begin
  with TabSet1, Pages[Index] do
  begin
    try
      Memo1.Lines.SaveToFile(Filename);
      Dirty := False;
    except on e:EWriteError do
      MessageDlg('Error writing file', mtError, [mbOk], 0);
    end;
  end;
end;
```

Listing 12-3 shows TabEdit's File-menu event handlers. The procedures use the OpenDialog and SaveDialog components, and call the procedures in Listing 12-2. Use this listing as a guide to adding Open, Save, and Save As commands to your own applications.

Listing 12-3: **TabEdit's File-menu event handlers**

```
{ File|Open command }
procedure TMainForm.FileOpenClick(Sender: TObject);
begin
  with Pages[TabSet1.TabIndex] do
  begin
    if Dirty then FileSaveClick(Sender);
    if {still} Dirty then Exit;  { File not saved }
    if FileOpenDialog.Execute then
```

```
            LoadFile(FileOpenDialog.Filename);
    end;
end;

{ File|Close command }
procedure TMainForm.FileCloseClick(Sender: TObject);
var
  W: Word;
begin
  with TabSet1, Pages[TabIndex] do
  begin
    if Dirty then
    begin
      W := MessageDlg(
        'Save changes to ' + Tabs[TabIndex] + '?',
      mtWarning, [mbYes, mbNo, mbCancel], 0);
      case W of
        mrYes: FileSaveClick(Sender);
        mrNo: Dirty := False;
        mrCancel: Exit;
      end;
    end;
    if {still} Dirty then Exit;   { File not saved }
    Page.Clear;
    Memo1.Clear;
    Filename := untitledName;
    Tabs[TabIndex] := Filename;
  end;
end;

{ File|Save command }
procedure TMainForm.FileSaveClick(Sender: TObject);
begin
  with TabSet1, Pages[TabIndex] do
  if Filename = untitledName then
    FileSaveAsClick(Sender)
  else
    SaveFile(TabIndex);
end;

{ File|Save As command }
procedure TMainForm.FileSaveAsClick(Sender: TObject);
begin
  with TabSet1, Pages[TabIndex] do
  if FileSaveDialog.Execute then
  begin
    SetFilename(FileSaveDialog.Filename);
    SaveFile(TabIndex);
  end;
end;
```

FileOpenClick saves the current file if Dirty is True, which indicates the user made changes to the file. After this chore, the procedure displays a FileOpenDialog by calling its Execute method. If the method returns True, then LoadFile attempts to read the dialog's selected Filename.

FileCloseClick prompts users to save any changes and closes the current file. FileSaveClick defaults to FileSaveAsClick if the current file is not named; otherwise, the procedure calls SaveFile to attempt to write the current file to disk. Neither of these procedures uses any dialog components.

FileSaveAsClick calls Execute for the FileSaveDialog object. If the method returns True, then the users selected a new filename (or gave permission to overwrite an existing file), and the program calls SaveFile to write the current file to disk. The SetFilename statement assigns the file's name to the page tab label.

Filters and multiple file types

In a program that opens different types of files, it's often best to limit the SaveDialog's filters to the same types of files as the one most recently opened. For example, if users open a text file, the SaveDialog might display only .txt files. If users open a bitmap, the SaveDialog would display .bmp files. This reminds users of the types of files they are opening and saving. If you instead program the same filters in both the OpenDialog and SaveDialog dialogs, users might imagine they can convert between file types simply by altering the extension (for example, by saving a .txt file as a .bmp file). Unless your application can perform such conversions, it's best not to imply that it can.

To reprogram the SaveDialog Filter, use the following statement after executing an OpenDialog object. When users next attempt to save the file, the SaveDialog displays only files with the same extension. For example, if you open a .bmp file, the resulting string assigned to the SaveDialog object's Filter property is Files *.bmp|(*.bmp):

```
SaveDialog1.Filter :=
  'Files (*'
  + ExtractFileExt(OpenDialog1.FileName)
  + ')|*'
  + ExtractFileExt(OpenDialog1.FileName);
```

Tip

Using the Format function and repeating arguments in square brackets, the preceding can be shortened by eliminating the duplicate call to ExtractFileExt. For example, this statement is equivalent to the preceding code:

```
SaveDialog1.Filter := Format(
  'Files (*.%s)|*.%0:s',
  [ExtractFileExt(OpenDialog1.Filename)]);
```

Creating a history list

OpenDialog and SaveDialog components have a TStrings proptery, HistoryList, that you can use to save recently selected filenames. This creates a history of filenames from which users can select the files they worked with earlier. You might even save the history list in a disk file for restoring the next time the application is started.

Creating a history list requires three steps:

1. Insert an OpenDialog or SaveDialog component object into a form.

2. Change the OpenDialog or SaveDialog FileEditStyle property to fsComboBox.

3. Add selected filenames to the OpenDialog or SaveDialog HistoryList property.

To complete Step 3, in the OnClick command or button event handler that opens or saves a file, execute the dialog and add a selected filename to the history list with code such as this:

```
with OpenDialog1 do
if Execute then
begin
  { Open file here }
  FileName := Lowercase(FileName);
  HistoryList.Add(FileName);
end;
```

You can do the same with a SaveDialog object. When the user next opens the dialog, the most recently selected files appear in the combobox edit window. (Try the preceding code in a button's OnClick event handler to see the effect. Be sure to set the dialog's FileEditStyle property to fsComboBox, or the history list does not appear.)

To limit the number of filenames in the HistoryList, declare a constant in the module:

```
const
  maxHistoryList = 6;
```

Then, use the following programming to insert filenames into the HistoryList. The most recently selected files appear at the top of the list; older files scroll off the bottom when the list reaches its maximum size:

```
with OpenDialog1 do
if Execute then
begin
  { Open file here }
  FileName := Lowercase(FileName);
```

```
with HistoryList do
begin
  if Count = maxHistoryList then
    Delete(Count - 1);
  HistoryList.Insert(0, FileName);
end;
end;
```

You might also want to include a command or option to erase the history list. To do that, use statements such as these:

```
OpenDialog1.HistoryList.Clear;
SaveDialog1.HistoryList.Clear;
```

Paged Dialogs

Even with today's high-resolution monitors, available space on screen is as rare as an empty lot in Manhattan. To get some additional real estate for controls and other objects, you can create multipage windows and dialog boxes. This can also help organize controls into categories that users select by choosing labeled tabs. The following sections suggest ways to create multipage windows with the TabSet, Notebook, and TabbedNotebook components.

Note   The components discussed in this section are on the Win3.1 palette, and are available for 16- and 32-bit Windows programs. Newer programs should use the PageControl, TabSheet, and TabControl components discussed later in this chapter. The information on the Win3.1 components discussed here, however, is still valuable if you need to support Windows 3.1, or if you are upgrading an older application to use the newer controls.

TabSet

Figure 12-2 shows a TabSet object in a test window. To create the figure, I clicked the Tabs property's ellipsis, and entered seven labels, Tab1, Tab2, . . ., Tab7. However, because there's only enough room for six of the seven labels, the component displays horizontal arrow buttons that users can click to scroll the TabSet left and right.

Figure 12-2: TabSet displays horizontal arrow buttons so users can scroll the tabs left and right if there isn't enough room for all tabs.

The TabEdit application uses a TabSet object, aligned to the bottom of the window, to create the illusion of a multipage Memo object. Actually, the program has only one Memo. To store multiple files in memory, the program uses a global Pages array of TPageRec records. Each TPageRec record contains a TStringList object (Page). When you select a tab to turn the page, the program assigns the selected string list to the Memo object.

Listing 12-4 shows the program's TabSet event handlers. In most cases, you need to respond to only two events — one generated before a Tab change and one generated after. The two events give your program the opportunity to detach the current page when a tab is about to change and then attach a new page after the change. The meaning of a page depends entirely on your application — the TabSet component merely gives you a controlled means for creating the multipage illusion.

Listing 12-4: TabSet's two event handlers from the TabEdit application

```
{ A tab is changing. Save Memo's text in a TStringList object }
procedure TMainForm.TabSet1Change(Sender: TObject; NewTab:
Integer;
  var AllowChange: Boolean);
begin
  with TabSet1, Pages[TabIndex] do
  begin
    Page.Clear;
    Page.Assign(Memo1.Lines);
  end;
end;

{ A tab has changed. Assign a TStringList object to Memo }
procedure TMainForm.TabSet1Click(Sender: TObject);
begin
  with TabSet1 do
    Memo1.Lines.Assign(Pages[TabIndex].Page);
end;
```

Procedure TabSet1Change first clears the current TStringList Page object. Next, the procedure calls Assign for Page, passing the Memo's Lines property (an object of type TStrings). This saves the Memo object's current contents in Page before the TabSet changes.

After the change, the TabSet1Click method again calls Assign. This time, however, the assignment goes in the opposite direction — from the Page TStringList indexed by TabIndex to Memo1's Lines TStrings list. Now, the Memo object displays the new page of text associated with the selected tab.

Notebook

The Notebook component provides a multipage container that is most often used in conjunction with a TabSet object. For a practical demonstration of the technique, try the Palette application on the CD-ROM in the Source\Palette directory. With just two event handlers, the program creates a tabbed toolbar, similar to Delphi's VCL palette. Figure 12-3 shows Palette's display. Click a page tab to change to another page of SpeedButtons. Select any SpeedButton to show its caption in the large Label. Listing 12-5 shows the program's source code.

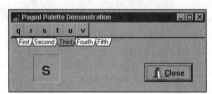

Figure 12-3: The Palette application demonstrates how to create a tabbed toolbar, similar to Delphi's VCL palette.

To conserve space in this chapter, I deleted most of the 36 SpeedButton object declarations from the TMainForm class.

Listing 12-5: **Palette\Main.pas**

```
unit Main;

interface

uses
  SysUtils, Windows, Messages, Classes, Graphics,
  Controls, Forms, Dialogs, Buttons, ExtCtrls, Tabs, StdCtrls;

type
  TMainForm = class(TForm)
    TabSet1: TTabSet;
    Notebook1: TNotebook;
    SpeedButton1: TSpeedButton;
```

```
    SpeedButton2: TSpeedButton;
{ ... }
    SpeedButton36: TSpeedButton;
    BitBtn1: TBitBtn;
    Label1: TLabel;
    Bevel1: TBevel;
    procedure TabSet1Click(Sender: TObject);
    procedure SpeedButton1Click(Sender: TObject);
  private
    { Private declarations }
  public
    { Public declarations }
  end;

var
  MainForm: TMainForm;

implementation

{$R *.DFM}

procedure TMainForm.TabSet1Click(Sender: TObject);
begin
  with TabSet1 do
  NoteBook1.ActivePage := Tabs[TabIndex];
end;

procedure TMainForm.SpeedButton1Click(Sender: TObject);
begin
  with Sender as TSpeedButton do
    Label1.Caption := Caption;
end;

end.
```

Follow these steps to recreate the Palette program and construct a tabbed toolbar using the Notebook component:

1. Insert a Notebook component into a form, and set its Align property to alTop. Change the Notebook's Height to 25.

2. Insert a TabSet component into the form. Set its Align property to alTop. This places the TabSet object directly beneath the Notebook.

3. Select TabSet1's Tabs property, and click the ellipsis button to run Delphi's String list editor. Enter labels for the toolbar's tabs, one label per line. (To recreate the example program, enter First, Second, Third, Fourth, and Fifth.)

4. Select Notebook1's Pages property, and click the ellipsis button to open Delphi's Notebook editor. Click the Edit button to modify the default page name to First. Then, click the Add button to add pages for the remaining tab labels. When associating a Notebook with a TabSet using the technique described here, each Notebook page should have a matching TabSet label.

5. The Notebook's ActivePage property equals the string name of the pages you entered in the preceding step. Change ActivePage to First. Insert SpeedButton objects into Notebook1 (click the mouse inside the Notebook1 object, and then drag each SpeedButton to its final position).

6. Repeat Step 5 for the other Notebook pages. Change ActivePage to Second, Third, . . . Fifth, and insert a few SpeedButtons into each page. You can label your SpeedButtons as I did in the demonstration, or assign them glyph bitmaps. Insert a Label object and select a large font size to show the selected button's caption.

7. When you are done preparing each Notebook page, set ActivePage to First and the TabSet's PageIndex property to zero. Create an OnClick event handler for all SpeedButton objects. Also, create an OnClick handler for TabSet1. Insert the statements in the listing. To turn the page on the toolbar, the TabSet1 handler assigns the tabbed label to Notebook1's ActivePage. The SpeedButton OnClick handler displays the selected button's caption.

 Tip To create a tabbed toolbar at the bottom of a window, reverse Steps 1 and 2 and set Align for both objects to alBottom.

TabbedNotebook

The primary difference between a TabbedNotebook and a pair of Notebook and TabSet objects is appearance. Use a TabbedNotebook to create multipage dialogs that look like file folders with selectable tabs along the top. Use the Notebook and TabSet components when you need more control over object positions, and when you want the flexibility of programming page-turning operations using separate components.

A TabbedNotebook is particularly useful for creating categorical options dialogs — for example, with printing options on one page, color setups on another, and general-purpose options on still another page. By dividing controls into categories, you can program an Options command that opens a single window, which users may find less confusing than multiple commands in an Options menu.

To use a TabbedNotebook object, insert it into a form. Usually, you want to set the object's Align property to alClient so the TabbedNotebook completely fills the window, but of course, that's up to you. Select the Pages property to create each labeled page using the same Notebook editor mentioned in the preceding section. On each page, insert the controls that you need (CheckBoxes, RadioButtons, and other objects).

At run time, you can display a specific page in two ways. Usually, you won't need to do that because users can select the pages they want. However, to display a page by number, assign a value to PageIndex. The first index is zero, so two represents the third page:

```
TabbedNotebook1.PageIndex := 2;   {Display page 3}
```

Or, to display a page by its labeled name, assign a string to ActivePage:

```
TabbedNotebook1.ActivePage := 'General options';
```

For a cleaner window in a complex options dialog with many pages, assign a value to TabsPerRow. For example, if your dialog has 12 pages, set TabsPerRow to 4 to stack folders in three rows of four. This seems to work, however, only in Delphi Versions 1 and 2. Versions 3 and 4 display only a single row of tabs (see the PageControl component in this chapter for a better way to create multipaged dialogs). This is because Delphi 3 abandoned the old 16-bit code for TTabbedNotebook, and replaced it with the Windows 32-bit Tabs control. This change updated the control's appearance, and also reduced its code-file size. As a consequence, however, the component can no longer specify the number of tabs per row and it is no longer possible to enable and disable individual tabs. The control is still capable of multiple tab rows — you just can't specify how many you want. These losses are extremely minor, and the tradeoffs in performance and memory savings are far greater than any disadvantages from these changes. (Thanks to Danny Thorpe for this information.)

Tip   Delphi automatically adjusts TabsPerRow so that all labels fit comfortably on their tabs. For this reason, you should assign a new value to TabsPerRow after creating all TabbedNotebook pages.

To change the default system font for tab labels, select a different font for the TabFont property. The Font property affects the font for control objects inserted into a TabbedNotebook. The two fonts may be different. For example, you can use italic text for tab labels and normal text for controls on the tabbed pages.

Component objects may belong to the form even when they appear to reside inside a TabbedNotebook. For example, insert a Close button into the form and drag it over the TabbedNotebook. The button appears on top of the notebook page, but it still belongs to the form. Because of its relationship to its parent object, the button remains visible for all notebook pages. This works even when the TabbedNotebook completely fills the form's client area.

After setting a TabbedNotebook's Align property to alClient, it is difficult to insert objects into the form, but here's an easy solution. Temporarily set Align to alNone. Select the Button or BitBtn (or other component you want to insert) in the VCL palette and then maximize the form window. Click the mouse pointer in the form background to insert your object, and drag the resulting button onto any TabbedNotebook page (it doesn't matter which one). Shrink the window back to normal size, and set the TabbedNotebook's Align property back to alClient. When you run the program, the button remains visible regardless of which page is active.

Or, hold down the Shift key when you click the form to drop the component. Shift-clicking drops the object into the parent of the target container (usually the form) rather than the container itself.

One common use for a TabbedNotebook is to hold Memo objects, one per page. Insert the Memos into the TabbedNotebook pages, and set the Memo Align properties to alClient. Because the TabbedNotebook owns the Memos, they fill the page but do not obscure the tabbed labels. This is a quick-and-dirty method for creating a multipage text editor, but you have to carefully program the module to perform operations on only the current page. For example, to copy text to the clipboard, inspect PageIndex to determine which Memo object to use:

```
case TabbedNotebook1.PageIndex of
  0: Memo1.CopyToClipboard;
  1: Memo2.CopyToClipboard;
  2: Memo3.CopyToClipboard;
end;
```

This works, but it is not the most elegant solution. Listing 12-6 shows a more general approach that works regardless of how many pages the TabbedNotebook object has. The program assigns to variable *P*, of type TComponent, the result of FindComponent, which searches for Memo objects using PageIndex to create the object names (Memo1, Memo2, . . ., Memo*N*). If the search succeeds, the program calls CopyToClipboard for the located Memo on the current page. You might use similar code in an Edit|Copy menu command or as a button's OnClick event handler.

Listing 12-6: **To copy selected Memo object text to the clipboard, use FindComponent to locate the Memo on the current TabbedNotebook page, and then call CopyToClipboard for that Memo.**

```
procedure TForm1.Copytoclipboard1Click(Sender: TObject);
var
  P: TComponent;
begin
  P := FindComponent('Memo' +
    IntToStr(TabbedNotebook1.PageIndex + 1));
  if P <> nil then
    TMemo(P).CopyToClipboard;
end;
```

Tip

Selecting a component with the Object Inspector's drop-down list automatically turns to the Notebook or TabbedNotebook page that contains the object.

Inserting pages at run time

On the CD-ROM

The AddPage application on the CD-ROM in the Source\AddPage directory shows how to add new pages to a TabbedNotebook object at run time. The program also demonstrates how to insert a control into a page—again, entirely under program control. Listing 12-7 shows the program's source code. Run AddPage and click the Add page button to insert new pages into the TabbedNotebook. Click Add control to insert a ListBox into the current page.

Listing 12-7: **AddPage\main.Pas**

```
unit Main;

interface

uses
    SysUtils, Windows,  Messages, Classes, Graphics,
    Controls, Forms, Dialogs, Buttons, StdCtrls, TabNotBk;

type
  TMainForm = class(TForm)
    TabbedNotebook1: TTabbedNotebook;
    AddPageButton: TButton;
    CloseBitBtn: TBitBtn;
    AddControlButton: TButton;
    procedure AddPageButtonClick(Sender: TObject);
    procedure AddControlButtonClick(Sender: TObject);
  private
    { Private declarations }
  public
    { Public declarations }
  end;

var
  MainForm: TMainForm;

implementation

{$R *.DFM}
```

(continued)

Listing 12-7 *(continued)*

```
{ Insert new page into TabbedNotebook }
procedure TMainForm.AddPageButtonClick(Sender: TObject);
begin
  with TabbedNotebook1 do
    Pages.Add(Format('Page %d',[Pages.Count-1]));
end;

{ Insert new control into current page }
procedure TMainForm.AddControlButtonClick(Sender: TObject);
var
  L: TListBox;
  P: TWinControl;
begin
  L := TListBox.Create(Self);
  with TabbedNotebook1 do
  begin
    P := Pages.Objects[PageIndex] as TWinControl;
    L.Parent := P;
    L.SetBounds(10, 10, 100, 100);
{ Insert page tab label into edit control for demonstration.
  You don't have to perform this step. }
    L.Items.Add(TTabPage(P).Caption);
  end;
end;

end.
```

Procedure AddPageButtonClick shows how to add a page to a TabbedNotebook object. Simply add a string to the Pages property. The procedure calls Format to create string labels such as Page 1, Page 2, . . ., Page *n*.

Procedure AddControlButtonClick shows how to add a new control object to the TabbedNotebook's current page. First, Create constructs the new control. Then, *P* is set to refer to the page, using the Objects array in the TabbedNotebook's Pages string list. The program assigns the page reference *P* as the control's parent, and then calls SetBounds to define the control's width, height, and position. (Other types of control objects require different kinds of initializations.) Finally, just to display something in the new control, the Add method adds the current page tab label to the newly inserted ListBox. You don't have to perform this final step.

Searching with Dialogs

Delphi's FindDialog and ReplaceDialog components are as easy to use as peanut butter. The sticky part, however, is writing find-and-replace code that works in conjunction with these modeless dialog boxes. After the following brief introductions, a sample application provides a shell that you can use for implementing Find and Replace commands.

Find dialog

The FindDialog component offers two methods and one event. To display the dialog window shown in Figure 12-4 and start a search, call the Execute method. Call CloseDialog to hide the dialog. To perform the actual search, write a handler for the OnFind event, generated when users click the Find Next button.

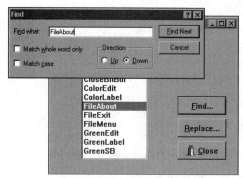

Figure 12-4: The FindDialog component displays this modeless dialog.

To obtain the text that users enter into the Find what edit control, use the FindDialog object's FindText property. You can also select various Options—for example, to hide or disable the Match case check box.

Find and replace dialog

As shown in Figure 12-5, the ReplaceDialog component is an expanded version of FindDialog, with a second edit control for entering replacement text. To FindDialog's members, ReplaceDialog adds another property, ReplaceText, which contains the text users enter into the Replace with edit window. Call Execute to display a ReplaceDialog object. Call CloseDialog to hide the dialog window.

ReplaceDialog recognizes two events. Create an OnFind event handler to search for text items. Create an OnReplace event handler to perform the actual replacement. Writing this code also requires a few tricks, as I explain in the next section.

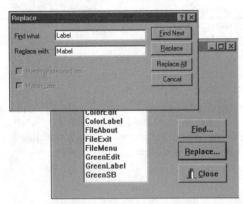

Figure 12-5: The ReplaceDialog component displays this modeless dialog.

Programming Find and Replace commands

Unfortunately, programming Find and Replace commands is a lot more difficult than inserting a couple of components into a form. To simplify the job, follow the plan outlined in the FindRepl application on the CD-ROM. Figure 12-6 shows the program's display. It lists some object names (cut from the SysColor utility) in a ListBox. Click the Find button to find items in the ListBox. Click Replace to replace items or partial items. Listing 12-8 shows how the program performs these operations.

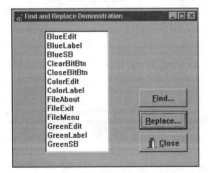

Figure 12-6: The FindRepl application outlines the programming needed for an application's Find and Replace commands.

Listing 12-8: FindRepl\Main.pas

```pascal
unit Main;

interface

uses
  SysUtils, Windows,  Messages, Classes, Graphics,
  Controls, Forms, Dialogs, StdCtrls, Buttons;

type
  TMainForm = class(TForm)
    ListBox1: TListBox;
    FindDialog: TFindDialog;
    FindBitBtn: TBitBtn;
    CloseBitBtn: TBitBtn;
    ReplaceBitBtn: TBitBtn;
    ReplaceDialog: TReplaceDialog;
    procedure FindBitBtnClick(Sender: TObject);
    procedure FindDialogFind(Sender: TObject);
    procedure ReplaceBitBtnClick(Sender: TObject);
    procedure ReplaceDialogFind(Sender: TObject);
    procedure ReplaceDialogReplace(Sender: TObject);
  private
    FindIndex, FoundPos, FoundLen: Integer;
    FoundItem: Boolean;
  public
  end;

var
  MainForm: TMainForm;

implementation

{$R *.DFM}

{ Begin a FindDialog operation }
procedure TMainForm.FindBitBtnClick(Sender: TObject);
begin
  FindDialog.Execute;
  FindIndex := 0;
  ListBox1.ItemIndex := -1;
end;

{ Continue a FindDialog operation }
procedure TMainForm.FindDialogFind(Sender: TObject);
var
```

(continued)

Listing 12-8 *(continued)*

```
    S: String;
begin
  while FindIndex < ListBox1.Items.Count do
  begin
    S := ListBox1.Items[FindIndex];
    Inc(FindIndex);
    if Pos(FindDialog.FindText, S) <> 0 then
    begin
      ListBox1.ItemIndex := FindIndex - 1;
      Exit;
    end;
  end;
  ShowMessage('No more matches!');
  FindDialog.CloseDialog;
end;

{ Start a ReplaceDialog operation }
procedure TMainForm.ReplaceBitBtnClick(Sender: TObject);
begin
  ReplaceDialog.Execute;
  FindIndex := 0;
  ListBox1.ItemIndex := - 1;
  FoundItem := False;
end;

{ Continue a ReplaceDialog operation }
procedure TMainForm.ReplaceDialogFind(Sender: TObject);
var
  S: String;
begin
  while FindIndex < ListBox1.Items.Count do
  begin
    S := ListBox1.Items[FindIndex];
    Inc(FindIndex);
    FoundPos := Pos(ReplaceDialog.FindText, S);
    if FoundPos <> 0 then
    begin
      ListBox1.ItemIndex := FindIndex - 1;
      FoundLen := Length(ReplaceDialog.FindText);
      FoundItem := True;
      Exit;
    end;
  end;
  ShowMessage('No more matches!');
  ReplaceDialog.CloseDialog;
end;
```

```
{ Perform replacement for a ReplaceDialog operation }
procedure TMainForm.ReplaceDialogReplace(Sender: TObject);
var
  S: String;
begin
  if frReplaceAll in ReplaceDialog.Options then
    ShowMessage('Replace All not implemented')
  else if not FoundItem then
    ShowMessage('Click Find to begin/continue search')
  else begin
    S := ListBox1.Items[FindIndex - 1];
    Delete(S, FoundPos, FoundLen);
    Insert(ReplaceDialog.ReplaceText, S, FoundPos);
    ListBox1.Items[FindIndex - 1] := S;
    FoundItem := False;
  end;
end;

end.
```

Programming a Find command is the easiest of the two tasks. First, insert an event handler for a command or button that begins a search. Call the FindDialog's Execute method and prepare global variables used to continue searching. For example, FindRepl starts a search with these statements:

```
FindDialog.Execute;
FindIndex := 0;
ListBox1.ItemIndex := -1;
```

The first line brings up the modeless dialog. The second line initializes a global variable used to indicate the ListBox line most recently searched. The last line sets ItemIndex in the ListBox object to –1 so that no lines are initially highlighted.

When you start searching by clicking the dialog's Find Next button, the FindDialogFind event handler performs the actual search using the global FindIndex to determine which ListBox item to examine. Function Pos examines whether the FindText property is found in the target string *S*, copied from the ListBox's Items. If Pos is nonzero, a match was found, and the assignment to ItemIndex highlights the matching item.

Notice the event handler exits after finding a match. This does not close the dialog — it merely returns control to the program so users can perform other actions. However, if the global FindIndex equals the count of items, the program calls ShowMessage to tell users the search is over. CloseDialog then hides the FindDialog window.

Writing the code for a replace command is more difficult. Start the search as for Find, but initialize any global variables you need for making replacements. (See ReplaceBitBtnClick in the listing.) You need a Boolean flag, such as FoundItem, to indicate that an item was found. Initialize this variable to False at the start of the search. Here's how the sample program responds to clicking the Replace button:

```
ReplaceDialog.Execute;
FindIndex := 0;
ListBox1.ItemIndex := -1;
FoundItem := False;
```

The first line calls Execute to display the modeless dialog box. The second line assigns zero to FindIndex, which represents the ListBox line being searched. The third line assigns –1 to the ListBox's ItemIndex property so that no lines are initially highlighted. The final line initializes the global Boolean flag, FoundItem, to False.

To finish the Replace command, you need two event handlers. The first (ReplaceDialogFind in the listing) is similar to the FindDialog's event handler. On finding a matching item, initialize global variables you need for performing a replacement. Set the FoundItem flag to True so that the second event handler can determine that it was called as the result of a matching search.

In that handler (see ReplaceDialogReplace), if FoundItem is True, the procedure executes its replacement statements. As the listing shows, you can also detect whether users clicked the Replace All button by testing whether constant frReplaceAll is in the dialog's Options set. Of course, the actual replacement code is unique to your program, but Delphi can't do everything (can it?).

Page Controls

Three relatively new components simplify the task of creating multipage dialogs and other windows. The three components are:

✦ **PageControl** — When you need to create a multipage dialog or window with separate sets of controls on each page, this component is probably the best choice.

✦ **TabSheet** — Each page in a PageControl dialog or window is a TabSheet component object. This component is not on the VCL palette — you create TabSheet objects by right-clicking inside a PageControl and selecting the New Page command from the resulting pop-up menu.

✦ **TabControl** — When you need a simpler, single-component, multipage dialog, use this Component instead of PageControl and TabSheet. The end results are visually similar, but the placement of objects on individual pages is your responsibility. TabControls are especially useful for creating multipage windows with the same controls on each page, but with different contents — a group of Edit boxes, for example, that change their text content depending on which page the user selects.

The following sections explain how to use each of these three components. The PageControl and TabControl components are located on the Win32 palette. TabSheet objects are created using the PageControl component as explained in the next section.

Figure 12-7 shows samples of PageControl and TabControl objects. The pages in a PageControl are objects of the TabSheet component. This figure is a screen shot of the PageTab demonstration, located in the Source\PageTab directory on the CD-ROM. Listing 12-9 shows the PageTab program's source code.

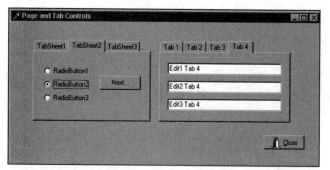

Figure 12-7: The PageTab demonstration program shows examples of the PageControl (left) and TabControl (right) components. Each page in the PageControl is a TabSheet object.

Listing 12-9: **PageTab\Main.pas**

```
unit Main;

interface

uses
  Windows, Messages, SysUtils, Classes, Graphics, Controls,
  Forms, Dialogs, StdCtrls, ComCtrls, Buttons;
```

(continued)

Listing 12-9 *(continued)*

```
type
  TMainForm = class(TForm)
    PageControl1: TPageControl;
    TabSheet1: TTabSheet;
    TabSheet2: TTabSheet;
    CheckBox1: TCheckBox;
    CheckBox2: TCheckBox;
    CheckBox3: TCheckBox;
    RadioButton1: TRadioButton;
    RadioButton2: TRadioButton;
    TabControl1: TTabControl;
    Edit1: TEdit;
    Edit2: TEdit;
    Edit3: TEdit;
    BitBtn1: TBitBtn;
    TabSheet3: TTabSheet;
    DateTimePicker1: TDateTimePicker;
    Button2: TButton;
    RadioButton3: TRadioButton;
    Button1: TButton;
    procedure TabControl1Change(Sender: TObject);
    procedure Button1Click(Sender: TObject);
    procedure Button2Click(Sender: TObject);
  private
    { Private declarations }
  public
    { Public declarations }
  end;

var
  MainForm: TMainForm;

implementation

{$R *.DFM}

procedure TMainForm.TabControl1Change(Sender: TObject);
var
  S: String;
begin
  S := IntToStr(TabControl1.TabIndex + 1);
  Edit1.Text := 'Edit1 Tab ' + S;
  Edit2.Text := 'Edit2 Tab ' + S;
  Edit3.Text := 'Edit3 Tab ' + S;
end;

procedure TMainForm.Button1Click(Sender: TObject);
```

```
begin
  PageControl1.ActivePage := TabSheet3;
end;

procedure TMainForm.Button2Click(Sender: TObject);
begin
  PageControl1.ActivePage := TabSheet1;
end;

end.
```

PageControl component

The PageControl component simplifies creating multipage dialogs with unique sets of controls on each page. To see an example of a PageControl object in action, load the PageTab.dpr project into Delphi from the Source\PageTab directory. The program displays PageControl (left) and TabControl (right) objects. Before running the program, notice that you can select the PageControl's tabs at design time, but that you cannot do this with the TabControl. This is because PageControl pages are TabSheet objects, and therefore, can be selected and modified using the Object Inspector. A TabControl, however, is a single object — its pages are mere illusions — and, therefore, you cannot select the individual tabs at design time.

Try the following steps to learn more about using the PageControl component:

1. Start a new application. Select the Win32 page tab on Delphi's VCL palette and click the PageControl component (second from the left). Click inside the form to deposit a PageControl object. The object initially looks like a blank panel.

2. To create pages in a PageControl, click the right mouse button inside the PageControl. Select New Page from the resulting pop-up menu. This creates a TabSheet object, adds that object to any others owned by this PageControl, and displays the page tab. Figure 12-8 shows the display after adding two pages.

3. Click the page tabs and notice that the Object Inspector window lists the properties for PageControl1. Click inside the PageControl window (below the page tabs) to select a page's TabSheet object. The Object Inspector then shows the TabSheet's properties.

4. To add a control to a PageControl page, select that page and then drop any control onto it. You can do this with just about any control, such as Buttons, CheckBoxes, Labels, StringGrids, and DateTimePickers. Although the controls reside on individual TabSheet pages, you access them as you do any other controls by referring to their names such as Button1 and CheckBox3. You do not have to use the PageControl object to access the controls it contains.

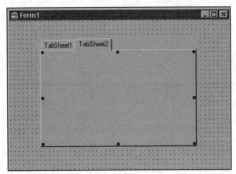

Figure 12-8: A PageControl component with two TabSheet objects

PageControl properties

The PageControl component provides several properties that you can use to customize the control in various ways. Using the sample PageControl from the preceding section (or you can just drop one into a blank form), try the following property settings:

✦ **ActivePage** — Set this to the name of the TabSheet object that you want to display as the initial active page. At run time, a *program* statement can also assign this value to change the active page under program control (see procedure Button2Click in Listing 12-9 for example).

✦ **DockSite** — Set to True to create a PageControl that can serve as a docking station, or dock site, for other controls. See "Creating Docking Controls" in this chapter for more information on creating docking sites, a new feature in Delphi 4.

✦ **Hint** — Enter text to display when the user rests the mouse cursor on the control for a moment or two. Use this property along with ShowHint to display the same hint text regardless of the active page. See the TabSheet Hint and ShowHint properties for more information.

✦ **HotTrack** — Set to True to provide visual feedback. When the user passes the mouse cursor over a page tab, its text dims briefly to show users they can click the mouse to select that tab.

✦ **MultiLine** — In complex PageControls with many pages, set this property to True to display the pages on two or more rows if they don't all fit on one row inside the defined window width. When this property is False, scroll arrows appear if there are too many pages than fit comfortably on one row — however, multiple rows are probably better in most cases.

✦ **MultiSelect** — This is an obscure property that works only when the tab style is set to tsButton or tsFlatButton. It appears to be a TabControl feature that has exposure in the page control, but selecting multiple pages doesn't seem to be an operation with much practical value. It isn't documented, and it doesn't seem to have much if any effect. Call this one a mystery.

✦ **OwnerDraw** — When this property is set to True, it is your responsibility to display text or graphics (or both) in each tab. To do this, create an OnDrawTab event handler and insert code to display text or bitmaps in the page tab area outlined by the procedure's Rect parameter. See "Creating owner draw PageControls" in this chapter for more information.

✦ **ScrollOpposite** — When a PageControl has numerous tabs, you can set ScrollOpposite to True or False to alter the way other tabs move out of the way when users select a particular tab. For example, in a PageControl with two rows of three tabs, if ScrollOpposite is True, selecting a tab in one row moves the other row to the bottom of the display (see Figure 12-9).

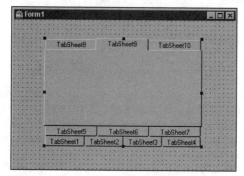

Figure 12-9: Setting the ScrollOpposite PageControl property to True causes multiple tabs to move to the opposite end of the control when users select a tab in another group.

✦ **ShowHint** — Set this property to True to display the text in the Hint property when the user rests the mouse cursor on the PageControl for a moment or two. To display different text depending on which page is active, set ShowHint to False and use the Hint and ShowHint properties in the TabSheet component (see the next two sections).

✦ **Style** — This property affects the way tabs are displayed (Figure 12-10 shows examples of each setting). Set to tsTabs for a control that looks like the page tabs on file folders; use tsButtons to display page tabs styled as Windows buttons; use tsFlatButtons to display page tabs without any borders, but sunken when selected. (Tip: When using the tsFlatButtons style, you probably should set HotTrack to True to display feedback in the form of raised buttons when the user passes the mouse cursor over the control's page tabs.)

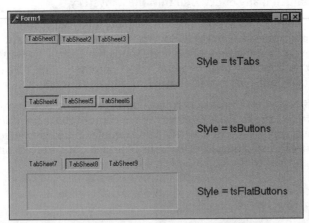

Figure 12-10: Use the PageControl's Style property to affect the way tabs are displayed.

✦ **TabPosition** — You can use this property to select whether to display page tabs at the top of the control (tpTop) or bottom (tpBottom). Page tabs are usually displayed at the top and many users expect to find them there. It's probably best not to change this property unless you have a good reason.

Tip

When a PageControl's Style property is set to tsButtons or tsFlatButtons, no border is shown around the control's individual pages. If you want a border, insert a Panel object into each page and then drop your controls onto the Panels. Or, save a window handle and use a Bevel object instead.

TabSheet component

Each page on a PageControl object is itself an object of the TTabSheet class. As I mentioned, the only way to create TabSheets is to right-click a PageControl and select the New Page command from the pop-up menu. To select a TabSheet object in a PageControl, click the page tab you want, and then click inside the control's body (below the page tabs if they are on top). You can then use the Object Inspector to make changes to individual TabSheet properties.

Tip

When setting properties for multiple TabSheets, it is difficult, but possible, to select them all at the same time. To do this, hold down the Shift key while clicking inside each page tab, then in each TabSheet (in the body of the control). After selecting the final TabSheet, while still holding down Shift, click any page tab to deselect the PageControl itself. You can then assign property values to all selected TabSheets—set the Cursor property to crCross for example.

TabSheet properties

The following are selected TabSheet properties that you might want to change when designing PageControl objects. To try these settings, drop a PageControl into a form, right-click inside the control, and select New Page to add one or more pages. Select the TabSheet page by clicking inside the body of the PageControl (below the page tabs), and then try out these property settings:

✦ **BorderWidth** — Set to a positive, nonzero value, to alter the width of the border around this TabSheet page.

✦ **Caption** — Type whatever text you want to appear in this page's tab. The tab width is automatically adjusted to accommodate the text. If the PageControl's OwnerDraw field is True, it is your responsibility to display the page tab's text.

✦ **Cursor** — Select one of the cursor shapes listed in this property's drop-down list. The cursor automatically changes when it passes over the page's body.

✦ **Hint** — Enter hint text to appear at the cursor position when it rests for a moment or two. Set ShowHint to True to display this Hint text.

✦ **PageIndex** — This field is automatically set to the index value of each TabSheet page. The first page index is zero, the next is one, and so on. If you change this value at design time, the other pages are adjusted accordingly, and the changed page is inserted into a new position. You might do this after creating a PageControl to alter the order of its individual pages, but in most cases, you won't need to enter values into this property.

Note

The online help incorrectly states that PageIndex is set to −1 when TabVisible is False. This is not so—the PageIndex value stays the same regardless of whether the TabSheet page is visible or not.

✦ **PopupMenu** — Add a PopupMenu object from the Standard palette to the form, and set this property to the object's name. Users can then right-click the mouse while pointing the cursor inside the TabSheet page to display a pop-up menu. All pages may use the same PopupMenu object, or each may have a different one. This technique is a great way to provide different sets of local commands depending on the active page.

✦ **ShowHint** — Set to True to display the text entered into the Hint property when the user rests the mouse cursor on this page for a moment or two. Use this and the Hint property to display a unique hint depending on the active page.

Tip

To display the same hint for all TabSheet pages, it is easier to set ShowHint to False, and ParentShowHint to True. Select the PageControl, enter your Hint text, and set that control's ShowHint to True.

✦ **TabVisible** — Set this property to False at run time to temporarily remove a tab sheet from a page control. This also sets the sheet's TabIndex property to –1. Resetting TabVisible to True again shows the tab sheet.

Tip

When TabVisible is set to False, it is no longer possible to select the TabSheet using the mouse because that page is no longer displayed. Instead, select this TabSheet from the Object Inspector's drop-down list. You can then reset TabVisible True to make the page visible again.

Creating owner-draw PageControls

To customize the display of page tab contents, you can create an owner-draw PageControl. This places the responsibility for displaying page tab text or graphics on your shoulders — a feature you might use, for example, to display page tabs using different fonts, or to display an icon.

On the
CD-ROM

Figure 12-11 shows an example of an owner-draw PageControl, to which I added 12 pages. The program displays the active page's tab text in italic, and also displays a small icon next to each tab label. Listing 12-10 shows this program's source code — it's on the CD-ROM in the Source\PageTabOD directory. To save room, I deleted a few lines that merely declare TabSheet and Label objects in the form's class — Delphi creates these declarations automatically and you can ignore them.

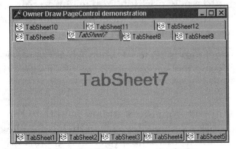

Figure 12-11: Using an owner-draw PageControl object, you can display page tab text using a different font (this example uses italic for the active page), and graphics such as the small icons shown here.

Listing 12-10: **PageTabOD\Main.pas**

```pascal
unit Main;

interface

uses
  Windows, Messages, SysUtils, Classes, Graphics, Controls,
  Forms, Dialogs, ComCtrls, Images, StdCtrls;

type
  TMainForm = class(TForm)
    PageControl1: TPageControl;
    TabSheet1: TTabSheet;
// TabSheet2 ... TabSheet 12 deleted
    ImageList1: TImageList;
    Label1: TLabel;
// Label2 ... Label12 deleted
    procedure PageControl1DrawTab(Control: TCustomTabControl;
      TabIndex: Integer; const Rect: TRect; Active: Boolean);
  private
    { Private declarations }
  public
    { Public declarations }
  end;

var
  MainForm: TMainForm;

implementation

{$R *.DFM}

procedure TMainForm.PageControl1DrawTab(
  Control: TCustomTabControl; TabIndex: Integer;
  const Rect: TRect; Active: Boolean);
begin
  with Control.Canvas do
  begin
    if active
      then Font.Style := [fsItalic]
      else Font.Style := [];
    TextRect(Rect, Rect.Left + 20, Rect.Top + 3,
      PageControl1.Pages[TabIndex].Caption);
    ImageList1.Draw(Control.Canvas,
      Rect.Left + 2, Rect.Top + 2, 0);
  end;
end;

end.
```

Follow these steps to create the PageTabOD demonstration listed here:

1. Start a new application.

2. Drop an ImageList component from the Win32 palette onto the form. Double-click the component object and click the Add button to add an icon image. I used the Sample.ico icon from the Source\Data directory on the CD-ROM, but you can use any other bitmap if you want.

3. Drop a PageControl component from the Win32 palette onto the form. Click the right mouse button inside the component and select New Page from the pop-up menu. Do this 12 times.

4. Optional: Drop a Label component onto each page of the PageControl object. To do this, select each tab and click inside the PageControl's body. This selects the TabSheet object that serves as a vessel for this page's controls (check the Object Inspector window to be sure you have selected a TabSheet object). Then, drop a Label object onto the TabSheet. This associates the label with the page—the label appears only when its page is active. Use this same method to drop any other types of controls onto PageControl pages.

5. Select the PageControl1 object. You can do this either by using the Object Inspector drop-down list, or by clicking any page tab. Make sure the Object Inspector lists PageControl1 at top.

6. Set Align to alClient so the PageControl fills the window's client area. This step is optional, but when creating paged dialogs, you usually use this setting.

7. Set MultiLine to True so that all page tabs are visible in multiple rows. Also set ScrollOpposite to True so that some rows move down to the bottom of the window.

8. Set OwnerDraw to True. At this point, the page tab labels become blank.

9. To display the icons and text in each page tab, you must create an event handler for the PageControl object. Be sure PageControl1 is still selected, and then click the Events tab in the Object Inspector. Double-click the OnDrawTab event to create a procedure, which you can fill in with the code from the listing.

When you run the completed program by pressing F9, the OnDrawTab event handler is called to draw the text and graphics for each page tab. The procedure and its parameters are declared as follows:

```
procedure TMainForm.PageControl1DrawTab(
    Control: TCustomTabControl; TabIndex: Integer;
    const Rect: TRect; Active: Boolean);
```

✦ **Control**—This refers to the object that forms the tab image. To draw inside this area, use the Control's Canvas property.

✦ **TabIndex** — This equals the index of the TabSheet object that forms the page, with zero for the first page, one for the next, and so on.

✦ **Rect** — The values in this record define the relative coordinates for drawing in the tab. Usually, you call methods in Canvas and pass Rect or its inner values, such as Rect.Left and Rect.Top, as arguments.

✦ **Active** — This is True if the page tab being drawn is the active one (the page tab that is selected at run time). If False, the procedure is drawing an inactive page — that is, one with its controls not visible.

The sample program uses these parameters to draw icons and text in each page tab. A *with* statement ensures that we are using the Canvas property associated with the page tab control and not for some other object:

```
with Control.Canvas do
begin
   // Call methods for the Control's Canvas
end;
```

The first step is to determine whether we are drawing the active page. If so, the program sets the Canvas's font style to italic; otherwise, the style is set to normal (no specific style constants), using the *if* statement:

```
if active
  then Font.Style := [fsItalic]
  else Font.Style := [];
```

To display the page tab captions, the program calls the TextRect method in Canvas:

```
TextRect(Rect, Rect.Left + 20, Rect.Top + 3,
   PageControl1.Pages[TabIndex].Caption);
```

The first three arguments to TextRect specify the full Rect, which defines the limits of where text is allowed to appear, and the left and top coordinates of the text string's upper-left pixel. The last argument is the text to display. This is taken from the PageControl object's Pages array, using the TabIndex value passed to the OnDrawTab event handler. This locates the TabSheet object that represents the page and its associated Caption property.

To draw the icons, the program calls the Draw method in the ImageList object that holds the icon image:

```
ImageList1.Draw(Control.Canvas,
   Rect.Left + 2, Rect.Top + 2, 0);
```

The first argument specifies that the page tab's Canvas is to be used to draw the image. The next two arguments specify the location of the image. The last argument is the image's index in the ImageList component object. Although the sample program draws the same icon in each page tab, it's easy to display different icons. Simply load the icon images into your ImageList object, and specify their index values to ImageList.Draw. (Tip: You can use the TabIndex parameter passed to the OnDrawTab event — that way, the image index values are the same as the TabSheet objects in the PageControl.)

Note   The widths of page tabs are automatically determined by how much text the OnDrawTab event handler displays.

TabControl component

A simpler way to create multipage dialogs and other controls is to use the TabControl component on the Win32 palette. Unlike the more sophisticated PageControl component, TabControl objects do not have separate pages, even though they appear that way. The pages in a TabControl are mere illusions. Users can select a TabControl's page tabs, just as they do a PageControl's — visually, the two objects look the same. However, because a TabControl has no actual pages, what is drawn in the body of the control is entirely up to you.

One practical use for a TabControl is to create data-entry forms with groups of controls whose content changes depending on the selected tab. For example, load the PageTab.dpr project file into Delphi — on the CD-ROM, this file is in the Source\PageTab directory. The TabControl object on the right (refer back to Figure 12-7) shows three Edit objects. Run the program by pressing F9, and select each of the four page tabs. The Edit controls stay put, but their content changes depending on the active page. Remember, however, there are no actual pages in this case — only the page tabs change appearance to indicate which area in the control is selected.

To enter text into the Edit objects, the sample program executes this procedure:

```
procedure TMainForm.TabControl1Change(Sender: TObject);
var
  S: String;
begin
  S := IntToStr(TabControl1.TabIndex + 1);
  Edit1.Text := 'Edit1 Tab ' + S;
  Edit2.Text := 'Edit2 Tab ' + S;
  Edit3.Text := 'Edit3 Tab ' + S;
end;
```

This code is purely for demonstration purposes, but it does illustrate how to modify a TabControl's objects depending on which page tab is selected. The procedure is an event handler for the TabControl's OnChange event, which is called when the user selects a page tab. To determine which tab is selected, use the TabControl object's TabIndex property. The first tab is numbered zero, the next is one, and so on. To number the labels shown in the Edit objects, the program adds one to this value and creates a string *S* for appending to the static text items shown. These are assigned to the Edit object Text properties. In a real program, you would use similar techniques to change the contents of the controls — by reading text information from a file, for example.

Tip

At design time, you can change a TabControl's TabIndex to activate a different tab. Unlike with a PageControl, a TabControl's tabs are not clickable at design time.

TabControl properties

TabControl properties are similar to PageControl's, so I won't list them separately (see "PageControl properties" in this chapter). The only significantly different property is Tabs, a TStrings object. Double-click this property value, or click its ellipsis button, to open Delphi's string-list editor. Each text line in this editor represents one page tab label. Simply type as many labels as you need to create the TabControl's page tabs.

Constraining Window Size

In past versions of Delphi, it wasn't possible to restrict window sizes (or at least, it wasn't easy). This often led to problems when users resized a window, covering some of its controls. The only option was to make the window fixed in size, but this is often too restrictive.

Delphi 4 adds a new property to the TControl class: constraints of type TSizeConstraints. You can use this property to set minimum and maximum widths and heights for most components descended from TControl. Even the form window itself can be constrained in size.

Using the Constraints property is easy. For a sample, start a new application and locate the Constraints property in the Object Inspector window for the application's Form1 object. Double-click the small plus sign to the left of Constraints. This opens the property's four subvalues: MaxHeight, MaxWidth, MinHeight, and MinWidth. These values are normally zero, which turns off all constraints. Enter any integer values into these properties to restrict a window or other control object's width and height. Values are positive integers representing the control sizes in pixels.

The Constraint demonstration program on the CD-ROM in the Source\Constraint directory shows how to create a constrained PageControl object. The goal in the demonstration is to ensure that users cannot shrink a dialog window so small that it obscures other controls such as CheckBoxes and RadioButtons. At the same time, we want to restrict the dialog from filling the screen, which wastes screen real estate and looks bad. Figure 12-12 shows the program's display — notice that the PageControl object fills the window. It is the PageControl that is constrained in size, but because the window owns the control, it too has the same constraints. This program's Main.pas source file has no significant code, so it's not listed here.

Figure 12-12: A constrained PageControl object constrains the size of its window, which ensures users can neither shrink the window and cover its controls nor maximize the window larger than a practical size.

Note With Constraints in effect, clicking the window's full screen button maximizes the window to its constrained maximum width and height, and also positions the window at the upper-left corner of the display. This might be disconcerting to users who expect the full screen button to cause a window to fill the display — you might want to add a note in your application's documentation about the effect of constrained window sizes.

To create the sample program on your own, follow these steps:

1. Drop a PageControl object onto a blank form. Click the right mouse button inside the PageControl and select New Page from the pop-up menu to add a few pages.

2. Drop some other controls into the PageControl's pages. It doesn't matter which controls you use. For the demonstration, I added three CheckBoxes to the first page, three RadioButtons to the second page, and a DateTimePicker to the third page.

3. Still in Delphi, size the window to the maximum you want. Note the values of the PageControl's Height and Width properties. (Be sure the Object Inspector displays properties for PageControl1 — if not, select that object in the Object Inspector's drop-down list.) Double-click the Constraints property, and enter the noted Height and Width values into MaxHeight and MaxWidth respectively.

4. Shrink the window to the minimum size that looks good and also does not cover any of the controls you added to the PageControl object. Repeat Step 3, but this time enter the noted Height and Width values into MinHeight and MaxHeight.

5. Run the program by pressing F9. Try sizing the window — it does not shrink or grow beyond the set limits. Also, click the full screen button and notice that the window grows only to its limited maximum size.

Adding controls to a constrained container such as PageControl resets its Constraints property values to zero. Program the Constraints property in these cases only after inserting all child controls into the parent container.

At run time, you can override a control's constraints using a new event handler provided for this purpose. You might do this to permit users to maximize a normally constrained window to full screen, perhaps as a program option that turns constraints on and off.

To try this event handler, reload the Constraint.dpr project from the CD-ROM's Source\Constraint directory into Delphi, and then follow these steps:

1. Select MainForm using the Object Inspector's drop-down list.

2. Click the Events tab on the Object Inspector window.

3. Double-click the OnConstrainedResize event to create a blank event handler. Fill in this handler's code using Listing 12-11 as a guide.

4. Run the program by pressing F9. Resize the window — it can now grow to full screen, but is still restricted from shrinking too small. Also try clicking the window's full screen button, which now functions normally.

Listing 12-11: Enter the code from this OnConstrainedResize event handler to the Constraint project to demonstrate how to override a window's constraints.

```
procedure TMainForm.FormConstrainedResize(Sender: TObject;
  var MinWidth, MinHeight, MaxWidth, MaxHeight: Integer);
begin
  MaxWidth := Screen.Width;
  MaxHeight := Screen.Height;
end;
```

This event is published only for the TForm, TScrollBox, and TPanel classes. Use it to override at run time the Constraints property values entered at design time. For example, as shown here, you can set the constrained control's MaxWidth and MaxHeight values to the global Screen object's Width and Height properties, thus allowing the window to be maximized to full screen.

Creating Docking Controls

As you probably know, you can dock various Delphi 4 windows together. For example, select View|Project Manager, and then click and drag its window into the code editor at either the left or right border. When the dragging outline changes size, release the mouse button and the window docks to the code editor. This is especially useful with high-resolution displays, where there's plenty of extra room to the left or right of the text editing area. To undock a window, click and drag it until its dragging outline changes back to normal size, and then release the mouse.

You can also create your own docking controls using Delphi 4 — earlier versions do not have this feature. To do this, you need two basic objects:

✦ A docking site object

✦ A dockable control object

A docking site object can be any component with a DockSite property. This includes the Form, Panel, PageControl, TabControl, ToolBar, CoolBar and other components. A docking site object must be able to own other controls — simple components such as Buttons and CheckBoxes cannot be docking sites.

A dockable control object is any component with the two properties: DragKind and DragMode. A few components have only DragMode — to be dockable, however, the control must have both properties. Examples of components that cannot be dockable are those on the Win3.1 palette, and those that do not have visual run time shapes such as Timer and MainMenu.

Tip   Most applications use Panel objects as docking sites. Dockable controls are typically those that hold other controls such as ToolBars, CoolBars, and PageControls.

Dockable windows are made possible by modifications made in Delphi 4 to the TControl and TWinControl classes. A docking site must be an object of a class descended from TWinControl. A dockable control must be an object of a class descended from TControl. The TWinControl class is itself descended from TControl; therefore, many docking site objects can also be dockable windows. A ToolBar, for example, can be a docking site for other windows, or it can be dockable on its own. It can even serve both duties — as a docking site for holding other windows, and as a dockable control that users can drag to attach or detach from a form.

Creating a docking site

You can create a docking site out of any control with a DockSite property. Simply set that property to true to allow the control to accept another window (called the docked client). A docking site is typically a Form, Panel, or CoolBar component, but it can be any other container with a DockSite property.

In most cases, you also want to set the docking site's AutoSize property to True. When DockSite and AutoSize are True, the control is not visible at run time until another control is docked to it. Normally, this is the preferred effect — the end user sees only the docked control outline, not the actual docking site.

Creating a dockable object

As mentioned, a dockable control object can be any component with both DragKind and DragMode properties. For example, a ToolBar can be made into a dockable control. To do that, set the ToolBar object's DragKind property to dkDock and its DragMode to dmAutomatic.

To take over docking control (which is rarely necessary), you can set DragKind to dkDrag (the default) and implement OnDragOver, OnEndDrag, and OnDragDrop event handlers. If DragMode is set to dmManual, call BeginDrag to start a dragging operation.

To set the type of object that can contain the dockable control when it is undocked from a docking site, set the FloatingDockSiteClass property to TMainForm (your application's form class descendent created by Delphi), or to another control. If, however, the dockable control is a descendent of TWinControl, this step isn't required, as undocking is automatic.

Expert-User Tips

✦ In cases where a class's multiple variables are not referenced in the program source code, you may delete all but one of those variables to save four bytes each in objects of the class. For example, suppose you deposit a couple dozen TSpeedButton objects onto a form, but you don't reference any of them explicitly in the program's source code. You can delete the button declarations from the form's class — this does not delete them from the form's .dfm file — and save four bytes for each deletion. You must leave at least one declaration of each type of variable so that the associated VCL code is linked into the final .exe code file.

✦ Modeless dialogs that are on display during lengthy operations may not react promptly enough to user input. This is a Windows limitation that you can usually work around inside loops by calling ProcessMessages for the global Application object. For example, write time-intensive loops like this:

```
while Flag do
begin
  PerformOperation;
  Application.ProcessMessages;
  Flag := ContinueOperation;
end;
```

✦ If you are familiar with Borland Pascal, you may have written code to transfer dialog information to and from application variables. In Delphi, declare variables in the dialog form's class, and either provide functions to return those variables, or access them directly through the class's public section. For example, follow these steps to demonstrate how to access a dialog's controls:

1. Insert a Button into a form (module Unit1). Select Delphi's New form SpeedButton or command and choose the Standard dialog box with buttons along the right border.

2. Insert a CheckBox into the second form (module Unit2).

3. Add Unit2 to Unit1's *uses* declaration. This permits the Button object's event handlers, and other code in the main form, to access the second module's public items.

4. Implement the Button's OnClick event handler in module Unit1 as follows. As the statements illustrate, you can directly access the Checked property in the dialog's CheckBox1 object. The dialog object itself stores its control values, and therefore, Borland Pascal's transfer mechanism isn't needed in Delphi applications:

```
with BtnRightDlg do
if ShowModal = mrOk then
  if CheckBox1.Checked then
    ShowMessage('Checkbox is enabled')
  else
    ShowMessage('Checkbox is disabled');
```

✦ In past versions of Delphi, you receive a GPF (general protection fault) immediately on running an application if you refer to a method in a form that does not yet exist. For example, in a program with a dialog box, you could not call YourDialog.AnyMethod in the main form's OnCreate event handler because YourDialog is not yet initialized. If you are still using an early version of Delphi, to repair the problem, move the statement to the form's OnActivate event handler and use a Boolean flag to indicate whether the dialog has been initialized. This problem does not appear to occur in Delphi 3 and later releases.

✦ Each page in a TabbedNotebook component is a TTabPage object. Refer to these objects through the Objects and Pages properties. For example, the following procedure displays the Caption of the first page tab in a TabbedNotebook object:

```
procedure TForm1.Button1Click(Sender: TObject);
var
  P: TTabPage;  { Reference to a TabbedNotebook page }
begin
  with TabbedNotebook1 do
    P := TTabPage(Pages.Objects[0]);  { P refers to page 1 }
    ShowMessage(P.Caption);  { Display page tab label }
end;
```

✦ To prevent users from selecting a specific page in a TabbedNotebook object, create a handler for the OnChange event, which has two parameters in addition to Sender: NewTab, representing the tab index that the user clicked; and AllowChange, which you can set to indicate whether that page is selectable. For example, in the TabbedNotebook object's OnChange handler, use this statement to disable the third page (the first page index equals zero):

```
if NewTab = 2 then
  AllowChange := False;
```

Projects to Try

12-1: Write a telephone dialer dialog. The window should look like a touch-tone phone. Return a phone number through ShowModal if users click the Dial button.

12-2: Add a ColorDialog component and command to the SysColor utility from the preceding chapter.

12-3: Advanced. Implement Find and Replace commands for a TStringList object.

12-4: Advanced. Use Notebook and TabSet components to create a multipage Options dialog. This takes a little more effort than using a TabbedNotebook as suggested in this chapter, but gives you extra flexibility. For example, you can place TabSets where you like, and if space is limited, you can take advantage of the TabSet component's capability to scroll tab labels horizontally.

Summary

✦ A dialog box is a program's voice and ears. In Delphi, any form window can have dialog characteristics for prompting users, displaying messages, and presenting options.

✦ Delphi encapsulates common Windows dialogs in the ColorDialog, FindDialog, FontDialog, OpenDialog, ReplaceDialog, and SaveDialog components. This chapter also discusses the related TabSet, Notebook, and TabbedNotebook components, which are handy for creating multipage dialog box windows.

✦ Dialogs can be modal (capture and retain the input focus) or modeless (capture, but do not retain the input focus). Call a form's ShowModal method to display a modal dialog. Call Show to display a modeless dialog window. To display common Windows dialogs, call their component Execute methods.

✦ You normally use the TabSet and Notebook components together to create the illusion of a tabbed panel. This chapter's TabEdit multipage text editor demonstrates this useful interface technique.

✦ You can also use TabSet and Notebook components to create tabbed toolbars, similar to Delphi's VCL palette. This chapter's Palette application explains the technique.

✦ The primary difference between a pair of TabSet and Notebook objects, and the TabbedNotebook component, is appearance. TabbedNotebooks look like stacked file folders with labeled tabs along the top. The TabbedNotebook component is especially suitable for creating multipage options dialogs.

✦ Writing Find and Replace commands is no simple task. Delphi's FindDialog and ReplaceDialog components provide standard tools for creating find and replace modeless dialogs, but it's up to you to supply the actual search-and-replace programming. This chapter's FindRepl application outlines the fundamental steps.

✦ Delphi's TextDemo demonstration (see file Search.pas in the Demos\Textdemo directory) contains a general-purpose text search routine that you can extract for Find and Replace operations.

✦ The relatively new PageControl component simplifies creating multipaged dialogs, such as typically displayed by an application's Options command. Each page of a PageControl is a TabSheet object, which holds controls such as Buttons and CheckBoxes associated with that page.

✦ The TabControl component is similar to PageControl in that it displays page tabs that users can select. However, a TabControl is a single object, and its pages are merely illusions. A typical use for a TabControl component is to create data-entry screens with sets of Edit controls whose content changes depending on which page tab the user selects.

✦ Use the new Constraints property to constrain a window or other control's width and height. To override constraints, implement an OnConstrainedResize event handler for a Form, ScrollBox, or Panel component.

✦ With Delphi 4, you can create your own docking windows. Any component such as Panel with a DockSite property can become a docking site. Set this property to True, and usually, also set AutoSize True so that the docking site is not visible at run time.

✦ To create a dockable control, set its DragKind property to dkDock and also set DragMode to dmAutomatic. At run time, users can click and drag the control to a dock site, and they can drag it off the dock site to undock the control.

This chapter concludes the investigation of Part II into user-interface construction techniques using Delphi components. In Part III, you consider the other side of the development coin—the internal tasks your application performs.

✦   ✦   ✦

The Application

Designing your program's user interface, the subject of this book up to now, is only half the game of writing successful software. The other half involves the guts of your program—that is, what it does that makes it unique from other programs. In this part, you learn techniques for developing *applications* that make use of the interface elements you learned about in Parts I and II.

Most applications fall into or use major elements from the subjects described in the chapters in this part. Before reading the upcoming chapters, you should be comfortable with Delphi's commands and windows, and you should fully understand the techniques of user interface programming— especially component properties and events—as explained in Part II.

In the following chapters, you learn how to create many different types of applications that use advanced-level components for graphics, animations, printer output, multiple document interfaces (MDI), clipboard data transfers, dynamic data exchange (DDE), object linking and embedding (OLE), ActiveX, charts and reports, and database management. Even though your own application is, of course, unique, it probably falls into one of the categories described in this part's chapters.

Developing Graphics Applications

Regardless of your artistic skills (mine never progressed much beyond crayons and chalk), with the help of Delphi's Canvas property, you can draw and paint any shape you can imagine. In addition, Delphi's graphics components, data types, procedures, and functions greatly simplify programming tasks such as working with bitmaps, and reading and writing metafiles.

In this chapter, I introduce Delphi's graphics components and techniques and explain how to use the extensive Canvas property, which many components provide for a general-purpose drawing surface. I also cover related graphics topics such as animation, graphics file handling, offscreen bitmaps, picture dialogs, and drag-and-drop objects.

Components

Following is a list of Delphi's graphics components:

✦ **Animate** — Use this component to add animation windows to a form or dialog. You can play standard .avi (audiovisual) files, and you can also select from standard Windows animations such as seen when copying and deleting files using the Explorer. Palette: Win32.

✦ **Image** — Use this component to import bitmaps, icons, and metafiles into a form. An Image object is a wrapper that contains a graphical figure in its Picture property. Palette: Additional.

✦ **MediaPlayer** — Use this full-featured, multimedia component to build animation graphics and sound software. As this chapter explains, with just a few strokes of the keyboard, you can build a functional .avi (audiovisual) video-file viewer. Palette: System.

✦ **OpenPictureDialog, SavePictureDialog** — These two components provide standard dialogs for opening and saving graphics files. Palette: Dialogs.

✦ **PaintBox** — Use this component to add drawing and painting capabilities to components such as Panel that don't have a Canvas property. You can also use a PaintBox object to restrict drawing to one or more rectangular areas in a form window. Palette: System.

✦ **Shape** — Use this component to create geometrical shapes such as filled and unfilled ellipses and rectangles. Choose the shape you want by setting a Shape object's Shape property (the property and component have the same name). Palette: Additional.

Introducing the Canvas

All graphics operations take place in the context of the Canvas property, which many components provide. For example, the form has a Canvas property, as do TBitmap, TComboBox, TListBox, TPaintBox, and others. The Canvas property embodies the Windows Graphics Device Interface (GDI), and it provides a device-independent surface for drawing graphical objects in windows. (The next chapter covers printing of graphics and text.) It's useful to think of the Canvas as a surface on which your program paints text and graphics — it isn't a "surface," but more like a conduit through which graphics commands flow to the display, where they become visual.

Note

For those who are familiar with Windows programming, Delphi's Canvas is an object-oriented encapsulation of a handle to a device context (HDC). To create graphics on a device, methods in the TCanvas class call Windows GDI functions.

Drawing with the Canvas

The Canvas property is a comprehensive, object-oriented wrapper for the Windows GDI. The Canvas, which is always ready to use, is an object in its own right, and its TCanvas class provides dozens of properties, methods, and events. Generally, you use a Canvas property in two ways:

✦ To configure graphical output by assigning colors, patterns, fonts, and other values to Canvas properties and subproperties.

✦ To produce visual shapes by calling graphical methods, some of which also provide supporting services such as determining the display pixel width of a string.

Note

See the next chapter for information about displaying and printing text with the Canvas text output methods.

The Canvas property is not available at design time in the Object Inspector window. To use the Canvas, you must write statements that assign values to Canvas properties and that call Canvas methods. For example, to draw a blue rectangle filled with yellow diagonal hatches in the form window, insert these statements into a form's OnPaint event handler:

```
with Canvas do
begin
  Pen.Color := clBlue;
  Brush.Color := clYellow;
  Brush.Style := bsDiagCross;
  Rectangle(10, 10, 100, 100);
end;
```

To enter this code, start a new application, select Form1 in the Object Inspector, click that window's Events page tab, and double-click in the value field of the OnPaint event. Add the preceding lines to the resulting event handler that Delphi creates, and then press F9 to compile and run the program.

This programming fragment uses a *with* statement that tells Delphi to use the properties and methods in Canvas. Because this statement appears in a TForm1 method, it is the form's Canvas that is being referenced, and therefore, output appears in the form — the program's main window in this case. The first three statements assign values to two Canvas properties: Pen and Brush, setting subproperties of those elements as shown. The final statement calls a Canvas method, Rectangle, to paint a graphics shape using the assigned values. To create most types of graphics, you use similar steps:

✦ Assign values to Canvas properties and subproperties

✦ Call Canvas methods to produce visual output

Drawing with Shapes

Delphi provides another way to create Shapes. Rather than call Canvas methods to draw shapes at run time, you can insert a Shape object into a form. The end results are visually the same, but the Shape component gives you the means to arrange graphics objects at design time by clicking and dragging and by assigning property values. For example, insert a Shape object from the Additional palette into the form from the preceding section, or use a fresh form. Select a Shape property value such as stRoundRect, or insert this statement into the form's OnCreate or another event handler:

```
Shape1.Shape := stRoundRect;
```

To change a Shape's color and pattern at design time, use the Object Inspector to assign values to its Brush and Pen subproperties. The Brush affects the shape's interior. The Pen affects the shape's outline. Try different settings, or assign values at run time with statements such as the following in the form's OnCreate or another event handler:

```
with Shape1 do
begin
  Shape := stRoundRect;
  Brush.Color := clLime;
  Brush.Style := bsCross;
  Pen.Color := clNavy;
  Pen.Width := 3;
end;
```

Because many components have a Canvas property, if graphics do not appear as expected, the cause may be a *with* statement that refers to an object's Canvas when you meant to use the form's property. Either don't use *with*, or use statements such as MainForm.Canvas.

Canvas properties

The Canvas property provides eight subproperties for configuring graphics. You can assign values to these properties only at run time, usually in a form's OnCreate or OnPaint event handler. Following are brief descriptions of each property:

✦ **Brush** — Provides the fill color and pattern for circle, rectangle, and polygon interiors, and also the background color for text. It has no effect on lines and text foreground color. Assign values to the Brush's Color and Style subproperties.

✦ **ClipRect** — Clips graphics inside this rectangle's boundaries. It is usually equal in size to the window's client area. You can assign new values to its Left, Top, Right, and Bottom Integer subvalues to clip graphical output to another region. (Hint: See the PaintBox component for an easier method.)

✦ **CopyMode** — Determines how to combine bits when calling a Canvas's CopyRect method, which you can use to copy one object's Canvas into another. For example, set CopyMode to cmNotSourceCopy to invert pixels before copying them to another Canvas.

✦ **Font** — Assigns subproperties to select font styles for text that you draw by calling the Canvas's TextOut and TextRect methods. This Font object is not related to the form's Font property — initialize Canvas.Font properties before drawing text.

✦ **Handle** — For GDI functions that require a handle to a device context, pass Canvas.Handle to an HDC parameter. This makes it possible to call GDI functions that Canvas does not encapsulate.

✦ **Pen** — Affects lines and outlines. You assign values to the Pen's Color, Style, Mode, and Width subproperties.

✦ **PenPos** — Gives the internal pen's location (PenPos.X, PenPos.Y) that determines where the next graphical output appears. Although Delphi permits assigning new values to PenPos, you should instead call the Canvas's MoveTo method to change the pen's internal location.

✦ **Pixels** — Provides a two-dimensional array to the Canvas's individual pixels. Each element of the array is a TColor value. For example, the expression Pixels[0,0] (use square brackets) returns the color of the pixel at coordinate (0,0). If you like to do graphics the hard way, you may also color individual pixels by assigning new color values to this array.

The Pixels property is a pseudo-array; it is not a bitmap. The TCanvas class translates references and assignments of Pixels[X,Y] into GDI GetPixel and SetPixel function calls. For this reason, using Pixels is one of the most inefficient methods available for creating graphics. Use Pixels only when you absolutely must have access to individual pixel colors.

Canvas methods and events

The Canvas property provides numerous methods that can help tame the madness every programmer experiences, sooner or later, with the Windows GDI. Several shape-producing methods such as Arc, Ellipse, FloodFill, Polygon, Rectangle, and RoundRect, correspond directly with GDI functions of the same names. After you become familiar with the general technique for calling Canvas methods, they are easy to use. For example, to draw an ellipse, insert statements such as these into an OnPaint event handler:

```
Canvas.Pen.Color := clMaroon;
Canvas.Brush.Color := clYellow;
Canvas.Ellipse(10, 20, 100, 100);
```

Assign values to Canvas properties before each use of the Canvas in an OnPaint event handler. For example, to draw a blue line, assign clBlue to the Canvas's Pen.Color subproperty, and then call the MoveTo and LineTo methods. You cannot preconfigure Canvas properties in a form's OnCreate event handler because OnPaint receives a device context from Windows, and this context is provided to your program via Canvas. Thus, the Canvas in OnPaint does not contain any property values assigned outside of the event handler.

The less obvious methods that you can call for a Canvas property include the following:

✦ **CopyRect**—Copies all or a portion of one Canvas to another. Set the CopyMode property to determine how pixels are combined in the final result. Look up CopyMode in Delphi's online help for settings you can use.

✦ **Draw**—Draws an object of the TGraphic class, which is the immediate ancestor of the TIcon, TBitmap, and TMetafile classes. You may pass any icon, bitmap, or metafile object to Draw.

✦ **DrawFocusRect**—Draws a rectangle using exclusive-OR logic. Call a second time with identical arguments to erase the rectangle. Use this method to draw drag-and-drop outlines.

✦ **FrameRect**—Draws an unfilled rectangle by using the current Pen, but ignoring the Canvas's brush. Use FrameRect rather than Rectangle when you want a plain outline without having to set Brush properties.

✦ **StretchDraw**—This is the same as Draw, but stretches or shrinks an icon, bitmap, or metafile to fit within a defined rectangle.

The Canvas property also recognizes two events that might be useful in special circumstances. In most applications, you won't need to provide handlers for them —just be aware of them in case you need their special services. The two events are:

✦ **OnChange**—Called after a Canvas property value has been changed

✦ **OnChanging**—Called immediately before a Canvas property changes

Because the Canvas property is not available at design time, you can't use the Object Inspector to create handlers for these two events. To use them, declare procedures in the form's class:

```
TForm1 = class(TForm)
  procedure MyOnChange(Sender: TObject);
  procedure MyOnChanging(Sender: TObject);
...
end;
```

Assign the procedure names to OnChange and OnChanging in the form's OnCreate event handler:

```
Canvas.OnChange := MyOnChange;
Canvas.OnChanging := MyOnChanging;
```

Implement the procedures to perform whatever actions you need. For example, write an OnChange event handler as follows (OnChanging is similar in design):

```
procedure TForm1.MyOnChange(Sender: TObject);
begin
  SavedPenColor := Canvas.Pen.Color;
end;
```

Caution

Delphi's smart Project Manager deletes the preceding declarations if the event handlers contain no statements or comments. When creating multiple event handlers, don't compile the program until after inserting at least one statement or comment into each handler's procedure.

Drawing and Painting

Windows applications draw individual shapes such as lines and filled rectangles. They paint graphical objects to maintain the illusion of overlapping windows on a desktop. A program may have to draw a shape only once, but it must always be ready to paint that shape if, for example, the user hides and then uncovers the application window.

A simple test demonstrates the difference between drawing and painting. Insert a Button object into a form. Create an OnClick event handler for the Button with the programming from Listing 13-1. Run the program and click the button to outline the button with a rounded red rectangle. Hide and uncover the window, and the rectangle disappears.

Listing 13-1: Use this OnClick event handler to demonstrate drawing and painting.

```
procedure TForm1.Button1Click(Sender: TObject);
var
  X1, Y1, X2, Y2: Integer;
begin
  Canvas.Pen.Color := clRed;
  Canvas.Pen.Width := 2;
  with Button1 do
  begin
    X1 := Left - 3; Y1 := Top - 3;
    X2 := Left + Width + 4; Y2 := Top + Height + 4;
    Canvas.RoundRect(X1, Y1, X2, Y2, 4, 4);
  end;
end;
```

Quit the test program and return to Delphi. Insert an OnPaint event handler for the form, and copy the statements and *var* declaration into that procedure. Delete the OnClick event handler. Now when you run the program, it outlines the Button from the start, and the outline does not disappear when you hide and uncover the window.

It's usually easiest (and safest) to delete a handler by removing its declarations and statements, leaving a bare *begin and end* block. Don't delete the entire procedure — this might confuse Delphi's code generator. For example, to remove the Button's OnClick event handler, reduce the procedure in Listing 13-1 to:

```
procedure TForm1.Button1Click(Sender: TObject);
begin
end;
```

When you next compile the source code file, Delphi's smart Project Manager deletes the procedure declaration and body along with any references to that procedure in object events.

In most cases, you can simply insert drawing statements into a form or a PaintBox OnPaint event handler. If you draw objects in other procedures, however, you must also provide code to recreate those objects in an OnPaint event. If you don't do that, your graphics vanish like smoke in the breeze when users cover and uncover the application's window.

Call the form's Invalidate method to inform Windows that the form (or control) needs to be repainted. Call the form's Update method to repaint immediately. For example, suppose your program has an OnPaint event handler that draws some graphics based on global variables. If those variables change, don't draw the new shape — instead, insert these statements to repaint the graphics by forcing an OnPaint event to occur:

```
MainForm.Invalidate;
MainForm.Update;      { optional }
```

Never do that inside an OnPaint event handler. The purpose of these statements is to cause an OnPaint event to occur — executing them inside OnPaint causes the program to endlessly repaint itself. Invalidate tells Windows that the object needs painting. Windows issues a wm_Paint message to the object when no other messages are pending. Update, which is optional, tells Windows to issue the wm_Paint message immediately.

The PaintBox component

Insert a PaintBox object into a form or another container such as a Panel to give it graphics capabilities. All coordinates are relative to the container. For example, insert a Panel into a form and stretch it a bit to make room for the PaintBox object. Select the PaintBox component from the System palette and click the mouse pointer inside the Panel. To reposition the combined object, simply drag the Panel —you don't have to also select the PaintBox.

You have just given a Panel new graphics capabilities. You might use this technique to draw shapes, bitmaps, and other graphics in a toolbar or a status line. For example, to draw a navy blue box inside the Panel, insert the following statements into PaintBox1's OnPaint event handler. (Be sure to create a handler for the PaintBox object, not for the form.) Here's the entire procedure for reference:

```
procedure TForm1.PaintBox1Paint(Sender: TObject);
begin
  with PaintBox1.Canvas do
  begin
    Pen.Color := clNavy;
    Rectangle(0, 0, 100, 100);
  end;
end;
```

Note

Notice the *with* statement refers to the PaintBox1 Canvas. If this statement referenced Canvas alone, it would refer to the form's Canvas rather than the PaintBox's. Always be aware all visual components have Canvas properties and be sure you are referring to the correct one so your graphics output goes where intended.

You can also use a PaintBox object to restrict drawing to a specific rectangle in a form or other container. To compartmentalize a form or container into multiple sections, you may insert as many PaintBoxes as you need.

Using Pens and Brushes

Every Canvas has Pen and Brush properties. The Pen specifies the color and style of lines, and also the outlines for shapes such as ellipses and rectangles. The Brush specifies shape interior colors and patterns. Pens have four significant properties:

   ✦ **Color**—Affects line and outline, but not shape interior colors. Assign any TColor value or constant such as clRed or clLime, to Pen.Color. To match desktop colors, assign a constant such as clWindow or clWindowText.

✦ **Mode** — Determines the logical method for drawing lines and outlines. Assign a constant such as pmBlack (always black) or pmNotCopy (inverse of Pen color) to Pen.Mode. Use pmXor so you can redraw a line to erase it and restore its former background.

✦ **Style** — Selects a solid, dashed, or dotted line style. For example, assign a constant such as psSolid or psDashDot to Pen.Style. In 16-bit Windows and Windows 95, lines with widths greater than one pixel are always solid. Windows 95 and Windows NT enable you to set the style of thick and thin lines.

✦ **Width** — Specifies the width in pixels of lines and outlines. In 16-bit Windows, this property must equal one (the default) to use a Pen Style other than psSolid.

For a complete list of Color, Mode, and Style constants, view those properties for the TPen class in Delphi's online help. Or, if you have Delphi's run-time library source code, browse the Graphics.pas file.

Brushes have three significant properties:

✦ **Bitmap** — Assigns a TBitmap object with a dimension up to 8 × 8 pixels. The brush replicates the Bitmap (like wallpaper) to fill interior shapes.

✦ **Color** — This is the same as Pen.

✦ **Style** — Specifies a pattern to use for painting interior shapes.

For example, assign a constant such as bsCross or bsFDiagonal to Brush.Style. Use bsSolid when assigning a Bitmap. To draw an outline shape with the background showing through, set Style to bsClear. For a complete list of Style constants, look up the Style property for the TBrush class in Delphi's online help.

Pens and Brushes have methods such as Create and Free that are common to many components. Pens and Brushes also have an OnChange event handler that you can use to notify the program of any changes to Pen and Brush properties, although using this event is rarely necessary.

The PolyFlow application on the CD-ROM is one of my oldest Pascal standard test programs. The files are in the Source\PolyFlow directory. PolyFlow is a good example of drawing versus painting; it also shows how to use a Timer object to create graphics animations. Figure 13-1 shows PolyFlow's display. Listing 13-2 lists the program's source code.

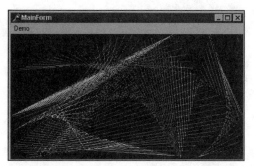

Figure 13-1: Polyflow, an old standard with a new Delphi interface, demonstrates drawing versus painting, and it shows how to use a Timer object to create graphics animations.

Listing 13-2: **PolyFlow\Main.pas**

```
unit Main;

interface

uses
  SysUtils, Windows, Messages, Classes, Graphics,
  Controls, Forms, Dialogs, Menus, ExtCtrls;

const
  maxIndex = 100;        { Maximum number of lines visible }
  dx1: Integer = 4;      { "Delta" values for controlling }
  dy1: Integer = 10;     {   the animation's personality.  }
  dx2: Integer = 3;
  dy2: Integer = 9;

type
  LineRec = record       { Line ends and color }
    X1, Y1, X2, Y2 : Integer;
    Color: TColor;
  end;

type
  TMainForm = class(TForm)
    MainMenu1: TMainMenu;
    Demo1: TMenuItem;
    Exit1: TMenuItem;
```

(continued)

Listing 13-2 *(continued)*

```
    Timer1: TTimer;
    procedure Exit1Click(Sender: TObject);
    procedure FormCreate(Sender: TObject);
    procedure Timer1Timer(Sender: TObject);
    procedure FormPaint(Sender: TObject);
    procedure FormResize(Sender: TObject);
  protected
    procedure CreateParams(var Params: TCreateParams);
      override;
  private
    LineArray: array[0 .. maxIndex _ 1] of LineRec;
    Index: Integer;      { Index for LineArray }
    Erasing: Boolean;    { True if erasing old lines }
    function Sign(N: Integer): Integer;
    procedure InitLineArray;
    procedure MakeNewLine(R: TRect; Index: Integer);
    procedure DrawLine(Index: Integer);
  public
    { Public declarations }
  end;

var
  MainForm: TMainForm;

implementation

{$R *.DFM}

procedure TMainForm.CreateParams(var Params: TCreateParams);
begin
  inherited CreateParams(params);
  with Params.WindowClass do
{ Repaint the window automatically when resized }
    Style := Style or cs_HRedraw or cs_VRedraw;
end;

{ Return _1 if n < 0 or +1 if n >= 0 }
function TMainForm.Sign(N: Integer): Integer;
begin
  if N < 0 then Sign :=  _1 else Sign := 1;
end;

{ Erase LineArray and set X1 to -1 as "no line" flag }
procedure TMainForm.InitLineArray;
var
  I: Integer;
begin
```

```
      Index := 0;
      Erasing := False;
      FillChar(LineArray, SizeOf(LineArray), 0);
      for I := 0 to maxIndex _ 1 do
        LineArray[I].X1 := _ 1;
  end;

{ Create new line, direction, and color }
procedure TMainForm.MakeNewLine(R: TRect; Index: Integer);
  procedure NewCoord(var C, Change: Integer; Max: Integer;
    var Color: TColor);
  var
    Temp: Integer;
  begin
    Temp := C + Change;
    if (Temp < 0) or (Temp > Max) then
    begin
      Change := Sign(-Change) * (3 + Random(12));
      repeat
        Color := RGB(Random(256), Random(256), Random(256));
        Color := GetNearestColor(Canvas.Handle, Color)
      until Color <> GetBkColor(Canvas.Handle);
    end else
      C := Temp;
  end;
begin
  with LineArray[Index] do
  begin
    NewCoord(X1, dx1, R.Right, Color);
    NewCoord(Y1, dy1, R.Bottom, Color);
    NewCoord(X2, dx2, R.Right, Color);
    NewCoord(Y2, dy2, R.Bottom, Color)
  end
end;

{ Draw or erase a line identified by Index }
procedure TMainForm.DrawLine(Index: Integer);
begin
  with Canvas, LineArray[Index] do
  begin
    Pen.Color := Color;
    MoveTo(X1, Y1);
    LineTo(X2, Y2);
  end;
end;

{ Draw some lines at each timer interval }
procedure TMainForm.Timer1Timer(Sender: TObject);
```

(continued)

Listing 13-2 *(continued)*

```
var
  R: TRect;
  I, OldIndex: Integer;
begin
  R := GetClientRect;
  for I := 1 to 10 do   { 10 = number of lines }
  begin
    OldIndex := Index;
    Inc(Index);
    if Index = maxIndex _ 1 then
    begin
      Index := 0;          { Wrap Index around to start }
      Erasing := True;   { True until window size changes }
    end;
    if Erasing then
      DrawLine(Index);   { Erase old line }
    LineArray[Index] := LineArray[OldIndex];
    MakeNewLine(R, Index);
    DrawLine(Index);      { Draw new line }
  end;
end;

{ Paint or repaint screen using data in LineArray }
procedure TMainForm.FormPaint(Sender: TObject);
var
  I: Integer;
begin
  with Canvas do
    for I := 0 to maxIndex _ 1 do
      if LineArray[I].X1 >= 0 then   { Draw non-flagged lines }
        DrawLine(I);
end;

{ Start new lines when window size changes }
procedure TMainForm.FormResize(Sender: TObject);
begin
  InitLineArray;    { Erase LineArray and reset globals }
end;

{ Initialize globals and LineArray }
procedure TMainForm.FormCreate(Sender: TObject);
begin
  with Canvas.Pen do
  begin
    Style := psSolid;
    Width := 1;
    Mode := pmXor;
```

```
    end;
    Randomize;
    InitLineArray;
end;

{ End program }
procedure TMainForm.Exit1Click(Sender: TObject);
begin
    Close;
end;

end.
```

PolyFlow's OnTimer event handler (see procedure Timer1Timer) draws ten lines of the animation. It could draw only one line, but this would slow the effect unacceptably. The form's OnPaint event handler redraws the entire window so that, when you hide it and then uncover it, the program restores the animation's current state. This is a typical Windows graphics technique — parts of the program draw shapes and store their parameters (see LineArray in the listing). To maintain the window, an OnPaint event handler uses those parameters to repaint the program's graphics.

Try running PolyFlow and cover a portion of its window. Notice that the Timer events continue running. In addition to creating animations, you can use this same technique to program other background processes, but be careful not to lock up the system by executing lengthy operations in a Timer event.

Graphics Programming Techniques

All form-based and graphical Delphi applications use the Graphics unit, which provides classes such as TPen, TBrush, TFont, TCanvas, and related declarations. This section covers some other classes and advanced graphics techniques such as bitmaps, graphics files, and how to create drag-and-drop objects.

Graphics class relationships

When you first begin to design your graphical program, you may be unsure whether to use the Image or Shape components or an object of the TPicture class. To decide on the best course for your program, first understand the relationships among the following classes:

✦ **TCanvas**—As mentioned, this class provides a painting surface on which you can draw and paint graphics by calling methods and assigning property values. You never create a stand-alone TCanvas object—you always use this class as the Canvas property of another object such as a PaintBox or a form.

✦ **TGraphic**—This class is the immediate ancestor for the TBitmap, TIcon, and TMetafile classes. You never create a stand-alone TGraphic object. Instead, you use this class as a parameter data type or as a component property. You may assign a bitmap, icon, or metafile object to any TGraphic parameter, variable, or property. TGraphic also serves as the abstract base class for all image data types in Delphi, including add-in classes such as JPEG (from the JPEG unit) plus other file formats.

✦ **TPicture**—This class creates a container that holds a TGraphic object, which can be a bitmap, an icon, or a metafile. TPicture's file-handling methods determine an image's type from its filename extension, which simplifies graphics file handling. You find the TPicture class used as the Picture property in other objects such as the Image component, and as a parameter data type. You can also create a stand-alone TPicture object—for example, to provide a container for a bitmap loaded from a disk file.

✦ **TGraphicsObject**—This class is the immediate ancestor for the TFont, TPen, and TBrush classes. Use TGraphicsObject as a procedure or function parameter data type so you can pass fonts, pens, or brushes as arguments to subroutines. You never create a stand-alone object of the TGraphicsObject class.

✦ **TGraphicControl**—This component class is the ancestor for the graphical component classes TSpeedButton, TTabButton (used by the TabbedNotebook component), TShape, TPaintBox, TImage, TBevel, and TCustomLabel (the immediate ancestor to TLabel). The TGraphicControl class provides a Canvas, which, for example, a SpeedButton uses to display its glyph bitmap. You probably do not need TGraphicControl in application development. It is valuable mostly for writing visual components that do not have associated window handles, and therefore take less memory than components that serve as interfaces for standard Windows elements such as buttons and check boxes. The Controls unit (not Graphics) declares TGraphicControl.

Drawing with components

To draw graphics, you may call Canvas methods and insert one of the following two components into a form or another container:

✦ **Image**—This component contains a Picture (TPicture class) object, which contains a Graphic property (TGraphic class). Because the TGraphic class is the ancestor to TBitmap, TIcon, and TMetafile, an Image component object can hold and display a bitmap, icon, or metafile referenced as Image.Picture.Graphic. Image can also handle third-party formats such as JPEG provided in the JPEG unit and TJPEGImage class.

✦ **Shape**—This component draws an image by calling Canvas methods. Use a Shape to draw and paint lines, rectangles, circles, and other objects.

The important difference between these two components is that an Image object contains a graphical image; a Shape object draws and paints a figure using an inherited Canvas. Use Image and Shape components to create graphics at design time. Use Canvas to draw and paint at run time.

To store graphical objects in memory, create an object of the TPicture class. You can also construct individual TBitmap, TIcon, and TMetafile objects, but it is often best to create a TPicture object that contains a bitmap, icon, or metafile image. For example, try the Button OnClick event handler in Listing 13-3, which loads and displays a bitmap file entirely at run time without using graphics components.

> **Listing 13-3: Try this Button OnClick event handler to load and display a bitmap file entirely under program control.**

```
procedure TForm1.BitBtn1Click(Sender: TObject);
var
  P: TPicture;
begin
  P := TPicture.Create;
  try
    P.LoadFromFile('C:\Windows\Clouds.bmp');
    Canvas.Draw(0, 0, P.Graphic);
  finally
    P.Free;
  end;
end;
```

Listing 13-3 demonstrates some key graphics techniques. Variable *P* is a TPicture object, constructed by calling TPicture.Create as the procedure's first statement. To ensure proper disposal of the resulting object, all statements that use *P* are inside a *try* block, and a *finally* block calls P.Free. This ensures that, if any exceptions occur inside the *try* block, the statement in the *finally* block is executed. Regardless of any errors that might occur, the memory occupied by the TPicture object is guaranteed to be properly disposed before the procedure ends.

Inside the *try* block, TPicture's LoadFromFile method reads a bitmap file (change the filename if you want). To display the image, the program calls the Canvas's Draw method, which Delphi defines as follows:

```
procedure Draw(X, Y: Integer; Graphic: Tgraphic);
```

✦ **X, Y**—Client-area coordinates relative to the object that provides the Canvas. Set these values to zero to display the image in the Canvas's upper left corner.

✦ **Graphic** — Pass a TBitmap, TIcon, or TMetaFile object to this parameter. Or, as the listing demonstrates, when using a TPicture object, pass its Graphic property.

Or, you can insert an Image component into a form and use its Picture property to load and display a bitmap. The following programming performs the identical tasks as in Listing 13-3:

```
with Image1 do
    Picture.LoadFromFile('C:\Windows\Clouds.Bmp');
```

The difference between the techniques is purely a design choice. If it is more convenient to use a component, the preceding code is the simplest approach, and it doesn't require you to construct and free objects or call a Canvas's Draw method. If you need to construct and use objects at run time, use the technique in Listing 13-3. However, TPicture does not use a window handle; TImage does. This makes TPicture the more memory-efficient choice.

Note

TImage is a class derived from TGraphicControl, and it therefore does not have a window handle. TDBImage, however, does have a window handle, a subtle distinction. See Chapter 17, Developing Database Applications, for more information on TDBImage and other database controls.

Metafile, bitmap, and icon files

Using the preceding information, you can construct an image file viewer that can display a metafile (.wmf), icon (.ico), or bitmap (.bmp) file, and copy any of those files to another directory. Figure 13-2 shows MetaMore's display opened to a Windows metafile supplied with Microsoft Office. The program, which is shown in Listing 13-4, can also read, display, and copy bitmap and icon files.

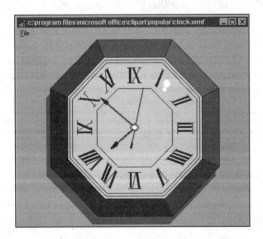

Figure 13-2: MetaMore can display any metafile, bitmap, or icon file.

Listing 13-4: **MetaMore\Main.pas**

```
unit Main;

interface

uses
  SysUtils, Windows, Messages, Classes, Graphics,
  Controls, Forms, Dialogs, Menus, ExtCtrls;

type
  TMainForm = class(TForm)
    Image1: TImage;
    MainMenu1: TMainMenu;
    FileMenu: TMenuItem;
    FileOpen: TMenuItem;
    N1: TMenuItem;
    FileExit: TMenuItem;
    OpenDialog1: TOpenDialog;
    SaveDialog1: TSaveDialog;
    FileSaveAs: TMenuItem;
    procedure FileOpenClick(Sender: TObject);
    procedure FileSaveAsClick(Sender: TObject);
    procedure FileExitClick(Sender: TObject);
  private
    { Private declarations }
  public
    { Public declarations }
  end;

var
  MainForm: TMainForm;

implementation

{$R *.DFM}

procedure TMainForm.FileOpenClick(Sender: TObject);
begin
  with OpenDialog1 do
  begin
    if Execute then
      Image1.Picture.LoadFromFile(Filename);
    Caption := Lowercase(Filename);
  end;
end;

procedure TMainForm.FileSaveAsClick(Sender: TObject);
```

(continued)

Listing 13-4 *(continued)*

```
begin
  with SaveDialog1 do
  begin
    Filename := Caption;
    if Execute then
      Image1.Picture.SaveToFile(Filename);
    Caption := Lowercase(Filename);
  end;
end;

procedure TMainForm.FileExitClick(Sender: TObject);
begin
  Close;
end;

end.
```

Caution   MetaMore cannot translate file types. For example, if you load a bitmap, you must save it as a bitmap.

MetaMore uses an Image component object, which is often the simplest approach. Alternatively, you could construct a Picture object as Listing 13-3 demonstrates. Or, you can create an object for a specific type of image file. For example, Listing 13-5 shows a Button OnClick event handler that creates a TMetaFile object and loads and displays a Windows metafile. (If you have Microsoft Office, you can find sample metafiles in the Program Files\Microsoft Office\Clipart\Popular and other directory paths.)

As with the TPicture class, this technique takes more programming than using an Image component, but uses less memory and fewer Windows resources. First, create the TMetaFile object by calling the class's Create method. Use the resulting object in a *try* block, and free it in a *finally* block. This ensures proper disposal in case an exception occurs.

Listing 13-5: Try this Button OnClick event handler to construct a TMetaFile obiect and load and display a Windows metafile.

```
procedure TForm1.Button1Click(Sender: TObject);
var
  MetaFile: TMetaFile;
begin
  MetaFile := TMetaFile.Create;
  try
```

```
    MetaFile.LoadFromFile(ôC:\msoffice\clipart\anchor.wmf');
    Canvas.Draw(0, 0, MetaFile);
  finally
    MetaFile.Free;
  end;
end;
```

To load a metafile, call the MetaFile object's LoadFromFile method (change the filename if necessary). Call the Canvas's Draw method to display the MetaFile. You can pass MetaFile to Draw because the TMetaFile class is a TGraphic descendent.

You can use the same programming in Listing 13-5 to load and display bitmap and icon files. Simply replace TMetaFile with TBitmap or TIcon, and load a file of the appropriate type. Use TPicture (see Listing 13-3) to load metafile, icon, and bitmap files based on the filename extension.

Instead of Draw, call StretchDraw to resize an image to fit within a defined rectangle. For example, to fill the window's client area with the MetaFile image, replace the Canvas.Draw statement in Listing 13-5 with this line:

```
    Canvas.StretchDraw(ClientRect, MetaFile);
```

Delphi defines StretchDraw as:

```
    procedure StretchDraw(const Rect: TRect; Graphic: Tgraphic);
```

- ✦ **Rect** — Defines a rectangular area for displaying an image. Assign values to this record's Left, Top, Right, and Bottom integers; or if more convenient, you can assign TPoint records to Rect's TopLeft and BottomRight members.

- ✦ **Graphic** — Any TBitmap, TIcon, or TMetaFile object. StretchDraw resizes the image to fit within Rect's defined area.

Bitmap resources

Unlike in conventional Windows programming, you won't use many resource objects in Delphi applications. One exception to this rule is a bitmap that you want to include with your application. You could distribute a separate bitmap file and use a TPicture or TBitmap object to load and display it. Or, you can create the bitmap as a resource (.res) using Delphi's Image Editor on the Tools menu.

After creating the resource file with a bitmap (let's assume you named it YOURBITS), bind the resource into the compiled .exe code file by inserting this directive in the module's implementation:

```
    {$R Yourbits.Res}
```

Use the programming in Listing 13-6 to create a bitmap object, and call the TBitmap method, LoadFromResourceName. Pass the application's instance handle (HInstance) and the name of the resource to load. This may be a 256-color bitmap. The string YOURBITS is the resource name that you assigned in the Image Editor. (The Yourbits.res file could be named something else — it doesn't have to be the same as the name of the resource it contains.) Call the Draw or StretchDraw (commented out) methods as shown in the sample listing.

Listing 13-6: This Button OnClick event handler demonstrates how to load and display a bitmap resource bound into the program's compiled .exe code file by Delphi's Image Editor.

```
procedure TForm1.Button1Click(Sender: TObject);
var
  YourBits: TBitmap;
begin
  YourBits := TBitmap.Create;
  try
    YourBits.LoadFromResourceName(HInstance,'YOURBITS');
    Canvas.Draw(0, 0, YourBits);
(*    Canvas.StretchDraw(ClientRect, YourBits); *)
  finally
    YourBits.Free;
  end;
end;
```

Offscreen bitmaps

The TBitmap class provides a Canvas property that you can use to draw offscreen. Simply construct a TBitmap object, and call methods in its Canvas property to draw on a virtual canvas that remains hidden from view. You can then display the resulting graphics all at once by calling methods such as Draw, StretchDraw, CopyRect, and BrushCopy for a form or PaintBox's Canvas. This technique is important in animations, as well as for hiding the details of a complex image's formation until the figure is complete.

Listing 13-7 demonstrates the basic techniques required to draw in an offscreen bitmap. To try the code, use the listing as a Button's OnClick event handler. The program draws a rectangle and ellipse offscreen and then displays the resulting image by calling CopyRect.

In Listing 13-7, the Source and Dest TRect records specify the size of the offscreen bitmap, as well as the location to which the image is copied onto the form. Create the bitmap object by calling TBitmap.Create. Assign Width and Height values to create a bitmap of the size you need.

To draw offscreen, call methods such as Rectangle and Ellipse, and assign values to Pen and Brush properties and subproperties. Be sure to call methods and make assignments for the bitmap's Canvas. When you are done creating your image, call a form or PaintBox Canvas method such as CopyRect to bring the offscreen image into view.

Calling TBitmap.Create creates a memory device context, which consumes Windows resources and time. In this example of a simple button click, the end result is quick enough, but for the best speed in a fast loop or a performance-critical OnPaint event handler, create the bitmap object in the form's OnCreate handler and destroy it in OnDestroy.

When using *with* statements, be especially careful that you draw into the intended Canvas. To draw offscreen, call methods for a TBitmap object's Canvas. Copy the offscreen image by calling a method for a form or PaintBox's Canvas.

Drag-and-drop objects

When you design a Delphi application, you click and drag component objects around in a form window. But how can you do the same for graphics shapes in your own applications? The answer requires a bit of programming which is not difficult to understand, but does require careful attention to detail, especially in mouse coordinate handling.

Listing 13-7: This Button OnClick event handler demonstrates how to draw into an offscreen bitmap.

```
procedure TForm1.BitBtn1Click(Sender: TObject);
var
  OffScreen: TBitmap;
  Dest, Source: TRect;
begin
  Source := Rect(0, 0, 255, 255);
  Dest := Rect(10, 10, 265, 265);
  OffScreen := TBitmap.Create;
  try
```

(continued)

Listing 13-7 *(continued)*

```
    OffScreen.Width := Source.Right + 1;
    OffScreen.Height := Source.Bottom + 1;
    with OffScreen.Canvas do
    begin
      Pen.Color := clRed;
      Brush.Color := clAppWorkSpace;
      Rectangle(0, 0, 255, 255);
      Ellipse(63, 63, 127, 127);
    end;
    Canvas.CopyRect(Dest, OffScreen.Canvas, Source);
  finally
    OffScreen.Free;
  end;
end;
```

On the
CD-ROM

For an example of drag-and-drop graphics, try the DragMe application on the CD-ROM. The files are in the Source\DragMe directory. As shown in Figure 13-3, the program displays three shapes: a yellow rounded rectangle, a red circle, and a blue square. Each figure is a Shape component object. Run the program and click and drag the objects around the application window. Listing 13-8 shows the steps needed to create this useful illusion, which you can put to work to make draggable any shape you can draw.

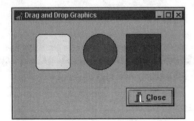

Figure 13-3: The DragMe application displays three Shape objects, which you can click and drag to move around the program's window.

Listing 13-8: **DragMe\Main.pas**

```pascal
unit Main;

interface

uses
  SysUtils, Windows, Messages, Classes, Graphics,
  Controls, Forms, Dialogs, ExtCtrls, StdCtrls, Buttons;

type
  TMainForm = class(TForm)
    Shape1: TShape;
    Shape2: TShape;
    Shape3: TShape;
    BitBtn1: TBitBtn;
    procedure ShapeMouseDown(Sender: TObject;
      Button: TMouseButton; Shift: TShiftState; X, Y: Integer);
    procedure ShapeMouseMove(Sender: TObject;
      Shift: TShiftState; X, Y: Integer);
    procedure ShapeMouseUp(Sender: TObject;
      Button: TMouseButton; Shift: TShiftState; X, Y: Integer);
    procedure FormCreate(Sender: TObject);
  private
    Dragging: Boolean;          // Drag operation in progress
    XOffset, YOffset: Integer;  // Offsets from shape upper left
    FocusRect: TRect;           // Dotted outline while dragging
    PS: TShape;                 // Reference to shape dragging
  public
    { Public declarations }
  end;

var
  MainForm: TMainForm;

implementation

{$R *.DFM}

procedure TMainForm.ShapeMouseDown(Sender: TObject;
  Button: TMouseButton; Shift: TShiftState; X, Y: Integer);
begin
  Dragging := True;        { Set dragging flag true }
  XOffset := X;            { Keep offsets from shape upper left }
  YOffset := Y;
  PS := Sender as TShape;  { Assign reference to shape }
  with PS do               { Create outline rectangle }
```

(continued)

Listing 13-8 *(continued)*

```
    FocusRect := Rect(Left, Top, Left + Width, Top + Height);
  Canvas.DrawFocusRect(FocusRect);  { Draw outline }
end;

procedure TMainForm.ShapeMouseMove(Sender: TObject;
  Shift: TShiftState; X, Y: Integer);
begin
  if Dragging then  { Move outline only if dragging }
  begin
    Canvas.DrawFocusRect(FocusRect);  { Erase outline }
    with FocusRect do
    begin  { Move outline rectangle }
      Left := (PS.Left + X) _ XOffset;
      Top := (PS.Top + Y) _ YOffset;
      Right := PS.Width + Left;
      Bottom := PS.Height + Top;
    end;
    Canvas.DrawFocusRect(FocusRect);
  end;
end;

procedure TMainForm.ShapeMouseUp(Sender: TObject;
  Button: TMouseButton; Shift: TShiftState; X, Y: Integer);
begin
  if Dragging then  { Move shape only if dragging }
  begin
    Canvas.DrawFocusRect(FocusRect);
    Dragging := False;
    with Sender as TShape do
    begin  { Move shape to new location }
      Left := (Left + X) _ XOffset;
      Top := (Top + Y) _ YOffset;
    end;
  end;
end;

procedure TMainForm.FormCreate(Sender: TObject);
begin
  Dragging := False;
end;

end.
```

DragMe declares five variables in the module's form class. Dragging is True during a drag-and-drop operation. XOffset and YOffset are the pixel coordinates of the mouse cursor relative to the Shape that is being dragged. These values make it possible to "pick up" the shape by clicking the mouse anywhere inside its borders. FocusRect is a TRect record with Left, Top, Right, and Bottom values that define the outline rectangle you see while clicking and dragging a shape. PS is a pointer to a shape, which the program uses to refer to the shape that is being dragged around.

Three event handlers implement dragging and dropping for any Shape object. When you click the mouse pointer inside a Shape, procedure ShapeMouseDown begins a drag-and-drop operation. First, the program sets the Dragging flag to True. It then saves the mouse x- and y-coordinate values in XOffset and YOffset. This marks the mouse location relative to the shape's upper-left corner. The program also saves the Sender parameter, type-cast to a TShape object, in PS for future reference to the shape being dragged. Using PS, the program assigns values to FocusRect for drawing the dotted outline during dragging with this statement:

```
Canvas.DrawFocusRect(FocusRect);  { Draw outline }
```

DrawFocusRect draws a dotted rectangular outline using exclusive-OR logic. Calling DrawFocusRect twice for the same TRect record erases the outline. When you move the mouse, if Dragging is True, the OnMouseMove event handler, ShapeMouseMove, calls DragFocusRect to erase the rectangle in its old position. The procedure then assigns new values to FocusRect's Left, Top, Right, and Bottom members. When reading this code, remember that the x and y mouse coordinate parameters are relative to the shape being dragged, not to the window or the screen. Thus, the new FocusRect position equals the shape's location (which hasn't changed) plus x and y, minus the offsets from the shape's upper left to the location where you clicked the mouse. Calling DrawFocusRect with these new values moves the outline as you drag the mouse.

When you release the mouse button, the third and final event handler, ShapeMouseUp, moves the shape to its new location. (Checking whether Dragging is true in this case is probably unnecessary because an OnMouseUp event can't occur without a prior OnMouseDown event, but it's always best to be careful.) Once again, the program calls DrawFocusRect, this time to erase the final outline. After setting the Dragging flag to False, it's a simple matter to move the shape by assigning new values to its Left and Top properties, completing the illusion of the shape hopping to the last-known position of the focus rectangle.

Remember that objects can share event handlers. For example, to add a new draggable shape to DragMe, simply insert a Shape object and set its OnMouseDown, OnMouseMove, and OnMouseUp events to the module's existing event handlers.

Picture Dialogs

You can use standard dialog components OpenDialog and SaveDialog to browse for and to prompt users for graphics filenames. However, two relatively new components, OpenPictureDialog and SavePictureDialog, provide dialogs specifically for browsing graphics files. The dialogs show previews of graphics images so users can see the files they are selecting before loading them into your application. (This preview is sometimes called a *thumbnail sketch,* although I don't see what my thumbnail has to do with it.)

OpenPictureDialog

On the
CD-ROM

Use the OpenPictureDialog component to prompt users for graphics filenames. By default, the dialog shows all .bmp (bitmap), .ico (icon), emf (enhanced metafile), and .wmf (Windows metafile) files in the selected directory. When the user selects one of these types of files, the dialog shows a preview of the image (see Figure 13-4). This figure shows the dialog that's displayed by the PicDialogs sample application on the CD-ROM in the Source\PicDialogs directory. Listing 13-9 shows the sample program's source code.

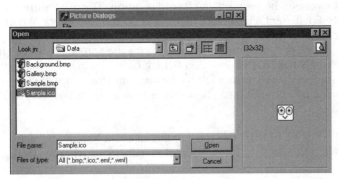

Figure 13-4: The OpenPictureDialog component prompts users for a graphics filename, and shows a preview of the selected image.

Listing 13-9: **PicDialogs\Main.pas**

```
unit Main;

interface

uses
```

```
  Windows, Messages, SysUtils, Classes, Graphics, Controls,
  Forms, Dialogs, Menus, ExtDlgs, ExtCtrls;

type
  TMainForm = class(TForm)
    Image1: TImage;
    OpenPictureDialog1: TOpenPictureDialog;
    SavePictureDialog1: TSavePictureDialog;
    MainMenu1: TMainMenu;
    File1: TMenuItem;
    Open1: TMenuItem;
    Save1: TMenuItem;
    N1: TMenuItem;
    Exit1: TMenuItem;
    procedure Open1Click(Sender: TObject);
    procedure Exit1Click(Sender: TObject);
    procedure Save1Click(Sender: TObject);
  private
    { Private declarations }
  public
    { Public declarations }
  end;

var
  MainForm: TMainForm;

implementation

{$R *.DFM}

procedure TMainForm.Open1Click(Sender: TObject);
begin
  with OpenPictureDialog1 do
  if Execute then
  begin
    Image1.Picture.LoadFromFile(Filename);
    Caption := Lowercase(Filename);
    Save1.Enabled := True; // Enable File|Save... command
  end;
end;

procedure TMainForm.Save1Click(Sender: TObject);
begin
  with SavePictureDialog1 do
  begin
    Filename := Caption;
    if Execute then
    begin
```

(continued)

Listing 13-9 *(continued)*

```
      Image1.Picture.SaveToFile(Filename);
      Caption := Lowercase(Filename);
    end;
  end;
end;

procedure TMainForm.Exit1Click(Sender: TObject);
begin
  Close;
end;

end.
```

To use the OpenPictureDialog, insert an object of that component into a form. Program an event handler such as Open1Click in the sample listing that executes when the user selects your program's Open command—from a menu, for example, or by clicking a button. At that point, call the OpenPictureDialog object's Execute command, which returns True only if the user selects a graphics file. In most cases, you use code such as the following:

```
with OpenPictureDialog1 do
if Execute then
begin
  // Use Filename property here to load file
end;
```

The *with* statement tells Delphi to use the OpenPictureDialog properties and methods by default. The *if* statement calls Execute, which if True, executes the statements between *begin* and *end*. Insert your programming here to use the Filename property, which holds the path name of the selected file. If Execute returns False, then the user clicked the Cancel button or pressed Esc to end the dialog, and your program should not load any file.

OpenPictureDialog properties

Following are some properties that you can modify to customize an OpenPictureDialog object:

✦ **DefaultExt**—Set this to the default filename extension, without a period, such as bmp or ico. This string is appended to a selected filename, unless that filename already ends with a registered extension. If the user selects a file with an unregistered extension (for example, the user types Anyfile rather than Anyfile.bmp), DefaultExt is appended to the filename. You might also set

DefaultExt in code to the default graphics extension for a graphics class such as TBitmap, using a statement such as:

```
OpenPictureDialog1.DefaultExt := GraphicExtension(TBitmap);
```

✦ **Files**—If the Options property includes the option ofAllowMultiSelect, then the Files property contains a string list of all selected files. Files.Count equals the number of selected files.

✦ **Filter**—This works the same as the Filter property in other file-open (and file-save) dialogs. Click the ellipsis next to this property to modify the default set of file filters, which by default, is set to the following list of strings in Table 13-1. The default settings are registered with the TGraphic class. You can add to these by calling TPicture.RegisterFileFormat.

✦ **FilterIndex**—Set this to the index of the string in the Filter string-list property that you want the dialog to use by default. This is the filename type that users see when they initially open the dialog. For example, using the default filters listed in the preceding table, setting FilterIndex to two selects Icons (*.ico) as the default filename filter. If FilterIndex is out of range, the first Filter string is used by default.

✦ **InitialDir**—Set this to the pathname of the directory you want users to see when they first open the dialog. If you don't set this field, the current directory is used by default.

✦ **Options**—You can select numerous options by assigning values to this set. For example, specify ofAllowMultiSelect to allow users to select more than one filename (see the Files property). I explain more about Options in the next section.

✦ **Title**—Assign the string you want the dialog to display in its window title bar. If you don't assign a string to this property, the dialog displays the word Open as its title. (The SavePictureDialog displays the word Save.)

Table 13-1
Default Filter Properties of the OpenPictureDialog and SavePictureDialog Components

Filter name	Filter
All (*.bmp;*.ico;*.emf;*.wmf)	*.bmp;*.ico;*.emf;*.wmf
Bitmaps (*.bmp)	*.bmp
Icons (*.ico)	*.ico
Enhanced Metafiles (*.emf)	*.emf
Metafiles (*.wmf)	*.wmf

OpenPictureDialog options

The OpenPictureDialog and SavePictureDialog components provide numerous options that you can select to customize how you want the dialog to appear and operate. The full set of options is declared as the Pascal enumerated data type:

```
TOpenOption = (ofReadOnly, ofOverwritePrompt, ofHideReadOnly,
  ofNoChangeDir, ofShowHelp, ofNoValidate, ofAllowMultiSelect,
  ofExtensionDifferent, ofPathMustExist, ofFileMustExist,
  ofCreatePrompt, ofShareAware, ofNoReadOnlyReturn,
  ofNoTestFileCreate, ofNoNetworkButton, ofNoLongNames,
  ofOldStyleDialog, ofNoDereferenceLinks);
TOpenOptions = set of TOpenOption;
```

Actually, that's two declarations. TOpenOption (singular) is the enumerated type — a variable of that type can be assigned any of the listed constants. TOpenOptions (plural) is declared as a Pascal set TOpenOption constants. A variable of the TOpenOptions type can be assigned zero, one, or more combinations of TOpenOption constants. For example, to specify the ofReadOnly and ofAllowMultiSelect options, the program can execute a statement such as:

```
OpenPictureDialog1.Options := [ofReadOnly, ofAllowMultiSelect];
```

To assign options at design time, select the OpenPictureDialog object and double-click the small plus sign to the left of the Options property in the Object Inspector. This opens these properties' subvalues, which are programmed as True/False properties corresponding to the TOpenOption enumerated constants. For example, to make the preceding assignment at design time, set the ofReadOnly and ofAllowMultiSelect properties to True.

Table 13-2 describes each option in alphabetic order. No options are specified for a new OpenPictureDialog or SavePictureDialog object.

Table 13-2
OpenPictureDialog and SavePictureDialog Component Options

Option	Description
ofAllowMultiSelect	Permit selection of one or more files. Selected filenames are returned in the Files property. Files.Count equals the number of selected filenames.
ofCreatePrompt	If the user enters the name of a file that does not exist, this option presents a dialog that asks whether a new file of that name should be created. Your code must create the actual file — this option merely manages the prompts; it doesn't create the file.

Option	Description

ofExtensionDifferent	This option operates as a True or False flag that indicates whether the filename extension is different from that set in the DefaultExt property. Use a statement such as:
	
	`if TOpenOption.ofExtensionDifferent in OpenPictureDialog1.Options`
	
	   `then..`
	
	to inspect whether this flag is included in the Options set.

ofFileMustExist	Use this option to have the dialog display an error message if the user attempts to enter the name of a file that does not exist. This option ensures that the returned Filename property equals the name of a file selected from a directory listing.
ofHideReadOnly	The picture dialogs normally have an Open As Read Only check box.
ofNoChangeDir	If you want the directory to be reset to its path before the dialog's Execute statement is called, include this option. If you don't include this option, the current directory is changed to whatever path the user selected.
ofNoDereferenceLinks	Normally, Windows shortcuts are dereferenced (translated) to the actual paths of the files to which the shortcuts refer. If you don't want this to happen, include this option. In that case, the returned Filename of a selected shortcut is set to that item's .lnk file, and it is up to you to determine the actual referenced file.
ofNoLongNames	Disables long filenames, and displays only old-style 8.3 (eight-character filename, three-character extension) names in the dialog directory pane.
ofNoNetworkButton	Obsolete. This option deletes the Network button from the file-selection dialog, which appears only if the ofOldStyleDialog option is also included.
ofNoReadOnlyReturn	If the user attempts to open a read-only file, this option causes the dialog to display an error message and refuse to return the selected file. Using this option ensures that a file can be written to (but be aware that the file state can be changed by another program in the meantime).
ofNoTestFileCreate	Use with extreme caution. Subverts network file protection allowing file saves in a shared network directory.

(continued)

Table 13-2 *(continued)*	
Option	**Description**
ofNoValidate	Normally, filenames are checked for any illegal characters. Use this option only if such characters are somehow used in the actual filenames.
ofOldStyleDialog	Reverts to an older style dialog (see also ofNoNetworkButton).
ofOverwritePrompt	For save dialogs only, this option displays an error message prompt that warns users they have selected an existing filename. If you use this option, you can be sure that users have answered Yes to the "Overwrite file?" prompt, and you can safely write to the selected file even if it already exists.
ofPathMustExist	If the user enters a directory path that does not exist, this option displays an error message and refuses to return the path in Filename.
ofReadOnly	Specifies that only files marked read-only can be returned by the dialog in the Filename property.
ofShareAware	Use with extreme caution. This option subverts file-share violations (users attempting to open a file in use, for example), and allows selection of files that are perhaps in the process of being modified by other users or programs.
ofShowHelp	Use this option to display a Help button. Also assign a HelpContext value to link to your help file's subject.

SavePictureDialog

On the CD-ROM

The SavePictureDialog is nearly the same as the OpenPictureDialog. Both components have identical properties and options, but of course, the SavePictureDialog component prompts users for filenames to save graphics files. The PicDialogs demonstration program on the CD-ROM in the Source\PicDialogs directory demonstrates how to use SavePictureDialog. (Refer back to Figure 13-4 and Listing 13-9.)

You use the SavePictureDialog component in much the same way as OpenPictureDialog. However, you might want to take one additional step as demonstrated by the following code, which shows how to respond to the program's Save command or button:

```
with SavePictureDialog1 do
begin
  Filename := Caption;
  if Execute then
  begin
    Image1.Picture.SaveToFile(Filename);
    Caption := Lowercase(Filename);
  end;
end;
```

This code, cut from the PicDialogs sample application, uses a *with* statement to specify that properties and methods belonging to SavePictureDialog1 object are to be used. The Filename property of that object is first set to the window's caption — this causes the dialog to display the current filename, which was saved in the window caption by the close-command's procedure (see Open1Click in the listing). Calling Execute brings up the dialog, and returns True only if the user selected filename and clicked the Save button. In that case, the Image object's SaveToFile method in the Picture property is called to write the file to disk. Because the user might have selected a different filename in which to save the file, the window caption is reset to the current Filename property of the SavePictureDialog1 object. This ensures that the selected filename and window caption always agree.

Animations

With Delphi components, it's easy to add animations to your programs. In this section, I explain the basics of using the Animate and MediaPlayer components. With Animate, you can add standard animations that give visual feedback to users during common operations such as copying and deleting files. You can also play any .avi (audiovisual) file. With MediaPlayer, you can build a full-featured .avi file viewer, as the sample VideoPlayer application in this section demonstrates.

The Animate component

On the
CD-ROM

The Animate component on the Win32 palette can play any AVI clip file to provide animated graphics in a window. You can also use this component to display common AVI clips provided with Windows such as displayed by Explorer during file operations. Figure 13-5 shows one of eight possible standard animations displayed by the Animator sample application on the CD-ROM in the Source\Animator directory. Load this program's project file, Animator.dpr, into Delphi and press F9 to compile and run the demonstration. Select one of the radio buttons to view a different animation. Click the Go button to run the animation; click Stop to halt. Listing 13-10 shows the Animator program's source code.

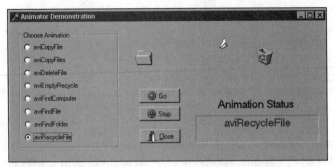

Figure 13-5: The Animator sample application demonstrates how to use an Animate object to run a standard Windows AVI clip, in this case, the "Recycle File" video.

Listing 13-10: **Animator\Main.pas**

```
unit Main;

interface

uses
  Windows, Messages, SysUtils, Classes, Graphics, Controls,
  Forms, Dialogs, StdCtrls, Buttons, ExtCtrls, ComCtrls;

type
  TMainForm = class(TForm)
    Animate1: TAnimate;
    RadioGroup1: TRadioGroup;
    GoBitBtn: TBitBtn;
    StopBitBtn: TBitBtn;
    BitBtn1: TBitBtn;
    StatusText: TStaticText;
    Label1: TLabel;
    procedure GoBitBtnClick(Sender: TObject);
    procedure StopBitBtnClick(Sender: TObject);
  private
    { Private declarations }
  public
    { Public declarations }
  end;

var
  MainForm: TMainForm;

implementation
```

```
{$R *.DFM}

{ Define array types for easier assignments of the
  Animate object's CommonAvi property, and also the
  StatusText object that shows which animation is running. }
type
  aviKindArray = array[0 .. 7] of TCommonAvi;
  aviStringArray = array[0 .. 7] of String;

{ Define constant arrays containing the TCommonAvi values
  in the same order they appear in the RadioGroup object,
  and also strings for displaying in the StatusText object
  that shows which animation is running. }
const

  aviKinds: aviKindArray =
    (aviCopyFile,
     aviCopyFiles,
     aviDeleteFile,
     aviEmptyRecycle,
     aviFindComputer,
     aviFindFile,
     aviFindFolder,
     aviRecycleFile);

  aviStrings: aviStringArray =
    ('aviCopyFile',
     'aviCopyFiles',
     'aviDeleteFile',
     'aviEmptyRecycle',
     'aviFindComputer',
     'aviFindFile',
     'aviFindFolder',
     'aviRecycleFile');

{ Start selected animation. This event handler is assigned
  to the OnClick event for both the Go button and the
  RadioGroup1. Clicking Go or clicking a radio button starts
  the animation immediately. }
procedure TMainForm.GoBitBtnClick(Sender: TObject);
var
  AnimIndex: Integer;  // Index of selected animation
begin
  AnimIndex := RadioGroup1.ItemIndex;
  with Animate1 do
  begin
    StatusText.Caption := aviStrings[AnimIndex];
```

(continued)

Listing 13-10 *(continued)*

```
     CommonAVI := aviKinds[AnimIndex];
     Play(1, FrameCount, 0);  // Start the animation
   end;
end;

{ Halt the animation when user clicks the Stop button. }
procedure TMainForm.StopBitBtnClick(Sender: TObject);
begin
  Animate1.Stop;
  StatusText.Caption := '(stopped)';
end;

end.
```

The Animator application shows how to select, start, and stop a standard Windows AVI clip using an Animate object. The GoBitBtnClick procedure is assigned to the OnClick event for both the Go button and the RadioGroup1 objects. As a result, clicking Go or selecting an animation type radio button starts playing that animation immediately.

The GoBitBtnClick procedure begins by assigning the ItemIndex of the RadioGroup1 object to a local Integer, just to make it simpler to use. This indicates which button of the group is currently selected. To show onscreen which animation is running, a StaticText object named StatusText is assigned a string label from a constant array, aviStrings, defined in the unit's implementation section. Using the same radio group index, the CommonAvi property of the Animate object is set to the selected animation name such as aviCopyFile or aviFindComputer. To play the animation, the program calls the Animate component's Play method using the statement:

```
  Play(1, FrameCount, 0);
```

The first two arguments indicate the range of frame numbers to play. The first frame is numbered one. FrameCount, a field in the Animate object, indicates the number of frames in the assigned AVI clip. The final argument equals the number of repititions. Set this value to zero, as done here, to repeat the animation until the Animate Stop method is called.

That happens in Animator when you click the Stop button. This calls the StopBitBtnClick event handler, which calls the Animate component's Stop method. To indicate that no animation is running, the procedure also sets the StatusText object's Caption to read '(stopped)'.

Animate properties

Following are selected Animate properties you can use to customize an Animate object:

✦ **Active** — Set this to True to begin playing an animation. Before setting Active True, however, you must select a standard AVI clip with the CommonAVI property, or enter the filename of an AVI video into the FileName field. Setting CommonAVI to aviNone, or clearing the FileName field, sets Active to False. You can also inspect Active at run time to determine whether an animation is running.

✦ **AutoSize** — Normally set this to True to automatically size the Animate object depending on the AVI clip's size. Set AutoSize False only if all clips are the same size, or you are playing only one clip. Tip: To determine how large to make the Animate object, set AutoSize True and select a CommonAVI or FileName. Set Active True to run the animation, then set Active and AutoSize to False. The Animate object is now set to the required size of the selected AVI clip.

✦ **Center** — Normally set this to True so the animation is centered in the Animate object's display space. Setting Center to False causes the animation to appear flush against the Animate object's top-left corner.

✦ **CommonAVI** — This property selects a standard Windows AVI clip. Set CommonAVI to one of the TCommonAvi enumerated constants aviNone, aviFindFolder, aviFindFile, aviFindComputer, aviCopyFiles, aviCopyFile, aviRecycleFile, aviEmptyRecycle, and aviDeleteFile.

✦ **FileName** — Enter the filename of an AVI video-only (no sound) clip file into this property. You may do this at design time, or at run time. This automatically sets CommonAVI to aviNone — you cannot choose both a common Windows AVI clip and a file at the same time; you may use one or the other property. The file must exist, and it must be a silent AVI clip. (See "The MediaPlayer component" in this chapter for information on how to play AVI sound clips and movies.)

✦ **FrameCount** — Equals the number of frames in the AVI clip. This value is read-only; it does not appear in the Object Inspector. FrameCount is updated automatically when the CommonAVI or FileName are assigned values.

✦ **Repetitions** — Set to the number of repetitions to play the clip when Active is True. A value of zero indicates the clip should play indefinitely until Active is set to False or the Animate.Stop method is called.

✦ **StartFrame** — Assign the starting frame to begin the animation. The first frame is numbered one. You don't need to set this field if your program calls the Play method.

✦ **StopFrame** — Assign the last frame of the animation to play. The number of frames is found in the read-only FrameCount field. You don't need to set this field if your program calls the Play method.

✦ **Timers** — When False (the default value), this property causes animations to run in a separate thread. When True, the property causes the animation to be controlled by a system timer. Normally, you can leave Timers set to False, but if you need to synchronize other events with an animation, you can change Timers to True. Use the Animate component's OnStart and OnStop events to control the synchronized activity.

✦ **Transparent** — Set to True to display the parent object's color as the animation's background. This is the usual value when displaying animations in a window. If Transparent is False, the animation background color is taken from the AVI clip.

The MediaPlayer component

The MediaPlayer component is a virtual home studio you can use to build multimedia software. I used a MediaPlayer object to create the VideoPlayer demonstration program on the CD-ROM (it's in the Source\VideoPlayer directory). This program can open and play any AVI sound clip, and it shows how to create features such as an auto-repeat option.

Figure 13-6 shows the VideoPlayer program playing an AVI clip that I found in the Windows\Help directory — several clips are stored there that are part of the Windows online help system. The one shown here is a video that demonstrates cutting and pasting. Listing 13-11 shows the VideoPlayer's source code. Some of the steps in the program have critical effects on the run-time results, so I added numerous comments in the listing to explain the statements. I explain more about how the program works after the listing.

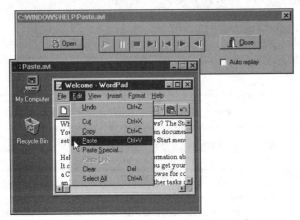

Figure 13-6: The VideoPlayer application on the CD-ROM can display any AVI sound and video clip. The clip shown here is Paste.avi from the Windows\Help directory.

Note

MediaPlayer is more than just a video player. It can function as a multimedia controller for a CD-ROM, MIDI sequencer, or a VCR. In this chapter, I explain how to use MediaPlayer to display AVI silent and sound clips, but the same component is capable of serving as a controller for numerous other types of multimedia. MediaPlayer can also play MPEG movies if the user has installed Microsoft's ActiveMovie software.

Listing 13-11: VideoPlayer.Main.pas

```
unit Main;

interface

uses
  Windows, Messages, SysUtils, Classes, Graphics, Controls,
  Forms, Dialogs, StdCtrls, Buttons, MPlayer, ComCtrls;

type
  TForm1 = class(TForm)
    MediaPlayer1: TMediaPlayer;
    OpenBitBtn: TBitBtn;
    BitBtn2: TBitBtn;
    OpenDialog1: TOpenDialog;
    AutoPlayCheckBox: TCheckBox;
    procedure OpenBitBtnClick(Sender: TObject);
    procedure MediaPlayer1Notify(Sender: TObject);
    procedure MediaPlayer1Click(Sender: TObject;
      Button: TMPBtnType; var DoDefault: Boolean);
    procedure AutoPlayCheckBoxClick(Sender: TObject);
  private
    { Private declarations }
  public
    { Public declarations }
  end;

var
  Form1: TForm1;

implementation

{$R *.DFM}

(* Note: Set the MediaPlayer1 object properties as follows
      AutoEnable      False     All buttons always enabled
      AutoOpen        True      Doesn't really matter
      AutoRewind      True      Rewinds media when it stops
      Other properties  Default settings
*)
```

(continued)

Listing 13-11 *(continued)*

```
{ Responds to user selection of the Open file button. }
{ Opens media file and starts playing immediately. }
{ Also sets the window caption to the filename. }
procedure TForm1.OpenBitBtnClick(Sender: TObject);
begin
  if OpenDialog1.Execute then
  begin
    Form1.Caption := OpenDialog1.FileName;
    MediaPlayer1.FileName := OpenDialog1.FileName;
    MediaPlayer1.Notify := True;   // Wants media event notify
    MediaPlayer1.Open;             // Opens assigned file
    MediaPlayer1.Frames := 1;      // Sets single step frames
    MediaPlayer1.Play;             // Start playing the file
  end;
end;

{ Responds to media event notifications. This gives us the
  chance to check whether the auto-replay checkbox is set, and
  if so, and if the media is stopped, to restart play. Despite
  the control's documentation, it is necessary to check whether
  Notify is true. Even if this flag is false, the procedure is
  called when the user clicks the stop button. }
procedure TForm1.MediaPlayer1Notify(Sender: TObject);
begin
  if (MediaPlayer1.Notify) and           // If flag is true
     (MediaPlayer1.Mode = mpStopped) and  // and playis stopped
     (AutoPlayCheckBox.Checked) then      // & checkbox enabled
  begin
    MediaPlayer1.Rewind;                  // rewind to start
    MediaPlayer1.Play;                    // and begin playing
  end;
  { You must set Notify to True so that the next media event
  generates a notification; otherwise, this procedure
    would be called only once. }
  MediaPlayer1.Notify := True;  // Request next notification
end;

{ Responds to user clicking in the MediaPlayer object. We need
  to check for this because, if the auto-replay checkbox is
  enabled, stopping the media would generate a notification,
  which would start playing again! In other words, this
  procedure allows the media to be stopped regardless of the
  auto-replay checkbox setting. }
procedure TForm1.MediaPlayer1Click(Sender: TObject;
  Button: TMPBtnType; var DoDefault: Boolean);
begin
  if (Button = btStop) or (Button = btPause) then
```

```
      MediaPlayer1.Notify := False    // Do not continue replay
    else
      MediaPlayer1.Notify := True;    // Replay if checkbox is set
  end;

{ Responds to user changing the state of the auto-replay
  checkbox. If the checkbox is being enabled, this procedure
  turns on notifications so that, when the media stops, the
  Notify event handler can restart the media playing. }
procedure TForm1.AutoPlayCheckBoxClick(Sender: TObject);
begin
  if AutoPlayCheckBox.Checked then
    MediaPlayer1.Notify := True;  // Triggers notifications
  end;

end.
```

Many factors are involved in successfully writing an AVI video player such as the VideoPlayer sample application listed here. The operating system version, the display hardware, the video drivers on the user's system, and the AVI file format all affect the outcome. Newer computer systems produce the best results — those with older hardware and early versions of Windows 95 may function poorly or not play AVI clips at all. In any case, the MediaPlayer component seems highly robust — I used VideoPlayer to play some damaged AVI clips that I could not view by any other means.

Onscreen, the MediaPlayer component is merely a toolbar of buttons that users can click to operate the object, like the buttons on a VCR. Figure 13-7 shows an unmodified MediaPlayer object inserted into a form. The nine buttons in left-to-right order are: Play, Pause, Stop, Next, Previous, Step, Back, Record, and Eject. Three properties affect button appearances. Use the ColoredButtons property to display individual buttons in color or black-and-white. Use EnabledButtons to enable or disable individual buttons (disabled buttons display in dim gray, and cannot be selected). Use the VisibleButtons property to indicate which buttons should be displayed. This is useful for hiding unwanted buttons — VideoPlayer, for example, hides the Record and Eject buttons which have no practical use in the program.

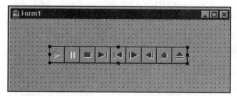

Figure 13-7: An unmodified MediaPlayer object with all its buttons

To start playing an AVI clip, use a dialog box or other means to prompt users for a filename. VideoPlayer demonstrates how to program this action in the event handler, OpenBitBtnClick, which executes when you click the Open button:

```
if OpenDialog1.Execute then
begin
   Form1.Caption := OpenDialog1.FileName;
   MediaPlayer1.FileName := OpenDialog1.FileName;
   MediaPlayer1.Notify := True;   // Wants media event notify
   MediaPlayer1.Open;             // Opens assigned file
   MediaPlayer1.Frames := 1;      // Sets single step frames
   MediaPlayer1.Play;             // Start playing the file
end;
```

Calling Execute brings up the OpenDialog window. The function returns True if the user selected a filename, in which case the statements between *begin* and *end* execute. To display which file is running, the first statement sets the form's window caption to the selected filename, taken from the OpenDialog1 object. This same name is assigned to the MediaPlayer1 object's FileName property—this prepares the file for viewing. To indicate that we want notifications of media events, the program sets Notify to True (more on this later).

After those two steps, the Open method loads the file into memory, but doesn't play it just yet. To indicate how many frames the step button should advance the video, Frames is set to one (this is normally set to ten percent of the number of frames in the video, but I prefer stepping one frame at a time). By the way, the Frames property is unpublished—you can set it at run time, but not in the Object Inspector.

To begin playing the AVI clip, the event handler calls the Play method for the MediaPlayer1 object. Unlike Animate, this version of Play has no arguments. Just call it to begin running the video. If the program doesn't call Play, users must click the Play button to begin running the AVI clip.

One of the tricky aspects of using the MediaPlayer component is responding to media notifications. By setting the Notify property to True, you specify that you want to receive these notifications, which are generated for various events that occur such as the starting and stopping of a video clip. To respond to these notifications, set Notify to True (you must do this using a program statement as shown in the preceding fragment), and create an OnNotify event handler for the MediaPlayer object. VideoPlayer's OnNotify event handler follows:

```
procedure TForm1.MediaPlayer1Notify(Sender: TObject);
begin
   if (MediaPlayer1.Notify) and            // If flag is true
      (MediaPlayer1.Mode = mpStopped) and  // and play's stopped
```

```
    (AutoPlayCheckBox.Checked) then        // & checkbox enabled
  begin
    MediaPlayer1.Rewind;                   // rewind to start
    MediaPlayer1.Play;                     // and begin playing
  end;
  MediaPlayer1.Notify := True;  // Request next notification
end;
```

The purpose of this code is to replay the current AVI clip if the user has checked the Auto replay check box. Because numerous notifications are received by this same procedure, the first step is to determine whether the video has stopped, in which case it is rewound and restarted from the beginning. If the Auto replay check box is not selected, the procedure does nothing, and therefore, the video stops at its end (or when the user clicks the Stop button).

Even though the program sets Notify to True, it is still necessary to check the Notify flag on entry to the OnNotify event handler. Tests indicate that notifications are still received at times even when Notify is False, perhaps because those events are generated during the time Notify is changing value. If Notify is True, VideoPlayer's OnNotify event handler inspects the Mode property to determine the state of the object. If that state equals mpStopped, then the user has halted play (or it has come to the end). If the AutoPlayCheckBox object is checked, the program rewinds and replays the current clip by calling the MediaPlayer's Rewind and Play methods.

Note   Notice that Notify is set to True just before OnNotify ends. This is necessary to request further notifications. If you don't want any more notifications, set Notify to False before the OnNotify event returns.

One wrinkle in the notification ointment is that, when the user stops the video, the action should halt immediately rather than restart from the beginning. As written, OnNotify repeats the current video if the Auto replay check box is selected — this would cause the AVI clip to repeat even if halted by clicking the controller's Stop button.

To fix this problem, an OnClick event handler for the MediaPlayer object checks whether the user has clicked the Stop button. Here's the completed procedure from the VideoPlayer application:

```
procedure TForm1.MediaPlayer1Click(Sender: TObject;
  Button: TMPBtnType; var DoDefault: Boolean);
begin
  if (Button = btStop) or (Button = btPause) then
    MediaPlayer1.Notify := False    // Do not continue replay
  else
    MediaPlayer1.Notify := True;    // Replay if checkbox is set
end;
```

The procedure receives three parameters. Sender is the object that was clicked (MediaPlayer1 in this case). Because there is only one such object, we can safely ignore this parameter. The Button parameter indicates which button was clicked. This is equal to one of the values: btBack, btEject, btNext, btPause, btPlay, btPrev, btRecord, btStep, or btStop. In the sample code, the program checks whether the user has clicked the Stop or Pause buttons. If so, Notify is set to False so that notifications are no longer received by the MediaPlayer's OnNotify handler, and therefore, auto-replay is disabled regardless of the check box's setting.

The final parameter, DoDefault, received by the MediaPlayer's OnClick event handler indicates whether your code or the component should execute standard actions. If DoDefault is True (the default), the component executes standard code for all buttons. Clicking Play, for example, causes MediaPlayer to call its own Play method.

If you do not want the component to call its own methods, set DoDefault to False in the MediaPlayer's OnClick event handler. This indicates to the component that your code has executed alternate statements for one or another button. For example, to single-step through an AVI clip's frames, you might use the following code in an OnClick event handler:

```
begin
  if Button = btStep then
  begin
    MediaPlayer1.Frames := 1;
    MediaPlayer1.Step;
    DoDefault := False;
  end;
  // Other buttons execute standard methods
end;
```

If the Button parameter indicates that the Step button was clicked, the program sets Frames to one and calls the MediaPlayer object's Step method. This advances the clip by one frame rather than by ten percent of the total number of frames, which is the standard setting. To indicate to MediaPlayer that the program has already responded to the Step button, DoDefault is set to False. Because DoDefault is True by default, after the OnClick event handler ends, the MediaPlayer object responds to other button clicks normally.

MediaPlayer properties

Following are some notes about selected MediaPlayer properties that you can use to customize this component object:

✦ **AutoEnable** — Set to True to enable and disable selected MediaPlayer buttons depending on the state of the multimedia device. For example, when this property is True, the Play button is disabled when no file is loaded. Set AutoEnable to False to enable all buttons all the time (this might seem backward until you think about it for a moment). VideoPlayer uses this setting.

✦ **AutoOpen** — Set to True to automatically open a file specified by FileName. If this property is False, you must call the Open method to open the file.

✦ **AutoRewind** — Set to True to rewind the multimedia file when it is finished. Clicking the Play button then restarts the media from its beginning.

✦ **DeviceType** — Use this property to specify what type of device or file the MediaPlayer object controls. The default value, dtAutoSelect, determines the type of device, and therefore the type of device driver to use, based on the selected filename extension as recorded in the Windows registry. To specify a particular type of device, you may set DeviceType to one of the values dtAVIVideo, dtCDAudio, dtDAT, dtDigitalVideo, dtMMMovie, dtOther, dtOverlay, dtScanner, dtSequencer, dtVCR, dtVideodisc, or dtWaveAudio.

✦ **Display** — Assigns the name of a windowed component such as a Panel or Form to this property. Output from the MediaPlayer object is then sent to this component. However, certain kinds of media always display in a separate window. As a result, the Display property is ignored for Animation, AVI Video (with sound), Digital Video, Overlay, and VCR media. (This book's reviewers tell me that AVI Video displays in-place for them; however, for some reason I haven't determined, my videos appear in a separate window despite this property's setting.)

✦ **FileName** — Assigns the name of the media file to open. If AutoOpen is true, changes to FileName automatically call the Open method.

✦ **Frames** — This property specifies the number of frames that the media is stepped when the user clicks the Step or Back buttons. Normally, Frames is set, after opening a media file, to ten percent of the number of frames in that file. Change this value *after* calling Open to alter the number of stepping frames.

✦ **Mode** — You typically examine this property in a MediaPlayer object's OnNotify event handler (be sure to set Notify to True so your procedure receives media notifications). Mode equals one of the self-explanatory values mpNotReady, mpStopped, mpPlaying, mpRecording, mpSeeking, mpPaused, or mpOpen.

Expert-User Tips

✦ If your graphical output doesn't appear as expected, make sure you have assigned a color value to the Canvas's Pen.Color property. If your image still doesn't appear, be sure you are drawing to the correct Canvas. Beware of *with* statements, which might cause statements to refer to the Canvas property in an object such as a bitmap instead of the intended form or PaintBox.

✦ Because of changes in the Windows 95 desktop, drawing on an icon — for example, to animate a minimized application — is no longer recommended. However, you can do this for Windows 3.1 applications by assigning a TIcon object to the Application.Icon property. The TIcon class is derived from TGraphic — use TIcon in the same way you use a TBitmap object.

✦ To delete an image such as a large bitmap associated with an Image component object, pass nil to the Picture property's Assign method. For example, the following statement clears any image data for Image1, which you might do to conserve memory:

```
Image1.Picture.Assign(nil);
```

✦ Calling a form's Update method after Invalidate is optional. However, you should always call Invalidate before calling Update. Calling Update alone does nothing. Calling Invalidate (and optionally Update) also generates an OnPaint event for any PaintBox objects in a form.

✦ Don't call Update too frequently, or you might cause your program to become sluggish. Windows consolidates multiple calls to Invalidate and issues a single wm_Paint message when all's quiet on the message front. Usually, this results in cleaner displays with as little flicker as possible. Use Update strictly to force an immediate screen update — prior to a lengthy calculation, for example, that might overly delay the next OnPaint event.

✦ Assignments to a TBitmap object's Height and Width properties cause the bitmap to be copied in memory. You may change a TBitmap object's dimensions at any time, but if you make an image smaller, any pixels outside of the new dimensions are permanently lost.

Projects to Try

13-1: Try inserting Image, Shape, and PaintBox objects into a Panel to create a graphical toolbar. You might use these objects along with the usual SpeedButtons and subpanels to dress up an application's toolbars and status lines.

13-2: Write an application that displays Delphi's Calendar.bmp file located in the directory C:\...\Images\Backgrnd. Add drag-and-drop icons that users can move into a day square — for example, to indicate a birthday or an appointment.

13-3: Write a utility program that displays all icon files in the C:\Delphi\Images\Icons directory.

13-4: Write a program that displays a bitmap file upside down. (Hint: Use an offscreen bitmap.)

13-5: Advanced. Develop animation procedures that display bitmaps stored in a TStringList's Objects array. (Hint: See Chapter 8's description of owner-draw controls and the GlyphLst project on the CD-ROM.)

13-6: Write a file copy utility that uses an Animate object to display the standard Windows animation (two folders with flying sheets that travel between them).

13-7: Using the VideoPlayer sample application as a guide, write an AudioPlayer program that can play WAV music files.

Summary

✦ Various components provide a Canvas property that you can use to paint graphics. Canvas is an object of the TCanvas class, which encapsulates the Windows Graphics Device Interface (GDI) and the concept of a handle to a device context.

✦ To configure graphical output, assign values to the Canvas Pen and Brush properties. To draw shapes, call methods in Canvas such as Rectangle and Ellipse.

✦ Applications draw individual shapes such as lines and rectangles. They paint graphical objects in response to an OnPaint event to maintain the illusion of overlapping windows on a desktop. This chapter's PolyFlow application demonstrates the differences between drawing and painting.

✦ Use the PaintBox component to provide a Canvas and add graphics capabilities to objects such as the Panel component. You can also use one or more PaintBox objects to restrict graphical output to a defined rectangular region in a form.

✦ TGraphic is the ancestor class for TBitmap, TIcon, and TMetafile. The TPicture class contains a TGraphic object. Your program may create TPicture objects to store graphical images in memory. Or, you can insert an Image component into a form, and use its Picture property for this same purpose. This also applies to TGraphic derived controls such as TJPEGImage and those that come from third-party component vendors.

✦ The TPicture class's file-handling methods, LoadFromFile and SaveToFile, determine the type of graphics image from the filename extension. A TPicture object can therefore read and write metafile, bitmap, and icon image files. It can also handle class descendents such as TJPEGImage and those from other component vendors.

✦ Call the Canvas Draw or StretchDraw methods to draw any TGraphic object (a metafile, bitmap, or icon). Use Draw to draw graphics in their defined sizes. Use StretchDraw to resize images to fit within a defined rectangle.

✦ The TBitmap class provides a Canvas property that you can use to draw complex images offscreen. Call a form or PaintBox's CopyRect or BrushCopy methods to draw the finished offscreen image.

✦ Create drag-and-drop Shape objects by implementing OnMouseDown, OnMouseMove, and OnMouseUp event handlers, as this chapter's DragMe application demonstrates.

✦ The Animate component can display silent AVI video clips, either loaded from a disk file, or selected from one of the standard Windows clips.

✦ The MediaPlayer component serves as a controller for various multimedia devices. This chapter explains how to use MediaPlayer to construct an AVI video file viewer.

In a graphical user interface, printing and displaying graphics are intimately related subjects. The next chapter covers Delphi's text and graphics printing capabilities.

✦   ✦   ✦

Developing Printer Applications

For printing text and graphics, many development systems require you to use archaic Windows "escape" commands that can make writing even simple printing modules as pleasant as a toothache. Fortunately, Delphi's printer-related components, procedures, and functions take the "hard" out of hard copy. It's about time somebody made printer application development this painless.

In this chapter, I explain how to display printer setup dialogs and how to use Delphi's Printers unit for printing text and graphics. I also suggest a technique for creating a print-preview command—a feature that all printer applications should provide so that users can inspect output on screen, rather than waste a small forest in discarded test pages.

Components

The following is a list of Delphi's printer-related components:

✦ **PrintDialog**—Use this component to prompt users at the start of a print job. The component encapsulates a standard Windows dialog that prompts users for pages to print and provides access to printer setup options. Palette: Dialogs.

✦ **PrinterSetupDialog**—Use this component to display one or more setup dialogs provided by installed printer drivers. You should always include this dialog in printer applications to give users a method for configuring printers or selecting among multiple printer devices and output ports. Palette: Dialogs.

✦ **TPrinter**—This component is not on the VCL palette, but is defined as a class in the Printers unit. Among its other members, the TPrinter class provides a Canvas property that gives you a WYSIWYG drawing surface for printing text and graphics. Palette: none.

Plain-Text Printing

Delphi applications can print text in two ways. In this section, I explain the simplest method—using Pascal's Write and Writeln (pronounced *write-line*) procedures along with a Text output file. That's not a disk file, but a file in the general programming sense as a destination for a stream of data. When you have only text to print, these are the techniques to use.

Note The following Write and Writeln techniques print text using TrueType and other graphics fonts, which you can style in bold or italic if you wish. Even though these techniques are strictly for printing text, the methods do not use the printer's native character set unless you have installed a generic text-only printer driver. Some newer printers map TrueType fonts directly to internal printer fonts, but for all practical purposes, this action is transparent.

The Printers unit

To every module that needs printing capabilities, add the Printers unit to the module's *uses* declaration. For example, start a new project and modify the main unit's *uses* declaration like this (the new addition is in bold):

```
uses
   Windows, Messages, SysUtils, Classes, Graphics, Controls,
   Forms, Dialogs, Printers;
```

The Printers unit provides a Printer object of the TPrinter component class. All printer output commands go through this object, which also provides useful information such as the pixels width and height of a page.

Tip This may be obvious, but the Printers unit is plural; its Printer object is singular. If you have trouble getting started printing, make sure you didn't mix up the words.

A bit later in this section, I describe each TPrinter class member. But first, let's take a look at a simple print job that demonstrates how to use the Printers unit and its Printer object. Connect your printer, turn it on, and follow these steps:

1. Start a new application. Switch to the code editor window, and at the top in the *uses* declaration, add Printers to the list of other units this module uses.

2. Insert a Button object from the Standard palette into the form and double-click the Button object to create an OnClick event handler.

3. Copy the programming from Listing 14-1 into the Button1Click procedure. The code demonstrates rudimentary text-printing techniques.

4. Compile and run the program by pressing F9. When the program window appears, click the button to print the following string at the top of the page (depending on what type of printer you have, the output might be very small):

```
Hello printer!
```

Listing 14-1: This Button OnClick event handler demonstrates rudimentary text-printing techniques.

```
procedure TForm1.Button1Click(Sender: TObject);
var
  FPrn: System.Text;
begin
  AssignPrn(FPrn);
  Rewrite(FPrn);
  try
    Writeln(FPrn, 'Hello printer!');
  finally
    CloseFile(FPrn);
  end;
end;
```

To provide a destination file to which the program sends text output, the procedure defines FPrn (you can name it something else) of type System.Text. Perform two steps to attach this file variable to Pascal's output procedures and to open it for business:

```
AssignPrn(FPrn);   { Attach file for output }
Rewrite(FPrn);     { Open the file }
```

The Printers unit provides AssignPrn to assign an output file and to provide an output buffer in memory. Rewrite is a standard Pascal procedure that opens a text file. After those two steps, you can call Writeln to print strings. (Those who know Pascal but develop exclusively for Windows may be unfamiliar with Write and Writeln, so I briefly review them here.) Calling Writeln prints a string and starts a new line. To handle any possible exceptions, use FPrn inside a *try* block:

```
try
  Writeln(FPrn, 'Plain text is plain and simple!');
  { ... insert other output statements here }
```

Close the printer, which finishes the print job and ejects any partially completed page, by calling CloseFile. For safety, insert this statement in a *finally block*, which is guaranteed to execute even if printing fails:

```
finally
  CloseFile(FPrn);
end;
```

Notice that *end* is required to terminate the *try-finally* statement, even though there is no matching *begin*. You can also use Writeln to print multiple values, integers, floating-point variables, and other simple data-type objects:

```
Writeln(FPrn, 'Number of components = ', ComponentCount);
```

Use Write to print text without starting a new line. For example, the following lines are equivalent to the single preceding statement:

```
Write(FPrn, 'Number of components = ');
Write(FPrn, ComponentCount);
Writeln(FPrn);   { Start new line }
```

Attempting to pass a printer output file that was assigned with AssignPrn to Read or Readln generates a run-time error exception. You cannot read data from a printer output device.

Control codes and fonts

Write and Writeln respond to four control codes, listed in Table 14-1, which you can use to send commands to the printer.

<table>
<tr><td colspan="2" align="center">Table 14-1
Write and Writeln's Four Control Codes</td></tr>
<tr><td>**Control Code**</td><td>**Command**</td></tr>
<tr><td>#9</td><td>Tab</td></tr>
<tr><td>#10</td><td>New Line</td></tr>
<tr><td>#13</td><td>Carriage Return</td></tr>
<tr><td>^L</td><td>New Page</td></tr>
</table>

You can embed these ASCII values in strings or print them with Write statements such as these:

```
Write(FPrn, #9);    { Tab }
Write(FPrn, #13);   { Flush output buffer }
Write(FPrn, #10);   { Flush and start new line }
Write(FPrn, ^L);    { Flush and start new page }
```

Write and Writeln expand tabs to eight times the average character width in pixels of the current font. When printing with a proportional font, this means you cannot use tabs to align nonnumerical columns with Write and Writeln. In most proportional fonts, however, digits are monospace in size, so you might want to use tab control codes to align purely numerical columns.

The Printer object provides a Canvas property that, among other talents, determines the printer's font, which defaults to System in 10 points. You can change the printer's font by assigning its name to the Canvas's Font.Name property. For example, use these statements to select the TrueType Courier New font in 12 points for subsequent Write and Writeln statements:

```
with Printer.Canvas do
begin
  Font.Name := 'Courier New';
  Font.Size := 12;
end;
```

You can add this code to the preceding example Button1Click event handler. Insert the five lines listed here just after the Rewrite statement (above the keyword *try*). Now when you press F9 to compile and run the program and click the button, the text is printed in monospace 12 points.

Caution When printing plain text using the techniques in this section, always call AssignPrn and Rewrite before changing Font property values in the Printer's Canvas.

The selected font affects character pixel height and width and, therefore, changes the number of lines per page (more on this later). You may use any installed font, but TrueType fonts are usually best for printing because the Windows GDI can render characters for any graphics print driver, even if it does not directly support TrueType.

You should also learn to use the Write and Writeln techniques described here to print on text-only printers such as those old hammer-head clunkers. (I kept my ancient NEC thimble printer on the floor and it still shook the room so badly I feared disk-head crashes every time I printed a listing.) If you must support a text-only printer, use the Control Panel to install the Windows Generic/Text Only driver and give it a whirl. There's no guarantee this will work, however, and for best results you should specify to your program's end users that a graphics printer is required for printing under Windows.

Printer statistics

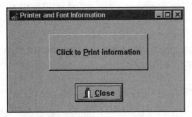

The PrnInfo application shown in Figure 14-1 prints statistics about your printer's capabilities and the current font. The program's files are on the CD-ROM in the Source\PrnInfo directory. The program also demonstrates how to determine the number of lines per page, which might be useful in some applications.

Figure 14-1: Click PrnInfo's large button for a printed report about your printer's resolution, driver, lines per page, and average characters per line.

To use the program, load the PrnInfo.dpr project file into Delphi, turn on your printer, press F9 to compile and run the program, and click the large button. Here's what PrnInfo printed for my system when I did that:

```
Device = HP DeskJet 720C Series on LPT1:
Font = Courier New
Font Size = 12 points
PageHeight = 3150 pixels
PageWidth = 2400 pixels
Extent.Cx = 6720 pixels
Extent.Cy = 53 pixels
Lines per page = 56
Chars per line = 80
```

Listing 14-2 shows the source code for PrnInfo.

Listing 14-2: **PrnInfo\Main.pas**

```
unit Main;

interface

uses
```

```
    SysUtils, Windows, Messages, Classes, Graphics,
    Controls, Forms, Dialogs, Printers, StdCtrls, Buttons;

type
  TMainForm = class(TForm)
    PrintButton: TButton;
    CloseBitBtn: TBitBtn;
    procedure PrintButtonClick(Sender: TObject);
  private
    { Private declarations }
  public
    { Public declarations }
  end;

var
  MainForm: TMainForm;

implementation

{$R *.DFM}

procedure TMainForm.PrintButtonClick(Sender: TObject);
var
  FPrn: System.Text;
  Extent: TSize;
  Metrics: TTextMetric;
  I, LinesPerPage, CharsPerLine, AverageWidth: Integer;
  S : String;
begin
  AssignPrn(FPrn);
  Rewrite(FPrn);

  with Printer.Canvas do
  begin
    Font.Name := 'Courier New';
    Font.Size := 12;
  end;

{ Fill test string with ASCII values 32 to 255 }
  try
(*    S[0] := Chr(224);     // This is no longer allowed *)
    SetLength(S, 224);      // Use this method instead
    for I := 32 to 255 do   // Fill string with test chars
      S[I - 31] := Chr(I);
    with Printer, Canvas do
    begin
    { Determine number of lines per page }
      GetTextExtentPoint(Handle, @S[1], Length(S), Extent);
```

(continued)

Listing 14-2 *(continued)*

```
        LinesPerPage := PageHeight div (Extent.Cy + 2);
        if PageHeight mod Extent.Cy <> 0 then
          Dec(LinesPerPage);
      { Determine average number of characters per line }
        GetTextMetrics(Handle, Metrics);
        AverageWidth := Metrics.tmAveCharWidth;
        CharsPerLine := PageWidth div AverageWidth;
      { Print the report }
        Writeln(FPrn, 'Device = ', Printers[PrinterIndex]);
        Writeln(FPrn, 'Font = ', Font.Name);
        Writeln(FPrn, 'Font Size = ', Font.Size, ' points');
        Writeln(FPrn, 'PageHeight = ', PageHeight, ' pixels');
        Writeln(FPrn, 'PageWidth = ', PageWidth, ' pixels');
        Writeln(FPrn, 'Extent.Cx = ', Extent.Cx, ' pixels');
        Writeln(FPrn, 'Extent.Cy = ', Extent.Cy, ' pixels');
        Writeln(FPrn, 'Lines per page = ', LinesPerPage);
        Writeln(FPrn, 'Chars per line = ', CharsPerLine);
    end;
  finally
    CloseFile(FPrn);
  end;
end;

end.
```

In the reported information, the Extent.Cx value equals the number of horizontal pixels that would be required to print the program's test string using the current font (set to Courier New, 12 point). PrnInfo does not print this string — it's used only to prepare the report. Extent.Cy equals the height in pixels of the test string. The number of lines per page is accurate only if you print all lines on the page with the same font. The number of characters per line is approximate for proportional fonts. These values are often critical in determining how much information fits on a page of output. Be sure to select a font name and size, as shown in the sample listing, before obtaining the information.

To display statistics about a different font, add statements such as the following immediately preceding the call to GetTextExtentPoint:

```
Font.Name := 'Arial';
Font.Size := 24;
```

PrnInfo demonstrates how to call Windows API functions that require a handle to a printer device context. Simply pass the Handle property of the Printer's Canvas to this parameter. For example, this calls GetTextExtentPoint:

```
GetTextExtentPoint(Handle, @S[1], Length(S), Extent);
```

To satisfy the function's PChar parameter, the statement passes the address of the test string's first character (@S[1]). A similar statement calls another API function, GetTextMetrics:

```
GetTextMetrics(Handle, Metrics);
```

Use these techniques and PrnInfo's reported values, only with the Write and Writeln text-printing methods described here. As I explain later in this chapter, other text-printing techniques give you better control over results, especially when printing graphics.

Printing string lists

To print a TStrings or TStringList object's text lines, use Writeln as described in this section. Add Printers to the module's *uses* directive and insert this code into a Button OnClick event handler to print a string list using a Memo object:

```
var
  FPrn: TextFile;
  I: Integer;
begin
  AssignPrn(FPrn);
  Rewrite(FPrn);
  try
    for I := 0 to Memo1.Lines.Count - 1 do
      Writeln(FPrn, Memo1.Lines[I]);
  finally
    CloseFile(FPrn);
  end;
end;
```

You can use this code to print any TStrings component property—for example, the Lines property in a Memo object as shown here or the Items property in a ListBox.

Printer dialogs

User-interface methods for printing vary among applications, but most programs use at least one of the following traditional file-menu commands. The four standard menu commands are:

✦ **File | Page Setup**... — Optional. Displays an application dialog that configures headers, page numbers, margins, and any other miscellaneous settings that you need. There aren't any standard methods for implementing this command, except that it should permit users to configure whatever items are unique to your application's printing features. For example, you might prompt users to enter a title string to print at the top of each page.

✦ **File | Print Preview**... — Optional. Displays simulated printout pages in a window. There aren't any standard ways to implement this command, but later in this chapter I suggest a technique that should work for most applications.

✦ **File | Print Setup**... — Displays the current printer driver's setup dialog, which typically includes an Options button that opens additional dialog boxes. This command should never print anything. Use a PrinterSetupDialog component to simplify implementing this command.

✦ **File | Print**... — Displays a print configuration dialog for users to enter the number of copies they want and a range of page numbers. If the user clicks the dialog's OK button, the program should begin printing immediately. This command's dialog box includes a Setup button that displays the same setup dialog as the File | Print Setup command. Use a PrinterDialog component to simplify implementing this command.

The first two commands are optional. File|Print Setup... and File|Print... are standard, although you can get away with only File|Print... in a pinch because this command permits access to the driver's setup dialog. However, most applications should implement at least the File|Print Setup... and File|Print... commands. The Lister application on the CD-ROM — and shown in Figure 14-2 and Listing 14-3 — demonstrates how to use Delphi's PrinterSetupDialog and PrintDialog components in writing a program's File|Print... and File|Print Setup... commands. The Lister program can print any .pas, .txt, or other text file. To demonstrate printing numerical data as well as text, Lister prefaces lines with line numbers. Printed text uses the 10-point Courier New font. All Lister files are on the CD-ROM in the Source\Lister directory.

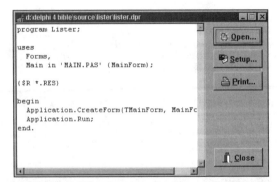

Figure 14-2: The Lister application prints any text file and demonstrates how to implement File|Print Setup and File|Print commands.

Listing 14-3: **Lister\Main.pas**

```pascal
unit Main;

interface

uses
  SysUtils, Windows, Messages, Classes, Graphics,
  Controls, Forms, Dialogs, StdCtrls, Buttons, Printers;

type
  TMainForm = class(TForm)
    Memo1: TMemo;
    SetupBitBtn: TBitBtn;
    PrintBitBtn: TBitBtn;
    CloseBitBtn: TBitBtn;
    OpenBitBtn: TBitBtn;
    OpenDialog1: TOpenDialog;
    PrintDialog1: TPrintDialog;
    PrinterSetupDialog1: TPrinterSetupDialog;
    procedure OpenBitBtnClick(Sender: TObject);
    procedure SetupBitBtnClick(Sender: TObject);
    procedure PrintBitBtnClick(Sender: TObject);
  private
    { Private declarations }
  public
    { Public declarations }
  end;

var
  MainForm: TMainForm;

implementation

{$R *.DFM}

procedure TMainForm.OpenBitBtnClick(Sender: TObject);
begin
  with OpenDialog1 do
  if Execute then
  begin
    Memo1.Lines.LoadFromFile(FileName);
    Caption := Lowercase(FileName);
  end;
end;

procedure TMainForm.SetupBitBtnClick(Sender: TObject);
```

(continued)

Listing 14-3 *(continued)*

```
begin
  PrinterSetupDialog1.Execute;
end;

procedure TMainForm.PrintBitBtnClick(Sender: TObject);
var
  FPrn: System.Text;    { Printer output text file }
  I: Integer;           { Memo1.Lines index }
  LCol: Integer;        { Line number column width }
begin
  if PrintDialog1.Execute then
  begin
    AssignPrn(FPrn);  { Direct Write/Writeln to FPrn }
    Rewrite(FPrn);    { Open printer output file }
    try
      Printer.Canvas.Font := Memo1.Font;  { Use Memo's font }
      with Memo1, Lines do
      begin  {Set line number column width for file size:}
        if Count < 10 then LCol := 1        {0 .. 9 lines    }
        else if Count < 100 then LCol := 2 {10 .. 99 lines  }
        else if Count < 1000 then LCol := 3 {100 .. 999 lines}
        else LCol := 4;                     { You must be kidding }
        for I := 0 to Count - 1 do
        begin
          Write(FPrn, I + 1:LCol, ': ');  { Print line number }
          Writeln(FPrn, Lines[I]);        { Print line }
        end;
      end;
    finally
      CloseFile(FPrn);  { Close printer output file }
    end;
  end;
end;

end.
```

To implement the File|Print Setup... command, as in the Lister program, insert a PrinterSetupDialog component object into the form. The object is represented by an icon, which does not appear at run time. Into a Button or menu command OnClick event handler, insert the statement:

```
PrinterSetupDialog1.Execute;
```

Or, you can perform another action if users close the setup dialog by selecting its OK button, although this is rarely necessary:

```
if PrinterSetupDialog1.Execute then
  { ... take action if user selected OK }
```

Implement a File|Print command similarly, but insert a PrintDialog component object (this also has no run-time appearance). Listing 14-4 shows the general layout of the command's OnClick event handler. Inside the *try* block, insert Write and Writeln statements as the Lister application's PrintBitBtnClick procedure demonstrates.

Listing 14-4: **Implement a File|Print command using this type of code.**

```
if PrintDialog1.Execute then
begin
  AssignPrn(FPrn);
  Rewrite(FPrn);
  try
    { ... Write text to FPrn }
  finally
    CloseFile(FPrn);
  end;
end;
```

In most cases, you use the same font for printing as you do for displaying text onscreen. When using a component such as Memo for displaying text, assign the object's Font to the Printer's Canvas with a statement such as the following, but be sure to open the output file beforehand:

```
Printer.Canvas.Font := Memo1.Font;
```

It's up to you to use any information supplied in the PrintDialog object. After calling Execute, use the Copies, FromPage, ToPage, and other property values in your *print* loop:

```
with PrintDialog1 do
for Copy := 1 to Copies do
  for Page := FromPage to ToPage do
    { ... Print pages here }
```

The TPrinter Class

Before getting to the next section, which explains how to print graphics and WYSIWYG text, scan the following explanations of TPrinter's properties and methods. You need a good understanding of these items when your printing needs extend beyond Delphi's Write and Writeln procedures.

Use the Printer object to refer to all properties and events mentioned in this section. For example, the expression Printer.Canvas accesses the Printer's Canvas object. To use these properties and methods, add Printers to your application module's *uses* directive.

TPrinter properties

The following is a list of TPrinter's properties:

✦ **Aborted** — This property becomes True if the user aborts printing, for example, by closing the Print Manager. Inspect this Boolean variable in your *print* loop to determine whether TPrinter's Abort method has been called, in which case you should end the loop immediately without calling EndDoc.

✦ **Canvas** — To print graphics and WYSIWYG text, assign values to the Canvas's Pen, Brush, and other properties and call its methods, exactly as you do for displaying graphics.

✦ **Capabilities** — This property lists the set of printer device driver capabilities. It is a set of the values pcCopies, pcOrientation, and pcCollation.

✦ **Copies** — Equals the number of copies that have been printed.

✦ **Fonts** — Shows a TStrings list of all fonts that the current printer supports. You may always print using TrueType fonts because the GDI can render TrueType characters even for older printer drivers that do not support TrueType. This shouldn't be a problem, however, for Windows 95, 98, and NT.

✦ **Handle** — Pass this value to any Windows API function that requires a handle to a device context (HDC) — for example, GetText Metrics.

✦ **Orientation** — This property has one of two values: poPortrait or poLandscape. You can assign these values before printing, or you can inspect them to determine page parameters.

✦ **PageHeight** — Equals the height of one printer page in pixels. This value can vary widely among printers.

✦ **PageNumber** — Equals the current page number. The meaning of a page is up to your application. The Printer object increments PageNumber every time you call the NewPage method. For plain-text printing, PageNumber is incremented when Writeln starts a new page.

✦ **PageWidth** — Equals the width of one printer page in pixels. This value can vary widely among printers.

✦ **PrinterIndex** — Equals the index of the current printer name in the Printers string list.

✦ **Printers** — Shows a TStrings string list of installed printers. The expression Printer.Printers[PrinterIndex] gives the name of the current printer.

✦ **Printing** — Equals True while printing is in progress.

✦ **Title** — Contains a string, which you may assign, that identifies the print task in the Print Manager or a network task header.

TPrinter methods

Following is a list of TPrinter's methods:

✦ **Abort** — You may call Abort to terminate a print job in progress. For example, you can display a modeless dialog box before your application enters its *print* loop. Use a global flag to indicate whether the user clicked the dialog's Abort button, and if so, call Printer.Abort and exit the *printer-output* loop. (Do not also call EndDoc.) Calling Abort sets the Printer.Aborted flag to True.

✦ **BeginDoc** — Call this before beginning a new print job. You do not have to call BeginDoc when using the Write and Writeln plain-text techniques described at the beginning of this chapter.

✦ **EndDoc** — Call this after finishing the print job. EndDoc flushes the output buffer and ejects the final page if necessary. Do not call EndDoc when using the Write and Writeln plain-text techniques. Also, do not call EndDoc after terminating a print job by calling Printer.Abort (this is less critical, however, in Delphi Versions 3 and 4 than it was in Delphi 1 and 2).

✦ **NewPage** — Call this procedure at any time to start a new page. The meaning and contents of a page are up to you and your program to provide. NewPage merely flushes the output buffer and ejects the current page.

Caution

Never construct an object of the TPrinter class. The Printers unit provides a Printer object of this class data type ready to use.

Graphics Printing

The text-printing techniques described in the preceding section represent a reasonable compromise between ease-of-use and results. When you need more control over output parameters — to more accurately position text on the page, for example, or to handle tabs for proportional fonts — you can use the following methods. In this section, I explain how to print forms, graphics, WYSIWYG text, and bitmaps. This section's font sampler application, FontSamp, also suggests a general-purpose technique for previewing printed output onscreen.

Printing forms

You might want to include a command that prints a snapshot of a form's onscreen appearance. This is easy to do — just call the form's Print method. You do not have to call any TPrinter methods, or add Printers to the module's *uses* declaration.

To print a form, insert a PrintDialog object into the form (it does not appear at run time or on the printed output), and then implement a Button or menu command's OnClick event handler with a statement such as this:

```
if PrintDialog1.Execute then
  Print;
```

To print a specific form by name, use this statement:

```
AboutBox.Print;
```

AboutBox is the Name property that you assign to the form object. Internally, the form component's Print method copies the current window's client area to an offscreen bitmap. The Print method then prints this bitmap by calling the Windows API StretchDIBits function. Assign one of three values to the form's PrintScale property to determine how the output is scaled. You can do this at run time or in the Object Inspector. The three PrintScale choices are:

✦ **poNone** — No scaling. The size of the printed form depends on the printer's resolution. Using this option to print forms on laser printers results in tiny windows that are cute, but unreadable (at least I can't see them). You rarely have use for this option.

✦ **poPrintToFit** — Scale to page size. The printed form fills the page in at least one direction (typically horizontally). This option is the most wasteful of printer ink, but when you want a form to fill the page, this is the right option to use.

✦ **poProportional** — Scale using printer's pixels-per-inch property. This results in the best-looking output, which at normal viewing distance, looks similar in size to the form's onscreen appearance. That's not to suggest the sizes match exactly; the printed output is simply a good compromise between readability and space.

Printing graphics objects

The techniques for printing graphics and WYSIWYG text — that is, text printed as graphics objects — requires different techniques than printing plain text with Write and Writeln statements. You use the same Printers unit and Printer object, but you call methods in the TPrinter class to begin and end a print job. You have to define the meaning of a page for your application and draw every output object. This takes more work, but provides the utmost control over results.

Listing 14-5 demonstrates the basic steps required to print the contents of an Image component. (This text is in file Print1.pas, on the CD-ROM, in the Source\PrintMisc directory.) You don't have to use the component, but it's useful for this demonstration. The three basic steps are as follows:

1. Call the Printer's BeginDoc procedure to begin printing.

2. Call methods for the Printer's Canvas. For example, call Draw to print a TGraphic object (a bitmap, an icon, or metafile), or you can call methods such as Ellipse and Rectangle. Whatever you deposit on the Printer's Canvas ends up on the printed page, within the limits of your printer's capabilities. For better error control, perform these steps inside a *try* block.

3. Call EndDoc when you are finished printing. For better error control, call EndDoc in a *finally* block.

Listing 14-5: **Follow this general plan to print graphics.**

```
procedure TForm1.Print1Click(Sender: TObject);
begin
  Printer.BeginDoc;
  try
    Printer.Canvas.Draw(0, 0, Image1.Picture.Graphic);
  finally
    Printer.EndDoc;
  end;
end;
```

To try the procedure in Listing 14-5, insert an Image component and a Button into a form. The size of the Image object is unimportant. Use the Image object's Picture property to load any bitmap file. Double-click the Button object to create an OnClick event handler for it, and replace the resulting procedure with the programming from the listing. Compile and run the program by pressing F9 and then click the button to print the bitmap.

Don't be concerned if the output is smaller than a Lilliputian flea. This happens because, unless you scale printed images according to the printer's resolution, the results use the printer's default resolution. This is an especially big problem with laser printers, which provide far greater resolution than current display screens. At 300 dots-per-inch or better, graphics output might be too small to be readable.

To scale images to better match the output device's resolution, call the Windows API GetDeviceCaps (that's Caps for capabilities) and request the logPixelsX and logPixelsY values for the Printer object's device context handle. This obtains the logical pixels-per-inch for the device, which, when divided by the form's PixelsPerInch property, scales the image to an appropriate size.

The actual number of pixels-per-inch for a specific device may differ from its logical values for many reasons, one of which is that Windows displays text onscreen larger than real life, so small point sizes are readable on low-resolution displays.

On the CD-ROM

Listing 14-6 improves on the procedure in Listing 14-5 by scaling the printed image according to the printer's resolution. Replace the test program's OnClick event handler with this listing, recompile, run, and print. The image size should now be closer to its onscreen appearance. Again, that's not to say the display and printed sizes match exactly; only that they appear similar at normal viewing distances. (On my system, holding the printed page about 2/3 the distance from my eyes to the screen makes the onscreen and on-paper images appear to be about the same size.) This text for Listing 14-6 is on the CD-ROM in the Source\PrintMisc directory, in file Print2.pas.

Listing 14-6: Use this code to scale an image according to the printer's resolution.

```
procedure TForm1.Button1Click(Sender: TObject);
var
  ScaleX, ScaleY: Integer;
  R: TRect;
begin
  Printer.BeginDoc;
  with Printer do
  try
    ScaleX :=
```

```
        GetDeviceCaps(Handle, logPixelsX) div PixelsPerInch;
      ScaleY :=
        GetDeviceCaps(Handle, logPixelsY) div PixelsPerInch;
      R := Rect(0, 0, Image1.Picture.Width * ScaleX,
        Image1.Picture.Height * ScaleY);
      Canvas.StretchDraw(R, Image1.Picture.Graphic);
    finally
      EndDoc;
    end;
  end;
```

The procedure in Listing 14-6 initializes two integer variables, ScaleX and ScaleY, to values equal to the printer's logical pixels-per-inch obtained by GetDeviceCaps divided by the form's PixelsPerInch property. There's only one such property because VGA display modes are square, and the number of pixels-per-inch should be the same vertically and horizontally. The same fact is not necessarily true for all output devices, however, which is why GetDeviceCaps provides values for x- and y-axes.

After setting ScaleX and ScaleY, the procedure creates a TRect record, R, of the output's dimensions. Multiplying the Image object's Picture.Width and Picture.Height by the scaling factors adjusts the rectangle to a comfortable fit. Finally, StretchDraw draws the bitmap by referring to the Picture's Graphic property.

Note

Printing actually begins when the program calls EndDoc or NewPage. Drawing to the Printer's Canvas property does not produce any output.

Printing bitmaps, icons, and metafiles

You don't have to use an Image component to print graphics. You can use the technique in Listing 14-6 to print bitmaps, icons, and metafiles. Construct a TPicture object (see the preceding chapter for instructions) and pass its Graphic property to the Printer Canvas's Draw or StretchDraw methods. Listing 14-7 shows how to use this technique to print the Sample.bmp file on the CD-ROM in the Source\Data directory. Modify the path name string as needed in the call to LoadFromFile. The text of this procedure in on the CD-ROM in the Source\PrintMisc directory in file Print2.pas.

Listings 14-6 and 14-7 produce the same results. Which technique to use depends on whether you want to use an Image component or construct a TPicture object under program control. Displaying the Image object is probably easier, so if you can't decide, use the method in Listing 14-6. However, Listing 14-7 is a little more efficient in its use of memory because the bitmap object exists only within the scope of the event handler.

Listing 14-7: **Use this code to print any bitmap, icon, or metafile without using an Image object.**

```
procedure TForm1.Button1Click(Sender: TObject);
var
  P: TPicture;
  ScaleX, ScaleY: Integer;
  R: TRect;
begin
  P := TPicture.Create;
  try
  // Modify the pathname string in the following statement
  // to load any .bmp, .ico, or metafile:
    P.LoadFromFile('D:\Delphi 4 Bible\Source\Data\Sample.bmp');
    Printer.BeginDoc;
    with Printer do
    try
      ScaleX :=
        GetDeviceCaps(Handle, logPixelsX) div PixelsPerInch;
      ScaleY :=
        GetDeviceCaps(Handle, logPixelsY) div PixelsPerInch;
      R := Rect(0, 0, P.Width * ScaleX, P.Height * ScaleY);
      Canvas.StretchDraw(R, P.Graphic);
    finally
      Printer.EndDoc;
    end;
  finally
    P.Free;
  end;
end;
```

Printing graphics shapes

To display and print graphics shapes, write a procedure that draws graphics and text to a Canvas object passed as an argument. Call your procedure to print on the Printer object's Canvas. Call the same procedure in a form's OnPaint event handler to display graphics. The trick is to scale the printed image so it comes out a reasonable onscreen and paper size. On the CD-ROM, the PrintGr application in the Source\PrintGr directory demonstrates how to display and print graphics shapes and text. Figure 14-3 shows PrintGr's display—nothing fancy, but adequate for the demonstration. Listing 14-8 lists the program's source code. Run the program, and select the File|Print... command to print.

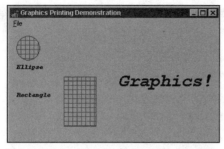

Figure 14-3: PrintGr demonstrates one way to display and print graphics shapes and text.

Listing 14-8: **PrintGr\Main.pas**

```
unit Main;

interface

uses
  SysUtils, Windows, Messages, Classes, Graphics,
  Controls, Forms, Dialogs, Menus, Printers;

type
  TMainForm = class(TForm)
    MainMenu1: TMainMenu;
    File1: TMenuItem;
    Print1: TMenuItem;
    N1: TMenuItem;
    Exit1: TMenuItem;
    PrintDialog1: TPrintDialog;
    procedure Print1Click(Sender: TObject);
    procedure FormPaint(Sender: TObject);
    procedure Exit1Click(Sender: TObject);
  private
    procedure PaintGraphics(C: TCanvas;
      ScaleX, ScaleY: Integer);
  public
    { Public declarations }
  end;

var
  MainForm: TMainForm;
```

(continued)

Listing 14-8 *(continued)*

```
implementation

{$R *.DFM}

procedure TMainForm.PaintGraphics(C: TCanvas;
  ScaleX, ScaleY: Integer);
var
  R: TRect;
  P: TPoint;

  function ScalePoint(X, Y: Integer): TPoint;
  begin
    Result := Point(X * ScaleX, Y * ScaleY);
  end;

  function ScaleRect(L, T, R, B: Integer): TRect;
  begin
    Result :=
      Rect(L * ScaleX, T * ScaleY, R * ScaleX, B * ScaleY);
  end;

begin
  with C do
  begin
    Pen.Color := clBlue;
    Brush.Color := clRed;
    Brush.Style := bsCross;
    Font.Name := 'Courier New';
    Font.Size := 8;
    Font.Style := [fsBold, fsItalic];
    R := ScaleRect(12, 12, 57, 57);
    Ellipse(R.Left, R.Top, R.Right, R.Bottom);
    R := ScaleRect(100, 85, 160, 174);
    Rectangle(R.Left, R.Top, R.Right, R.Bottom);
    P := ScalePoint(12, 60);
    TextOut(P.X, P.Y, 'Ellipse');
    P := ScalePoint(12, 110);
    TextOut(P.X, P.Y, 'Rectangle');
    Font.Size := 24;
    Font.Style := [fsBold, fsItalic];
    P := ScalePoint(200, 75);
    TextOut(P.X, P.Y, 'Graphics!');
  end;
```

```
end;

procedure TMainForm.Print1Click(Sender: TObject);
var
  ScaleX, ScaleY: Integer;
begin
  if PrintDialog1.Execute then
  Printer.BeginDoc;
  try
    ScaleX := GetDeviceCaps(Printer.Canvas.Handle,
      logPixelsX) div PixelsPerInch;
    ScaleY := GetDeviceCaps(Printer.Canvas.Handle,
      logPixelsY) div PixelsPerInch;
    PaintGraphics(Printer.Canvas, ScaleX, ScaleY);
  finally
    Printer.EndDoc;
  end;
end;

procedure TMainForm.FormPaint(Sender: TObject);
begin
  PaintGraphics(Canvas, 1, 1);
end;

procedure TMainForm.Exit1Click(Sender: TObject);
begin
  Close;
end;

end.
```

The program calls procedure PaintGraphics to display and print its shapes and text. The procedure declares three parameters: a TCanvas, and two Integers, ScaleX and ScaleY, for scaling coordinates.

Two functions perform the scaling. ScalePoint multiplies x and y by the scaling factors and returns a TPoint record. ScaleRect does the same, but returns a TRect record. PaintGraphics shows how to use these functions. For example, to paint an ellipse, the program executes these statements:

```
R := ScaleRect(12, 12, 57, 57);
Ellipse(R.Left, R.Top, R.Right, R.Bottom);
```

Calling ScaleRect adjusts the coordinates to account for the greater resolution of most printers. However, this isn't the only way to perform scaling—the next section demonstrates another technique.

Creating a print-preview command

Although the term WYSIWYG has come to define hard-copy quality, to a
programmer, producing WYSIWYG output is largely a matter of relative positioning.
Unless the display and printer resolutions match exactly, it's physically impossible
to produce the same onscreen and printed graphics, but with careful programming
and scaleable TrueType fonts, the results are good enough for most applications.

The final program in this chapter demonstrates WYSIWYG output, and reveals a few
more printing techniques, such as multipage printing and how to implement a print-
preview window. The program, FontSamp, displays a list of fonts. To try out the program, load the FontSamp.dpr project file from the CD-ROM in the Source\FontSamp
directory. Press F9 to compile and run and then select one or more font names. You
can also click the Select all button to choose all fonts and then click Print to print
sampler pages of each selected font in a variety of sizes and styles. (Watch out – if
you have a lot of fonts on your system, this might produce a virtual bible of printed
pages!) Click Preview to view sampler pages before printing. Figure 14-4 shows the
program's main display. Select one or more font names from the list box. Click Print
to print samples of each font. Click Preview to view sample pages before printing.
Figure 14-5 then shows the preview window.

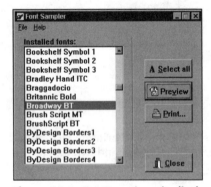

Figure 14-4: FontSamp's main display

FontSamp's print-preview window displays TrueType fonts such as Arial more accurately than bitmapped fonts such as Courier. Maximize the print-preview window for
best results.

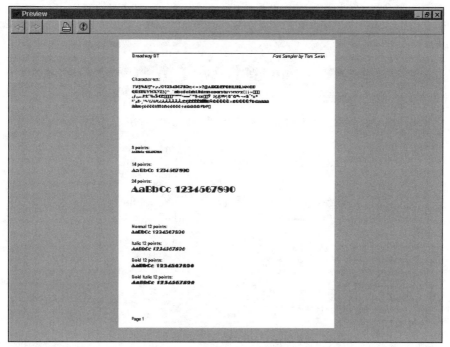

Figure 14-5: FontSamp's print-preview window showing the TrueType font Broadway BT

Delphi's TBitmap class simplifies the steps needed to create a print-preview window. FontSamp creates a TBitmap object with its width and height set to the same ratio as an $8^1/_2 \times 11$-inch page. To preview printed output, the program draws onto the bitmap's Canvas. To print, the program draws onto the Printer's Canvas. The result is a true visual representation of the program's printed output.

Almost.

In practice, it's difficult at best to match printed output exactly in a small bitmap. Non-TrueType fonts are particularly ornery and don't resize well. One plan that seems to work, but doesn't require months of coding, is to program all coordinates as floating-point values that represent inches. (You could use metric measurements just as well.) This plan keeps the program neat and simple. For example, to print text at midpage, assuming an 11-inch vertical dimension, you select a y-coordinate of 6.5 inches. All you need are some simple functions to convert inches to pixels based on the Canvas's logical resolution.

Three modules in FontSamp fulfill this plan: Main, Preview, and DrawPage. Listing 14-9 shows the Main module's Preview and Print button OnClick event handlers.

Listing 14-9: FontSamp\Main.pas Preview and Print button OnClick event handlers

```
procedure TMainForm.PreviewBitBtnClick(Sender: TObject);
begin
  if PreviewForm.ShowModal = mrOk then
    PrintBitBtn.Click;  { Preview's print button }
end;

{ This is the procedure that prints the pages }
procedure TMainForm.PrintBitBtnClick(Sender: TObject);
var
  PpiX, PpiY, Page, FirstPage, LastPage: Integer;

  { Initialize PrintDialog1 object}
  procedure InitPrintDialog;
  begin
    with PrintDialog1 do
    begin
      MinPage := 1;
      MaxPage := FontListBox.SelCount;
      FromPage := MinPage;
      ToPage := MaxPage;
    end;
  end;

  { Initialize printing variables }
  procedure InitParameters;
  begin
  { Do our own scaling based on Page width and height. This
  seems to be more reliable than GetDeviceCaps. }
    PpiX := Trunc(Printer.PageWidth / 8.5);
    PpiY := Trunc(Printer.PageHeight / 11.0);
  { Set FirstPage and LastPage }
    if PrintDialog1.PrintRange = prAllPages then
    begin
      FirstPage := 1;
      LastPage := FontListBox.SelCount;
    end else
    begin
      FirstPage := PrintDialog1.FromPage;
      LastPage := PrintDialog1.ToPage;
    end;
  end;
```

```
begin
  InitPrintDialog;
  if PrintDialog1.Execute then
  begin
    Printer.BeginDoc;
    try
      InitParameters;
      for Page := FirstPage to LastPage do
      begin
        DrawOnePage(Printer.Canvas, FontListBox, Page,
          Printer.PageWidth, Printer.PageHeight, False,
          PpiX, PpiY);
        if page < LastPage then
          Printer.NewPage;
      end;
    finally
      Printer.EndDoc;
    end;
  end;

end;
```

The Preview button's OnClick event handler displays the Preview window by calling ShowModal. If that function returns mrOk, the user clicked the preview's Print speed button. To print, the procedure calls the Print button's Click method.

The Print button's OnClick event handler calls two local procedures to initialize the print dialog and other parameters. Set the PrintDialog1 object's MinPage and MaxPage properties to the page range. In this case, there's one font sampler per page, so the maximum page number equals FontListBox.SelCount. Set FromPage and ToPage to these same values so they appear in the print dialog's edit windows.

To initialize printing, procedure InitParameters sets variables PpiX and PpiY equal to the number of logical pixels-per-inch for the assumed page size of $8\frac{1}{2} \times 11$ inches. Doing the calculations this way seems more accurate than calling GetDeviceCaps. The procedure inspects the PrintDialog1 object's PrintRange property. If this equals the constant prAllPages, the user clicked the dialog's All radio button; otherwise, the user may have modified the page range and you can get these values from ToPage and FromPage as shown.

Following these initializations, the program is ready for printing. A *for* loop handles this by calling a procedure, DrawOnePage (in the DrawPage module) with various arguments. The most important argument is the first, Printer.Canvas, which directs output to the printer. Printer.PageWidth and Printer.PageHeight give DrawOnePage the output's boundaries for a single page. Calling Printer.NewPage ejects each page after drawing.

The Preview module in Listing 14-10 also calls DrawOnePage to simulate printed pages. This module is relatively short, so I list it in full here.

Listing 14-10: **FontSamp\Preview.pas**

```
unit Preview;

interface

uses
  SysUtils, Windows, Messages, Classes, Graphics,
  Controls, Forms, Dialogs, StdCtrls, Buttons, ExtCtrls,
  DrawPage;

type
  TPreviewForm = class(TForm)
    ToolBar: TPanel;
    LeftPageSB: TSpeedButton;
    RightPageSB: TSpeedButton;
    PrintSB: TSpeedButton;
    CloseSB: TSpeedButton;
    procedure FormCreate(Sender: TObject);
    procedure FormResize(Sender: TObject);
    procedure FormPaint(Sender: TObject);
    procedure FormDestroy(Sender: TObject);
    procedure CloseSBClick(Sender: TObject);
    procedure PrintSBClick(Sender: TObject);
    procedure FormActivate(Sender: TObject);
    procedure LeftPageSBClick(Sender: TObject);
    procedure RightPageSBClick(Sender: TObject);
  private
    PreBits: TBitmap;         { Preview bitmap with canvas }
    PpiX, PpiY: Integer;      { Logical pixels per inch }
    Page: Integer;           { One font sampler per page }
    procedure InitGlobals;    { Initialize global variables }
  public
    FontListBox: TListBox;    { Reference to form's ListBox }
  end;

var
  PreviewForm: TPreviewForm;

implementation

uses Main;

{$R *.DFM}
```

```
const
  border = 10;        { Top and bottom preview bitmap borders }

{ Create form and a bitmap to represent the preview page }
procedure TPreviewForm.FormCreate(Sender: TObject);
begin
  FontListBox := nil;
  PreBits := TBitmap.Create;
end;

{ Initialize global variables and window size }
procedure TPreviewForm.InitGlobals;
begin
  PreBits.Width :=
    ClientWidth div 2; {Bitmap width = @bf1/2 client width }
  PreBits.Height :=
    Round(1.3 * PreBits.Width);   { 1.3 = 8@bf1/2 x 11 ratio }
  PpiX :=
    Round(PreBits.Width / 8.5);     { Logical pixels per inch }
  PpiY :=
    Round(PreBits.Height / 11.0);  { Logical pixels per inch }
  if WindowState <> wsMaximized then    { Adjust window bottom }
    ClientHeight :=
      ToolBar.Height + PreBits.Height + border * 2;
end;

{ Tip: OnResize is called before OnActivate, but
only if the form is NOT maximized, in which case FormResize
is never called. Don't use OnResize as your only
display initializer—also initialize in OnActivate. }
procedure TPreviewForm.FormResize(Sender: TObject);
begin
  InitGlobals;
  DrawOnePage(PreBits.Canvas, FontListBox, Page, {Redraw page}
    PreBits.Width, Height, True, PpiX, PpiY);
  Invalidate;
end;

{ Because the program does its own scaling, we can call Draw
instead of StretchDraw as some previewers do. This keeps the
display fast and keeps the text looking as WYSIWYG as possible}

procedure TPreviewForm.FormPaint(Sender: TObject);
begin
  Canvas.Draw(ClientWidth div 4,
    ToolBar.Height + border, PreBits);
end;
```

(continued)

Listing 14-10 *(continued)*

```
procedure TPreviewForm.FormDestroy(Sender: TObject);
begin
  PreBits.Free;
end;

procedure TPreviewForm.CloseSBClick(Sender: TObject);
begin
  ModalResult := mrCancel;
end;

procedure TPreviewForm.PrintSBClick(Sender: TObject);
begin
  ModalResult := mrOk;
end;

{ This procedure prepares the FontListBox, and it draws
the first page (or a blank if no font is selected). The
procedure also enables and disables the toolbar SpeedButtons }
procedure TPreviewForm.FormActivate(Sender: TObject);
begin
{ If you don't assign a ListBox to PreviewForm.FontListBox,
this statement picks up the ListBox from the parent form. }
  if FontListBox = nil then
    FontListBox := MainForm.FontListBox;
{ Draw first page }
  Page := 1;
  InitGlobals;
  DrawOnePage(PreBits.Canvas, FontListBox, Page,
    PreBits.Width, Height, True, PpiX, PpiY);
{ Enable / disable speed buttons in toolbar }
  with FontListBox do
  begin
    LeftPageSB.Enabled := SelCount > 1;
    RightPageSB.Enabled := SelCount > 1;
    PrintSB.Enabled := SelCount > 0;
  end;
end;

{ Display previous page }
procedure TPreviewForm.LeftPageSBClick(Sender: TObject);
begin
  if Page > 1 then
  begin
    Dec(Page);
    DrawOnePage(PreBits.Canvas, FontListBox, Page,
      PreBits.Width, Height, True, PpiX, PpiY);
    Invalidate;
  end;
end;
```

```
{ Display next page }
procedure TPreviewForm.RightPageSBClick(Sender: TObject);
begin
  if Page < FontListBox.SelCount then
  begin
    Inc(Page);
    DrawOnePage(PreBits.Canvas, FontListBox, Page,
      PreBits.Width, Height, True, PpiX, PpiY);
    Invalidate;
  end;
end;

end.
```

The Preview module declares several variables private to the TPreviewForm class. PreBits, a TBitmap object, represents one page of the preview. PpiX and PpiY are the logical pixels-per-inch of this bitmap. Page is the page number. FontListBox is a reference to the parent form's FontListBox. Procedure InitGlobals initializes these variables.

The Preview form creates the PreBits bitmap in an OnCreate event handler. Procedure InitGlobals shows how to perform some necessary calculations for the simulated output page. Assigning values to PreBits.Width and PreBits.Height sizes the bitmap relative to the Preview form window, but in the ratio of the $8^{1}/_{2} \times 11$-inch page size. The program sets PpiX and PpiY to the logical pixels-per-inch for this same page size — this is not equal to the pixels-per-inch of the screen or the form window, but of the bitmap that simulates the output page. Finally, unless the window is maximized, the program assigns an adjusted value to the form's ClientHeight property. This moves the window bottom so the Preview bitmap page is always completely visible. Try resizing the Preview window and watch how the window bottom seeks its own level.

Skip down to the OnPaint event handler, FormPaint. To display a preview page, the program passes the PreBits bitmap to the Canvas's Draw method. This keeps the output fast. A print-preview command could form a bitmap in real size and then use StretchDraw to display that bitmap in a window. This is easier to program, but gives poor results.

Because the program uses Draw, it has to redraw each page when:

✦ The Preview window first appears

✦ The window changes size

✦ The user requests a different page

The OnResize event handler, FormResize, initializes global variables according to the current window size and calls DrawOnePage to form the preview output. To draw on the offscreen bitmap, the program passes PreBits.Canvas to DrawOnePage. It then calls Invalidate, which causes Windows to issue a wm_Paint message to the window. This leads to an OnPaint event, which as you've seen, draws the bitmap by calling the Canvas.Draw method (the one in the form's Canvas, not the bitmap's).

When the Preview form is first activated, its OnActivate event handler initializes some values such as the FontListBox reference and the Page number. It then calls DrawOnePage to form the first output page. It is unnecessary to call Invalidate to force an OnPaint event, this occurs automatically after OnActivate. The OnActivate handler also enables and disables the Preview window's SpeedButtons depending on the number of selected fonts (FontListBox.SelCount).

The FormActivate procedure assigns FontListBox to the MainForm's FontListBox. This assignment does not create a second list box. Use *nil,* as shown here as a flag, to indicate whether a reference such as FontListBox has been initialized. For example, you could insert two or more ListBox objects with different font sets in them and assign references to them to PreviewForm.FontListBox. Or, you can have the module detect that FontListBox is *nil*, in which case it picks up the parent's FontListBox by default. (FontListBox is initialized to *nil* in the form's OnCreate event handler.) This is a good example of defensive programming — the module works correctly regardless of whether another module initializes the public FontListBox variable.

Finally, the OnClick event handlers for the toolbar's previous- and next-page SpeedButtons are in the Preview module. The procedures simply increment or decrement the Page variable and call DrawOnePage to form the bitmap. As I explained, calling Invalidate forces an OnPaint event to occur, which draws the new bitmap on the Preview form's Canvas.

As you may have surmised by now, DrawOnePage is the glue that holds this program's graphical output together. Listing 14-11 shows the module, DrawPage, that implements this procedure.

Listing 14-11: **FontSamp\DrawPage.pas**

```
unit Drawpage;

interface

uses SysUtils, Graphics, StdCtrls;

{ Call DrawOnePage to form each sampler page either during
printing or for previewing with an offscreen bitmap. }
```

```
procedure DrawOnePage(
  Canvas: TCanvas;      { Printer or TBitmap Canvas for preview }
  FontListBox: TListBox; { Fonts with multiple selections }
  Page,                 { Page number (FontList selection index) }
  PageWidth,            { Unscaled page width in pixels }
  PageHeight: Integer;  { Unscaled page height in pixels }
  Previewing: Boolean;  { True if previewing; else printing }
  PpiX, PpiY: Integer   { Pixels per inch on X- and Y- axes }
);

implementation

uses Main;

var
  C: TCanvas;
  FontName, HeaderName: String;
  PixelsPerInchX, PixelsPerInchY: Integer;
  Preview: Boolean;

{ Return selected font at index }
function SelectedFont(ListBox: TListBox;
  Index: Integer): String;
var
  I: Integer;
begin
  with ListBox do
  for I := 0 to Items.Count - 1 do
  if Selected[I] then
  begin
    Dec(Index);
    if Index <= 0 then
    begin
      Result := Items[I];
      Exit;
    end;
  end;
  Result := 'System';
end;

{ Assign font name, style, and size to Canvas font }
procedure SetFont(const Name: String; Style: TFontStyles;
  Size: Integer);
begin
{ Adjust point size for preview page's logical pixels per
inch relative to the form's actual pixels per inch. This allows
the program to draw into the bitmap with TextOut, and then
display the bitmap in real size with Canvas.Draw. Some print
previewers use StretchDraw, which produces relatively poor
results.}
```

(continued)

Listing 14-11 *(continued)*

```
  if Preview then
    Size := Round(Size *
      (PixelsPerInchY / MainForm.PixelsPerInch));
{ Assign parameters to Canvas C Font property }
  C.Font.Name := Name;
  C.Font.Style := Style;
  C.Font.Size := Size;
end;

{ Return pixel width of Name in inches }
function InchWidth(const Name: String): Double;
begin
  Result := C.TextWidth(Name);
  Result := Result / PixelsPerInchX;
end;

{ Return pixel height of Name in inches }
function InchHeight(const Name: String): Double;
begin
  Result := C.TextHeight(Name);
  Result := Result / PixelsPerInchY;
end;

{ Write string S at inch coordinates X and Y }
procedure TextAtInch(X, Y: Double; const S: String);
var
  Px, Py: Integer;
begin
  Px := Round(X * PixelsPerInchX);
  Py := Round(Y * PixelsPerInchY);
  C.TextOut(Px, Py, S);
end;

{ Draw a line at inch coordinates X1, Y1, X2, Y2 }
procedure LineAtInch(X1, Y1, X2, Y2: Double);
var
  Px1, Py1, Px2, Py2: Integer;
begin
  Px1 := Round(X1 * PixelsPerInchX);
  Py1 := Round(Y1 * PixelsPerInchY);
  Px2 := Round(X2 * PixelsPerInchX);
  Py2 := Round(Y2 * PixelsPerInchY);
  C.MoveTo(Px1, Py1);
  C.LineTo(Px2, Py2);
end;

{ Draw header at top of page }
```

```
procedure DrawHeader(const Name: String);
var
  S: String[24];
begin
  SetFont(HeaderName, [fsBold], 12);
  TextAtInch(0.5, 0.5, Name);
  SetFont(HeaderName, [fsItalic], 12);
  S := 'Font Sampler by Tom Swan';
  TextAtInch(8.0 - InchWidth(S), 0.5, S);
  LineAtInch(0.5, 0.5, 8.0, 0.5);
end;

{ Draw footer at bottom of page }
procedure DrawFooter(Page: Integer);
begin
  SetFont(HeaderName, [], 12);
  TextAtInch(0.5, 10.5, 'Page ' + IntToStr(Page));
end;

{ Draw sample character set (ASCII 32-255) }
procedure DrawCharacterSet;
var
  H: Double;
  procedure DrawOneLine(J, K: Integer);
  var
    I: Integer;
    S: String;
  begin
    S := '';
    for I := J to K do
      S := S + Chr(I);
    TextAtInch(0.5, H, S);
    H := H + InchHeight('M');
  end;
begin
  SetFont(HeaderName, [fsBold], 12);
  TextAtInch(0.5, 1.4, 'Character set:');
  SetFont(FontName, [], 10);
  H := 1.5 + InchHeight('M');
  DrawOneLine(32, 80);
  DrawOneLine(81, 129);
  DrawOneLine(130, 178);
  DrawOneLine(179, 227);
  DrawOneLIne(228, 256);
end;

{ Draw sample text in 8, 14, and 24 point sizes }
procedure DrawPointSamples;
var
```

(continued)

Listing 14-11 *(continued)*

```
    H, M: Double;
    procedure DrawOneSample(Pts: Integer);
    begin
      SetFont(HeaderName, [fsBold], 12);
      TextAtInch(0.5, H, IntToStr(Pts) + ' points:');
      M := InchHeight('M');
      H := H + M;
      SetFont(FontName, [], Pts);
      TextAtInch(0.5, H, 'AaBbCc 1234567890');
      H := H + M * 2;
    end;
  begin
    H := 4.0;
    DrawOneSample(8);
    DrawOneSample(14);
    DrawOneSample(24);
  end;

  { Draw normal, italic, bold, and bold-italic samples }
  procedure DrawNormBoldItal;
  var
    H, M: Double;
    procedure DrawOneLine(const S: String; Style: TFontStyles);
    begin
      SetFont(HeaderName, [fsBold], 12);
      TextAtInch(0.5, H, S);
      M := InchHeight('M');
      H := H + M;
      SetFont(FontName, Style, 12);
      TextAtInch(0.5, H, 'AaBbCc 1234567890');
      H := H + M * 2;
    end;
  begin
    H := 7.0;
    DrawOneLine('Normal 12 points:', []);
    DrawOneLine('Italic 12 points:', [fsItalic]);
    DrawOneLine('Bold 12 points:', [fsBold]);
    DrawOneLine('Bold Italic 12 points:', [fsBold, fsItalic]);
  end;

  { Printing and preview code calls this procedure to draw
  each page. See declaration at top of file for descriptions
  of the parameters. }
  procedure DrawOnePage(Canvas: TCanvas; FontListBox: TListBox;
    Page, PageWidth, PageHeight: Integer; Previewing: Boolean;
    PpiX, PpiY: Integer);
  begin
```

```
  { Save some parameters in global variables for easy access }
    C := Canvas;
    C.Pen.Color := clBlack;
    PixelsPerInchX := PpiX;
    PixelsPerInchY := PpiY;
    Preview := Previewing;
  { Draw the font samples on the Canvas (Printer or Preview) }
    with Canvas do
    begin
      FillRect(ClipRect);      { Erase page }
      if (FontListBox = nil) or (FontListBox.SelCount < 1) then
        Exit;  { Display / print blank page if no font selected }
      FontName := SelectedFont(FontListBox, Page);
      HeaderName := 'Arial';
      DrawHeader(FontName);  { These statements draw the }
      DrawFooter(Page);      { header, footer, and font samples }
      DrawCharacterSet;
      DrawPointSamples;
      DrawNormBoldItal;
    end;
  end;

end.
```

It's totally up to you to decide how to implement your program's drawing procedures, but I usually consign them to a separate module. In addition to making the program easier to maintain, separating graphics statements has helped me to port several programs to multiple operating systems, which tend to have different drawing commands. The DrawPage module has a single public procedure, DrawOnePage, which as you've seen, FontSamp calls to print and preview sampler pages.

In your own applications, design the preview and drawing modules before implementing the program's printing commands. This saves paper and forces you to think carefully about how you scale output for different resolutions. Because I followed this plan in writing FontSamp, its printing commands worked the first time I tried them. (Okay, maybe it was the third time, but anyway, the printing commands seemed easier to construct because I had already solved the hard problems in the Preview and DrawPage modules.)

I don't explain all of the DrawPage module's code, which does not contain any printing statements. However, the importance of the module is that it draws on a Canvas, regardless of its type. Therefore, the program can pass to DrawOnePage the Printer's Canvas to print, or the PreBits bitmap's Canvas to draw preview pages offscreen.

Programming would be nice and neat if the preceding statement were always 100 percent true. In practice, however, achieving WYSIWYG output is not so simple. I needed a flag, Previewing, to determine whether the module was printing or previewing. Procedure SetFont uses this flag to reduce font point size when previewing, which is necessary because text would normally be rendered for the window's scale (not the scale of the simulated bitmap page). To get around this problem, the program could draw fonts in their real sizes and call StretchDraw to paint the resulting bitmap. But, as I mentioned, the results are poor and they display slowly.

Expert-User Tips

✦ If text does not print in the expected size, make sure your code calls Print.BeginDoc before changing the Printer Canvas Font and its subproperties.

✦ You must eventually call CloseFile for a System.Text variable passed to AssignPrn. Attempting to assign a second output file without closing a currently assigned file raises an exception.

✦ When printing plain text, watch for the Printer object's PageNumber property to change after each call to Writeln. When PageNumber advances, a new page has been started. Rather than calculate the number of lines per page as this chapter suggests, you can use this technique to write a header line at the top of each new page.

✦ Allow a small border in printed output. Many printers lose sharpness at the extreme ranges as represented by the Printer object's PageHeight and PageWidth properties.

✦ Assign a string to the Printer object's Title property to identify a print job in the Windows Print Manager and on network page headers.

✦ To create an abort printing dialog, use a separate form and call its Show method to display it. Have the form set a global variable to True as a flag that indicates the user clicked an Abort button. Check for this flag inside your program's *printer output* loop and if the flag is True, call the Printer.Abort method to cancel printing. You do not also have to call EndDoc in that case.

✦ To detect whether a print job was aborted (for example, by a *print* loop calling Printer.Abort), inspect the read-only Printer.Aborted flag.

Projects to Try

14-1: Improve the Lister demonstration by adding a menu command for selecting font, style, and size, and for making line numbers optional. You might also implement a File | Page Setup command to configure headers, page numbers, and so on. Simply print these items as you do other text using Write and Writeln. (Hint: Use the method demonstrated by the PrnInfo application to calculate the number of lines per page.)

14-2: Changing fonts in PrnInfo causes the program to print its report in that same font, which can cause problems — for example, if you select a large point size or a symbolic font. Revise this feature (well, maybe it's a bug) by writing a procedure that returns printer statistics for any font, style, and point size. Then, use your procedure to print the report in a standard font.

14-3: Write a utility to determine the number of lines per page for every installed font. Print a report of this information.

14-4: Design a printer diagnostic program that prints a test pattern. This program is useful for checking edge sharpness, text appearance, line straightness, and other useful information.

14-5: **Advanced.** Design and implement a Delphi project documenter that prints all .pas files in the current directory as well as the .dpr project file. Also print icons and bitmap files.

Summary

✦ Use the PrintDialog and PrinterSetupDialog components to prompt users to print and to provide access to installed printer device driver setups.

✦ The TPrinter component, which is not on the VCL palette, provides printing capabilities. Add Printers to your program's *uses* directive. You can then assign values to the global Printer object's properties, and call methods such as Printer.BeginDoc and Printer.NewPage. You never create an object of the TPrinter class. Instead, use the Printer object provided by the Printers unit.

✦ Two ways to print exist: For plain-text printing, use a Text file along with Pascal's Write and Writeln procedures. For graphics and WYSIWYG text printing, use the Printer object's Canvas. Call BeginDoc to start a print job. Draw on the Canvas as you do to display graphics in a window. Call NewPage to eject a page. Call EndDoc to end printing.

✦ To print a form, call its Print method, which paints the form's client area on an offscreen bitmap. The method uses the Printer object's BeginDoc and EndDoc techniques to print the resulting bitmap.

✦ Create a print-preview command by separating graphics output statements in a module, or a procedure such as DrawOnePage in the FontSamp application. To print, pass the Printer's Canvas to the procedure. To draw simulated preview pages, pass a TBitmap's Canvas and draw the bitmap using the form's Canvas.Draw method (not the bitmap's).

The Multiple Document Interface, or MDI, has been one of Windows' controversial features among programmers since day one. MDI isn't appropriate for all programs, but it is useful for creating multipage windows using a standard interface, as explained in the next chapter.

✦   ✦   ✦

Developing MDI Applications

Windows developers enjoy a love/hate relationship
with the MDI, or Multiple Document Interface. In fact,
most programmers love to hate it. But the MDI isn't as poorly
conceived as many claim. When you need a framework for
managing multiple documents, with one data block per
window, the MDI offers a standard interface that's easy to use
and, with Delphi's help, mostly straightforward to program.

This chapter explains how to use Delphi forms to construct
MDI main and child windows. I also explain related topics
such as how to create a Window menu with window-
management commands, how to subclass a form to create
child windows, how to add window titles to the Window menu,
and how to merge child- and main-window menus.

Components

The following are some of Delphi's components for developing
MDI applications:

+ **TForm** — This component, which is the same as the one
used in Single Document Interface (SDI) applications, is
not on the VCL palette. MDI applications use objects of
the TForm class for main and child windows. Set the
main window's FormStyle property to fsMDIForm. For
child windows, set this property to fsMDIChild and
follow the instructions in this chapter to construct child
windows at run time — in response to a File | Open
command, for example. Palette: none.

✦ **MainMenu**—Every MDI application's main form window must have a MainMenu component object, introduced in Chapter 5. Most MDI MainMenu objects have File and Window menu items, although you are free to name your menus as you want. MDI child windows may also have MainMenu objects for merging into the main-window menu. Palette: Standard.

Note   Pronounce MDI as "M," "D," "I," to avoid confusing it with MIDI, the musical instrument device interface. MDI and MIDI are unrelated.

Fundamentals of MDI Programming

Every MDI application has three basic parts:

✦ The MDI main-window form

✦ One or more document MDI child-window forms

✦ The MDI main menu

Unlike in conventional Windows programming, a Delphi form object takes the place of the standard MDI frame and client windows. Classically, the frame window is the visible one; the client window is a kind of silent partner that handles global operations, creates child windows, and performs message services. In Delphi applications, the frame and client windows still exist, but you rarely use them. For all practical purposes, you can treat the frame and the client as one window, represented to your program as the main-window form.

Document child windows are also forms, but unlike windows such as an AboutBoxdialog that you insert into a module, MDI child windows cannot stray out of their backyard. They are restricted to appearing inside the main window's client area. When you minimize a child window, its icon displays inside the main window, not on the Windows Start bar.

Except for these differences, MDI main and child windows are similar to single-window application forms. In MDI applications, you can insert toolbars, status lines, component objects and graphics, and use all other Delphi programming techniques. Typically, however, the MDI is most advantageous in applications that work with multiple documents.

Note   The MDI is often considered a file-handling system, but an application's child windows do not have to be associated with disk files. You can also use the MDI to construct multiwindow applications of other kinds. The term *document* in this chapter refers to any information that can be displayed in a window, not necessarily data in a document disk file.

MDI main-window form

Follow these steps to create the main window for an MDI application:

1. Start a new application.

2. Assign a Name such as MainForm to the form.

3. Set the FormStyle property to fsMDIForm.

4. Save the project in a new directory. Name the unit module Main.pas; name the project as you like (use the name MDITest if you are following along).

Only the main-window form may have its FormStyle set to fsMDIForm, and there can be only one such window per application. To ensure that the window's form object is automatically created, select Project I Options…, and verify that MainForm is shown in the Main form list box and is listed under Auto-create forms.

This is all you need to do to create an MDI application's main window. You can now proceed to the next section to create your program's child windows and menu.

Note

To try the techniques in this chapter, start a new application using the File|New Application menu command, or use File|New… and select Application in the New page of templates. Do not select MDI Application under Projects. This application template prepares a new MDI project with default menus, a child window form, and event handlers. Later in this chapter, I explain how to use the MDI project template, but for most demonstrations in this chapter, you can simply create a blank single-window application and then follow the numbered steps.

Adding MDI child-window forms

Every MDI application also needs at least one child-window form and unit. Follow these steps to add an MDI child window to a new MDI application:

1. Start a new application by selecting the File I New Application command. Change Form1's Name property, using the Object Inspector, to MainForm. Change MainForm's FormStyle property to fsMDIForm.

2. Select File I Save All (or click the Save All speed button, the one that shows a stack of disks). Change Unit1.pas's name to Main.pas and save. Change Project1.dpr to MDITest.dpr and save.

3. Choose File I New Form or click the New form SpeedButton. This creates a new form object named Form1 by default. (It is named Form1 and not Form2 because you changed the other form's name to MainForm.) Resize the Form1 window to make it easier to select (it is initially the same size as MainForm and probably covers that window completely).

4. Use the Object Inspector to change Form1's Name property to ChildForm. Set FormStyle to fsMDIChild.

5. Select File | Save All (or click the Save All speed button). You are prompted for a filename for ChildForm's unit module. Change this name from its default, Unit1.pas, to Child.pas, and select the Save button.

6. Select Project | Options to open the Project Options dialog. Highlight the ChildForm object listed in the left pane, and click the single-line, right-arrow button to move the object from the Auto-create forms list to the Available forms list. If you don't perform these steps, a child window is created automatically when the program starts. Nothing is technically wrong with that, but the result may confuse users who expect to open and create child windows using commands such as File | New and File | Open. Most MDI applications create their child windows under program control, not automatically when the program runs. Close the Project Options dialog.

The preceding steps complete the creation of a bare-bones MDI shell. You can now insert programming into the shell for constructing child windows in response to commands such as File | New and File | Open. The next section explains how to write this code.

Tip

MDI application child windows do not all have to be of the same type. If your application needs different types of child windows, simply add as many additional forms as you need by repeating Steps 3 to 5. Create a unique Name for each new form and set FormStyle to fsMDIChild. Save the project using the File|Save All command and enter a unique name for the unit's .pas file—for example, you might name your child windows Child1Form and Child2Form and save them as files named Child1.pas and Child2.pas. For more information on creating multiple types of child-window forms, see "Working with different-type child windows" in this chapter.

At this point, if you are following along, among other files in your project directory you can find these three Pascal modules:

✦ **Child.pas**—This is the child-window form's unit module. The module typically contains programming specific to the type of document or other information provided by the child window. A child window may also have a menu, which is normally merged into the main form's menu.

✦ **Main.pas**—This is the main-window form's unit module. Insert event handlers in this unit for any objects in the main-window form, as well as for menu items. Typically, at least one event handler in this module should create instances of the program's child windows. For details on writing this code, see "Child Windows" and "Creating child window instances" later in this chapter.

✦ **MDITest.dpr**—This is the program's project file. It rarely needs any modification for MDI applications.

Tip

Make a copy of your project directory now and use the MDITest.dpr project to try out various programming techniques in this chapter.

Creating an MDI main menu

Every MDI application must have a main menu object. At least one command in this menu should create child-window form objects — typically, this is the File|New command. Follow the next steps to create the menu for the MDITest application that you created in the preceding sections. Open the MDITest.dpr project, if necessary, and then follow these steps:

1. Insert a MainMenu component object from the Standard palette into MainForm. (Be sure to select MainForm, not ChildForm.) Double-click the MainMenu object to open Delphi's Menu Designer.

2. Type **&File** (the ampersand indicates that the following letter, *F*, is the menu hot key). Press Enter and the Menu Designer creates the File menu. Click File in the Menu Designer — this selects the TMenuItem object (File1) in the Object Inspector. Change the Name property for File1 to FileMenu.

3. Still using Menu Designer, add &New, &Open..., and &Save... commands to the File menu. To do this, click below the File menu title and just type the commands. Each command is created as a TMenuItem object. For this chapter, I use the default object names New1, Open1, and Save1, but if you prefer, you can select each object using the Menu Designer and change their Name properties in the Object Inspector window. The menu now has File|New, File|Open..., and File|Save... commands, the minimum probably required by all MDI applications. (The section "Creating child window instances" in this chapter describes how to write code for constructing child window objects, and opening and saving documents, when users select these menu commands.)

4. Still using Menu Designer, create a second menu named Window. To do this, click next to File and type **&Window**. Select the Window menu (click it in Menu Designer), and using the Object Inspector window, change the Name property of this TMenuItem object from its default, Window1, to WindowMenu.

5. Back in the Menu Designer again, click below Window, and enter three commands for this menu: **&Cascade, &Tile,** and **&Arrange All**. As with the File menu's commands, you could select each of these command objects and change their Name properties, but for this demonstration, we use the default Delphi object names Cascade1, Tile1, and Arrange1. To learn how to write event handlers for these and other Window menu commands, see the section "Using Window menu commands" in this chapter. Figure 15-1 shows the Menu Designer and the developing MDI menu at this point.

Main MDI window

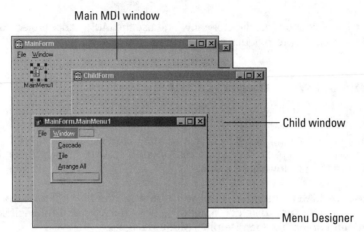

Child window

Menu Designer

Figure 15-1: Delphi's Menu Designer with suggested menu items for an MDI application

6. Close the Menu Designer or shove it aside, and select MainForm (press F12 or use View I Project Manager to find MainForm). Use the Object Inspector to set MainForm's WindowMenu property to the TMenuItem, WindowMenu. To do this, click the arrow next to the WindowMenu property and select WindowMenu from the resulting list of objects available to the form. This setting causes the application to automatically list the titles of open child windows in the designated menu — you don't have to write any code to make this happen.

Of course, the exact menu commands in your application depend on your program's needs. At the very minimum, however, an MDI application should have commands to create and open document child windows, and a menu, usually named Window, for listing the titles of open windows.

You may assign to a form's WindowMenu property only a top-level menu object — in other words, a TMenuItem object that represents a menu item in the main window's menu bar. Do not assign a menu command object such as Open1 or Save1 to this property.

Child-window forms may also have MainMenu objects. When users activate an instance of the child window, its menu commands automatically merge into the main form's menu according to the menu items' GroupIndex property. See "Merging menus" in this chapter for instructions on merging MDI menus.

Accessing child windows

Three Form component properties provide access to child windows, and you use them in most MDI applications. Throughout this chapter are numerous examples of each of these three properties:

✦ **ActiveMDIChild** — A reference to the currently active child window. If no children exist, ActiveMDIChild is *nil*. This property is a reference to a TForm object, therefore, you often need to cast ActiveMDIChild to the child window's class such as TChildForm.

✦ **MDIChildCount** — The integer count of child windows that the MDI parent window owns. If no children exist, MDIChildCount is zero.

✦ **MDIChildren** — An array of TForm object references to all child windows owned by the MDI parent window. The expression MDIChildren[0] references the first child window in the array; the expression MDIChildren[MCIChildCount - 1] references the last child window.

If ActiveMDIChild is *nil*, or if MDIChildCount equals zero, no child windows are present. In such cases, the program should not refer to the MDIChildren array, although doing so does not necessarily generate an exception. Specifically, the expression MDIChildren[0] is *nil* when MDIChildCount equals zero.

Child Windows

A child window in an MDI application operates much like the main window in a single-window application. Child windows can have component objects such as Memos and Buttons. Typically, a child window displays a document — for example, a text file or a bitmap. Users can open multiple child windows, arrange them in cascaded or tiled order, and minimize them to icons. Child windows may have toolbars and status lines, but traditionally, these kinds of objects usually appear in the main window.

Selecting a child window can also, optionally, merge commands into the application's main menu. This technique is especially useful when you are using multiple types of child windows, each with its own command requirements. The following section discusses these child-window programming techniques and lists an MDI application shell that you can use to begin new programs.

Same-type child windows

The MDIDemo application on the CD-ROM in the Source\MDIDemo directory demonstrates how to create same-type MDI child windows. The program shows how to program common menu commands such as File|New, File|Open..., Window|Cascade, and Window|Tile. Figure 15-2 shows the program's display with a few sample windows open. (Windows 95, 98, and NT show minimized child windows by stacking their window headers along the main window's bottom border.)

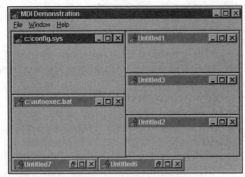

Figure 15-2: The MDIDemo application demonstrates same-type, child-window programming.

Listing 15-1 shows the MDIDemo application's Child.pas module. In this demonstration, the child window displays no real data, so the module is simplistic. However, it shows the bare-minimum procedures a child window typically provides.

Listing 15-1: **MDIDemo\Child.pas**

```
unit Child;

interface

uses
  Windows, Messages, SysUtils, Classes, Graphics, Controls,
  Forms, Dialogs, StdCtrls;

type
  TChildForm = class(TForm)
    procedure FormClose(Sender: TObject;
      var Action: TCloseAction);
```

```
    private
    { Private declarations }
    public
    { Public declarations }
      procedure LoadData(const FileName: String); virtual;
      procedure SaveData(const FileName: String); virtual;
    end;

var
  ChildForm: TChildForm;

implementation

{$R *.DFM}

procedure TChildForm.FormClose(Sender: TObject;
  var Action: TCloseAction);
begin
  Action := caFree;
end;

procedure TChildForm.LoadData(const FileName: String);
begin
  ShowMessage('LoadData from ' + FileName);
  Caption := LowerCase(FileName);
end;

procedure TChildForm.SaveData(const FileName: String);
begin
  ShowMessage('SaveData to ' + FileName);
  Caption := LowerCase(FileName);
end;

end.
```

The child-window module can provide procedures to load and save document data. Procedures such as LoadData and SaveData are declared as public members of the TChildForm class. The reason for making them public is so that the main module's Open and Save commands can call them.

The sample listing also declares LoadData and SaveData virtual. As a result, another module can inherit the TChildForm class and override the procedures. For example, you can add another child-window form to the program and base the form's class on TChildForm, rather than the usual TForm. You can then write LoadData and SaveData procedures for reading and writing the module's specific data. Inheriting a class this way is often called *subclassing a form*, a technique demonstrated later in this chapter.

Tip   You should always provide an OnClose event handler for each type of child window. Set the Action parameter to caFree so the application disposes of the child-window object when you close its window. If you don't set Action to caFree, closing the window minimizes it in the main window's client area.

In addition to OnClose, you may also want to write an OnCloseQuery event handler to warn users when they close a window with unsaved data. In the procedure, set CanClose to False to prevent the window from closing; set CanClose to True if the window may close. See "Closing a Window" in Chapter 3 for more information about OnClose and OnCloseQuery events. MDI application main windows can't close, thus the application can't end, unless all child windows can close. This desirable feature helps prevent loss of data — for example, accidentally tossing out changes in a child window that is hidden by another window.

MDIDemo's sample LoadData and SaveData procedures do not read or write any real files, so feel free to play with the program's Open..., Save, and Save As... commands. To confirm that the program calls the procedures at the proper times, ShowMessage displays a dialog with the current filename. Typically, when child windows display file documents, the LoadData and SaveData procedures should also assign the current filename to the child form's Caption. This displays the filename and its path in the window title bar.

You can easily modify MDIDemo to read and write real data. For example, insert a Memo object into ChildForm (if you don't see this window, open MDIDemo.dpr, select the View|Project Manager command, click the plus sign next to Child, and double-click ChildForm). Set the new Memo1 object's Align property to alClient, which causes the object to completely fill its window. Select an appropriate font property if you wish, delete "Memo1" from the Lines property (click the ellipsis to open the editor), and set ScrollBars to ssBoth.

To reprogram the ChildForm module, using the Project Manager, open the Child.pas file and select it in the code editor. In place of the ShowMessage statements from Listing 15-1, insert the following commands to read and write text files:

```
{ Replace ShowMessage statement in LoadData with: }
Memo1.Lines.LoadFromFile(FileName);

{ Replace ShowMessage statement in SaveData with: }
Memo1.Lines.SaveToFile(FileName);
```

You have just constructed an MDI text editor!

Press F9 to compile and run the modified program. Select the File|New or File|Open commands to open a child window, into which you can type text or make changes. Use File|Save or File|Save As... to save your changes to disk.

Caution

The preceding code makes MDIDemo a "live" application. Changes that you make to files and save to disk are permanent. If you are just playing around, save copies of any files you edit.

Long path names can look messy in window Captions, and you may want to use the ExtractFileName function to assign filenames to child-window title bars without the drive and path information. To do this, add SysUtils to the module's *uses* statement, and declare a String variable in the TChildForm class. Assign the full filename to the string variable for use in input and output statements and assign to the window's Caption property the result of function ExtractFileName from the SysUtils unit. Look up "file management routines" in Delphi's online help for more information on this and other file functions.

Creating child window instances

On the CD-ROM

Listing 15-2 shows MDIDemo's TMainForm class declaration and the File menu's OnClick event handlers. This portion of the listing demonstrates how to create new instances of the TChildForm class. Because MDIDemo's main module is lengthy, I present it in pieces. To inspect the full listing, load the MDIDemo.dpr project into Delphi from the CD-ROM in the Source\MDIDemo directory.

Listing 15-2: **MDIDemo's File menu OnClick event handlers**

```
unit Main;

interface

uses
  Windows, Messages, SysUtils, Classes, Graphics, Controls,
  Forms, Dialogs, Menus, Child;

type
  TMainForm = class(TForm)
    MainMenu1: TMainMenu;
    FileMenu: TMenuItem;
    FileOpen: TMenuItem;
    FileSave: TMenuItem;
    FileSaveAs: TMenuItem;
    FileNew: TMenuItem;
    N1: TMenuItem;
    FileExit: TMenuItem;
    WindowMenu: TMenuItem;
    WindowCascade: TMenuItem;
    WindowTile: TMenuItem;
    WindowArrangeIcons: TMenuItem;
```

(continued)

Listing 15-2 *(continued)*

```pascal
    N2: TMenuItem;
    WindowCloseAll: TMenuItem;
    WindowMinimizeAll: TMenuItem;
    HelpMenu: TMenuItem;
    HelpAbout: TMenuItem;
    OpenDialog: TOpenDialog;
    FileClose: TMenuItem;
    N3: TMenuItem;
    SaveDialog: TSaveDialog;
    procedure FileNewClick(Sender: TObject);
    procedure FileOpenClick(Sender: TObject);
    procedure FileCloseClick(Sender: TObject);
    procedure FileSaveClick(Sender: TObject);
    procedure FileSaveAsClick(Sender: TObject);
    procedure FileExitClick(Sender: TObject);
    procedure WindowCascadeClick(Sender: TObject);
    procedure WindowTileClick(Sender: TObject);
    procedure WindowArrangeIconsClick(Sender: TObject);
    procedure WindowMinimizeAllClick(Sender: TObject);
    procedure WindowCloseAllClick(Sender: TObject);
    procedure HelpAboutClick(Sender: TObject);
    procedure FileMenuClick(Sender: TObject);
    procedure WindowMenuClick(Sender: TObject);
  private
  {- Private declarations }
    procedure CreateChild(const Name: string);
  public
  {- Public declarations }
  end;

var
  MainForm: TMainForm;

implementation

{$R *.DFM}

const
  maxChildren = 10;   { Optional: No maximum required }

procedure TMainForm.CreateChild(const Name: String);
var
  Child: TChildForm;
begin
  Child := TChildForm.Create(Application);
  Child.Caption := Name;
end;
```

```pascal
procedure TMainForm.FileNewClick(Sender: TObject);
begin
  CreateChild('Untitled' + IntToStr(MDIChildCount + 1));
end;

procedure TMainForm.FileOpenClick(Sender: TObject);
begin
  if OpenDialog.Execute then
  begin
    CreateChild(Lowercase(OpenDialog.FileName));
    with ActiveMDIChild as TChildForm do
      LoadData(OpenDialog.FileName);
  end;
end;

procedure TMainForm.FileCloseClick(Sender: TObject);
begin
  if ActiveMDIChild <> nil then
    ActiveMDIChild.Close;
end;

procedure TMainForm.FileSaveClick(Sender: TObject);
begin
  if Pos('Untitled', ActiveMDIChild.Caption) = 1 then
    FileSaveAsClick(Sender)
  else with ActiveMDIChild as TChildForm do
    SaveData(Caption);
end;

procedure TMainForm.FileSaveAsClick(Sender: TObject);
var
  FExt: String;
begin
  with SaveDialog do
  begin
    FileName := ActiveMDIChild.Caption;
    FExt := ExtractFileExt(FileName);
    if Length(FExt) = 0 then
      FExt := '.*';
    Filter := 'Files (*' + FExt + ')|*' + FExt;
    if Execute then
    with ActiveMDIChild as TChildForm do
      SaveData(FileName);
  end;
end;

procedure TMainForm.FileExitClick(Sender: TObject);
begin
  Close;
end;
```

The CreateChild procedure, declared as a private member of the TMainForm class, creates instances of the TChildForm class. Privately declared items are accessible only from methods in the class. This helps ensure that other modules do not indiscriminately call procedures and functions that perform critical services. The CreateChild procedure also shows how to create a form object at run time. To do that, declare a variable of the class type:

```
var
   Child: TChildForm;
```

Next, in the procedure body, call the class's Create method with Application as an argument. Assign the resulting object to the variable:

```
Child := TChildForm.Create(Application);
```

The reason for passing Application, and not MainForm, to Create is because Application represents the MDI's frame window, which is the real window that owns the child window. MainForm is a kind of stepparent to its children.

The program's File|New event handler, procedure FileNewClick, calls CreateChild. The File|Open handler does the same, but also calls the Child.pas module's LoadData public procedure. However, these are only suggested techniques for constructing child windows and loading data from files; you are free to code the modules as you want.

Use the MainForm object's ActiveMDIChild property to perform operations on the current child window. This property equals *nil* if no child windows are present, and you should always check for this condition before using the property. For example, the sample program's File|Close event handler, procedure FileCloseClick, closes the active child window with the statement:

```
if ActiveMDIChild <> nil then
   ActiveMDIChild.Close;
```

Never use an unrestricted statement such as the following, which generates an exception if no child windows exist. This happens because the statement may attempt to call a method (Close) for a *nil* reference:

```
ActiveMDIChild.Close;  /// ???
```

As I suggested, the child module should perform its own data-save verification in OnClose and OnCloseQuery event handlers. The window does not actually close unless the child object verifies that it can close—an example of sound object-oriented programming.

MainForm's FileSaveClick and FileSaveAsClick procedures call the SaveData procedure for the active child-window object. If the window caption is Untitled, FileSaveClick defaults to FileSaveAsClick; otherwise, the code calls SaveData with the current filename, picked up from the window caption. FileSaveAsClick uses the technique suggested in Chapter 12 to limit SaveDialog files to those with the same extension as the current window's.

Finally in this portion of the listing, the MainForm's File | Exit event handler, procedure FileExitClick, simply calls Close. It can do this because the parent object attempts to close and free all of its child windows. However, the application ends only if all children can close.

Using Window menu commands

Most MDI applications provide a Window menu, which performs operations on child windows such as cascading, tiling, and arranging icons in the main window's client area. Listing 15-3 shows MDIDemo's Window menu OnClick event handlers and demonstrates how to write custom window commands such as Close all, which Delphi doesn't provide.

Listing 15-3: **MDIDemo's Window menu OnClick event handlers**

```
procedure TMainForm.WindowCascadeClick(Sender: TObject);
begin
  Cascade;
end;

procedure TMainForm.WindowTileClick(Sender: TObject);
begin
  Tile;
end;

procedure TMainForm.WindowArrangeIconsClick(Sender: TObject);
begin
  ArrangeIcons;
end;

procedure TMainForm.WindowMinimizeAllClick(Sender: TObject);
var
  I: Integer;
begin
  for I := MDIChildCount - 1 downto 0 do
    MDIChildren[I].WindowState := wsMinimized;
end;
```

(continued)

Listing 15-3 *(continued)*

```
procedure TMainForm.WindowCloseAllClick(Sender: TObject);
var
  I: Integer;
begin
  for I := 0 to MDIChildCount - 1 do
    MDIChildren[I].Close;
end;
```

The first three procedures implement standard Window menu commands: Cascade, Tile, and Arrange icons. Because these are so common, the TForm class provides the necessary code in its Cascade, Tile, and ArrangeIcons methods. Simply call these methods in response to the appropriate menu commands. You may also call these methods at other times — for example, in response to a toolbar SpeedButton's OnClick event.

Two other standard commands you can add to the Window menu are Next and Previous. Simply call the main form's Next and Previous methods. However, you may want to disable these commands if only one window uses statements such as the following in the Window menu's OnClick event handler (assume WindowNext and WindowPrevious are TMenuItem objects):

```
WindowNext.Enabled := MDIChildCount > 1;
WindowPrevious.Enabled := WindowNext.Enabled;
```

In addition to standard Window menu commands, you can write new commands to perform operations on all child windows. For example, MDIDemo implements a Window|Minimize all command with this *for* loop:

```
for I := MDIChildCount - 1 downto 0 do
  MDIChildren[I].WindowState := wsMinimized;
```

To make the icons come out in a sensible order, the *for* loop counts down from the last child window to the first. Use the main-window form's MDIChildren array to access each child window. The array's elements are of type TForm, so unless you are using an inherited method or property such as WindowState as shown here, you need to use a type-cast expression to call methods and use properties in your child-window class. For example, the following calls a fictitious YourMethod procedure for the first child window:

```
if MDIChildCount > 0 then
  TChildForm(MDIChildren[0]).YourMethod;
```

Alternatively, use a *with* statement such as this:

```
if MDIChildCount > 0 then
with MDIChildren[0] as TChildForm do
  YourMethod;
```

A properly designed MDI application should always check for at least one child-window object before performing actions through the MDIChildren array. Either check whether MDIChildCount is greater than zero, or test whether ActiveMDIChild is not *nil*.

Although not all MDI applications provide a Window|Close all command, maybe they should. I tend to open lots of windows as I work on various projects, and it's helpful to have a method for shutting down all windows without having to close them one by one. MDIDemo performs this action in procedure WindowCloseAllClick, which executes the following *for* loop to close the windows in first-to-last order:

```
for I := MDIChildCount - 1 downto 0 do
  MDIChildren[I].Close;
```

Internally, MDIChildren is implemented as a TList object, therefore, it is permissible to perform operations such as the preceding that affect the number of child windows.

Miscellaneous MDI commands

Listing 15-4 shows the remainder of MDIDemo's Main.pas source code module.

Listing 15-4: **MDIDemo's miscellaneous procedures**

```
procedure TMainForm.HelpAboutClick(Sender: TObject);
begin
  AboutForm.ShowModal;
end;

procedure TMainForm.FileMenuClick(Sender: TObject);
begin
  FileNew.Enabled := MDIChildCount < maxChildren;
  FileOpen.Enabled := FileNew.Enabled;
  FileClose.Enabled := MDIChildCount > 0;
  FileSave.Enabled := FileClose.Enabled;
  FileSaveAs.Enabled := FileClose.Enabled;
```

(continued)

Listing 15-4 *(continued)*

```
end;

procedure TMainForm.WindowMenuClick(Sender: TObject);
var
  I: Integer;
begin
  with WindowMenu do
  for I := 0 to Count - 1 do
    with Items[I] as TMenuItem do
      Enabled := MDIChildCount > 0;
end;

end.
```

The HelpAboutClick procedure displays the program's AboutBox dialog, which isn't shown here. Procedures FileMenuClick and WindowMenuClick are the OnClick event handlers for the FileMenu and WindowMenu objects. The program calls these procedures when users open the menus. The procedures enable and disable commands based on program conditions. For example, File | New is disabled when MDIChildCount equals maxChildren, which effectively limits the number of child windows that users can open. All Window menu commands are disabled when no child windows are present. If you add Next and Previous commands as suggested, you should enable them separately if MDIChildCount is greater than one.

Note

You needn't limit the number of child windows. I included this feature in MDIDemo just to show the programming. MDI applications may have as many child windows as memory and other resources allow.

Working with different-type child windows

On the
CD-ROM

An MDI application's child windows may be of different types. For each type of child window, add a new form to the project and add programming to the main module to construct window instances. For example, try the following steps to add to MDIDemo a child window that can display bitmap files. (The completed program is on the CD-ROM in the Source\MDIDemo2 directory. If you don't want to make these modifications yourself, open the MDIDemo2.dpr project file in that directory to view the finished files with Delphi. These steps assume you are modifying the original project in Source\MDIDemo.)

1. Open the MDIDemo.dpr project file. Add another module to MDIDemo by selecting File | New Form or clicking the New Form SpeedButton.

2. Change the new form's Name property from Form1 to ChildBmpForm. Set FormStyle to fsMDIChild. Choose Project | Options and move ChildBmpForm from the list of Auto-create forms to the list of Available forms. The right panel should list two forms: ChildForm and ChildBmpForm. The left panel should list MainForm and AboutForm. Close the Project Options dialog by clicking OK.

3. Save the project by selecting File | Save All. When prompted for a filename, enter **Childbmp.pas** in place of the default name, Unit1.pas.

4. Select the ChildBmp form by clicking inside its window. Switch to the Object Inspector, click Events, and double-click the space to the right of OnClose to create a handler for this event. Type a statement that assigns caFree to Action. This frees the form object when you close the child window. If you don't perform this step, closing the window minimizes it in the main window's client area — this is allowable, but is usually not what you want. The OnClose event handler procedure should look like this:

```
procedure TChildBmpForm.FormClose(Sender: TObject;
  var Action: TCloseAction);
begin
  Action := caFree;
end;
```

5. Insert an Image component object from the Additional palette into the ChildBmp form. Set the Image1 object's Align property to alClient so it fills the window and set the Image1 Stretch property to True. These changes fill the child window with the loaded image at run time and size the image to fit the child window's client area.

6. Switch to the code editor and select the ChildBmp unit. Add Child into the *uses* statement at the top of the module. This is necessary because we want the new form class to inherit (build upon) the original Child form. The completed *uses* statement should look something like this (change in bold):

```
uses
  Windows, Messages, SysUtils, Classes, Graphics, Controls,
  Forms, Dialogs, Child;
```

7. While still in the code editor for ChildBmp, change the TChildBmpForm's base class from TForm to TChildForm. This causes TChildBmpForm to inherit the properties and methods from TChildForm, a technique called *subclassing a form*. TChildBmpForm's modified class declaration should now look like this (change in bold):

```
type
  TChildBmpForm = class(TChildForm)
  ...
```

8. Add LoadData and SaveData procedures to the TChildBmpForm class. Designate the procedures with the *override* directive, which tells Delphi to replace the virtual methods inherited from TChildForm. Insert these declarations below the *public* keyword in the TChildBmpForm class declaration:

```
public
   procedure LoadData(const FileName: String); override;
   procedure SaveData(const FileName: String); override;
```

9. Implement those two procedures in the ChildBmp module's implementation section. Listing 15-5 shows the completed code, which you can use as a guide to completing your own program if you are following along. This listing, along with others for this section, is in the Source\MDIDemo2 directory on the CD-ROM.

10. Select the ChildBmpForm object in the Object Inspector, click the Events page tab, and double-click the space to the right of the OnCreate event. Enter the code from the FormCreate procedure in Listing 15-5. This frees the inherited Memo1 object, which would otherwise conflict with the Image1 object in the new class. (Listing 15-5 and others in this section are on the CD-ROM in the Source\MDIDemo2 directory.)

Listing 15-5: **The completed ChildBmp module source code**

```
unit Childbmp;

interface

uses
   Windows, Messages, SysUtils, Classes, Graphics, Controls,
   Forms, Dialogs, Child, ExtCtrls;

type
   TChildBmpForm = class(TChildForm)
     Image1: TImage;
     procedure FormClose(Sender: TObject;
       var Action: TCloseAction);
     procedure FormCreate(Sender: TObject);
   private
     { Private declarations }
   public
     { Public declarations }
     procedure LoadData(const FileName: String); override;
     procedure SaveData(const FileName: String); override;
   end;

var
```

```
    ChildBmpForm: TChildBmpForm;

implementation

{$R *.DFM}

procedure TChildBmpForm.FormClose(Sender: TObject;
  var Action: TCloseAction);
begin
  Action := caFree;
end;

procedure TChildBmpForm.LoadData(const FileName: String);
begin
  Image1.Picture.LoadFromFile(FileName);
  Caption := LowerCase(FileName);
end;

procedure TChildBmpForm.SaveData(const FileName: String);
begin
  Image1.Picture.SaveToFile(FileName);
  Caption := LowerCase(FileName);
end;

procedure TChildBmpForm.FormCreate(Sender: TObject);
begin
  inherited;
  Memo1.Free;
end;

end.
```

Note

The reason for freeing Memo1 in the FormCreate method is to prevent this object from conflicting with the Image1 object in the new TChildBmpForm class. This illustrates one potential problem with subclassing windows — the new class might add objects that conflict with objects in its ancestor. See Project 15-6 for suggestions on how to improve the program's class hierarchy.

The final step in modifying MDIDemo to read and write bitmap files is to reprogram the Main module so it can construct instances of the bitmap child class. To do that, select the Main module in the code editor (use View | Project Manager to open MainForm.pas if the Main module is not visible). Add ChildBmp to the Main module's *uses* statement, which should look something like this:

```
uses
  Windows, Messages, SysUtils, Classes, Graphics, Controls,
  Forms, Dialogs, Menus, Child, ChildBmp;
```

On the
CD-ROM

Rewrite the CreateChild procedure as shown in Listing 15-6. (This text is in the Source\MDIDemo2 directory on the CD-ROM.) Press F9 to compile and run the modified program. Open a bitmap file. (If you added a Memo object to the Child module as suggested, you can also open text files.) The program constructs the proper type of window based on the filename extension.

Listing 15-6: The Main module's reprogrammed CreateChild procedure for the modified MDIDemo application; also adds ChildBmp to the module's uses statement

```
procedure TMainForm.CreateChild(const Name: String);
var
  Child: TChildForm;
  FExt: String;
begin
  FExt := ExtractFileExt(Name);
  if FExt = '.bmp' then
    Child := TChildBmpForm.Create(Application)
  else
    Child := TChildForm.Create(Application);
  Child.Caption := Name;
end;
```

In the new CreateChild procedure, if the file extension is .bmp, the program constructs a TChildBmpForm child window; otherwise, it constructs a TChildForm object. Because LoadData and SaveData are virtual procedures (refer to Listings 15-1 and 15-5), the type of child-window object determines what type of data is loaded.

To better understand the value of using virtual methods in subclassed forms, see the Main module's FileOpenClick procedure in Listing 15-2. If the child window is a TChildForm object, the procedure calls the original LoadData procedure. If the window is a TChildBmpForm object, the procedure calls the overridden method. These calls are directed not by explicit code in the program, but by the types of child-window objects referenced by ActiveMDIChild. This is sound object-oriented programming — the child-window objects determine the kind of data that is appropriate to load and save.

Because of the program's object-oriented design, it's relatively easy to add other types of child windows. Simply create and program a new form module as you did TChildBmpForm. Derive the new form class from TChildForm and write LoadData and SaveData procedures. Modify CreateChild in the Main module to construct instances of your new class, and you're done.

Merging menus

Especially in MDI applications with multiple types of child windows, you may want to modify menu commands or even add menus, depending on which type of child window is active. This is easy to do, but requires attention to some details that may not be obvious.

In the parent window — the one with FormStyle set to fsMDIForm — the MainMenu object should contain global commands that apply generally to all child windows. For example, the parent window's menu normally provides a Window menu with Cascade, Tile, and other commands that affect all windows, regardless of type. The main window's menu should also have commands such as File|New, File|Open..., and File|Close that open and close child windows.

In each child window that requires unique commands, or that needs to change menu items based on various conditions, you can insert another MainMenu object. I like to name these objects according to the module — ChildFormMenu or ChildBmpFormMenu, for example. Insert commands into these MainMenu objects for merging with the parent window's menu.

Menu merging in MDI applications is automatic for any child window that has a MainMenu object. For this reason, you should set all MainMenu objects' AutoMerge properties to False. Technically speaking, only the parent window's AutoMerge property must be False. The child window's MainMenu AutoMerge values are ignored, but set them all False anyway.

Tip   See Chapter 5 for instructions on merging menus in non-MDI applications. Only non-MDI applications use the AutoMerge property.

Next, assign GroupIndex values to specific menu items. These values determine where to insert menus and whether to replace a menu item or add new commands. When merging, the application uses GroupIndex values according to the following rules:

✦ Menu items with the same GroupIndex values are replaced. For example, if a MainMenu item has a GroupIndex of ten, any menu items in a child window's MainMenu with that same GroupIndex replace the parent items.

✦ Menu items with unique GroupIndex values are inserted. Assign higher values to insert menu items in the child window to the right of lower-valued items in the parent. Assign lower values to insert menu items to the left of parent items.

In addition to merging menus, you can also call TMenuItem methods to enable and disable menu items, to insert or change commands, and to perform other menu tricks. For example, a child window can add a check mark to an Options|Save command with a statement such as this:

```
MainForm.OptionsSave.Checked := True;
```

The trick here is gaining access to the MainForm object from inside the Child module. Do that by adding Main (or another unit name) to a *uses* clause in the Child module. To prevent a circular reference, you must do this in the child's implementation, not in the *uses* clause in the interface part. Because the Main module's *uses* clause already refers to the Child module, referring back to Main in the child causes the circular reference, which Object Pascal does not allow. In the Child module, locate the implementation keyword and form-loading directive, and add a *uses* clause as shown here. You can then access menu items in the MainForm object:

```
implementation
{$R *.DFM}
uses Main;
```

Circular unit references occur when two modules — call them Chicken and Egg — refer to each other in their interface sections' *uses* statements. Object Pascal does not permit this because of the possibility that module Chicken uses a declaration from module Egg, which might require a declaration from module Chicken. To resolve the Chicken-and-Egg paradox, add the secondary module to a *uses* statement in the primary module's interface section; add the primary module to a *uses* statement in the secondary module's implementation section. Unit interfaces may not circularly refer to each other, but their implementations may do so without restriction.

Other MDI Techniques

While writing this chapter, I came across many MDI tidbits among the source code examples I examined. The following are some other MDI techniques you might find useful.

Accessing client and frame windows

It may be necessary at times to gain access to the MDI application's client and frame windows. You probably won't need to use these techniques unless you call Windows API functions that require window handles. Delphi's TForm class should provide adequate services for most MDI applications.

Use the ClientHandle property in the main form object to refer to the client window. In classic MDI programming, this window provides global operations — such as message handling — that apply to all child windows.

Note   The ClientHandle value, of type HWnd (window handle), is valid only in forms with FormStyle set to fsMDIForm.

You can refer to the frame window by using the main form's Handle property. This value always references the window handle of the form in both MDI and non-MDI applications. In a form with FormStyle equal to fsMDIForm, the Handle property refers to the MDI frame window.

Using the MDI Application Template

For rapid programming of MDI prototypes, use Delphi's MDI Application Template. First, create an empty directory for storing the project files. Next, select File|New..., click the Projects page tab in the New Items dialog window, and choose MDI Application. Click OK and then in the directory selector dialog that pops up, change to the new directory where you want to store the project's files.

Close the directory dialog window, and Delphi constructs an MDI application with a status panel, a toolbar, and a menu with File, Edit, Window, and Help items. Figure 15-3 shows the resulting form window on top of the Child and About windows that the template also creates.

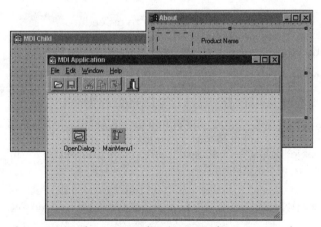

Figure 15-3: The MDI Application Template creates a form with a status panel, a toolbar, and a main menu. It also creates Child and About windows, shown here partially obscured behind the main form.

The following notes help you get started using the MDI Application template:

✦ The ChildWin.pas module declares the TMDIChild class. You might add LoadData and SaveData procedures to this class, or you can read and write data in the Main module. If your application has only one type of child window, you can add the programming to Main; otherwise, make each window class responsible for its own input and output, and base additional window classes on TMDIChild.

✦ By default, the Application is named MDIApp. To rename it, select File | Save Project as, and enter a new filename. Save and compile the project. You can then delete all MDIApp.* files from the project directory.

✦ The Main.pas module declares the TMainForm class. Hint: Review the class declarations in this module for various object names. Some names, such as Edit1, are defaults; others, such as SaveBtn, are named according to use. The template's naming conventions are not the same as the applications in this book. You may change them, but if you do so, you must change them every place they occur. It is not enough, for example, to change an object's Name property—you must also globally search and replace that object name in any statements that refer to it. Delphi automatically updates only object name declarations; it does not search for and replace object names used in statements.

✦ Select View | Project Manager and highlight ChildWin to open the child window's unit and form. You can then insert any objects you want into the child window, create a merged menu, and write code for child-window commands.

✦ In the Main module, add data-loading statements to procedure FileOpenItemClick. As I mentioned, you can read files directly, or you might call a LoadData procedure for the ActiveMDIChild window.

✦ Insert a SaveDialog object into the main form, and write code to save data in the FileSaveItemClick and FileSaveAsItemClick procedures. Or, you might call a SaveData procedure that you add to the child window's class.

✦ Optionally, program Cut, Copy, and Paste commands by calling clipboard procedures. For example, you can insert a Memo object into the ChildWin form, and call the object's CutToClipboard method. See Chapter 16 for more information on clipboard programming.

✦ Insert an OnCloseQuery event handler into the ChildWin module. Set CanClose to False to prevent users from closing windows without saving changes.

Expert-User Tips

✦ Only one window in an MDI application may have its FormStyle set to fsMDIForm. This window must be the application's main window (use Project ⏐ Options if necessary to designate which form is the main one).

✦ If the program's child windows appear as stand-alone windows on the desktop, instead of appearing inside the main window, the child form's FormStyle property is probably not set correctly. (In past versions of Delphi and Windows, this problem could lead to a general protection fault, but that no longer seems to be the case.) All child-window forms must have their FormStyle property set to fsMDIChild. The program's main window must have its FormStyle set to fsMDIForm, and only one window per application may have that setting.

✦ If you don't want a child window to appear automatically when you run the application, choose Options ⏐ Project and move the child window to the list of Available forms. However, nothing is technically wrong with having the application automatically create the first child window. For example, an MDI text editor could offer users a blank window at startup. The application could create additional child windows as explained in this chapter — only the first window is automatically constructed when the program begins.

✦ If closing an MDI application's child window causes it to minimize, make sure the child-window module has an OnClose event handler that sets Action to caFree. If you don't assign this value to Action, the application does not free the child-window object when the window closes. This is not an error, however, and it can be a useful design technique.

✦ When constructing forms and other objects at run time (such as the TChildForm objects in this chapter), remember to assign the constructed object instance into the instance variable — don't call the Create method using the uninitialized instance variable. For example, this is a typical error:

```
var
  Child: TChildForm;
begin
  Child.Create(Application);  {???}
...
```

The faulty statement literally attempts to have the child give birth to itself, which, fortunately for the world's population, even real children cannot do. The statement always causes an "access violation" fault because Child has not been initialized and calling an uninitialized object's methods is a programming error (though not a compiling error). Use the following code to call the class Create method and assign the resulting object to the Child reference:

```
var
  Child: TChildForm; // Or, you may use TForm as the type
begin
  Child := TChildForm.Create(Application);
```

✦ You are not required to save references to child-window objects. Merely creating a child instance with Application as the parent constructs the child window. The parent is responsible for maintaining and freeing the resulting objects. As a demonstration of this principle, you can shorten the CreateChild procedure in MDIDemo's Main module to the following. However, this makes it more difficult to perform operations on newborn children such as assigning Caption strings:

```
procedure TMainForm.CreateChild(const Name: String);
begin
  TChildForm.Create(Application);
end;
```

✦ In MDI applications with multiple types of child windows, name the unit modules ChildXXX.pas, where XXX is the document filename extension. For example, use Childtxt.pas for .txt files or Childbmp.pas for .bmp files. Of course, you can name the modules as you want, but this is a useful convention for identifying modules by their file types.

✦ Menu merging is automatic in MDI applications. Set all MainMenu AutoMerge properties to False. The parent MDI window's AutoMerge property must be False. Use the AutoMerge property to perform menu merging only in non-MDI applications.

✦ Avoid dropping components into the MDI main form. Lightweight controls like TLabel won't be drawn at all, and normal window handle controls (like TButton) might not work correctly when dropped into the client area of an MDI main form. This is due to quirks in the Windows MDI interface. Top- or bottom-aligned TPanels, however, are acceptable. Insert other control objects into child-window forms or into Panel objects.

Projects to Try

15-1: Add a metafile child window to MDIDemo.

15-2: Write a file-view application that works with a variety of file types.

15-3: Design a File | Save All command that calls a virtual SaveData procedure in a child-window class.

15-4: Advanced. Add a Window|Restore command to the MDIDemo application. The command should restore child windows to their former positions and sizes following a Tile, Cascade, or Minimize all command. Remember to use object-oriented programming. Child-window objects should be capable of restoring themselves to a saved position and size. Don't burden the parent; put your kids to work.

15-5: Write an MDI text editor using the MDI Application template. The results don't have to be fancy, but the exercise can help you understand various template naming conventions.

15-6: Advanced. Convert MDIDemo into an improved MDI Application template. Insert virtual methods such as LoadData and SaveData in the TChildForm class. Don't create objects of that class; instead, subclass new forms based on TChildForm and write LoadData and SaveData replacement procedures to read and write specific types of files. Ideally, to program a new application, you add a new child-window form, write LoadData and SaveData procedures, and construct child instances in the Main module.

Summary

✦ MDI applications use Delphi's TForm component, which is not on the VCL palette, to construct main and child windows. The main window takes the place of the frame and client windows used in classic Windows programming.

✦ Every MDI application has three basic parts: a main-window form, one or more document child-window forms, and a main menu. Use the main form's WindowMenu property to designate a top-level menu item for listing window titles.

✦ Set the main form's FormStyle property to fsMDIForm. There can be only one such form per application. In all child windows, set FormStyle to fsMDIChild. You may create as many types of child windows as your application needs.

✦ To construct a child window at run time, call the window class's Create method. Pass Application to Create's parent-object parameter.

✦ Every child window should implement OnClose and OnCloseQuery event handlers. Use these events to warn users about unsaved data when they attempt to close windows.

✦ The main form's ActiveMDIChild property refers to the current child window. If this property is *nil*, no child windows exist. Always check whether ActiveMDIChild is *nil* before using this property to call methods and assign property values.

✦ The main form's MDIChildCount property equals the number of child windows. If MDIChildCount is zero, no child windows exist.

✦ The MDIChildren array provides indexed access to all child windows owned by the application.

✦ Child-window MainMenu objects automatically merge with the main form's MainMenu. Use the GroupIndex property to control merging.

✦ The main form's Handle refers to the MDI application's frame window. The ClientHandle property refers to the client window. Most MDI applications do not need to use these properties.

✦ Use the MDI Application project template to rapidly create MDI projects with default menus, a toolbar, and a status line.

Transferring data from one application to another is one of the murkiest subjects in Windows programming. The next chapter helps you wade through the swamplands of clipboard, DDE, and OLE data transfer techniques. It also takes a look at using and creating ActiveX controls with Delphi.

✦   ✦   ✦

Developing with the Clipboard, DDE, and OLE

S haring data among applications is like making a horse drink water. You can lead your code to a multitasking or networked environment, but it takes some extra coaxing to make it share information with other programs.

Windows provides three basic methods for sharing data: the clipboard, Dynamic Data Exchange (DDE), and Object Linking and Embedding (OLE). Which method to use depends on your application's needs and the type of data you have to share. In this chapter, I explain how to use the clipboard to transfer text and graphics, how to use DDE to establish links with programs such as Microsoft Excel and Word, and how to link and embed OLE objects in Delphi applications.

Components

The following is a list of Delphi's components for developing with the clipboard, DDE, and OLE:

✦ **DdeClientConv** — A DDE client application (an application that receives data from a DDE server) uses this component to establish a link, called a *conversation*, with the server. Every client application has at least one of these objects. Palette: System.

✦ **DdeClientItem** — In addition to a DdeClientConv object, a DDE client application uses one or more DdeClientItem objects as containers that receive data from the server. Every client application has at least one of these objects for each DdeClientConv object. Palette: System.

✦ **DdeServerConv**—A DDE server application (an application that sends data to a DDE client) can use this component to originate a DDE conversation. Most server applications use at least one of these objects, but it is possible to originate a conversation without the DdeServerConv component. Palette: System.

✦ **DdeServerItem**—A DDE server application uses one or more of these objects to send data to the client. The DdeServerItem object may or may not be associated with a DdeServerConv object, but it usually is. Palette: System.

✦ **OleContainer**—Use this object to construct an OLE container application that can hold objects from OLE servers. For example, using OleContainer, your application documents can combine Excel spreadsheets, Word documents, and Visio Express drawings. Users can edit data in these objects directly from your application. Palette: System.

Clipboard Transfers

As most Windows users know, an Edit menu's Cut, Copy, and Paste commands transfer data to and from the Windows clipboard. Probably the most common use for these commands is for shuffling text between applications, or even within the same program, but the clipboard can handle transfers of data in countless other formats. For example, users can cut and paste bitmaps between graphics programs.

Delphi's Edit, MaskEdit, and Memo components (as well as the database components TDBEdit, TDBImage, and TDBMemo) support single-statement text clipboard transfers. To transfer object data, simply call methods CutToClipboard, CopyToClipboard, and PasteToClipboard, usually in response to the user selecting a menu command or clicking a button. For example, to cut selected text from a Memo component, use the statement:

```
Memo1.CutToClipboard;
```

The other two procedures are equally simple to use:

```
Memo1.CopyToClipboard;
Memo1.PasteFromClipboard;
```

Tip   For text-based components, only selected text is copied or cut to the clipboard. To copy or cut all of an object's text, call Memo1.SelectAll before performing the clipboard operation.

The TClipboard Class

To cut, copy, and paste nontext data, use the TClipboard class in the Clipbrd unit (note the abbreviated spelling). Because TClipboard is not a component on the VCL palette, to use the class you must add the unit's name to the module's *uses* declaration. Modify that declaration as follows (change in bold):

```
uses
  Windows, Messages, SysUtils, Classes, Graphics, Controls,
  Forms, Dialogs, Clipbrd;
```

TClipboard Pproperties

The TClipboard class provides the following properties:

✦ **AsText** — Use this string property to copy and paste text to and from the clipboard. To copy a string to the clipboard, assign a Pascal string to AsText. To receive a string, use AsText in a statement. To read and write lengthier clipboard text, you can also use the SetTextBuf and GetTextBuf TClipboard methods, but because Object Pascal strings can now be virtually unlimited in length, these methods are not as useful as they once were. On a related topic, if the clipboard contains text — it's always wise to check this before pasting — the following *if* statement expression is true:

```
if Clipboard.HasFormat(cf_Text) then ...
```

✦ **FormatCount** — This integer property equals the number of elements in the Formats array, described next. Valid array index expressions range from Formats[0] to Formats[FormatCount - 1]. Always use FormatCount to prevent index range errors when using the Formats array.

✦ **Formats** — This is an array of Word values that represent the clipboard's registered data types or formats. The FormatCount property equals the number of elements in the Formats array. Table 16-1 lists standard clipboard format constants from Windows.pas provided with Delphi's source files. The constants are in uppercase in the file, but you may type them in lowercase if you prefer.

Additional formats

The Clipbrd unit registers two clipboard formats in addition to the standards listed in Table 16-1. The unit does this by executing these statements in any program that uses Clipbrd:

```
cf_Picture := RegisterClipboardFormat('Delphi Picture');
cf_Component := RegisterClipboardFormat('Delphi Component');
```

Table 16-1 Clipboard Formats from WinTypes.pas	
Constant	**Format Value**
CF_TEXT	1
CF_BITMAP	2
CF_METAFILEPICT	3
CF_SYLK	4
CF_DIF	5
CF_TIFF	6
CF_OEMTEXT	7
CF_DIB	8
CF_PALETTE	9
CF_PENDATA	10
CF_RIFF	11
CF_WAVE	12
CF_UNICODETEXT	13
CF_ENHMETAFILE	14
CF_HDROP	15

Use the cf_Picture and cf_Component variables, along with the Clipboard's HasFormat, function to determine if the clipboard currently contains a TGraphics picture (an icon, a bitmap, or a metafile) or another kind of component object. Delphi itself uses cf_Component to cut and paste component objects in forms, but it's unlikely applications need to use this variable.

This is an example of registering a custom clipboard format, which you can do in your own applications. For example, use these techniques to register a special structure's format to transfer data of that type to other applications using the clipboard.

TClipboard methods

Call methods in the TClipboard class to cut, copy, and paste data, and also to perform miscellaneous clipboard operations. The Clipbrd unit provides a Clipboard object that's ready to use—you do not have to construct an object of the

TClipboard class. Simply add Clipbrd to the module's *uses* directive. You can do this by modifying the module's *uses* declaration, or you can add a new *uses* clause in the module's implementation. For example, add the following text (shown in bold):

```
implementation
uses Clipbrd;
```

Be aware of how the Clipbrd unit is spelled. Don't do as I do—type **uses Clipboard**, and then waste ten minutes wondering why my program doesn't compile.

Using the Clipbrd unit this way makes its public declarations available to procedures and functions in the module's implementation section. For example, in a procedure or function, a statement can call the Clipbrd unit's HasFormat method like this:

```
if Clipboard.HasFormat(cf_Bitmap) then
  // ... copy bitmap from clipboard
```

Notice the call to HasFormat is in reference to the Clipboard object, which is already initialized and ready for use. If you don't want to type **Clipboard** over and over, you can use a *with* statement as in this fragment:

```
with Clipboard do
begin
  if HasFormat(cf_Bitmap) then
    // ... copy bitmap from clipboard
  else if HasFormat(cf_Text) then
    // ... copy text from clipboard
end;
```

The following are brief descriptions of key TClipboard methods that you can call in reference to the Clipboard object:

✦ **Assign** — To copy graphics to the clipboard, pass to Assign any TGraphic, TBitmap, TPicture, or TMetafile object or object property.

✦ **Clear** — Clears any data in the clipboard. You don't usually have to call this method, because assigning new information to the clipboard performs an automatic Clear. However, you might call Clear just before the program ends if the clipboard has a large amount of data. Prompt the user about whether the clipboard should be cleared.

✦ **Close** — Closes the clipboard following a call to Open. Each Open statement should have a corresponding Close. You don't have to call Open and Close unless you access the clipboard by calling Windows API functions. Methods in the Clipboard object open and close the clipboard automatically as needed.

✦ **GetAsHandle** — Returns a Windows handle to clipboard data. Use this only if you need to call Windows API functions that require handles, or when converting conventionally written programs to Delphi. Most applications don't need to use this function.

✦ **GetComponent** — Retrieves a Delphi component object from the clipboard. For more information on using GetComponent and SetComponent see, "Component objects and the clipboard," in this chapter.

✦ **GetTextBuf** — This function retrieves text from the clipboard as a null-terminated buffer. In the past, this method was used to work with large amounts of text. But today, because Pascal strings have no length limit, you can more simply use the AsText property to retrieve clipboard text. See "Text and the clipboard" in this chapter for more information on using GetTextBuf and SetTextBuf.

✦ **HasFormat** — Returns True if the clipboard has data in the format specified by a Word argument passed to HasFormat. See Table 16-1 for standard constant values to use with this function. Always call HasFormat before copying information from the clipboard into an application object or other variable.

✦ **Open** — You need to open the clipboard by calling this method only if you call Windows API functions to access the clipboard. All methods in the Clipboard object open the clipboard automatically as needed. Caution: Calling Open temporarily prevents other tasks from using the clipboard. Each call to Open should have a corresponding call to Close.

✦ **SetAsHandle** — Assigns data to the clipboard using a Windows handle. See GetAsHandle. Most applications don't need to call this method.

✦ **SetComponent** — Assigns a component object to the clipboard. See GetComponent and "Component objects and the clipboard" in this chapter for more information.

✦ **SetTextBuf** — Assigns null-terminated text data to the clipboard. Use this function to work with large amounts of text stored in Char arrays. See also GetTextBuf. Because Pascal strings are now virtually unlimited in length, most applications can simply assign strings to the Clipboard's AsText property rather than calling SetTextBuf and GetTextBuf.

Text and the clipboard

It's easy to transfer text to and from the clipboard and text-based components such as Memo and Edit. Using the Pascal dynamic string data type, you simply assign any Text property to the Clipboard's AsText property, and you're done. However, a few items are worth extra consideration.

To demonstrate these aspects of text and the clipboard, the following steps use a Memo component for convenience. Although you can more easily perform similar operations by calling the Memo component's CopyToClipboard, CutToClipboard, and PasteFromClipboard methods, the following steps introduce important programming techniques that you can apply to other types of clipboard data transfers. Follow these steps:

1. Start a new application. Add a *uses* declaration for Clipbrd just after the *implementation* keyword in the application's form unit. The declaration should look like this (new text in bold):

```
implementation
uses Clipbrd;
```

2. Insert a Memo object from the Standard palette into the form. Select the Memo1 object and set its ScrollBars property to ssBoth. You can enlarge the Memo1 object if you want.

3. Insert two Button objects into the form. Change the first button's Name property to CopyButton and its Caption to Copy. Change the second button's Name to PasteButton and its Caption to Paste. Figure 16-1 shows the program's window so far:

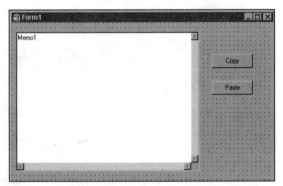

Figure 16-1: The clipboard test's Form window with a Memo and two Button objects

4. Double-click the Copy button to create a handler for its OnClick event. Insert the code from Listing 16-1 into the procedure. On the CD-ROM, this text is in the Clip1.pas file in the Source\Clipboard directory.

5. Double-click the Paste button to create a handler for its OnClick event. Insert the code from Listing 16-2 into the procedure. On the CD-ROM, this text is in the Clip1.pas file in the Source\Clipboard directory.

6. Run the test program and use the Windows Notepad utility to open a text file. Select all lines, and choose Edit I Copy to transfer the text to the clipboard. Switch back to the test program, and click the Paste button to copy the clipboard text to the Memo object. Click Copy to copy the text to the clipboard. Delete the text, and click Paste to verify that the program pastes the clipboard to the Memo object. You can also switch back to the Notepad, and choose Edit I Paste to insert the copied text from the clipboard.

Listing 16-1: **Copy button OnClick event handler**

```
procedure TForm1.CopyButtonClick(Sender: TObject);
begin
  with Memo1 do
  begin
    if SelLength = 0 then      // If no text selected,
      SelectAll;               // select all lines of Memo1.
    if SelLength = 0 then      // If still no text selected,
      Exit;                    // Memo1 is empty—exit now.
    Clipboard.Clear;
    Clipboard.AsText := Memo1.Text;
  end;
end;
```

Listing 16-2: **Paste button OnClick event handler**

```
procedure TForm1.PasteButtonClick(Sender: TObject);
begin
  if Clipboard.HasFormat(CF_TEXT) then
    Memo1.Text := Clipboard.AsText;
end;
```

An obsolete clipboard text technique

An older technique for working with clipboard text is still available. You might use this method if you are writing code for Windows 3.1, or if you have an early version of Delphi. You can also use the information in this section as a guide to upgrading older software that uses this now obsolete technique for storing clipboard text in character arrays.

Call the Clipboard's SetTextBuf method to copy large text buffers to the clipboard. For example, if Buffer is a PChar pointer to a null-terminated string buffer, this statement copies the text to the clipboard:

```
Clipboard.SetTextBuf(Buffer);
```

To retrieve text from the clipboard, allocate memory for a buffer and call the Clipboard's GetTextBuf function, which returns the number of characters copied:

```
Buffer := StrAlloc(1024);
Len := Clipboard.GetTextBuf(Buffer, 1024);
```

Unfortunately, GetTextBuf requires you to determine in advance the size of the text buffer, but the Clipbrd unit provides no method for determining that size. To demonstrate one way around this problem, follow the steps in the preceding section to create a test program with a Memo and two Button objects named CopyButton and PasteButton. Instead of using the Button OnClick event handlers in the preceding listing, use the code from Listing 16-3 and Listing 16-4. This text is in the Clip2.pas file on the CD-ROM in the Source\Clipboard directory.

Listing 16-3: This OnClick event handler demonstrates how to use the Clipboard's SetTextBuf method to copy a null-terminated string buffer to the clipboard.

```
{ Copy null-terminated text buffer to clipboard }
procedure TForm1.CopyButtonClick(Sender: TObject);
var
  P: PChar;  { Pointer to character buffer }
begin
  with Memo1 do
  begin
    if SelLength = 0 then    // If no text selected,
      SelectAll;             // select all lines of Memo1.
    if SelLength = 0 then    // If still no text selected,
      Exit;                  // Memo1 is empty—exit now.
    P := StrAlloc(SelLength + 1); // Allocate char buffer
    try
      GetTextBuf(P, SelLength + 1); // Copy text to buffer
      Clipboard.SetTextBuf(P); //Copy text buffer to clipboard
    finally
      StrDispose(P);  // Dispose of character buffer
    end;
  end;
end;
```

Listing 16-4: **This OnClick event handler demonstrates an alternative to the Clipboard's GetTextBuf method, which requires you to determine the buffer size in advance.**

```
{ Copy null-terminated text buffer from clipboard }
procedure TForm1.PasteButtonClick(Sender: TObject);
var
  Data: THandle;
  DataPtr: PChar;
  P: PChar;
begin
  Clipboard.Open;
  try
    Data := GetClipboardData(cf_Text);
    if Data = 0 then Exit;
    DataPtr := GlobalLock(Data);
    try
      P := StrNew(DataPtr);
      Memo1.SetTextBuf(P);
    finally
      GlobalUnlock(Data);
      StrDispose(P);
    end;
  finally
    Clipboard.Close;
  end;
end;
```

Listing 16-3 checks that the Memo1 object has some selected text — if not, the procedure calls SelectAll. This step is optional, but makes it easy to copy all of a document to the clipboard without requiring users to select every character. StrAlloc prepares a buffer into which GetTextBuf copies the Memo1 object's text. The program then calls the Clipboard's SetTextBuf to copy that buffer to the Windows clipboard.

When performing memory allocations, it's always wise to insert subsequent statements into *try-finally* blocks. As Listing 16-1 demonstrates, the memory allocated to *P* is disposed by StrDispose regardless of whether any statement in the *try* block raises an exception.

Listing 16-4 works around the Clipboard's lack of a method for determining how much text the clipboard holds. Instead of calling GetTextBuf to retrieve text from the clipboard, the procedure calls Windows API functions to obtain that data in raw, binary form via the Windows API function, GetClipboardData. The procedure's inner *try* block calls StrNew to allocate memory to a PChar pointer *P*, and then copy the clipboard data block as a null-terminated string to that memory. For demonstration only, the procedure passes the string to the Memo component.

Caution

When using the clipboard transfer method in Listing 16-4, you must call Open and Close as shown because the procedure bypasses the Clipboard object's methods. Remember, the techniques in this section demonstrate obsolete methods — don't use them in new applications.

Graphics and the clipboard

You can use the Clipboard's Assign method to cut, copy, and paste TGraphics objects such as found in an Image component's Picture property. To demonstrate the technique, start a new application and add a *uses* declaration to the unit's implementation as follows (change in bold):

```
implementation
uses Clipbrd;
```

Insert two Image objects from the Additional palette and a Button from the Standard palette into a form. Set the Stretch property for both Image objects to True. Double-click the Button and insert the following statements between *begin* and *end* in the object's OnClick event handler. (You would normally perform these operations in separate places in the program, or in separate applications. For the demonstration, however, I perform both transfers at once.)

```
Clipboard.Assign(Image1.Picture);   // Copy to clipboard
if Clipboard.HasFormat(cf_Picture) then
  Image2.Picture.Assign(Clipboard); // Copy from clipboard
```

Still in Delphi, select the Image1 object and use its Picture property to load an icon, a bitmap, or a Windows metafile. Run the program by pressing F9, and then click the button to transfer the image from Image1 to Image2 via the Windows clipboard. Both Image objects should now show the same graphics.

The first statement calls the Clipboard's Assign method to copy a TGraphics property (Image1.Picture) to the clipboard. The second statement verifies that the clipboard has a cf_Picture object, and if so, calls Image2's Picture.Assign method, passing Clipboard as an argument. Although you may use Clipboard as an argument to Assign this way, you should always test as shown here by calling HasFormation whether the clipboard data is in the expected format. For example, to receive a bitmap image copied to the clipboard by another application such as the Windows Paint utility, use code such as:

```
if Clipboard.HasFormat(cf_Bitmap) then
   Image2.Picture.Bitmap.Assign(Clipboard)
else
   Image2.Picture.Bitmap.Assign(nil);
```

Using the Picture property enables the object to work with icon, bitmap, and metafile data. This also enables the object to work with any add-in TGraphic class such as TJPEGImage from the JPEGunit. Calling Assign for a TBitmap object is more restrictive, but either technique is acceptable.

Component objects and the clipboard

Call the Clipboard's SetComponent method to copy any component object to the clipboard. Call the Clipboard's GetComponent method, in either the same or in another application, to paste a visual component object from the clipboard.

Internally, SetComponent and GetComponent use a memory stream to copy components to and from memory. To retrieve a component, in addition to calling GetComponent you have to register the component's class with Delphi's memory-streaming system. An example of component clipboard transfers explains the basic techniques. Follow these steps to create a test application:

1. Start a new application and add a *uses* declaration to the unit's implementation as follows (change in bold):

   ```
   implementation
   uses Clipbrd;
   ```

2. From Delphi's Standard palette, insert a Button and a ScrollBar (the object to be copied) into a form. Create an OnClick event handler by double-clicking Button1, and insert the following statement between *begin* and *end* to copy the ScrollBar object to the clipboard when you click the Button:

   ```
   Clipboard.SetComponent(ScrollBar1);
   ```

3. Compile and run the application by pressing F9, and then click the button. This copies the ScrollBar1 object to the Windows clipboard. Exit the program to get back to Delphi. Save the application in a temporary directory (select File|Save All and use the default filenames).

4. Start a new application, and insert a Button object into the form, and as before, add a *uses* declaration to the unit's implementation as follows (change in bold):

   ```
   implementation
   uses Clipbrd;
   ```

5. Double-click Button1 to create an OnClick event handler, and insert the following statement between *begin* and *end:*

```
if Clipboard.HasFormat(cf_Component) then
   Clipboard.GetComponent(Self, Self);
```

6. Scroll the code editor to the final *end* in the unit module, and just above that line, insert the following initialization statement. The unit should end (including the final *end* with period) as shown here (your typing is in bold):

```
initialization
   RegisterClasses([TScrollBar]);
end.
```

7. Press F9 to compile and run the second application, and click the button to copy the ScrollBar object from the clipboard and paste it into the form. (If this doesn't work, you may have copied something else to the clipboard while writing the second application. In that case, rerun the saved first application using the Windows Explorer, and then from Delphi, run the second and click the button.)

The Clipboard's GetComponent function requires two arguments that represent the pasted object's owner and parent. Although these arguments are often the same as in the preceding demonstration, they are different when you are pasting components into a container such as a GroupBox. In that case, the form is usually the owner and the GroupBox is the parent of the pasted object, and you might use code such as:

```
if Clipboard.HasFormat(cf_Component) then
   Clipboard.GetComponent(Self, GroupBox1);
```

Note   In the preceding fragments, I assume the statements are in an event handler for the form or an object in that form, in which case, Self refers to the form object.

By the way, the preceding examples introduce a rarely needed, but useful, Object Pascal programming technique. To perform initializations for any unit module one time when the application begins, insert statements between the keyword *initialization* and the final *end* of a unit. This replaces the old style *begin-end* initialization section in units, which Delphi still supports. In new units, use the new format as shown here:

```
unit AnyUnit;
...
initialization   { same as begin }
   // Statements to perform when application begins.
end.
```

You may use *begin* or *initialization,* but the latter helps the compiler to locate mismatched pairs of *begin* and *end* keywords elsewhere in the module, so *initialization* is preferred.

Dynamic Data Exchange

The Windows clipboard works well enough, but it's as primitive as a cork bulletin board on which users cut, copy, and paste information by tacking up notes and tearing off telephone number tabs. Like a bulletin board, the clipboard requires its participants to voluntarily transfer information.

The Windows Dynamic Data Exchange (DDE) protocols work more like a modern bulletin board or Internet Web site accessed via modems. To transfer data, two applications, known as the client and the server, start a conversation through which data may flow. After the applications establish a conversation, DDE transfers can occur automatically, or one application can request data from the other.

A DDE conversation takes two to tango. The data sender is called the *server application.* The data receiver is called the *client application.* If you find these terms confusing, just remember that the server serves data to clients. However, a DDE conversation is a two-way street, and during a conversation, data can flow in either direction, blurring the distinction between client and server.

DDE is suitable for dynamically updating information among multiple applications. For example, with DDE, you can write a program that automatically updates a graphics image as users enter data into a spreadsheet. Or, you might use DDE to construct multiple applications that share information.

Tip   DDE can help prevent destruction of data by inexperienced users. For example, you can write a client application to display the results of spreadsheet calculations. However, users cannot use the client application to modify the original spreadsheet formulas.

Understanding Delphi's DDE components

Use Delphi's four DDE components — DdeClientConv, DdeClientItem, DdeServerConv, and DdeServerItem — to construct client and server applications that can communicate using DDE. *Conv* stands for conversation, which represents the established link between two DDE-aware tasks. You can start a DDE conversation when you design the application, or you can link a client and a server at run time.

The DdeClientConv component operates something like a modem that receives a call from another computer. A client conversation object "picks up the phone" to establish a link with the remote system that originated the call. Most DDE applications need only one DdeClientConv object, although you may use multiple objects to establish more than one communication path.

The DdeClientItem component represents the data that comes in through the modem over the conversation path. An application that receives multiple types of data might have many DdeClientItem objects associated with the same DdeClientConv. However, a client application typically needs only one DdeClientConv and one associated DdeClientItem object.

In the server application — in other words, the data sender — use a DdeServerConv object to initiate a conversation. You normally need only one DdeServerConv object per application, but you may use several to establish multiple conversations. Insert one or more DdeServerItem objects to represent the data to send to clients. Most DDE server applications need only one DdeServerConv and one associated DdeServerItem object.

Tip   To send and receive DDE information in the same application, insert DdeServer and DdeClient objects into the project's form window. This is also useful for testing DDE concepts.

Examining DDE conversation terms

Three terms define a DDE conversation and the data items that flow between two or more applications. These terms are:

✦ **Service** — Identifies the server, usually by its executable filename minus the .exe extension. In some cases, however, a DDE Service is a different identifier. In a Delphi client application, the Service is always the server's filename minus .exe.

✦ **Topic** — Identifies a unit of data such as a filename, or a window caption. There are no set rules about what a Topic means. In Delphi applications, however, a Topic is either the server application's main-window caption, or the name of a DdeServerItem object in the server.

✦ **Item** — Identifies an element of text data sent by a server to a client application. The text may be any practical length, but most DDE transfers are small. For larger blocks of text, especially those organized into lines, Delphi's DDE components represent Items as TStrings string lists.

Establishing client-server conversations

As an example of using DDE, in this section you construct simple client-server applications that transfer text between two Edit control objects. Typing data in the server's Edit window automatically updates the client's Edit object. Typing in the client's Edit window, however, does not update the server — an example of a typical one-way DDE conversation.

On the CD-ROM

Listings of the programming in this and the next few sections are in the Source\Dde1 subdirectory on the CD-ROM.

Writing the server

Unless you already have a DDE server application, it's usually best to develop the server before writing the client. At a minimum, a server application requires a DdeServerItem object and some data to send to clients. Follow these steps to create a simple server that sends an Edit object's text to a client application. Except where noted, I use default component object names, which help clarify the relationships among the DDE objects.

1. Create a new disk directory to hold the project files. Start a new application and set Form1's Name property to ServerForm. Set the form's Caption property to Server1.

2. Select File|Save All and save the project in the new directory. Name the unit module Server.pas and the project Server1.dpr.

3. Insert a DdeServerItem object from the System VCL palette into the form. The server sends data through this object. Also, insert three objects: Edit, Button, and BitBtn. Set Button1's Caption to Edit Copy. Change BitBtn1's Kind property to bkClose. Arrange and size the form window to resemble Figure 16-2.

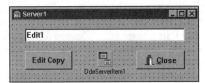

Figure 16-2: Server1's form window in Delphi

4. Create a handler for the Edit1 object's OnChange event. Insert the statement from Listing 16-5, procedure Edit1Change, to assign the Edit1 object's Text property to DdeServerItem1's Text. When Edit1's text changes, this sends the text to any client applications that have established a link with the server.

5. Create a handler for the Button1 object's OnClick event. Insert the statement from Listing 16-5, procedure Button1Click, to call DdeServerItem1's CopyToClipboard method. This informs client applications of the server's Service and Topic names. You use this information in writing the client application.

Listing 16-5: **Dde1\Server.pas**

```
unit Server;

interface

uses
  Windows, Messages, Classes, Graphics, Controls,
  Forms, Dialogs, StdCtrls, DdeMan, Buttons;

type
  TServerForm = class(TForm)
    DdeServerItem1: TDdeServerItem;
    Edit1: TEdit;
    Button1: TButton;
    BitBtn1: TBitBtn;
    procedure Edit1Change(Sender: TObject);
    procedure Button1Click(Sender: TObject);
  private
    { Private declarations }
  public
    { Public declarations }
  end;

var
  ServerForm: TServerForm;

implementation

{$R *.DFM}

procedure TServerForm.Edit1Change(Sender: TObject);
begin
  DdeServerItem1.Text := Edit1.Text;
end;

procedure TServerForm.Button1Click(Sender: TObject);
begin
  DdeServerItem1.CopyToClipboard;
end;

end.
```

Writing the client

I've been known to talk to myself, but my conversations tend to be more interesting when I chatter with at least one other person. Likewise, every server application needs one or more clients to engage in a conversation and transmit data. Follow these steps to construct a client application to obtain text items from the server created in the preceding section. In Step 2, be sure to save the project files in the same directory as the server.

1. Start a new application. Name the form ClientForm, and change its Caption to Client1.

2. Use File|Save All to save the project files in the same directory that holds the Server1 project. Name the unit module Client.pas and the project Client1.dpr.

3. Insert a DdeClientConv object from the System VCL palette into the form. Also, insert a DdeClientItem object. Unlike servers, client applications need conversation and item objects to establish a conversation with a server and to receive data items. To provide a place for displaying received data, insert a standard Edit object into the form. Also, insert a BitBtn and change its Kind property to bkClose. Make the client form resemble Figure 16-3. You might want to move the form down so it doesn't exactly overlap the server window.

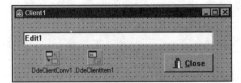

Figure 16-3: Client1's form window

4. Select the DdeClientItem1 object (the icon without the arrows), and set its DdeConv property to DdeClientConv1. This establishes the relationship between the conversation and the item object, and it tells DdeClientItem1 from where to receive its data.

5. Use the Windows Explorer to run the Server1 application. (You need to run both applications, which you can't do from inside Delphi.) Click the Edit Copy button to copy the server's Service and Topic names to the clipboard. You may leave Server1 running for the rest of these steps.

6. Return to Delphi. Select the DdeClientConv1 object (the icon with the arrows), and click the ellipsis button next to the DdeService or DdeTopic properties (it doesn't matter which one). Click the resulting DDE Info dialog's Paste Link button. You should see the strings SERVER1 and Server1 in the two edit

windows. If not, switch to Server1, click Edit Copy, and then immediately switch back to Delphi and try again. If you know a server's Service and Topic strings, you can enter them into the dialog, but this causes an attempt to execute the server, and the two strings must be valid or Delphi rejects them. Click OK to close the DDE Info dialog.

7. Create a handler for the form's OnCreate event, and insert the programming from Listing 16-6 to assign the name of the server's DdeServerItem1 object to the DdeItem property in the client's DdeClientItem1 object. The client has now specified the Service (SERVER1), Topic (Server1), and Item (DdeServerItem1) strings that a DDE conversation requires. You can specify the Service and Topic at design time, but you normally assign the Item at run time because, if the DdeClientConv object's ConnectMode property is set to ddeAutomatic (the default value), the DdeServerItem1 and Text properties in the DdeClientItem1 object are subject to change via the established link. Because of DDE's interactive nature, this fact is true even at design time.

8. Finally, create a handler for the DdeClientItem1 object's OnChange event, which occurs when new information comes in from the server. Insert the statement from Listing 16-6 to assign the DdeClientItem1 object's Text (representing the received data) to the Edit1 object's Text property.

9. Save the project. Press F9 to compile and run Client1. If Server1 is not already running, this also starts the server. Make both the Client1 and Server1 windows visible. Enter text into Server1's Edit1 window—you should see your typing in the Client1 Edit1 object. However, text entered into Client1 is not reflected back to the server because this is a one-way conversation.

Note

If you experience difficulties establishing a DDE conversation, either quit Delphi or start a new project and run the client and server applications using the Windows Explorer, or the Taskbar. For unknown reasons, running a client application in Delphi's Debug mode seems to not always establish a conversation correctly with the server. Also try running the server before starting the client, which might be necessary if the server's executable file is not in a system PATH directory.

Listing 16-6: **Dde1\Client.pas**

```
unit Client;

interface

uses
  Windows, Messages, Classes, Graphics, Controls,
  Forms, Dialogs, DdeMan, StdCtrls, Buttons;
```

(continued)

Listing 16-6 *(continued)*

```
type
  TClientForm = class(TForm)
    DdeClientItem1: TDdeClientItem;
    DdeClientConv1: TDdeClientConv;
    Edit1: TEdit;
    BitBtn1: TBitBtn;
    procedure FormCreate(Sender: TObject);
    procedure DdeClientItem1Change(Sender: TObject);
  private
    { Private declarations }
  public
    { Public declarations }
  end;

var
  ClientForm: TClientForm;

implementation

{$R *.DFM}

procedure TClientForm.FormCreate(Sender: TObject);
begin
  DdeClientItem1.DdeItem := 'DdeServerItem1';
end;

procedure TClientForm.DdeClientItem1Change(Sender: TObject);
begin
  Edit1.Text := DdeClientItem1.Text;
end;

end.
```

Establishing conversations at run time

The preceding section demonstrated how to establish a DDE conversation by specifying Service and Topic strings in the Object Inspector. You can also start a DDE conversation at run time, which may sometimes be more convenient, especially if your program gabs with many servers over multiple conversation paths.

Establishing a DDE conversation at run time is entirely the client application's job. You write the server application no differently than in the preceding demonstration. The client initializes the DDE Service and Topic names and specifies the name of a data item to receive from the server. Because the program performs these jobs in code, it also has to call one or two methods to link to a server.

For example, you can convert the preceding Client1 application to initialize a conversation at run time by deleting the DdeService and DdeTopic strings from the DdeClientConv1 object. Optionally set ConnectMode to ddeManual, and then modify the form's OnCreate event handler to match Listing 16-7. (The listing is from a modified client application in directory Source\Dde2 on the CD-ROM.)

> **Listing 16-7: This modified OnCreate event handler shows how to establish a DDE conversation at run time.**

```
procedure TClientForm.FormCreate(Sender: TObject);
begin
  if DdeClientConv1.SetLink('SERVER2', 'Server2') then
  begin
    DdeClientItem1.DdeItem := 'DdeServerItem1';
    if DdeClientConv1.ConnectMode = ddeManual then
      DdeClientConv1.OpenLink;
  end;
end;
```

The modified OnCreate event handler calls SetLink for the DdeClientConv1 object. The two strings initialize the DdeService and DdeTopic properties respectively— never simply assign strings to these properties; always call SetLink to initialize them. SetLink returns True if it was able to link to the specified server. Also, assign an item name to the DdeItem property in the DdeClientItem1 object. Finally, if the DdeClientConv1's ConnectMode is ddeManual, call OpenLink to begin the conversation. If ConnectMode is ddeAutomatic, SetLink calls OpenLink automatically.

Determining the service and topic

To determine the Service and the Topic of a DDE server application, follow these steps:

1. Run the application.

2. Select some data.

3. Choose Edit⏐Copy. (Try this with Microsoft Excel.)

4. Switch to Delphi.

5. Insert a DdeClientConv object into a form.

6. Click the ellipsis button next to the DdeService property.

7. Click Paste Link in the DDE Info dialog.

This should display the Service and Topic strings that the server pasted to the Windows clipboard. However, this technique does not tell you the names of data items, which you need to complete the client application. Consult the server's documentation, or contact the software vendor, but be prepared to put on your gumshoes and do some detective work to determine the server's item names. Item names typically specify data addresses, offsets, or other locations. For example, a spreadsheet application's items are usually cell ranges; a database's items might be record field names.

Receiving data from a DDE server

A DDE client application receives data from a server through a DdeClientItem object. Implement the object's OnChange event handler to respond to new data that comes in from the server. For example, the OnChange event handler in Listing 16-6 assigns the Text property from the DdeClientItem1 object to an Edit object's Text.

For longer blocks of text data, especially when organized into lines, use the DdeClientItem's Lines property, an object of the TStrings type. For example, to receive a multiline text item over a DDE conversation, use code such as the following, which assigns the received text to a Memo object's Lines property:

```
with ddeClientItem1 do
  Memo1.Lines := ddeClientItem1.Lines;
```

Most DDE applications receive data automatically through a DdeClientItem's OnChange event. However, a client application can also request specific data from a server — a specified cell in a spreadsheet, for example. To request a specific item of data, call the DdeClientConv object's RequestData function, which returns a PChar pointer to a null-terminated string. For example, this code fragment requests the DdeServerItem1 item and assigns the resulting null-terminated string to a Label object's caption. Always call StrDispose to dispose of the memory that RequestData allocates to incoming data:

```
var
  P: PChar;
begin
  P := DdeClientConv.RequestData('DdeServerItem1');
```

```
        if P <> nil then
        try
            Label1.Caption := StrPas(P);
        finally
            StrDispose(P);
        end;
    end;
```

Sending data to a DDE server

Sending data to a DDE client is usually a simple matter of assigning strings to a DdeServerItem object's Text or Lines properties. This automatically sends the data to any clients with which the server is holding a conversation. Alternatively, a client application can reverse roles and send data to a server. To do that, call methods PokeData (single strings) or PokeDataLines (large text blocks or multiple lines) for the client's DdeClientConv object. Each function returns True if successful. Pass two string arguments to PokeData: the name of the DdeServerItem to which you want to send data and the text to send:

```
with DdeClientConv1 do
    if not PokeData('DdeServerItem1', 'I''d rather go sailing')
then
    ShowMessage('Poke failed');
```

Use PokeDataLines the same way, but pass a TStrings object or a TStringList object as the second argument. Poking works only if the server voluntarily accepts poked data. In Delphi applications, you must also create a handler for the DdeServerItem's OnPokeData event, triggered when a client attempts to poke data to the cooperating server. In the event handler, the poked data is available through the DdeServerItem's Text or Lines properties.

Using DDE macros

If a server supports macros, a client application can send macro commands to perform operations in the server. For example, a Delphi DDE client application can use this technique to send and execute a macro for a Microsoft Word document.

In pure Delphi applications, the meaning of a macro is up to you to define. If your server does support macros, however, you can use components to send and receive macro commands. To do this, the server's DdeServerConv object implements a handler for an OnExecuteMacro event. When this event occurs, your server should execute the macro commands in the DdeServerItem Lines property. (Although you could also use the Text property, you usually use Lines, because a macro is probably composed of multiple lines.)

On the client side of the coin, call ExecuteMacro or ExecuteMacroLines for a DdeClientConv object. You normally use ExecuteMacroLines to send a multiline macro command to a server for execution. If that command is in a TStringList object named Macro, use this code to send it to the server:

```
with DdeClientConv1 do
  if not ExecuteMacroLines(Macro, True) then
    ShowMessage('Macro failed');
```

ExecuteMacro and ExecuteMacroLines return True if successful. The first argument to ExecuteMacro is a PChar pointer to a string; it's a TStrings or TStringList object for ExecuteMacroLines. The second argument is True if you want the program to wait for the server to execute the macro; set the second argument to False to enable the client to continue while the server does whatever it does with the posted macro.

Examining a DDE example program

As a final demonstration of DDE conversations, the CD-ROM's DdeColor directory contains two applications, CServer and CClient, that send and receive color information via a DDE conversation. Figure 16-4 shows CServer's display. Figure 16-5 shows CClient's window.

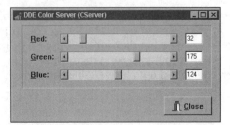

Figure 16-4: CServer sends color information to any client applications that establish a DDE conversation with CServer.

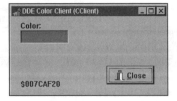

Figure 16-5: CClient starts a conversation with the server and automatically receives color information over the link.

To compile the programs, follow these steps:

1. Switch to a copy of the Source\DdeColor directory on the CD-ROM.

2. Load the CServer.dpr project file into Delphi.

3. Press Ctrl+F9 to compile, but not run, the program.

4. Load CClient.dpr from the same directory, and again press Ctrl+F9 to compile.

5. Close all files in Delphi.

6. Using Windows Explorer, run CClient.exe.

This also starts CServer, unless it's already running (minimize other windows if the program's window does not become visible). Use the server's scroll bars to update the sample color in the client application.

> **Note**
>
> For best results, always run compiled DDE applications using Explorer. You may run DDE programs from inside Delphi, but I've had trouble establishing the communication links on occasion. Before wasting time debugging your programs, try running them outside of Delphi. (The situation should be much improved in Delphi 4 than it was in Delphi 2, and you well might never experience these troubles.)

The example server has three scroll bars that you can adjust to create a color value composed of red, green, and blue byte values from 0–255. The server makes the selected color available to any client applications that establish a conversation with the server. The example client automatically receives the server's color values, which the program samples in a disabled Edit object. A Label object displays the color's value in hexadecimal. Colors that match Delphi's standards, such as cl_White and cl_Fuschia, are displayed by name.

A significant difference in the CServer application is the use of a DdeServerConv object to initiate a conversation. Use this object to specify a DDE Topic that is not equal to the server's window caption. In CServer, for example, the DdeServerConv object is named ColorServer. The corresponding DdeServerItem object specifies ColorServer in its ServerConv property — this tells the server item how to send data over a conversation. In the CClient application, the DdeTopic property of the DdeClientConv1 object is also set to ColorServer.

> **On the CD-ROM**
>
> Listing 16-8 shows how the CClient application receives, from the server, a text item that represents a color value in hexadecimal. This fragment is from the CClient application in the Source\DdeColor directory on the CD-ROM. Safely converting this text to a binary color, however, requires careful programming.

Listing 16-8: The CClient application receiving a text item from the server

```
procedure TMainForm.DdeClientItem1Change(Sender: TObject);
var
  S: String;
  C: TColor;
begin
  with DdeClientItem1 do
  begin
    if Length(Text) = 0 then
      S := '$0'   { Default string }
    else
      S := Text;  { String from server }
    try
    { Delete trailing blanks }
      while S[Length(S)] = asciiBlank do
        System.Delete(S, Length(S), 1);
      C := StringToColor(S);              { Convert to color }
      ColorValueLabel.Caption := S;       { Assign to label }
      Edit1.Color := C;                   { Show color }
    except
      ShowMessage('Bad color format from server');
    end;
  end;
end;
```

Received text may be zero length, in which case the OnChange event handler for the DdeClientItem1 object sets a string variable to the default $0. (In Object Pascal, hexadecimal string values are prefaced with a dollar sign.) Otherwise, the program assigns the incoming Text to string *S*. This string may have trailing blanks, which can cause the StringToColor function to generate an exception. A *while* loop therefore removes any trailing blanks. Notice that the program calls Delete prefaced with System. This is necessary because Delete is also a method in numerous Delphi components. To call the string Delete method in system, you usually use the form System.Delete as shown here.

Note

Some servers may send control codes in their text data. Set the FormatChars property to True for the client application's DdeClientConv object. This strips backspace (#8), tab (#9), line feed (#10), and carriage return (#13) control codes from received text.

Object Linking and Embedding

The most sophisticated data-sharing technique available in Windows is known as Object Linking and Embedding, or OLE. The key advantage that OLE offers is a shift from an application-oriented view of computing to one that centers on documents. Computer users work with data, and placing the emphasis on documents as objects is more natural for many users. With OLE, users can also combine information in unforeseen ways. For example, a word processor document can contain graphical images created by software unknown to the word processor's author. OLE makes it possible for users, not just software designers, to create new types of documents that are not limited to a single application-specific format.

Another use for OLE is to access objects in other applications — Microsoft Word, for example. This is possible because OLE 2 is based on the Common Object Model, or COM. These objects provide an interface that any application can use to access properties and methods in the objects, regardless of the language that was used to create them. COM objects, and therefore, OLE objects, are constructed from a binary model to which Delphi provides full access.

As with DDE, OLE requires two cooperating applications — a client and a server. The client application is known as an OLE container. The server provides commands for editing specific types of data. The container receives objects from an OLE server, either directly, by way of the Windows clipboard, or by dragging and dropping files from the Windows Explorer. For example, as an OLE server, an audio-wave form editor could provide commands for creating sound documents that an OLE container could store along with text that describes the sound. The container provides generic commands for creating new sound-and-text documents, but the OLE servers provide the commands for creating, editing, and viewing or playing the individual pieces of data.

Creating OLE objects

An application can create an OLE object from any type that is registered with the Windows registry. For example, you can create an OLE object in Microsoft Word, and then use that object to call methods that write text, select fonts, print pages, and save documents in disk files. Your applications can perform similar tasks with other OLE applications servers — Microsoft Excel, for instance.

To create an OLE object, call the CreateOleObject function in Delphi's ComObj unit. Add a *uses* declaration to import this unit into a unit, usually in the implementation section:

```
implementation
uses ComObj;
```

Caution

Numerous online and printed references provided with Delphi incorrectly tell you to use the OleAuto unit. To call CreateOleObject, you must use ComObj as shown here.

The ComObj unit declares CreateOleObject and its parameters as follows:

```
function CreateOleObject(const ClassName: string): IDispatch;
```

✦ **ClassName** — This is the name of the registered class — Word.Basic or Word.Document, for example — of which you want to create an OLE object.

✦ **IDispatch** — If successful, CreateOleObject returns an object of type IDispatch, an interface declaration based on IUnknown, both of which are declared in Delphi's System.pas unit. The IDisplatch object is typically assigned to a Variant, which is then used to make calls to methods and to access properties in the OLE object.

A couple of example programs demonstrate how to use CreateOleObject. In each program, commands create a Microsoft Word document, insert text into the document, print it, and save it in a .doc file on disk. These steps outline the basic techniques required to create and use OLE objects — you might use similar programming to output an application's text in a document format more familiar to the user. For example, a database system could prepare reports and save them in Microsoft Word or Excel documents, all without requiring users to open those applications.

Note

The reason this section has two example programs is that Microsoft, in its infinite wisdom, replaced Word Basic — the long-time macro language of Word and Excel — with Visual Basic in Microsoft Office 97. This means that most commands, macros, and OLE code no longer works with Word 97. The fundamentals of creating OLE objects are unchanged, but the details are completely different. If you have Word for Windows 95 or an earlier version, look up Word Basic commands using the program's online help. If you have the newer Word 97, start the Visual Basic Editor using the Tools|Macro... command, and then click the Object Browser toolbar button to gain access to a searchable online help system for Visual Basic.

Sample OLE object for Word 95 and earlier

On the CD-ROM

If you have Word 95 or an earlier version, load the OleWord1.dpr project file from the CD-ROM in the Source\OleWord1 directory into Delphi. (Use OleWord2 if you have Word 97 or later.) Start Word now if you want to see the created document. If Word isn't running, it is executed as a silent server. In that case, the document is still created and printed, but Word must be running for you to see the document text as it is inserted. Also, turn on your printer — if you don't have one, you receive an error message from the operating system (this does no harm, but you can delete the V.FilePrint; statement to avoid it).

Press F9 to compile and run the program, and then click its button to create a Word document, insert the text "Hello from Delphi," print the page, and save the document as C:\Hold.doc. (This is a name I typically use for temporary files.) Listing 16-9 shows the program's source code.

Listing 16-9: **OleWord1\Main.pas**

```
unit Main;

interface

uses
  Windows, Messages, SysUtils, Classes, Graphics, Controls,
  Forms, Dialogs, StdCtrls;

type
  TMainForm = class(TForm)
    Button1: TButton;
    procedure Button1Click(Sender: TObject);
  private
    { Private declarations }
  public
    { Public declarations }
  end;

var
  MainForm: TMainForm;

implementation

uses ComObj;    // Declares the CreateOleObject function

{$R *.DFM}

{ This procedure works with Microsoft Word 95 and
  earlier versions. It does *not* work with the
  newer Word 97, which now uses Visual Basic in
  place of Word Basic. }
procedure TMainForm.Button1Click(Sender: TObject);
var
  V: Variant;
begin
  V := CreateOleObject('Word.Basic');
  V.Insert('Hello from Delphi');
  V.FilePrint;
  V.FileSaveAs('C:\Hold.doc');
end;

end.
```

Caution You must have Microsoft Word 95 or an earlier version installed and running to use the OleWord1 sample application. See OleWord2 in this chapter if you have Word 97 or a later version.

The program's display is simplistic, so it is not shown here. When the program runs, it displays a large button. Click it to create, print, and save a Word document. The program's OnClick event handler demonstrates how to use the CreateOleObject function. As I mentioned, you must add a *uses* declaration to gain access to this function — you could add the unit name to the module's main *uses* declaration at top, or you can add a new *uses* declaration as shown in the listing just after the module's *implementation* keyword.

To hold the results of CreateOleObject, declare a variable of type Variant like this:

```
var
  V: Variant;
```

A Variant is a special data type that, in essence, can be any actual type of object. For example, a Variant can hold an integer value, a floating-point number, or a string. It can also hold OLE objects — or, to be more precise, an IDispatch object such as returned by the CreateOleObject function. Variant objects perform automatic type conversion so that, if one holds an integer and you assign it to a string, the integer's value is automatically converted to text.

Caution Variants might seem magical, and it's natural to be tempted to use them extensively. However, they are bulky and slow — each Variant is at least 16 bytes in length, regardless of type — and the code associated with Variant operations takes a lot longer to run than code performed on native data types. Don't use Variants except when you absolutely must have them — to hold OLE objects, for example.

After declaring a Variant, call CreateOleObject and assign the result to the Variant. You can then call methods and access properties in the OLE object. For example, the following two lines create a Word Basic object and then call that language's Insert method to insert some text into a Word document:

```
V := CreateOleObject('Word.Basic');
V.Insert('Hello from Delphi');
```

You might wonder, how does the compiler know that Word.Basic has a method named Insert? The answer is: it doesn't. When using variants, the Delphi compiler relaxes most of its syntax checking rules and enables you to type anything in reference to a Variant object. The following statement compiles perfectly well:

```
V.NoSuchMethod('Any parameter', 123);
```

even though Word Basic has no such method named NoSuchMethod. When you run the program, however, you receive an error message to that effect when the program attempts to call this method in the OLE Word object.

This process is an example of *late binding*—meaning that, rather than resolving calls to methods and other references during compilation, the resolution for Variants occurs at run time. When the program calls CreateOleObject, if successful, that object provides, via its interface, a list of available methods and properties. This is how it is possible for statements such as V.Insert to work.

The other two statements in the sample program's OnClick event handler demonstrate two more Word Basic calls. These statements:

```
V.FilePrint;
V.FileSaveAs('C:\Hold.doc');
```

call FilePrint to print the document text and FileSaveAs to save it to the named file. All of these actions take place within the OLE object inside Microsoft Word.

Note

You can't run any old application by creating an OLE object. The application must be an OLE server such as Word or Excel that is specifically designed to respond to requests from OLE client applications such as the demonstration programs in this chapter.

Sample OLE object for Word 97 and later

On the CD-ROM

If you have Word 97 or a later version, load the OleWord2.dpr project file from the CD-ROM in the Source\OleWord2 directory into Delphi. Start Word—it must be running for this demonstration to work properly. Also turn on your printer—if you don't have one, you receive an error message from the operating system (this does no harm, but you can delete the V.PrintOut; statement to avoid it).

Press F9 to compile and run the program, and then click its button to create a Word document, insert the text "Hello from Delphi," print the page, and save the document as C:\Hold.doc. Listing 16-10 shows the program's source code.

Caution

You must have Microsoft Word 97 or a later version installed and running to use the OleWord2 sample application. See OleWord1 in this chapter if you have Word 95 or an earlier version.

Listing 16-10: OleWord2\Main.pas

```pascal
unit Main;

interface

uses
  Windows, Messages, SysUtils, Classes, Graphics, Controls,
  Forms, Dialogs, StdCtrls;

type
  TMainForm = class(TForm)
    Button1: TButton;
    procedure Button1Click(Sender: TObject);
  private
    { Private declarations }
  public
    { Public declarations }
  end;

var
  MainForm: TMainForm;

implementation

uses ComObj;   // Declares the CreateOleObject function

{$R *.DFM}

{ This procedure works with the newer Word 97,
  which uses Visual Basic in place of the standard
  Word Basic as its controlling language. }
procedure TMainForm.Button1Click(Sender: TObject);
var
  V, X: Variant;
  S: String;
begin
  V := CreateOleObject('Word.Document');
  X := V.Range(0, 0);
  X.InsertBefore('Hello from Delphi');
  X.Font.Name := 'Arial';
  X.Font.Size := 18;
  X.InsertParagraphAfter;
  V.Printout;
  V.SaveAs('C:\Hold.doc');
end;

end.
```

This edition of the sample OLE object program is similar to the preceding one, but it demonstrates how to call methods and access property values in Visual Basic, which replaces Word Basic in Microsoft software products. Unfortunately, most commands are different. So to support both versions of Word, you need separate applications or an option to select the correct procedures.

The process of creating an OLE object for Word 97 is similar to the process for Word 95, but instead of Word.Basic, CreateOleObject now requests an object of type Word.Document. As before, declare a Variant (*V* in the sample procedure), and then call CreateOleObject like this:

```
V := CreateOleObject('Word.Document');
```

Passing Word.Document as a string argument ensures that the latest installed version of Word is used to create the OLE object. You may reference a specific software release by attaching its major version number. For example, this also works:

```
V := CreateOleObject('Word.Document.8');
```

After creating the OLE object, the program can make calls to its methods. Remember, however, the methods and properties are different in Word Basic and Visual Basic. Worse, the required steps for performing various operations are now also different. For example, to insert some text now requires at least three commands such as:

```
X := V.Range(0, 0);
X.InsertBefore('Hello from Delphi');
...
X.InsertParagraphAfter;
```

The call to Range prevents replacing any selected text, which in this case isn't strictly necessary, but is recommended in the Visual Basic programming guide. The ellipsis shows where other commands can go to alter aspects of the inserted text, which is selected by default. The sample program uses this place to select a font name and size with the statements:

```
X.Font.Name := 'Arial';
X.Font.Size := 18;
```

Calling InsertParagraphAfter starts a new paragraph and is roughly equivalent to pressing Enter when typing a document. To print the inserted text and save it in a file, the sample program executes two more Visual Basic commands:

```
V.Printout;
V.SaveAs('C:\Hold.doc');
```

There isn't room here to go into Visual Basic programming in detail. For more information, look up Visual Basic syntax and programming tips in Word 97's online help.

Using CreateOleObject

The preceding two sample applications demonstrated how to call CreateOleObject. The function creates one object, which is not initialized, using the class name that is passed as a string parameter. This class name must be registered in the Windows registry. Save the result of the function in a Variant. For example, call the function like this to create a Word document:

```
V := CreateOleObject('Word.Document');
```

The string Word.Document is actually a representation of the Class ID (CLSID), which is also sometimes called a GUID (gooey ID). This ID is a lengthy hexadecimal key that is statistically guaranteed to be unique. (If any two GUIDs ever do conflict, the result is, no doubt, a sticky mess.) Using the Regedit.exe utility in C:\Windows, you can look up the CLSIDs for installed programs. When I did this, I searched the HKEY_CLASSES_ROOT (the root entry for registered classes and their keys) for Word.Document, which displayed the following CLSID:

```
"{00020906-0000-0000-C000-000000000046}"
```

This is the *same* CLSID for Word.Document.8, which explains why either designation works for the purpose of creating an OLE object. If, in the future, I install a newer version of Word, I expect that Word.Document's CLSID will be updated in the Windows registry.

The CreateOleObject function is declared in Delphi's ComObj.pas file as follows:

```
function CreateOleObject(const ClassName: string): IDispatch;
```

The function returns an object of type IDispatch, which is declared as an interface derived from IUnknown:

```
IDispatch = interface(IUnknown)
  ['{00020400-0000-0000-C000-000000000046}']
  function GetTypeInfoCount(out Count: Integer): HResult;
    stdcall;
  function GetTypeInfo(Index, LocaleID: Integer;
    out TypeInfo): HResult; stdcall;
  function GetIDsOfNames(const IID: TGUID; Names: Pointer;
    NameCount, LocaleID: Integer; DispIDs: Pointer): HResult;
    stdcall;
  function Invoke(DispID: Integer; const IID: TGUID;
```

```
      LocaleID: Integer; Flags: Word; var Params;
      VarResult, ExcepInfo, ArgErr: Pointer): HResult; stdcall;
    end;
```

This declaration uses some odd syntax that you won't find in many other places in Delphi. There's no need to understand every detail here; just be aware that when you call CreateOleObject, you get back an object of type IDispatch. That object refers to the OLE object that resides in its own host application. All calls to that object, via the object's OLE interface, are made by calling the Invoke function in IDispatch.

It's not really necessary to understand these and other nuts-and-bolts issues regarding the registry and CLSID values. However, before delving too deeply into the muddy waters of OLE programming, you should understand that OLE objects exist in their registered programs and that your application's object is really of type IDispatch. Because you can't tell until run time what interface an OLE application provides, you must use a Variant to make calls to the OLE object through IDispatch. If you run into trouble, use the Windows Regedit utility to browse the names of available objects that your applications can create, and to debug problems. If a registered object doesn't have a CLSID, you can't create an OLE object for it, and even if it does, there's no guarantee that passing the object class name to CreateOleObject works. (There's an entry for Word.Basic on my system's registry, but CreateOleObject still can't create an OLE object of that type.)

Be extremely cautious when using the Regedit program. Browsing is okay, but even small changes to the Windows registry could have far-reaching, even disastrous results. For safety, use Regedit's Registry|Export Registry File... command to create a text backup of the entire registry. You can then use Registry|Import Registry File... to load the saved registry. Also see the Regedit help topic "Restoring the registry" for steps that you can use to restore a damaged registry.

CreateOleObject returns a reference to the identifier of the interface that can be used to communicate with the object. For CreateOleObject this interface is of type IDispatch. To create a COM object that is not an IDispatch interface, use CreateComObject.

Writing an OLE container application

The preceding sections demonstrate only one way to use OLE. Another way is to create a *container* application that communicates with an OLE server. With this technique, you can link and embed server documents in your application. For example, an OLE container can create, load, edit, and save a Microsoft Excel document. Because Excel is a full-featured OLE server application, your Delphi program can call on Excel to create spreadsheet documents, all from inside your own program's window.

Linking and embedding documents of various types — especially when those types are not known at design time — is a great way to enable users to decide how they wish to store information on their computers. You can also use linking and embedding as a way to provide sophisticated commands in your programs with very little programming. Rather than spend half of next year creating a text editor for users to enter and edit documents, you can simply provide an OLE container and enable your program's users to create text documents using their favorite editor — whether that's Microsoft Word or WordPerfect.

In this section, I explain how to create a general-purpose OLE container application using the OleContainer component from the System palette. The sample program demonstrates how to implement *in-place editing,* whereby the program's menus and toolbars are replaced by the OLE server. When you open an Excel spreadsheet, Microsoft Excel's menus and toolbars appear inside the Delphi application. Likewise, when you open a Word document, Microsoft Word's menus and tools replace the Delphi application's interface. The sample program also shows how to enable users to embed documents as icons in the application, in which case opening them brings up their server applications in separate windows.

To provide for OLE in-place editing, a Delphi application should contain:

✦ One OleContainer object for each OLE object in the container

✦ A MainMenu object

✦ A toolbar Panel object (optional)

✦ A statusbar Panel object (optional)

With these items, the server can insert its own menus, toolbar SpeedButtons, and status messages into the container. For example, when editing an embedded or linked Microsoft Word object in a container, Word's menus augment the container's menus. Users see the familar word-processor's commands, but they are still running the container — they don't have to explicitly switch to or run the server.

For a server to use a container's toolbar Panel, its Align property must equal either alBottom, alLeft, alRight, or alTop, and Locked must be False. Also, the container should probably use the MDI interface to manage the main window's client area and to provide child windows for document editing. It is possible to use a single-window application as an OLE container client, but the MDI interface is more sensible because it enables users to create child-window documents of any server type.

To create an OLE container, insert an instance of the OleContainer component into a form. The resulting object looks like a Panel with an indented surface. In it, the user can insert an OLE object, displayed as an icon or in its full likeness. Try these steps to write a bare-bones OLE container application that demonstrates the fundamentals of working with OLE objects:

1. Start a new application and insert an OleContainer object from the System VCL palette into Form1's window.

2. Insert a MainMenu object from the Standard palette. Double-click the menu icon, and enter two menus: **File and Edit**. Set the Edit menu's GroupIndex property to one. In the File menu, insert an Exit command. In Edit, insert the command Insert Object....

3. Quit the Menu Designer and select File | Exit from the form's menu bar. Enter **Close**; between *begin* and *end* in the menu-command's event handler. Select Edit | Insert Object... from the form's menu bar, and enter the programming from Listing 16-11. The text is from the Source\OleCont\Main.pas file on the CD-ROM.

Listing 16-11: This procedure demonstrates the required steps for inserting an OLE object into an OleContainer component.

```
procedure TMainForm.InsertObject1Click(Sender: TObject);
begin
   with OleContainer1 do
   begin
      if InsertObjectDialog then
         DoVerb(PrimaryVerb);
   end;
end;
```

The event handler for the Edit | Insert Object... command shows the most basic way to use an OleContainer object. Call the object's InsertObjectDialog method, which displays the dialog shown in Figure 16-6. The user can select the type of OLE object to create — a Bitmap for example — and also choose whether to insert a full image of the object or display it as an icon. Users can also select an icon to depict the file. All of these actions take place at the operating system level — your code simply calls InsertObjectDialog to start the ball rolling.

If that function returns True, then the user has selected an object to create. To finish the job and insert the OLE object into the OleContainer component in the Delphi application, call DoVerb and pass PrimaryVerb as an argument. The DoVerb method performs an action for the OLE object. The PrimaryVerb is the default action listed for this type of object — usually, this verb creates and initializes a new object.

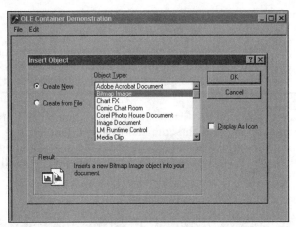

Figure 16-6: The Insert Object Dialog displayed by an OleContainer object

Figure 16-7 shows the OleCont application after I created a bitmap file in response to the dialog shown in Figure 16-6. The Windows Paint utility—an OLE server—replaces the Delphi application's menus and display with its own. With only a little programming, the sample program provides full graphics file editing capabilities to users. Figure 16-8 shows the same program, but this time editing a Microsoft Excel Chart document. Don't you wish all programming could be this easy?

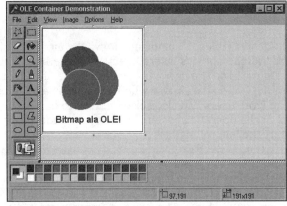

Figure 16-7: The OleCont application editing a bitmap file using Windows Paint

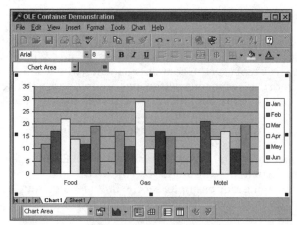

Figure 16-8: The same OleCont application, but this time editing a Microsoft Excel Chart document

Listing 16-12 shows the programming that used to be required in Delphi 1 for creating embedded OLE documents. Although the OleContainer component is used in the same way, the programming is very different and is shown here only for comparison purposes. Do not use these techniques in new applications. See Listing 16-11 for the correct methods to use for embedding OLE objects in container applications.

Listing 16-12: Embedding an OLE object in an OleContainer object in Delphi 1 required using code like this.

```
procedure TForm1.Insertobject1Click(Sender: TObject);
var
  P: Pointer;
begin
  if InsertOLEObjectDlg(Form1, 0, P) then
  begin
    OleContainer1.PInitInfo := P;
    ReleaseOleInitInfo(P);
  end;
end;
```

OLE menu merging

To support OLE 2.0 in-place editing, the container application's MainMenu object assigns standard values to top-level menu item GroupIndex properties. When users edit an object, the OLE 2.0 server replaces the container's menus with a subset of its own commands. The server replaces menus with equal GroupIndexes; it inserts menus to the left of menus with higher GroupIndexes. The server also provides Update and Exit to Container or similar commands, usually in the File menu, for saving new or modified objects back to the container application.

Table 16-2 lists suggested top-level menus and commands for an OLE container application. Set the top-level menu item's GroupIndex to the values in the table to enable OLE 2.0 server menu merging. For example, set the Edit menu's GroupIndex to one so the server can replace this menu with its own commands.

Table 16-2 Suggested OLE 2.0 Container Application Menus and GroupIndex Property Values		
Menu	*Suggested commands*	*GroupIndex*
File	New, Open, Exit	0
Edit	Insert object, Paste special, Object (set Enabled to false)	1
Object	Deactivate	2
View	none	3
Window	Cascade, Tile, Arrange icons	4
Help	none	5

Tip You do not have to set every menu item's GroupIndex value. Assign values only to top-level menu items.

Assign the name of your application's Object menu, with a GroupIndex value of two, to the form's ObjectMenuItem property. In a single-document application, assign this property for the main form. In an MDI application, assign the property in your program's child-window form. By making this assignment, the OleContainer object in the form automatically makes object-editing commands available for selected objects.

Use GroupIndex values other than those in Table 16-2 to prevent OLE 2.0 server applications from replacing your application menus. For example, if you assign a value of nine to all top-level menu GroupIndex properties, the server's menu items are added to your application's menu commands. To reduce the potential for confusion (two Edit menus, for example), if you employ this trick, your application should not use any of the menu names listed in the table.

OLE and the clipboard

You should add a Paste Special command to your application's Edit menu so users can paste OLE objects from the Windows clipboard. Not all OLE server applications can copy objects to the clipboard, but this command enables users to paste objects for those that do. You need a Paste Special command to separate it from your application's normal Edit|Paste operation.

To implement a Paste Special command, call the OleContainer component's PasteSpecialDialog. Usually, you also want to check whether the container currently has a document, in which case users should be prompted whether to discard it. Listing 16-13 shows the general layout of a Paste|Special command's event handler.

Listing 16-13: Implement a Paste|Special command using code like this.

```
procedure TMainForm.PasteSpecial1Click(Sender: TObject);
begin
  if (OleContainer1.State = osEmpty) or
     (MessageDlg('Delete current OLE object?',
       mtConfirmation, mbOkCancel, 0) = mrOk) then
  if OleContainer1.PasteSpecialDialog then
  begin
    // ... Enable Cut, Copy, and Paste buttons here
  end;
end;
```

This sample code is similar to that in the Delphi demonstration program, OleSdi found in the Demos\Olectnrs directory. The State property is first checked to determine whether the OleContainer object is empty. If not, a message dialog prompts the user for permission to delete the current OLE object. If the user answers Yes, the program calls PasteSpecialDialog, which handles the rest of the required tasks. The ellipsis shows where you might insert code to enable various menu commands or buttons now that the user has pasted an object into the container. For example, if you have a CopyButton object, you might execute this code:

```
CopyButton.Enabled := True;
```

Be aware that not all OLE servers can paste objects, and rather than enable a Paste button or menu command, it's best to use the CanPaste property in the container. This property is True if the OLE server enables pasting. Enable a PasteButton object using code such as:

```
PasteButton.Enabled := OleContainer1.CanPaste;
```

Expert-User Tips

✦ In programs that paste large objects such as bitmaps to the clipboard, you may want to give users the chance to clear the clipboard before the program ends. This can help conserve memory. For example, insert a prompt such as "Clear large bitmap on clipboard?" into a main form's OnClose event handler, and call Clipboard.Clear if the user answers Yes.

✦ Although DDE can transfer only text data, that text may represent numeric values, filenames, or structures of bytes represented as hexadecimal strings. It may take some creative programming to use DDE to transfer binary objects, but if you can figure out how to represent your data as text, DDE can carry the information.

✦ When communicating with servers that do not use their filenames as the Service, in the client application's DdeClientConv object, set DdeService to the identifier obtained from the server's documentation. Set ServiceApplication to the server's filename. The client can then start the server if ConnectMode, also in the DdeClientConv object, is set to ddeAutomatic.

✦ To add scroll bars to OLE objects, insert an instance of the OleContainer component into a ScrollBox. To make the scroll bars visible, set the Range subproperties of VertScrollBar and HorzScrollBar to values greater than the ScrollBox's Width and Height, respectively.

✦ To prevent editing of an OLE object, set the OleContainer's Auto-Activate property to aaManual. With this setting, the application must set the Active property to True to enable editing.

✦ When programming single-window OLE container applications, you might have better luck with your program's display if you place the OleContainer object into a Panel. Set the Panel object's Align property to alClient, and then drop the OleContainer object into the Panel. You don't need to do this if your application uses the MDI multiwindow design because, in that case, each child window has a separate OleContainer.

Projects to Try

16-1: Write your own Clipboard viewer that supports standard formats as well as TPicture and TComponent objects.

16-2: Write a DDE server application that creates a letter in Microsoft Word or another word processor. Your program might offer several different types of business and personal letter formats.

16-3: Write a DDE client application that prints labels or names and addresses entered into a Microsoft Excel or other spreadsheet application.

16-4: Advanced. Write a read-only OLE container application that links two or more documents from OLE server applications on your system — a worksheet and a word-processor document, for example.

Summary

✦ The Windows clipboard, though primitive, is the easiest method for sharing data among applications. The clipboard requires the voluntary cooperation of two applications (or two processes in the same application).

✦ Dynamic Data Exchange, or DDE, offers a more sophisticated method for sharing text data. To use DDE, a client and a server application establish a conversation through which data can flow. Data normally flows from the server to the client, but the applications can reverse their roles and pass data in the other direction.

✦ Object Linking and Embedding, or OLE, shifts the focus from the application to the document, which many users find more natural. Also, with OLE, users can build new document types in ways not foreseen by application designers.

✦ An OLE container application links or embeds objects. An OLE server application provides editing and other commands for specific kinds of objects. Use Delphi's OleContainer component to construct OLE container applications.

Every computer needs a good database system, and as you discover in the next chapter, Delphi offers database development tools that are as good as they come.

✦   ✦   ✦

Developing Database Applications

Delphi is truly a one-stop shop for Windows programming but, as this chapter explains, Delphi is also a database developer's dream come true. With Delphi, you can create, edit, and write software for just about all types of desktop databases such as dBASE, Paradox, and ODBC systems like Microsoft Access. You can also develop sophisticated client-server applications for remote data servers operating on the smallest PC network up to the largest of mainframes. I believe in never saying never, but here it is anyway—with Delphi, it's likely you won't ever need another database management system.

In this chapter, I explain how to get started with Delphi's database components and how you can use them to create and use databases in a variety of formats. After you master a few basics, you learn how to perform searches with SQL (structured query language) and how to create relational database applications based on the master-detail table model.

Note

All versions of Delphi include the Borland Database Engine (BDE), which provides a complete set of programming tools for many popular desktop database systems such as dBase and Paradox. Delphi's Client-Server edition includes the BDE, and it provides access to remote database servers such as Oracle, Sybase, Microsoft SQL Server, and Informix. The Client-Server edition of Delphi also comes with components for developing remote client-server applications. You may use any edition of Delphi with this chapter.

Components

Delphi's database components are:

✦ **BatchMove** — Performs batched operations on records and tables, such as duplicating a dataset, appending records from one dataset to another, and updating or deleting records that match a specified argument. Palette: Data Access.

✦ **Database** — Provides additional database services such as server logins and local aliases. Delphi creates Database objects automatically as needed, but you can create them explicitly if necessary. Palette: Data Access.

✦ **DataSource** — Connects dataset components such as Table and Query with data-aware components such as DBEdit and DBMemo. Every database application needs at least one DataSource object. Palette: Data Access.

✦ **DBChart** — A full-featured component for creating visual charts from database information. The next chapter explains how to use the DBChart component. Palette: Data Controls.

✦ **DBCheckBox** — A data-aware CheckBox component. Palette: Data Controls.

✦ **DBComboBox** — A data-aware ComboBox component. Palette: Data Controls.

✦ **DBCtrlGrid** — A scrollable set of panels each representing one database record. Each panel may contain one or more data-aware control objects. Typically used along with a DBNavigator object for a nontraditional (nontable) view of data. Also see the DBGrid component. Palette: Data Controls.

✦ **DBEdit** — A data-aware Edit single-line text-entry component. Palette: Data Controls.

✦ **DBGrid** — A data-aware, row-and-column grid that displays database records, one record per row. Typically used along with a DBNavigator object for a traditional table-like view of data. Palette: Data Controls.

✦ **DBImage** — A data-aware graphical Image component. Typically used to display Blobs (binary large objects) that contain bitmap images. Palette: Data Controls.

✦ **DBListBox** — A data-aware ListBox component. Palette: Data Controls.

✦ **DBLookupComboBox** — A data-aware ComboBox component with the capability to search a lookup table. Early versions of Delphi named this component DBLookupCombo. Palette: Data Controls.

✦ **DBLookupListBox** — A data-aware ListBox component with the capability to search a lookup table. Early versions of Delphi named this component DBLookupList. Palette: Data Controls.

✦ **DBMemo** — A data-aware Memo multiline text-entry component. Palette: Data Controls.

✦ **DBNavigator** — A sophisticated database browsing and editing tool. This component is to database programming what a remote control is to a video recorder. Users click DBNavigator buttons to move through database records, insert new records, delete records, and perform other navigational operations. Palette: Data Controls.

✦ **DBRadioGroup** — A data-aware RadioGroup component. Palette: Data Controls.

✦ **DBRichEdit** — Similar to a DBMemo control, the DBRichEdit component can display and enable editing of text data stored in rich-text format (RTF). Palette: Data Controls.

✦ **DBText** — A data-aware, read-only text component for displaying database information that you don't want users to edit. (Note: Use the standard Label component, not DBText, to label input fields on data-entry screens.) Palette: Data Controls.

✦ **Query** — Issues SQL statements to the BDE or to an SQL server. Palette: Data Access.

✦ **Session** — All database connections take place in the context of a Session object, which manages those connections. Delphi automatically creates a global Session object for all database applications; however, you may add Session components to an application to provide multiple sessions, which you might do for example to access tables in different network locations. Palette: Data Access.

✦ **StoredProc** — Enables applications to execute stored procedures on a database server. Unless you are developing client-server database applications, you probably won't need to use this component. Typical stored procedures include commands for obtaining information on locked processes and the logon IDs of database users. However, the exact procedures available depend on the server. Palette: Data Access.

✦ **Table** — Gives applications access to databases through the BDE. This component is usually associated with a DataSource object, which connects the Table with data-aware controls. Most database applications have at least one Table object. Palette: Data Access.

✦ **UpdateSQL** — This component is provided to developers who need to perform updates on read-only datasets returned by an SQL server. Using UpdateSQL, it is possible to perform INSERT, UPDATE, and DELETE commands even though the dataset is marked read-only (this can happen, for example, when an application queries multiple tables, even though the tables themselves are not read-only). You need this component only if you experience this kind of trouble; otherwise, use Query. Palette: Data Access.

Note   Data-aware controls resemble their data-blind cousins, but can use information from databases. For example, a DBListBox is similar to a plain ListBox, but it can obtain its information from a database Table through a DataSource object.

Early versions of Delphi provided the Report component in the Data Access palette. This component, which provided access to Borland's ReportSmith database report generator, is no longer available. For constructing database reports, use the components on the QReport (Quick Report) palette. QReport components (and the TDBChart component) are discussed in the next chapter.

Database Development

Delphi's database components put an object-oriented face on database application development. Even more important, database components standardize access to databases in a variety of formats. This means your applications can access data in dBASE files, Paradox tables, Microsoft Access and other Open Database Connectivity (ODBC) systems, or if you have the Client-Server edition, through remote SQL servers. Best of all, you can use all other Delphi components, interface techniques, and Object Pascal programming in your database applications.

Using the Database Form Wizard

You can develop database applications using the same tools and techniques described throughout this book. A database application differs from other Windows software only in its capability to read and write information in database tables. In terms of the program's user interface, you develop the application's form as you do any other window.

However, a typical database form may require numerous edit controls, labels, and grids, as well as components that provide the necessary links to database tables. It can be tedious to program all of these objects individually, and to get a leg up on new database applications, you can instead use the Database Form Wizard template. (This takes the place of Delphi's Database Form Expert command on the Help menu in early releases.) To use the new wizard, start a new application with File|New..., click the Business page tab, and select Database Form Wizard.

The Database Form Wizard is an interactive tool for constructing database forms. In a nutshell, you answer various prompts and select options that the wizard offers. When you're done, the wizard creates a brand-new form complete with all database components in their proper places. You can move these components and make other modifications to the final form, but in many cases, the end results require only a little polishing to create a finished application.

Follow these steps to create a database form for a table in a sample database supplied with Delphi (or you can use another database table if you have one):

1. Select File | New... to start a new application. Select the Business page tab, and double-click Database Form Wizard (see Figure 17-1).

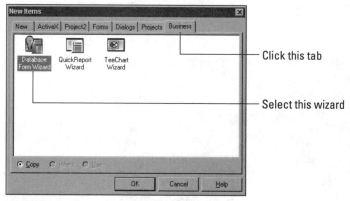

Figure 17-1: The Database Form Wizard is on the Business page of the New Items dialog.

2. The wizard presents several dialog-box pages, with options for creating a variety of forms. On the first page, choose Create a simple form and Create a form using TTable objects (see Figure 17-2). These are the default settings.

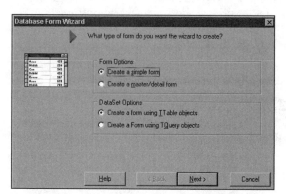

Figure 17-2: The initial page of the Database Form Wizard.

3. Click the Next button to move to the next page. (At any time, you can click Prev to return to previous pages if you make a mistake, or if you change your mind about a previous selection.)

4. Select a table by opening the ComboBox labeled Drive or Alias Name. Select DBDEMOS or another database alias if available on your system. In the Table Name list, you should now see the names of tables that make up the DBDEMOS database. Choose ANIMALS.DBF or another table (see Figure 17-3), and then click Next to move to the next page.

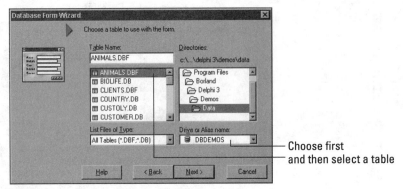

Figure 17-3: Select a database alias and table name using the Database Form Wizard.

5. The wizard now lists the fields available in the selected table. Click the double-arrow button to move all fields to the Selected list, or you can Shift+click and Ctrl+click individual fields and use the single-arrow buttons (see Figure 17-4). Drag-and-drop, or click the up and down arrows, to arrange your selected fields in any order, and then click Next to move to the next page.

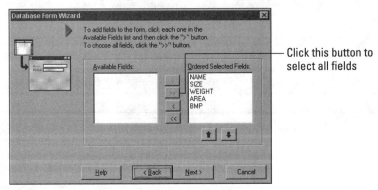

Figure 17-4: Choose the fields you want to use.

6. Choose a layout option: Horizontal for side-by-side data-entry controls, Vertical to place each control under the preceding one, or Grid to create a spreadsheet-like appearance for viewing and editing multiple records, one per row. If you are following along, choose In a grid (see Figure 17-5), and then click Next to move to the next page.

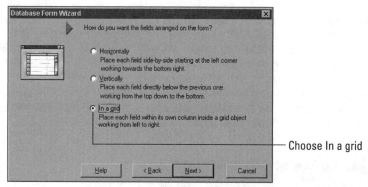

Figure 17-5: Choose a layout option such as In a grid.

7. The final wizard page offers you the choice of creating only a Form with all components, or a Form and DataModule, with nonvisual components in the data module. (This differs from earlier wizards which did not use data modules.) If you are following along, make sure the Generate a main form check box is selected, and choose the Form and DataModule option (see Figure 17-6). Click the Finish button (formerly named Create), to generate the new database form.

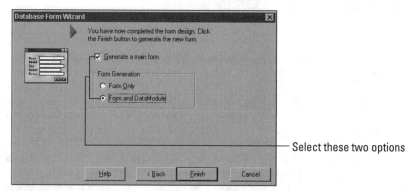

Figure 17-6: This is the final Database Form Wizard dialog page.

On the final wizard dialog page, if you disable the Generate a main form check box, you need to insert programming to display the generated form—by calling ShowModal, for example. With the check box selected, the new form is designated as the program's main one, and you may use the Project Manager to delete the new project's old main form, which is blank and serves no purpose.

You can now press F9 to compile and run the database application. Figure 17-7 shows the program's window. Although you added no programming, it is a fully functional database application! At the top is a DBNavigator object with buttons for browsing records, adding new rows, deleting records, and so on. Feel free to use these controls, but be aware that any changes you make are immediately stored in the database. For example, you might change the Area for Angel Fish from Computer Aquariums to Tropical Waters (let's hope some Angel Fish still live in the wild). Quit, and rerun the program to verify that your editing stuck.

NAME	SIZE	WEIGHT	AREA	BMP
Angel Fish	2	2	Computer Aquariums	(BLOB)
Boa	10	8	South America	(BLOB)
Critters	30	20	Screen Savers	(BLOB)
House Cat	10	5	New Orleans	(BLOB)
Ocelot	40	35	Africa and Asia	(BLOB)
Parrot	5	5	South America	(BLOB)
Tetras	2	2	Fish Bowls	(BLOB)

Figure 17-7: The sample database application created by the helpful Database Form Wizard and the steps in this section for the DBDEMOS database alias and the Animals.dbf table

If you try the preceding steps, one problem you may notice is that bitmap data fields do not display as graphics, but are instead identified as Blobs (Binary Large Objects). This occurs because the DBGrid component, used if you selected the wizard's grid layout, doesn't know how to display graphics. We fix this problem later by inserting a DBImage control into a project. The wizard doesn't do this automatically.

Although DBNavigator is easy to program, some users may find its complexity intimidating at first. The component comes with built-in help hints, which you can enable by setting the ShowHint property to True. This enables default hints, which you can change if necessary by editing the Hints property.

DBNavigator is a powerful control, and you should be careful not to delete records or make any drastic changes, which become permanent when you move the highlighted field to another row or record. Before doing that, however, you can undo any editing by selecting the *X* button. Clicking the check mark button posts the current record to the database. The plus and minus buttons add and delete records. The circular arrow refreshes the data by reloading from the table. The other buttons browse through the table's records.

Tip

To insert additional database forms into an application, select the Database|Form Wizard... command. This runs the same wizard that you selected with File|New... on the New Items Business page.

Database terms and components

Before creating databases and writing applications to access database information, it's important that you understand three related terms as used in database programming and by the BDE. These are:

✦ **Table** — This is an individual, flat-file data source, which you can think of as having rows (records) and columns (fields). One field in the table is the primary key on which the information in the flat file is indexed. Tables may also be indexed on secondary keys. A table is often called a *dataset*.

✦ **Query** — Similar to a Table, a Query presents SQL datasets in a navigable, scrollable format. Although it is possible to use a Table to access SQL data, using a Query object simplifies this task, especially when data comes from SQL servers (the Query object also helps lighten network traffic.) You can also use Query objects to create logical unions of dissimilar datasets (Tables can't do this), and you can join data from different sources such as Paradox and SQL tables.

✦ **Database** — This is a collection of one or more tables (usually at least two). When one table refers to another through a key value in a specified field, the result is known as a relational database.

✦ **Alias** — This is a name registered with the BDE that hides actual disk drives and path names that locate database files. Always use aliases to refer to databases; never hard code file and path names in your applications. By using aliases, you can move your database files to other locations — or transfer them to a networked directory — and all of your applications work without modification.

Creating a new database

Although it's possible to use Delphi to write an application that can create new databases, Inprise Corporation's crack programmers have already done that job for you in the Database Desktop, which is provided with Delphi. Use this utility to construct new database tables, to modify the fields in existing databases, to view database information, and to create aliases for data sources. Professional and Client-Server editions of Delphi also provide database explorers that you can use to browse tables and their structures. If you have one of these Delphi editions, select the explorer from the Database menu. Figure 17-8 shows Database Desktop viewing the DBDEMOS Customer.db table. Use Database Desktop, provided with all Delphi editions, to create and modify database tables in a variety of formats. Some editions of Delphi also provide a database explorer utility such as SQL Explorer. Figure 17-9 shows SQL Explorer viewing the structure of the same table used in Figure 17-8. (SQL Explorer is provided only with Delphi's Client-Server edition; Professional editions include a similar Explorer without SQL capabilities).

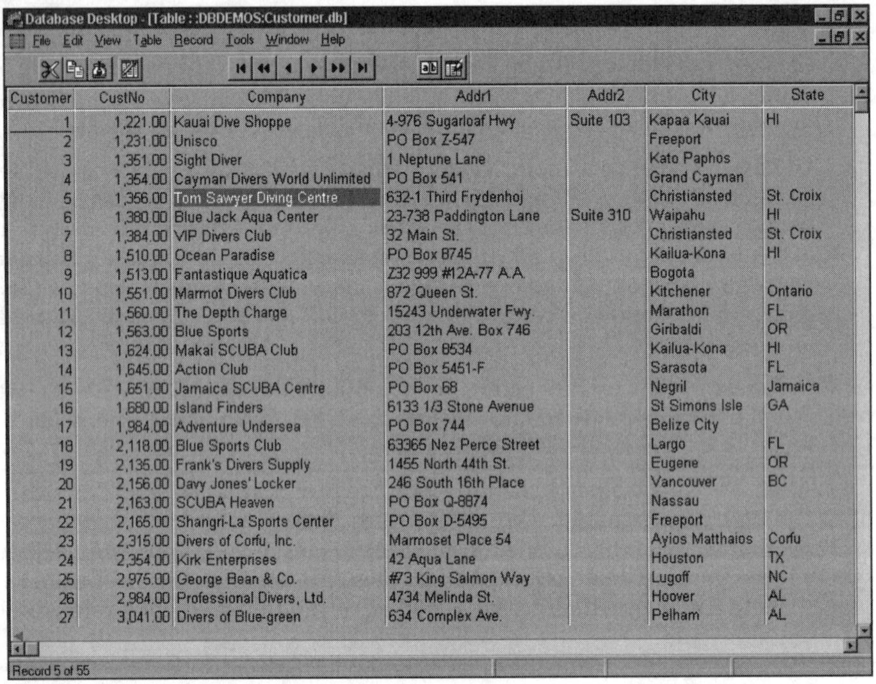

Customer	CustNo	Company	Addr1	Addr2	City	State
1	1,221.00	Kauai Dive Shoppe	4-976 Sugarloaf Hwy	Suite 103	Kapaa Kauai	HI
2	1,231.00	Unisco	PO Box Z-547		Freeport	
3	1,351.00	Sight Diver	1 Neptune Lane		Kato Paphos	
4	1,354.00	Cayman Divers World Unlimited	PO Box 541		Grand Cayman	
5	1,356.00	Tom Sawyer Diving Centre	632-1 Third Frydenhoj		Christiansted	St. Croix
6	1,380.00	Blue Jack Aqua Center	23-738 Paddington Lane	Suite 310	Waipahu	HI
7	1,384.00	VIP Divers Club	32 Main St.		Christiansted	St. Croix
8	1,510.00	Ocean Paradise	PO Box 8745		Kailua-Kona	HI
9	1,513.00	Fantastique Aquatica	Z32 999 #12A-77 A.A.		Bogota	
10	1,551.00	Marmot Divers Club	872 Queen St.		Kitchener	Ontario
11	1,560.00	The Depth Charge	15243 Underwater Fwy.		Marathon	FL
12	1,563.00	Blue Sports	203 12th Ave. Box 746		Giribaldi	OR
13	1,624.00	Makai SCUBA Club	PO Box 8534		Kailua-Kona	HI
14	1,645.00	Action Club	PO Box 5451-F		Sarasota	FL
15	1,651.00	Jamaica SCUBA Centre	PO Box 68		Negril	Jamaica
16	1,680.00	Island Finders	6133 1/3 Stone Avenue		St Simons Isle	GA
17	1,984.00	Adventure Undersea	PO Box 744		Belize City	
18	2,118.00	Blue Sports Club	63365 Nez Perce Street		Largo	FL
19	2,135.00	Frank's Divers Supply	1455 North 44th St.		Eugene	OR
20	2,156.00	Davy Jones' Locker	246 South 16th Place		Vancouver	BC
21	2,163.00	SCUBA Heaven	PO Box Q-8874		Nassau	
22	2,165.00	Shangri-La Sports Center	PO Box D-5495		Freeport	
23	2,315.00	Divers of Corfu, Inc.	Marmoset Place 54		Ayios Matthaios	Corfu
24	2,354.00	Kirk Enterprises	42 Aqua Lane		Houston	TX
25	2,975.00	George Bean & Co.	#73 King Salmon Way		Lugoff	NC
26	2,984.00	Professional Divers, Ltd.	4734 Melinda St.		Hoover	AL
27	3,041.00	Divers of Blue-green	634 Complex Ave.		Pelham	AL

Figure 17-8: This figure shows Database Desktop viewing the contents of the DBDEMOS Customer.db file provided with Delphi.

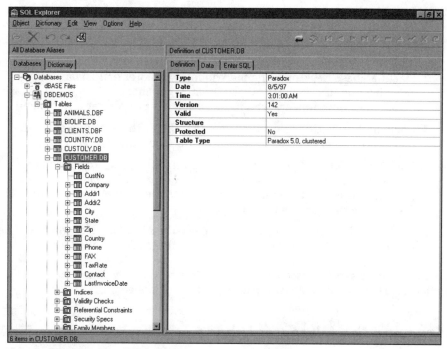

Figure 17-9: This figure shows SQL Explorer viewing the structure of the DBDEMOS Customer.db file provided with Delphi.

Note Database Desktop is a stand-alone application—you can run it from Delphi's Tools menu or from Delphi's installation directory. SQL Explorer is integral to Delphi and can only be run by selecting the Database|Explore command.

To create a new database, the first step is defining a place to store your information, and assigning an alias that refers to this location. You have two choices: you can create a new, empty database, or you can use the sample files on this book's CD-ROM. To use the sample files, follow the next numbered steps. To create an empty, new database, skip to "Creating the Wines database."

Using the Wines database

Follow these steps to use the sample Wines database files on the CD-ROM in the Source\WinesDemo directory:

1. Copy the Source\Data\Wines directory and its two files, Wines.px and Wines.db, to a new directory named C:\Database\Wines. You may use a different drive letter and path name, but the innermost directory should be named Wines.

2. Start Database Desktop using the Windows Explorer or Taskbar, or by selecting Delphi's Tools|Database Desktop command. When the Database Desktop window appears, choose the Tools|Alias Manager... command.

3. Click the New button to create a new alias. Enter the alias name, **WINES**, and make sure Driver Type is set to STANDARD (the default).

4. Click the Browse button, and in the resulting Directory Browser dialog, choose the drive letter and directories to locate the C:\Database\Wines path (or, you can simply type that path name into the Directories edit box). Click OK to close the Directory Browser dialog.

5. Click Keep New and then click OK to close the Alias Manager window. When asked whether to save Public Aliases in IDAPI32.CFG, answer Yes.

The following section describes how to create a new, empty Wines database. If you followed the preceding steps, skip to "Database Components."

Creating the Wines database

The following notes explain how to create a new, empty Wines database. This helps you learn how to use Database Desktop to create your own database tables.

The first step is to create a place to store the files. The exact file and directory names are up to you, but on my system, I used the Windows Explorer to create a directory, D:\Database\Wines (you can use a different drive letter and path name if you prefer). After creating the directory, follow these steps to create an alias for the database path, and to create the table files:

1. Start Database Desktop using the Windows Explorer or Taskbar, or by selecting Delphi's Tools|Database Desktop command. When the Database Desktop window appears, choose the Tools|Alias Manager... command.

2. Click the New button to create a new alias. Enter the alias name — it can be any string, but is usually the same as the directory or network file in which the database is located. For example, enter **WINES** as an alias for a database you might use for keeping track of a wine cellar's inventory.

3. Set Driver Type to STANDARD (the default value) unless you are creating a client-server database, in which case you may select INTRBASE. (On a minimum Delphi installation, only STANDARD is available.)

4. Click the Browse button, and pull down the "Drive (or Alias)" ComboBox control. Choose D: (or the drive letter you used to create the Wines directory), and then double-click Database followed by Wines in the path list box above. The Directories field should read "D:\Database\Wines."

5. Click the OK button to close the directory browser. Figure 17-10 shows the Database Desktop display at this stage. Click OK and answer Yes when prompted whether to save the public aliases in IDAPI32.CFG. You can now refer to the WINES alias in Delphi applications rather than hard code drive and path names to this database.

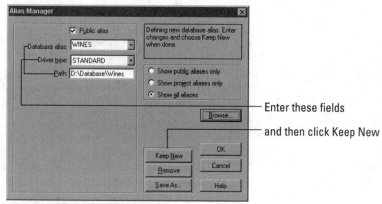

Figure 17-10: The WINES alias and path registered by Database Desktop

Registering the WINES alias and creating a place to store the files does not create the actual files for storing database information. To do that, follow the next steps, which create a flat-file database for a simple wine-cellar inventory:

1. Start Database Desktop if it is not already running.

2. Select File|New and choose the Table... submenu command. You see a list of available database formats. Select Paradox 7, the default. (When creating a new database, Paradox is probably the best choice — it offers the most numbers of field data types and also sophisticated key indexing capabilities. Of course, you may choose any other database format such as dBASE or Intrbase if you prefer.)

3. You now see the main entry screen for inserting and editing fields. Enter field names, types (press the space bar for a list), a size for alphabetic fields, and an asterisk (you can type any character) to indicate a primary key field on which the database is indexed. Table 17-1 lists some sample fields. (This is only a demonstration, and a real wine-cellar database would have many more fields.) Figure 17-11 shows the completed database table structure in Database Desktop.

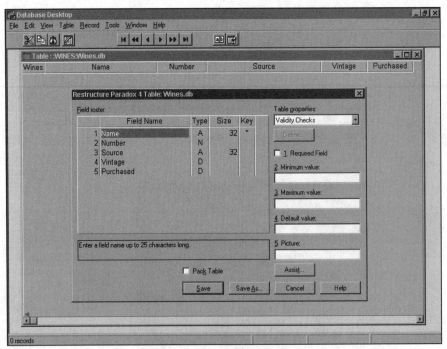

Figure 17-11: The completed Wines.db database table structure in Database Desktop

4. After entering your fields, click the Save As button. Enter **Wines** into the Filename edit box, and then choose an alias for referring to the new database table. Select the WINES alias that you created earlier (WINES), and then click Save to create the table and any associated files such as indexes depending on the database driver you selected in Step 2. If you are following along, you should now have two files, Wines.db and Wines.px in the \Database\Wines directory.

Database Components

After creating a new database or choosing an existing one for which you have registered an alias, you are ready to write a Delphi application to insert, edit, and view the database's information. As mentioned, one way to begin is to use the Database Form Wizard (use File|New...., click the Business page tab, and double-click Database Form Wizard).

Table 17-1
Sample Wine-Cellar Database Fields

Field name	Type	Size	Key
Name	Alpha	32	*
Number	Number		
Source	Alpha	32	
Vintage	Date		
Purchased	Date		

However, as explained next, you may construct database applications from scratch by inserting component objects into a form. You don't have to use the wizard. Performing these steps yourself also teaches you about what various database components do and how they interact. Even if you plan to use the Database Form Wizard, you must understand these relationships to successfully program database applications.

Tip

Because Delphi generates numerous files that you don't need to deploy to end users with your finished applications, it's probably best to create separate directories for databases and their applications.

Data Access components

The components on the Data Access palette provide access to database tables. Think of Data Access components as *gateways* to database information. In most cases, you need instances of the two components, Table and DataSource. The other Data Access components perform SQL operations such as lookups (Query), and execute global operations such as updating all fields in matching records (BatchMove). The Database and Session components are used automatically as needed to organize access to database tables — you won't need these components unless you are creating advanced software to perform tasks such as accessing multiple communication links. You probably won't need the StoredProc and UpdateSQL components unless you are developing client-server databases.

Note

Early versions of Delphi included the ReportSmith program and the Report component for generating database reports. These items are replaced by the extensive report-generation components on the QReport palette. See the next chapter for more information on these components and also the TDBChart component.

The first component you normally insert into a form is a Table. This object creates a bridge between an application and a database alias as shown in Figure 17-12. In addition to a Table, you need a DataSource object, which links data-aware controls to the database. The DataSource object feeds data to and from other objects and the Table. The Table object handles the actual transactions for the database.

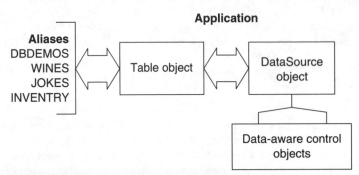

Figure 17-12: A Table object forms a bridge between the application and a database, identified by a registered alias. A Data Source object links the Table with data-aware controls such as DBEdit and DBNavigator.

These actions between a Table, DataSource, and a data-aware control, take place courtesy of the Borland Database Engine (BDE), which performs the real work of reading and writing data in the proper format. The data-aware controls might be additionally linked to create interactive data-entry screens. For example, linking a DBNavigator object to a DataSource, which is connected to a Table, creates a browsing toolbar that you can use to view, edit, insert, and delete records displayed in DBEdit and other control windows. Until you get used to which objects link to others, these relationships may seem overly complex. However, after you create one or two sample applications, you find that data-entry screens fit together as easily as a child's building blocks.

Follow these steps to create Table, DataSource, and data-aware control objects for entering and viewing information in the sample wine-cellar database (you can also use these instructions with any other database on your system):

1. Start a new application by selecting File | New Application. This time, I don't use the Database Form Wizard — I construct the necessary code the hard way.

2. Insert Table and DataSource objects from the Data Access palette into the form. These are displayed as icons that do not appear at run time. I use Delphi's default Names for all objects in this demonstration, but in your own programs, you may want to assign descriptive Name properties to the objects. (I strongly suggest using the words Table and Source in these names. For example, MasterTable and NamesSource are good object names.)

Tip

You can place nonvisual components such as Tables and DataSources into a data module rather than in a visible form window. You can also use data modules to build common database-access modules that multiple applications can share. See "Using Data Modules" in this chapter for more information.

3. Select the Table1 object, and in the Object Inspector's Properties, click the arrow next to the DatabaseName property. This drops down a list of registered database names and aliases. Select WINES or another listed name.

4. Remember that a database may be composed of one or more tables, also called datasets. Even though our sample wine-cellar database has only one dataset table, in addition to a DatabaseName alias, you also have to specify a TableName. Select the TableName property for the Table1 object, and choose Wines.db or another table name. Remember: All Table objects must specify DatabaseName and TableName properties.

5. Next, select the DataSource1 object. Link it to Table1 by selecting Table1 from the DataSet property's drop-down list. With this step, you have completed the bare-minimum requirements for connecting an application to a database, and you can now insert data-aware controls in the form for viewing and editing database information. Remember: All DataSource objects must be linked through the DataSet property to a Table object.

6. One component you almost always use is DBNavigator. Select that component from the Data Controls palette, and insert it into the form at a convenient location, somewhere near the top border. Specify the DataSource1 object for the DBNavigator's DataSource property. This tells the data-aware control where to get its data. Because the dataset is not open at this time, setting the DataSource property causes the DBNavigator's buttons to be disabled. Remember: All data-aware controls must be linked via the DataSource property to a DataSource object.

7. To provide a platform for viewing and editing database information, insert a DBGrid object from the Data Controls palette into the form. Specify DataSource1 as the DBGrid1 object's DataSource property. Resize and position the controls and the window as you want. Figure 17-13 shows the developing application's form window at this stage in Delphi.

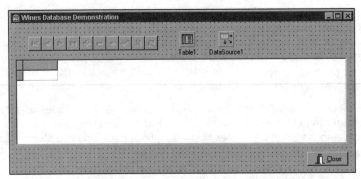

Figure 17-13: The developing form shows the bare-minimum components required for a typical database application.

8. Now get ready for some magic. Select the Table1 object, and double-click the Active property to change its value to True. This opens the database table inside the developing application—you don't have to run the program. You see the database table's field names in the DBGrid object, and if the table has any information, you see that as well. The DBGrid object is now an *active control,* and the database is open at this time. It's convenient to have live data available when designing database applications—for example, you can more easily size components to display a table's information—but you may set Active to False to close the table. In that case, you can insert the following assignment into the form's OnCreate event handler (or another procedure) to open the database and table at run time:

```
Table1.Open;  // Open database and table
```

Caution

Database Desktop cannot restructure a table that is open. If you cannot open a table using Database Desktop, switch back to Delphi and set the Table object's Active field to False. Or, save and close your application, and then try using Database Desktop again.

9. Figure 17-14 shows the completed WinesDemo application.

On the CD-ROM

In many cases, you use a DBGrid object to view and edit database table information. But this isn't the only way to go—you can also build data-entry forms using a variety of data-aware controls. For example, using DBEdit objects, you can build a database entry form that shows one record at a time. Figure 17-15 shows one possible arrangement of controls for the Wines.db table. The finished application is on the CD-ROM in the Source\WinesEntry directory—open the WinesEntry.dpr project file in that directory and press F9 to compile and run the program. (The program has no user programming, and is not listed here.)

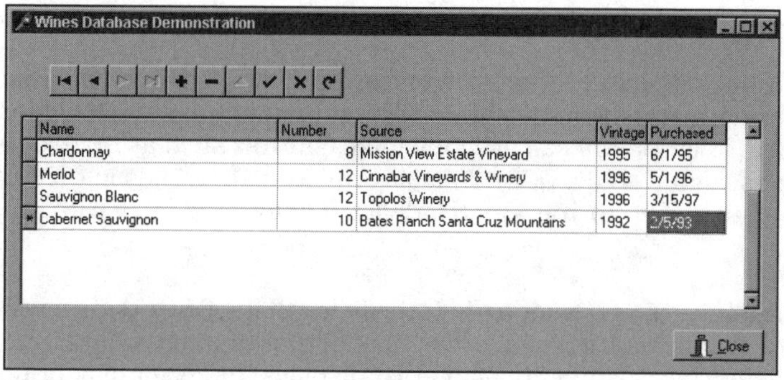

Figure 17-14: This is the completed WinesDemo application.

To create the WinesEntry program shown in the figure, I added Table and DataSource objects to a new form. I then selected the Table, and I set its DatabaseName property to the WINES alias and its TableName property to Wines.db. I selected the DataSource object and set its DataSet property to Table1. After these steps, I inserted a DBNavigator control and five DBEdit objects along with Labels and a Button as shown in Figure 17-14. The DBNavigator and DBEdit objects' DataSource field is set to DataSource1. Each DBEdit object's DataField property is set to a different field name in the Wine.db table. Finally, I selected the Table1 object and changed its Active property to True. I then pressed F9 to compile and run the finished program.

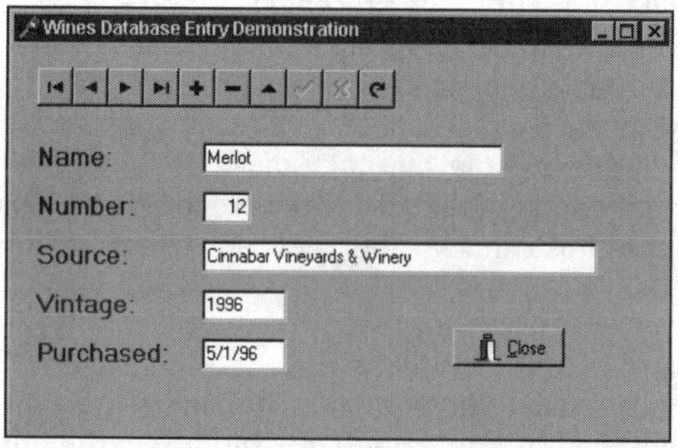

Figure 17-15: In place of DBGrid, this version of the Wines database application uses DBEdit fields to edit and display database information one record at a time.

Data-aware controls

When designing data-entry forms, you must decide which fields you want to display in which positions. You have two basic choices: you can use a DBGrid for a row-and-column display, or you can use individual controls such as DBText, DBEdit, and DBMemo for selected fields. DBGrid displays all available fields in their physical order by default. It's up to you which individual fields to display with other data-aware controls.

Many times, however, you want to limit the fields that a DBGrid displays, or you may want to change their column order. In addition, you may want to create a *calculated field.* This is a phantom field that displays the result of a formula using values in other cells. You can carry out these tasks by modifying the virtual fields that the Table component provides from the dataset's physical fields. A virtual field could display a portion or modified version of a physical field — for example, a person's last name or the full spelling of a state abbreviation.

To perform these types of actions, rather than use the physical fields in a table, you can instruct the Table component to build a set of field objects that, in essence, overlay physical dataset columns. Some columns can directly translate from the physical column to the overlay — you can, for example, tell the Table component to use a Name field as it exists in the dataset. Other columns can be whatever you like. These "phantom" columns might calculate values based on other fields, or they might display information formatted in some special way using the raw data from the table.

Try these concepts using the Wines database from the preceding section — or you can use the Database Form Wizard to create a sample application for any dataset table. To edit the table's fields, double-click the Table1 object in the form. (The completed files for this section are on the CD-ROM in the Source\WinesCalc directory.) As shown in Figures 17-16 and 17-17, double-clicking a Table object displays the component's Fields editor which begins as an empty window labeled in this case Mainform.Table1. Right-click while pointing the cursor to this window. This pops up a menu with two enabled commands:

✦ **Add Fields** — Use this command to add physical dataset columns to the Table object. If, for example, you want to use a Name field as it is in the dataset file, use Add Fields to select it. If you do not add a field, it is hidden in the final output — in a DBGrid object, for example. Each added field is represented as an object in the form's class. Figure 17-16 shows the Add Fields dialog.

Figure 17-16: Add Fields dialog

✦ **New Field**—Use this command to create new, phantom fields, which can be one of three types: Data, Calculated, or Lookup. *Data fields* are usually translated from raw data in the dataset file. For example, you might create a data field to display raw uppercase strings in uppercase and lowercase. *Calculated fields* trigger an event handler that you can use to perform calculations (or any other operation) using other field values. A calculated field, for instance, might display the number of elapsed days between two dates (more on this later). The third type of New Field you can create is called a *lookup field*. This obtains information from another dataset—the name of a company, for example, given a customer ID number. Each new field is represented as an object in the form's class. Figure 17-17 shows the New Field dialog.

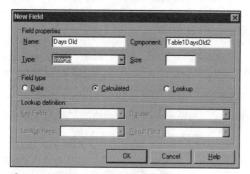

Figure 17-17: New Field dialog

To create the sample WinesCalc demonstration, which shows how to create calculated fields, I double-clicked the Table1 object in a copy of the WinesDemo application, and then used the Add Fields command to add the Name, Source, Vintage, and Purchased columns to the Table1 object. Because I did not select the Number field, it is hidden in the final grid. (See Figure 17-16).

I next used the New Field command to create a calculated field named Days Old, of type Integer. In the program, this field is represented as the Table1DaysOld object of type TIntegerField. (See Figure 17-17).

Note   The changes you make with the Fields editor do not modify the physical dataset, so don't be nervous about experimenting. Use the Add button to reinstate any fields you deleted. (Try this: Click Clear all, and answer Yes to the prompt that asks if you want to delete all field components. Then click Add and OK to add the fields back again. As you can see, deletions are not permanent.) Each field is declared in the form as a component of a dataset field type—TStringField, TFloatField, TDateField, and others. Using the Fields editor reprograms these object declarations.

Each field in a Table dataset becomes an object in the form's class. Use the Object Inspector to modify the properties of these objects the same way you program values for other component objects. For example, if you are following along, select the Table1Name object in the Object Inspector's drop-down list, and change the object's ReadOnly property to True. Users are then unable to make changes to values in this field.

Tip   To select a field object, double-click the Table component in the form, and select the object by its column name. Or, you can select the object using the Object Inspector's drop-down list. Either way, after selecting an object, use the Object Inspector window to modify the field object's properties.

The Fields editor programs the number, the names, and the types of data fields that a Table component makes available to a DataSource object. It is still your responsibility to perform the actual calculations, or to insert values into any virtual fields that you add. Adding a field using the Fields editor does not create a new column in the dataset table—use Database Desktop to make changes to a table's physical information. The Fields editor reshapes that information for use in the application.

For example, given a dataset with two Date fields, you might want to display the number of days between them. It would be pointless to store this information in the database because it could potentially change every day for every record. This is a perfect example of the kind of field that the application should calculate. Follow these steps:

1. Reinsert a DBGrid object, if necessary, into the sample application and set its DataSource property to DataSource1. Set Table1's Active property to True to display the sample database in the grid. Repeat the instructions in the preceding section if you experience trouble, or if you didn't save the project.

2. Double-click the Table1 object to open the Fields editor. Right-click while pointing to the editor window, and select the Add Fields command. Choose

the Name, Source, Vintage, and Purchased fields. (You may use a different database for these steps — any dataset with at least one date field is fine.) Refer back to Figure 17-16. Click OK to close this window.

Tip

If you add a field by mistake, right-click to bring up the editor's pop-up menu and select Delete to delete the field. This deletes only the object that represents the field. The actual dataset in the file is never changed.

3. Right-click pointing into the Fields editor and select the New Field command (refer back to Figure 17-17). Enter a Name such as **Days Old** for the new field, which must differ from other field names. As shown in Figure 17-17, you see the component object name (Table1DaysOld) in the second edit window. This is the name of the object as declared in the form's class — you can modify the automatically generated name at this time, or you can use the Object Inspector later on to change the object's Name property.

4. Select a Field type for this new virtual field. In this example, IntegerField is appropriate. This option designates the data type, such as TStringField and TIntegerField, for declaring the object in the form class. (Each field becomes a component object in the form.)

5. Be sure the Calculated radio button is selected, and then click OK to add the new field to the Table1 object. You can then close the Fields editor or shove its window aside. Notice that the DBGrid object now displays a new column labeled Days Old. (Drag the vertical bar to the right of the Name column to shorten this field and make the other columns visible if necessary.) Also examine the form's class declaration, which now includes an object declaration for the new virtual field:

```
Table1DaysOld: TIntegerField;
```

6. It's up to you to provide the programming that calculates the new field's value. Do that by selecting the Table1DaysOld object using the Object Inspector's drop-down list. (You cannot select this component in the form because dataset fields have no visual representation.) Select the Object Inspector's Events page, and then double-click the OnGetText event to create an empty event handler procedure. Enter the following code into the procedure (the entire procedure is listed here for reference — if you are following along, you need to enter only the single statement between *begin* and *end*):

```
{ Calculate the Days Old virtual field using today's
  date (returned by the SysUtils Date function) and
  the value of the database table's Purchased value. }
procedure TMainForm.Table1DaysOldGetText(Sender: TField;
  var Text: String; DisplayText: Boolean);
begin
  Text := FloatToStr(Date - Table1Purchased.Value);
end;
```

7. Press F9 to compile and run the program and display the calculated fields. The completed WinesCalc sample application is on the CD-ROM in the Source\WinesCals directory.

Data-aware controls trigger the OnGetText event to obtain a field's information. In the event handler in the above code, assign to the Text parameter the data you want to display. In this example, the program calculates the number of days between today and the Purchased date field. The Date function from the SysUtils unit returns today's date as a floating-point value. The Purchased field is referenced through the Value property of the field object, Table1Purchased. This is one of the objects you added to the Table component using the Fields editor's Add Field command.

The type of a field object's Value property depends on the object — in this case, for TDateField objects, Value is a floating-point data type. To calculate the number of days that have elapsed between today and the field value, the program simply subtracts their values and passes the result to Delphi's FloatToStr function. This result is assigned to the variable Text parameter, which is used to display the calculated value in the DBGrid object. Figure 17-18 shows the final program with the calculated Days Old column at far right in the database grid.

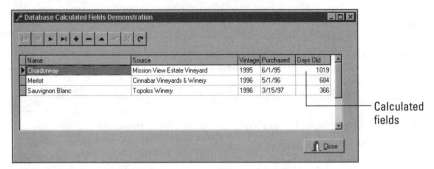

Calculated fields

Figure 17-18: Final WinesCalc application with the calculated Days Old column

Tip

Calculated fields that generate exceptions may create an endless loop of error messages. If you can't seem to get rid of the errors — which is common because closing the error dialog attempts to redisplay the window, which recalculates the faulty field, which generates another exception — switch over to Delphi, select Tools|Environment Options..., and in the Debugger page of the resulting dialog, select Delphi Exceptions and select the User Program button under Handled By. (In Delphi 3 and earlier versions, the equivalent option was the Break on Exception check box, selected by the Environment|Tools Options command.) Because you are running the program in the Delphi debugger, setting this option works even for an executing application. This should halt the endless errors and return you to Delphi. You may also have to select

Program Reset (Ctrl+F2) in the Run menu. Don't reboot until you try these recovery steps. Eventually, however, you still may have to reboot, but ending the process ought to reclaim any orphaned memory blocks if you are using Windows 95 or 98. You probably would not have to reboot under Windows NT, which provides superior memory handling. Note that this technique works only when you run an application from inside Delphi.

The Blob

One of my favorite horror movies of old is *The Blob,* a black-and-white screamer featuring a monster whose slimy goo quickly reduces its victims to sizzling stains on the ground. Judging from this movie's quality, its operating budget was probably not much more than the cost of a case of gelatin and a can of lighter fluid. I happen to suspect this because those are the materials we used to create our own blobs in the alley. Don't tell my mother.

Fortunately, Delphi's Blob fields aren't so horrific, and not nearly as gooey. In case you've forgotten, this kind of Blob is an acronym for a *Binary Large Object.* In a database table, a Blob field can store any kind of data, but is typically used for graphics images. For example, a real estate database might use Blob fields to store pictures of properties for sale.

The Fishy application on the CD-ROM, in the Source\Fishy directory, demonstrates how to use Blob fields. Figure 17-19 shows the Fishy application's display. Listing 17-1 shows the program's source code. To compile and run the program, you must have installed Delphi's demo files, specifically the ones in the Demos\Data path. There should be a DBDEMOS alias registered for this database. If you can't get the Fishy application to work, use Database Desktop as explained in this chapter to locate the DBDEMOS alias. If you can't find this alias, reinstall Delphi.

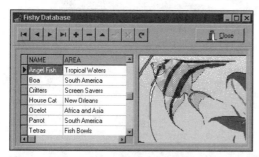

Figure 17-19: The Fishy application demonstrates Delphi's capability to read and write Blob fields in databases. In this case, the Blob is the bitmap image shown at right in the program's window.

Listing 17-1: **Fishy\Main.pas**

```pascal
unit Main;

interface

uses
  SysUtils, Windows, Messages, Classes, Graphics, Controls,
  Dialogs, StdCtrls, Forms, DBCtrls, DB, DBGrids, DBTables,
  Grids, Buttons, ExtCtrls;

type
  TMainForm = class(TForm)
    ScrollBox: TScrollBox;
    DBNavigator: TDBNavigator;
    Panel1: TPanel;
    DataSource1: TDataSource;
    Panel2: TPanel;
    Table1: TTable;
    DBImage1: TDBImage;
    DBGrid1: TDBGrid;
    Table1NAME: TStringField;
    Table1AREA: TStringField;
    Table1BMP: TBlobField;
    BitBtn1: TBitBtn;
    procedure FormCreate(Sender: TObject);
    procedure DBImage1DblClick(Sender: TObject);
  private
    { private declarations }
  public
    { public declarations }
  end;

var
  MainForm: TMainForm;

implementation

{$R *.DFM}

{- Open the Table1 dataset }
procedure TMainForm.FormCreate(Sender: TObject);
begin
  Table1.Open;
end;

{- Respond to double-click in Blob image }
procedure TMainForm.DBImage1DblClick(Sender: TObject);
begin
```

```
    with DBImage1.Picture do
        ShowMessage('W=' + IntToStr(Width) +
            ' H=' + IntToStr(Height));
    end;

    end.
```

There's not much to the Fishy application's listing — most of the program is handled by its component objects. To create the program, I used the Database Form Wizard, opened the DBDEMOS alias, and selected the Animals.dbf file. After the wizard created the form, I shuffled the components around and I added a DBImage object to display the bitmap Blob field, labeled BMP in the Animals dataset table. Tip: To try your hand at creating your own version of this program, set the DBImage object's DataSource property to DataSource1, and set DataField to BMP. The rest is straightforward.

To illustrate how you can program interactive events for database information, the Fishy program implements an OnDblClick event for the DBImage1 object. I used the code shown at the end of the listing to determine how large to make the final Blob window (200×160 in this case). Run the program, and then double-click a Blob image to see these values. In a more extensive application, you might implement this same event to load a bitmap image, or to run a bitmap editor for creating and modifying bitmap images stored in databases. Use DBImage1.Picture as shown in the sample listing to access the bitmap.

Structured Query Language

The structured query language (SQL) is an industry-standard data access and manipulation language, first developed in 1986 by The American National Standards Institute (ANSI). Because it has no control structures, SQL is not correctly thought of as a programming language. However, SQL defines program-like commands such as SELECT, JOIN, and UPDATE for performing operations on database tables. SQL is archaic and difficult to use, but almost all databases support at least a subset of the language, so you can benefit from knowing how to use it.

Note

Some pronounce SQL as "sequel"; others say "S, Q, L." Many more call it other terms I wouldn't dare repeat here.

Because Delphi and the BDE perform most database services, unless you are developing client-server applications for remote SQL databases, you probably need to learn only one SQL command: SELECT. As I explain in this section, you can use this command to perform many different types of searches on the information stored in database tables.

The BDE supports a subset of the SQL standard for Paradox, dBase, Oracle, and other databases. If your database tables are in one of the supported formats, you may use the self-explanatory SQL commands SELECT, INSERT, UPDATE, and DELETE to perform these operations. Other SQL servers provide additional commands — consult your server's documentation for the exact commands you can use.

The Query component

Database applications use a Query component to issue SQL statements to a database. You need one Query object for each database to which you post SQL commands. In Delphi applications, you mostly use Query objects to perform searches based on arguments such as "all persons with brown eyes who were born on Tuesday and belong to a bowling league" and other earth-shaking criteria.

An instance of the Query component resembles a Table object because the Query component provides a gateway to a database through a registered alias. In addition to a Query component, you need a DataSource object to link Queries with data-aware controls. The controls typically show the results of executed SQL commands.

Building an SQL editor

On the CD-ROM

The SQLPlay application on the CD-ROM, in the Source\SQLPlay directory, provides a starting place for building an editor to issue SQL commands to a selected database. This shows how to issue and respond to SQL commands using the Query component. The program also demonstrates how to interrogate the BDE for all database aliases and table names — you want to do this in your own applications to provide a means for users to select available database tables.

Run the SQLPlay application now by loading SQLPlay.dpr into Delphi and pressing F9. Figure 17-20 shows the program's main window before opening any database tables.

Click SQLPlay's Open button to display the dialog box shown in Figure 17-21. Use this dialog to select a database and table such as DBDEMOS and CUSTOMER, and then click OK to return to the program's main window.

Enter SQL commands into the Memo box below the DBGrid object that shows database information. Click Perform to execute your commands. For example, open the DBDEMOS database and the Customer table. Then, edit the Memo window's command to the following lines, which search for all customers in California. Click Perform or press Alt+P to issue the SQL command for the database table:

```
Select * From CUSTOMER
  where State="CA"
```

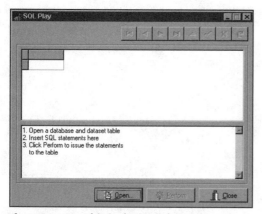

Figure 17-20: This is the SQLPlay program's display before opening a database table.

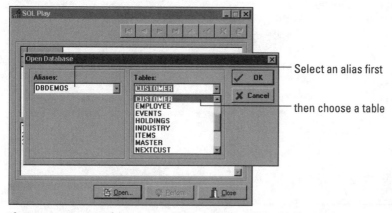

Select an alias first

then choose a table

Figure 17-21: SQLPlay's Open dialog lists available database aliases and tables.

Listing 17-2 shows SQLPlay's dialog module, Open.pas. This unit demonstrates how to obtain all registered database aliases and their dataset table names and how to present that information in drop-down lists from which users can select a database table to edit and view.

Listing 17-2: **SQLPlay\Open.pas**

```pascal
unit Open;

interface

uses
  Windows, Messages, SysUtils, Classes, Graphics, Controls,
  Forms, Dialogs, StdCtrls, Buttons, ExtCtrls, Db, DbTables;

type
  TOpenForm = class(TForm)
    OKBtn: TBitBtn;
    CancelBtn: TBitBtn;
    Bevel1: TBevel;
    ComboBox1: TComboBox;
    Label1: TLabel;
    Bevel2: TBevel;
    Label2: TLabel;
    ComboBox2: TComboBox;
    procedure FormActivate(Sender: TObject);
    procedure ComboBox1Change(Sender: TObject);
  private
    { Private declarations }
  public
    { Public declarations }
  end;

var
  OpenForm: TOpenForm;

implementation

{$R *.DFM}

procedure TOpenForm.FormActivate(Sender: TObject);
begin
  Session.GetAliasNames(ComboBox1.Items);
end;

procedure TOpenForm.ComboBox1Change(Sender: TObject);
begin
  Session.GetTableNames(ComboBox1.Text, '*.*',
    False, False, ComboBox2.Items);
  ComboBox2.ItemIndex := 0;
end;

end.
```

On the form's activation (see procedure FormActivate, the event handler for this form's OnActivate event), the dialog box unit calls GetAliasNames to obtain a string list of database aliases from the BDE. This method—and several others—are provided by the TSession class. To use this object, add Db to the module's *uses* clause, and call TSession methods in reference to the Session object, which Delphi creates automatically for all database applications. GetAliasNames clears and inserts alias names into a TStrings property or a TStringList object. Here, the program uses the method to initialize ComboBox1's items.

Because the table names depend on which alias the user selects, the second ComboBox object cannot be initialized in FormActivate. Instead, after the user selects a database, the ComboBox1Change procedure—triggered when the control's edit window changes—calls another TSession method, GetTableNames, to fill in ComboBox2's information. TSession declares GetTableNames and its five parameters as follows:

```
procedure GetTableNames(const DatabaseName, Pattern: string;
   Extensions, SystemTables: Boolean; List: Tstrings);
```

✦ **DatabaseName**—This is the name of a database or alias such as DBDEMOS.

✦ **Pattern**—Set this to a filename filter such as *.db to restrict table names to matching files.

✦ **Extensions**—Set to True if you want the returned names to include filename extensions. This parameter is meaningful only for desktop database applications.

✦ **SystemTables**—Set to True to obtain system tables as well as to use datasets from a remote server. This parameter is meaningful only for client-server database applications.

✦ **List**—Pass any TStrings property or TStringList object to this parameter. GetTableNames clears the list and inserts dataset table names into the list. The sample application uses this parameter to initialize ComboBox2's Items property, an object of type TStrings. Setting that object's ItemIndex to zero displays the first listed entry in the combo box's edit window.

Listing 17-3 shows SQLPlay's main module, which performs the SQL commands and displays selected database tables. After the listing, I explain how the main form's component objects cooperate to show the results of a database search in the DBGrid object (you can use the same methods for any data-aware controls).

Listing 17-3: **SQLPlay\Main.pas**

```pascal
unit Main;

interface

uses
  SysUtils, Windows, Messages, Classes, Graphics, Controls,
  Forms, Dialogs, StdCtrls, Buttons, ExtCtrls, Grids,
  DBGrids, DBCtrls, DB, DBTables, Open;

type
  TMainForm = class(TForm)
    DataSource1: TDataSource;
    DBNavigator1: TDBNavigator;
    DBGrid1: TDBGrid;
    Memo1: TMemo;
    Bevel1: TBevel;
    PerformBitBtn: TBitBtn;
    CloseBitBtn: TBitBtn;
    OpenBitBtn: TBitBtn;
    Query1: TQuery;
    procedure OpenBitBtnClick(Sender: TObject);
    procedure PerformBitBtnClick(Sender: TObject);
    procedure FormClose(Sender: TObject;
      var Action: TCloseAction);
  private
    { Private declarations }
  public
    { Public declarations }
  end;

var
  MainForm: TMainForm;

implementation

{$R *.DFM}

procedure TMainForm.OpenBitBtnClick(Sender: TObject);
begin
  if OpenForm.ShowModal = mrOk then
  begin
    Query1.Close;
    try
      Query1.DatabaseName := OpenForm.ComboBox1.Text;
      Query1.SQL.Clear;
      Query1.SQL.Add('Select * From ' +
        OpenForm.ComboBox2.Text);
```

```
        Memo1.Lines := Query1.SQL;
        Query1.Open;
        Memo1.SetFocus;
        PerformBitBtn.Enabled := True;
      except;
        ShowMessage('Unable to open database');
      end;
    end;
end;

procedure TMainForm.PerformBitBtnClick(Sender: TObject);
begin
  Query1.Close;
  try
    Query1.SQL := Memo1.Lines;
    Query1.Open;
  except
    ShowMessage('Invalid query');
  end;
end;

procedure TMainForm.FormClose(Sender: TObject;
  var Action: TCloseAction);
begin
  Query1.Close;
end;

end.
```

In the main program's listing, procedure OpenBitBtnClick displays OpenForm's window by calling ShowModal. If the user ends the dialog by clicking OK, the program closes the Query1 object to prepare for opening a new database. Query objects operate like Tables, but they can also execute SQL statements. This takes a few setup statements. First, the program assigns DatabaseName from the dialog's ComboBox1 edit window. Then, two statements are needed to clear the current SQL string list in the Query object, and call Add to insert a statement such as:

```
Select * From Animals
```

The SQL Select command searches a dataset such as Animals for matching entries. The asterisk selects all columns (or fields) of the Animals table. Because no WHERE clause was used to restrict the selection of rows, all rows (or records) in the Animals table are included in the result set. To enable you to edit the SQL commands, the program assigns Query1's SQL property to a Memo object. The program then calls Open for Query1, which issues the SQL statement to the dataset.

Note

Calling Open for a Query object issues only the Select SQL command. For other SQL commands such as Insert and Delete, call the ExecSQL method.

The PerformBitBtnClick procedure executes the SQL commands that you enter into the Memo window. First, the program closes the Query1 object. (Always close Queries and Tables before making significant changes to their properties.) Assign a TStrings or TStringList object to the SQL property, and then Open the database to issue the command, which in this example must be Select.

To experiment with SQLPlay, run the program and open the DBDEMOS database. Select the HOLDINGS dataset table. Click OK to get back to the program's main window, and click inside the Memo pad. Edit the default SQL statement to the following, and press Alt+P to perform the command, which searches the dataset for all holdings in which shares are greater than 10,000:

```
Select * From HOLDINGS
where shares >10000
```

You can continue to refine a search. For example, add another restriction, as follows, below the preceding two lines to display shares greater than 10,000 and having a purchase price more than $50. Figure 17-22 shows the resulting window. (The SQLPlay application on the CD-ROM demonstrates how to issue and respond to SQL commands.)

```
and pur_Price > 50
```

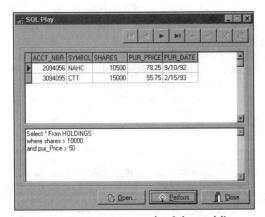

Figure 17-22: Here, a search of the Holdings DBDEMOS table is shown for records with shares greater than 10000, and purchase price greater than $50.

Note   After opening a database with SQLPlay's Open button, you may choose another dataset table without reopening the dialog. For example, replace all lines in the Memo window with Select * From Animals, and press Alt+P to open the Animals table and display all of its records.

Master-Detail Databases

Most databases are relational, which simply means they have two or more tables that are related by common fields. For example, a Customer table might have an ID field that is also used in the Purchases table to identify each purchase that a specific customer has made. This setup is called a one-to-many relationship. Individual records are uniquely identified by a key (the ID field) in the master table (Customer). One or more related records are linked to customers in the detail table (Purchases). This relationship is called the *master-detail model*.

Understanding the master-detail model

Delphi comes with several useful examples of master-detail database tables. For a sample, run the SQLPlay application from the preceding section and open the DBDEMOS database alias. Select the MASTER table and click OK to return to the main window. The DBGrid object lists various stocks, each uniquely identified by a primary key named SYMBOL.

Now, enter this SQL statement into the Memo window:

```
Select * From HOLDINGS
where SYMBOL = "SMC"
```

Press Alt+P to perform the statement and select all HOLDINGS with the symbol SMC. The master table has only one such entry; the detail table may have several records, one for each purchase of this particular stock. Figure 17-23 shows SQLPlay's window after performing this search.

Programming master-detail applications

The MasterSource and MasterFields properties of the Table component define master-detail relationships in Delphi database applications. Use these properties as follows:

✦ **MasterSource** — For the detail Table object, assign the name of a DataSource component object linked to a master Table. Leave this property blank in the master Table object.

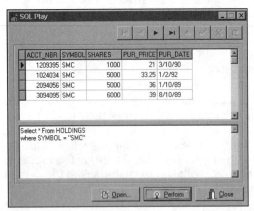

Figure 17-23: SQLPlay after searching HOLDINGS on the common SYMBOL field

✦ **MasterFields** — Also for the detail Table object, assign a string with one or more field names to this property, which defines the field (column) over which two tables are connected or joined.

You may specify multiple fields separated by semicolons in the MasterField's string. Here are some sample assignments that show the possible formats:

```
DetailTable.MasterFields := 'Symbol';
DetailTable.MasterFields := 'Symbol;Exchange';
```

Contrary to some accounts, you don't have to specify MasterFields in the master table. Assign a string to this property only in the detail Table object. In addition, specify the detail table's IndexFieldNames or IndexName properties. Always use IndexName when possible because it produces faster lookups. Specify IndexFieldNames when no index exists for the joined field.

For an example of how to create a master-detail database application, run the Master program on the CD-ROM in the Source\Master directory. This program uses the Master and Holdings tables from the DBDEMOS database supplied with Delphi. Figure 17-24 shows the program's display. Click the DBNavigator buttons to browse the Master table and display entries from Holdings with matching Symbol fields. The following code shows the only significant programming in this application: the form's OnCreate event handler, which opens the two database Table objects. Components and their properties take care of all other aspects of this program's operation — a powerful demonstration of Delphi's visual programming capabilities.

```
procedure TMainForm.FormCreate(Sender: TObject);
begin
  MasterTable.Open;
  DetailTable.Open;
end;
```

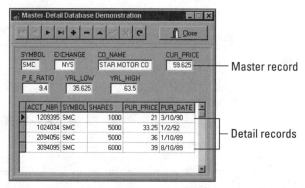

Figure 17-24: Click the DBNavigator buttons to view stocks from the Master table and show any holdings of those stocks in the DBGrid from the detail Holdings table.

Table 17-2 shows significant property values for the Master program's Table and DataSource objects. In general, every master-detail relationship needs two pairs of these objects related by the properties shown in the table. The table also shows a sample data-aware control (EditSYMBOL) linked to MasterSource, and the DetailDBGrid object linked to DetailSource. These items represent the minimum required elements of a master-detail database application. (By the way, I used the Database Form Wizard to begin this application, which I modified by renaming components, inserting the DBGrid object, and making minor adjustments to the display.)

Using Data Modules

It's not uncommon for numerous applications to access the same dataset tables. For example, in a company with an extensive database, you might be required to create dozens of applications for searching, reporting, sorting, and massaging database information. In such cases, it's often a good idea to create a Data Module that defines the rules and regulations for accessing dataset tables. By installing the Data Module in Delphi's Object Repository, you and other programmers can easily begin new database applications.

Table 17-2
The Master Application's Table and DataSource Properties

Component	Name	Property	Value
Table	MasterTable	DatabaseName	DBDEMOS
		TableName	master.dbf
DataSource	MasterSource	DataSet	MasterTable
Table	DetailTable	DatabaseName	DBDEMOS
		IndexName	SYMBOL
		MasterFields	SYMBOL
		MasterSource	MasterSource
		TableName	holdings.dbf
DataSource	DetailSource	DataSet	DetailTable
DBEdit	EditSymbol	DataField	SYMBOL
		DataSource	MasterSource
DBGrid	DetailDBGrid	DataSource	DetailSource

A typical Data Module contains Table, Query, DataSource, and other components that define the database alias, table name, and other properties. Any number of applications can add the Data Module to their project files, and begin using the database tables instantly. This organization also keeps the nonvisual database components in a separate, invisible window, rather than cluttering the design-time form. But the real advantage of using Data Modules is providing multiple applications with the raw materials needed for accessing the database. What's more, if the rules and regulations change—as they so often do—you can simply update the Data Module components and recompile your applications rather than having to reprogram umpteen Table and DataSource objects in each of your programs.

Note   For an introduction on using Data Modules and the Object Repository, see Chapter 3, Introducing Forms, under the section titled "Form Templates."

Follow these steps to create a Data Module for the Wines database in this chapter, and to install it in Delphi's Object Repository (the resulting files are not on the CD-ROM—you must create them to use the information in this section):

1. Provide a directory to store the files. Start a new application, and then select the File | New Data Module command.

2. Use the Object Inspector to change the name of the Data Module to WinesDataModule. You may save all files at this point to establish the target directory — rename the file associated with the Data Module (Unit2.pas in this example) to something sensible such as WinesDM.pas.

3. Bring up the WinesDataModule window again (use the View | Window List command if you can't find it). Into this window, drop a DataSource and a Table component from the Data Access palette. Change the Name property of the DataSource1 object to WinesDataSource. Change the Name property of the Table1 object to WinesTable. Figure 17-25 shows the Data Module window at this stage. The Form1 window is blank and won't be used (however, you could develop it into a test program for this Data Module).

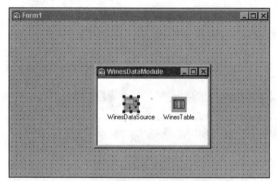

Figure 17-25: The WinesDataModule window with DataSource and Table components

4. You next develop the rules for accessing the database using the Data Module components. First, select the WinesTable object, and in the Object Inspector, click the down arrow next to the DatabaseName property, and select WINES. Similarly, select Wines.db for the TableName property.

5. Select the WinesDataSource object in the Data Module. Then, using the Object Inspectory, set the DataSet property to WinesTable.

6. Save all files by selecting File | Save All or clicking the Save All speed button.

The preceding steps complete the programming of the sample Data Module. In your own applications, you are free to add additional components and set other properties to access your database tables. Although the sample uses only two components, a more complex Data Module might have numerous Table, DataSource, and other database component objects for accessing a variety of database tables.

Tip

Don't bother setting a Table object's Active property to True. This is changed to False when you store the Data Module in the Object Repository.

To make the Data Module available to other applications, add it to Delphi's Object Repository. (I explain how to delete the entry, so don't hesitate to try this out.) Follow these steps to add the Data Module from the preceding steps to the Object Repository:

1. Make the WinesDataModule window visible (use View⎮Window List if necessary to locate the window). Right-click while pointing the mouse cursor inside this window. This brings up a pop-up menu. Select the Add to Repository... command. Figure 17-26 shows the resulting dialog.

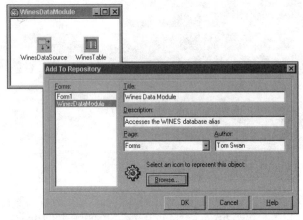

Figure 17-26: The Add to Repository dialog

2. Select WinesDataModule in the list of Forms (it should be selected by default). Enter a Title and Description, and select a Page where you want the Data Module to appear when you select File⎮New.... You can also fill in the Author field and click Browse to select an icon file for displaying an image in the New Items dialog. (I used a sample icon supplied with Delphi in the Images\Icons directory.) Figure 17-26 shows the values I filled in.

3. Click OK to close the Add to Repository dialog. If you did not save the added module, you are prompted to do so before it is incorporated into Delphi's repository.

You can now use the Data Module in any application. This is simple to do — just select it using the File I New... command. Try these steps to test out the Wines Data Module:

1. Start a new application.

2. Select File I New... and click the Forms page tab in the New Items dialog. You should see the newly added Wines Data Module (see Figure 17-27).

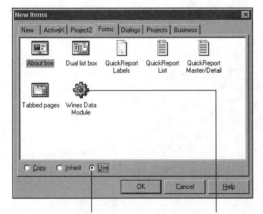

First choose the Use button   and then double-click this icon

Figure 17-27: Select the newly added Wines Data Module from the New Items dialog.

3. Click the button labeled Use near the bottom of the dialog window (refer to Figure 17-27). See the note following these steps for an explanation of the three possible ways to incorporate the module: Copy, Inherit, and Use.

4. Double-click the Wines Data Module icon. This opens a Data Module window in the current application and adds its Pascal source code unit to the code editor window.

5. Switch to the code editor window, and select Unit1 (the source code for the program's main form). Locate the *uses* declaration at the top of the display and modify it as follows (change in bold). This change makes the Data Module, WinesDM (this is the name you saved the module's Pascal source code), available to the main form's unit. Alternatively, you could use Delphi's File I Use Unit command to make this change automatically, but to the host unit's implementation section rather than the interface as shown here:

```
uses
   Windows, Messages, SysUtils, Classes, Graphics, Controls,
   Forms, Dialogs, WinesDM;
```

6. Add DBNavigator and DBGrid components from the Data Controls palette to the main form window. Select both objects (Shift+click each object). In the Object Inspector window, set the DataSource property for both objects to the following (this is the only selection in this example):

```
WinesDataModule.WinesDataSource
```

7. Switch back to the Wines Data Module window (use View\|Window List... if you can't find it). Select the WinesTable object, and use the Object Inspector to set the Active property to True. This opens the Wines database and shows live data in the DBNavigator and DBGrid windows (see Figure 17-28).

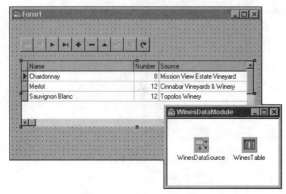

Figure 17-28: This sample program, created by following the numbered steps in this section, uses the Wines Data Module to access the Wines database.

The sample application you just built using the Wines Data Module demonstrates a great way to share database access objects among multiple applications. You don't need Table and DataSource objects in the sample program's main form because these are provided in the Data Module. Other applications can use the same Data Module objects to gain access to the Wines database. If those objects need to be changed — for example, to alter the database alias, table name, or to add phantom fields as explained in this chapter using the Fields editor — you simply recompile your applications to incorporate the changes.

Note

Items in the Object Repository can be added to a project using three options: Copy, Inherit, and Use. (Not all options are available for every type of item — projects, for example, can only be copied.) When you copy an Object Repository item, Delphi makes a complete copy of that item's files in your project's directory. Any changes you make to the item exist only for that copy. When you inherit an item, Delphi builds a new class based on the item's class. With this option, you can make changes to your class, but by recompiling, inherit any changes made to the item in the Object Repository. When you use an item, Delphi simply refers to its files wherever they are stored. Any changes made to the item are reflected in your application when it is compiled. Database Data Modules are typically best inherited or used.

Database Programming Issues

The following sections describes some miscellaneous items about database programming with Delphi that you might find helpful.

TDataSet CacheBlobs property

The TDataSet class now provides a property, CacheBlobs, which you can set True or False. *CacheBlobs* is inherited by all class descendents of TDataSet, such as TBDEDataSet, TTable, TQuery, and TStoredProc.

Set CacheBlobs to True to hold in memory as many Blob fields as possible, even when the associated records are not in memory. Set CacheBlobs to False to discard Blob fields from memory along with other database records.

Normally, CacheBlobs is True. This dramatically improves performance especially in programs that display bitmaps from Blob fields. When the user returns to a record with a cached Blob, it is loaded from memory rather than from the database table on disk or across a network.

When CacheBlobs is False, Blobs are read from the table or network along with other dataset information. If your program does *not* display Blob bitmaps, you can set CacheBlobs to False and improve the program's memory usage. Otherwise, leave CacheBlobs set to True.

TDBDataSet versus TDataSet

In Delphi 4, the TDataSet class is no longer dependent on the BDE. This change has no effect on existing applications, and does not affect the use of TDBDataSet (from which TTable, TQuery, and TStoredProc are derived). However, it is now possible to create TDataSet classes that do not need the BDE for accessing databases. You can, for example, create your own TDataSet class to access a database server without going through the BDE — the BDE does not even have to be installed on the end user's system.

Creating a TDataSet class is a complex job and requires advanced programming skills. The class is abstract, meaning that it cannot be instantiated as an object. To use the new TDataSet class, you must derive a new class and provide the code for its abstract methods. How to do that exactly depends on your database server, and is beyond the scope of this book.

If you need to create your own TDataSet derived class, you can get a head start by studying how Inprise Corporation implements the TBDEDataSet and TDBDataSet classes. Essentially, you need to create similar classes that call your database driver's subroutines rather than using BDE API calls. After completing these steps, which are nontrivial, to say the least, you can build a TTable-like class and use it in your applications. All data-aware controls and DataSource objects work with your derived TDataSet class. This includes TClientDataSet, which is much more simply implemented than TBDEDataSet.

TField IsBlob property

All fields in dataset tables are represented in a Delphi program as objects of the TField class. Type-specific classes such as TStringField and TIntegerField are derived from the TField class.

A relatively new Boolean True or False function, IsBlob, returns True if a TField object is a Blob (remember, this is a Binary Large Object). The function is declared as:

```
class function IsBlob: Boolean; override;
```

In a procedure that declares a TField parameter, you can call IsBlob to determine whether the field is a Blob. This can simplify the task of displaying bitmaps versus displaying text and other values. For example, after using the Fields editor, you can select a TField object from the Object Inspector and create an event handler for an event such as OnGetText. (To open the Fields editor, double-click a Table object, right-click inside the Fields editor window, and use the Add Fields and New Field commands as explained in this chapter).

The event handler can detect whether a field is a Blob and take appropriate action. You might program the event handler along the following lines (this assumes you have written a DisplayAsBlob procedure to display a TBlobField as a bitmap, perhaps with the help of an Image component object in the form):

```
procedure TMainForm.Table1YourFieldNameGetText(Sender: TField;
  var Text: String; DisplayText: Boolean);
begin
```

```
  if Sender.IsBlob then
  begin
    DisplayAsBlob(Sender as TBlobField);
    Text := '';
     else
       Text := Sender.AsString;
end;
```

Expert-User Tips

✦ Consider using DDE to share data among multiple database applications. This is more efficient (and is certainly more user-friendly) than writing data to temporary disk files, which is a common practice. See Chapter 16 for instructions on establishing DDE conversations.

✦ Although mentioned a few times in this chapter, the advice bears repeating — always register alias names using the Database Desktop — never hard code database drive and path name information in your applications. Although this is possible to do, hard-coded path names restrict you from moving database files to new locations, other hard drives, or networks. If you use aliases to access your database tables, you never lose track of where they are when, for example, they must be moved to a new and larger hard drive.

✦ The Database Form Wizard creates a secondary form for a fresh application. To use this form as the program's main window, click the Project Manager's Options button, and specify the form under Main form. You can then use the Project Manager to delete the project's blank form.

✦ The Windows ODBC driver for Access is designed for use with Microsoft Office. To create Access database applications with Delphi, you must acquire the full ODBC Desktop Driver. The driver is available from Microsoft and on the ODBC SDK, which includes drivers for Access, Btrieve, dBASE, Excel, Fox, Paradox, and Text databases.

✦ To distribute a database application, you need to supply your program's .exe code file (plus any supporting data files) and the Inprise Corporation Database Engine. See the Redist.txt file provided with Delphi for information on the necessary files to provide your end users.

Projects to Try

17-1: Write a single-table name-and-address database application. Or think up some other simple application. Use the Database Form Wizard to create a suitable viewer and editor.

17-2: Expand your name-and-address database to include a unique identifying number for each record. Program additional tables and develop master-detail relationships. For example, rather than store important dates such as birthdays and anniversaries directly in the master records, create a Dates detail table linked to the master names. With this setup, any name can have a potentially unlimited number of important dates. You save disk space as well, by not reserving space in records for which you don't need to record dates.

17-3: Use this chapter's SQLPlay application to explore other datasets in Delphi's supplied DBDEMOS database. Experiment with SQL Select commands to search for records with specified field values.

17-4: Try other Database Form Wizard options. For example, you can use the Expert to create master-detail relationships, and to insert Query objects for performing searches.

Summary

✦ Delphi's database components fall into two categories: Data Access components provide gateways and links between the application and databases; Data Controls components include data-aware controls and other objects for displaying and editing data fields, and for navigating through database records.

✦ Delphi's Desktop, Professional, and Client-Server editions include the Borland Database Engine (BDE), which provides a complete set of API programming functions for many popular database systems including dBASE, Paradox, and ODBC systems such as Microsoft Access and Btrieve. Delphi's Client-Server edition includes all of the Desktop edition's features plus it provides access to remote database servers such as Oracle, Sybase, Microsoft SQL Server, Interbase, and Informix.

✦ The new TDataSet component no longer depends on the BDE. Advanced programmers can now derive a new class from TDataSet to call functions in a foreign database server without installing or using the BDE. This is not necessary for most applications.

✦ For a head start on creating a new database application, use the Database Form Wizard command located on Delphi's Database menu (this used to be titled the Database Form Expert and was located on the Help menu). The Database Form Wizard creates a form with Data Access and Data Controls components that you can modify after generating the form.

✦ A table is equivalent to one dataset, conceptually a row-and-column collection of data cells. Rows are equivalent to records; columns are equivalent to fields. A database is a collection of one or more tables. An alias is a name that hides drive, network, path, and filename information for actual database directories and files. Always use aliases to refer to databases; that way, your applications work without recompilation if you move the database files to other directories, or if you install them over a network after you test your code.

✦ Most database applications need a Table and a DataSource object. A Table provides a gateway to a database table (best referenced with an alias). A DataSource object links a Table with one or more Data Controls objects.

✦ Use the Database Desktop to create and modify database tables. You can also view and edit database information using this extensive program, which serves as a front end to the BDE.

✦ BDE supports a subset of standard SQL commands (Select, Insert, Update, and Delete) for Paradox, dBASE, Oracle, and other database formats. You may use the full language with other servers depending on their SQL support.

✦ The Query component executes SQL statements. Because Delphi's database components offer much of what SQL can do, you probably need to use only the SQL Select command — to perform searches, for example, and to restrict datasets to records that match various arguments.

✦ A master-detail database application joins two database tables using a common field such as a customer number or a stock market trading symbol. The master-detail model requires two pairs of related Table and DataSource objects.

✦ Consider placing your Table, DataSource, and other Data Access components in a Data Module, and then installing it in Delphi's Object Repository. Multiple applications can then inherit or use the Data Module to gain access to database tables.

The next chapter continues the story of database programming. Coming up, you learn how to develop reports and charts using database information.

✦   ✦   ✦

Developing Charts and Reports

Anybody can store data in a computer, but it takes real skill to extract information from a database and present it in usable form. It is the *view* of data that makes information interesting and useful. Database programmers and system managers probably spend more time developing applications for viewing and printing charts and reports than any other types of software.

Delphi makes those tasks easy. As you discover in this chapter, Delphi's TeeChart 4 library, created by David Berneda, provides numerous types of charts for displaying data visually. Delphi's QuickReport 3 library, created by Allan Lochert, provides a versatile editor and component library for developing all sorts of printed reports. Delphi 4 provides complete, standard versions of each library, with components installed on the VCL palette, ready to use.

In this chapter, I cover basic and intermediate programming techniques for the TeeChart and QuickReport component libraries to create professional, knock-your-socks-off printouts from information stored in database tables.

Delphi 4 comes supplied with standard editions of the TeeChart and QuickReport component libraries, covered in this chapter.

Components

Delphi's components covered in this chapter are:

✦ **Chart** — Use this component to create charts from data stored in files, or entered directly into a program. Palette: Additional.

✦ **DBChart** — Use this component to create charts from data stored in database tables. Palette: Data Controls.

✦ **DecisionGraph** — This component creates graphs from cross-tabulated database data. Palette: Decision Cube.

✦ **QRBand** — Reports are made up of bands, each of which is an object of this component. Palette: QReport.

✦ **QRChart** — Use this component to insert charts into database reports. Palette: QReport.

✦ **QRChildBand** — This component extends a report's regular bands. It is used for creating expanding bands with other components that move or also expand, and for bands that span multiple pages. Palette: QReport.

✦ **QRDBImage** — Use this component to insert an Image object into a report, usually one that is associated with a Blob field in a database table. Palette: QReport.

✦ **QRDBRichText** — Use this component to insert a database table rich text object into a report. Palette: QReport.

✦ **QRDBText** — Use this component to print most types of database table fields in text form. This is true not only for text fields, but also for numeric fields, date fields, currency fields, and others. Palette: QReport.

✦ **QRExpr** — Use this component to create expressions, for example, to calculate the value of a report entry using other database table fields. Palette: QReport.

✦ **QRImage** — Use this component to insert a bitmap or other type of image such as an icon into a report. This component supports all of the same image types as the Image component. Palette: QReport.

✦ **QRLabel** — Use this component to insert a static label into a report. Palette: QReport.

✦ **QRMemo** — Use this component to insert multiline text objects into a report. Palette: QReport.

✦ **QRPreview** — Use this component to provide a preview of a report. Rather than use this component, however, it is often easier to call the QuickRep component's Preview method. Palette: QReport.

✦ **QRRichText**—Use this component to insert a rich text object into a report. Palette: QReport.

✦ **QRShape**—Use this component to insert a graphics shape such as a rectangle or circle into a report. Palette: QReport.

✦ **QRSubDetail**—Use this component to link multiple datasets into a report. Typically, you do this to print reports of databases that use the master-detail model. Palette: QReport.

✦ **QRSysData**—Use this component to insert various system objects such as the current date and time, page numbers, and other miscellaneous items into a report, usually in a header band. Palette: QReport.

✦ **QuickRep**—Use this component to create a new report. The component's Bands property inserts various types of bands, which hold database fields and other types of objects to print in the finished report. Palette: QReport.

Many QR (QuickReport) components are built from Data Control components. Others are built from nondatabase controls. For example, the QRImage component can insert a bitmap into a report; QRDBImage does the same, but receives its data from a database table field (in this case, probably a Blob, or Binary Large Object, field).

Creating Charts with TeeChart

Each of the many different types of charts in the TeeChart library is created from a series of data points. Each series is itself an object owned by the chart. Figure 18-1 shows the TeeChart Gallery dialog from which you select the type of series you want to use in a chart. Each chart series has numerous options for customizing the results however you wish. You can add labels, adjust colors, select various borders, specify 3D effects, and choose among many other options.

Click the Gallery's 3D check box to view two- and three-dimensional versions of available charts.

Full documentation for the TeeChart library is provided in a Delphi installation directory. (Because I am using a prerelease version of Delphi 4, I don't know at this time where the documentation file will be located, but in Delphi 3, it was in the directory path Delphi 3\TeeChart.) Open the TChartVx.doc file (x equals the version number) using Microsoft Word or a Word viewer. Full online help is also available—select any TeeChart component or other item in a Delphi form window and press F1 for more information.

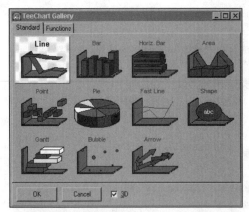

Figure 18-1: To select the type of chart series you want, choose an icon from the TeeChart Gallery. Each chart can be displayed in two- or three-dimensional formats.

Getting started with charts

The easiest way to get started using the TeeChart library is to create a few simple charts. Start Delphi and then follow these steps (you don't have to save the project):

1. Start a new application.

2. Click Delphi's Additional page tab on the VCL palette.

3. Click the Chart icon (it looks like a small pie chart), and then click inside the form window to deposit a new, empty Chart object. The form window on your display looks like Figure 18-2.

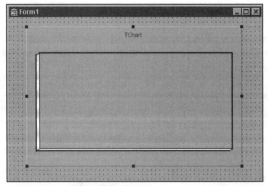

Figure 18-2: Use the Chart component to create a new, empty Chart in a form window.

Note

The TChart class is derived from Delphi's TPanel component class, and therefore, a Chart object is literally an enhanced Panel. Among other things, this means you can insert other objects such as Buttons and CheckBoxes into a Chart object. See Chapter 7 for more information on the Panel component.

4. Right-click while pointing the mouse cursor inside the Chart object. This brings up the Chart's local menu. Select the Edit Chart... command to open TeeChart's extensive chart editor. (Another way to open the editor is to double-click the Chart object.)

5. Click the editor's Add button to add a series object to the chart. This brings up the TeeChart Gallery dialog shown in Figure 18-1. Select the Pie series from the Gallery, and then click OK or press Enter to close the Gallery dialog window. Move the editor window aside so you can see the form and Chart object. As Figure 18-3 shows, TeeChart displays a sample chart of the selected type with random data points added to the series.

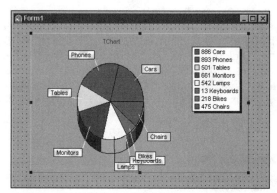

Figure 18-3: TeeChart shows your selected chart in Delphi with random data points.

Note

When you create a new chart, the TeeChart library automatically supplies random data points so you can see an example of the finished product. This data is not displayed at run time. When you run the program, the chart uses your own data, which can come from a variety of sources. This feature helps you design good-looking charts, and it's also a great way to learn your way around the TeeChart library.

Try some of the other chart series types in the TeeChart Gallery (refer back to Figure 18-1). Repeat the preceding steps starting with Step 4, and select the Add button to add additional series objects. A chart can have multiple series of the same type — for comparing data points such as stock market prices, for example, with multiple lines in an x and y grid. A chart might also combine series of different types — for instance, to show bar and line charts in the same grid, perhaps to compare historical against new information.

Use the TeeChart editor's Change button to change the type of chart displayed for a selected series — for example, to change a bar chart to a point diagram. Click the editor's Delete button to delete a selected series (this displays a confirming prompt dialog in case you clicked Delete by accident). Try these options now to become familiar with them.

Note   Many TeeChart editor options differ depending on the type of series you select for your chart. If the figures in this chapter differ from those you see on screen, you probably selected a different type of series — a Bar chart instead of a Line diagram, for instance.

Also select some of the page tabs in the TeeChart editor (see Figure 18-4). This opens various pages in the editor window for customizing charts. As you can see by selecting a few tabs, dozens upon dozens of options exist for selecting colors, chart styles, and features. Try this: click the General tab and disable the 3D check box to convert a three-dimensional chart into a two-dimensional one. Also try this: click the Legend tab and disable the Visible check box to turn off the legend panel, which lists the pie chart's values (this is the small, white background window shown at upper-right in Figure 18-3).

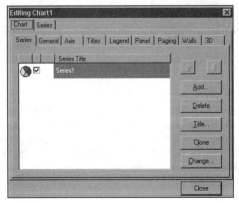

Figure 18-4: The TeeChart editor provides numerous options for creating and editing charts.

Notice the TeeChart editor has two rows of page tabs. These topmost tabs select one of the two major areas in the editor. These are:

✦ **Chart** — Select the editor's topmost tab labeled Chart, and then select page tabs on the second row to make changes to the chart's properties. For example, click the Titles tab and enter chart titles. Notice that your changes are instantly reflected in the displayed sample chart.

✦ **Series** — Click the Series tab on top of the editor, and then choose a series object from the drop-down list. You can then select the second row's tabs to make changes to series properties. If you are following along, click Series now on the top row, select the Series1 object, click the Marks tab on the second row, and choose one of the following buttons under Style: choose Value to show only data point values, Percent to show percents, Label & Percent to show both text labels and percents for each data point, and so on.

Another way to select chart properties is to select the Chart object (close the TeeChart editor first), and then use the Object Inspector window to customize your chart's properties just as you do for other Delphi components. Most properties are available in both the TeeChart editor and Object Inspector. You can use whichever method you want, but you'll probably discover that the editor is easier to use because of the way it organizes properties and options into dialog pages. The Object Inspector merely presents most of the same items in one grand window, which can make it difficult to locate the items you need.

Note

The TeeChart editor has far too many options and features to cover in this single chapter. By following the suggested steps outlined here, however, you can learn how to use other options on your own. I also explain more about specific chart options in the next several sections.

Printing and exporting charts

The TeeChart library provides full printing and print-preview features, which you can provide to end users at run time. You can use these same features in Delphi to print sample charts. In addition, you can save any chart in a graphics file for incorporating into other documents, or for transmitting over the Internet.

Printing charts in Delphi

To print a chart in Delphi, right-click inside the Chart object, and select the Print Preview... command from the local pop-up menu. (Follow the steps in the preceding section to create a sample chart if you need one.) The command displays the TeeChart Print Preview window shown in Figure 18-5.

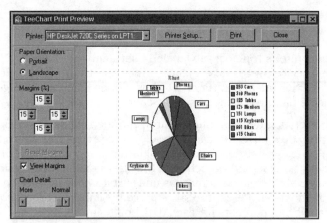

Figure 18-5: The TeeChart Print Preview window

The Print Preview window shows the chart as it appears when printed. Use the various options to select Portrait or Landscape orientation, to adjust margins, and to adjust the chart detail (the exact effect depends on the type of chart — grab and slide the Chart Detail scroll button to see how it changes the image).

You can also use the mouse to click and drag the dotted line margins and to move the chart around on the page. Try this now — click the mouse inside the preview window and drag to alter the chart's layout and size.

When you are finished adjusting the chart and selecting options (also click the Printer Setup... button to select your printer's output options), click the Print button to print. You can then click the Close button to close the Print Preview window.

When you close the Print Preview window, all settings revert back to their defaults. Don't close the window until after you are finished printing your chart.

Printing charts at run time

Your program's users can bring up the Print Preview window, and use all of the options described in the preceding section. To try this, add a Button object to the form, and double-click it to create a handler for its OnClick event. Switch to Delphi's code editor window, and locate the *implementation* keyword. Add a *uses* statement as follows (changes in bold):

```
implementation
{$R *.DFM}
uses
  TeePrevi;
```

This makes the TeePrevi (TeeChart Print Preview) unit available to the module. You can now program the Button's event handler as follows:

```
procedure TForm.Button1Click(Sender: TObject);
begin
  ChartPreview(Form1, Chart1);
end;
```

Call the TeePrevi unit's ChartPreview procedure and pass the chart's form (Form1 here) and chart (Chart1) objects as arguments. This displays the Print Preview window shown in Figure 18-5. The unit completely handles all printing options — no other code needs to be written. When the user closes the window, the program continues normally.

Exporting charts in Delphi

To export a chart in Delphi, right-click inside the chart object to open the TeeChart pop-up menu (if necessary, create a sample chart as explained in this chapter). Select the Export Chart... command, which displays the dialog window shown in Figure 18-6.

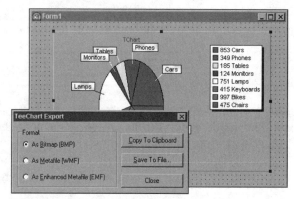

Figure 18-6: Use the TeeChart Export dialog to copy a chart image to the Windows clipboard, or to save it in an image file.

The TeeChart Export dialog presents three format options for copying a chart to the Windows clipboard, or for saving a chart in a disk file. The three formats are:

✦ **As Bitmap (BMP)** — Use this option to save a chart in a bitmap file, the size of which depends on the chart size.

✦ **As Metafile (WMF)** — Use this option to save a chart in a standard Windows metafile. This is not an image, but a set of commands that draw the image exactly the same as in the original program. Metafiles use only a small amount of disk space, and they are easily scaled to new display dimensions. Use this option if your images need to be viewed by Windows 3.1 users.

✦ **As Enhanced Metafile (EMF)** — Use this option to save a chart in an enhanced Windows metafile. This is similar to a standard metafile, but can be viewed only by Windows 95, 98, and NT users. Enhanced metafiles are superior in many respects, including accuracy of reproduction and scaling, than standard metafiles. Enhanced metafiles use 32-bit coordinates; standard metafiles use 16-bit coordinates. For best results, use enhanced metafiles whenever possible.

After selecting one of the three format options, click the Copy to Clipboard button to copy the image to the Windows clipboard. You can then switch to another program such as a text editor and paste the image into a document (assuming, of course, the program can handle images in the selected format). Click the Save to File... button to bring up a dialog that you can use to enter a target filename, and to select an output directory.

Exporting charts at run time

To export a chart at run time, call one of the following three TChart methods:

```
SaveToBitmapFile(const Filename: String);
SaveToMetafile(const Filename: String);
SaveToMetafileEnh(const Filename: String);
```

To each method, pass the name of the file, which may include drive and path name information. The filename extension should match the file type — this is not added automatically. For example, to save a chart as a Windows bitmap, use a statement such as:

```
Chart1.SaveToBitmapFile('C:\Test.bmp');
```

Note

Some editions of the TeeChart online help incorrectly name the preceding procedure SaveToBitmap. The correct name is SaveToBitmapFile.

Call the other functions similarly. The following two statements save a chart as a Windows metafile and as an enhanced Windows metafile. As before, it's your responsibility to specify the correct filename extension for the type of file you create:

```
Chart1.SaveToMetafile('C:\Test.wmf');
Chart1.SaveToMetafileEnh('C:\Test.emf');
```

Understanding chart data sources

As the preceding sections demonstrate, it's easy to create a chart with the TeeChart library. But selecting the best type of chart for a particular series of data points is often the most difficult and time-consuming part of the charting task. To create a successful chart, you need to carefully consider the source of your data, the information it represents, and your goal in providing a visual representation of that information.

To help you get started developing charts for your own data, the following sections present realistic chart examples using three basic types of data sources:

✦ **Program data**—Use this data source to create a chart using data that you type directly into the program's source code. This data could be fixed—to display a chart of historical information for example—or it might be calculated using program functions.

✦ **File data**—Use this data source to create a chart with data stored in a disk file. The type of file is up to you. It might be a file of data downloaded from the Internet, or it could be a text file with information that you enter or that you cut and paste from another document.

✦ **Database data**—Use this data source to create a chart using data loaded from a database table. At a minimum, you also need to use DataSource and Table components to connect to your database. (See Chapter 17 for information on these and other Delphi database components.)

The following sections describe how to program charts using data from each of these three sources. Sample programs in each section also demonstrate additional charting techniques.

Charts from program data

One way to provide data for a chart is to type it directly into the program's source code. Or, you might use this method to display information provided by various procedures such as operating system functions. For these types of data, use the Chart component on the Additional palette.

Drop a Chart object onto a form, double-click it and select Edit Chart... to open the TeeChart editor. Click the Add button to create one or more series objects and to select the type of chart to display. You can also select various options for the chart at this time.

After you are done designing your chart, add program statements to supply it with real data. To insert the data, call the Add, AddX, AddY, or AddXY methods for your series objects to add data points. For example, the following statement adds AValue (assumed to be a double variable) to the Series1 object, sets this data point's label to the string 'Value', and specifies that the Chart object should select an appropriate color:

```
Series1.Add(AValue, 'Value', clTeeColor);
```

In place of clTeeColor, you can use any TColor value such as clBlue or clRed, or you can specify colors in hexadecimal. (Look up TColor using Delphi's online help for more information; also see Chapter 13, Developing Graphics Applications.)

The MemInfo sample application on the CD-ROM in the Source\MemInfo directory demonstrates how to add program data to a chart. Figure 18-7 shows the program's display, a bar chart of the program's memory use as reported by Delphi's System.GetHeapStatus function. To run the program, load the MemInfo.dpr project file into Delphi and press F9. When the program window appears, click the ShowInfo button to display various memory use values. You might add this program's form to your own projects to debug memory problems, or simply to review memory use. Listing 18-1 shows the program's source code.

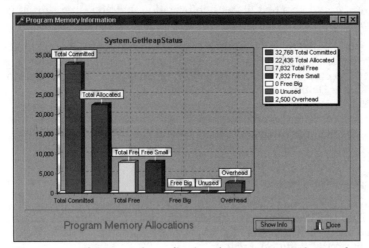

Figure 18-7: The MemInfo application shows a program's use of memory and also demonstrates how to add program data to a chart.

Listing 18-1: **MemInfo\Main.pas**

```
unit Main;

interface

uses
  Windows, Messages, SysUtils, Classes, Graphics, Controls,
  Forms, Dialogs, StdCtrls, TeEngine, Series, ExtCtrls,
  TeeProcs, Chart, Buttons;
```

```
type
  TMainForm = class(TForm)
    Chart1: TChart;
    Button1: TButton;
    Series1: TBarSeries;
    BitBtn1: TBitBtn;
    Label1: TLabel;
    procedure Button1Click(Sender: TObject);
  private
    { Private declarations }
  public
    { Public declarations }
  end;

var
  MainForm: TMainForm;

implementation

{$R *.DFM}

var
  HeapStatus: THeapStatus;

procedure TMainForm.Button1Click(Sender: TObject);
begin
  HeapStatus := System.GetHeapStatus;
  with Series1, HeapStatus do
  begin
//    Add(TotalAddrSpace, 'Total address space', clTeeColor);
//    Add(TotalUncommitted, 'Total Uncommitted', clTeeColor);
    Add(TotalCommitted, 'Total Committed', clTeeColor);
    Add(TotalAllocated, 'Total Allocated', clTeeColor);
    Add(TotalFree, 'Total Free', clTeeColor);
    Add(FreeSmall, 'Free Small', clTeeColor);
    Add(FreeBig, 'Free Big', clTeeColor);
    Add(Unused, 'Unused', clTeeColor);
    Add(Overhead, 'Overhead', clTeeColor);
  end;
end;

end.
```

To obtain memory use values, the MemInfo program calls the GetHeapStatus function in Delphi's System unit. This function returns a record of type THeapStatus, declared as a variable in MemInfo's implementation section. The following statement fills in the HeapStatus record with values such as TotalCommitted and TotalAllocated, that represent the program's memory use. (See Delphi's online help for information about each variable in the THeapStatus record.)

```
HeapStatus := System.GetHeapStatus;
```

To add the returned values to the chart's Series1 object, the Show Info button's OnClick event handler calls the Add method. For example, this statement adds the TotalFree value to the chart:

```
Add(TotalFree, 'Total Free', clTeeColor);
```

This creates a new bar for the value in HeapStatus.TotalFree and labels it with the string shown. The color value clTeeColor tells the chart to select a color automatically for this data point. The other data points are added similarly.

Note MemInfo does not display bars for two GetHeapStatus values, TotalAddrSpace and TotalUncommitted. These are global system values, which do not directly relate to the other program-memory values shown in the sample chart. This is a good example of when too much information might be more harmful than informative, so I commented out the two statements near the beginning of the Button event handler.

The Add method used in MemInfo is appropriate for simple bar charts. It's also good for creating pie charts because these show data as percentages of some whole — for comparing populations of cities, for example, or for showing the relative number of products in a factory inventory. Other types of charts such as line drawings depict information grafted onto an x and y coordinate grid. For these types of charts, you sometimes have x or y values, or you might have both. To add data points for these types of series, call the AddX, AddY, or AddXY procedures. The following statement adds YValue (a double variable assumed to be declared by the program), labels the y axis with the string 'Y-Label', and colors the display of this data red:

```
Series1.AddY(YValue, 'Y-Label', clRed);
```

The x coordinate for this data point is automatically calculated using the values selected with the TeeChart editor's Chart|Axis page of options. Similarly, if you have an x value, call AddX to create a new data point for a series:

```
Series1.AddX(XValue, 'X-Label', clWhite);
```

Finally, if you have two values to chart as an *x* and *y* position in the grid, call AddXY using a statement such as:

```
Series1.AddXY(XValue, YValue, 'X-Label', clBlue);
```

Charts from file data

Probably the most common data source for charts comes from information stored in files. The main problem in reading this data is knowing or figuring out the file format. It might be a text file downloaded from the Internet, or it might contain values stored in binary. If you know or can determine the file format, you can write a procedure to load the data into memory and then call the Add, AddY, AddX, or AddXY methods to insert data points into a chart's series.

As a real-life demonstration of the problems involved in reading data files, the MayTemp sample application on the CD-ROM in the Source\MayTemp directory displays a graph of numeric data that I downloaded from the Internet Web site `http://www-mfl.nhc.noaa.gov`. This accesses the National Weather Service's office in Miami Florida, which provides weather forecasts, charts, and other information. In this case, I was interested in climate data for Key West, Florida, for the month of May, especially the average high and low temperatures. This data is located in the /climate/Key-West_May_Climat.html file, shown in its original form in Figure 18-8 as displayed on my system using Internet Explorer. As you may realize, the Internet is loaded (some say it's overstuffed) with interesting data like this.

Readers with sharp eyes might notice that the original data is labeled "MAY" but is subtitled "January 1871 - 1996." Apparently, this is a mistake (this is May, not January, data), which I have reported to the NWS. This also goes to show that, when downloading data from the Internet, it's a good idea to question the validity of information received.

Getting the raw data was the easy part—moving that data from the Internet to a file and then into a Delphi program for display as a visual graph took a little more work. I first selected the raw data in Internet Explorer's window, pressed Ctrl+C to copy the text to the clipboard, and then opened the Windows Notepad utility. Pressing Ctrl+V pasted the information into Notepad. After deleting extraneous text, I saved the data in a text file named KeyWestMayClimate.txt. This file, shown here in Listing 18-2, is on the CD-ROM in the Source\Data directory. (Also included for reference in that directory is the Key-West_May_Climat.html file, which you can load into your Internet browser if you want to practice massaging the data on your own.)

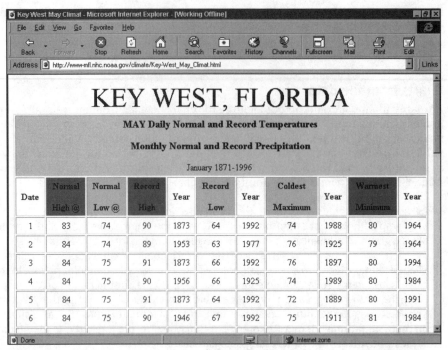

Figure 18-8: The original climate data from the National Weather Service for Key West, Florida for the month of May (the January label is apparently a mistake) from 1871 to 1996.

Listing 18-2: **Data\KeyWestMayClimate.txt**

```
 1  83  74  90  1873  64  1992  74  1988  80  1964
 2  84  74  89  1953  63  1977  76  1925  79  1964
 3  84  75  91  1873  66  1992  76  1897  80  1994
 4  84  75  90  1956  66  1925  74  1989  80  1984
 5  84  75  91  1873  64  1992  72  1889  80  1991
 6  84  75  90  1946  67  1992  75  1911  81  1984
 7  84  75  89  1956  66  1954  76  1903  80  1991
 8  84  75  91  1873  65  1988  74  1898  80  1991
 9  84  75  92  1873  64  1992  76  1928  80  1978
10  85  75  90  1873  66  1960  75  1891  80  1995
11  85  76  90  1873  64  1944  77  1891  80  1995
12  85  76  90  1926  68  1944  77  1900  80  1996
13  85  76  90  1995  66  1888  76  1900  81  1995
14  85  76  90  1878  65  1917  74  1900  81  1995
15  85  76  90  1991  68  1932  76  1917  81  1994
16  85  76  90  1991  66  1951  76  1977  82  1994
```

17	85	76	92	1878	66	1951	78	1880	81	1989
18	85	76	92	1881	67	1951	77	1904	81	1995
19	85	77	92	1881	68	1917	77	1904	82	1995
20	86	77	91	1886	68	1911	76	1875	81	1995
21	86	77	91	1935	68	1901	74	1875	80	1885
22	86	77	92	1935	68	1940	76	1921	82	1985
23	86	77	92	1873	69	1940	77	1892	80	1995
24	86	77	92	1873	68	1900	78	1883	82	1985
25	86	77	91	1989	70	1913	78	1982	82	1995
26	86	77	91	1989	68	1992	81	1879	81	1995
27	86	77	90	1989	70	1894	79	1880	81	1995
28	86	77	92	1953	68	1916	77	1901	81	1924
29	86	77	91	1952	68	1926	78	1918	81	1995
30	86	78	92	1949	67	1932	76	1960	82	1915
31	87	78	93	1881	70	1934	79	1960	82	1985

The data shown here in text form is typical. Lines are not perfectly aligned, and the columns are unlabeled. In this case, the original data tells us what the values are, so it's not difficult to read them into program variables. Because this is a text file, Object Pascal's Read procedure is probably the best way to load the data and display it visually. Figure 18-9 shows the finished chart, displayed by the MayTemp application on the CD-ROM in the Source\MayTemp directory. Load the MayTemp.dpr project file into Delphi, and press F9 to compile and run. Listing 18-3 shows the program's source code.

The MayTemp program reads the data file KeyWestMayClimate.txt located in the Source\Data directory on the CD-ROM. If the program fails to run properly, make sure the current directory is Source\MayTemp, or modify the path name in the program's FileName constant.

MayTemp uses standard Object Pascal techniques for opening a text file and reading its information. To do this at run time, the program uses an OnActivate event handler for the form. This ensures that the data is loaded and properly added to the chart's series objects, when the program starts, but before the window becomes visible.

The event handler, TMainForm.FormActivate, declares integer variables for each data value — one variable per item on each row (see Figure 18-2). To read the file data into these variables, the procedure also declares a file variable:

```
var
  F: TextFile;
```

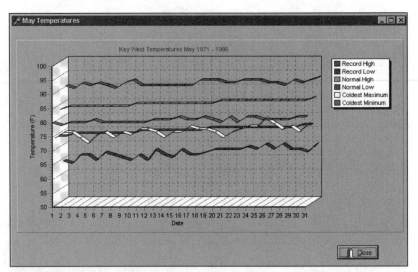

Figure 18-9: The finished chart, showing the temperature data from the raw information from Listing 18-2

Listing 18-3: **MayTemp\Main.pas**

```
unit Main;

interface

uses
  Windows, Messages, SysUtils, Classes, Graphics, Controls,
  Forms, Dialogs, TeEngine, Series, ExtCtrls, TeeProcs, Chart,
  StdCtrls, Buttons;

type
  TMainForm = class(TForm)
    Chart1: TChart;
    Series1: TLineSeries;
    Series2: TLineSeries;
    Series4: TLineSeries;
    Series5: TLineSeries;
    Series6: TLineSeries;
    Series3: TLineSeries;
    BitBtn1: TBitBtn;
    procedure FormActivate(Sender: TObject);
  private
    { Private declarations }
  public
```

```
        { Public declarations }
    end;

var
    MainForm: TMainForm;

implementation

{$R *.DFM}

{ Change the following path name if your data file is
  in another location. The path name is relative to the
  current directory, which is assumed to be at the
  same level as \Data\. }

const
    FileName = '..\Data\KeyWestMayClimate.txt';

{ The following procedure is called when the form is first
  activated. At that time, the program opens the data file,
  reads its values, and adds them to the chart's series
  objects. }

procedure TMainForm.FormActivate(Sender: TObject);
var
    F: TextFile;                        // File variable
    Date: Integer;                      // First column in file data
    NormalHigh : Integer;               // Next column
    NormalLow : Integer;                // and so on ...
    RecordHigh : Integer;
    RecordHighYear : Integer;
    RecordLow : Integer;
    RecordLowYear : Integer;
    ColdestMaximum : Integer;
    ColdestMaximumYear : Integer;
    WarmestMaximum : Integer;           // ... down to the
    WarmestMaximumYear : Integer;       // Last column in file data
begin
    AssignFile(F, FileName);    // Initialize file variable
    Reset(F);                   // Open the file
    while not Eof(F) do         // Loop until the end of the file
    begin
      Read(F,                   // Read one row of data
        Date,                   // into the individual variables.
        NormalHigh,
        NormalLow,
        RecordHigh,
```

(continued)

Listing 18-3 *(continued)*

```
        RecordHighYear,
        RecordLow,
        RecordLowYear,
        ColdestMaximum,
        ColdestMaximumYear,
        WarmestMaximum,
        WarmestMaximumYear);    // End of Read statement

      { One row of file data has been loaded at this point. The
        following statements add the data points to each of the
        line chart's six series objects. The empty string
        arguments can be used to label data points. These
        strings aren't used here because the X axis of this
        sample chart already shows day values (1, 2, ..., 31). }

      Series1.AddXY(Date, NormalHigh, '', clTeeColor);
      Series2.AddXY(Date, NormalLow, '', clTeeColor);
      Series3.AddXY(Date, RecordHigh, '', clTeeColor);
      Series4.AddXY(Date, RecordLow, '', clTeeColor);
      Series5.AddXY(Date, ColdestMaximum, '', clTeeColor);
      Series6.AddXY(Date, WarmestMaximum, '', clTeeColor);

    end;
  end;

  end.
```

Two statements initialize this variable using the constant FileName string, and open the file to prepare for reading its data:

```
AssignFile(F, FileName);
Reset(F);
```

Following these steps, a *while* statement continues to execute until all rows of data are loaded into the program's variables. This fragment, for example, shows how the program loads the first value in each row, representing the date (1, 2, 3, ..., 31):

```
while not Eof(F) do
begin
  Read(F,
   Date,
 ...
end;
```

The other variables are loaded similarly, with a single Read statement, by listing them separated by commas.

Tip

Use Pascal's Read procedure to read individual values on the same original text line into separate variables. Use Readln to read an entire line as a string.

After loading each row of data, the program inserts most of the values into the chart's series. In this case, the chart has six series objects, one for each line displayed in the final graph (see Figure 18-9). Each data point is added by calling the TeeChart AddXY method. For example, the following two statements insert the NormalHigh and NormalLow values into their respective series objects:

```
Series1.AddXY(Date, NormalHigh, '', clTeeColor);
Series2.AddXY(Date, NormalLow, '', clTeeColor);
```

The first argument, Date, is the same for both data points — the *x* axis in this case represents the day of the month. The next argument is the value to use for this data point. The null string isn't needed because the chart already displays temperature values along the *y* axis. The final argument tells the chart to use the preprogrammed color for this data point.

Tip

TeeChart's random data for the chart in the MayTemp application does not produce a good-looking chart at design time. This happens because the random values fall outside of the restricted *x* and *y* coordinate ranges that I needed to use for this chart. To turn off random data generation, I opened the TeeChart editor, clicked the Series page tab, and selected each series object from the drop-down list. For each series, I selected the Data Source page tab and then No Data from the drop-down list of data source options. You might want to inspect this area of the TeeChart editor in case you need to turn off random data generation for your own charts.

Charts from database data

The third and final way to obtain data for charts is to load field values from database tables. This technique uses components such as Table and DataSource, explained in Chapter 17, to open a database table. Instead of the Chart component used so far, however, to load data from the database table, use the DBChart component located on Delphi's Data Controls palette. DBChart works exactly the same as Chart, except that its data comes from a database table. All other features and options are the same as described in the preceding sections.

On the
CD-ROM

On the CD-ROM, the WinesChart application demonstrates how to create a chart from database information. This program is in the Source\WinesChart directory. Figure 18-10 shows the program's display using the sample Wines database in the Source\Data directory on the CD-ROM. Listing 18-4 shows the program's source code.

Note

If WinesChart doesn't run on your system, the likely cause is a missing WINES database alias. To create this alias, select Tools|Database Desktop, and then in the desktop program, choose Tools|Alias Manager.... Click the New button, and enter **WINES** as the alias name. Set the associated directory to the Source\Data\Wines directory from the CD-ROM. Click Keep New and then select OK. Answer Yes, when prompted whether to save public aliases. You should now be able to run WinesChart successfully. Also see Chapter 17 for more information on setting and using database aliases.

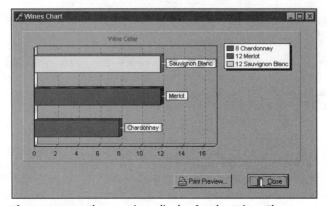

Figure 18-10: The run-time display for the WinesChart program demonstrates how to read information from a database table and display it as a chart.

Listing 18-4: **WinesChart\Main.pas**

```
unit Main;

interface

uses
  Windows, Messages, SysUtils, Classes, Graphics, Controls,
Forms, Dialogs,
  StdCtrls, Buttons, TeEngine, Series, ExtCtrls, TeeProcs,
Chart, DBChart,
  Db, DBTables;

type
  TMainForm = class(TForm)
    Table1: TTable;
```

```
    DataSource1: TDataSource;
    DBChart1: TDBChart;
    Series1: THorizBarSeries;
    BitBtn1: TBitBtn;
    BitBtn2: TBitBtn;
    procedure BitBtn2Click(Sender: TObject);
  private
    { Private declarations }
  public
    { Public declarations }
  end;

var
  MainForm: TMainForm;

implementation

{$R *.DFM}

uses
  TeePrevi;

procedure TMainForm.BitBtn2Click(Sender: TObject);
begin
  ChartPreview(MainForm, DBChart1);
end;

end.
```

To create the WinesChart application, follow these steps:

1. Drop Table and DataSource objects into a form, along with a DBChart object. Also insert two buttons, labeled Print Preview... and Close as in Figure 18-11, which shows the finished form window in Delphi.

2. Set the Table1 object's DatabaseName property to WINES. Set TableName to Wines.db. Then, change Active to True.

3. Set the DataSource1 object's DataSet property to Table1.

4. Select the DBChart1 object, and right-click the mouse to bring up TeeChart's local menu. Select Edit Chart... to display the TeeChart editor.

5. Click the editor's Add button and choose the Horiz. Bar chart series. Click OK. You should see random sample data displayed in the chart.

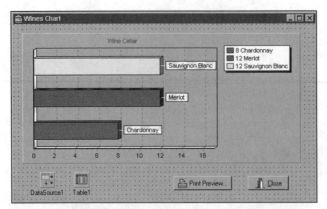

Figure 18-11: The design-time display for the WinesChart form window also shows the DataSource1 and Table1 objects that connect the program to the Wines database.

6. To link the chart to the WINES database, select the TeeChart editor's Series page tab at the top of the window. Because there is only one series object, it is already selected (in your own programs, if you use multiple series objects, select each one from the drop-down list and then repeat the next step).

7. Click the Data Source tab in the TeeChart editor. Open the drop-down list below the second row of page tabs and select the Dataset entry. Similarly, set the Dataset edit box to Table1. These steps link the chart to the database table. To specify which fields to display, select Name for the Label edit box and Number for Bar. These values specify a chart depicting the number of bottles in the wine cellar labeled by each bottle's Name field. Figure 18-12 shows the TeeChart editor with the Series | Data Source page filled in.

8. Close the TeeChart editor to view the finished chart in the form window, showing the information extracted from the WINES database. You don't have to run the program — because you set the Table1 object's Active property to True, the data is live inside Delphi.

To finish the program, you can change the chart's titles and select other properties. In fact, this would be a good place for you to begin experimenting with various chart options. The program's listing (see Listing 18-4) shows how to program the Print Preview... button as explained earlier in this chapter.

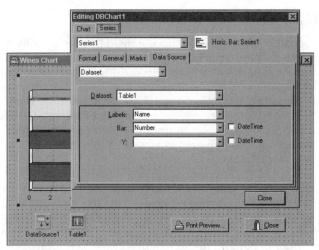

Figure 18-12: Use the TeeChart editor to connect a chart series to a database Table, in this case, for the sample WINES database.

Creating Reports with QuickReport

Today's computer printers seem to work fairly well, but this wasn't always so. Not long ago, just getting a printer to print *anything* was a major accomplishment for many computer users. But now, most ink jet and laser printers are reliable work horses. However, making them gallop exactly as you want can still take much trial and error.

Delphi's QuickReport library can greatly simplify your application's printout requirements, especially if you need to prepare printed reports from file or database data. The library comes with an easy-to-use editor that simplifies page layout. There's also a handy print-preview feature that shows on screen exactly how the finished printout will appear, and which you can also use to save reports in disk files.

Note

Full documentation for the QuickReport library is provided in a Delphi installation directory. (Because I am using a prerelease version of Delphi 4, I don't know the path name for this directory, but in Delphi 3, the path was Delphi 3\Quickrpt.) Open the Qrptxman.doc file (*x* equals the version number) using Microsoft Word or a Word viewer. Full online help is also available — select any QuickReport component or other item and press F1 for more information.

Getting started with reports

QuickReport is a *banded report generator*. In a nutshell, this means you create a report by inserting one or more band objects into a blank page, an object of the QuickRep component. Into each band, you drop various items that you want to appear on the report, such as titles, the date and time, page numbers, database record fields, summary totals, and other items. When you print the report, QuickReport fills the bands with information and replicates them as necessary to produce the finished product. For example, on each page, QuickReport automatically increments a page number object, and it fills record fields with information extracted from database tables.

As you work with QuickReport, you discover that its bands and their objects are highly intelligent (as far as programming objects go, that is). In most cases, you can design good-looking reports simply by creating a few bands and dropping objects onto them. You need little, if any, programming. A handy print-preview feature, which you can use either in Delphi's designer mode or in the run-time application, makes it easy to view the report's layout without wasting paper. When you have all your ducks in the rows where you want them, simply click the print-preview's Print speed button to send the result on its way to your printer. You can also save reports in disk files and then reload them into QuickReport's print-preview window for printing.

On the CD-ROM

To demonstrate how to use QuickReport components, follow the steps in this and the next several sections. Even if you don't have a printer, you can follow these step-by-step instructions to learn how to design a report. (The finished application, Report1, is on the CD-ROM in the Source\Report1 directory. To use this program, or to create it by following the steps here, you must have installed Delphi's database demonstration files, identified as the DBDEMOS alias.) Start a new application and then follow these steps:

1. Click the Data Access page tab, select the Table component and drop it onto the form. Select the DataSource component and drop it next to Table1. The exact locations don't matter — neither component appears in the finished application.

2. Click the Table1 component, and then click the Properties tab in Delphi's Object Inspector window. Set three properties as follows: DatabaseName to DBDEMOS, TableName to Parts.db, and Active to True.

Note

If DBDEMOS is not listed in the drop-down list of Table1's DatabaseName property, you need to reinstall Delphi and start over. Or, you can select any other database and table available on your system, and then specify whatever fields are available in place of those suggested here. Also see Chapter 17 for more information on using database components.

3. Click the DataSource1 component and, using Object Inspector, set its DataSet property to Table1.

4. Select Delphi's QReport page tab on the VCL palette, and click the first icon at the left, QuickRep. Click inside the form window to create a bare report object, named QuickRep1 by default. Figure 18-13 shows the form window in design mode so far. The grid and its row and column numbers that you see onscreen are for laying out the report's elements, and do not appear in the finished report.

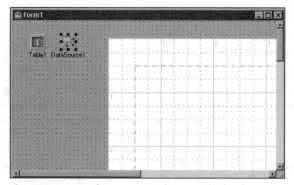

Figure 18-13: A bare report object with database components

5. Click inside the bare report object, and then in the Object Inspector window, double-click the small plus sign to the left of the Bands property. This opens a list of subproperties, each one a True or False setting that, if True, creates a band of that type in the report object.

6. Set the HasDetail subproperty to True. This creates a band object in the report. If you look closely, you can see the faint word "Detail" inside this band. This identifies the type of band, but is not printed in the finished report. The QuickRep1 object with a band object is shown in Figure 18-14. (Look on your screen for "Detail" inside the band. This text is probably too small to see in the printed figure.)

7. Make sure QuickRep1 is still selected (it is listed in the Object Inspector's drop-down list at top), and set the DataSet property to Table1. The report object is now linked with the database components from which information is extracted to produce the finished report.

8. Click inside the Detail band to select it, and notice that the Object Inspector displays the band object's name, DetailBand1. QuickReport replicates the Detail band in the finished report to print rows of information.

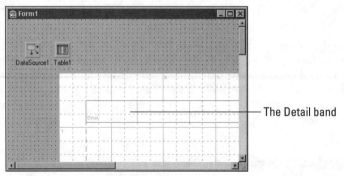

Figure 18-14: The QuickRep1 object with a band object

9. To provide that information, drop some detail objects onto the band. Locate the QRDBText speed button in the VCL's QReport palette. (Numerous icons are found in this section of Delphi — pause the mouse cursor over each button and wait a moment to see its name. This helps you to find the specific component needed.) Click the QRDBText component, and then click inside the report's Detail band. You can drag the resulting text object (labeled QRDBText1) to whatever position you want inside the Detail band — somewhere to the left in the band is fine.

10. Make sure QRDBText1 is selected, and then in the Object Inspector window, set two properties as follows: DataSet to Table1 and DataField to PartNo. These steps specify that the first column in the report lists the item's part number. Notice that the band shows the selected field name.

11. Repeat Step 9 to add additional database table fields to the report's Detail band. For example, again select the QRDBText component in the palette, and click in the Detail band to create QRDBText2. Set this object's DataSet to Table1, but this time, set DataField to Description. Add additional QRDBText components for the table's Cost, ListPrice, OnHand, and OnOrder fields. Resize the form window as necessary to expose more of the developing report. Figure 18-15 shows the finished Detail band.

Tip

Depending on the type of field you print in a column, you might want to set its Alignment property differently. For example, the Description column in the sample report probably should set Alignment to taLeftJustify. The other numeric fields probably look best set to taRightJustify. You probably have to fiddle with these and other properties, and you may need to adjust the column positions, to get the final results you want.

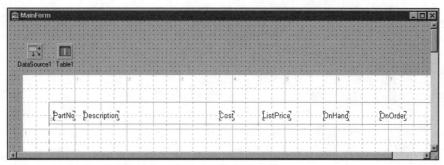

Figure 18-15: The finished sample Detail band. Each QRDBText object represents a database table field to be printed in the finished report.

12. If you are following along, save the application now. You continue to develop this report in the coming sections. Use the default unit and project names, and save them in any temporary directory.

Caution   A report band is a container object. This means that, if you delete a band, you also delete the objects in the band. Most important: never switch off a band by setting the QuickRep object's Bands subproperty to False, or you have to reinsert all the objects you so carefully inserted into that band. For safety, after creating each band and inserting objects into it, save your project.

The preceding steps produce a complete report, which is ready for viewing and printing. To try these steps, right-click inside the QuickRep1 object (*don't* click inside the Detail band, however). Select the Preview command from the local pop-up menu to view the report as designed so far. Figure 18-16 shows the results.

Note   Although you are trying QuickReport's preview and printing commands inside Delphi, your application's end users see the exact same preview dialog window. Later in this chapter, I explain how to provide this feature in your finished applications.

Try out the buttons on the print-preview page. Click Zoom to display the full page (the text, however, might not be readable), click Zoom to 100 percent for a close onscreen representation of the printed report (this option is useful for carefully positioning objects before printing). Click the arrow buttons to page through the report. Click Printer setup to prepare your printer's options; click Print to print (printing starts immediately — it does not display a print-properties dialog, so be sure to select Printer setup beforehand). Two other buttons, Save and Open, save the current report in a disk file and reload previously saved reports. Click the Close button to return to the chart's form page.

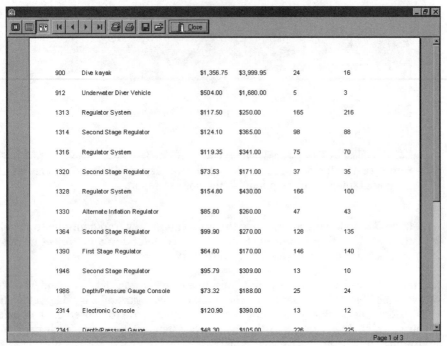

900	Dive kayak	$1,356.75	$3,999.95	24	16
912	Underwater Diver Vehicle	$504.00	$1,680.00	5	3
1313	Regulator System	$117.50	$250.00	165	216
1314	Second Stage Regulator	$124.10	$365.00	98	88
1316	Regulator System	$119.35	$341.00	75	70
1320	Second Stage Regulator	$73.53	$171.00	37	35
1328	Regulator System	$154.80	$430.00	166	100
1330	Alternate Inflation Regulator	$85.80	$260.00	47	43
1364	Second Stage Regulator	$99.90	$270.00	128	135
1390	First Stage Regulator	$64.60	$170.00	146	140
1946	Second Stage Regulator	$95.79	$309.00	13	10
1986	Depth/Pressure Gauge Console	$73.32	$188.00	25	24
2314	Electronic Console	$120.90	$390.00	13	12
2341	Depth/Pressure Gauge	$48.30	$105.00	226	225

Page 1 of 3

Figure 18-16: QuickReport's print Preview command displays the report as it will appear on the printed page.

Printing column headers

So far, our report looks okay, but the columns are not identified, and most of the information on the finished output is meaningless (see Figure 18-16). Each column needs a label, best printed using a different font to make the column header stand out.

A column header is simply a group of QRLabel objects, which can show any text you want. These objects are much like Delphi's Label components, but are designed to be inserted into a QuickRep object's bands. Because, in this case, the column header should print only at the top of each page, you need to create a different report band to hold it. If you put labels into a Detail band, they are repeated for each new line of the output (this might be useful in some cases, but it's not the effect needed here).

If you are still viewing QuickReport's print-preview window, close it to return to Delphi, and then follow these steps to add column headers to the report (again, the finished report application is on the CD-ROM in the Source\Report1 directory):

1. Select the QuickRep1 object (its name should appear in the Object Inspector window). Double-click the plus sign next to the Bands property, and set the HasColumnHeader property to True. This adds another band to the QuickRep1 object, faintly labeled Column Header (this text does not appear in the finished report). Figure 18-17 shows the report with its new Column Header band.

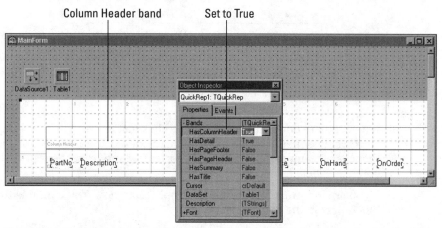

Figure 18-17: Set HasColumnHeader to True to add a Column Header band, which prints column labels on each page of the finished report.

2. Select the QRLabel component from the VCL QReport palette, and click inside the Column Header band to insert a label, named QRLabel1 by default. Drag the QRLabel1 object to above the column that needs a label, and then use the Object Inspector to enter the label's text into the Caption property. You can type any text you want — it doesn't have to match the column's field name. Figure 18-18 shows the completed Column Header band with QRLabel objects atop each column.

3. It's usually best to print column headers using a different font. You may select fonts for each individual QRLabel (and most other) QuickReport components using their Font properties. However, to change the font for the entire band, select the Column Header band (the Object Inspector window's drop-down list shows ColumnHeaderBand1), and then click the ellipsis next to the Font property. In the resulting font selection dialog, select Bold. You may also choose output colors, font family names, point sizes, and make other changes to the selected font and its characteristics.

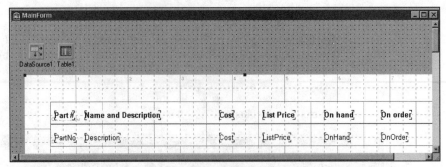

Figure 18-18: The completed Column Header band labels each column with a QRLabel object.

4. When you are done labeling columns, click inside the QuickRep1 object (don't click inside either of the two bands), and choose the Preview command from the local pop-up menu. You can then preview and print the report with all columns labeled.

5. If you are following along, save the application now. You continue to develop this report in the coming sections.

Tip

All objects take on the font characteristics of their parent container. The bands use the report's font, the objects in the bands use the band's fonts, and so on. To change the font for the entire report, select the QuickRep object and set its Font property. You can then modify the Font properties for individual bands and the objects they contain.

Printing system information

You probably want to add system information to the report's pages. This information might display a report title, the current date and time, and a page number. As you did with the report's field and column labels, to add system information, you simply create another type of band into which you drop QuickReport components.

Close the QuickReport preview window if it is open, and return to Delphi. Then, follow these steps to add a title, date and time, and page number to the report:

1. Select the QuickRep1 object, and double-click the plus sign to the left of the Bands property. Set the HasPageHeader property to True. This adds a third band to the report, as shown in Figure 18-19. As with the other bands, the faint text Page Header shows up only at design time, not in the printed output. (You might have to look on your screen to see this text.)

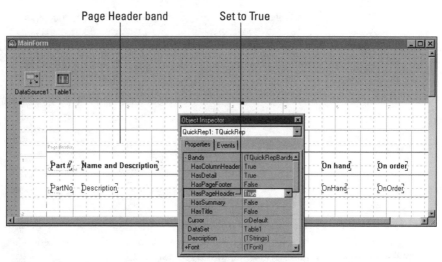

Page Header band   Set to True

Figure 18-19: Create a Page Header band to print titles, dates and times, page numbers, and other information at the top of each page.

2. Objects in a Page Header band are usually QRLabel or QRSysData objects. To add a title to the top of the page, select the QRLabel component from the QReport VCL palette, and click inside the Page Header band to create the QRLabel7 object. Set its Caption property, and select a font size, style, and color using the Font property. (I used Arial, 14 points, Bold Italic, and deep-sea Navy blue. After all, this report is for a dive shop's inventory.)

3. Select the QRSysData component, and drop two of them into the Page Header band. Each of these components can display various types of fixed, system information. Select each object, and set the Data property to the type of information you want — in this case, I set the first object to qrsDateTime and the second to qrs PageNumber. Position the components as you wish. Figure 18-20 shows the report with its completed Page Header band.

4. If you are following along, save the application now. You continue to develop this report in the coming sections.

As you did before, right-click inside the QuickRep1 object (but not inside a band), and then select the Preview command. As Figure 18-21 shows, the finished report is beginning to shape up nicely, but a few more items can be added to polish it some more.

QRLabel object   QRSysData objects

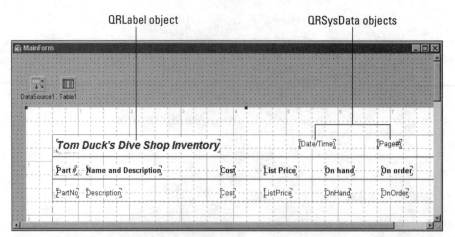

Figure 18-20: The completed Page Header band with a QRLabel title and QRSysData objects showing the date and time, and page number.

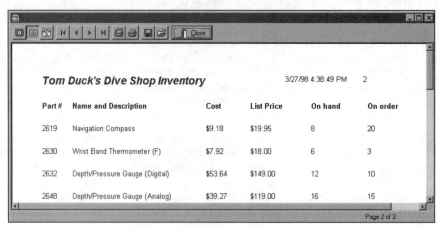

Figure 18-21: The (almost) finished report with page title, date and time, page number, column headers, and database information.

Tip

Rather than use a Page Header band to print the report title, you might set the Bands subproperty, HasTitle, to True. You can then add a title label to the Title Band—this band is printed only on the first page.

To print information at the bottom of each page, set the QuickRep object's Bands subproperty, HasFooter, to True. Use the resulting band just like the Header Band described in this section. Of course, the objects you insert into this band are printed at the bottom rather than the top of each page.

Summing columns

To total the values in a numerical column and to provide other summary information, you need to add one additional band and a couple of components to the report. For example, the developing report (refer back to Figure 18-21) might sum the values in the On Hand and On Order columns. For demonstration purposes, I also show a total for the List Price column, although that doesn't seem useful in this case. However, the total value of the dive shop's inventory would be highly useful to know, so I do include that in the final report.

To add a summary band to the report, close the QuickReport preview dialog window if it is open, and get back to Delphi. Then, follow these steps:

1. Select the QuickRep1 object, and in the Object Inspector, double-click the Bands property. Set the subproperty HasSummary to True. Figure 18-22 shows the growing report object with its new band. As with other bands, the faint label Summary appears only in Delphi, not in the finished printout.

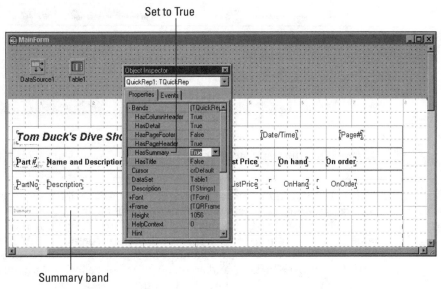

Figure 18-22: Add a Summary band to the report to print column totals and other summary information at the end of the report.

2. The Summary band appears at the end of the chart, after the last row of data. You may add various QuickReport objects to this band. In this case, we need two types: QRLabel objects to identify the summary values and QRExpr objects to perform the calculatations. (The QRExpr icon is neatly labeled $E = mc^{\#2}$.) Deposit two QRLabel objects onto the Summary band and four QRExpr objects. Click and drag the Summary band outline to enlarge it, and arrange the objects as shown in Figure 18-23. Set the QRLabel Caption properties as shown in the figure, and use the Font property to select an output color (I merely changed the text style to bold).

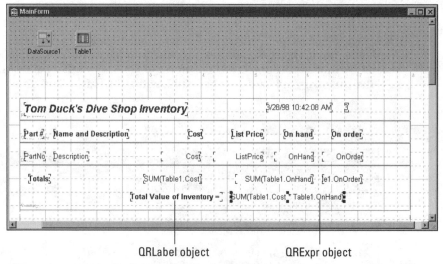

QRLabel object   QRExpr object

Figure 18-23: The completed Summary band with QRLabel and QRExpr objects

3. To calculate the summary values, select each QRExpr object, and set each Expression property as follows. These expressions are displayed in the designed form and in the finished report, they are replaced by the calculated values. Notice that to refer to a specific field in the database table, the expressions refer to the form's Table1 object using dot-notation plus the name of the field (Cost, OnHand, and so on). This is not Pascal programming — the expression text is evaluated by QuickReport:

```
Sum(Table1.Cost)
Sum(Table1.OnHand)
Sum(Table1.OnOrder)
Sum(Table1.Cost * Table1.OnHand)
```

QuickReport Expression Builder

Rather than type expressions into QRExpr Expression properties, you can click this property's ellipsis to open the QuickReport Expression Builder. See Figure 18-24. To use the editor, choose a Function, and click Add in the left panel. For example, choose SUM. Next, select a Dataset object (there's only one in this example, Table1), and choose a Field such as Cost. Click Add in the right panel to add this field to the expression. Optionally click an Operator in the far right panel, and then select another Field such as OnHand. Finally, click OK to complete the expression, which is shown in the bottom window. When you are satisfied, click OK again to enter the expression into the QRExpr Expression property and return to designing the form.

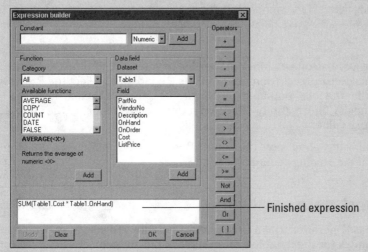

Figure 18-24: Rather than enter QRExpr Expression properties by typing, you can use the QuickReport Expression Builder to create expressions.

4. In addition to setting QRExpr Expression properties, you probably also want to enter a Mask property to configure the printed value. You may also want to do the same for the QRDBText objects in the Detail band — Masks give you better control over column alignment, and they enable you to specify the number of decimal places in numeric values. The following are the mask properties used in the sample report and examples of their results:

```
#,###.00              2,609.20
$#,###,###.00         $24,891.05
####                  43
```

Masks

In a mask, a hatch-character (#) represents any digit, but is printed only if the value has a digit in this position. A zero represents any digit, and is always printed even if the value has no digit there. Commas indicate the separator you want to use in large values.

The type of mask differs depending on the type of data field. TDateField, TDateTimeField, and TTimeField objects are formatted by calling Delphi's DateTimeToStr function. For these components, if no Mask property is entered, the output conforms to the settings in the Windows initialization file, Win.ini, in the [International] section.

TBCDField, TCurrencyField, and TFloatField objects are formatted by calling Delphi's FloatToTextFmt function. For these components, if no Mask or Display format is entered, the value is formatted using the field's Currency property.

5. After setting Expression and Mask properties in your QRExpr objects, right-click the QuickRep1 object (don't click inside a band), and select the Preview command from the local pop-up menu. Figure 18-25 shows the finished report's summary information with column totals and a report of the shop's total inventory value.

6. If you are following along, save the application now. You continue to develop this report in the coming sections.

Sorting report data

Sorting is a database operation, not a QuickReport function. To sort a report, you merely select an index for the database table and print. If an index doesn't exist for the field by which you want to sort a database table, use Database Desktop to create one.

Tip

But, you might wonder, what if you can't create a new index because your database tables are read-only, or they are available only via a remote server? In such cases, I suggest you print the report to a disk text file, and then sort the text lines. If you have special sorting requirements, you can write code to do the sorting, or if you merely want an alphabetical or numerical sort, you can do as I do. Load the text into your word processor and use the program's Sort command. You can then print the sorted text file. This is usually much easier than trying to sort actual database records.

To sort our sample dive shop report by item description, close the QuickReport preview window if it is open, and return to Delphi. Follow these steps:

1. Select the Table1 object. In the Object Inspector (press F11 if it isn't visible), click the down arrow next to the IndexName property. This displays the available field indexes. Select ByDescription (see Figure 18-25).

Select Table ─┐   ┌─Choose index name

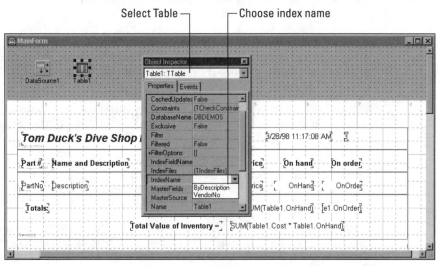

Figure 18-25: Sorting is a database, not a report, operation. To sort a report, select its Table object and select an index listed in the IndexName property.

2. Right-click the QuickRep1 object (but not inside a band) and select Preview to view and print the finished report.

3. If you are following along, save the application now. You need it one more time in the next section.

Printing reports at run time

Until now, you have developed, previewed, and printed reports entirely from within Delphi. If you merely need to create database reports for yourself, this is perfectly acceptable — you don't have to write a scrap of code or finish the application. However, you might want to provide report generation capabilities for your application's end users, and give them all the same previewing and printing features introduced in this chapter.

On the CD-ROM

Follow the next steps to finish the sample Report1 application and to add Buttons for previewing and printing the finished report. The finished program is on the CD-ROM in the Source\Report1 directory. You may load the Report1.dpr project file into Delphi, or if you are following along, close the QuickReport preview window if it is open, get back to Delphi, and follow these steps:

1. Add two BitBtn objects from the Additional VCL palette to the form, and set their Caption properties to Preview... and Print. (You may also add a third BitBtn and set its Kind property to bkClose to provide a quick way for users to exit the application.)

2. Optionally load bitmaps into the Glyph properties for each button. I used the Report.bmp and Print.bmp images supplied with Delphi in the installation directory, Images\Buttons.

3. Double-click BitBtn1 to create an OnClick event handler for the Preview... button. Fill in the procedure using Listing 18-5 as a guide. Double-click BitBtn2 to create a second OnClick event handler for the Print button. Fill in this procedure also using Listing 18-5 as a guide.

4. Press F9 to compile and run the program. Figure 18-26 shows the program's finished display. Click the Preview... button to bring up the QuickReport Preview window. Click Print to print the final report — printing starts as soon as you click this button. If you try this, you see a progress indicator on screen (seen Figure 18-27) while the printout is being created and sent to the printer. You also see data flash by in the report's various components.

Listing 18-5: **Report1\Main.pas (BitBtn OnClick event handlers)**

```
{ Respond to click of the Preview... button }
procedure TMainForm.BitBtn1Click(Sender: TObject);
begin
  QuickRep1.Preview;
end;

{ Respond to click of the Print button }
procedure TMainForm.BitBtn2Click(Sender: TObject);
begin
  QuickRep1.Print;
end;
```

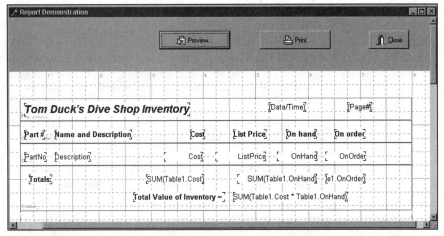

Figure 18-26: The Report1 application's finished display with Preview... and Print buttons

Figure 18-27: During printing, users see this progress indicator.

Expert-User Tips

✦ While using the TeeChart editor, click the Chart and General page tabs, and then click the Print Preview... button to preview and print the chart. Or, you can click Export to write charts to disk metafile or bitmap files. These buttons are much easier to use while designing a chart than exiting the TeeChart editor and right-clicking inside the chart object to preview the chart.

✦ To enter fixed chart axis labels, such as used in this chapter's MayTemp application, open the TeeChart editor, select the Chart page tab, and click the Axis subpage. Inside this page is yet another series of page tabs. Select Scales and disable the Automatic check box. Next, click each of the two Change... buttons and enter the maximum and minimum values to show on the axis selected at left. (Make sure the Visible check box is enabled, or your changes won't be shown in the finished chart.) If you want to set only a minimum or maximum, click that value's Change button, and enable the other's Auto check box.

✦ If you try the preceding tip, do not check the Automatic check box again, or you will have to disable it and re-enter your maximum and minimum scale values.

✦ To prevent report objects from overprinting one another, set their AutoSize properties to True. Also click and drag the individual objects (QRDBText, QRExpr, QRLabel, and others) to size them. Use the Mask property to configure output formats.

✦ It's possible to have a report object stretch to have its band stretch vertically if there is not enough room to print the object's text. To do this, set AutoStretch to True. However, only one component per band should have this property set to True — if more than one object is set to automatically stretch, the end results might be unpredictable (not to mention unreadable).

✦ The sample Report1 application in this chapter has Preview... and Print commands. However, because the QuickReport preview window has its own Print button, it might not be necessary to add a Print command to your applications — calling the QuickRep Preview method provides all viewing and printing services.

✦ To print reports in the background, instead of calling the QuickRep Print method, call PrintBackground. This enables users to continue using the program while printing lengthy reports. You must have a 32-bit version of Delphi (Version 2 or later) to use PrintBackground.

✦ To add a chart to a printed report, select the QRChart object from the QReport VCL palette, and insert this object into a report band. Even though the QRChart component is on the QReport palette, this is a TeeChart object, and is documented further in TeeChart's online documentation files.

 ## Projects to Try

18-1: Modify the MayTemp project to load other files of temperature data. For example, your program might use a File | Open command, or a button, to display a file-open dialog. Enable users to open a temperature file and view the data in the program's line chart.

18-2: Add a print-preview menu command or button to one of the chart example programs in this chapter, MemInfo or MayTemp.

18-3: Add a command to the WinesChart sample application to save its chart in a bitmap file. Display a file-save dialog to enable the user to select an output filename and directory.

18-4: Create printed reports for the MayTemp, MemInfo, and WinesChart sample applications in this chapter.

Summary

✦ The TeeChart library provides extensive charting capabilities. A complete version of the TeeChart library is provided with Delphi. A professional edition with full source code and additional components is available from the product's distributor, teeMach.

✦ Select a chart series to create various types of charts such as pie charts and bar charts. A chart object may have one or more series objects, which may be of the same or different types.

✦ Right-click inside a Chart object and select Print Preview... to print and preview charts inside Delphi.

✦ To preview a chart at run time, which also gives users the capability of printing the chart, add TeePrevi to the unit's *uses* declaration, and call the ChartPreview procedure as demonstrated in this chapter's WinesChart sample application. (This is on the CD-ROM in the Source\WinesChart directory.)

✦ The QuickReport library provides extensive report generation capabilities. A complete version of the QuickReport library is provided with Delphi. A professional edition with full source code and additional components is available from the product's distributor, QuSoft.

✦ QuickReport is a "banded report generator." To create a report, drop a QuickRep object onto a form. Use this object's Bands property to create bands. Drop individual objects into these bands to program the report. Very little, if any, programming is required to create even the most extensive types of reports.

In the next and final part of the book, you look at advanced topics in Delphi and Object Pascal programming, including exceptions, component construction, and such subjects as writing DLLs, using Delph's command-line tools, writing application-level event handlers, and more.

✦　　✦　　✦

Advanced Techniques

After creating an application's interface and programming, many programmers ship the beast out the door and never look back. But the most successful developers take the time to add finishing touches using advanced Delphi techniques that can turn a merely good application into a great piece of software.

The chapters in Part IV cover advanced Delphi programming techniques. You find explanations on how to handle errors gracefully with exceptions, how to construct custom components and ActiveX controls, and how to hone your Delphi skills with programming tips and techniques — including an introduction to writing Internet applications.

Handling Exceptions

Dealing with errors is one of the dirty necessities of a software developer's life. There's no getting around this duty — if your applications fail due to an error condition, your software will be as popular as a fur coat in the tropics during a heat wave. A robust application handles all possible conditions that might cause the program to halt or to produce incorrect results.

Such conditions are called *exceptions* and handling them is the subject of this chapter. Object Pascal provides a highly sophisticated exception-handling mechanism, and every Delphi application has default exception handlers that display error messages and prevent the program from halting unexpectedly if an exception occurs. By incorporating additional exception handling, you can further tailor your application's responses to unexpected conditions and, when trouble brews, perform essential cleanup chores such as freeing allocated memory, saving critical data, and closing files.

Introducing Exceptions

Experienced developers incorporate error handling into their projects during the development cycle. Object Pascal's exception handling is an object-oriented technique that minimizes the hassle of writing this code. Exceptions facilitate developing code and its error handling together, and as you learn in this chapter, exception handlers tend not to get in the way of the program's algorithms the way other techniques do. If you have wished for better error control methods than deeply nested *if* statements, Boolean flags, and special function return values, exception handling is right up your alley.

Where do exceptions originate?

Exceptions can arise from a number of different sources. For example, your program can generate exceptions for abnormal conditions. Delphi components can generate exceptions for a variety of events such as assigning an out-of-range value to a property, or attempting to index a nonexistent array element.

Run-time library procedures and functions can also produce exceptions. Executing a math expression that performs an illegal operation such as dividing by zero guarantees an exception. Other examples of exception-producing operations include referencing a *nil* pointer, allocating more memory than the largest available free block, and executing an illegal type-cast expression.

Potentially, then, every statement in a program may lead to an exception. However, some statements are relatively safe, and a large part of your task in writing robust code is deciding which statements need protection and which ones can do no harm. This chapter's examples explore typical cases that can help you make these decisions for your own programs.

However, this doesn't mean you have to write statements to handle every possible exception. Delphi's global exception handler, which is added to every application, automatically handles exceptions by displaying a dialog box with a description of the problem and the location of the faulty statement. This default response is adequate for test programs and examples such as most of those in this book, but you need to write exception handlers to deal with your program's unique requirements.

Some of the types of operations that can raise exceptions involve the following:

✦ File handling

✦ Memory allocations

✦ Windows resources

✦ Objects and forms you create at run time

✦ Hardware and operating system conflicts

Exceptional keywords

Object Pascal provides several keywords specifically for creating and handling exceptions. These keywords are *try, except, on-do-else, finally, raise,* and *at.* You meet all of them in this chapter. Don't try to use these words for other purposes.

Note Earlier Borland and Turbo Pascal compilers do not recognize Object Pascal's exception keywords. Exception handling is new to Delphi's Object Pascal compiler.

A few good terms

In the preceding paragraphs, I've loosely used a few new terms such as *exception* and *handler* without explaining their meanings. The following are more formal definitions of these and other terms and phrases that you need to know before using exceptions in your applications:

✦ **Exception** — An unusual or unexpected condition that interrupts the normal flow of a program.

✦ **Raising an exception** — The notification of an unusual or unexpected condition. Component methods, run-time library subroutines, expressions, hardware faults — even assigning an illegal value to a component property — can potentially raise exceptions. Your application also can raise an exception on detecting a condition that requires special handling. Use the *raise* keyword to raise an exception.

✦ **Exception handler** — Code that resolves the condition that raised an exception. This code should restore the system to a stable condition so the program may continue to run normally.

✦ **Exception instance** — An object of a class usually derived from the Exception class defined in the SysUtils unit. The exception instance typically contains information that describes the nature of an exceptional condition. Raising an exception allocates memory for an exception instance. Handling the exception automatically frees the allocated memory.

✦ **Try block** — One or more statements, preceded by the keyword *try*, for which you want to handle exceptions or for which you want to free a resource such as a memory allocation.

✦ **Except block** — One or more statements that handle exceptions raised by statements in a preceding *try* block. *Except* blocks begin with the keyword *except,* and may optionally contain *on-do-else* clauses. The *except* block must immediately follow a *try* block.

✦ **Finally block** — One or more statements that must execute to free allocated memory, close files, or perform other critical tasks in the event of an exception raised by statements in a preceding *try* block. *Finally* blocks begin with the keyword *finally* and they must immediately follow a *try* block. *Finally* blocks do not handle exceptions — only *except* blocks can do that.

✦ **Protected-statement block** — One or more statements that have specific handlers for any exceptions those statements might raise. A *protected-statement* block is composed of a pair of *try* and *except* blocks.

✦ **Protected-resource block** — One or more statements that have specific deallocation handlers for any exceptions the use of a resource might raise. Examples of resources include memory allocations, Windows resources, and files. A *protected-resource* block is composed of a pair of *try* and *finally* blocks.

✦ **Robust application** — A program that uses protected-statement and protected-resource blocks to handle all possible error conditions that might occur, and to safely deallocate resources.

Note

Remember this rule: *A robust application takes only time; it leaves no footprints.* The goal in using exceptions is to write robust code that gracefully handles all possible error conditions.

Protected-statement blocks

The protected-statement block is your basic tool for handling exceptions. Listing 19-1 shows a schematic for creating a protected-statement block using the *try* and *except* keywords. Notice that the block ends with the keyword *end* and a semicolon. Comments indicate the types of statements you may insert in various positions. (This listing is for information only and is not on the CD-ROM.)

Listing 19-1: **A schematic for creating a protected-statement block**

```
{ Unprotected statements }
try
   { Protected statements that may raise an exception}
except
   { Statements to handle any raised exceptions }
end;
{ More unprotected statements }
```

Try a real-life example to learn how to use the schematic in Listing 19-1 and create a protected-statement block. Follow these steps:

1. Start a new application.

2. Insert a Button object into the form.

3. Double-click Button1, and use Listing 19-2 as a guide to writing an OnClick event handler with a protected-statement block. This listing text is in file Except1.pas on the CD-ROM in the Source\ExceptMisc directory.

4. Compile and run the program by pressing F9. Click the program's button to force an exception to occur. Figure 19-1 shows the message dialog displayed by the exception handler's ShowMessage statement you see when you click the button.

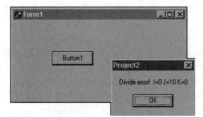

Figure 19-1: The Except1.pas OnClick procedure displays this message when it handles the divide-by-zero exception.

Listing 19-2: **ExceptMisc\Except1.pas. This OnClick Button event handler demonstrates how to create a protected-statement block using *try* and *except*.**

```
procedure TForm1.Button1Click(Sender: TObject);
var
  I, J, K: Integer;
begin
  I := 0;
  J := 10;
  try
    K := J div I;
  except
    ShowMessage(
     'Divide error! '+
     ' I=' + IntToStr(I) +
     ' J=' + IntToStr(J) +
     ' K=' + IntToStr(K) );
  end;
end;
```

Tip

When testing exceptions, it's probably best to close Delphi's message-spy utility WinSight32 if it is running. If you are using Delphi 4, select Tools|Debugger options, select the language exceptions pages, and uncheck the "Stop on Delphi Exceptions" check box. If you are using Delphi 3, choose the Preferences page tab, and disable the Break on Exception check box. Also see "Environmental Considerations" in this chapter for advice on using these options for debugging a program's exception handling. While learning how to use exceptions, however, it's best to disable these extra exception-reporting devices. This way, you see exactly how the program responds on the end user's system. (Alternatively, you can compile the program and run its .exe code file using Windows Explorer.)

The procedure in Listing 19-2 performs the mathematical equivalent of eating peas with a knife. The expression *J div I* attempts to divide ten by zero, which causes the Object Pascal run-time library to raise an exception. However, because the expression is in a *try* block, the procedure handles the exception by displaying a message. The ShowMessage statement in the *except* block executes only if one or more statements in the preceding *try* block fail. The program exercises total control over any exceptional conditions—if the program enters the *except* block, *K's* value is undefined. Of course, this is only a simplistic example, but in deeply nested, complex code, such knowledge is priceless.

To demonstrate what happens when unprotected statements raise exceptions, delete *try*, *except*, and the first *end* from Listing 19-2. Leave the other statements as they are, and then press F9 to compile and run the modified program. Click the button to view the dialog box that Delphi's default exception handler displays, shown in Figure 19-2. This experiment shows that even if you don't use protected-statement blocks, all exceptions are eventually handled. The default response to those exceptions may be inadequate for a commercial-grade application, but at least the program doesn't explode in a puff of smoke. A default response is always better than none.

On the CD-ROM

When an exception occurs in a *try* block, execution immediately jumps to the first statement in the *except* block. Other statements in the *try* block do not execute after the one that raised the exception, and this fact can have important consequences. For instance, consider the protected block in Listing 19-3, which you can insert into a Button object's OnClick event handler as in the preceding test. (The procedure is on the CD-ROM in file Except2.pas in the Source\ExceptMisc directory.) If any of the division expressions fail for any reason, execution immediately jumps to ShowMessage, after which the procedure continues normally following the protected block's *end*. For example, if the second division fails, which it will with the values assigned to the procedure variables, the third statement in the *try* block does not execute. Figure 19-3 shows the message dialog displayed by the procedure's ShowMessage statement.

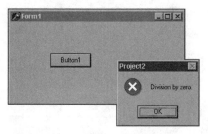

Figure 19-2: A Delphi application's default exception handler displays this dialog box for any unhandled exceptions.

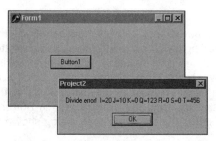

Figure 19-3: The Except2.pas OnClick event handler displays this message when an exception occurs.

Listing 19-3: ExceptMisc\Except2.pas. If any one of the three division statements raises an exception, execution immediately jumps to ShowMessage.

```
procedure TForm1.Button1Click(Sender: TObject);
var
  I, J, K, Q, R, S, T: Integer;
begin
  I := 20; J := 10; Q := 123; T := 456;
  try
    K := (I div J) - 2;
    R := Q div K;   // ???
    S := T div R;
  except
```

(continued)

Listing 19-3 *(continued)*

```
    ShowMessage(
      'Divide error! '+
      ' I=' + IntToStr(I) +
      ' J=' + IntToStr(J) +
      ' K=' + IntToStr(K) +
      ' Q=' + IntToStr(Q) +
      ' R=' + IntToStr(R) +
      ' S=' + IntToStr(S) +
      ' T=' + IntToStr(T) );
  end;
end;
```

On the
CD-ROM

Listing 19-3 demonstrates one of the key advantages of exception handling—the elimination of repetitive error checks preceding or following individual, related statements. It's useful to compare the non-exception error-handling equivalent, of which there are countless variations. Listing 19-4 shows a typical messy case. Don't ever write code like this. (The procedure is on the CD-ROM in file Except3.pas in the Source\ExceptMisc directory. You can test it by using the procedure as a Button's OnClick event handler.) The procedure displays the same message dialog shown in Figure 19-3.

Listing 19-4: **ExceptMisc\Except3.pas. With exception handling, you never need to write messy code like this.**

```
procedure TForm1.Button1Click(Sender: TObject);
var
  I, J, K, Q, R, S, T: Integer;
  { Sub-procedure for displaying error message }
  procedure ReportError;
  begin
    ShowMessage(
      'Divide error! '+
      ' I=' + IntToStr(I) +
      ' J=' + IntToStr(J) +
      ' K=' + IntToStr(K) +
      ' Q=' + IntToStr(Q) +
      ' R=' + IntToStr(R) +
      ' S=' + IntToStr(S) +
      ' T=' + IntToStr(T) );
  end;
```

```
begin
  I := 20; J := 10; Q := 123; T := 456;
  if J = 0 then ReportError else
  begin
    K := (I div J) - 2;
    if K = 0 then ReportError else
    begin
      R := Q div K;
      if R = 0 then ReportError else
      begin
        S := T div R;
      end;
    end;
  end;
end;
```

Typical questions

The following three points answer some typical questions you might have about how protected-statement blocks affect program flow:

✦ If a statement in an *except* block handles an exception, the procedure or function continues normally after the protected block's end.

✦ If no statement handles an exception, the current procedure or function immediately exits, and the exception passes up through the call chain until it finds a suitable handler.

✦ Unhandled exceptions eventually reach the application's default exception handler, which displays a dialog box and message. The default exception handler is a catchall for any exceptions for which you do not provide a handler. You do not have to write a default exception handler — Delphi automatically attaches it to every compiled application. Later in this chapter, I explain how to replace the default handler with your own code, which is rarely necessary, but might be useful in advanced projects.

Protected-resource blocks

Displaying error messages is only one aspect of exception handling. A robust application must also restore stability when disaster strikes. For example, if a disk error occurs or if the system runs low on gas, the application must free any allocated memory blocks that might needlessly occupy space until the user reboots. A robust program gracefully recovers from errors by closing open files, deallocating Windows resources, and doing all that's possible to restore order in the midst of chaos.

Use the *try* and *finally* keywords to create protected-resource blocks. Listing 19-5 shows the basic schematic, which closely resembles a protected-statement block. In fact, the only difference is the word *finally* in place of *except*. However, despite an apparent similarity, protected-resource blocks differ greatly in operation from protected-statement blocks. (This listing's text is for illustration only and is not on the CD-ROM.)

Listing 19-5: A schematic for creating a protected-resource block

```
{ Allocate memory or other resource}
try
   { Statements that may raise an exception }
finally
   { Free the resource-guaranteed to execute!}
end;
{ Continue if no exceptions occurred in the try block }
```

Statements in the *finally* block always execute, regardless of whether any statements in the *try* block raise an exception. Typically, the statements in the *finally* block free memory, close files, and perform other must-do operations that restore stability to the system when an exception occurs.

Caution   Statements outside a *try* block that raise an exception immediately cause the procedure or function to exit, skipping the *finally* block. To guarantee execution of the *finally* block, place in the *try* block all statements that might raise an exception and leave an allocated resource dangling.

A common confusion with protected-resource blocks is where to place a statement that allocates a resource. Even though this may raise an exception (for example, if a memory allocation fails due to a shortage of RAM), the allocation statement does not belong in the *try* block. This rule is critical! One way to remember the rule is to keep in mind that the purpose of a *finally* block is to deallocate a resource, and you don't want to deallocate something that wasn't allocated in the first place. Therefore, you should place the allocating statement before the *try* block. Inside that block, insert any statements that might raise an exception, causing the procedure or function to exit and leaving the allocated resource dangling somewhere in memory until the user reboots.

A simple example explains this important technique, and shows how to use protected-resource blocks to guard against dangling resources, which can eventually choke the RAM out of your system. Disappearing icons, text that strangely reverts to the System font, an unresponsive keyboard, and a general sluggishness are the symptoms of a resource leak, usually caused by dangling memory and other resource allocations.

Try these steps:

1. Start a new application.

2. Insert a Button object into the form.

3. Double-click the Button to create an OnClick event handler, and fill in the procedure using Listing 19-6 as a guide. (This text is on the CD-ROM in the Except4.pas file in the Source\ExceptMisc directory.)

4. Press F9 to compile and run the program, and then click the button to test what happens if an exception occurs in a procedure that allocates a block of memory. Figures 19-4 and 19-5 show the message dialogs you see in turn when running the test procedure.

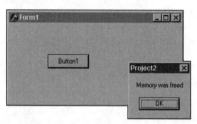

Figure 19-4: Even though an exception occurs in the Except4.pas test procedure, this message dialog and the one shown in Figure 19-5 prove that the allocated memory is properly freed.

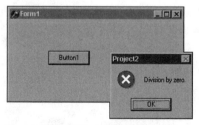

Figure 19-5: Except4.pas displays this dialog after you close the one shown in Figure 19-4.

Listing 19-6: ExceptMisc\Except4.pas. This OnClick Button event handler demonstrates how to create a protected-resource block using *try* and *finally*.

```
procedure TForm1.Button1Click(Sender: TObject);
var
  I, J, K: Integer;
  P: Pointer;
begin
  I := 0;
  J := 10;
  GetMem(P, 4098);  // Allocate memory resource
  try
    K := J div I;    // Raises an exception!
    ShowMessage('Results: ' +
      ' I=' + IntToStr(I) +
      ' J=' + IntToStr(J) +
      ' K=' + IntToStr(K) );
  finally
    FreeMem(P, 4098);  // Guaranteed to execute
    ShowMessage('Memory was freed');
  end;
end;
```

Listing 19-6 resembles the protected-statement block, but adds a memory allocation statement that calls GetMem to reserve 4,098 bytes of RAM. Notice this statement (as well as the obviously harmless integer variable assignments) are placed outside the *try* block. Inside the *try* block is the potentially faulty division expression. If that division were not inside *try*, and if that statement's execution raised an exception, the procedure would immediately end, leaving the allocated memory block lost in space.

The *finally* block guards against that blunder by calling FreeMem regardless of whether the division raises an exception. (Assign two to *I* and rerun the test to prove this.) The final ShowMessage statement is just for demonstration — in practice, *finally* blocks usually carry out their services in silence.

Note

Remember: The statements in a *finally* block are guaranteed to execute even if any exceptions are raised in the preceding *try* block.

A *finally* block does not handle exceptions — only an *except* block can do that. A *finally* block merely guarantees execution of statements regardless of whether any statements in the preceding *try* block raise an exception. In this case, the exception is not handled, and therefore, when you run the sample code in Listing 19-6, Delphi's default exception handler displays an error message dialog. As the next section explains, however, it's possible for a procedure to have protected-statement and protected-resource blocks.

Nested *try-except* and *try-finally* blocks

If you are just getting started with exception handling, you may wonder how you can handle exceptions and protect resource allocations in the same procedure. The trick is to remember that these are entirely separate operations, and you cannot merge *try-except* and *try-finally* blocks. There is no such animal as a *try-except-finally* block in Delphi's Object Pascal.

However, you can nest a *try-except* block inside a *try-finally* block to handle exceptions and to prevent dangling resources. Listing 19-7 shows the basic schematic for accomplishing this additional level of protection. (This code is for illustration only and is not on the CD-ROM.)

Listing 19-7: **A schematic for creating nested protected-statement and protected-resource blocks**

```
{ Allocate resource }
try
  try
    { Statements that might raise exceptions }
  except
    { Statements that handle exceptions }
  end;
finally
  { Free the resource }
end;
```

You need to use nested *try-except* and *try-finally* blocks as illustrated in Listing 19-7 only when the *except* block handles a specific type of exception, in which case, other types of exceptions might cause the procedure to end prematurely. In this and preceding examples, the *except* block handles all exceptions that occur in the preceding *try* block. As I explain later in this chapter, however, you usually trap specific exceptions, and allow others to pass upwards in the call chain, perhaps reaching Delphi's default exception handlers. In the absence of a *try-finally* block, those other exceptions, because they are not handled in the procedure, would cause the memory allocation not to be freed.

Later in this chapter, I explain how to handle specific types of exceptions using *on-do* statements. For now, Listing 19-8 shows an executable example of the schematic in Listing 19-7. Listing 19-9 shows this same code with the nested *try-except* block banished to a callable function, which is somewhat less efficient, but eliminates the nesting that some developers find confusing. Try both of these procedures as you did before by inserting Buttons into a form and creating OnClick event handlers. Press F9 to compile and run, and then click the button. The program's messages prove that the allocated memory is freed even though an exception occurs. The two listings are in files Except5.pas and Except6.pas located on the CD-ROM in the Source\ExceptMisc directory.

Listing 19-8's Button OnClick event handler demonstrates how to nest a *try-except* block inside a *try-finally* block to handle exceptions and to prevent dangling resources.

Listing 19-8: **ExceptMisc\Except5.pas**

```
procedure TForm1.Button1Click(Sender: TObject);
var
  I, J, K: Integer;
  P: Pointer;
begin
  I := 0;
  J := 10;
  GetMem(P, 4098);
  try
    try
      K := J div I;
      ShowMessage('Results: K=' + IntToStr(K));
    except
      ShowMessage('Divide error! ' +
        ' I=' + IntToStr(I) +
        ' J=' + IntToStr(J) );
    end;
  finally
    FreeMem(P, 4098);
    ShowMessage('Memory was freed');
  end;
end;
```

Listing 19-9's function and OnClick event handler is operationally identical to the code in Listing 19-8, but it places the nested *try-except* block inside a callable function, GetInt. The result is a cleaner OnClick procedure at the expense of an additional function call.

Listing 19-9: **ExceptMisc\Except6.pas**

```
function GetInt: Integer;
var
  I, J, K: Integer;
begin
  I := 0;
  J := 10;
  try
    K := J div I;  // Raises an exception
    Result := K;    // Assign function result (doesn't execute)
    ShowMessage('Results: K=' + IntToStr(K));
  except
    Result := 0;    // Assign function result on error
    ShowMessage('Divide error! ' +
    ' I=' + IntToStr(I) +
    ' J=' + IntToStr(J) );
  end;
end;

procedure TForm1.Button1Click(Sender: TObject);
var
  K: Integer;
  P: Pointer;
begin
  GetMem(P, 4098);  // Allocate memory resource
  try
    K := GetInt;    // Might cause an exception
  finally
    FreeMem(P, 4098);  // Guaranteed to execute
    ShowMessage('Memory was freed');
  end;
end;
```

Listing 19-9 demonstrates how exception handling decouples a program's normal statements from its error-handling logic. For example, delete *try, except,* all statements in the *except* block, and the first *end* from the GetInt function. The stripped function looks like this:

```
begin
  I := 0;
  J := 10;
  K := J div I;  // Raises an exception and exits procedure!
  Result := K;
  ShowMessage('Results: K=' + IntToStr(K));
end;
```

Press F9 to compile and rerun the program, and then click the button to force an exception to occur. The Button's OnClick event handler still frees the allocated memory even though the function no longer handles the exception raised by the faulty division. If the OnClick event handler did not use *try-finally*, GetInt's exception would cause the OnClick procedure to end, leaving the allocated memory dangling.

Handling and Raising Exceptions

The preceding sections introduce most of the exception-handling techniques needed to write robust Delphi applications. In this part, you go beyond the basics to learn how to handle specific types of exceptions, and how to raise and reraise exceptions of your own. First, however, you need to consider some environmental options that affect how your development system responds to exceptions.

An environmental consideration when developing applications — and especially for debugging exception handlers — is whether to have Delphi halt a program when an exception occurs. To enable this feature, choose the Tools | Environment Options... command. If you are using Delphi 3, choose the Preferences page tab, and enable the Break on Exception check box. If you are using Delphi 4, select Tools | Debugger options, select the language exceptions page, and uncheck the Stop on Delphi Exceptions check box.

Note   Some of the commands noted here differ depending on your version of Delphi. If you are using Delphi Version 1, select Environment|Options; for Version 2, select Tools|Options, and then follow the preceding instructions for Delphi Version 3.

Try running an exception-test program (one containing Listing 19-2's event handler, for example) with this option on and off. When enabled, the option displays a full report of any exceptions, and the program halts at the statement that caused the problem. Figure 19-6 shows the resulting dialog box that Delphi displays. The offending line that caused the problem is highlighted in Delphi's code editor window. It's important to understand that Delphi itself, not the application's default exception handler, displays this dialog window. You must run your program inside Delphi (in other words, in debug mode) to see it. Your application's end users never see this dialog.

If you are following along, read the dialog's information, and click the OK button. Examine the highlighted statement that raised the exception. The program is still running, but is paused at the offending statement. Press F9 to continue running, or you can press F8 or F7 to single-step the program starting from this location.

Tip   Even though you are looking at your program's code in Delphi, the program is still running in debug mode. You must run and exit the program before you can continue to develop the application.

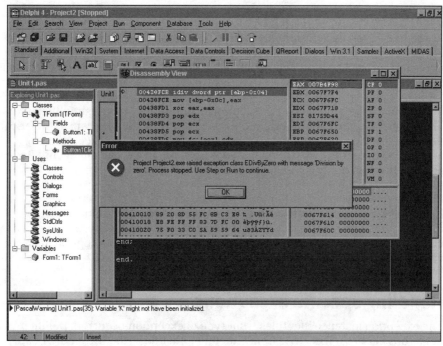

Figure 19-6: When exceptions are handled by the debugger, and an exception occurs, the program is paused and Delphi displays a dialog box similar to this one.

To follow along, press F9 now. You are switched back to the program window, and depending on the example you are running, you see one or more message dialogs that are displayed by the program itself. The first time you try these steps, the multitude of dialogs might be confusing, but after you understand the different levels of exception handling that are taking place, the information is invaluable in chasing down bugs — especially any errors in your own exception handlers.

When exceptions are handled by the Delphi debugger, you can run the compiled application using Windows Explorer to test how the finished program responds to errors outside of Delphi. Run your code inside Delphi for information on exceptions in addition to any exception handling your application provides.

Note

To continue with this chapter, you may elect to have the debugger handle exceptions, but you need to press F9 once to continue running the program at each exception occurrence. If you find this troublesome, turn off debugger exception handling. If you are using Delphi 3, choose the Preferences page tab, and disable the Break on Exception check box.

The exception instance

As mentioned, an exception is an event or condition that interrupts the normal flow of a program. Physically, however, an exception is an object of a class, usually derived from the Exception class defined in the SysUtils unit. This object is called the *exception instance*.

Raising an exception creates an exception instance. If a statement in the *except* part of a protected-statement block handles the exception, the program automatically destroys the exception instance. If no statement handles the exception, the application passes the exception instance upwards in the call chain until finding a suitable handler, or until reaching the default exception handler.

The only safe way to destroy an exception instance is to handle the exception. Handling an exception destroys the exception instance automatically. In the following sections, you learn how to reference exception instances. Never write code to free or destroy these objects. Attempting to free an exception instance causes a fatal application error.

Handling specific exceptions

The exception instance identifies what type of exception occurred. Delphi provides numerous classes, all derived from Exception, that describe the nature of specific problems. You may use this information to refine your program's response to exceptions, and you may write exception handlers that are triggered by specific kinds of problems. To accomplish these tasks, use an *on-do* statement inside an *except* block.

The *on-do* statement performs two services: it identifies a specific kind of exception, and it can provide a reference to the exception instance. Typically, the exception instance provides information about what kind of problem occurred. Your program can use this information to resolve the problem and to display helpful notes to users.

Referencing an exception instance

The Except1 sample application on the CD ROM in the Source\Except1 directory demonstrates how to use *on-do* to reference an exception instance. Figure 19-7 shows the program's window and the dialog displayed when you click the button. This forces an exception to occur by attempting to assign illegal values to the window's two scrollbar controls. Listing 19-10 shows the Button object's OnClick event handler.

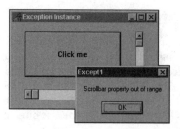

Figure 19-7: Clicking Except1's button forces an exception and displays the dialog box shown here.

Listing 19-10: **Except1\Main.pas (Button1 object's OnClick event handler)**

```
procedure TMainForm.Button1Click(Sender: TObject);
begin
  try
    ScrollBar1.SetParams(0, 500, 0);
    ScrollBar2.SetParams(0, 500, 0);
  except
    on E: Exception do
      ShowMessage(E.Message);
  end;
end;
```

The program calls SetParams for the two scrollbars, but to force an exception to occur, it purposely reverses the Min and Max arguments. The ScrollBar component specifies that Min must be less than or equal to Max, and the first call to SetParams therefore raises the exception.

In the *except* block, an *on-do* statement declares a variable *E* of the Exception class. (You can use any name, but *E* is convenient.) This statement does not create a new Exception instance; it simply creates a reference (*E*) to the exception instance that describes the problem. The program uses *E*'s Message string property to display a meaningful message in a dialog box.

However, trapping every type of exception this way is not usually the best course of action. A better plan is to trap specific exceptions, and allow others to pass through normally. This way, your code responds to exceptions it is prepared to handle—a bad parameter, for example, or a divide-by-zero error—but allows Delphi's default exception handlers to take care of more serious problems such as an out-of-memory fault.

On the
CD-ROM

Trapping specific types of exceptions

You can use *on-do* to trap specific types of exceptions. For example to handle divide-by-zero exceptions, but allow another handler higher in the call chain to handle other exception types, use *on-do* as follows. Specify the exception class you need in the *on-do* statement, as shown in Listing 19-11. This is the same code from Listing 19-2, but this time, specifically handles only the exception EDivByZero. On the CD-ROM, the procedure text is in file Except7.pas in the Source\ExceptMisc directory.

Listing 19-11: This OnClick Button event handler demonstrates how to create a protected-statement block using *try* and *except* for a specific type of exception.

```
procedure TForm1.Button1Click(Sender: TObject);
var
  I, J, K: Integer;
begin
  I := 0;
  J := 10;
  try
    K := J div I;
  except
    on E: EDivByZero do
    begin
      ShowMessage(E.Message +
        ' I=' + IntToStr(I) +
        ' J=' + IntToStr(J) +
        ' K=' + IntToStr(K) );
    end;
  end;
end;
```

Notice the ShowMessage statement first displays E.Message, which is declared in all exception objects as a String property. You don't have to display this string, but it is included in all exception objects, and in most cases, an error dialog should show it somewhere.

Examining the exception classes

Following is a list of exception classes defined in various Delphi units. This is not a comprehensive list, but includes most of the types of exceptions you are likely to respond to or raise in your own applications. All classes in the table are derived, not necessarily directly, from the Exception class. Use them as Listing 19-11 demonstrates. For example, to trap an EPrinter error, use code such as this:

```
try
  { Printer operations }
except
  on E: EPrinter do
    ShowMessage(E.Message);  // Display printer error message
end;
```

✦ **EAbort** — Silent exception raised by calling Abort.

✦ **EAbstractError** — Raised if a statement attempts to call an abstract method. Delphi displays a warning if your code creates an instance of a class with one or more abstract methods. The only time you will receive an EAbstractError exception is if you ignore this warning.

✦ **EAccessViolation** — Indicates one of three invalid memory access errors: using a *nil* pointer, writing to a code memory page, accessing a non-allocated memory page. Don't raise this exception explicitly.

✦ **EArrayError** — Indicates one of three illegal array operations: an out-of-range index, attempting to add an item to a fixed size array, inserting an item into a sorted array. See also EBitsError.

✦ **EAssertionFailed** — Raised by Assert when passed a False Boolean expression.

✦ **EBitsError** — Indicates one of two illegal Boolean array (using the TBits class) operations: a negative or out-of-range index value.

✦ **EClassNotFound** — This exception is raised when the program attempts to read an object of a class that is not linked in the application (for example, its declaration was deleted from a form's source code module, or the program attempted to read an unknown object from a stream).

✦ **EComponentError** — Raised on any errors during a component's registration. Also raised if the program attempts to obtain a component's COM interface if that component does not support COM. See Chapter 20 for information on constructing and registering components.

✦ **EControlC** — Console applications only. This exception is raised if the program user presses Ctrl+C. This exception is never raised in a Windows application.

✦ **EConvertError**—Raised for conversion errors such as attempting to convert a string with a non-numeric character into an integer by calling StrToInt.

✦ **EDatabaseError**—General database error exception raised by Data Access and Data Controls components. For more specific database exceptions, search Delphi's online help for EDB. exception classes, for example, EDBClient and EDBEditError.

✦ **EDateTimeError**—Raised by invalid dates and times entered into a TDateTimePicker object.

✦ **EDivByZero**—Integer attempt to divide by zero.

✦ **EFCreateError**—Indicates a file-creation error.

✦ **EFilerError**—Raised for problems during file-stream operations.

✦ **EFOpenError**—Indicates a file-open error.

✦ **EInOutError**—File input/output error. The exception instance ErrorCode Integer field holds the I/O error code. This exception is raised only in code compiled with the {$I+} switch in effect (this is the default setting). Error codes are: 2-file not found, 3-invalid filename, 4-too many open files, 5-access denied, 100-end of file, 101-disk full, and 106-invalid input. Other error codes are possible—see Microsoft's MS-DOS Technical Reference manual and various Win32 documentation sources.

✦ **EIntError**—Base class for integer math exceptions. Never created as an exception object, but may be used to trap all integer-operation errors. To create specific integer exception objects, use instead the derived exception classes EDivByZero, ERangeError, and EIntOverflow.

✦ **EIntfCastError**—Raised when a statement attempts to cast an inappropriate class with the *as* operator.

✦ **EIntOverflow**—Integer overflow.

✦ **EInvalidArgument**—An out-of-range value in a financial accounting function in the Math unit.

✦ **EInvalidCast**—Invalid type-cast expression.

✦ **EInvalidGraphic**—Raised when the program attempts to open an unrecognized graphics file (for example, mistakenly opening a text file as a bitmap).

✦ **EInvalidGraphicOperation**—Indicates an illegal graphics operation such as attempting to change the size of an icon.

✦ **EInvalidGridOperation**—Raised for illegal grid-component operations such as attempting to access a non-existent cell.

✦ **EInvalidOp** — Invalid floating-point math processor operation. This exception is raised for undefined math errors when, for example, the CPU detects an undefined instruction, attempts to perform an invalid operation, or if the processor math stack overflows.

✦ **EInvalidOperation** — Indicates an invalid operation on a component, specifically one that requires a window handle for a component whose Parent property is unassigned. Can also occur for illegal drag-and-drop operations.

✦ **EInvalidPointer** — Invalid pointer — for example, attempting to use a *nil* pointer or disposing an allocated memory block more than once.

✦ **EMathError** — Base class for floating-point math exceptions. Never used directly as an exception object. Use instead the derived exception classes EInvalidArgument, EInvalidOp, EOverflow, EUnderflow, and EZeroDivide.

✦ **EMCIDeviceError** — Raised for problems with a Media Control Interface (MCI) driver.

✦ **EMenuError** — Indicates an illegal operation on a menu — for example, a statement that incorrectly affects a menu object.

✦ **ENoResultSet** — Raised by Query database objects used with no SELECT statement provided.

✦ **EOleCtrlError** — Raised on a failed attempt to link to an ActiveX control.

✦ **EOleException** — Raised on any failures with IDispatch method calls.

✦ **EOleSysError** — Raised if the IDispatch invoke method fails.

✦ **EOutOfMemory** — Unable to fulfill requested memory allocation.

✦ **EOutOfResources** — Raised on failed attempt to create a Windows handle.

✦ **EOverflow** — Floating-point overflow (value too large).

✦ **EPackageError** — Raised for any errors involving packages.

✦ **EPrinter** — Indicates an error occurred during printing.

✦ **EPrivilege** — Raised for processor privilege faults such as an attempt to execute an instruction that is not permitted at the current privilege level.

✦ **EPropertyError** — Raised if a property value cannot be set, for example, if it is out of range or an illegal data type.

✦ **EPropReadOnly** — Indicates an illegal attempt to write to a read-only property using OLE automation.

✦ **EPropWriteOnly** — Indicates an illegal attempt to read from a write-only property using OLE automation.

✦ **ERangeError**—Value out of range for an array or short-string indexing operation, and also for assignments to scalar and subrange variables. This exception is not raised for long strings. It requires the program to be compiled with the {$R+} switch in effect, which is typically done only during debugging. The default setting {$R-} turns off range checking, and prevents this type of exception from being raised.

✦ **EReadError**—Raised for a faulty attempt to read stream data, and also if Delphi is unable to read a property value during a form object's creation.

✦ **ERegistryException**—Indicates a failure with an operation performed on the Windows registry such as trying to modify an area of the registry with insufficient user privileges.

✦ **EResNotFound**—Raised if a specified resource such as an icon is not found. A typical cause of this problem is an accidentally deleted or commented-out {$R *.DFM} directive in the implementation section of a form unit's source code module.

✦ **ESocketError**—Indicates a failure with a Windows socket object.

✦ **EStackOverflow**—Raised when the current thread's stack grows into the "final guard page," which indicates that the program is soon to run out of memory. Typical causes of this problem are extremely large local variables in procedures and functions and also in deeply nested recursive subroutines. (Move large variables outside of procedures and functions.)

✦ **EStreamError**—Base class for file-streaming errors. However, an object of this class might be created if a stream cannot be allocated.

✦ **EStringListError**—Indicates an error with a string-list operation such as an invalid index applied to a list-box.

✦ **EThread**—Indicates a thread-synchronization problem.

✦ **ETreeViewError**—Raised when an illegal index is used with the TreeView component.

✦ **EUnderflow**—Floating-point math underflow (value too small).

✦ **EVariantError**—Indicates an error with a variant data type such as an invalid type-cast expression, or an out-of-range index.

✦ **EWin32Error**—This exception is raised if a Windows error is detected. The default exception handler displays a dialog box listing the error code value and message string. You can use the SysUtils Win32Check function along with this exception to fetch the message string from the operating system.

✦ **EWriteError**—Raised for file-stream write errors.

✦ **EZeroDivide**—Floating-point attempt to divide by zero.

Finding Exception Class Properties

Look up specific types of exceptions in Delphi's online help, and then search for their declarations. This tells you what types of properties in addition to Message an exception class declares. For example, the SysUtils unit defines EInOutError like this:

```
EInOutError = class(Exception)
public
   ErrorCode: Integer;
end;
```

This declaration tells you that, in addition to a Message property which all exceptions provide, EInOutError also provides an ErrorCode field. The Sysutils.pas source code file is located in Delphi's installation directory Source\Rtl\Sys. Specific exception classes are declared in many other Delphi source code files.

You can also use these classes for pure identification purposes without creating a reference to the exception instance. For example, replace the *on-do* statement in Listing 19-11 with the following:

```
on EDivByZero do
  ShowMessage('Divide error');
```

The first line compares the exception instance's class with EDivByZero, and if the object is of that class, calls ShowMessage. Exceptions of other types travel upwards through the call chain. Use this technique if you don't need to refer to the exception instance. Or, use this code:

```
on E: EDivByZero do
  ShowMessage(E.Message);
```

to reference the exception instance *E* and display its contained message string.

Handling multiple exceptions

The *except* block may respond to more than one type of exception. For instance, the following code fragment shows how to handle three types of exception objects; others continue up the chain until they find a handler:

```
on EDivByZero do
  ...;
on EInOutError do
  ...;
on EOutOfMemory do
  ...;
```

You can also declare exception instances to access various other information provided with specific exception types. For example, the following code fragment traps three types of exceptions, and defines an exception instance *E* for each type:

```
try
  {Statements that might raise one of the following exceptions}
except
  on E: EDivByZero do
    ShowMessage(E.Message + ' (I = 0)');
  on E: EInOutError do
    with E do
      ShowMessage(Message + ' #:' + IntToStr(ErrorCode));
  on E: EOutOfMemory do
  begin
    ShowMessage(E.Message);
// free reserved memory here
  end;
end;
```

Each exception handler in the preceding fragment uses the information in the object *E* differently. The first handler traps integer divide-by-zero errors, and displays *E*'s Message property along with an attached literal string that provides a little more information about what went wrong.

The second exception handler traps I/O errors. It uses a *with* statement to access *E*'s properties, and displays the E.Message string along with the E.Errorcode variable declared for the EInOutError exception class. This value is converted to a string with a call to Delphi's IntToStr function.

The third exception handler traps out-of-memory errors. It displays E.Message. The comment indicates a good place to free a reserved block of memory that a program might allocate to provide some additional memory, if only for the purpose of allowing the user to exit gracefully from the application, or to terminate the operation that caused the out-of-memory condition.

Caution   When you use *on-do* to handle specific exception classes, the presence of other types of unhandled exceptions causes the current procedure or function to exit immediately. In such cases, use a *try-finally* block to free allocated memory, close files, and perform other must-do operations.

Raising a new exception

Many exceptions are raised automatically — a divide-by-zero error, for example. But you may also raise your own exceptions to report errors or unusual conditions.

Use the *raise* keyword to raise a new exception. Following *raise,* create an exception instance of the Exception or any derived class. Assuming the program has a Boolean variable ErrorFlag that, if True, indicates a problem, the program might raise an exception with code such as this:

```
if ErrorFlag then
  raise Exception.Create('Error');
```

In place of Exception, you may use most of the previously listed classes. You can also raise exceptions of your own classes, but more on that later. The results of this code are identical in every way to exceptions raised by components, math expressions, hardware faults, or any other source. You can write exception handlers for the exceptions your code raises, or you can let the application's default exception handlers catch them.

Note

Raising an exception immediately searches for the nearest exception handler in the procedure or function that calls *raise*. If the procedure or function itself has no handlers, *raise* effectively exits the subroutine.

Caution

For a demonstration of raising exceptions, run the Except2 demonstration on the CD-ROM in the Source\Except2 directory, and then enter a value from 0 to 99 in the Edit window. Figure 19-8 shows the program's display. Click the I'm Done button to end the program. Run the program again and this time enter an illegal value such as 100. As you can see, this raises an exception that prevents the program from closing. Delphi's default exception handlers take care of reporting the problem. Listing 19-12 shows the button's OnClick event handler.

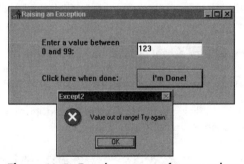

Figure 19-8: Entering an out-of-range value in the Except2's Edit window raises an exception that prevents the program from closing.

Listing 19-12: **Except2\Main.pas (Button OnClick event handler)**

```
procedure TMainForm.Button1Click(Sender: TObject);
var
  N: Integer;
begin
  N := StrToInt(Edit1.Text);
  if (N < 0) or (N > 99) then
    raise ERangeError.Create('Value out of range! Try again')
  else begin
    ShowMessage('Success! Click Ok to end program');
    Close;
  end;
end;
```

In the Button object's OnClick event handler, StrToInt converts the Edit1 object's Text property to an integer value, and assigns that value to *N*. The subsequent *if* statement raises an exception if *N* is not within the range of 0 to 99. Following the *raise* keyword, the program creates an exception instance of the ERangeError class. In this program, the default exception handler receives the ERangeError object and displays the message in a dialog box.

Less obvious is the fact that the sample event handler might fail due to another type of exception: a conversion error raised by calling StrToInt. Run the program again and enter **3.14159** or your name into the Edit window, and then click the button. This time you see a different message such as *3.14159 is not a valid Integer value*. This is displayed by Delphi's default exception handler. Most important, the exception raised by StrToInt causes the event handler to exit immediately, which skips the rest of the procedure's code.

A better version of this event handler uses a *try-except* block to handle this type of situation, and to give users a chance to correct bad input, no matter what the cause. You may also have noticed that you have to press Tab or click the mouse to get back to the Edit window after closing the error message dialog. With exceptions, we can do better. Listing 19-13 shows the final OnClick event handler extracted from the Except3 project on the CD-ROM in the Source\Except3 directory.

The revised procedure uses a nested procedure to display an error message plus the words *Try again*. It also calls the Edit1 object's SetFocus method to make it easier for users to enter another value after reading the error message. The main body of the procedure raises an exception if *N* is out of range. It also uses a *try* block so that other types of exceptions such as might be raised by the call to StrToInt are also handled. The *except* block shows how to handle two types of problems: conversion errors raised by StrToInt, and integer errors raised by the procedure itself. In both cases, the *on-do* statements call the nested Handler to display the message and set the focus back to the Edit control. Any other types of problems are still passed on to Delphi's default exception handlers.

Listing 19-13: Except3\Main.pas (Button OnClick event handler)

```
procedure TMainForm.Button1Click(Sender: TObject);
var
  N: Integer; S: String;
  // Nested exception handler
  procedure Handler(Message: String);
  begin
    ShowMessage(Message + ' Try again.');
    Edit1.SetFocus;
  end;
begin
  try
    N := StrToInt(Edit1.Text);
    if (N < 0) or (N > 99) then
      raise ERangeError.Create('Value out of range!')
    else begin
      ShowMessage('Success! Click Ok to end program');
      Close;
    end;
  except
    on E: EIntError do Handler(E.Message);
    on E: EConvertError do Handler(E.Message);
  end;
end;
```

Tip   The Handler procedure does not have to be nested inside another procedure. It can be declared as a separate procedure, or as a class method. You might do that, for example, so that multiple procedures can call the same handler.

Reraising an exception

As you develop your application, you write numerous procedures and functions that provide exception handlers, and you may often want to add new capabilities to this existing code. For example, you might have a program that closes a file in the event of a disk error. Another module might need to handle that same exception for its own purposes. Rather than close the file in two different places—a poor programming practice that complicates future maintenance—the secondary exception handler can reraise the exception. This keeps the exception alive so that, after the secondary handler performs its actions, the exception object travels up the call chain to reach other handlers that watch for it.

If you are familiar with object-oriented programming, you might think of reraising an exception as a kind of run-time subclassing. An exception handler can augment other handlers by trapping specific types of exceptions, performing some action, and then reraising the exception to keep it alive for additional handling. This is similar to the way a method in a derived class calls an inherited method to augment what that code does.

To handle an exception and not destroy the exception instance, use the *raise* keyword alone with no argument. Do this for all types of exceptions by using code such as the following (the comment shows where to put one or more statements that might raise the original exception):

```
try
  { Statements that might raise an exception }
except
  ShowMessage('OOPs!');
  raise;  { Reraise the exception }
end;
```

If any statement in the *try* block raises an exception, execution jumps to ShowMessage. After that, the use of *raise* with no argument reraises the exception. Running this code would display two messages: the first by ShowMessage, and the second by the application's default exception handler. (Some exceptions are silent, however, and don't display any message—more on this later.)

Caution   The preceding code traps all exceptions, which is generally unwise, and could lead to deep trouble—not handling an out-of-memory condition properly, for example. However, because this code also reraises all exceptions, Delphi's default exception handlers still get the opportunity to take care of critical problems. Except in rare circumstances when you have excellent reasons for breaking this rule, always call *raise* as shown here in an *except* block that traps all exceptions.

To reraise a specific type of exception, use similar code, but insert *raise* into an *on-do* statement. For example, this code fragment:

```
try
{ Statements that might raise an exception }
except
  on E: EOverflow do
  begin
    ShowMessage('OOPs!');
    raise;  { Reraise specific exception }
  end;
end;
```

traps instances of the EOverflow class, displays a message, and then reraises the same exception. Other exceptions that occur in the *try* block's statements exit the procedure or function immediately, skipping the *except* block.

Note   Reraising an exception immediately exits the procedure or function that calls *raise*.

Creating Exception Classes

When you need to raise an exception, you can choose one of Delphi's classes derived from Exception (refer to the previous list) or you can create your own exception classes. You may derive your class from Exception, or you can create a fresh class of your own design — it doesn't have to be based on Exception.

Derive your exception class from Exception if you want the application's default handlers to trap any unhandled exceptions of your class. Generally speaking, this is the best plan. However, you can create a fresh class of your own design if you do not want the default handlers to recognize your exceptions.

Caution   Any unhandled exceptions of a class not derived from Exception cause a fatal application error. Your code *must* handle all occurrences of an exception not based on the Exception class.

Custom exception classes

Custom exception classes are useful for collecting information about problems that occur in your program. For example, a math procedure that performs some sort of calculation might pass back illegal variable values in an object of a custom exception class. In the program's *except* block, a statement can display those values. This gives your program's users information they can use to repair a problem — entering correct values into a dialog box, for instance. Nobody appreciates an error message such as "File I/O error." A message such as "Filename contains the illegal character @" is far more informative. You can use custom exception classes to create this type of error message. Custom exception classes are also highly useful for debugging.

The simplest method for creating a custom exception class is to define a new class type based on Exception. For example, insert the following *type* declaration into a unit's interface (it can go in the implementation, but you probably want to make the class available to other modules so they can create and handle exceptions of the new class):

```
type
    TCustomException = class(Exception);
```

The new class simply provides a unique class name for identifying a specific type of problem — the class doesn't need a body. With this declaration, you can raise exceptions of the TCustomException class, and trap errors of that specific type. For example, you might insert this statement into a Button's OnClick event handler:

```
raise TCustomException.Create('Custom exception');
```

When you run the program and click the button, Delphi's default exception handlers receive the exception instance and display the message. Your own exception handlers can also trap TCustomException objects using code such as:

```
try
{ Statements that might raise an exception }
except
  on E: TCustomException do
    ShowMessage(E.Message);
end;
```

This is similar to other examples in this chapter; the only difference is that the code traps only exceptions of the TCustomException class. Other types of exceptions pass upwards in the call chain until they find a handler or reach Delphi's default exception handlers.

One reason to create your own exception class is to store values that provide additional information about an error. For example, suppose you want the program to detect if users click inside a graphics shape that the program draws. Because the shape is not an object, you must detect all mouse clicks in the form window and respond appropriately — exiting the application, for example, only if the user clicks inside a specified shape. You could, of course, do this using Delphi components, but the problem demonstrates a good use for custom exceptions.

The MouseExcept application on the CD-ROM in the Source\MouseExcept directory demonstrates how to create and use a custom exception. Figure 19-9 shows the program's display. Listing 19-14 shows the program's source code.

Click here to force the exception

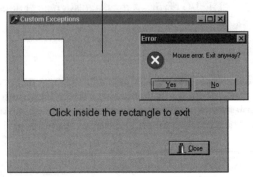

Figure 19-9: The MouseExcept application demonstrates creating and using a custom exception. Click inside the small rectangle to exit the program; click elsewhere in the window to raise an exception.

Listing 19-14: **MouseExcept\Main.pas**

```pascal
unit Main;

interface

uses
  Windows, Messages, SysUtils, Classes, Graphics, Controls,
  Forms, Dialogs, StdCtrls, Buttons, ExtCtrls;

type
  TMainForm = class(TForm)
    BitBtn1: TBitBtn;
    Label1: TLabel;
    procedure FormMouseDown(Sender: TObject;
      Button: TMouseButton; Shift: TShiftState; X, Y: Integer);
    procedure FormPaint(Sender: TObject);
  private
    { Private declarations }
    procedure CheckMouseLocation(X, Y: Integer);
    procedure ExitOnClick(X, Y: Integer);
  public
    { Public declarations }
  end;

var
  MainForm: TMainForm;

implementation

{$R *.DFM}

const
  rLeft   = 25;
  rTop    = 25;
  rRight  = 100;
  rBottom = 100;

type
  TMouseException = class(Exception)
    X, Y: Integer;
    constructor Create(const Msg: string; XX, YY: Integer);
  end;

constructor TMouseException.Create(const Msg: string;
  XX, YY: Integer);
begin
  X := XX;    // Save X and Y values in object
  Y := YY;
```

continued

Listing 19-14 *(continued)*

```
  Message :=   // Create message string
    Msg + ' (X=' + IntToStr(X) + ', Y=' + IntToStr(Y) + ')';
end;

procedure TMainForm.CheckMouseLocation(X, Y: Integer);
begin
  if (X < rLeft) or (X > rRight) or
     (Y < rTop)  or (Y > rBottom) then
    raise
      TMouseException.Create('Mouse location error', X, Y);
end;

procedure TMainForm.ExitOnClick(X, Y: Integer);
begin
  try
    CheckMouseLocation(X, Y);  // Bad values raise exception
    Close;                     // Exit the program
  except
    on TMouseException do
    begin
      if MessageDlg('Mouse error. Exit anyway?',
        mtError, [mbYes, mbNo], 0) = mrYes
      then
        Close
      else
        raise;
    end;
  end;
end;

procedure TMainForm.FormMouseDown(Sender: TObject;
  Button: TMouseButton; Shift: TShiftState; X, Y: Integer);
begin
  ExitOnClick(X, Y);
end;

procedure TMainForm.FormPaint(Sender: TObject);
begin
  Canvas.Rectangle(rLeft, rTop, rRight, rBottom);
end;

end.
```

The MouseExcept program's OnPaint event handler for the main form paints a small rectangle using constant values declared in the unit's implementation. When you click the mouse anywhere in the window, the OnMouseDown event handler, FormMouseDown, receives the mouse cursor's x and y coordinate values. This procedure calls ExitOnClick, passing those same x and y values as arguments. ExitOnClick is a public procedure that I added to the form's class and implemented as shown in the listing.

ExitOnClick executes two statements in a *try* block. First, it calls a second procedure added to the class, CheckMouseLocation, which tests whether x and y are inside the rectangle. The procedure also calls Close to exit the program. Because CheckMouseLocation raises an exception if any problems are detected with x and y, the Close statement is skipped if the user clicks outside of the rectangle. In that event, the procedure's *except* block displays an error message and asks whether to exit the program anyway. I programmed the procedure this way so that, if you answer No to the message dialog, the *except* block reraises the exception. The test program therefore demonstrates both the program's own response to the custom exception and shows what happens when Delphi's default exception handlers receive that same object.

That object is defined as an instance of a class that the program itself declares as follows:

```
type
  TMouseException = class(Exception)
    X, Y: Integer;
    constructor Create(const Msg: string; XX, YY: Integer);
  end;
```

TMouseException is derived from Delphi's Exception class. In addition to the items inherited from Exception, TMouseException adds integer members X and Y, and declares a constructor, which is called to initialize objects of the class. The constructor is programmed like this:

```
constructor TMouseException.Create(const Msg: string;
  XX, YY: Integer);
begin
  X := XX;    // Save X and Y values in object
  Y := YY;
  Message :=  // Create message string
    Msg + ' (X=' + IntToStr(X) + ', Y=' + IntToStr(Y) + ')';
end;
```

The first two statements in the constructor save the values of the XX and YY parameters in the *X* and *Y* members declared in TMouseException. The Message string, which is inherited from Exception, is assigned a message that includes these two values.

To understand how the custom exception class is used, take a look at the CheckMouseLocation procedure. If *X* or *Y* are outside of the rectangle that the program draws, this procedure raises an exception object of the TMouseException class using the statement:

```
raise
   TMouseException.Create('Mouse location error', X, Y);
```

This creates a TMouseException object, which saves the *x* and *y* values of the errant cursor location, and immediately exits CheckMouseLocation. Back in ExitOnClick, if this exception is raised, the Close statement is skipped and the *except* block takes over control.

Although this example program might seem overly complex to perform its operations, in a more extensive application with many graphics images, a class such as TMouseException can greatly simplify the code. Without a custom exception class, the program might use numerous hard-to-follow condition *if* statements to test mouse locations, making debugging difficult. Concentrating all error handling in a custom exception class, and by using *try-except* blocks to detect errors, keeps the code lean and improves its robustness.

Nonderived exception classes

You can also create entirely new exception classes that are not based on Exception. The simplest case is a class that has no body. Because it is a base class, however, its declaration must end with the keyword *end* and a semicolon. This is one of the rare places in Object Pascal where an *end* is not required to have a matching *begin*. For example, start a new application and insert this *type* declaration into the unit's implementation or interface:

```
type
  TBareException = class
  end;
```

Next, insert a Button object into the form, and create an empty OnClick event handler by double-clicking that event in the Object Inspector window. Program the event handler as follows:

```
procedure TForm1.Button1Click(Sender: TObject);
begin
  raise TBareException.Create;
```

```
end;
```

Calling the class's Create method constructs an object of the class, which is raised as an exception. When you compile and run the program by pressing F9, clicking the button executes this code and raises the exception. Delphi's default exception handler receives this object, and displays the message dialog in Figure 19-10.

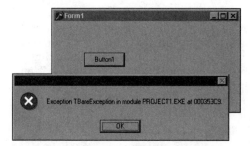

Figure 19-10: Delphi's default exception handler displays this message for an exception object of a class not derived from Exception.

Note   Because all classes derive from TObject, even a spanking-new base class comes with Create and Free methods already built in.

If you use this technique, it's probably best to handle all instances of your exception class, and you might also want to install your own default exception handler as described later in this chapter. The class could declare additional variables and methods — it's up to you what to put into your custom exception classes.

The Exception base class

By basing your exception classes on Exception, your classes inherit a wealth of members. For example, the Exception base class provides a number of methods for constructing exception objects in different ways. All of these constructors are named beginning with *Create,* and they all have the singular purpose of creating an error message string out of different sorts of arguments. You may call these constructors to create exception instances of your derived classes, or you may call them for Exception objects or for any of the derived classes listed earlier in this chapter. I run through Exception's constructors briefly here — one of them is sure to suit your needs.

The simplest Create is the one you've already seen. Pass a string variable or constant as an error message:

```
raise Exception.Create('Trouble in Paradise');
```

Tip

Insert the preceding statement into a Button object's OnClick event handler, run the program, and click the button to see the results. Do the same for the other examples in this section.

To create a message that contains additional information — variable values, for instance — call the alternate constructor CreateFmt. To the constructor, pass a string with formatting commands plus a set of values to insert in the string. (For help with these techniques, see "Using the Format Function" in Chapter 7, and also look up Format in Delphi's online help.) For example, this statement raises an exception with an error message that displays two integer values:

```
raise Exception.CreateFmt('Error: X=%d Y=%d', [X, Y]);
```

As a result of this statement, users see an error message such as the following:

```
Error: X=-1 Y=12
```

When constructing exception objects this way, you might want to use Delphi's set of error message resource strings in the SysConst unit. Table 19-1 lists the constants in this table and shows their associated strings. They are linked into all applications anyway, so you might as well use them rather than define your own similar strings. To use them, add a *uses* declaration to the unit's implementation:

```
uses
  SysConst;
```

Next, raise an exception using one of the defined constants:

```
raise Exception.Create(SDiskFull);
```

Note

Early versions of Delphi defined in the SysUtils unit the constants in Table 19-1 as resource integer identifiers, which you could pass to the CreateRes Exception class constructor. These constants are now defined as resource strings in the SysConst unit. CreateRes is still available, however, for creating Exception objects that load error message strings from a Windows string resource table — however, this method is probably inappropriate for most Delphi applications. (Resources in general are more useful in conventional Windows programming using C and C++.)

Table 19-1
The SysConst Unit Defines These Standard Error Messages, Which You Can Use to Create Your Own Exception Class Objects.

Identifier	String
SinvalidInteger	'"%s" is not a valid integer value';
SinvalidFloat	'"%s" is not a valid floating point value';
SinvalidDate	'"%s" is not a valid date';
SinvalidTime	'"%s" is not a valid time';
SinvalidDateTime	'"%s" is not a valid date and time';
StimeEncodeError	'Invalid argument to time encode';
SDateEncodeError	'Invalid argument to date encode';
SOutOfMemory	'Out of memory';
SinOutError	'I/O error %d';
SfileNotFound	'File not found';
SinvalidFilename	'Invalid filename';
StooManyOpenFiles	'Too many open files';
SAccessDenied	'File access denied';
SEndOfFile	'Read beyond end of file';
SDiskFull	'Disk full';
SinvalidInput	'Invalid numeric input';
SDivByZero	'Division by zero';
SRangeError	'Range check error';
SintOverflow	'Integer overflow';
SinvalidOp	'Invalid floating point operation';
SZeroDivide	'Floating point division by zero';
SOverflow	'Floating point overflow';
SUnderflow	'Floating point underflow';
SinvalidPointer	'Invalid pointer operation';
SinvalidCast	'Invalid class typecast';
SAccessViolation	'Access violation at address %p. %s of address %p';
SStackOverflow	'Stack overflow';
SControlC	'Control-C hit';

Continued

Table 19-1

Identifier	String
SPrivilege	'Privileged instruction';
SOperationAborted	'Operation aborted';
SException	'Exception %s in module %s at %p.'#$0A'%s%s';
SExceptTitle	'Application Error';
SinvalidFormat	'Format "%s" invalid or incompatible with argument';
SArgumentMissing	'No argument for format "%s"';
SinvalidVarCast	'Invalid variant type conversion';
SinvalidVarOp	'Invalid variant operation';
SDispatchError	'Variant method calls not supported';
SReadAccess	'Read';
SWriteAccess	'Write';
SResultTooLong	'Format result longer than 4096 characters';
SFormatTooLong	'Format string too long';
SVarArrayCreate	'Error creating variant array';
SVarNotArray	'Variant is not an array';
SVarArrayBounds	'Variant array index out of bounds';
SExternalException	'External exception %x';
SAssertionFailed	'Assertion failed';
SIntfCastError	'Interface not supported';
SAssertError	'%s (%s, line %d)';
SAbstractError	'Abstract Error';
SModuleAccessViolation	'Access violation at address %p in module ''%s''. %s of address %p';
SCannotReadPackageInfo	'Cannot access package information for package ''%s''';
sErrorLoadingPackage	'Can''t load package %s.'#13#10'%s';
SInvalidPackageFile	'Invalid package file ''%s''';
SInvalidPackageHandle	'Invalid package handle';
SDuplicatePackageUnit	'Cannot load package ''%s.'' It contains unit ''%s,''' + ';which is also contained in package ''%s''';

Identifier	String
SWin32Error	`'Win32 Error. Code: %d.'#10'%s';`
SUnkWin32Error	`'A Win32 API function failed';`
SNL	`'Application is not licensed to use this feature';`

The remaining Exception constructors are variations on the preceding themes. Following are examples of them all. CreateResFmt loads a string-table resource with an embedded %s string-formatting command (notice that you must pass a string set to this constructor). CreateHelp adds a help-context identifier (it's up to your exception handler to use it). CreateFmtHelp combines a formatting string with a help-context identifier. CreateResHelp combines a string-table resource with a help-context identifier. CreateResFmtHelp puts the whole ball of wax together with a resource string containing formatting codes such as %s or %d and a help-context identifier:

```
raise Exception.CreateResFmt(SInvalidInteger, [IntToStr(N)]);
raise Exception.CreateHelp('Whoops, sorry', 123);
raise Exception.CreateFmtHelp('Error N=%d', [N], 123);
raise Exception.CreateResHelp(SFileNotFound, 123);
raise Exception.CreateResFmtHelp(SInvalidInteger, [S], 123);
```

Other Exceptional Techniques

The following sections discuss advanced exception techniques that are useful in special — or should I say *exceptional* — circumstances.

Silent exceptions

A *silent exception* is one that has no apparent effect on a program. However, it is useful in aborting deeply nested processes. The silent exception instance is an object of the EAbort class, which is derived from Exception. Delphi's default exception handler is programmed not to display any error messages when it receives an EAbort exception. Instead, the default handler merely destroys the exception instance and returns control to the program.

Call the Abort procedure to raise an exception of the EAbort class. For example, a *while* loop that inspects a NormalCondition Boolean flag could also inspect another flag, SpecialConditionFlag, and abort the loop by calling Abort (I made up the flag names — they represent any kind of conditions your program needs to monitor):

```
while NormalCondition do
begin
  if SpecialConditionFlag = False then
    Abort;
end;
```

Calling Abort is equivalent to raising an EAbort exception, which you may do the hard way in order to pass a string message along with the object (because the exception is normally silent, however, the program never displays this string):

```
raise EAbort.Create('Operation aborted');
```

The importance of this technique is that it produces no onscreen effect. The loop ends silently by raising an exception of the EAbort class, which the default exception handler receives and returns normal control to the program. Passing a string this way in the silent exception can be useful for debugging. For example, if your program includes an exception handler, that handler may respond to EAbort just as it does for any other exceptions. Alternatively, if you do *not* want to recognize silent exceptions (so that they remain silent), use the following *try-except* block, which handles the exception but calls ShowMessage only if the exception is not of the EAbort class:

```
try
  { Statements that may call Abort }
except
  on E: Exception do
    if not (E is EAbort) then
      ShowMessage(E.Message);
  raise;
end;
```

Replacing the default exception handler

For truly advanced work, you can get out the pick and shovel and excavate a custom default exception handler that operates on the Application object level. This technique provides access to all unhandled exceptions, which can be useful for debugging the application's exception-handling capabilities as well as replacing the default handler's dialog box with a more descriptive display.

Even if you don't need to write a default exception handler for your application, you may want to try the technique in this section. Being capable of trapping unhandled exceptions on the application level is potentially valuable for debugging your program's error handling. The sample application in this section uses this method to maintain a list of all unhandled exceptions during the course of the program. Such a list could be invaluable for tracking down the source of difficult problems.

The TApplication component provides a procedure, HandleException, that processes any unhandled exceptions that arise during a program's execution. You should not attempt to override this method — that would completely sidestep Delphi's default exception handlers, and would almost surely lead to serious trouble. Instead, to augment the default handler, you may provide a procedure for the Application object's OnException event. The HandleException method calls the OnException procedure, if one is assigned, instead of displaying a default error message.

On the
CD-ROM

Figure 19-11 shows the ExList application's display. All unhandled exceptions pass
through the new handler, which in this program adds the error messages to a ListBox
component. This provides a complete tracking of unhandled exceptions in the application. The program is on the CD-ROM in the Source\ExList directory. Run this program
and click the three Exception buttons to generate three types of exceptions. After you
close the resulting default dialog box, the program adds the exception error messages
to the form's ListBox. Clicking Exception1 raises a divide-by-zero exception. Clicking
Exception2 raises a file-not-found exception. Clicking Exception3 converts all listed
strings to uppercase — but the programming contains an intentional bug that raises an
index-out-of-bounds exception. Listing 19-15 shows the program's source code.

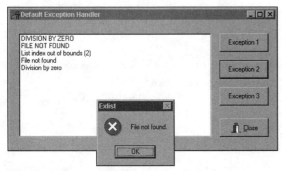

Figure 19-11: The ExList application demonstrates
how to write a default exception handler.

Listing 19-15: **ExList\Main.pas**

```
unit Main;

interface

uses
  Windows, SysUtils, Messages, Classes, Graphics, Controls,
  Forms, Dialogs, Buttons, StdCtrls;

type
  TMainForm = class(TForm)
    ListBox1: TListBox;
    Button1: TButton;
    Button2: TButton;
    Button3: TButton;
    BitBtn1: TBitBtn;
    procedure FormCreate(Sender: TObject);
    procedure Button1Click(Sender: TObject);
    procedure Button2Click(Sender: TObject);
```

(continued)

Listing 19-15 *(continued)*

```pascal
    procedure Button3Click(Sender: TObject);
  private
    { Private declarations }
  public
{ 1. Declare the OnException event handler }
    procedure NewOnException(Sender: TObject;
      E: Exception);
    { Public declarations }
  end;

var
  MainForm: TMainForm;

implementation

{$R *.DFM}

{ 2. Implement the OnException event handler }
procedure TMainForm.NewOnException(Sender: TObject;
  E: Exception);
begin
  Application.ShowException(E);
  ListBox1.Items.Add(E.Message);
end;

{ 3. Assign the event handler to Application.OnException }
procedure TMainForm.FormCreate(Sender: TObject);
begin
  Application.OnException := NewOnException;
end;

{ Raise a divide-by-zero exception }
procedure TMainForm.Button1Click(Sender: TObject);
var
  I, J, K: Integer;
begin
  I := 0;
  J := 10;
  try
    K := J div I;  { Divide by zero! }
    { The following statement doesn't execute, but it is
      needed so the optimizer in Object Pascal, which notices
      that K isn't used in this procedure, doesn't strip
      out the preceding statement. Smart compiler. }
    ShowMessage('K=' + IntToStr(K));
  except
    raise;
```

```
    end;
end;

{ Raise a file-not-found exception }
procedure TMainForm.Button2Click(Sender: TObject);
var
  T: TextFile;
begin
  AssignFile(T, 'XXXX.$$$');
  Reset(T);  { Open a non-existent file! }
  try
    { You would normally use T here }
  finally
    CloseFile(T);  { For safety's sake }
  end;
end;

{ Raise an index-out-of-bounds exception }
procedure TMainForm.Button3Click(Sender: TObject);
var
  I: Integer;
begin
  with ListBox1.Items do
  for I := 0 to Count do  { Should be Count - 1! }
    Strings[I] := Uppercase(Strings[I]);
  end;

end.
```

It's more work to assign an Application event handler than creating one, say, for a Button object's OnClick event. This is because the Application object is not accessible to Delphi's Object Inspector. To create the OnException event handler therefore requires three steps, numbered in comments in the listing (these comments are in bold to make them easier to find). The steps are:

1. Declare the OnException event handler in the form's class. It must have the parameters shown in the listing, although the procedure name is up to you.

2. Implement the OnException event handler. Remember to preface its name with the form class name and a period.

3. Assign the event handler to Application.OnException. The Application object's HandleException method checks whether the program has assigned a procedure to OnException. If so, HandleException calls the procedure for any unhandled exceptions it receives.

Note   A custom OnException event handler receives only exceptions derived from the Exception class except for EAbort exceptions, which remain silent.

You may perform whatever actions you want in the OnException handler. In the sample program (see Step 2), the first statement calls the Application's ShowException method. This is what the default handler already does. In addition, the program uses the Add method for the ListBox1's Items string list to keep a copy of each error message. Notice that the event handler receives the exception object as parameter *E*. (This object is destroyed elsewhere; you don't have to free it.)

You may silence the default event handler by deleting the call to Application.ShowException. Don't do this indiscriminately, however, as it could hide a serious defect in your code. Your OnException event handler probably should display some kind of message on receiving unhandled exceptions.

Expert-User Tips

✦ One way to think of exceptions is to consider them as a means for returning multiple types of objects from procedures and functions. Technically speaking, you could raise exceptions to pass objects around and use *try-except* blocks to catch those objects. I don't recommend that you go overboard using exceptions this way. The overhead would be at least 100 if not 1,000 times the performance cost of simply returning a value from a function, but it is helpful to understand that using them for error control is voluntary. The meaning of exception objects, especially those of your own classes, is up to you to define.

✦ The default HandleException method in TApplication sends the Windows message wm_CancelMode to release the mouse if it had been captured at the time the exception occurred. This also causes list boxes, combo boxes, drop-down lists, and menus to close.

✦ When constructing hierarchies of exception classes, carefully place any *on-do* statements that refer to your classes to handle exception objects of most-derived Exception classes first. Consider the following code, which is similar to other examples in the chapter (the ShowMessage statement merely uses *K* so that Object Pascal's optimizer does not delete the preceding division statement):

```
try
  K := J div I;
  ShowMessage('K=' + IntToStr(K));
```

```
except
  on E: EDivByZero do  // This must come first!
    ShowMessage('Divide error');
  on E: EIntError do    // Trap all other EIntErrors here
    ShowMessage('Other integer math error');
end;
```

✦ This code uses two *on-do* statements (you can have as many as you need in an *except* block). The first statement traps EDivByZero exceptions, perhaps to do something special with those types of errors. The second traps all other exceptions derived from the EIntError class, which is also the base class for EDivByZero. It would be a mistake to reverse the *on-do* statements because if the ancestor-class exceptions are trapped first, they would include EDivByZero exceptions (which are derived from Exception) and the special Divide error code would never be executed.

✦ A Delphi application has two default exception handlers. One is provided by the VCL and it protects every window procedure through which message traffic passes. This handler traps unhandled exceptions, displays an error message, and continues executing the program. The other default exception handler is in the RTL (run-time library), provided by the SysUtils unit. This handler is below the VCL default handler, so seeing it in action is unlikely. When this handler traps an exception, it displays a detailed message (with exception address information for debugging), and then terminates the application. These exceptions are not recoverable.

Projects to Try

18-1: Rewrite Listing 19-13 to call a function that converts Edit1's Text property to an integer value. This demonstrates how, with exceptions, you can make major modifications to a program and remain confident of its error-handling logic.

18-2: Replace the default Application exception handler with your own version that displays a more helpful dialog box. For example, your dialog might include a Help button that users can click for information about specific types of exceptions.

18-3: Convert the ExList application into a module that you can incorporate into any application for debugging unhandled exceptions. Add a command to your module to save the list of exception messages in a text file.

Summary

✦ Experienced developers incorporate error-handling code into their programs as they write them. Delphi's exception-handling mechanisms make this relatively easy to do.

✦ Exceptions can arise from a number of sources. Components, mathematical expressions, file input/output operations, memory shortages, and other events can raise exceptions. You can also raise an exception to notify your application of a problem.

✦ Protected-statement blocks use the *try-except* keywords to handle exceptions that statements in the *try* part might raise.

✦ Protected-resource blocks use the *try-finally* keywords to execute must-do code such as freeing allocated memory even if an exception occurs for a statement in the *try* block.

✦ An exception is an object of a class, usually derived from Exception, that describes the nature of an exception. Raising an exception creates this object. Handling the exception destroys it. You must never explicitly free an exception instance.

✦ Use *on-do* statements in an *except* block to handle specific types of exceptions. When using this technique, remember that any unhandled exceptions of types not mentioned in *on-do* statements cause the current procedure or function to exit after the *except* block. Use *try-finally* blocks to clean up any resource allocations in such cases.

✦ To raise an exception, call *raise* with a newly created exception instance. To reraise an exception after handling it in an *except* block, call *raise* with no arguments.

✦ You may create your own exception classes, either from scratch, or by deriving them from Exception. In most cases, you should derive your exception classes from Exception because Delphi's default exception handlers recognize only exceptions of these types.

✦ The Exception class provides a number of Create constructors for creating error messages from strings, values, and string-table resources.

✦ Call Abort to raise a silent exception of the EAbort class. The default exception handlers do not display an error-message dialog for EAbort exceptions.

✦ Augment the default exception handler by declaring, implementing, and assigning an OnException event handler in your program's TForm derived class. See the ExList application on the CD-ROM for instructions. Use this technique to debug your program's unhandled exceptions, or to replace the default error-message dialog.

The next chapter presents tips and fundamental techniques for readers interested in writing custom components and ActiveX controls.

✦   ✦   ✦

Constructing Custom Components

✦ ✦ ✦ ✦

In This Chapter

Components

Introducing
components

Introducing
packages

Developing a
component

Understanding
component design

Creating ActiveX
controls

✦ ✦ ✦ ✦

As you acquire new Delphi skills, you may begin to
wonder how components actually work. Or, perhaps
you have a great idea for a hyperactive confabulator that
would make a super visual component. Most Delphi
developers never need to build a custom component, but if
you are interested in this advanced subject, this chapter helps
you get started in component design.

In the following sections, you learn about the parts of a
component and how they interact with Delphi's development
environment. You can create, test, and install new components
into Delphi's component palette, and you can take a look at
several key component construction techniques. You can also
convert one of the components in this chapter to an ActiveX
control. After reading this chapter, you are prepared to go
beyond the basics in component design, a subject that could
easily fill a book of this size.

Introducing Components

A component is an Object Pascal class that conforms to
certain rules and regulations. You can build a component from
an existing one, and you can construct a component from
scratch. Most often, however, you base your components on
those that come with Delphi. For example, if you want to add
some spice to button objects, you can base a new component
on Delphi's TButton class and stir in whatever new ingredients
you like.

The following are some of the reasons you may want to construct custom components. These are not hard-and-fast rules — they are merely suggestions that may help you decide whether you need to construct a custom component:

✦ You need to modify an existing component for a special purpose — for example, you need an Image component that can load a bitmap from a hardware device your company is developing. By basing your component on Image, all of that component's properties, methods, and events are available to your enhanced design. You may derive new components from TButton, TListBox, or any other component class. This also makes good use of object-oriented inheritance. The new class *inherits* the capabilities of its base class rather than copying or modifying existing code. Inheritance helps you better organize your component libraries, and also facilitates maintenance.

✦ You want to create a Delphi component interface for a Windows custom control. Usually, you can derive this kind of component from TWinControl, which provides basic properties, methods, and events that are common to all Windows controls.

✦ You want to create an entirely new component out of thin air. This can take some effort, but you can save yourself a lot of time by basing the component on TCustomControl, which provides a GDI Canvas along with properties, methods, and events common to all components.

✦ Your application has special graphics requirements, and you want to construct a component that provides these capabilities. Most graphics components are based on the TGraphicControl class. A sample module in this chapter uses this method to create a BarChart component that displays (you guessed it) a bar chart from a set of data points managed by a string list.

✦ You want to create a nonvisual component — one that does not appear on the component palette. You've met a few instances of nonvisual components — the TClipboard class, for example. These are relatively rare, but they take advantage of component construction techniques, such as published properties, that can contribute greatly to a program's reliability and ease of maintenance.

Component authors and component users

Throughout this book so far, you have been a component user. By the time you finish this chapter, you can also be a component author. Component users create multiple objects from components at design time by inserting them into a form window, and at run time, by calling their Create methods. Component authors create new component classes from which users may create one or more objects at design time and at run time.

Another difference between component users and component authors concerns access to a component's elements. As a component user, you have only restricted rights of access to a component's innards. For example, you can read and write only published properties, and you can create events only for those actions the component makes available in the Object Inspector window.

As a component author, you have no such restrictions. You decide which properties to publish and how to create the actions your components need. All of your component's elements are available to your program (except for private members of base classes, which as you probably know, are accessible only in those classes), and you can gain access to protected elements in existing components that are hands-off for users. In return for this freedom, you accept a greater responsibility for writing robust code. Errors on the component level tend to have more serious consequences than application errors.

Creating your own components:

✦ Provides access to restricted parts of components

✦ Makes it possible to add and modify existing component properties, methods, and events

✦ Requires a good working knowledge of Object Pascal, object-oriented programming, and exception handling

Aim to make your components safe to use, even by rank beginners. If a component requires a certain item, it should provide a default value in case users don't supply one. Never assume that users know how to deploy your components correctly. Ideally, users should be able to do anything with a component without causing serious harm.

A few good terms

The following are definitions of terms that you need to know for constructing custom components. The glossary conforms to the use of these terms in other published information about Delphi, but I've tried to be more rigorous here (and throughout the book) on subtle meanings of related words such as object and class, or declaration and definition. These and other hair-splitting distinctions are much more important to component authors than to users:

✦ **Declaration** — A statement of an a item's name, type, and parameters.

✦ **Definition** — The creation or implementation of a declared item.

✦ **Class** — The declaration of a new type that encapsulates data and code for operating on that data. Conceptually, a class resembles a simple data type such as Object Pascal's Integer type. Class names traditionally begin with T (TButton, for example).

✦ **Instance** — The definition in memory of a class variable. A program may define as many instances of a class as it needs. Conceptually, an instance is similar to a variable of a simple data type such as Integer. You may define as many Integer variables as your program needs, but only one Integer data type. In that same sense, you may define as many class instances as your program needs. (Some rare classes, however, might restrict you to creating only one instance. For example, there can be only one TApplication instance in any application.)

✦ **Component** — A class derived directly or indirectly from TComponent with special access paths to its data, published properties, and other features that conform to Delphi's requirements for a visual or nonvisual component. You declare and implement components in Object Pascal units.

✦ **Object** — Same as instance. In past versions of Borland Pascal, an object was what a class is in Delphi, leading to much confusion in currently published books and manuals. In this book, I use the word object strictly to mean an instance of a class or other type. It is correct, in other words, to call an Integer variable an object. Typically, however, an object is an instance of a class.

✦ **Access specifier** — One of the keywords — *private, protected, public,* or *published* — that divide a class declaration into sections. Program statements have varying degrees of access rights to declarations, based on their access specifiers. Private declarations are for use only in the unit that declares the class; protected declarations are also available to derived classes; public declarations are available to all users; and published declarations are properties that define access rules for class data and, for components installed in the VCL palette, appear in the Object Inspector window.

✦ **Field** — A variable declared in a class.

✦ **Method** — A procedure or function declared in a class.

✦ **Method implementation** — The body of a method, including any variables and statements that perform the method's actions.

✦ **Property** — A published field that typically specifies methods for reading and writing the field's value; also, a published event handler such as OnClick.

✦ **Event** — A pointer to a user-supplied procedure for specific objects. Contrast this to a method, which performs the identical operations for all objects of the method's class. An event property enables an object to delegate actions to another object, which can potentially perform widely varying operations for the same type of event. For example, two Buttons could respond differently to an OnClick event, but the TButton's Hide method works the same for all Button objects.

✦ **Unit** — A Pascal module stored and compiled separately from other modules. A unit may contain one or more components. However, you may install only entire units, including all of their components, on the component palette. To install individual components, they must be in separate units.

✦ **Interface part** — Publicly shareable declarations and definitions in a unit; preceded by the *interface* keyword.

✦ **Implementation part** — Private nonshareable declarations and definitions in a unit; preceded by the *implementation* keyword.

✦ **Initialization part** — Statements executed when the module is loaded into memory; preceded by the *initialization* keyword and terminated by the keyword *end* and a period.

✦ **Visual component** — A component with a run-time visual representation. Some components such as the TClipboard class are nonvisual, but they are still components in every other way. Visual components may or may not appear on the palette. For example, TForm is a visual component, but is not available on the palette.

Note

You probably realize this by now, but for those who skipped ahead to this chapter, in this book I refer to components on the component palette by their hint-text names — Button, ListBox, and others. Those components' classes are named TButton and TListBox. When prefaced with a capital *T*, a name refers to a class declaration; without the *T*, it refers to the component as used in Delphi's form designer.

Component class hierarchy

Most new components are based on existing component classes. A derived component inherits all of the properties, methods, and events from its ancestor component. To master component construction, you need to become intimately familiar with Delphi's component library and the methods it provides to derived components. Figure 20-1 shows the hierarchy of the classes that typically serve as ancestor components. Use this figure to explore the properties, methods, and events that your derived components inherit. Try never to reinvent capabilities that you can inherit from another component class. Of course, the hierarchy shown here is not complete. You receive the complete tree diagram with Delphi.

To become an expert component author, you need Delphi's run-time library source files (however, you don't need them for this chapter). The source files include all of the programming for the visual component library, and you can learn numerous tricks and techniques by browsing through the files.

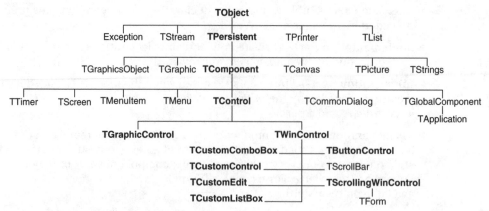

Figure 20-1: Delphi component class hierarchy

Introducing Packages

Before developing a new component, you need to be familiar with packages. A package encapsulates compiled units, which typically provide the inner workings for components such as Buttons and ListBoxes. Creating a package for those units accomplishes two key tasks:

✦ It enables multiple applications to share VCL and other component code, rather than requiring each application to have its own separate copy of that code.

✦ It provides a vehicle for installing components into Delphi's palette. With packages, it is not necessary to recompile the entire VCL, as it was in some previous versions of Delphi, to install a component into the palette.

Although both of these features use packages, they are distinctly different and use different package formats. For this reason, two kinds of packages exist:

✦ **Run-time packages** — used to provide component code that multiple Delphi applications can share.

✦ **Design-time package** — used to install components into the Delphi palette, and provide a link to the associated run-time packages.

This section explains the general concepts of how to create and use run-time and design-time packages. You need to understand at least the basics of packages to create new components intended for installation on Delphi's palette.

Tip To enable run-time packages, use Project|Options, select the Packages page tab, and enable the Build with run-time packages check box. You can then build your application to share code in units that are referenced by packages. With this option disabled, the unit code is copied directly to the finished .exe code file.

Creating a package is easy. First, create, test, and debug the units you want to install in a package. Run-time packages are the simplest to create, so it's best to start there. Locate one or more units you want to install in a package, and then follow these steps:

1. Start a new application. This could become your unit or component's test program, but if you don't need one, you can close and ignore the application's unit and project files.

2. Select File|New... and click the New page tab. Double-click the Package icon to start Delphi's Package Editor.

3. The New Package dialog asks for a filename and description. Click the Browse button to open a standard file dialog, and change to the directory where you want to store the package files. Enter a filename into this dialog with no filename extension, for example, TestPkg. Press Enter, and Delphi inserts the path and filename plus the extension .dpk into the filename box. Enter a description if you want — this is optional, but shows up in various places, so it's usually a good idea to enter one.

4. Click the New Package dialog's OK button. This brings up Delphi's Package Editor window. To add a unit to the package, click the Add button, and browse to the unit's .pas source code file. Notice that you add source code files, not the compiled unit files, to packages. Click OK or press Enter to return to the Package Editor. Click Add again for as many units as you want to add to the package.

5. When you are done adding units, click the editor's Requires page tab. This shows the packages containing the units that other units in the new package need. At a minimum, your packages need to refer to VCL40 which contains the VCL units. To add other packages, click the Add button and enter or browse to another package file.

6. When you are done adding contained units and required packages, click the Options button. Click the Description page tab, and select one or both of the check boxes labeled Usage options. For this demonstration, enable only the Runtime package option. For creating and installing components into Delphi's palette, you normally enable both options. Edit the other options as necessary for your units and components. Click OK to close the Package Options dialog.

Those steps complete the design of a new package. (Inserting components into packages and the Delphi palette requires some additional steps, which I explain in a bit.) You are now ready to compile and use your new package. Click the Compile button to compile the package, and all of its units. This creates the .bpl package file in the specified directory.

To view your package's source code, right click inside the Package Editor window, and select the View Package Source command. This opens the package in Delphi's code editor window. Ignoring a lengthy series of compilation options, which are automatically inserted into the text, a package is merely a simple affair that looks like this:

```
package TestPkg;
{$R *.RES}
{$ALIGN ON}
{$ASSERTIONS ON}
...
{$DESCRIPTION 'Test runtime package'}
{$DESIGNONLY}
{$IMPLICITBUILD ON}

requires
  vcl40;

contains
  Clrform;

end.
```

I replaced most of the compilation directives with an ellipsis — you see the full set when you view your own package source code.

Packages are specially compiled DLLs. To distinguish them from other .dll files, the package filename extension is .bpl. A package source file contains three fundamental items:

   ✦ The keyword *package* and its name followed by a semicolon

   ✦ A *requires* declaration that lists other packages required by this one

   ✦ A *contains* declaration that lists the units to be encapsulated in this package

Note

Although an application is linked to run-time packages, the program's modules must still add the units they require to a *uses* declaration. Compiling with run-time packages tells the application only where to find its component code. The application source files must still import the units they require by listing the unit names in a *uses* declaration.

Components that you want to install on the Delphi palette must be compiled using packages. The steps for doing this are similar to those described previously for run-time packages, but you normally select both Runtime and Design-time package output for components. This creates two packages: one for use at run time for applications that use the packaged components, and one for use at design time to enable the component on the VCL palette.

It might seem redundant to have two different kinds of packages, but actually, design-time packages merely refer to run-time packages. A design-time package is merely a shell—the actual unit code is always in a run-time package. This means that you can distribute run-time packages with your applications, and also provide design-time packages to programmers who need to use your components by selecting them from Delphi's VCL palette.

To open a package file for recompiling, use the File\|Open command, and view files of type Delphi package source (*.dpk).

Note
To use a design-time package—which you must do for all components installed on the VCL—you must have the appropriate design-time package *and* its associated run-time package.

The next section explains how to create a new component, insert it into a package, and install the component on Delphi's VCL palette in the Samples category.

Developing a Component

In the following sections, you construct two components that demonstrate component programming and the process of installing a finished component into Delphi's component palette. These steps are all reversible, so don't hesitate to play.

First, you create a simple component just to demonstrate some of the required steps. After that, you construct a more complex component that demonstrates more about properties, methods, and events, plus techniques for registration, debugging, and installation.

First steps

Components require different programming techniques than applications. You can program components from scratch using Delphi's code editor, but because components to be installed on the VCL palette require installation in a package, it's highly recommended that you use Delphi's Package Editor to create the component unit. You must use this editor anyway to compile and install the component into the palette, so you might as well use it to create the unit.

Follow these steps to subclass the standard Button component as a new component named TDingButton. This new component creates a button that, when clicked, rings the computer's chime. This test demonstrates two important aspects of component construction: inheriting the capabilities of an existing component on which you build a new one, and using packages to install a component into the VCL palette.

On the CD-ROM

The sample Source\Ding directory on the CD-ROM contains all the files for this section. If you don't want to create your own component by following the steps listed here, simply open the Ding package file, and use the Package Editor to compile and install the component into Delphi. However, for a better understanding of the process, I urge you to create a fresh directory and follow these steps to build your own TDing class.

1. Create a directory (I named mine Ding) to hold the component and test program files. Start a new application. Name the form MainForm. Select File|Save all..., and save Unit1 as Main.pas, and the project as TestDing.dpr in your directory. The project serves as a test platform for the custom component.

2. Select File|New... and click the New page tab. Double-click the Package icon.

3. Using the New Package dialog box, click Browse and verify that the directory from Step 1 is current. Enter **DingPkg** into the filename field, and click Open (which, it seems to me, is misnamed and should be OK, because we are creating a new file, not opening an existing one). This inserts the path and filename DingPkg.dpk into the New Package dialog. Optionally enter a description such as "Button with a bell," and click OK to continue.

4. The Package Editor is now running. Click the Add button, and when the Add dialog appears, click the New Component page tab. This opens another dialog into which you specify your component's characteristics. Enter or select from drop-down lists the following information:

   • Ancestor type: TButton

   • Class name: TDingButton

   • Palette page: Samples (the default)

   • Unit file name: C:\...\Ding\DingButton.pas (automatically entered)

   • Search path: (should include default paths plus the one for Ding)

5. Click OK to create the new component shell. This pops you back to the Package Editor. Click the Requires page tab and specify any packages required by this one. In this example, the default vcl340 package is all that's needed. In your own components, you might need to add additional packages to this list.

6. Click the Options button and enable both Design and Runtime check boxes. You may fiddle with the other options, but for this demonstration, the default values are fine. Click OK to get back to the Package Editor.

7. Click the Compile button to compile the package and its component unit. This simply ensures that the package and unit are in the correct formats. When you are ready to install the finished component, click Compile one last time, and then click Install to insert the component into the palette. But, don't do that yet — first, we need to program what our new component does.

Listing 20-1 shows the finished DingButton.pas file. Switch to Delphi's code editor window, and select the DingButton page tab. Use the listing as a guide to fill in the component shell you created with the preceding steps.

Listing 20-1: **Ding\DingButton.pas**

```
unit DingButton;

interface

uses
  Windows, Messages, SysUtils, Classes, Graphics, Controls,
  Forms, Dialogs, StdCtrls;

type
  TDingButton = class(TButton)
  private
    { Private declarations }
  protected
    { Protected declarations }
  public
    procedure Click; override;
    { Public declarations }
  published
    { Published declarations }
  end;

procedure Register;

implementation

procedure Register;
begin
  RegisterComponents('Samples', [TDingButton]);
end;
```

(continued)

Listing 20-1 *(continued)*

```
procedure TDing.Click;
begin
  MessageBeep(0);
  inherited Click;
end;


end.
```

The finished program adds only a few lines to the component template. To provide a bell sound when users click the button, I declared procedure Click in the TDing class with an override directive:

```
procedure Click; override;
```

The TButton class on which TDing is based provides a Click procedure along with numerous other properties and methods. The override declaration tells the compiler that the new component replaces the inherited Click with its own programming. In addition to declaring the method, you also have to implement it by writing the procedure's body. In this example, the replacement Click method executes two commands:

```
MessageBeep(0);
inherited Click;
```

The first line sounds a tone by calling the Windows API MessageBeep function. The second line calls the inherited Click procedure to perform TButton's actions, which include executing the OnClick event handler if one is assigned.

When overriding a method, you almost always call the *inherited* method. This is how you build new capabilities into a component while retaining what its methods already do. You are not required to call an inherited method, but if you don't, your program may skip an important initialization buried somewhere in an ancestor class. For safety, always call the inherited method in replacement procedures and functions unless you have an excellent reason for not doing so.

Notice that the DingButton.pas module includes a Register procedure that is not a member of the TDing class. Delphi calls this procedure as part of its component palette installation process. Follow these steps to install the new component (afterward, I explain how to delete the component, so don't be nervous about trying this):

1. Get back to the Package Editor window. If you can't find it, select View | Window List... and select Package Editor to bring this window to the front.

2. Click the Compile button. This compiles the package and its associated unit. Remember, you must compile the package — compiling only the unit separately does not properly create the package.

3. If you received no errors in Step 2, click Install to install the new component into the VCL palette. You should receive a message such as: "Package D:\...\DingPkg.bpl has been installed. The following new component(s) have been registered: TDingButton." Click the OK button to close this message window.

Click the Samples page tab on Delphi's VCL palette. The new button is there, ready for use. To test out the new component, you can create a new application, or for convenience in testing future updates, simply use the existing application you created at the beginning of the entire process. To use that application, open the Project Manager if necessary and make the Main form visible. Insert a DingButton object into the form. Notice that Delphi names this object DingButton1. Also notice that, if you pause the cursor over the component icon, Delphi displays its name in a pop-up window.

Press F9 to compile the application. Click DingButton to ring your computer's bell. You might want to save all files at this stage before continuing.

To delete a component, use Component | Configure Palette..., select a category at left (Samples for example), select the component to remove (Ding in this case), and then click Delete.

Properties, methods, and events

Writing custom components involves programming three main elements that are present in every component class: properties, methods, and events. In this and the next several sections, you develop, test, and install a more extensive component that uses all three of these elements. The finished result, BarChart, displays a bar chart from a set of data points managed by a string list. Figure 20-2 shows a sample of the component in use.

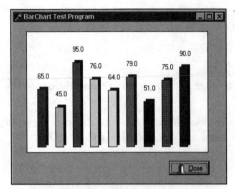

Figure 20-2: An example of the BarChart component that you develop, test, and install into Delphi.

If you don't want to create your own custom component, copy the Source\BarChart directory from the CD-ROM, select Component|Install Packages, click Add, and browse to the BarChart directory on your hard drive. Select BarPkg.bpl, and click OK twice. However, I urge you to follow the step-by-step instructions here, which better explain how to create and install your own custom components. (You can still copy the program text from the CD-ROM to save time.)

To create the BarChart component, follow these steps:

1. Create a new BarChart directory. Start a new application, name the form MainForm, and save all files. Save Unit1.pas as Main.pas, and save the project as Bartest.dpr. As with the Ding button, Bartest serves as a test bed for the custom BarChart component.

2. Select File|New..., click the New page tab, and double-click the Package icon. Into the resulting New Package dialog, click Browse, change to the BarChart directory (it probably is already current), and enter **BarPkg** into the File name field. Click Open (again, this button would be more sensibly labeled OK) to return to the New Package dialog. You should see ...\BarChart\BarPkg.dpk in the File name edit box. Enter BarChart Component into the Description field and click OK.

3. You now see the Package Editor. Click the Add speed button, and then select the New Component page tab. Set the fields in this dialog page as follows:

   • Ancestor type: TGraphicControl

   • Class name: TBarChart

   • Palette page: Samples (the default)

- Unit file name: C:\...\BarChart\BarChart.pas (Double-check this entry — it might be set to the Ding directory from the preceding section. If so, change it to BarChart.)

- Search path: (should include default paths plus the one for BarChart; delete the entry for the Ding path if necessary)

4. Click OK to create the new component shell, and return to the Package Editor. Click the Requires page tab and specify any packages required by this one. As with Ding, the default vcl40 package is all that's needed. In your own components, you might need to add additional packages to this list.

5. Click the Options button and enable both Design and Runtime check boxes. The other option default values are fine. Click OK to get back to the Package Editor.

6. Click the Compile button to compile the package and its component unit. This simply ensures that the package and unit are in the correct formats. When you are ready to install the finished component, click Compile one last time, and then click Install to insert the component into the palette. But, don't do that yet — as with the Ding button, first we need to program what our new component does.

7. Switch to Delphi's code editor window, and select the BarChart page tab. Copy the programming from the CD-ROM in file BarChart.pas located in the Source\BarChart directory. The rest of this chapter explains this listing's statements — for now, use the entire text to replace the blank BarChart.pas unit in the code editor.

The preceding steps complete the programming for the BarChart component. You can now compile the component and install its package into the VCL palette. After that, you can use the component just as you do others. To complete the custom component and test it, follow these steps:

1. Get back to the Package Editor window. If you can't find it, select View | Window List... and select Package Editor to bring this window to the front.

2. Click the Compile button. This compiles the package and its associated unit. Remember, you must compile the package — compiling only the unit separately does not properly create the package.

3. Click Install to install the new component into the VCL palette. You should receive a message such as: "Package C:\...\BarPkg.bpl has been installed. The following new component(s) have been registered: TBarChart." Click the OK button to close this message window.

4. Try out the new component. Click the Main page tab in the code editor window, and press F12 to bring up the testbed's form. Click the Samples VCL palette tab, and select the BarChart component. Click in the form to insert a BarChart object.

5. With BarChart1 selected, click the ellipsis next to its Data property. This brings up Delphi's string-list editor. Enter floating-point values between 0 and 100, one entry per line (32.9, 12.3, 75.0, 98.7, and so on).

6. Click the string-list editor's OK button to return to the form and view the chart displayed by the custom BarChart component. Figure 20-2 shows the sample BarChart you see on screen. (You don't have to run or save the test program, although you may do so if you wish.)

The TBarChart component class

Listing 20-2 shows the interface section of the BarChart.pas unit, including the TBarChart class declaration. As you can see, the Barchart unit uses several other Delphi unit modules, and you may add other unit names to the *uses* declaration. Because you are not programming a form, when programming a component, Delphi can't automatically add unit names to *uses* as it does for applications. If you call a function or procedure, or if you attempt to construct an object of a class, and you receive an Unknown identifier error, look up the identifier's type in Delphi's online help and add the item's unit to the *uses* directive at the top of the unit module. You may also add a private *uses* declaration to the unit's implementation.

Unlike most other project listings in this book, BarChart's is listed in this chapter in pieces. I explain each piece as we go along. Of course, the entire BarChart.pas listing is on the CD-ROM in the Source\BarChart directory.

Listing 20-2: **Barchart\BarChart.pas interface**

```
unit Barchart;

interface

uses
  Windows, Messages, SysUtils, Classes, Graphics, Controls,
  Forms, Dialogs;

type
  TBarChart = class(TGraphicControl)
  private
    FPen: TPen;
    FBrush: TBrush;
    FData: TStrings;
```

```
    FLabels: Boolean;
    XBase, YBase: Integer;
    XIncrement, YIncrement: Integer;
    procedure SetPen(Value: TPen);
    procedure SetBrush(Value: TBrush);
    procedure SetData(Value: TStrings);
    procedure SetLabels(Value: Boolean);
    function YData(N: Integer): Integer;
  protected
    procedure Paint; override;
  public
    constructor Create(AOwner: TComponent); override;
    destructor Destroy; override;
  published
    procedure StyleChanged(Sender: TObject);
    property Pen: TPen read FPen write SetPen;
    property Brush: TBrush read FBrush write SetBrush;
    property Data: TStrings read FData write SetData;
    property Labels: Boolean read FLabels write SetLabels;
    property DragCursor;
    property DragMode;
    property Enabled;
    property ParentShowHint;
    property ShowHint;
    property Visible;
    property OnDragDrop;
    property OnDragOver;
    property OnEndDrag;
    property OnMouseDown;
    property OnMouseMove;
    property OnMouseUp;
  end;

procedure Register;
```

TBarChart (the derived class) inherits the properties, methods, and events from TGraphicControl (the ancestor class). As you can see from Figure 20-1, the ancestor class is derived from four other classes: TControl, TComponent, TPersistent, and TObject. Therefore, TBarChart inherits all of the properties, methods, and events from those classes. As they used to say to me at the airline counter before I learned how to travel light, "That's a lot of baggage!" But don't fret that this needlessly bloats your new class. Because numerous components are also derived from these same classes, all the inherited methods and events are probably hanging around somewhere in your application anyway. Inheriting them just means the new class gains access to them—inheriting is not the same as copying.

The TBarChart class begins with several private declarations. All fields and methods following the keyword *private* are strictly for use by the unit that declares the class. No other unit anywhere—component or application—may refer to any of the class's private declarations. This is an example of data hiding, which experienced programmers realize is one of the keys to successful software development. Bugs are often caused by the indiscriminate use of data, and hiding sensitive items (such as the BarChart's FData string list) guarantees that if any bugs show up with this field, the trouble must be in this module, because only this module can refer to FData. Data hiding also frees the developer to modify a class's code without worry that those changes affect other modules.

However, the TBarChart class needs to make the FData string list available so that component users can supply new data for bar chart objects. The class does this by publishing the field, which specifies access methods that control how users read and write sensitive data—but more on this later. First, I want to explain TBarChart's other private parts.

Private data fields that are to be published are traditionally prefaced with the letter *F*. Though not required, this convention helps you keep track of private and published names. For example, FData's published property name is Data. In component programming, you must be able to distinguish between a field's private and published names.

The TBarChart class declares fields FPen, FBrush, FData, and FLabels. Try these properties in the sample program. For example, double-click the Brush property in the Object Inspector window, and change its Color subvalue. Also, toggle the Labels property from True to False to erase the data point labels above the bars.

TBarChart also declares a few miscellaneous variables just for convenience. By declaring these variables after the *private* access specifier, you can be sure that no other module can affect TBarChart objects except through the access methods that the class specifically provides.

In addition to fields, the class's private section also declares five methods: four procedures and one function. The *Set* procedures assign values to their respective fields. SetPen assigns a value to FPen, SetBrush assigns a value to FBrush, and so on. In a moment, you learn how published properties use these methods to write their associated field values. The YData function returns an integer coordinate for a data point indexed by N.

Here again, all of these methods are *private* to the class. This means that only statements in this unit may call them. No other modules may call SetPen or SetLabels. This restricts the use of the component, and helps prevent bugs. However, because the properties are *public*, assignments to them using the Object Inspector do call SetPen and SetLabels.

Tip In a class's private, protected, and public sections, field declarations must precede method and property declarations.

Following its private section, the TBarChart class declares a replacement procedure, Paint, in a protected section. TBarChart inherits Paint from its ancestor class, and to replace that method, it must end the declaration with the override directive. Methods and fields declared in a protected section are one cut above those in a private section. The unit may use these elements, as may any classes derived from TBarChart.

However, the component's users cannot directly call the protected Paint. This provides a measure of safety because Paint is called in response to the window receiving a wm_Paint message. The new class replaces Paint so it can draw a bar chart, but it would be a mistake for applications to call this procedure directly. You may declare fields, methods, and properties in a class's protected section.

The TBarChart class declares two other methods: a constructor Create, and a destructor Destroy. Both are inherited, and both need an override directive. They are declared in the class's public section so that users may call them. If you didn't put Create in the public section, programs would have no way to construct TBarChart objects. You may declare fields, methods, and properties in a public section. Any statement anywhere in the application that uses TBarChart may call public methods, and read and write any public data fields.

Finally in the TBarChart class is a lengthy section preceded by the access specifier *published*. In this section are the names of properties that you want Delphi to make available in the Object Inspector window for objects of the class. Any methods declared here are *public* (StyleChanged, for example), but you normally publish only the names of data fields and events.

Some of TBarChart's published properties are new; others are inherited from an ancestor class. For example, the Visible property is available in all visual components. If you don't want the component's users to change Visible's value, don't publish it. It's up to you to decide which properties to publish, but you generally publish most inherited ones, especially those such as Enabled and Visible that users expect to find in the Object Inspector.

Properties that are new to TBarChart use a different type of property declaration that specifies an access path to data. For example, look closely at the Pen property's published declaration:

```
property Pen: TPen read FPen write SetPen;
```

A colon follows the property name Pen, after which an expression states the property's data type (TPen), and its read and write access methods. Object Pascal statements can directly assign TPen values, so the read access method is simply the FPen data field's name. The *write* method, however, is a private method in the class, SetPen. This means that all assignments to the Pen property actually call SetPen.

The other properties use similar programming. By publishing them and providing read and write access methods, you carefully control the use of the component's data. TBarChart is only a relatively simple example, but in a more complex situation, this control is invaluable. For example, you might program a Set method to prevent users from assigning illegal or out-of-range values to variables.

Other ways to publish properties are available. If you provide only a *read* method, the property is effectively read-only. You may also create a write-only property for restricting sensitive fields such as a password or an encryption key, but such uses are rare. A property statement may also have additional commands for default values and specifying whether the property is to be stored in a form file. These techniques go beyond this chapter's introduction, but you can read about them in Delphi's online help and the Developer's Guide. (Rumor has it that the final release of Delphi 4 may not include the printed Developer's Guide. If so, search Delphi's online help for "Component Writer's Guide" for this information.)

The final line of the Barchart unit's interface declares a procedure that all component units must have for installation onto the palette. The Component Expert inserts this declaration for you, but if you write a component from scratch, you must remember to enter the line:

```
procedure Register;
```

Delphi calls Register when you install the component on the palette. A unit that lacks a Register procedure cannot be installed. Register is called only when the component is linked into the palette. A program must never call Register, which the Delphi linker removes from applications that use the component module.

Component class registration

Listing 20-3 shows the Barchart unit's Register implementation. The procedure calls RegisterComponents, which requires two arguments: a component palette page name, and a set of component classes in the unit. Surround one or more class names with square brackets to create the *set* argument.

Listing 20-3: Barchart Unit's Register procedure implementation

```
{ Delphi calls this to install component onto the palette }
procedure Register;
begin
  RegisterComponents('Samples', [TBarChart]);
end;
```

If your unit has multiple component classes, insert them into the component name set, separated by commas. For example, in a unit with three classes, you might call RegisterComponents like this:

```
RegisterComponents('Samples', [THisCtrl, THerCtrl, TYourCtrl]);
```

Or, you may call RegisterComponents multiple times. These statements are operationally the same as the preceding single statement, but are slightly easier to edit in case you have to change how many components the unit registers. Also use this form to install components on different palette pages (you still have to bracket the component names):

```
RegisterComponents('Dialogs', [THisCtrl]);
RegisterComponents('Additional', [THerCtrl]);
RegisterComponents('Samples', [THisCtrl]);
```

You don't have to register every class in a unit; only those that you want to install on the component palette. A unit may also provide procedures, functions, variables, classes, and nonvisual components that don't need to be selected from the palette at design time.

Component initialization

A component's Create constructor initializes objects of the component class. Every component must have a Create constructor. If your component has nothing to initialize, you don't need to override the Create constructor that you inherit from an ancestor class, but it's the rare component that doesn't have to perform some initializations.

Likewise, most every component needs a Destroy destructor to free any resources allocated to component objects. For example, if you create an object or allocate some memory in the component's constructor, you must insert a corresponding deallocation statement in the destructor. Failing to do this is sure to cause an eventual loss of memory (the so-called memory leak error). Listing 20-4 shows TBarChart's constructor and destructor implementations.

Listing 20-4: TBarChart's constructor and destructor implementations

```
{ Create component instance at runtime AND design time }
constructor TBarChart.Create(AOwner: TComponent);
begin
  inherited Create(AOwner);
  Width := 65;
  Height := 65;
  FPen := TPen.Create;
  FPen.OnChange := StyleChanged;
  FBrush := TBrush.Create;
  FBrush.OnChange := StyleChanged;
  FData := TStringList.Create;
  FLabels := True;
end;

{ Destroy component instance at runtime AND design time }
destructor TBarChart.Destroy;
begin
  FPen.Free;
  FBrush.Free;
  FData.Free;
  inherited Destroy;
end;
```

Create should always call its inherited constructor, usually as the first step. Unlike inherited methods, you must call the inherited Create constructor. Never skip this step, or the object is not initialized! After calling the inherited Create, the constructor assigns values to the Width and Height properties, inherited from the ancestor class. These values determine the initial appearance of the object when users insert it into a form.

Next, the constructor creates the FPen, FBrush, and FData fields, which are all objects of Delphi classes. This is a good example of how a component unit may access the class's private declarations. In addition to creating the fields, the program assigns a procedure, StyleChanged, to the FPen and FBrush OnChange event. Using the Object Inspector to assign values to those fields calls StyleChanged, which invalidates the window (try it with a sample project). Because of this, when users change the Brush property's color, for example, the effect is immediate.

As a last step, the component specifies a default value for the Boolean field, FLabels. The published property statement in the class declaration may specify this same value to prevent writing this field to the form file if the property value matches. Because the constructor assigns this value, there's no reason to waste space writing the default value to the form file. To do this, change the property's declaration to the following (this is one line, although it's shown here as two):

```
property Labels: Boolean read FLabels write SetLabels
default True;
```

As I mentioned, the class destructor must free any allocated resources. TBarChart's destructor, Destroy, does this by calling Free for the FPen, FBrush, and FData fields that the constructor created. As a last step, the destructor calls its inherited Destroy. Components must do this so that any ancestor class allocations are also freed. Never skip this step.

Any exceptions that occur in the constructor leave the object partially initialized. You should program destructors to handle this possibility — for example, by checking whether pointers are initialized before freeing memory allocated to them.

A component's class constructor is called not only at run time, but also when the user inserts a component object into a form. Likewise, if the user deletes the object or closes the form or the project, the program calls the component's destructor. Other methods may be called as well — for example, to make assignments to properties. Component objects are alive at run time and during application development.

Visual component painting

To make their grand appearances on Delphi's stage, visual components override an inherited Paint method. The method calls Canvas functions, sets pen and brush colors, and does whatever is necessary to draw the component object.

Delphi takes care of providing handles, clicking and dragging, resizing, and other design-time features. All you need to do is decide how you want your component objects to look. Listing 20-5 shows the implementation of TBarChart's Paint method along with supporting constants and the YData function, which converts data points to *y* coordinate values for drawing the chart's bars.

Paint calls Windows GDI functions through the services of the Canvas object inherited from TGraphicControl. To draw the BarChart's window — what the user initially sees when inserting a BarChart object into a form — Paint assigns the Canvas Pen and Brush colors using the data fields FPen and FBrush, which the user can program in the Object Inspector. After preparing a few variables, Paint calls Rectangle and, like magic, a white box appears in the form. This is all you need to do to give components their design-time appearance.

Listing 20-5: **TBarChart's Paint method implementation and supporting players**

```
const
{ Fixed constants }
  numClrs = 16;            { Number of colors in colorArray }
  spaceAtBottom = 10;      { Reserved pixels below chart }
  spaceAtLeft = 20;        { Reserved pixels at left of chart }
  spaceAtTop = 40;         { Reserved pixels above chart }
  spaceAtRight = 20;       { Reserved pixels at right of chart }
  yScaleMax = 100.0;       { Maximum Y scale value }
  yScaleIncrement = 10.0;  { Increment for Y scale markers }
{ Typed constants }
  spaceVertical: Integer = spaceAtTop + spaceAtBottom;
  spaceHorizontal: Integer = spaceAtLeft + spaceAtRight;
  yScale: Integer = Trunc(yScaleMax / yScaleIncrement);
{ Array of colors used to draw topmost bars }
  colorArray: array[0 .. numClrs _ 1] of TColor = (
    $0000000, $0FFFFFF, $0FF0000, $000FF00,
    $00000FF, $0FFFF00, $000FFFF, $0FF00FF,
    $0880000, $0008800, $0000088, $0888800,
    $0008888, $0880088, $0448844, $0884488
  );

{ Return Y-coordinate for data point N }
function TBarChart.YData(N: Integer): Integer;
var
  F: Double;
begin
  F := (StrToFloat(FData[N]) / yScaleIncrement) * yIncrement;
  Result := YBase _ Round(F);
end;

{ Paint component shape at runtime AND design time }
procedure TBarChart.Paint;
var
  XMax, YMax: Integer;
  Width1, WidthD2: Integer;
  I, X1, Y1, X2, Y2: Integer;
begin
  with Canvas do
  begin
  { Erase background }
    Pen.Color := FPen.Color;
    Brush.Color := FBrush.Color;
    X1 := Pen.Width div 2;
    Y1 := X1;
    XMax := Width _ Pen.Width + 1;
    YMax := Height _ Pen.Width + 1;
```

```
      Rectangle(X1, Y1, X1 + XMax, Y1 + YMax);
      if FData.Count = 0 then Exit;
   { Initialize variables }
      try
        XIncrement := (XMax _ spaceHorizontal) div FData.Count;
        YIncrement := (YMax _ spaceVertical) div yScale;
        Width1 := XIncrement div 2;
        WidthD2 := Width1 div 2;
        XBase := spaceAtLeft + WidthD2;
        YBase := YMax _ spaceAtBottom;
        Canvas.Font := Self.Font;
   { Draw barchart }
        for I := 0 to FData.Count _ 1 do
        begin
          X1 := spaceAtLeft + (XIncrement * I);
          Y1 := YData(I);
          X2 := X1 + Width1;
          Y2 := YBase;
          if FLabels then
          begin
            Brush.Color := FBrush.Color;
            TextOut(X1, Y1 _ 30, FData.Strings[I]);
          end;
          Brush.Color := clBlack;
          Rectangle(X1 + 4, Y1 _ 4, X2 + 4, Y2 _ 4);
          Brush.Color := colorArray[(I + 2) mod numClrs];
          Rectangle(X1, Y1, X2, Y2);
        end;
      except
        ShowMessage('Error in data point ' + IntToStr(I));
        FData.Clear;
        Invalidate;
      end;
   end;
 end;
```

Of course, your component probably needs to do more than display a simple box. The rest of TBarChart's Paint method draws the bars and text labels (if FLabels is True). This part of the program covers two important concerns. One, if FData.Count is zero, there are no data points in the Data property's string list. Paint exits in this case to prevent a divide-by-zero error. The second concern is exception handling, which Paint provides by inserting its math and drawing commands in a *try* block.

Despite this level of protection, any exceptions that occur in a Paint method can cause an endless loop — an anomaly that TBarChart works around in its *except* block. If an error occurs in the *try* block, Delphi displays a dialog box, which when closed, causes the underlying window to become invalid, which causes Windows to issue another wm_Paint, which reenters the Paint method, which generates another exception, and so on until the cows come home. (They never did when this happened to me — maybe we don't have any cows around here.)

For this reason, TBarChart handles any exceptions by displaying an error message, clearing the FData string list, and invalidating the window. Try this by inserting some bad data such as XYZ or another string into the Data property. You receive an error message that tells you the faulty data point index (the first index is zero as it is for all string lists), and the object clears.

Rather than clear Data, which is probably not the best response, the program might display a message or a symbol of some kind inside the object, or it could set a flag that the program could inspect. You might want to experiment with these alternative responses in the *except* block.

Component property access methods

Listing 20-6 shows the rest of TBarChart's programming. These procedures implement the property access methods for the FPen, FBrush, FData, and FLabels fields.

Listing 20-6: TBarChart's property access method implementations

```
{ Local event handler redraws shape when necessary }
procedure TBarChart.StyleChanged(Sender: TObject);
begin
  Invalidate;
end;

{ Assign new brush data to FBrush field }
procedure TBarChart.SetBrush(Value: TBrush);
begin
  FBrush.Assign(Value);
end;

{ Assign new pen data to FPen field }
procedure TBarChart.SetPen(Value: TPen);
begin
  FPen.Assign(Value);
end;

{ Assign new string list to FData field }
procedure TBarChart.SetData(Value: TStrings);
begin
  FData.Assign(Value);
```

```
      Invalidate;
end;

{ Assign new Boolean value to FLabels field }
procedure TBarChart.SetLabels(Value: Boolean);
begin
   if FLabels <> Value then   { Exit if no change needed }
   begin
     FLabels := Value;  { Assign to FLabels, NOT Labels ! }
     Invalidate;  { Redraw component to add/remove labels }
   end;
end;

end.
```

The StyleChanged procedure calls Invalidate so that Windows issues a wm_Paint message for the object's window. This eventually leads to a call to Paint, which erases and redraws the bar chart image. The program doesn't call StyleChanged; it assigns the procedure to the TPen and TBrush OnChange event. Any changes to the Pen and Brush properties, therefore, redraw the object.

Procedures SetBrush, SetPen, and SetData operate similarly. They each receive a parameter of their field type, which they pass to the field's Assign method. You can be sure that Assign does whatever is necessary to dispose of any existing resources before accepting the new data. For example, assigning a new Pen disposes of the Windows pen resource (if one exists) referenced by the FPen field.

Notice that SetData, which assigns the Data string list property, calls Invalidate to redraw the window. This is because the TStrings class does not provide an OnChange event; if it did, you could assign StyleChanged as for the Pen and Brush properties.

In a property access method, checking whether a value is the same as the new value can help prevent annoying flicker, especially for complex visual components such as BarChart. If SetLabels assigned the new value and called Invalidate, the object would flutter every time users highlighted the Labels property in the Object Inspector.

SetLabels assigns a user value to the FLabel's Boolean switch. This procedure demonstrates a common design for property access methods. Conventionally, the method first checks whether the Value is the same as the object's field. If so, there is nothing to do, and the procedure exits. Otherwise, the program assigns Value to the FLabels field, and invalidates the window to redraw it and remove or insert the data point labels.

Never assign values to properties in a property access method. Assign values only to data fields, usually declared in the class's private section. Ignoring this rule can cause a stack overflow, and may shut down Delphi and possibly Windows. In the example listing, SetLabels is the access method that the program calls for assignments to the Labels property. If SetLabels were to assign a value to Labels, the program would call SetLabels recursively until the stack blows. Be very careful when writing property access methods to assign values only to actual data fields in the class.

Caution   Assigning values to properties in a property access method can cause a so-called infinite recursion, leading to a stack overflow. Of course, the recursion isn't actually infinite because it halts the system, but never mind the terminology SNAFU. Just don't do this!

Understanding Component Design

The remainder of this chapter provides tips that are useful in understanding component design techniques. As I mentioned, component construction could easily fill a book of this size, so the following is necessarily incomplete. However, I've tried to touch on subjects that are of key interest to component authors, and that suggest topics to search for in other sources.

Custom components

In the VCL, you come across components with the word Custom in their names. For example, TCustomEdit is derived from TWinControl in the StdCtrls unit using the declaration:

```
TCustomEdit = class(TWinControl)
...
end;
```

Immediately following, you find this declaration for the TEdit component, the one that applications use:

```
TEdit = class(TCustomEdit)
...
end;
```

The reason for having two classes instead of just TEdit is to provide you with a raw edit-control class with no published properties (actually, there is one, TabStop, which gets a default value of True). Components with Custom in their names publish no (or only essential) properties. They may also contain abstract method declarations that a derived class is expected to implement.

If you derive your components from TEdit, all of its published properties become published in the derived class. If you instead derive your class from TCustomEdit, which provides the actual programming for TEdit, you decide which properties to publish. The derived class also implements any abstract methods.

Component debugging

Debugging and testing components is complicated by the fact that you are using the very development system into which you want to install the component. Delphi can compile only projects for debugging — to debug components, you must install them on the component palette and write a test application. When that's not convenient, you can take one of two approaches:

✦ Develop your component *as* an application, and then convert it to a component. I created the TBarChart component using this method. The original program, not listed here, displayed a bar chart using a class derived from TGraphicControl. I then copied this code into the final component unit.

✦ Include a component unit in a test project, and construct objects of the component's class in a procedure or function. You have to run the program to view the component, but this method helps you to debug your code before installing the component on the palette.

To experiment with the second technique — which is essential for creating and testing complex components — copy the BarChart.pas file from the CD-ROM's Source\ BarChart directory to a new, empty directory. Follow these steps to create a test program that creates a BarChart object entirely under program control. Listing 20-7 demonstrates how to construct an object at run time for a component not on the component palette.

1. Start a new application. Name the form MainForm, and set its Caption to Test BarChart Component. Save the project in the same directory that contains the copy of BarChart.pas. (In practice, the directories may be different, but it's easier to use the same one for this demonstration.) Name the unit Main.pas and the project BarTest.prj.

2. Add BarChart to the Main unit's *uses* directive.

3. Rather than use the BarChart component on the VCL palette (when testing a new component, it probably won't be), declare an object of the BarChart class manually. Do that by typing *object* declarations into the form's class — just as Delphi does automatically for finished components. For example, enter the following declaration in the TMainForm class's public section (change in bold):

```
TMainForm = class(TForm)
private
  { Private declarations }
public
  BarChart1: TBarChart;
end;
```

4. Create a handler for the form's OnCreate event (or you may use any event handler — a Button's OnClick, for example). Create the component instances you need. This takes a minimum of two steps: (1) Call Create to construct the object, and (2) Assign a parent object to the object's Parent field. Usually, you can use Self as arguments in both tasks. Self refers to the form object (because this is a method of the form's class), and you probably want to have the form own the object (Step 1) and serve as its parent (Step 2). For example, use these statements to create a BarChart object:

```
BarChart1 := TBarChart.Create(Self);
BarChart1.Parent := Self;
```

5. You also have to initialize other fields such as Left, Right, Width, and Height, which determine the object's position and size. In addition, you need to add statements to assign any required data — the BarChart object's Data string list, for example. Listing 20-7 shows the finished unit, stored as Main2.pas in the Source\BarChart directory on the CD-ROM. This file demonstrates how to construct an object at run time for a component not on the component palette. Use this file to create a test project for the BarChart component class.

Listing 20-7: Barchart\Main2.Pas. Use this file to create a test project for the BarChart component class.

```
unit Main;

interface

uses
   Windows, Messages, SysUtils, Classes, Graphics, Controls,
   Forms, Dialogs, BarChart;

type
   TMainForm = class(TForm)
     procedure FormCreate(Sender: TObject);
   private
     { Private declarations }
   public
     BarChart1: TBarChart;
   end;

var
   MainForm: TMainForm;

implementation

{$R *.DFM}
```

```
procedure TMainForm.FormCreate(Sender: TObject);
begin
  BarChart1 := TBarChart.Create(Self);
  BarChart1.Parent := Self;
  with BarChart1 do
  begin
    Left := 20;
    Top := 20;
    Width := 375;
    Height := 200;
    Data.Add('65.0');
    Data.Add('45.0');
    Data.Add('95.0');
    Data.Add('76.0');
    Data.Add('51.0');
    Data.Add('90.0');
  end;
end;

end.
```

Do not insert data fields or method declarations in the default *published* section of a form class (the section immediately following the class declaration up to the first access specifier, usually private). If you modify the default published section, you receive an error message because this is where Delphi declares objects and event handlers. Consider a class's default published section hands-off for your own declarations.

Class properties

A property may be any data type except a file. However, a property cannot be a Pascal array, because properties are not real fields and access to them is controlled by read and write methods. You may, however, create array-like properties that call methods to read and write their elements. (For more information, see "Array properties" in this chapter.) Except for these restrictions, a property may publish any kind of field.

Events are actually data fields of the TNotifyEvent or a similar type. An event is a pointer to a user-supplied method. However, an event is not itself a method, and therefore, publishing an event actually publishes a data field (the pointer), not code.

Properties appear to the component user as fields, but they are actually encapsulated methods for reading and writing other data fields, which are normally private to the component class. Properties may also be calculated. For example, you can write a property access method that computes a property value from other data fields. However, be careful not to introduce too many dependencies among calculated properties, or the order in which they are initialized becomes critical, a fact that can complicate future maintainence.

Publishing properties makes available run-time type information about the class that Delphi uses in several ways. For example, the Object Inspector uses run-time type information to display and edit property values, which are stored in a .dfm form file. After compiling this chapter's BarTest project, open the Main.dfm file to view how Delphi stores properties. Listing 20-8 shows a sample file. I deleted some lines to keep the listing short — use Delphi to open the file to inspect the whole shebang.

Listing 20-8: **Barchart\Main.dfm form file for the BarTest project**

```
object MainForm: TMainForm
  Left = 200
  Top = 95
  Width = 435
  Height = 300
...
  object BarChart1: TBarChart
    Left = 24
    Top = 16
    Width = 377
    Height = 209
    Hint = 'BarChart component'
    Brush.Color = clSilver
    Data.Strings = (
      '65.0'
      '45.0'
...
      '90.0')
    Labels = True
    ParentShowHint = False
    ShowHint = True
  end
end
```

That looks like Pascal, but it isn't. A form file contains property values as entered into the Object Inspector window. Delphi loads the property values after it calls the component's constructor, which gets first crack at initializing property values.

Property values can be initialized in one more way. After calling the component's constructor and loading property values from the form file (or its image bound into the compiled .exe code file), Delphi calls a virtual Loaded method that you can override. Place this declaration in the component class's protected section:

```
procedure Loaded; override;
```

Implement the procedure to perform any additional initializations for the object. These initializations take priority over any values assigned in the constructor or from the form file (in other words, by the Object Inspector). Users can still set properties using the Object Inspector, but when they run the program, Loaded is called again, so don't replace any values you want users to have access to.

Loaded is useful for providing default values for properties that users may decide to leave blank or that don't have form-file values. The Loaded function is also a good place to adjust a fixed-size component's dimensions. For example, the DBNavigator component uses this technique to initialize default hint-text strings if the user doesn't enter any into the Hints field; it also makes minor adjustments to the object's size and position.

Always call the inherited Loaded method in your replacement procedure, or you may skip an important initialization required by an ancestor class. Loaded is also the only chance you get to access any associated objects (siblings, child objects, or linked objects) during the loading process. For example, a data-aware component cannot use its DataSource property until Loaded is called.

Note

The Loaded method is not part of the construction sequence of a component; it is part of the streaming sequence. Because of this, you should never put critical code into an inherited Loaded method because it is not called if the component is constructed dynamically at run time rather than being loaded from a form stream.

Array properties

Properties may not be Pascal arrays, but you can create an array property that is used just like an array. Array properties are especially valuable for creating advanced data structures such as associative and sparse arrays. Like all properties, an array property provides access methods for reading and writing data. The property's class can choose any method for the actual data storage. For example, this is how the TStrings property provides access to string data using array indexing, but internally, links strings efficiently into a list.

Array properties may also use any kind of data type for indexes. You can create an array indexed on floating-point values or strings. Common Pascal arrays may use only ordinal indexes such as integers, characters, and enumerated constants.

Listing 20-9 is a DOS-prompt application that demonstrates how to program array properties. You may use the same technique in a component, but as this program illustrates, you can also publish array properties as protected members of any class. On the CD-ROM, this program is in the Source\Daynames directory, in the ArrayP.pas file. To run the program, click the Windows Start button, and select Programs|MS DOS Prompt; then change to the Daynames directory, and enter **Arrayp**.

Listing 20-9: **Daynames\ArrayP.pas**

```
program ArrayProperties;

uses SysUtils;

type

  TDayNames = class
  private
    function GetName(N: Integer): String;
  protected
    property DayStr[N: Integer]: String read GetName; default;
  end;

function TDayNames.GetName(N: Integer): String;
begin
  if (N < 0) or (N > 6) then
    raise ERangeError.Create('Array index out of range');
  case N of
    0: Result := 'Sunday';
    1: Result := 'Monday';
    2: Result := 'Tuesday';
    3: Result := 'Wednesday';
    4: Result := 'Thursday';
    5: Result := 'Friday';
    6: Result := 'Saturday';
  end;
end;

var
  DayNames: TDayNames;
  I: Integer;

begin
  DayNames := TDayNames.Create;
  try
    Writeln('Default property (DayNames[I])');
    for I := 0 to 6 do
```

```
      Writeln(DayNames[I]);
      Writeln;
      Writeln('Named property (DayNames.DayStr[I])');
      for I := 6 downto 0 do
        Writeln(DayNames.DayStr[I]);
    finally
      DayNames.Free;
    end;
end.
```

Note   For more information on using Delphi's command-line DOS-prompt compiler, see Chapter 21.

The example program creates a small class, TDayNames, that provides the days of the week as a pseudo-string array. The class declares a private function, GetName, that's used as the pseudo-string array's read-access method. The class's protected section declares that access method as a property, DayStr, followed by square brackets containing an integer argument. This argument could be any data type, even a string. Following the closing bracket are a colon, the data type of the array elements, and the read-access method, GetName.

Ending the property declaration with *default* sets this property as the class's default. This means that users of class objects can treat the object as though it were the property. Only one property of any class may be the default. For example, the program's first *for* loop uses the DayNames object as though it were an array:

```
for I := 0 to 6 do
  Writeln(DayNames[I]);
```

You can also refer to the property as a field in the object:

```
for I := 6 downto 0 do
  Writeln(DayNames.DayStr[I]);
```

The TStrings class uses this same method to provide access to its strings using an expression such as Items[I] or Items.Strings[I], which are the same because Strings is the default property of TStrings.

When the program uses an expression such as DayNames[I], the compiler generates a call to the designated read-access method, in this example, function GetName. In the listing, GetName first checks whether the index is in range—if not, it raises an ERangeError exception. Insert this statement into the main program's *try* block to test the exception:

```
Writeln(DayNames[7]);   { ??? }
```

Function GetNames uses a *case* statement to return a day-name string for the index values zero to six. Because the sample class is read-only, it does not provide a write-access method, but this is equally easy to do. Declare the write-access method, which must have an index value parameter (it can be any type, but here it is Integer), as follows:

```
procedure SetName(N: Integer; const S: String);
```

Next, add write SetName to the property declaration:

```
property DayStr[N: Integer]: String read GetName write SetName;
default;
```

Implement procedure SetName to store its passed string at the specified index. For example, you might insert the string into a list and record the index value in an object. The read-access method would then search the list for this index and return the associated string — an example of an associative, sparse array. Only entered strings are stored on the list; unused index positions occupy no space.

Noncomponent classes such as TDayNames may not publish properties, but can declare them in a protected or public section as demonstrated here. This is a useful technique for controlling access to data fields.

Creating ActiveX Controls

Any Delphi component can easily be converted into an ActiveX control. That control is then usable in development systems such as Visual Basic, Microsoft Access, Paradox for Windows, and other software that supports the ActiveX protocol. You can also use your ActiveX controls in Delphi and in Borland's C++ Builder, although if you have the original control as a component, it's best used in its native form in Delphi.

As an ActiveX control, a Delphi component is encased in a shell that controls communication between the control and the outside world. This interface conforms to Microsoft's ActiveX specifications, and as far as the user of the control is concerned, it appears no different from any other ActiveX control. Inside, however, the control is a Delphi component embedded like a plum in pudding.

How to create an ActiveX control

To create an ActiveX control takes several steps:

1. Design and test your component as explained in this chapter.

2. Run Delphi's ActiveX Control Wizard to convert your component into an ActiveX control.

3. Optionally, run the ActiveX Property Page Wizard. This step creates a property page that enables users to view and edit the control's properties, which is not necessary if all you want to do is deploy the control, for example, to an Internet browser. If you take this step, you also associate the property page with the ActiveX control.

4. After compilation, the control is registered with Windows. All ActiveX controls must be registered before they can be used.

When you create an ActiveX control from a component, Delphi automatically creates a type library that describes the control's interface. This library, stored in a .tlb file, is used by development systems to access the control's properties, methods, and events. The library is incorporated into any other control or code file that uses the ActiveX control when you compile that control or application.

Converting DingButton to an ActiveX control

Follow these steps to convert this chapter's DingButton component into an ActiveX control:

1. Choose File | New... and select the ActiveX page tab from the New Items dialog box (see Figure 20-3).

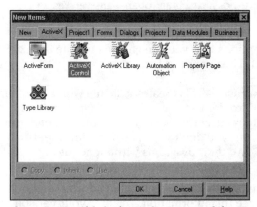

Figure 20-3: This is the ActiveX page of the New Items dialog.

2. Double-click the ActiveX Control icon. This displays the ActiveX Control Wizard dialog shown in Figure 20-4.

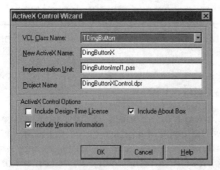

Figure 20-4: Select the component to convert to an ActiveX control.

3. Select the component to convert to an ActiveX control from the VCL Class Name drop-down list. When you do this, Delphi fills in the other fields, which you may edit if you want. For example, you may enter a different ActiveX Name and Implementation Unit, which contains the source code for the component's ActiveX interface wrapper. Click OK when you are done.

Note   ActiveX controls must be compiled as part of an ActiveX library project. At this point, Delphi warns you if you have no such library open—answer Yes to create a new library and continue.

Steps 2 and 3 provide three options that you can enable (see the check boxes at the bottom of the dialog window). These options are:

✦ **Include Design-Time License** — This creates a .lic file with a key that is required to open the control for use in a software design environment. Check this option if you want to restrict the use of your control to end users (such as in an Internet browser), but you don't want software developers to incorporate the control into their programs without acquiring a design-time license from you.

✦ **Include Version Information** — This adds version information to the control's .ocx file. The users can see this information. To enter your version information, select Project⏐Options... and choose the VersionInfo page tab.

✦ **Include About Box** — This creates an about-box dialog unit, which is added to the ActiveX library project. You may edit this about-box dialog as you do any other Delphi form. For example, choose it in the code editor window and press F12 to bring up the associated visual form. You can then add Buttons, Labels, and other components to the about-box dialog, which is displayed in the user's development environment.

After selecting the various options available for creating an ActiveX control, you can edit and program the resulting units in the library project. When you are done, select Project I Build all... to compile the control. This creates an .ocx file on disk that contains the ActiveX control.

Using the ActiveX control

After building the ActiveX control, you must register it with Windows to make the control available to other applications (including Delphi). This is easy to do — simply choose the Run I Register ActiveX Server command. An ActiveX library project must be open for this command to be enabled.

Delphi registers the control (or controls) in the current ActiveX library project. When done, Delphi displays an information dialog that tells you the operation was carried out successfully. The control is now available for use; however, it is not yet installed in Delphi's palette. To do that, you must perform one additional step.

> **Tip**
>
> To remove an ActiveX control from the system, open its project file and choose Run|Unregister ActiveX Server. This removes the control from the Windows registry.

To use the ActiveX control as a component in Delphi, select the Component I Import ActiveX Control... command. This brings up the Import ActiveX Control dialog shown in Figure 20-5. The dialog lists all ActiveX controls registered with Windows.

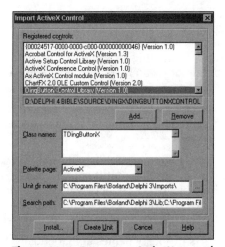

Figure 20-5: Import an ActiveX control into Delphi using the Import ActiveX Control dialog.

Select one of the registered controls to import into Delphi. You may select which palette page to install the control, but this is usually best set to the default, ActiveX. Click the Install button to import the ActiveX control into Delphi.

Note   The steps in this section are purely for demonstration. Because importing an ActiveX control into Delphi in effect creates a Delphi component shell around the ActiveX control, it is nothing short of ludicrous to perform this action on an ActiveX control that is in reality a wrapper around a Delphi component. This creates an end result with more layers than puff pastry — in all cases, it's best to use native Delphi components with Delphi. However, you may use the steps outlined in this section to import other ActiveX controls into Delphi for use as components.

Expert-User Tips

✦ You can provide online help for your components. When users select your component and press F1, Delphi initiates an online help search indexed on the keyword class_<name>, where <name> is your component's class name. For more information, see the online help topic "Merging Your Help into Delphi."

✦ Removing a component from the component palette does not affect any compiled applications that use that component. However, the component must be installed before you can load any project that uses it.

✦ To create a property that is available only at run time, but is not visible in the Object Inspector window, place the property declaration in the class's public section, but don't publish it. (Actually, it's not possible to declare a public, published property, which would create conflicting access paths to the associated field. A property can be public or it can be published; it can never be both.)

✦ Delphi can compile only projects. To compile a unit under development, use it in a test project. Delphi compiles modified data component units as necessary when you install them.

✦ Properties may be in a class's protected, public, or published sections. You may declare properties in a class's private section, but it is pointless to do so because the class's unit already has full access to all private data fields. The purpose of a property is to provide controlled access to private and protected data.

✦ The Object Inspector automatically sorts property names alphabetically. You may declare properties in any order in the class. This has no effect on their order in the Object Inspector.

✦ The VCL stores properties in their declared order, but loading occurs in whatever order the data exists in the form's .dfm file. That order may be the same as the property declaration order, but it can be different. For example, users can edit the form file as text and change property values and their orders. Never build components that rely on property loading order.

✦ Properties may be any data type except files, but there are additional restrictions on what kinds of properties a class can publish. You can't publish Pascal arrays, for example, nor can you publish read-only or write-only properties because the Object Inspector must read and write them. Published properties may also not use Pascal's Real or Extended data types. For floating-point properties, use Single, Double, or Comp.

✦ Standard run-time packages are named somewhat haphazardly. For example, VCL40.bpl, INET40bpl, and TEEDB40.bpl are all run-time packages. The only way to know this fact about the files is from their filename extensions.

✦ Most design-time packages are named in a more consistent fashion. For example, DCLSTD40.bpl and DCLDB40.bpl are design-time packages. Unfortunately, this design is broken by IBEVNT40bpl, although this is a package for the IBEventAlerter component in the Samples palette, and as a sample, is strictly "use at your own risk." Borland does not support sample components, and these have changed and even disappeared in some cases over Delphi's life.

✦ Run-time packages are typically stored in C:\Windows\System. With few exceptions, design-time packages are typically stored in Delphi's \Bin directory.

✦ It's important to understand the difference between the list of packages required by the new package and the list of units to be contained in the new package. The first rule refers to external units — for example, one that contains a subroutine that a new package unit needs. The second rule refers to the units that are to be contained in the new package. A package encapsulates those units, in much the same way that a class encapsulates its data and code.

✦ A design-time package is simply one that lists the names of other run-time packages in its *requires* declaration.

✦ Compiling a package automatically compiles any of its units whose source files have changed (that is, are out of date) since the previous compilation. To compile your packaged units, therefore, always compile the package. Compiling the individual units does not update them in the package.

Projects to Try

20-1: Create a Date and Time component that you can insert into a form. Add an alarm feature that rings a bell or pops up a message. You might use a string-list data field to enter alarm dates and times.

20-2: Add a Font property to the TBarChart component. Initialize the Font to the form's font (see the Paint method's assignment to Canvas.Font for a hint on how to do that).

20-3: Improve TBarChart's exception handling. Rather than delete data points if an exception occurs, try one of the other suggested responses. For example, you might display a bomb symbol instead of a dialog box, or you might test individual data points for validity in some other way.

20-4: Create a bitmapped version of the RadioButton component with a custom symbol (a diamond, for example) in place of the usual black dot.

20-5: Advanced. Create an animated icon component that displays a sequence of bitmaps. You might use the component to display animations during lengthy file, printing, and other operations.

20-6: Advanced. Add an array property to the TBarChart class that publishes the unit's currently static color array. This array provides 16 color values for drawing successive bars. (For more than 16 bars, the colors repeat.) Improve the BarChart component by making it possible for users to edit these color values.

20-7: Convert this chapter's BarChart component into an ActiveX control.

Summary

✦ Writing your own components is no simple task, but offers advanced programmers additional tools and capabilities not available to application developers. You can base new components on any supplied with Delphi, or you can construct entirely new ones.

✦ A component is a special class declaration and unit that conform to Delphi's requirements for visual components. To be installed on the VCL palette, a component must be inserted into a package. Use the File|New... command and the Packages item to create a new package.

✦ Components publish properties to provide access methods for reading and writing class data fields. Users can view and edit published properties that have write-access methods in the Object Inspector window.

✦ Components require constructor and destructor methods. Visual components implement a Paint method to create their on-screen appearance, both in the form at design time, and in the running program.

✦ To debug components, create them under program control rather than installing them on the component palette. This makes it possible to use Delphi's debugger to single-step the component's programming and to insert breakpoints and inspect variables.

✦ Properties may be any data types except files and Pascal arrays. You may create an array property that calls read and write access methods, but that is used as an array. Use this technique to create associative and sparse array data structures.

✦ You can use the ActiveX Control Wizard to convert any Delphi component into an ActiveX control. You can also import any ActiveX control into Delphi for use as a component. However, it is always best to use native Delphi components with Delphi.

Everybody loves a bargain, and I hope you find something of exceptional value in the next chapter, which collects tips, tricks, and techniques for sharpening your Delphi programming skills.

✦   ✦   ✦

Honing Your Delphi Skills

In This Chapter

Components

Command-line tools

CRT applications

Useful functions

Run-time type information

Online help

Dynamic Link Libraries

Application and message event handlers

File streams

Internet applications

Still more tips

I'm always on the prowl for wild new ideas, and as I wrote this book, I collected several hot tips and tricks for this final chapter. The following grab bag has absolutely no order or theme, but you're sure to find numerous hints and suggestions that can help sharpen your Delphi programming skills.

Topics in this chapter include how to use Delphi's command-line tools, a few useful functions, tips on creating and using online help, how to create and use dynamic link libraries, how to insert forms and other components into a DLL, and how to use run-time type information. You can also find information on application event handlers, file streams, multithreaded applications, and Pascal programming tidbits such as method overloading, dynamic arrays, and default parameters.

Command-Line Tools

Delphi comes with command-line tools that you can use to build Windows applications. The results are the same as with the integrated environment, but the command-line tools permit development using third-party editors rather than the Delphi environment. You can also select esoteric compiler options and produce linker map files for use during debugging. Command-line tools are also valuable for creating short test programs and for learning Pascal programming techniques from text books.

On the CD-ROM

The first step in using Delphi's command-line tools is to get to a command-line prompt. You can either quit Windows (use the Start button's Shut Down command and select "Restart in MS-DOS mode." Or, if you don't want to quit Windows, open a DOS prompt window using Start|Programs. Enter **path** to check whether Delphi's \bin (binaries) directory is on the system path. If not, run the Delpath.bat batch file in Listing 21-1. This is in the Source\Misc directory on this book's CD-ROM. You might have to modify the path string depending on your version of Delphi and where you installed it.

Listing 21-1: **Misc\Delpath.bat**

```
@echo off
rem
rem delpath.bat—Configure PATH for Delphi command line
rem
set path=%path%;"C:\Program Files\Borland\Delphi 4\bin"
echo Configured for Delphi command line
path
```

You can now compile stand-alone CRT applications, and complete Delphi Windows projects. For example, with the \bin directory on the path, use the DOS window to change to any Delphi project directory. To try this, change to a copy of this book's Polyflow application. From a DOS prompt, enter a command such as:

```
cd "\Delphi 4 Bible\Source\polyflow"
```

Notice the quote marks, required for multiple-word directories with blanks such as Delphi 4 Bible. To compile the application, run the dcc32 (Delphi command-line 32-bit compiler) from the DOS prompt. This runs the Borland Pascal compiler. The compiler looks for. pas files by default, so to compile a Windows application, you must supply the .dpr filename extension. Enter the text in bold that follows. Your screen should resemble the lines shown here, although the version numbers and copyright dates might differ:

```
D:\Delphi 4 Bible\Source\Polyflow>dcc32 polyflow.dpr
Borland Delphi for Version 12.0  Copyright (c) 1983,98 Inprise
Corporation
Polyflow.dpr(14)
15 lines, 0.75 seconds, 149128 bytes code, 4397 bytes data.
```

Assuming you did not receive any compiler errors, you can now type **Polyflow** and press Enter to run the program. Use this method to compile projects for which you want to select options with the command-line compiler and linker. For a list of available options, type **dcc32** and press Enter. For example, to compile a program and define a conditional symbol, you might enter a command such as this:

```
dcc32 -DDEBUGMODE polyflow.dpr
```

Caution   If you attempt to compile an older application written using Delphi 1, you may receive an error that the project's 16-bit resource file is incompatible with Delphi's 32-bit linker. This might happen even after you have upgraded and successfully compiled the application using Delphi's integrated environment. The only way I've found to get around this problem is to build a new application and then cut and paste the old source files into the project.

CRT Applications

Early versions of Delphi provided a CRT application for writing text-only test programs. This was necessary because 16-bit Windows 3.1 did not support console applications, as does 32-bit Windows 95, 98, and NT. The Crt application template is no longer available, nor is the WinCrt unit that provided DOS-like output in a graphical window. However, with newer versions of Delphi, you can use the following steps to create a stand-alone CRT console application that runs from a DOS prompt. (WinCrt never worked all that well, so its demise is no great loss.)

A CRT application is simply a text-only program that doesn't require a form and doesn't use components. A CRT application is the economy model—it costs you little in time and effort, but it gets you where you're going in a hurry.

Creating a CRT application

Use CRT applications to test Object Pascal programming methods, to experiment with algorithms, and to run plain-text examples from Pascal tutorials. To create a CRT application, I suggest the following steps. There might be other ways to achieve the same end results, but I find this method to be the easiest:

1. Review the preceding section to set the system PATH to include Delphi's \bin directory. Although it is possible to compile CRT applications from inside Delphi's integrated environment, compiling stand-alone CRT applications is generally easier from a DOS prompt. To follow along, open a DOS prompt window now and run the Delpath batch file listed in the preceding section (reminder: on the CD-ROM, this batch file is in the Source\Misc directory).

2. Get back to Delphi. Close all existing files, and select File I New.... Click the New page tab in the New Items dialog, and choose the Text template. This creates a new file, File1.txt, in the code editor.

3. To inform Delphi that the new file contains Pascal statements, immediately save it with a .pas filename extension. This enables syntax-highlighting, and makes Code Insights available (see Chapter 1).

4. Enter your program, and save it. You may use most any Pascal program, but if you don't have one, copy the text from Listing 21-2. This file is on the CD-ROM in the Source\Keytest directory.

5. Return to the DOS prompt window. Enter **dcc32 -cc keytest** to compile your program — you do not have to type the .pas filename extension, but doing so does no harm.

Caution

When compiling stand-alone CRT applications, don't forget to specify the -cc option. This tells the compiler to enable command-line input and output rather than use Windows functions.

Listing 21-2: Keytest\Keytest.pas. A sample CRT application that you can use to test the keyboard and experiment with Delphi's command-line tools. Press Ctrl+C to quit.

```
program KeyTest;
var
  Ch: Char;
begin
  Writeln('Keyboard tester. Press <key>+Enter.');
  Writeln('To quit, press Ctrl+C,');
  Writeln('or close the window.');
  Writeln;  { Output a blank line }
  repeat
    Read(Ch);               { Read from keyboard }
    Writeln(Ord(Ch):4);   { Show its value }
  until False;  { That is, "forever." }
end.
```

Note

It's possible to generate a console application using Project|Options..., selecting Linker, and enabling the Generate Console Application check box. This is also a neat trick to enable Writeln debugging statements that display values or note various program operations during development. However, it's probably easier to compile and run pure CRT console applications from a command-line prompt.

If you discover that running a Delphi Windows application opens a DOS window, this option is probably enabled. Uncheck it, and recompile to fix the problem.

If you already have a Pascal source code file, you may, of course, use Delphi's code editor to view and modify the program's statements. Simply use File|Open... to open the file (make sure Files of type specifies *.pas as one of the recognized filename extensions). After saving your changes, use the command-line compiler as explained to compile the program, which you can run from the DOS prompt. If you prefer, you may use another text editor to view, create, and edit CRT source code files — several good ones are on the market. (I've always liked multi-Edit from American Cybernetics. View their Web site at www.multiedit.com.)

Use Write, Writeln, Read, and Readln for input and output in CRT applications. For example, define a string variable, and try this short program to prompt users for input and then display the response (this text is not on the CD-ROM):

```
program Yourname;
var
  S: String;
begin
  Write('Hi! What''s your name? ');
  Readln(S);
  Writeln('Your name is ', S);
end.
```

Caution

If you receive "Runtime error 103" when you attempt to run the preceding CRT application, you probably forgot to compile with the *-cc* option.

A powerful function

Although Delphi's Object Pascal Math unit provides a Power function that can raise a floating-point base value to a floating-point exponent, this function incorrectly enables the value zero to be raised to a fractional power ($0^{0.5}$ for example). This section presents a custom Power function that raises an exception for this and other illegal power operations. To use it in your own code, copy the constant, exception class type, and function from the listing in this section to any module, and call Power as the program's Test procedure demonstrates.

I've published versions of Power elsewhere, but I included a new version of it here to demonstrate how math functions can use exception handling to report errors. For instance, it is illegal to raise a negative base to a fractional exponent or to raise zero to a nonzero exponent less than one. The Power function here raises an EPower exception for both of these and other kinds of booboos. Run the program to demonstrate how the Test procedure deals with these kinds of errors.

On the CD-ROM

To do this, open a command-line prompt window, and if you haven't done so yet, run the Delpath.bat batch file as explained earlier in this chapter. Change to a copy of the Source\Power directory from the CD-ROM, and enter **dcc32 -cc powertest** to compile the program. Enter **powertest** to run the demonstration. Figure 21-1 shows the program's text output that you see onscreen. Listing 21-3 shows the program's source code. Compile and run this test program from a DOS prompt.

You may run CRT applications using Windows Explorer, but this causes the DOS window to close as soon as the application ends. To prevent this problem, open a DOS prompt window using the Start menu's Programs command. Change to the Source\Power directory and type **PowerTest** to run the test program.

Figure 21-1: Running the PowerTest program displays this output in a DOS prompt window.

Listing 21-3: Power\PowerTest.pas. This program contains the function Power, which can raise a floating-point base to a floating-point exponent.

```pascal
program PowerTest;

uses SysUtils;

const
  sFmt = 'Exception raised in Power function. Base=%f Exp=%f';

type
{ Declare exception class }
  EPower = class(EMathError);

{ Return Base raised to Exponent }
function Power(Base, Exponent: Double): Double;
  function F(B, E: Double): Double;
  begin
    Result := Exp(E * Ln(B));
  end;
begin
  if Base = 0.0 then
    if Exponent = 0.0 then
      Result := 1.0
    else if Exponent < 1.0 then
```

```
          raise EPower.CreateFmt(sFmt, [Base, Exponent])
      else
        Result := 0.0
    else if Base > 0.0 then
      Result := F(Base, Exponent)
    else if Frac(Exponent) = 0.0 then
      if Odd(Trunc(Exponent)) then
        Result := -F(-Base, Exponent)
      else
        Result :=  F(-Base, Exponent )
    else raise EPower.CreateFmt(sFmt, [Base, Exponent]);
end; { Power }

{ Test procedure }
procedure Test(Base, Exponent: Double);
begin
  try
    Writeln(Base:8:3, ' ^ ', Exponent:8:3, ' = ',
      Power(Base, Exponent));
  except
    on E: EPower do
      Writeln(E.Message);
  end;
end;

{ The following is the CRT application's main body. It
  merely calls the test procedure with various values. The
  final four values intentionally test the Power function's
  exceptions. }
begin
  test( 7,    3  );
  test( 7,   -3  );
  test(-7,    3  );
  test(-7,   -3  );
  test( 7,    3.5);
  test( 7,   -3.5);
  test( 7.2,  3  );
  test( 7.2, -3  );
  test(-7.2,  3  );
  test(-7.2, -3  );
  test( 7.2,  3.5);
  test( 7.2, -3.5);
{ These four tests produce *expected* exceptions }
  test(-7,    3.5);
  test(-7,   -3.5);
  test(-7.2,  3.5);
  test(-7.2, -3.5);
  test( 0,    0.5);
end.
```

The Power function raises an exception of the EPower class, derived from the general-purpose EMathError class in Delphi's SysUtils unit. The EMathError class is in turn derived from the Exception base class. (See Chapter 19 for more information about programming with exceptions.)

To use the Power function, you must provide access to the Delphi exception classes. To do that, add the SysUtils unit to your program's *uses* directive (Delphi can do this automatically if you are incorporating the Power function into a Windows application). Copy the code from Listing 21-5 into your program, minus the *program* and *uses* declarations, and the final *end*.

In addition to providing a useful math function, Power also demonstrates a good way to create mathematical exceptions that show offending values. For example, to raise an exception, Power executes the statement:

```
raise EPower.CreateFmt(sFmt, [Base, Exponent])
```

The CreateFmt function, inherited from Exception, takes two arguments: a string with embedded formatting commands, and a set of values enclosed in square brackets. When an exception occurs, EPower's Message field contains a string that shows the values that caused the error. For example, the test program displays an exception's error message such as:

```
Exception raised in Power function. Base=-7.20 Exp=3.50
```

A Few Useful Functions

Every programmer has a library of subroutines that have proven their value over the years. Following are some useful additions you can make to your library.

Callback functions

A *callback function* is a subroutine in your program that Windows calls. A typical use for a callback function is to enumerate a list of items, such as the titles and handles for all windows, or the names of available fonts. The following examples demonstrate both techniques.

Listing 21-4 is the Main.pas file for the EnumWin project on the CD-ROM located in the Source\EnumWin directory. Load the program's project file into Delphi, and then press F9 to compile and run. As Figure 21-2 shows, the program lists all windows currently alive (that is, known to Windows). Of course the window titles you see probably differ from those shown here. In addition to showing how to find window titles, the program demonstrates the correct way to access all windows, which you might do for a variety of reasons — for example, to determine whether the current application is already running, to send a message to all windows, or to enable users to switch to a specific window.

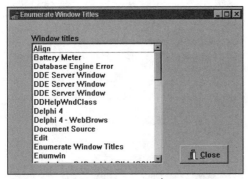

Figure 21-2: The EnumWin program uses a callback function to list all "alive" windows.

Listing 21-4: **EnumWin\Main.pas**

```
unit Main;

interface

uses
  Windows, SysUtils, Classes, Graphics, Controls,
  Forms, Dialogs, StdCtrls, Buttons;

type
  TMainForm = class(TForm)
    ListBox1: TListBox;
    Label1: TLabel;
    BitBtn1: TBitBtn;
    procedure FormCreate(Sender: TObject);
  private
    { Private declarations }
  public
    { Public declarations }
  end;

var
```

(continued)

Listing 21-4 *(continued)*

```
  MainForm: TMainForm;

implementation

{$R *.DFM}

{ Windows calls this function, passing in Handle a reference
  to each alive window. Param is not used in this example. }
function EnumWinProc(Handle: HWnd; Param: Longint): Boolean;
  Stdcall;  { Use this, not export, in Windows 95, 98 & NT }
var
  Sz: array[0 .. 132] of Char; {Holds result of GetWindowText}
begin
  Result := True;  { Always successful }
  { Call Windows to obtain each window's caption, and then
    add the returned string to the form's ListBox. }
  if GetWindowText(Handle, Sz, Sizeof(Sz)) <> 0 then
    MainForm.ListBox1.Items.Add(StrPas(Sz));
end;

{ Enumerate all alive windows by passing to Windows the
  address of the preceding callback function. }
procedure TMainForm.FormCreate(Sender: TObject);
begin
  EnumWindows(@EnumWinProc, 0);  { 0 is an unused parameter }
end;

end.
```

The sample program uses a single ListBox object to hold the list of window titles. To fill the ListBox with this information, I created an OnCreate event handler for the application's form. The procedure, FormCreate, executes the single statement:

```
EnumWindows(@EnumWinProc, 0);  { 0 is an unused parameter }
```

EnumWindows is a Windows procedure that receives two arguments: the address of a callback function, and an optional parameter of integer (or Longint) length — that is, any 32-bit object such as a pointer. This example doesn't use the second argument, so I set it to zero. Another program might use it to pass the address of a data object to the callback function.

Callback functions must be declared correctly, and this is especially critical because the compiler does not check their syntax. Carefully consult all possible sources of documentation to determine the correct syntax for the callback function you want to use. (The Windows.pas in Delphi's Source\Rtl\Win directory is invaluable for this.) In the sample program, the callback function is declared as:

```
function EnumWinProc(Handle: HWnd; Param: Longint): Boolean;
  Stdcall;
```

Note

In 16-bit Windows, this would be declared differently, using an Export designator. In 32-bit Windows 95 and NT, Export should be changed to Stdcall. This ensures parameters are passed in the correct order.

The EnumWinProc receives two parameters: a Handle that refers to one window, and a Param, which, as I mentioned, is not used in this case. The function returns a Boolean True or False result. Typically, EnumWinProc returns True to continue iterating all alive windows until finished, but it could return False to stop the ball rolling.

Remember, EnumWinProc is not a Windows function. It is a function in your program that Windows calls. Because of this, Windows cares only about the location (the address) of the function — its name is unimportant. If you want to rename EnumWinProc to HumptyDumptySatOnAWall, that's up to you. Windows doesn't care. I mention this because, in various published listings, you often see Windows callback functions spelled differently.

The code inside the callback function sets the function Result to True, and then calls the Windows GetWindowText function using the following *if* statement:

```
if GetWindowText(Handle, Sz, Sizeof(Sz)) <> 0 then
    MainForm.ListBox1.Items.Add(StrPas(Sz));
```

This code passes to GetWindowText the window Handle and two additional arguments: a place to store the window's caption, and the size of that variable. For simplicity, I created a 133-byte Char array, which is large enough to hold a caption of 132 characters. That should be large enough for any conceivable window title. The Sizeof function passes the size in bytes to GetWindowText, which is programmed never to store more information in the string object than specified.

If GetWindowText returns True, then a window's title is to be found in the Sz variable, which is added to the form's ListBox object. Notice MainForm is referenced to identify the ListBox1 object. This is necessary because the callback function is not a member of the application's TMainForm class.

Procedure instances

16-bit Windows required fancy footwork to call procedures and functions in your application's code. In the past, it was necessary to create a *procedure instance*, also known as a *thunk*, to use a stand-alone callback function. This is no longer necessary with Windows 95, 98, and NT, which can call application functions directly.

To demonstrate both techniques, Listing 21-5 shows the main source code for the Enumfon project. On the CD-ROM, you can find the program's files in the Source\Enumfon directory. Running the program lists all available font names — you might use similar programming to fill a list box from which users can select a font. I upgraded this program from an earlier one written for Windows 3.1. So you can compare the old and new techniques, rather than completely revamp the code, I inserted conditional compilation directives. This way, the project can compile with all versions of Delphi and Windows. If you need to upgrade older applications, you might use similar techniques to preserve 16-bit compatibility. Figure 21-3 shows the program's display.

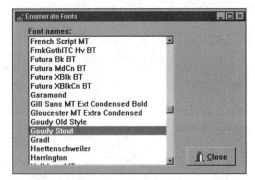

Figure 21-3: The Enumfon application lists available font names.

Listing 21-5: Enumfon\Main.pas. This program demonstrates how to enumerate font names using 16-bit and 32-bit versions of Delphi and Windows.

```
unit Main;

interface

uses
    Windows, SysUtils, Classes, Graphics, Controls,
```

```
    Forms, Dialogs, StdCtrls, Buttons;

type
  TMainForm = class(TForm)
    ListBox1: TListBox;
    Label1: TLabel;
    BitBtn1: TBitBtn;
    procedure FormCreate(Sender: TObject);
  private
    { Private declarations }
  public
    { Public declarations }
  end;

var
  MainForm: TMainForm;

implementation

{$R *.DFM}

{ ======================================================== }

{$IFDEF VER80}  // Delphi 1.x, 16-bit Windows only

function EnumFontsProc(var LogFont: TLogFont;
  var TextMetric: TTextMetric; FontType: Integer;
  Data: TListBox): Integer; export;
begin
  with TStrings(Data) do
    Add(StrPas(LogFont.lfFaceName));
  Result := 1;  { Continue enumeration until done }
end;

procedure TMainForm.FormCreate(Sender: TObject);
var
  Proc: TFarProc;
begin
  Proc := MakeProcInstance(@EnumFontsProc, HInstance);
  try
    EnumFonts(Canvas.Handle, nil,Proc,Pointer(ListBox1.Items));
  finally
    FreeProcInstance(Proc);
  end;
end;

{ ======================================================== }
```

(continued)

Listing 21-5 *(continued)*

```
{$ELSE}  // Delphi 2 and higher, 32-bit Windows 95, 98, and NT

function EnumFontsProc(var LogFont: TLogFont;
  var TextMetric: TTextMetric; FontType: Integer;
  Data: Pointer): Integer; stdcall;
var
  TheList: TStrings;
begin
  TheList := TStrings(Data);  // Get StringList passed in Data
  TheList.Add(LogFont.lfFaceName);  // Add font's name
  Result := 1;                 // Continue until done
end;

procedure TMainForm.FormCreate(Sender: TObject);
var
  DC: HDC;
begin
  DC := GetDC(0);  // Get a device context handle
  try
    EnumFonts(DC, nil, @EnumFontsProc,
      Pointer(ListBox1.Items));  // Pass data to callback fn
  finally
    ReleaseDC(0, DC);  // Release system resource
  end;
end;


{$ENDIF}

{ ============================================================ }

(*
{ The next procedure is *far* simpler than either of
  the preceding methods, and it also works with all versions
  of Delphi and Windows! Remember: Don't work harder than
  you have to; rather than call Windows subroutines and use
  callback functions, look for a Delphi component that
  does what you want. You can probably find one! }

procedure TMainForm.FormCreate(Sender: TObject);
begin
  Listbox1.Items := Screen.Fonts;
end;
*)

end.
```

Getting font-name information

Before you read the discussion of the callback functions used in Enumfon, look at the simple procedure at the end of the listing inside comment brackets. The FormCreate procedure (it could be another event handler or subroutine) shows the easiest method for getting font-name information. Simply assign Screen.Fonts to a TStringList object such as the Items property in a ListBox. This statement:

```
Listbox1.Items := Screen.Fonts;
```

illustrates one of the tenets of Delphi programming: Always use objects and component methods whenever possible. Don't make your life complicated by needlessly calling Windows API subroutines and using callback functions needlessly.

Another reason to use objects is that Delphi's VCL contains code that works around some obscure and little-known 32-bit Windows oddities. For example, the standard Windows EnumFonts function doesn't consistently return all available font names, particularly on non-Western locales such as Japan. The VCL's TScreen class works around this problem by calling EnumFontFamilies to provide a more complete list than the stock EnumFonts. Delphi's VCL contains numerous other fixes of which you can take advantage merely by using objects rather than calling Windows API functions.

Enumfon demonstrates three techniques for listing font names, two of which make use of Windows callback functions. The first demonstrated function is for Windows 3.1 16-bit applications; the second is for Windows 95, 98, and NT 32-bit applications.

If you must use callback functions, the following are two ways to complicate your program's code and, most likely, your programming life. Of course, legitimate reasons do exist for creating callback functions such as enumerating windows and using obscure Windows techniques not provided by Delphi components. But I want to stress that the following techniques are to be reserved for times when no other alternative exists.

In 16-bit Windows, you declare a callback function such as EnumFontsProc using the *export* keyword. To call the function, it is necessary first to create a procedure instance, which serves as a conduit for calls from Windows back to application code. To do this, the program calls MakeProcInstance for a given function, and then passes the result of this to the Windows function we want. Here's the basic outline:

```
Proc := MakeProcInstance(@EnumFontsProc, HInstance);
try
  EnumFonts(Canvas.Handle, nil, Proc,
    Pointer(ListBox1.Items));
finally
  FreeProcInstance(Proc);
end;
```

First, MakeProcInstance is called to create a thunk of type TFarProc for the callback function, EnumFontsProc in this example. This thunk is passed to EnumFonts, along with a device context handle (borrowed from Canvas for convenience), and a pointer to a TStringList object. Of course, Windows knows nothing about TStringList objects — the final parameter, which is always optional, is passed blindly to our callback function for our program's own use. It is essential to use a *try-finally* block, as shown here, so that the procedure instance is freed regardless of whether any exceptions occur during the call to EnumFonts. You can expect grave problems to develop sooner or later (probably sooner) if you don't clean up Windows resources in this way.

On the surface, the corresponding 32-bit technique appears similar, but is actually worlds apart from the preceding outdated method. (In the listing, refer to the code following the comment for "Delphi 2 and higher.") The EnumFontsProc callback function is declared similarly, although I show a more generally correct way to pass a Data parameter as a Pointer object. In other words, Data points to whatever data is passed to the callback function. The function result is the same, an Integer. But notice that sStdcall is used instead of export. This is important. Make sure your own callback functions always use sStdcall.

Inside the callback function, a temporary variable, TheList, is initialized using the Data pointer passed as a parameter. This does not copy the StringList object; it merely makes TheList refer to that object for easier reference in subsequent statements. For example, to add each font name, the program calls the TStringList.Add method. Windows has already provided the font's name in the LogFont parameter, so this is all that is needed to add each name to the program's ListBox. As before, a Result of one is passed back to continue the process until Windows has passed all fonts.

The program's OnCreate event handler for the main form shows how a 32-bit program prepares for using a callback function. I could have borrowed Canvas.Handle for a device context, but instead, I show here another way to obtain the necessary object. Call GetDC for a new device context, and pass it to EnumFonts along with *nil* (an unused parameter), the address of our callback function, and a pointer to the StringList object to hold the font names.

Once again, a *try-finally* block is needed to ensure that the device context is properly freed if any exceptions are raised in the call to EnumFonts or during execution of the callback function. By borrowing Canvas.Handle, however, the code can be simplified to the following. I wrote the longer version to illustrate the proper way to deal with system resources such as device context handles. Unless you need to do that, use this shorter version:

```
procedure TMainForm.FormCreate(Sender: TObject);
begin
  EnumFonts(Canvas.Handle, nil, @EnumFontsProc,
    Pointer(ListBox1.Items));  // Pass data to callback fn
end;
```

To review, the key differences between the 16-bit and 32-bit techniques are:

✦ The 16-bit callback function is declared with the *export* keyword; the 32-bit version uses sStdcall in place of *export*.

✦ The 16-bit callback function cannot be passed directly to a Windows function such as EnumFonts. You must first create a procedure instance by calling MakeProcInstance, and pass this result to the callback function. You must also be sure to free the procedure instance.

✦ Windows 95, 98, and NT can call application functions directly, and there is no need to call MakeProcInstance. Simply pass the address of the function as demonstrated in the sample Enumfon application.

Tip

You may still call MakeProcInstance and FreeProcInstance in 32-bit applications; however, these Windows functions now simply return without executing any code. For a fast conversion of 16-bit to 32-bit code, you might be able to simply replace *export* with sStdcall and recompile. Note, I said "might." For best results, upgrade your programs to pass callback function addresses directly as shown here.

Enumfon uses conditional compilation directives to compile differently depending on the version of Delphi you are using. Different versions of Enumfonts procedures are encased in these directives, which are useful for creating projects that compile for all Delphi versions:

```
{$IFDEF VER80}  // Delphi 1.x
...
{$ELSE}         // Delphi 2.x +
...
{$ENDIF}
```

Date and time functions

Object Pascal's System unit, which all applications use, defines the TDateTime data type as equivalent to Float. There are a baker's dozen plus an extra helping of procedures and functions that use TDateTime for just about any date and time operation you could possibly need.

The integer part of a TDateTime variable equals the number of days that have passed since December 30, 1899. (This matches the OLE Variant date format — Delphi 1.0 calculated dates starting from the year 0001.) TDateTime stores the time as the variable's fractional part, equal to the proportion of the day starting from midnight that has passed. For example, 0.75 represents 6:00 p.m. — three fourths of the day past midnight. (Impress your family tonight; announce it's past 0.95 hours and time for bed.)

Use Object Pascal's Trunc function to extract the day part of a TDateTime value. Given two TDateTime variables Date1 and Date2, the following statement assigns to an integer *N* the number of days between the two dates. Because it's the absolute value of the subtraction that matters, it doesn't matter which date you specify first:

```
N := abs(Trunc(Date1) - Trunc(Date2));
```

Another nifty date and time function is IncMonth in the SysUtils unit. This function returns a TDateTime value equal to a date that is a certain number of months forward or back from a specified date. For example, passing July 31 to IncMonth and requesting one month ahead returns August 30. You might use the function to program monthly chores — printing a report at the end of each month, for example.

The IncMonth function, and its parameters, are declared as:

```
function IncMonth(const Date: TDateTime;
  NumberOfMonths: Integer): TDateTime;
```

✦ **Date: TDateTime** — Pass any date to this parameter — the time doesn't matter, only the date. (Use the StrToDate function to convert dates in string format to TDateTime values.)

✦ **NumberOfMonths**: Integer — Pass the number of months by which to increment Date. Pass a negative value to decrement the Date.

The IncMonth function returns a TDateTime object equal to the number of months forward or back from the specified date. For example, insert a ListBox and a Button into a form, and double-click the Button to create an OnClick event handler. Complete this procedure using the code in Listing 21-6, which is located on the CD-ROM in file Date1.pas in the Source\Misc directory. Run the program and click the button to fill the ListBox with dates from 1/31/97 to 1/31/99. When you inspect that list, you see it correctly contains all month end dates such as 2/28/97 and 11/30/98.

Listing 21-6: **Misc\Date1.pas**

```
procedure TForm1.Button1Click(Sender: TObject);
var
  D1, D2: TDateTime;  // Date variables
  I: Integer;         // for-loop variable
begin
  D1 := StrToDate('1/31/98');
  for I := -12 to 12 do
  begin
    D2 := IncMonth(D1, I);
    ListBox1.Items.Add(DateToStr(D2));
  end;
end;
```

Note The IncMonth function is correctly programmed to handle dates in the next millenium. For example, it correctly returns the date 2/29/00 because the year 2000 is a rare century-boundary leap year. Using IncMonth and other Delphi date and time functions can help you avoid "millenium bugs" in your applications.

Run-Time Type Information

A compiler obviously can determine from the program's source code the types of objects it creates. But for objects created at run time, the source code may not be available, and objects must contain *run-time type information* (RTTI) that describes what they are. This is a controversial subject in object-oriented programming, and currently few, if any, standards exist on the best format to use for run-time object identification. COM (Common Object Model) objects come close; but not all objects conform to COM.

RTTI declarations are in the Typinfo.pas file located in Delphi's \...\Source\Vcl directory. Inprise Corporation has warned programmers that RTTI declarations will change in future Delphi releases, and they've made good on that promise. For easier upgrades, be careful to isolate your uses of this information.

On the CD-ROM As an example of how to use the Typinfo unit, the CD-ROM contains Inidata.pas, written by this book's technical reviewer, Danny Thorpe, Senior Engineer, Delphi R&D, for Inprise Corporation. Danny's unit uses object RTTI to write object property values in Windows initialization (.ini) files. Using this nifty unit, you can write all of a dialog box's check box, edit window, radio button, and other controls to an .ini file, and easily read those values back. Here are some notes from Danny that describe his unit:

"RTTI enables developers to write code that works with objects in a generic manner by figuring out at run time exactly what attributes an object has. Compiled code is often referred to as *early bound* because all linkage and access decisions are made at compile time. RTTI enables you to create code that is *late bound*, which means linkage and access is determined at run time.

"The IniData unit can write user data contained in any form or component. The purpose of the unit is to load and store only the user data that a component contains. The unit is built on some assumptions that are unrelated to RTTI—such as the fact that a component has only one important property containing user data, and that this property is a simple one (not a list or class, for example). If you want to store everything in a form, simply write it to a stream. IniData is for more precision work."

For a demonstration of how to use Inidata.pas, load into Delphi the Options project on the CD-ROM in the Source\Options directory. Run the program, and select its options on the sample dialog box's three TabbedNotebook pages. Figure 21-4 shows the program's display. Click the Save button to save the options to Test.ini in the C:\Windows directory. Quit and rerun to load the options from disk. Here's a sample Test.ini file that I created:

```
[TMainForm]
CheckBox1=cbUnchecked
CheckBox2=cbGrayed
CheckBox3=cbChecked
RadioButton1=False
RadioButton2=False
RadioButton3=True
Edit1=Delphi 4 Bible
Edit2=IDG Books Worldwide, Inc.
```

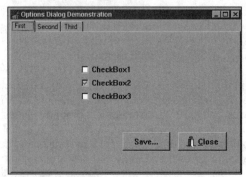

Figure 21-4: The Options application demonstrates how to use the Inidata unit to read and write object properties in .ini files.

The .ini file's section header equals the form's class name. Each item is a named component object, with a value equal to one component property. (You can save only one object property.) The project's Main.pas file in Listing 21-7 shows how to use the Inidata unit. This file is on the CD-ROM in the Source\Options directory.

Listing 21-7: **Options\Main.pas. This program demonstrates how to use the Inidata.pas unit, which is stored in the Source\Initdata directory.**

```
unit Main;

interface

uses
  Windows, SysUtils, Classes, Graphics, Controls,
  Forms, Dialogs, Inidata, StdCtrls, Buttons, TabNotBk,
  IniFiles, ComCtrls;

type
  TMainForm = class(TForm)
    TabbedNotebook1: TTabbedNotebook;
    CheckBox1: TCheckBox;
    CheckBox2: TCheckBox;
    CheckBox3: TCheckBox;
    RadioButton1: TRadioButton;
    RadioButton2: TRadioButton;
    RadioButton3: TRadioButton;
    Edit1: TEdit;
    Edit2: TEdit;
    BitBtn1: TBitBtn;
    BitBtn2: TBitBtn;
    procedure FormCreate(Sender: TObject);
    procedure BitBtn1Click(Sender: TObject);
  private
    procedure LoadOptions;
    procedure SaveOptions;
  public
    { Public declarations }
  end;

var
  MainForm: TMainForm;

implementation

{$R *.DFM}

procedure TMainForm.LoadOptions;
var
  IniFile: TIniFile;
begin
```

(continued)

Listing 21-7 *(continued)*

```
  IniFile := TIniFile.Create('test.ini');
  try
    LoadDataFromINI(MainForm, IniFile);
  finally
    IniFile.Free;
  end;
end;

procedure TMainForm.SaveOptions;
var
  IniFile: TIniFile;
begin
  IniFile := TIniFile.Create('test.ini');
  try
    SaveDataToINI(MainForm, IniFile);
  finally
    IniFile.Free;
  end;
end;

procedure TMainForm.FormCreate(Sender: TObject);
begin
  RegisterINIDataProp('TCheckBox', 'State');
  RegisterINIDataProp('TRadioButton', 'Checked');
  RegisterINIDataProp('TEdit', 'Text');
  LoadOptions;
end;

procedure TMainForm.BitBtn1Click(Sender: TObject);
begin
  SaveOptions;
end;

end.
```

The sample program's OnCreate event handler registers component classes and
one property to read and write in the .ini file. For example, to register the
TRadioButton component, FormCreate executes the statement:

```
RegisterINIDataProp('TRadioButton', 'Checked');
```

Because TCheckBox components can have three states, you have to register the
State, not the Checked, property. You can also register the Edit component using
these statements:

```
RegisterINIDataProp('TRadioButton', 'Checked');
RegisterINIDataProp('TEdit', 'Text');
```

Examine the LoadOptions and SaveOptions procedures for examples of how to read and write object properties to the .ini file. LoadOptions creates a TIniFile object, and calls LoadDataFromINI in the Inidata unit to read saved properties into MainForm's objects. SaveOptions similarly calls SaveDataToINI to create or update the .ini file.

Online Help

Creating a Windows online help file by hand is to documentation what assembly language is to programming. The steps are tedious, the process is error prone, and the results are likely to make you long for the good old days when users didn't expect software to be so helpful.

Before stepping out on the online help limb, I urge you to search for a help file generator that can construct Windows .hlp files more or less automatically. I can't recommend a specific program because I haven't used them extensively. However, they generally provide an input system for entering context-sensitive search strings, index values, keywords, footnotes, titles, and text. A compiler of sorts reads this information and spits out the .hlp file.

Note

Today's software is also gradually incorporating .html files for providing online help in the form of a World Wide Web style page. In fact, the Windows interface itself is expected to gravitate towards a Web-like user interface. Regardless of whether this happens, the intricacies of providing online help aren't getting any simpler.

Delphi comes with a version of Microsoft's Help Workshop, which you can use to construct your program's online help files (in .hlp format). The program is located in Delphi's Help\Tools directory, and it includes its own online reference in the Hcw.hlp file. Browse this file to get started using Help Workshop.

Whatever method you decide to use, after creating the .hlp file, assign its filename to the Application object's HelpFile property. You have to do this at run time (in a form's OnCreate event handler, for example). Enter a statement such as this:

```
Application.HelpFile := 'HelpMe.Hlp';
```

To provide specific help for objects in a form, assign help context index values. These are integer values. For example, using the Object Inspector, assign 1003 to a Button object's HelpContext property. You can assign help context values at run time, but you'll normally make the assignments when you design the form and as you add components to the window.

Not waiting too long to assign help context values is probably best. Do this as you create your application's forms, and keep track of the context values you use. Values may be negative. You might want to devise a systematic method for organizing indexes. For example, assign specific ranges such as 1000 . . . 1999 to a specific form.

Help context values cannot easily be dynamically updated, and you must keep account of the values that you assign. Good help generators do this automatically, but when creating online help manually, you need a spreadsheet or a database to record topics, context-sensitive strings, context index values, and keywords.

To open the help file to a specific topic, call the HelpContext method for the Application object. For example, use a statement such as:

```
Application.HelpContext(Button1.HelpContext);
```

Or, to jump to a subject indexed by a context-sensitive string, call HelpJump like this:

```
Application.HelpJump('Subject');
```

HelpJump returns a Boolean True or False value, depending on whether the Application has a help file assigned. You might display an error message if HelpJump returns False:

```
if not Application.HelpJump('Subject') then
   ShowMessage('Unable to open help file');
```

Your application must have at least one HelpContext value equal to the help file's Contents page index. If you don't assign a nonzero value to at least the main form's HelpContext property, the user cannot press F1 to bring up context-sensitive online help.

Because packages introduce the possibility that dialogs and other user-interface elements bundled into an application have no access to the host application help system, Inprise Corporation added a HelpFile property to TForm in Delphi 3. When a form window is active and the user requests help by pressing F1, the VCL satisfies the help request using the form's HelpFile property if assigned; otherwise, the VCL uses the TApplication.HelpFile property for this application.

Dynamic Link Libraries

A Dynamic Link Library, or DLL, is a kind of dynamic subroutine package that resides in a separate code file, and that applications (and other tasks) can share. Most of Windows is distributed among DLL files, custom control libraries are often supplied as DLLs, and you can develop other kinds of libraries with functions to share among multiple applications.

Using Delphi, you can write and use your own DLLs, and you can call functions in DLLs developed with other systems. You can place component objects into forms, and stuff the window into a DLL. Other applications, even those not developed with Delphi, can use the DLL—it's a complete package wrapped into a shareable code file library.

Creating a DLL

As a Delphi project, a DLL is a library with exported procedures and functions that other applications can call. Except for its exported subroutines, everything else inside a DLL is locked up as tight as an armored car. One of the key jobs in creating a new DLL, then, is deciding how to provide access to its contents.

One of the controversial questions that speeds around the information highway is whether a DLL can construct a form and other component objects. The answer is, Yes absolutely! In fact, this is one of the primary reasons for writing a Delphi DLL. You may place a form and any Delphi components into a DLL. Any program written in any other Windows development system can load the DLL to display the form. This is a great way for combining Delphi's capabilities with other systems such as C, C++, and Visual Basic. (However, ActiveX controls offer another way.)

On the
CD-ROM

When creating a new DLL, first test the form and its components as a common Delphi application. Create, write, and test this project as you do any other. As an example, the ColorDll application on the CD-ROM in the Source\ColorDll directory creates the foreground and background color grid dialog in Figure 21-5. The entire dialog is in a separate DLL that other applications can use. The figure shows that a Delphi DLL may have form objects and any other component instances that you can use in applications.

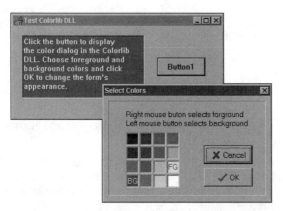

Figure 21-5: The Colorlib DLL displays this color selection dialog, using a ColorGrid component object.

All of the following files are on the CD-ROM in the Source\Colordll directory. Copy the directory to your hard drive, and then open the Colorlib project in Delphi. Press Ctrl+F9 to compile the DLL. This is not an executable program, and attempting to run it by pressing F9 produces an error message. There's no harm done if this happens, and it is still compiled normally.

To write the program, I first developed the color dialog as a common Delphi application. When I was satisfied, I modified the source code files as follows. You can use these steps to convert any Delphi project into a DLL:

1. Name the form unit something like ClrForm and the project ColorLib, or whatever you want to call the final DLL. Save the project as you normally do.

2. Declare a procedure or function in the form unit's interface section — not in the form's class. Users of the DLL call this subroutine to gain access to the library. You may declare as many access routines as your DLL needs. For example, Clrform.pas declares function FBGetColors as follows. So that other languages may call the function, declare only Windows data types (WordBool, for example, rather than Pascal's Boolean). Follow the declaration with the keyword *export*, which tells the compiler to make this function available to the DLL's users:

```
function FBGetColors(var FColor, BColor: TColor): WordBool;
export;
```

3. Implement the access procedure or function. Listing 21-8 shows the final result for the sample color selection dialog. I explain this part of the program after these steps.

4. After you are finished writing the form unit, convert the application project into a DLL. To do this, select the View | Project Source command to open the .dpr project file. Switch to that page in the unit text editor, and make the following changes.

5. Change *program* to *library*.

6. Delete Forms from the *uses* directive. (Projects need this unit for calling Application methods. DLLs are not applications, and their project files don't need the Forms unit. However, the DLL's other units may reference Forms — a DLL is not restricted from using Forms.)

7. Between the {$R} resource directive and the final line of the project's *uses* directive, add the word *exports,* followed by the name of the unit's access procedure or function — FBGetColors in this example. You may insert one or more subroutine names here.

8. Delete all statements between *begin* and *end,* leaving the initialization code block empty. Listing 21-9 shows the final result for the ColorLib project.

9. Press Ctrl+F9 to compile and create the .dll code file. You cannot run a DLL, so if you press F9 by mistake, you receive an error message. This still compiles the DLL, however, and does no harm.

Listing 21-8: **Colordll\Clrform.pas**.

```
unit Clrform;

interface

uses
  Windows, SysUtils, Classes, Graphics, Controls,
  Forms, Dialogs, StdCtrls, Buttons, ColorGrd, ExtCtrls;

type
  TColorForm = class(TForm)
    ColorGrid: TColorGrid;
    Label1: TLabel;
    Label2: TLabel;
    CancelBitBtn: TBitBtn;
    OkBitBtn: TBitBtn;
    Bevel1: TBevel;
    procedure CancelBitBtnClick(Sender: TObject);
    procedure OkBitBtnClick(Sender: TObject);
  private
    { Private declarations }
  public
    { Public declarations }
  end;

var
  ColorForm: TColorForm;

function FBGetColors(var FColor, BColor: TColor): WordBool;
  export;

implementation

{$R *.DFM}
```

(continued)

Listing 21-8 *(continued)*

```
{ Exit dialog via Cancel button }
procedure TColorForm.CancelBitBtnClick(Sender: TObject);
begin
  ModalResult := mrCancel;
end;

{ Exit dialog via Ok button }
procedure TColorForm.OkBitBtnClick(Sender: TObject);
begin
  ModalResult := mrOk;
end;

{ Get foreground and background colors }
function FBGetColors(var FColor, BColor: TColor): WordBool;
begin
  Result := False;
  ColorForm := TColorForm.Create(Application);
  try
    if ColorForm.ShowModal = mrOk then
    with ColorForm do
    begin
      FColor := ColorGrid.ForegroundColor;
      BColor := ColorGrid.BackgroundColor;
      Result := True;
    end;
  finally
    ColorForm.Free;
  end;
end;

end.
```

Listing 21-9: Colordll\Colorlib.dpr. To convert an application project to a DLL, modify its .dpr file as illustrated here.

```
library Colorlib;

{ Important note about DLL memory management: ShareMem must be
  the first unit in your library's USES clause AND your
  project's (select View-Project Source) USES clause if your
  DLL exports any procedures or functions that pass strings as
```

```
  parameters or function results. This applies to all strings
  passed to and from your DLL—even those that are nested in
  records and classes. ShareMem is the interface unit to the
  BORLNDMM.DLL shared memory manager, which must be deployed
  along with your DLL. To avoid using BORLNDMM.DLL, pass string
  information using PChar or ShortString parameters. }

uses
// ShareMem,      { Not required in this example }
   SysUtils,
   Classes,
   Clrform in 'CLRFORM.PAS' {ColorForm};

exports
   FBGetColors;

{$R *.RES}

begin
end.
```

Newer versions of Delphi provide a DLL project template that you can use to create new DLLs from scratch. Use File|New..., click the New page tab, and choose the DLL template. Although it's more work to follow the steps listed here, I typically develop DLLs as stand-alone applications for test purposes, and then convert the code to DLLs for sharing among applications.

In the DLL's unit, Clrform.pas, the access function FBColors shows how a DLL creates a form object. The function returns WordBool (Windows' Boolean data type) to indicate whether the user closed the dialog by clicking OK (True) or Cancel (False). First, the function initializes its return value to False. Next, it constructs a ColorForm object by calling the TColorForm class's Create method. Because you converted the application into a DLL, it no longer creates its form automatically, and the function has to do this under program control.

Tip   Always use a *try-finally* block as Clrform.pas demonstrates to guarantee that, even if an exception occurs, the form object is deleted.

Inside the *try* block, the program calls ColorForm's ShowModal method, which returns the value assigned to ModalResult by the dialog's OK and Cancel Button OnClick event handlers. If ShowModal returns mrOk, the program assigns the ColorGrid object's foreground and background colors to the access function's variable parameters. This passes the dialog's information back to the host program. To indicate success, the program assigns True to the function result.

Caution   If your DLL passes any string parameters or function results, or if it uses dynamic arrays, you must use the ShareMem unit *first* in the DLL and the application *uses* directive. The test program shown here doesn't need this unit, but I added it as a comment to show where it goes. This rule applies even to strings that are encased in a record or class object. If you pass string data by any means to and from a DLL, add ShareMem to the *uses* clause as shown here. Remember to do this in both the DLL and the application that uses it.

The *finally* block calls ColorForm's Free method to destroy the form object and all of its components. This returns system memory to its state at the beginning of the function. You must be especially careful in a DLL to create and free objects properly, or you can easily introduce a memory leak (which makes the floor all sticky and is a real mess to clean up).

For safety, exported routines in a DLL should be wrapped in an unqualified *try-except* block. This prevents any exceptions escaping from the DLL's scope, which is dangerous because exception handling is nonstandard across application boundaries. There's no telling what could happen to an exception if one escapes from the DLL and goes bouncing around Windows. One way to handle critical errors is for the DLL exception handler to call a function supplied by the program that uses the DLL. This callback function could raise an application exception, which can report the problem. This solution keeps any exceptions within their respective domains — DLL exceptions stay in the DLL; application exceptions stay in the application.

Using a DLL

If you are following along, you now have Colorlib.dll in a directory. Next, you create a sample application that calls the DLL's access function to display a color selection dialog. Just for fun, the sample application colors its Memo object's background and foreground using the returned color values.

On the CD-ROM   You may create the application yourself, or load the sample Testdll project from a copy of the CD-ROM's Colordll directory. Listing 21-10 shows the Testdll.pas source code, which demonstrates how a Delphi application loads and uses a DLL.

Listing 21-10: **Colordll\Testdll.pas. This program demonstrates how to load and use the Colorlib DLL from the preceding section.**

```
unit Main;

interface

uses
//  ShareMem,  { Not required by this example }
  Windows, SysUtils, Classes, Graphics, Controls,
  Forms, Dialogs, StdCtrls;

type
  TMainForm = class(TForm)
    Button1: TButton;
    Memo1: TMemo;
    procedure Button1Click(Sender: TObject);
  private
    { Private declarations }
  public
    { Public declarations }
  end;

var
  MainForm: TMainForm;

implementation

{$R *.DFM}

{ Declare external function in the Colorlib.Dll }
function FBGetColors(var FColor, BColor: TColor): WordBool;
far;
  external 'Colorlib';

{ Activate color dialog in the Colorlib.Dll }
procedure TMainForm.Button1Click(Sender: TObject);
var
  FColor, BColor: TColor;
begin
  FColor := Font.Color;    { Form's text color }
  BColor := Color;         { Window background color }
  if FBGetColors(FColor, BColor) then  { Call DLL ! }
  begin
    Memo1.Color := BColor;        { Assign window color }
    Memo1.Font.Color := FColor;  { Assign text color }
  end;
end;

end.
```

In the host application (the one that uses the DLL), declare the same access procedure or function that the DLL's unit declares. As Testdll.pas shows, however, use a slightly different form. Declare the function *far*. Technically speaking, you don't have to do that if you are sure your code will be compiled using a 32-bit version of Delphi, but I include the *far* keyword anyway. So call me finicky. Also declare the function *external*, followed by the string name of the DLL (minus the .dll extension if that's what it is). This tells the compiler that the program will import the function, which as you recall, the DLL exports.

The final step is the easiest. Simply call the *access* function as the sample program's OnClick button event handler demonstrates. The DLL opens the dialog form window, and fully controls all component objects and whatnot. If the function returns True, the program uses the selected color values passed back via the two TColor variable parameters.

Application and Message Event Handlers

The TApplication class provides a number of events for which you can write handlers. Because the Application object is not visible in the form, and TApplication is not available on the VCL palette, you have to use a different technique to create these handlers. Perform these steps:

✦ Declare the handler in the form class's private or public section (usually private). Do not declare handlers preceding the *private* keyword where Delphi automatically generates component object declarations and methods.

✦ Implement the handler by writing a procedure. Preface the procedure name with the form's class name. In general, use the same format Delphi uses when it creates event handlers for objects you select using the Object Inspector window's Events page tab.

✦ Assign the handler to an Application event property: OnActivate, OnDeactivate, OnException, OnHelp, OnHint, OnIdle, or OnMessage.

TApplication event handlers

Follow these steps for an example of assigning Application event handlers. The sample program demonstrates a highly useful technique that you can use to perform background processing without using a Timer object:

1. Create a new application. Insert a Label and a Memo object into the form.

2. Add the following two declarations to the TForm1 class's private section. *X* is an integer (initialized to zero automatically when the form is created) the AppOnIdle event handler increments and displays in the Label's Caption. The event handler must have the parameters and general form shown here, but you can name it as you like — search specific events for the required formats of their handler procedures:

```
X: Integer;
procedure AppOnIdle(Sender: TObject; var Done: Boolean);
```

3. Implement the AppOnIdle procedure by inserting the following lines into the unit's implementation section. Notice that the form's class name precedes the procedure name separated by a period. The event handler increments the private *X* variable and displays it by converting *X* to a string and assigning the result to the Label's Caption:

```
procedure TForm1.AppOnIdle(Sender: TObject; var Done:
Boolean);
begin
   Inc(X);
   Label1.Caption := IntToStr(X);
end;
```

4. To connect the event handler with TApplication's OnIdle event, assign the handler's procedure name to the event. You may do this at any place in the program, but you most often do it in a form's OnCreate event handler. Select the form and double-click its OnCreate event value to create this handler, and insert the following assignment statement:

```
Application.OnIdle := AppOnIdle;
```

5. Run the program, which continually updates the Label, even while you enter text into the Memo window.

Note

Although I used a Label object for this demonstration, changing the Label caption (as this book's technical editor pointed out) causes the Label window to be invalidated, leading to a wm__Paint message that ends the idle state prematurely. Less intrusive activities include calling MessageBeep, writing output to a file, or sending a message to another application.

Trap a Windows message by creating a handler for Application.OnMessage. This can help you fine-tune the application's responses to various messages, or provide services for messages not normally recognized. Declare an OnMessage event handler as follows:

```
procedure AppOnMessage(var Msg: TMsg; var Handled: Boolean);
```

✦ **Msg** — A record of type TMsg that contains the window handle, the message value, parameters, the time the message was posted, and cursor coordinates. These values depend on the specific message received.

✦ **Handled** — If your OnMessage event handler handles a message, set this parameter to True. If you don't handle a message, or if you want to retain its default actions, set Handled to False.

Tens of thousands of messages *per second* fly through TApplicationOnMessage. Be extremely careful of what you do in this message handler event, or you can easily slow your application's performance to a snail's pace.

Subclassing Windows messages

Another way to handle Windows messages is by writing a method indexed to a specific message constant. For example, you can use this technique to subclass a menu item's response to a command selection. The program's form can watch for the command message, perform some additional processing when it comes down the line, and pass the message on to perform its usual activity.

Try the following steps to subclass a File menu's Exit command, and display a message with Yes and No buttons that users can click to end the program or abort the command's selection:

1. Start a new application. Insert a MainMenu object. Double-click the object, and use Delphi's Menu Designer to create a File menu with an Exit command.

2. Select the File|Exit command in the form, and enter **Close;** into the command's event handler.

3. Run the program, and select File|Exit to test that this closes the program window.

4. You now subclass the Exit command's event handler by trapping its wm__Command Windows message, issued when you select the command. Insert the following message handler declaration into the TForm1 class's protected or public section. The procedure traditionally has the same name as the message, minus the underscore in the constant of the same name. The procedure receives a TWMCommand variable containing information about this type of Windows message:

```
procedure WMCommand(var Message: TWMCommand);
  message wm_Command;
```

5. Implement WMCommand as follows. Insert the procedure into the unit's implementation section:

```
procedure TForm1.WMCommand(var Message: TWMCommand);
begin
  if Message.ItemId = Exit1.Command then
  begin
    if MessageDlg('Quit program?', mtConfirmation,
      [mbYes, mbNo], 0) = mrNo then
    begin
      Message.Result := 1;   { Message was handled }
      Exit;                  { Exit without calling inherited
}
    end;
  end;
//  inherited WMCommand(Message);  { Old style }
  inherited;                 { Call inherited method }
  Message.Result := 1;       { Indicate message was handled }
end;
```

6. Run the program, and select File | Exit. If you answer Yes, the program ends; if you answer No, the program continues. This kind of prompt can be provided in other ways, but the importance of the technique demonstrated here is that the form class intercepts a Windows message to provide additional programming, or to replace that message's actions.

The WMCommand message event handler inspects the ItemId field in the Message record. This field equals the command value, automatically assigned to TMenuItem.Command properties when you design a Menu object. Use the object's property to find this value as demonstrated here for Exit1.Command.

To process an intercepted message normally, call *inherited* as shown here. In past Delphi versions, it was necessary to call an inherited procedure by name. This is no longer required — just use the *inherited* keyword as in the sample. Calling *inherited* is optional, but if you don't do this, you can wipe out an entire level of operations for a specific message. If you want to completely replace your code's response to a particular message, then you do not have to call *inherited*. Normally, however, you should do so.

Note   Windows message handlers such as WMCommand are now declared private to their class — TForm for example. Derived classes may not explicitly call or refer to an ancestor class's private declarations. On a technical level, this is why you must now use *inherited* with no argument as was required in the past.

Set the Message parameter's Result field to zero to indicate a message was not handled. Set Result to one if you handle a message. In this case, Result's value doesn't matter because the inherited procedure probably sets it, but I included the assignments anyway.

You can use the technique described here to override any message handler in a class. Look up the declaration in the unit's interface file (Forms.pas, for example, in Delphi's Source\Vcl directory), and copy the declaration to your form class. Implement the procedure — remember to preface its name with the class name and a period.

Overriding WinProc

There's yet another way to get to the messages that whiz around Windows and its myriad tasks. You can override the low-level window procedure, WinProc, which performs message handling for forms. Do that by declaring the following procedure in the form class's protected or public section:

```
procedure WndProc(Var Message: TMessage); override;
```

The NonClien application on the CD-ROM demonstrates how to trap messages by overriding (subclassing) a form's window procedure. Listing 21-11 shows the program's source code. The program intercepts left-mouse button double-clicks in the window's title bar, part of the window's "nonclient" area. Delphi normally ignores nonclient messages — which are named wm_NC . . . — but you can trap these messages by overriding the form's window procedure as shown here.

Under Windows 95, it is no longer possible to subclass right-mouse button double-clicks in the window's nonclient area. Double-clicking the right mouse button opens the window's system menu. You can still subclass the left-mouse button double-click event. For reference, the listing shows the former code that subclassed both buttons. However, only the left button works.

To override the form's window procedure, declare WndProc (it must be named that) as shown either in the form class's protected or public section. WndProc receives a single parameter of type TMessage that describes the message's content. Insert an override directive at the end of the declaration.

Listing 21-11: **Nonclien\Main.pas**

```
unit Main;

interface

uses
  SysUtils, WinTypes, WinProcs, Messages, Classes, Graphics,
Controls,
  Forms, Dialogs, StdCtrls;

type
  TMainForm = class(TForm)
    Label1: TLabel;
  private
    { Private declarations }
  public
    procedure WndProc(Var Message: TMessage); override;
    { Public declarations }
  end;

var
  MainForm: TMainForm;

implementation

{$R *.DFM}

procedure TMainForm.WndProc(var Message: TMessage);
begin
  with Message do
  case Msg of
    wm_NCLButtonDblClk:
      ShowMessage('Nonclient left button click');  // Obsolete!
    wm_NCRButtonDblClk:
      ShowMessage('Nonclient right button click');
  end;
  inherited WndProc(Message);
end;

end.
```

Implement the overridden window procedure by examining the Msg field in the Message variable. Msg equals a Windows message constant. Most often, you'll use a *case* statement, as in the sample listing, to compare Msg with one or more Windows messages — in this case, the two nonclient double-click messages. Remember, only one of these now works — wm_ NCLButtonDblClk is obsolete, at least for the purposes of subclassing the event. Call the inherited WndProc to process other messages, or you may set Message.Result to nonzero and call Exit to indicate that you have handled a message. However, you should pass most messages onto the inherited method for default processing.

To anticipate a question from the lowest-of-the-low systems programmers out there, yes it is possible to tap into the message stream even earlier than WinProc — that is, before the messages get to the form. If you scan the public Delphi archives, you may come across a method for doing this that attaches a window procedure to the Application's Handle using SetWindowLong. If so, ignore that advice — there's an easier way. Simply create an Application.OnMessage event handler to obtain messages at their point of arrival into the real application window. The TApplication class's ProcessMessages function — the so-called message loop in a Delphi application — triggers the OnMessage event for all messages except wm_Quit. Application.OnMessage processes only messages that are posted to the application's message queue for any window in that application. A component's WndProc method handles all messages delivered to that component's window handle via PostMessage and SendMessage.

File Streams

Delphi includes an object-oriented file-streaming system that you can use to read and write data, components, and other objects in disk files. Listing 21-12 demonstrates how to use the TStream and TFileStream classes to write a Button object to a disk file, and then read it back. The application also demonstrates how to create a component object entirely under program control. Run the program, and then click Create to create a button and display it on the form. Click Write to stream the button to a disk file named Test.stm (you can name the file anything you like, and the filename doesn't have to end with .stm). Clicking Write destroys the button object and removes it from the window. Click Read to read the object back from the file stream.

The Main unit defines a TButton object, *B*, to be streamed to and from a disk file. Look for this declaration in the unit's implementation section. To identify on screen whether the button came from the program or the stream, two event handlers BOnClick1 and BOnClick2 display different messages using the ShowMessage procedure. Procedure EnableButtons enables and disables the Create, Write, and Read buttons to suggest a correct order of operation. This prevents, for example, creating or reading more than one Button object at a time, which this simple demonstration is not designed to do.

Listing 21-12: **Compstrm\Main.pas**

```
unit Main;

interface

uses
  SysUtils, WinTypes, WinProcs, Messages, Classes, Graphics,
Controls,
  Forms, Dialogs, Buttons, StdCtrls;

type
  TMainForm = class(TForm)
    CreateButton: TButton;
    WriteButton: TButton;
    ReadButton: TButton;
    CloseBitBtn: TBitBtn;
    procedure FormCreate(Sender: TObject);
    procedure CreateButtonClick(Sender: TObject);
    procedure WriteButtonClick(Sender: TObject);
    procedure ReadButtonClick(Sender: TObject);
    procedure FormDestroy(Sender: TObject);
  private
    { Private declarations }
    procedure EnableButtons;
    procedure BOnClick1(Sender: TObject);
    procedure BOnClick2(Sender: TObject);
  public
    { Public declarations }
  end;

var
  MainForm: TMainForm;

implementation

{$R *.DFM}

const
  fileName = 'Test.stm';   { The stream's filename }

var
  B: TButton;   { Object to be streamed to and from disk }

{ OnClick event handler before writing Button to stream }
procedure TMainForm.BOnClick1(Sender: TObject);
begin
```

(continued)

Listing 21-12 *(continued)*

```
  ShowMessage('Thanks. I needed that!');
end;

{ OnClick event handler after reading Button from stream }
procedure TMainForm.BOnClick2(Sender: TObject);
begin
  ShowMessage('Hello. It''s nice to be back!');
end;

{ Enable and disable buttons depending on whether the Button
object and Test.Strm file exist }
procedure TMainForm.EnableButtons;
begin
  CreateButton.Enabled := False;  { Disable all buttons }
  WriteButton.Enabled := False;
  ReadButton.Enabled := False;
  if B <> nil then
    WriteButton.Enabled := True    { Write if B exists }
  else begin
    CreateButton.Enabled := True; { Create if B doesn't exist}
    if FileExists(fileName) then
      ReadButton.Enabled := True   { Allow read if file exists }
  end;
end;

{ Initialize other buttons to control clicking order }
procedure TMainForm.FormCreate(Sender: TObject);
begin
  EnableButtons;
end;

{ Create Button object entirely under program control }
procedure TMainForm.CreateButtonClick(Sender: TObject);
begin
  B := TButton.Create(Self);       { Create the Button object }
  B.Parent := Self;                { Assign parent object }
  B.Left := 240;                   { Assign left position }
  B.Top := 72;                     { Assign top position }
  B.Caption := 'Click me!';        { Assign label }
  B.OnClick := BOnClick1;          { Assign first event handler }
  EnableButtons;                   { Update operation order }
end;

{ Write Button object to file stream, and then destroy it }
procedure TMainForm.WriteButtonClick(Sender: TObject);
var
  Stream: TStream;
```

```
begin
{ Create a new disk file stream }
  Stream := TFileStream.Create(fileName, fmCreate);
  try
    Stream.WriteComponent(B);       { Write Button object }
    B.Free;                         { Destroy Button object }
    B := nil; { Prevent form's OnDestroy from Freeing again }
    EnableButtons;                  { Update operation order }
  finally
    Stream.Free;  { Destroy the file stream object }
  end;
end;

{ Read Button object from stream }
procedure TMainForm.ReadButtonClick(Sender: TObject);
var
  Stream: TStream;
begin
{ Create stream object in read-only mode }
  Stream := TFileStream.Create(fileName, fmOpenRead);
  try
    B := TButton(Stream.ReadComponent(nil)); {Read & Create B}
    B.Parent := Self;          { Always assign parent! }
    B.OnClick := BOnClick2;    { Assign second event handler }
    EnableButtons;             { Update operation order }
  finally
    Stream.Free;  { Destroy the file stream object }
  end;
end;

{ Destroy button if user closes app before completing test }
procedure TMainForm.FormDestroy(Sender: TObject);
begin
  if B <> nil then B.Free;
end;

{ Register the TButton class with Delphi stream system }
begin
  RegisterClass(TButton);
end.
```

The CreateButtonClick event handler creates a new button object by calling the TButton class's Create constructor and assigning the resulting object reference to *B*. To make the object visible, it must have a Parent, which in this case is the main form (referenced by Self in a form class's method such as this one). Most objects also need Left and Top values to position them — you may also set the object's Width and Height, but these and other properties have default values. So that the button does something when you click it, the procedure assigns BOnClick1 to the button object's OnClick event.

The WriteButtonClick procedure demonstrates how to create a new disk file stream. Do that by calling TFileStream's Create constructor with two arguments, a filename and a mode constant such as fmCreate, and save the resulting object reference in a TStream or TFileStream variable. Table 21-1 lists other mode constants you can pass to TFileStream.Create.

Table 21-1 TFileStream.Create Mode Constants	
Constant	Effect
fmOpenRead	Open file for reading
fmOpenWrite	Open file for writing
fmOpenReadWrite	Open file for reading and writing
fmShareExclusive	Open file for application's exclusive use
fmShareDenyWrite	Prevent other applications from writing to file
fmShareDenyRead	Prevent other applications from reading from file
fmShareDenyNone	Allow other applications to read and write file
fmCreate	Create a new file and open for writing

Use logical OR expressions to combine file mode constants. For example, the following expression opens a file for reading and writing, but prevents other applications from writing to the file as long as it remains open:

```
fmOpenReadWrite or fmOpenDenyWrite
```

Call TStream's WriteComponent method to write a component object to the stream. You may write as many components as you need, and they may be of the same or of different types. After writing the Button object, the sample application destroys it and sets its reference, *B,* to *nil.* If you close the application, this prevents the form's OnDestroy event handler from freeing the same object again, which would cause a General Protection Fault (GPF).

The WriteButtonClick procedure uses a *try-finally* block to ensure that the Stream object is freed even if an exception occurs — due to a write-protected disk error, for example. Always use *try-finally* this way in your procedures and functions that create TFileStream objects.

Procedure ReadButtonClick reads the streamed object from disk. Again, the first step calls TFileStream's Create constructor, but this time using the fmOpenRead mode. This statement reads the object from the file stream and assigns it to *B*:

```
B := TButton(Stream.ReadComponent(nil));
```

Call the TStream ReadComponent method to read one component from the file stream. Pass a component reference to ReadComponent to read an object into an existing one, or pass *nil* as in this example to have ReadComponent construct an entirely new object. ReadComponent returns type TComponent, so you have to use a type-cast to assign the result to a specific type of component reference such as *B*.

After reading an object from a stream, be sure to give it a Parent — this information is not saved in the stream because a different form or the same one at a different location in memory might own the object. You will also have to reassign any event handlers. As a general rule, any specific address information (event handlers, references to other objects, and the Parent property) is not streamed because this information is likely to be different after reading the objects.

Before an application can read and write component objects in file streams, it has to register their classes with Delphi's file-streaming mechanism. You may do this in the form's OnCreate event handler, but to ensure that the job is carried out as early as possible, add the *initialization* keyword preceding the unit's *end* statement. In between, insert calls to RegisterClass for each class for which this module will stream objects. Register classes, not objects.

Internet Applications

Delphi's Client/Server edition comes with a complete set of components for developing Internet and Intranet applications. (An intranet is a network that resembles the Internet in its protocols and organization, but is restricted to a local group of computers — all systems, for example, in a company.) These components are useful, not only for accessing Internet and intranet sites, but also for developing remote-access database software. For example, Inprise Corporation uses Delphi components in its bug-reporting application that is made available to software testers.

Internet components

Delphi provides a set of components for Internet and intranet programming. The Client/Server edition provides additional components as shown in Figure 21-6. Because few readers of this book will have the more expensive Client/Server edition, I introduce here only the components provided with Delphi Professional.

| Standard | Additional | Win32 | System | Internet | Data Access | Data Controls | Decision Cube | QReport | Dialogs | Win 3.1 | Samples | ActiveX | MIDAS |

Figure 21-6: Delphi Client/Server Internet components

Note

Inprise Corporation's Internet components have undergone some changes since the prior release. The ActiveX-based FTP, NNTP, and other components are replaced in Delphi 4 with native VCL equivalent components created by NetMasters. This change should not affect class names used in prior versions; however, my prerelease copy of Delphi did not include every class, although Inprise Corporation assures me the final release of Internet components and classes will be compatible with prior versions.

Delphi's Internet components have no visual run-time images, and are shown as icons in the form window. (You might want to deposit them into a data module as described in Chapter 17, Developing Database Applications.) All components are ActiveX controls encased in Delphi component wrappers. In order of their appearance onscreen, Delphi's Internet ActiveX control components are:

✦ **FTP (Internet File Transfer Protocol)** — Transfers files and data between a remote and local computer.

✦ **HTML (Hypertext Markup Language)** — Provides an HTML document viewer. Can also be used for parsing, but not displaying, HTML document commands.

✦ **HTTP (Hypertext Transport Protocol)** — Retrieves HTTP documents without browsing or image processing capabilities.

✦ **NNTP (Network News Transfer Protocol)** — Provides for newsgroup news reading and posting.

✦ **POP (Post Office Protocol)** — Gets mail from UNIX or other types of servers that support the POP3.

✦ **SMTP (Simple Mail Transfer Protocol)** — Accesses SMTP mail servers and provides for mail posting.

✦ **TCP (Transmission Control Protocol)** — For Client/Server applications needing TCP network services.

✦ **UDP (User Datagram Protocol)** — Implements WinSock for Client/Server applications. Can also send and receive UDP data.

Delphi's Internet applications

Delphi provides several sample applications that demonstrate how to use Internet components. For a quick introduction to Internet programming, try the sample Web browser located in Delphi's Demos\Internet\Html directory. This program shows how to create an entire Web browser using only a single HTML component. Load the Webbrows.dpr project file in that directory into Delphi, and press F9 to compile and run. Figure 21-7 shows the program's window after connecting to Borland's Web site (www.borland.com).

Figure 21-7: Delphi's sample Web browser demonstrates Internet programming with components.

To request an HTML document over the Internet, simply drop an HTML component onto a form, and program an event handler to call the component's RequestDoc method like this:

```
HTML1.RequestDoc(URLs.text);
```

This assumes URLs is a ComboBox or other component with a text property that is set to the URL you want. You can also pass a literal string to RequestDoc:

```
HTML1.RequestDoc('www.inprise.com');
```

An HTML component object is useful for obtaining the source text of an HTML document. To do this, connect to the site by calling RequestDoc, and then access the HTML document's SourceText property. This is a string list which contains the raw text of the document. Delphi's sample Web browser uses the SourceText property to display the HTML source in a window, adding the text to a Memo using the statements:

```
Memo1.Lines.Clear;
Memo1.Lines.Add(HTML1.SourceText);
```

Two HTML events are useful for detecting the start and stop of a document's retrieval. Select the HTML object and click the Events tab on the Object Inspector. Then, double-click the OnBeginRetrieval and OnEndRetrieval events to create handlers for each. The two events are:

✦ **OnBeginRetrieval**—Called when document loading begins

✦ **OnEndRetrieval**—Called when document loading ends

The sample Web browser uses these two events to enable and disable the program's Cancel button. (Obviously, a Cancel operation is not needed after the document is fully loaded.) You might think of other good uses for these events—starting a progress bar, for example, or simply displaying a message on screen that tells users a document is loading.

Of course, you can use several more Internet components and numerous other properties and events to develop Internet applications. Space limitations prevent going into more detail here, but the preceding introduction can at least help you to get started.

Still More Tips

I found the following tidbits, which were floating around in my notes along with some DOS batch files to be useful while using and learning about Delphi. Maybe you will, too.

Reducing code file size

The following are two surefire techniques that can reduce code file size, often drastically:

✦ Switch off debug information, which is written to the .exe code file for use during debugging sessions. Select Project | Options... and click the Linker page tab. Switch off the Include TD32 debug info check box. This prevents the compiler from transferring debug information to the code file.

✦ Use run-time packages. Normally, Delphi creates a complete .exe code file that contains all of your application's code plus all code for components in the VCL. This makes the code file convenient for distributing because you have to provide only the one file to end users. However, multiple copies of the application code file contain wasteful copies of the VCL. Eliminate this waste by selecting Project I Options..., click the Packages page tab, and switch on the check box labeled Build with run-time packages. This simple option can reduce the size of your code file by 235K or more. However, because the packages must be available to run the program, any disk space savings are realized only if you have multiple Delphi applications on the same system.

For both methods, rebuild your application to reduce the finished .exe code file. It's important to rebuild so that all modules are recompiled. You might also have to "touch" the application in some way to force relinking — move the form over by one pixel, for example. Do not simply press F9 to compile and run the application as you normally do. To create the finished .exe code file, select Project I Build all.

Run-time packages also reduce memory usage. Because a package is nothing more than a specially compiled DLL, its code is shared among all concurrently running Delphi applications.

Note

When using packages, you must provide them to your end users — for example, the VCL40.bpl file. This and other required .bpl files should be copied to your end user's C:\Windows\System directory.

Focus changes

In some versions of Delphi, it is not recommended to perform any actions that cause a focus change in an event handler that is itself involved in a focus change. For example, attempting to display a message dialog in an OnExit event for an Edit component can cause the program to lose the capability to tab to other controls.

This problem no longer exists in Delphi 3 and later versions. To find out if your system exhibits the behavior, place some Edit objects into a form, and call ShowMessage for one object's OnExit event. Run the program and tab from control to control. After you close the message dialog, you might have trouble shifting the focus to other controls — giving the dialog box the focus interferes with the process of giving the next control the focus, which is what OnExit was doing when you interrupted it. For example, pressing Tab after closing the dialog probably does not move the focus to the next Edit window as expected. This problem isn't going to blow up your programs, but if you seem to have trouble tabbing among controls in a window, this is the likely cause.

Multiple program instances

As you probably know, you can run multiple instances of some Windows programs, but others restrict you to running them only once. Microsoft dictates that new instances of an application be started when users run them a second or another time. This edict, however, can lead to big trouble. Just try running two instances of Microsoft Word—when I do this, I receive an error message the Normal.dot document template is in use by another application. Presumably, this is the original instance of Word.

Ideally, rather than toeing the line, you should decide whether it is appropriate for your application to run as a single instance, or as multiple instances when users restart the program. The trick for doing this is not simple, but is possible by modifying a Delphi project's source code. Follow these steps to try out the technique:

1. Start a new application. You want to save its files on disk so you can run the compiled .exe code file from the Windows Explorer. (You can't run multiple program instances from inside Delphi.) Create a directory for the project. Save the unit and project files using their default filenames.

2. Select View | Project Source to open the program's project file. As you can see, the project is actually the program's main Pascal program.

3. Add the Dialogs and Windows units to the project file's *uses* directive. I do this just below the Forms unit, but the positioning is probably not critical.

4. Modify the project's statements between *begin* and *end* using Listing 21-13 as a guide. The sample code listed here assumes the application's main form is named TForm1. If you change the form's name, you must update all references to it. Delphi does not do this automatically as it does in the form's unit source file.

5. Save the project to establish its directory, and then press Ctrl+F9 to compile. Close all files. Switch to the Windows Explorer, and run the Project1.exe code file. Without closing the window, run the program again—this time you see a message that the program is already running. Close the message dialog to switch automatically back to the first program instance.

Note
I find I must close the application files before I can run two instances of the program. This might be a consequence of calling FindWindow when the application's source files are open in Delphi because the window class of the form in Delphi is named TForm1.

Listing 21-13: Use this listing as a guide to modifying a project to prevent it from running multiple times.

```
program Project1;

uses
  Forms,
  Dialogs,
  Windows,
  Unit1 in 'Unit1.pas' {Form1};

{$R *.RES}

begin
  HPrevInst := FindWindow('TForm1', nil);
  if HPrevInst = 0 then
  begin
    Application.Initialize;
    Application.CreateForm(TForm1, Form1);
    Application.Run;
  end else
  begin
    ShowMessage('Application is already running');
    Windows.SetFocus(HPrevInst);
    Windows.SetForegroundWindow(HPrevInst);
  end;
end.
```

In the past, Windows set HPrevInst to the handle of an existing program instance. This is no longer done; however, we can duplicate the step by calling FindWindow as shown. The first parameter passed to FindWindow is the window's class name. The second parameter, which isn't used here, represents the window caption. This assumes the class name identifies the application absolutely and the form object hasn't been created yet by the application.

The modified project inspects HPrevInst, which if equal to zero indicates that this is the first time the program has been executed. Running the application searches for a window, and sets HPrevInst to the application's instance handle. If this handle is nonzero, the project's *else* statements display a message and call the Windows API SetFocus function to give the first instance the input focus. To display the instance's window requires also calling SetForegroundWindow as shown.

Notice that SetFocus and SetForegroundWindow are called in direct reference to the Windows unit, in which the two functions are declared. This is not strictly necessary, but because other Delphi components have SetFocus methods, prefacing the calls with Windows ensures that the program calls the proper method. You can do this with any unit, by the way, to resolve duplicate method and other object name conflicts.

Tip   To switch silently to the first program instance, delete the ShowMessage statement.

Some useful DOS batch files

Do you still type commands at the DOS prompt as often as I do? I'm a die-hard Windows fan, but there are times when I know how to get a job done in a text-only window and nothing else works as well. I'm also always writing batch files to perform various operations in a DOS window. The following are some I've found especially useful with Delphi.

On the CD-ROM   Listing 21-14 shows the Clean.bat file from the CD-ROM in the Source directory. Run this program to erase all but the essential files in a Delphi project. Listing 21-15 is part of the Cleanall.bat file you can run to delete wasteful files after you compile this book's example programs. To use these programs, copy them to the directory that contains your project subdirectories. Run Cleanall to clean all directories. Or, run Clean to clean individual ones like this:

```
Clean Polyflow
```

Listing 21-14: **Clean.bat**

```
@echo off
rem
rem CLEAN.BAT
rem Delete files created by Delphi
rem Called by CLEANALL.BAT
rem Input %1==subdirectory where clean.bat is stored
rem
rem ex. call clean Polyflow
rem
if "%1"=="" goto ERROR
if exist %1\NUL goto CONTINUE
goto ERROR
:CONTINUE
cd %1
echo Cleaning %1
rem
rem Add new files to delete here:
```

```
rem
if exist *.bak del *.bak
if exist *.~*  del *.~*
if exist *.dsk del *.dsk
if exist *.dsm del *.dsm
REM if exist *.exe del *.exe
rem
rem Go back to directory that has clean.bat
rem
:REPEAT
cd ..
if exist clean.bat goto END
goto REPEAT
:ERROR
echo.
echo Error cleaning: %1
echo No such directory
pause
:END
```

Listing 21-15: **Cleanall.bat (partial listing—full program on disk)**

```
@echo off
rem
rem cleanall.bat—call clean.bat for all source directories
rem
echo working...
if exist *.bak del *.bak
call clean aboutex
call clean addpage
call clean barchart
call clean bitview
call clean bitview2
...
echo done
:END
```

For safety, I commented out the instruction in Clean.bat that erases .exe code files. If you enable this line, be extremely careful not to erase other applications on your hard drive. You should not install Clean or Cleanall in a global Path directory. Also, you may want to keep one or another type of file. See Chapter 1, section "Filename Extensions," for descriptions of files Delphi creates.

Default parameters

Delphi 4 adds default parameters to Object Pascal. This feature, borrowed from C++, provides default values to procedure and function parameters. For example, suppose you have a procedure with three parameters declared as:

```
procedure CallMe(A: Integer; B: Double; C: String);
```

To call this procedure in a *program* statement, you must supply argument values for the three parameters:

```
CallMe(10, 3.14159. 'Message from a flounder');
```

Suppose, however, some calls of the procedure do not need to supply values to the String parameter. Without default parameters, you have to write code such as:

```
CallMe(10, 2.2, '');
CallMe(20, 3.3, '');
CallMe(30, 4.4, '');
```

In each case, you need to supply a null string to CallMe, even though this parameter is not used. Default parameter values help simplify this kind of code. Declare the default parameter as follows:

```
procedure CallMe(A: Integer; B: Double; C: String = '');
```

The default value assigned to parameter *C* tells the compiler to use this value if none is explicitly supplied. With this declaration in place, the preceding three calls to the procedure can now be written like this:

```
CallMe(10, 2.2);
CallMe(20, 3.3);
CallMe(30, 4.4);
```

Default values can be assigned to any parameter, but they must come last in the declaration. You cannot, for example, use a declaration such as:

```
procedure X(A: Integer = 0; B: Double); // ???
```

This doesn't compile because default parameter values must always be last. In this case, you could reverse the order of the parameters, or supply a default value also for *B*:

```
procedure X(A: Integer = 0; B: Double = 3.14159);
```

Default parameters simplify some kinds of statements, and help ensure all parameters have known values. One disadvantage to using default parameter values is the way they obscure the actual arguments passed to procedures and functions. For example, the three preceding calls to CallMe give no indication that a null string argument is passed as a secret third argument. Good comments, however, easily eliminate this objection.

Method overloading

Delphi 4 adds another popular feature borrowed from C++ — method *overloading*. This permits two or more procedures or functions to have identical names, but operate as distinctly different subroutines. The simple rule is: an overloaded method must differ in at least one parameter type. As long as you satisfy that rule, you may overload the same method as often as necessary.

Method overloading helps you create understandable code that conforms to object-oriented goals. You can, for instance, develop a set of procedures all named ShowItem that displays some kind of graphic figure. You can then write a statement such as

```
ShowItem(X);
```

where *X* might be a known object of many different types. This is simpler and easier to maintain than writing multiple procedures named ShowIntegerItem, ShowGraphicsItem, ShowImageItem, and so on.

Method overloading example

As another more complete example, suppose you want to develop a procedure to initialize dynamic arrays of various types. First, you declare the dynamic array types as follows:

```
type
  TIntArray = array of Integer;
  TFloatArray = array of Double;
  TStringArray = array of String;
```

Next, define variables of the three arrays:

```
var
  IntArray1: TIntArray;
  FloatArray1: TFloatArray;
  StringArray1: TStringArray;
```

These two code fragments show, by the way, a practical use for declaring array types. We need to create actual arrays of the three types, and we need to declare procedure parameters of those same types. The three procedures are declared something like this (inside a class's public section for example):

```
public
procedure InitIntArray(A: TIntArray; V: Integer);
procedure InitFloatArray(A: TFloatArray; V: Double);
procedure InitStringArray(A: TStringArray; V: String);
```

Each procedure is implemented to assign value *V* to each array position, thus setting all array elements to a known value. The first procedure might be implemented as:

```
var
  I: Integer;
begin
  for I := 0 to High(A) do
    A[I] := V;
end;
```

After writing this much of the code, you can call the array initializing procedures with statements such as:

```
InitIntArray(IntArray1, 0);
InitFloatArray(FloatArray1, 1.0);
InitStringArray(StringArray1, 'Msg:');
```

This works, but it's messy. With method overloading, a single procedure name can be designated for all types of array initializations. To do this, change all procedure names to be the same, and add the *overload* key word after the declaration:

```
procedure InitArray(A: TIntArray; V: Integer); overload;
procedure InitArray(A: TFloatArray; V: Double); overload;
procedure InitArray(A: TStringArray; V: String); overload;
```

The three procedures can have the same names because their declarations differ in at least one parameter type. Implement each procedure (you must implement all three separately) as before, using the same declarations shown here. To call the procedures, use code such as this:

```
InitArray(IntArray1, 0);
InitArray(FloatArray1, 1.0);
InitArray(StringArray1, 'Msg:');
```

There's nothing magical going on here. Internally, there are still three distinct procedures. But, rather than distinguish among them by name, with method overloading, it is possible to differentiate the procedures by the data passed as arguments. This clarifies the code and makes it easy to add new InitArray procedures for other data types.

Note

> A valid overloaded method must have at least one parameter type that differs from other methods of the same name or the methods must have different numbers of parameters. It is the type and number of parameters that matters. The parameter names are immaterial.

Method overloading and default parameters

You might use default parameter values with overloaded methods. For example, the *V* parameter in the preceding declarations might be assigned a default value using declarations such as:

```
procedure InitArray(A: TIntArray; V: Integer = 0); overload;
procedure InitArray(A: TFloatArray; V: Double = 1.1); overload;
procedure InitArray(A: TStringArray; V: String = ''); overload;
```

Now, it is possible to initialize arrays of the declared types with statements like these:

```
InitArray(IntArray1);
InitArray(FloatArray1);
InitArray(StringArray1);
```

Method overloading, along with default parameter values, often produces code like this that is simple and clear. It is also easier to remember method names without having to look up their declarations. ("Hmmm, was that procedure named InitFloatArray or InitDoubleArray? Or maybe it was InitFPArray.")

On the other hand, combining method overloading with default parameter values can lead to ambiguous code that doesn't compile.

```
procedure F(Height: Integer; D: Double = 0.0); overload;
procedure F(Width: Integer); overload;   // ???
```

This gives the compiler a dilemma because it isn't always possible to determine which procedure a statement is intended to call. This statement, for example:

```
F(10);   // ???
```

does not compile. Because of the default parameter value in the first declaration, the statement might call either procedure. To fix the problem, you must either, not assign a default parameter value to *D*, or you must rename the second procedure (to F2, for example).

Method overloading and class constructors

Method overloading is valuable in creating class constructors. In past versions of Object Pascal, multiple constructors must be named differently. For example, a typical class in the VCL might declare the following two constructors:

```
constructor Create(AOwner: TComponent); override;
constructor CreateNew(AOwner: TComponent; Flag: Integer);
   virtual;
```

With method overloading, the second constructor can be named Create because it has one more parameter than the first constructor. To overload the two constructors, change their names to Create and add the *overload* keyword. The new declarations are:

```
constructor Create(AOwner: TComponent); overload; override;
constructor Create(AOwner: TComponent; Flag: Integer);
   virtual; overload;
```

This greatly simplifies the construction of class objects because the correct constructor is now called based on the context of its use rather than by its explicit name. For example, these statements construct objects of the class:

```
Obj1 := TForm.Create(AOwner);
Obj2 := TForm.Create(AOwner, 1);
```

The first statement calls the first constructor, which overrides its inherited Create method. The second statement calls the second constructor because it supplies an integer argument to that constructor's Flag parameter.

Method overriding versus overloading

One difficulty you may encounter with overloaded methods is when a declaration of a method hides an original inherited method of the same name. To say that another way, there is a potential conflict between *overriding* an inherited method and *overloading* one. Delphi's online help gives an example similar to the following. Your code declares two classes. Here's the first:

```
FirstClass = class
public
   procedure X(I: Integer); virtual;
end;
```

The second class is derived from the first:

```
SecondClass = class(FirstClass)
public
   procedure X(S: string);
end;
```

These kinds of declarations are commonly used to replace a procedure (*X* in the demonstration) in a derived class. The replacement procedure in SecondClass declares a parameter of a different type than its inherited method. Therefore, only the first of the following two calls to *X* compiles:

```
var
   AnObject: SecondClass;
begin
   AnObject.X('Testing');
   AnObject.X(123);  // ???
end;
```

The second call to *X* fails to compile because the redeclaration of the inherited method hides the original declaration that declares an Integer parameter. Method overloading makes it possible to resolve this kind of conflict. The new classes are declared as follows:

```
FirstClass = class
public
   procedure X(I: Integer); virtual; overload;
end;
SecondClass = class(FirstClass)
public
   procedure X(S: string); overload;
end;
```

The only difference is the use of the *overload* keyword. Because the two procedures are overloaded, the procedure calls to *X* now compile because the compiler can distinguish between the two procedures from their different parameter types.

Because inheriting a method and changing its parameters, but not its name, hides the original declaration — in this example, *X* in SecondClass hides the *X* in FirstClass — the compiler issues a warning. To eliminate this warning, use the *reintroduce* keyword in the second declaration like this:

```
SecondClass = class(FirstClass)
public
   procedure X(S: string); reintroduce;
end;
```

This tells the compiler that you intend to obscure the original *X* and that you do not expect the new declaration to overload the method. The end result is the same, but simply avoids the compiler warning.

Method overloading and forward declarations

Object Pascal's *forward* declaration keyword is used a little differently now that the language has method overloading. In the past, you could declare a procedure or function *forward,* thus indicating its implementation comes later on in the source code file. For example,

```
// Declare forward procedure
procedure X(D: Double); forward;
...  // Code may call X here
// Implement the procedure
procedure X;
begin
  // Code for X
end;
```

The *forward* declaration gives the compiler all the information it needs to enable statements to call *X* ahead of the location in the source file where *X* is implemented. However, if you intend to overload *X* with a second, distinct procedure also named *X* but without parameters, the preceding code is ambiguous. Adding the *overload* keyword to the first declaration causes the compiler to create a new and separate parameterless procedure named *X*, which is possibly not what you want. To resolve this conflict, Object Pascal now permits you to redeclare the *forward* procedure with parameters. For example, to overload *X* with a parameterless version, and to implement the version of *X* with a Double parameter, you can write declarations such as:

```
// Declare overloaded forward procedure
procedure X(D: Double); overload; forward;
...
// Implement an overloaded, distinct procedure
procedure X; overload;
begin
end;
// Implement forward declaration
procedure X(D: Double); overload;
begin
end;
```

This would not be possible if *forward* implementations could not have parameter declarations. The parameterless *X* in this example is a distinctly separate procedure from the *forward* procedure *X* that declares a Double parameter.

Dynamic arrays

Delphi 4 adds dynamic arrays to Object Pascal. A dynamic array declares its type, but not its size. The actual array is created at run time by a program statement. Contrast a dynamic array with Pascal's common static array. For instance, this variable declaration:

```
var
  IntArray : array[1 .. 100] of Integer;
```

creates an array in memory of 100 integers. As a dynamic array, IntArray is first declared without a range of index values in brackets:

```
var
  IntArray : array of Integer;
```

This states that IntArray's type is an array of Integer values. To use the array, a *program* statement must allocate space to the array for holding those values.

The second, and preferred, method for creating dynamic arrays is to call the SetLength procedure, which in the past was used only to change the lengths of strings (both the short and long varieties). Use SetLength to initialize a dynamic array as follows:

```
begin
  SetLength(IntArray, 100);
  ...
end;
```

After allocating space to the array, you can use it just as you do the static variety. As with strings, you do not need to free the allocated space. However, you can remove a dynamic array's memory space by setting its length to zero with the statement:

```
begin
  SetLength(IntArray, 0);
  ...
end;
```

Another choice is to assign *nil* to the array variable. The preceding code can be simplified to this:

```
IntArray := nil;
```

You may declare a dynamic array of any type. For example, this declares a dynamic array of strings:

```
var
  StrArray : array of string;
```

You can also declare multidimensional dynamic arrays, which are literally "arrays of arrays." For example, the static definition:

```
var
  Grid: array[1 .. 10, 1 .. 25] of Double;
```

creates a two-dimensional static array with 10 rows and 25 columns of Double floating-point values. As a dynamic array, the array can be declared like this:

```
var
  Grid: array of array of Double;
begin
  Grid := New(Grid, 10, 25);
  ...
end;
```

Or, rather than use New, you can use SetLength as follows:

```
SetLength(Grid, 10, 25);
```

Either way, the Grid is allocated space for a two-dimensional, 10×25, array of Double floating-point values.

Unlike static arrays, dynamic arrays do not have to be rectangular. In other words, the rows and columns of a two- or more dimension array do not have to be of the same size. After setting the length or using New as described, you can reallocate any row or column with code such as:

```
begin
  SetLength(Grid, 10, 25);
  SetLength(Grid[2], 12);
  ...
end;
```

The first statement allocates to Grid a rectangular 10×25 array of Double values. The second statement reallocates the third row of that array, shrinking it to 12 values. The original row is disposed automatically. It is also possible to allocate only the rows of a multidimensional array. For example, the following creates a *triangular array,* in which the columns vary in size from one to *n* elements. (Conceptually, this looks like one of those mileage calculators on a road map that shows distances between various cities.) Examine this code:

```
var
  Triangle: array of Integer;
```

```
    I: Integer;
begin
  SetLength(Triangle, 10);  // Allocate 10 rows
  for I := 1 to 10 do
    SetLength(Triangle[I], I);
  ...
end;
```

Regardless of how you allocate space to dynamic arrays, they are always indexed from zero to one less than their size in elements. For safety, use the Low and High functions to obtain the legal bounds of a dynamic array. For example, in this fragment:

```
var
  IntArray: array of Integer;
  I: Integer;
begin
  SetLength(IntArray, 100);
  for I := Low(IntArray) to High(IntArray) do
    IntArray[I] := I;
end;
```

For a dynamic array, Low(X) always returns zero, so the preceding loop can be written safely as:

```
for I := 0 to High(IntArray) do
...
```

This is always the best way to prevent a boundary error — indexing a nonexistent array element beyond the highest allocated spot. The High function returns the number of elements in the array minus one.

Caution

Do not subtract one from High(X). The function returns a number that is one less than the number of elements in a dynamic array *X*.

Be careful when copying dynamic arrays — they do not work like strings. For example, if you have two arrays of the exact same type and size, you can assign one array to the other, as shown here:

```
var
  A, B: array of Double;
begin
  SetLength(A, 100);
  ... // Use array A
  B := A;  // Copy A to B which must be equal types
  ... // Use arrays A & B
end;
```

This code declares two dynamic arrays of Double floating-point values. The first array, *A*, is allocated space in memory, and used (see first comment). The assignment statement copies array *A* to *B*; however, because *A* and *B* are merely references (pointers), the statement causes *A* and *B* to address the same block of memory. It does not create two distinct arrays. Because arrays are reference counted, this is acceptable. However, unlike strings, dynamic arrays do not use copy-on-write algorithms.

Reference counting keeps track of how many pointers address the same block of memory. Only when the final pointer is disposed is the addressed memory actually returned to the heap. The copy-on-write algorithm ensures that, if a change is made to memory that is addressed by two or more pointers, a fresh copy of the memory is first made before that change is allowed. Thus, if you copy one string to another, only one string actually exists in memory until you make a change to one of the addressed strings. This is not the case with dynamic arrays. For example, following the assignment statement in the preceding example, this code:

```
A[1] := 3.14159;
```

also changes B[1] to the value of pi.

Dynamic array sizes can change at run time. In fact, this is one of the key advantages to dynamic arrays. This code, for example, creates an array of Double values, uses the array (see first comment), and then calls the Copy function to resize the array:

```
var
  Values: array of Double;
begin
  SetLength(Values, 100);
  ... // Use array Values here
  Values := Copy(Values, 500);
  ... // Use larger array here
end;
```

In this code, Values is a dynamic array of Double floating-point values. The first statement in the program prepares Values to hold 100 elements. The second statement calls the Copy function to create a larger array of 500 elements, and copies the existing values to the new array. After this, the original array is disposed.

Note　During a call to Copy, two arrays exist in memory—one of the original size and one of the new size. If you need to conserve memory use, be aware of this when calling Copy to reallocate array space.

In cases where many actual arrays are needed of the same type, you can create a dynamic array data type using code such as the following:

```
type
  TIntArray = array of Integer;
  TFloatArray = array of Single;
```

```
var
  IntArray1: TIntArray;
  IntArray2: TIntArray;
  FloatArray1: TFloatArray;
begin
  SetLength(IntArray1, 100);
  SetLength(IntArray2, 200);
  SetLength(FloatArray1, 300);
  ...
end;
```

Two dynamic array types are declared: TIntArray and TDoubleArray. Variables are then defined using the data types and allocated space using SetLength. The advantage of this technique is the ease of globally modifying the underlying array type. For example, in the preceding code, you can change the type of TFloatArray like this:

```
type
  ...
  TFloatArray = array of Double;
```

This is the only change required to modify all actual dynamic arrays of type TFloatArray from single-precision to double-precision floating-point elements.

Final Note

This is the last section in the book, but it's not the end of the line. In fact, your experiences (and mine) with Delphi are just beginning. Delphi's popularity has zoomed skyward since I began writing this book and its precursor, *Foundations of Delphi Development*. Software developers worldwide are adopting Delphi at a tremendous pace as more and more discover the value of visual, object-oriented programming that really works.

If you have read through most of this book, you now have a firm foundation in Delphi development techniques. I hope you have enjoyed the journey. Now it's your turn. Dig through the online help and the printed references. Learn to teach yourself new topics by writing short test programs. Browse the VCL source code library for hints on component construction. Join the Delphi Internet newsgroup, `forums.inprise.com`. Write favorable letters about the author to the publisher. And above all, have fun. Good luck!

✦   ✦   ✦

How to Use the CD-ROM

The CD-ROM inside the back cover contains all sample projects described in this book. Copy the files from any CD-ROM directory to an empty directory on your hard drive and then open the copied project with Delphi's File|Open... or File|Open Project... commands. Browse to any directory and open the .dpr file — there is only one in most project directory paths. If you don't see a .dpr file, make sure the Open dialog's Files of Type box displays Delphi file (*.pas, *.dpr). Not all sample directories, however, contain projects. For these, there are no .dpr files to open.

Using the Listings

All listings in the book are located in named directories on the CD-ROM. None of these files is compressed. To use the files, copy any subdirectory from the Source directory to your hard drive. Or, if you have the room, copy the entire Source directory to a hard drive letter such as C:\ or D:\.

Note

Some readers have requested that I organize sample applications by chapter number. This is a useful convention in some cases, but in *Delphi 4 Bible,* several different chapters refer to the same applications. For this reason, all sample applications are stored in directories named the same as their project names. For example, the SysColor demonstration's files are located in the Source\SysColor directory.

Although most directories contain full Delphi projects, some such as Misc contain .pas or other files. Use Delphi's File| Open... command to view these files.

Running and Compiling Programs

All programs are compiled. If you just want to run them, use the Windows Explorer program to execute any .exe code file. You may execute most programs directly from the CD-ROM. However, those programs that write to disk files must first be copied to your hard drive or another writeable device.

To compile a program, you must first copy its directory to your hard drive. If you attempt to compile a program directly to the CD-ROM, Delphi will display an error message when it attempts to write to the .exe code file. If, after copying a directory to your hard drive you still have trouble compiling, the target files might be marked Read-Only. See "Unmarking Read-Only Files" next for more help.

Unmarking Read-Only Files

Copying CD-ROM files might set their Read-Only attribute flags, which will prevent writing to the .exe and .dcu code files. If, when compiling a program you receive an error that a file is in use or marked read-only, follow these steps to correct the problem:

1. Copy the Source directory from the CD-ROM to your hard drive directory C:\, D:\, or other.

2. Open a command-line prompt (MS-DOS) window.

3. Enter C: or D: (or another letter) to change to the Source drive.

4. Enter the command **CD \Source** to change to the Source directory.

5. Type the command **ATTRIB -r *.* /S** to turn off all Read-Only flags.

6. If you receive a "sharing violation" error in Step 4, exit Delphi and try Step 4 again.

✦   ✦   ✦

Index

(continued)

(continued)

(continued)

IDG BOOKS WORLDWIDE, INC. END-USER LICENSE AGREEMENT

4. **Restrictions On Use of Individual Programs.** You must follow the individual requirements and restrictions detailed for each individual program in Appendix A of this Book. These limitations are also contained in the individual license agreements recorded on the Software Media. These limitations may include a requirement that after using the program for a specified period of time, the user must pay a registration fee or discontinue use. By opening the Software packet(s), you will be agreeing to abide by the licenses and restrictions for these individual programs that are detailed in Appendix A and on the Software Media. None of the material on this Software Media or listed in this Book may ever be redistributed, in original or modified form, for commercial purposes.

5. **Limited Warranty.**

   (a) IDGB warrants that the Software and Software Media are free from defects in materials and workmanship under normal use for a period of sixty (60) days from the date of purchase of this Book. If IDGB receives notification within the warranty period of defects in materials or workmanship, IDGB will replace the defective Software Media.

   (b) IDGB AND THE AUTHOR OF THE BOOK DISCLAIM ALL OTHER WARRANTIES, EXPRESS OR IMPLIED, INCLUDING WITHOUT LIMITATION IMPLIED WARRANTIES OF MERCHANTABILITY AND FITNESS FOR A PARTICULAR PURPOSE, WITH RESPECT TO THE SOFTWARE, THE PROGRAMS, THE SOURCE CODE CONTAINED THEREIN, AND/OR THE TECHNIQUES DESCRIBED IN THIS BOOK. IDGB DOES NOT WARRANT THAT THE FUNCTIONS CONTAINED IN THE SOFTWARE WILL MEET YOUR REQUIREMENTS OR THAT THE OPERATION OF THE SOFTWARE WILL BE ERROR FREE.

   (c) This limited warranty gives you specific legal rights, and you may have other rights that vary from jurisdiction to jurisdiction.

6. **Remedies.**

   (a) IDGB's entire liability and your exclusive remedy for defects in materials and workmanship shall be limited to replacement of the Software Media, which may be returned to IDGB with a copy of your receipt at the following address: Software Media Fulfillment Department, Attn.: *Delphi 4 Bible*, IDG Books Worldwide, Inc., 7260 Shadeland Station, Ste. 100, Indianapolis, IN 46256, or call 1-800-762-2974. Please allow three to four weeks for delivery. This Limited Warranty is void if failure of the Software Media has resulted from accident, abuse, or misapplication. Any replacement Software Media will be warranted for the remainder of the original warranty period or thirty (30) days, whichever is longer.

(b) In no event shall IDGB or the author be liable for any damages whatsoever (including without limitation damages for loss of business profits, business interruption, loss of business information, or any other pecuniary loss) arising from the use of or inability to use the Book or the Software, even if IDGB has been advised of the possibility of such damages.

(c) Because some jurisdictions do not allow the exclusion or limitation of liability for consequential or incidental damages, the above limitation or exclusion may not apply to you.

7. **U.S. Government Restricted Rights.** Use, duplication, or disclosure of the Software by the U.S. Government is subject to restrictions stated in paragraph (c)(1)(ii) of the Rights in Technical Data and Computer Software clause of DFARS 252.227-7013, and in subparagraphs (a) through (d) of the Commercial Computer — Restricted Rights clause at FAR 52.227-19, and in similar clauses in the NASA FAR supplement, when applicable.

8. **General.** This Agreement constitutes the entire understanding of the parties and revokes and supersedes all prior agreements, oral or written, between them and may not be modified or amended except in a writing signed by both parties hereto that specifically refers to this Agreement. This Agreement shall take precedence over any other documents that may be in conflict herewith. If any one or more provisions contained in this Agreement are held by any court or tribunal to be invalid, illegal, or otherwise unenforceable, each and every other provision shall remain in full force and effect.

CD-ROM Installation Instructions

The CD-ROM inside the back cover contains all sample projects described in this book. All programs are compiled. If you just want to run them, use the Windows Explorer program to execute any .exe code file. You may execute most programs directly from the CD-ROM. However, those programs that write to disk files must first be copied to your hard drive or another writeable device.

To do this, copy the files from any CD-ROM directory to an empty directory on your hard drive and then open the copied project with Delphi's File|Open... or File|Open Project... commands. Browse to any directory and open the .dpr file — only one is in most project directory paths. If you don't see a .dpr file, make sure the Open dialog's Files of Type box displays Delphi file (*.pas, *.dpr). Not all sample directories contain projects. For these, there are no .dpr files to open.

To compile a program, you must first copy its directory to your hard drive. If you attempt to compile a program directly to the CD-ROM, Delphi will display an error message when it attempts to write to the .exe code file. If, after copying a directory to your hard drive, you still have trouble compiling, the target files might be marked Read-Only. See Appendix A for more help on this subject.

✦   ✦   ✦